The Book of

Amazing History

Publications International, Ltd.

Contents

✳ ✳ ✳ ✳

These Events
Bear Repeating

* * * *

WHY ARE WE SO intrigued by history? Do we long to be a part of a different age? Do we wish we were part of great events as they happened? History affects every aspect of our lives, whether we are educators, engineers, or entertainers. Flip through this book and relive the momentous events of years past:

* Humans have an amazing capacity for invention. Turn to pages 29, 47, and 512 to find out which enterprising individuals eased communication through the inventions of radio, Braille, and television (respectively).

* Humans also have a magnificent creative capacity. Turn to pages 194, 205, and 480 to read about the most fascinating treasures the world has ever known.

* People are capable of immense goodness. Turn to pages 35 and 367 to read more about individuals who took it upon themselves to aid those threatened by slavery and the Holocaust.

* People also, however, are capable of unspeakable cruelty and greed. Turn to pages 81, 155, and 622 to read more about those who would stop at nothing to add to their own treasure stores.

* Humans have a great capacity to overcome seemingly insurmountable odds. Turn to pages 139, 284, and 408 for stories of heroism and sacrifice.

These events will probably not actually be repeated. The atrocities will not be repeated because by keeping them in our sights, we now know better. The best events are part of the past, but they are also what paved the way for the best of our current times.

Chapter 1

Voyages of Discovery

When Things Really Got Rolling

It's not difficult to see how important the wheel is to human civilization. The hard part is figuring out who came up with it first.

✳　✳　✳　✳

THE WHEEL IS a simple tool, but determining when it was invented is anything but simple. Many accounts assert that it was invented in Asia around 8000 B.C. but fail to elaborate.

Our most solid early evidence of the wheel comes from the excavations at the Sumerian city of Ur (in present-day Iraq) and date to about 3500 B.C. We have no idea who invented Sumer's wheel, but we know its function: pottery. One key to civilization is the production of agricultural excess that can be bartered for other goods and services. Without good storage for that excess, varmints will infest it.

The Bronocice Pot, found in Polish digs from the Funnel/Beaker culture, also dates to 3500 B.C. Could the Funnel/Beaker people have caught wind of the wheel from Sumer or vice versa? It's doubtful. As the bird flies, it's about 1,200 miles from South Poland to Mesopotamia. Each culture probably invented the wheel independently.

✳ **Some historians believe Ur's famous ziggurat was the biblical Tower of Babel.**

Greatest Shortcuts

The construction of such great canals as the Suez and the Panama cost vast amounts of money and required incredible feats of engineering. But the benefits we reap today remind us that it was all worth it.

✳ ✳ ✳ ✳

IN SEPTEMBER 1513, Vasco Núñez de Balboa left the Spanish colony of Darién on the Caribbean coast of the narrow Panamanian isthmus to climb the highest mountain in the area—to literally see what he could see. Upon reaching the summit, he gazed westward and became the first European to see the eastern shores of the Pacific Ocean.

From there, Balboa led a party of conquistadors toward his discovery. They labored across rugged ridges and hacked their way through dense jungles, sweating bullets under their metal breastplates each step of the way. It took four days for Balboa and his men to complete the 40-mile trek to the beach.

Balboa's journey would have been much easier if the Panama Canal had been built beforehand.

For 2,500 years, civilizations have carved canals through land to make water transportation easier and cheaper. History's first great navigational canal was built by the Persian emperor Darius I between 510 and 520 B.C. and linked the Nile River with the Red Sea. A generation later, the Chinese began their reign as the world's greatest canal builders, a distinction they would hold for 1,000 years—until the Europeans began building canals using technology developed centuries earlier during the construction of the world's longest artificial waterway: the 1,100-mile Grand Canal of China.

It's been a long time since a "great" canal was built anywhere in the world. Here's a brief look at the most recent three.

The Erie Canal: Clinton's Big Ditch

At the turn of the 19th century, Americans were eyeing new areas of settlement west of the Appalachians. But westward overland routes were slow and the cost of moving goods along them was exorbitant.

The idea of opening the West by building a canal linking the Great Lakes with the eastern seaboard had been floated since the mid-1700s. It finally became more than wishful thinking in 1817, when construction of the Erie Canal began.

Citing its $7-million price tag, detractors labeled the canal "Clinton's Big Ditch," in reference to its biggest proponent, New York governor Dewitt Clinton. When completed in 1825, however, the Erie Canal was hailed as the "Eighth Wonder of the World." It cut 363 miles through thick forest and swamp to link Lake Erie at Buffalo with the Hudson River at Albany. The Erie Canal fulfilled its promise, becoming a favored pathway for the great migration westward by slashing transportation costs a whopping 95 percent and bringing unprecedented prosperity to the towns along its route.

The Suez Canal: Grand Triumph

The centuries-old dream of a canal linking the Mediterranean and the Red Sea became reality in 1859, when French diplomat Ferdinand de Lesseps stuck the first shovel in the ground to commence the building of the Suez Canal.

Over the next ten years, 2.4 million laborers would move 97 million cubic yards of earth and build a 100-mile Sinai shortcut that made the 10,000-mile sea journey from Europe around Africa to India unnecessary.

De Lesseps convinced an old friend, Egypt's King Said, to grant him a concession to build and operate the canal for 99 years. French investors eagerly bankrolled three-quarters of the project. Said had to kick in the rest to keep the project afloat because others, particularly the British, rejected it as financial lunacy. Their criticisms were seemingly justified when the canal's final cost rang in at double the original estimate.

The Suez dramatically expanded world trade by reducing transportation time and cost. De Lesseps was proclaimed the world's greatest canal digger. The British, leery of France's new backdoor to their Indian empire, spent the next 20 years trying to wrest control of the Suez from their imperial rival.

The Panama Canal: Attempt Number One

When it came time to build the next great canal half a world away in Panama, everyone turned to de Lesseps to dig it.

But here de Lesseps was in over his head. Suez was a walk in the park compared to Panama. In the Suez, flat land at sea level had allowed de Lesseps to build a lockless channel. A canal in Panama, however, would have to slice through the multiple elevations of the Continental Divide.

In 1880, de Lesseps began a nine-year effort to dig a sea-level canal through the mountains. This strategy, combined with financial mismanagement and the deaths of some 22,000 workers from disease and landslides, killed de Lessep's scheme. Panama had crushed the hero of Suez.

The Panama Canal: A Masterpiece!

The idea of a Panama canal, however, persevered. In 1903, the United States, under the expansionist, big-stick leadership of Theodore Roosevelt, bought out the French and assumed control of the project. Using raised-lock engineering and disease-control methods that included spraying oil on mosquito breeding grounds to eliminate malaria and yellow fever, the Americans completed the canal in 1914.

The Panama Canal, the last of the world's great canals, made sailing from New York to San Francisco a breeze. A trip that once covered 14,000 miles and involved circumnavigating the treacherous tip of South America was now a mere 6,000-mile pleasure cruise.

The Old Salt Mine

In ancient times, salt was extremely hard to come by. Vital to the preservation of food, the tanning of hides, and even the production of gunpowder, salt was fought over and even traded for slaves.

❋   ❋   ❋   ❋

SALT CAN BE obtained through several different production methods, including primitive solar evaporation, mining, and complex refining techniques. The most common method of obtaining salt is by mining. Many countries have salt mines, and one of the oldest such mines can be found near Kraków, Poland. Salt was first mined in the area around 1044. During the Middle Ages, salt was one of Poland's chief exports.

Eight miles southeast of Kraków is the tiny town of Wieliczka. Founded in 1290, the town is built atop one of the world's oldest salt mine operations. Legend has it that the mine was a wedding gift presented to the Polish Prince Wstydliwy from his bride-to-be, the Hungarian Princess Kinga.

Tons of salt have been taken from the ground under the town over the course of 700 years. Though the mine ceased operation in the late 1990s, the site was designated a United Nations Educational, Scientific and Cultural Organization (UNESCO) World Heritage Cultural site in 1978 and now operates as a tourist attraction.

The mine consists of nine levels, more than 120 miles of tunnels, and more than 2,000 chambers. At its deepest, it rests 1,073 feet below the surface. Visitors to the site travel a two-mile route that winds through three levels of the mine. On display are several chapels, life-size statues, and scenes replicating famous pieces of art, including Leonardo da Vinci's Last Supper—all carved out of salt. A sanatorium and museum complex are also housed underground.

Groundbreaking Scientific Theories

As knowledge of the world becomes more complex, scientific breakthroughs become increasingly difficult to achieve. Here are a few examples of those whose work blazed a trail.

✳ ✳ ✳ ✳

Discovery of Cell Nuclei

HERE'S A QUICK scientific refresher: The fundamental unit of any living organism is the cell. Some organisms, such as bacteria and algae have only one cell. Others—people, for instance—have trillions of cells. Humans, plants, animals, bugs, and some single-celled organisms all have one thing in common, though: Each one of our cells has a nucleus. Robert Brown, a Scottish botanist, was the first to make this discovery.

Born in 1773, Brown studied medicine at the University of Edinburgh. Shortly after his graduation, he worked for five years as an army surgeon. Best known for traveling to distant lands and discovering hundreds of new plant species, Brown rose to prominence as a leading expert in botanic research. In 1831, while studying how herbs and orchids become fertilized, he noticed that each plant cell he studied had a structure in common. Brown decided to call this the *nucleus* of the cell, after the Latin word meaning "kernel," or "little nut."

Brown wasn't the first to see the nucleus of a cell. That credit went to the guy who perfected the microscope, Dutch scientist Antonie van Leeuwenhoek. Brown, however, was the first to recognize the nucleus's significance as the regulator of cellular activity. Brown's observations, research, and theories brought him much notoriety and fortune.

Genetics According to Mendel

Do you know why a person might have her mom's red hair and not her dad's blond hair? How about why someone has hazel eyes like Grandpa, even though Mom and Dad both have dark brown eyes? An Austrian-born geneticist named Johann Mendel, or Gregor Johann Mendel—the name by which he's more widely known—started to figure it out. Before Mendel, scientists didn't quite know how traits were passed from one generation to the next. There were several theories floating around, but most relied heavily on guesswork and didn't follow disciplined scientific methods to form their conclusions. Mendel changed that.

Mendel was born in 1822, the second of three children. He took an early interest in beekeeping and gardening, which guided his studies later in life. After joining a monastery and becoming a monk, Johann took the name Gregor and began studying the genetic variations of plants. He focused on the ordinary garden pea. After rigorous experimentation—on about 29,000 peas—and countless statistical and mathematical conclusions, Mendel discovered that peas pass their genetic traits to their offspring in a very specific way. How long would it take to count 29,000 peas, perform experiments, watch them grow, take notes on observations, and write a book about it? That's dedication!

Like most groundbreaking science throughout history, Mendel's theories weren't widely accepted when he published his work. In fact, his theories all but faded into history after his death in 1884. However, some 20 years later, other scientists discovered Mendel's work and replicated his experiments. Suddenly, everyone flocked to his ideas. Mendel's discovery became known as "Mendel's Laws of Inheritance" and laid the foundation for modern genetics.

Vitamins According to Funk

What's the deal with food packages listing all the important vitamins the food contains? Even something as sugary-good and delicious as breakfast cereal contains several "essential vitamins." What are these things? Let's turn the time machine back to 1911 and focus on a Polish biochemist by the name of Casimir Funk, the pioneer of vitamins.

The first part of the word *vitamin* comes from the Latin word for "life"; Funk knew that it would represent these life-giving, ammonia-based chemical compounds that he had discovered. These compounds can prevent diseases, help keep the body working in tip-top condition, and encourage healthy growth. Vitamins are essential for all multicelled life-forms to grow healthy and strong.

In Japan, it was discovered that a disease called beriberi, which attacks the nervous system, the heart, and the digestive system, was less likely to be contracted by those who ate lots of brown rice. No one knew why. Funk began experimenting by feeding rice to two groups of pigeons. He fed one group rice with its outer coating still on, and the other group rice with its coating removed. Funk discovered that the pigeons that ate the rice with the coating removed contracted beriberi, while the others remained healthy. After concentrating the nutrients he found in the coating of the rice, he labeled this concentration a *vitamine* in 1911.

Funk published a paper on his findings in 1912. His work was well received, especially by those suffering from beriberi and other diseases caused by vitamin deficiencies. He wasn't the only one to publish research on these nutrients at the time, but his was the most thorough and widely accepted.

The Discovery of DNA Structure

Deoxyribonucleic acid—DNA for short—is the substance in the cell nucleus that contains a living organism's genetic information. Although scientists have known about DNA since the 1860s, no one knew what it looked like. Imagine trying to find your way around a building without knowing anything about its appearance, inside or outside. You might know it's made of brick, but what shape is it? Where are the stairs and

the elevator? James Watson and Francis Crick wanted to answer those very same questions about DNA—the building block of life.

Watson and Crick were molecular biologists from the United States and Great Britain, respectively. In the 1950s, they built their first model of DNA from metal and wire at Cambridge University in England. Watson and Crick gathered information from all over the place. They attended lectures, read scientific papers, looked at X-rays, and did their own experiments before deciding that building a model was the best way to approach the challenge. Unfortunately, their model failed. It failed so badly that the head of their department told them to cease all DNA research. But the pair couldn't let it go.

A breakthrough came in 1953 when a competing scientist, also frustrated in trying to discover the structure of DNA, shared his work (and his partner's, without her knowledge) with Watson and Crick. The new insight caused them to take a huge leap in thought. It had been widely accepted that DNA probably had two strands that wrapped around each other like a staircase. This is the double helix. Watson and Crick theorized that one side of the strand wound upward and the other side downward, with matching chemicals (base pairs) holding the two helices together. Discovering how the four base pair chemicals—adenine with thymine and cytosine with guanine—fit together was the final step in unlocking the mystery.

The structure of DNA is one of the most important discoveries of the last 100 years. It has influenced everything from food to medication to technology. In 1962, Watson, Crick, and Maurice Wilkins (the scientist who shared the work of his partner, Rosalind Franklin) won the Nobel Prize for Physiology/Medicine. Franklin did not receive the Nobel Prize, but only because the award is reserved for the living—Franklin had died four years earlier.

Napoleon and the Civil War

The infamous general even impacted the all-American war.

✳   ✳   ✳   ✳

IN THE MID-19TH century, French General Napoleon Bonaparte was regarded as one of the greatest military geniuses in history. Everyone wanted to emulate his tactics. Civil War generals on both sides had been trained at West Point, and one of their primary textbooks was a volume on Napoleonic tactics written by Antoine Henri de Jomini. Many of these officers absolutely revered the French general and emperor. Thomas J. Jackson, who was later nicknamed "Stonewall," even traveled to Europe to study Napoleonic battlefields.

Building on Napoleon's Ideas

Outflanking was one of the most important Napoleonic principles taught to Civil War generals. When an attacking force gets around the side of its enemy, it forces the defender to turn its lines to face the attacker, rush reinforcements to that side, and disrupt the battle plan. How did Sherman conquer Atlanta? Not by facing the rebel army head on, but by executing a string of flanking maneuvers that forced the rebels to fall back slowly until Atlanta was vulnerable.

Sherman took another page from Napoleon's playbook during his March to the Sea across Georgia. The general fed his army by ransacking farms along the way; living off the land was Napoleon's strategy for maintaining an army far from home.

Not all the general's tactics worked, though. He advised keeping troops in straight formation. That's fine for enemies with bad aim, but Civil War rifles were more accurate than Napoleonic muskets, and soldiers lined up in neat formation were sitting ducks for sharpshooters. Overall, though, Napoleon's lessons made Civil War armies much more effective—and deadly—than previous American forces had been.

Words for the Ages

"Engines of war have long since reached their limits, and I see no further hope of any improvement in the art."

—FRONTINUS, A.D. 90

"The crowd, which follows me with admiration, would run with the same eagerness were I marching to the Guillotine."

—NAPOLEON BONAPARTE

"We are continually faced by great opportunities brilliantly disguised as insolvable problems."

—BENJAMIN FRANKLIN

"The Pope! How many divisions has he got?"

—JOSEPH STALIN, 1935, ON BEING ASKED TO SUPPORT CATHOLICISM IN RUSSIA

"Sleep is like a drug. Take too much at a time and it makes you dopey. You lose time and opportunities."

—THOMAS EDISON

"Today we have . . . the transmission of sight for the first time. . . . Human genius has now destroyed the impediment of distance . . . in a manner hitherto unknown."

—HERBERT HOOVER, DURING THE FIRST LONG-DISTANCE TRANSMISSION
OF A LIVE PICTURE AND VOICE (APRIL 9, 1927)

"Anyone who has never made a mistake has never tried anything new."

—ALBERT EINSTEIN

"But who prays for Satan? Who, in eighteen centuries, has had the common humanity to pray for the one sinner that needed it most?"

—MARK TWAIN

"The man who dies rich . . . dies disgraced.""

—ANDREW CARNEGIE

"My toast would be, may our country be always successful, but whether successful or otherwise, always right."

—JOHN QUINCY ADAMS

Worth the Paper It's Printed On: The History of Paper

Three cheers for Ts'ai Lun! Without him, there would be no daily gazette. Without him, there would be no dollar bills. Without him, there would be no fantastic historical diaries. Without him, no one could read this very book. Thanks to this gentleman from Lei-Yang, China, the world enjoys the gift of paper.

✳　✳　✳　✳

Where's the Paper, Boy?

Ts'ai Lun's invention of paper dates to A.D. 105. However, paperlike papyrus had been produced in Egypt for more than 3,000 years prior. The word *paper* is even derived from *papyrus*. Ancient Egyptians developed it by hammering strips of the papyrus plant into a unified sheet for writing. The Egyptians even sold it to the Greeks and Romans until around 300 B.C. With their papyrus supply cut off, Greeks and Romans turned to parchment, which is made from the skins of a variety of animals.

Paper on a Roll

Ts'ai Lun was a member of the imperial court who became fascinated with the way wasps made their nests. Using that knowledge as a starting point, he took a mash of wood pulp and spread it across a coarse cloth screen. The dried fibers formed a sheet of pliable paper that could be peeled off and written on.

The new material quickly became a staple for official government business, for wrapping, and for envelopes. By the 7th century A.D., the Chinese had even invented toilet paper. A Chinese scholar at the time showed good judgment, observing, "Paper on which there are quotations or . . . the names of sages, I dare not use for toilet purposes."

Paper Goes International

The art of papermaking remained in Asia for several centuries, spreading to Korea and Japan. Around A.D. 1000, papermaking reached the Middle East. Arabians used linen fibers in place of wood pulp, creating a higher-quality paper. These superior products were in high demand, and exports increased. In this way, the art of papermaking reached Europe and flourished—particularly in Italy—by the 13th century.

The Italians took their papermaking very seriously, using machinery and standardized processes to turn out large amounts of top-notch paper. They used water power to run paper mills, created higher-quality drying screens, and improved the sizing process. A new coating was also developed to improve paper strength and reduce water absorbancy.

(Don't) Stop the Presses!

When a German named Johannes Gutenberg developed the movable type printing press in the mid-1400s, the world of papermaking was changed forever. Books that were once hand-copied were now available in a mass-produced format. As the appetite for new books grew, so did the need for paper.

The New World was introduced to papermaking in the late 1600s, when the first paper mill was built in Mexico. A German immigrant named William Rittenhouse started the first paper plant in the British colonies in Philadelphia in 1690. In less than a century, 20 mills were producing paper in the colonies.

All the News(paper) That's Fit to Print

Much of the paper being produced in the mills was made from old rags, clothing, and other textiles, making a thick paper.

Around 1840, a Canadian named Charles Fenerty used a fine wood pulp to create a thin, inexpensive paper known as "newsprint." However, he didn't pursue a patent for his work and his claim of invention was lost to others. Still, Fenerty's invention enabled newspapers to be printed more frequently.

It's in the Bag

Paper has proved to be a versatile material in uses that go far beyond writing and printing. Following the Civil War, veteran Charles Stilwell returned to his home in Ohio and became a mechanical engineer. He noticed that paper bags used to carry groceries were not well made and wouldn't stand up on their own. He solved the problem, patenting a machine in 1883 that made paper grocery bags with a flat bottom and pleated sides. The style remains largely unchanged in the paper bags used today.

If Ts'ai Lun were still alive, he would most likely be amazed by how widespread his humble invention has become. In the modern world, it is virtually impossible to pass a day without picking up a book, a newspaper, an envelope, or a box. Readers, writers, shippers, and even shoppers owe him a debt of gratitude for making their world an easier place in which to live.

* Canada and the United States are the world's largest producers of paper and paper products.

* According to the Environmental Protection Agency, the average American uses approximately one 100-foot-tall Douglas fir tree in paper and wood products each year.

* Recycling just one ton of paper saves 17 trees.

* Americans take toilet paper very seriously. In one *Tonight Show* monologue in 1973, Johnny Carson cracked a joke about a toilet paper shortage. Concerned citizens across the country stocked up on toilet paper that very night.

Poisoned Puddings and Puritanism: Harvard's Early Days

Today, Harvard is famed for a vast endowment, but its early days were marked by a struggle to get by with quarter-bushels of wheat donated by local farmers.

✳ ✳ ✳ ✳

THE GENERAL COURT of Massachusetts allotted 400 pounds for a college across the Charles River from Boston in what became known as Cambridge, Massachusetts. The school was named for John Harvard, a clergyman from England's Cambridge University, which at the time was known to be a hotbed of Puritanism—the severe, idealistic faith opposed to the dominant Church of England.

John Harvard's family had known William Shakespeare. When the plague felled his brothers and his father, John inherited a considerable estate, including the Queen's Head Tavern. After immigrating to Boston, he became a preacher in Charleston, Massachusetts, but his career was short. In 1638, at the age of 31, he died of consumption, having bequeathed money and his personal library to the planned college.

The School's Scandalous First Leader

The tiny college soon faced its first crisis. In its earliest years, Harvard featured a student body of nine, a "yard" liberated from cows, and a single, hated instructor.

Harvard's 30-year-old schoolmaster, Nathaniel Eaton, was known to beat wayward students. Other students charged Eaton's wife, Elizabeth, of putting goat dung into their corn-meal porridge, or "hasty pudding." (Harvard's theatrical society is named for the dish.) Finally, Master Eaton went too far and was hauled into court after clubbing a scholar with a walnut-tree cudgel. He was also accused of embezzling 100 pounds (then an ample sum).

In 1639, Eaton and his wife were sent packing. Master Eaton returned to England, was made a vicar, then died in debtor's prison. Following the Eaton affair, Harvard's reputation lay in tatters; its operations were suspended, and its students were scattered.

Comeback Under the First President

In 1640, the colony's founders were desperate for educational cachet. They offered the post of Harvard president to Henry Dunster, a new arrival from England and another graduate of Cambridge University.

The energetic Dunster tapped into the colony's inherent educational edge. Many of the new Puritan arrivals had studied at the Oxford and Cambridge academies: Some 130 alumni of the two schools were in New England by 1646. Dunster himself was a leading scholar in biblical tongues such as Hebrew.

Led primarily by a Protestant culture that stressed reading the Bible, Boston set up the first free grammar school in 1635; within 12 years, every town in Massachusetts was required by law to have one. Harvard's new president mandated a four-year graduation requirement and rode out angry students who protested over a commencement fee. Dunster obtained Harvard's charter and authored the school's "Rules and Precepts." He bankrolled the facilities through donations of livestock and, over the course of 13 years, some 250 pounds of wheat. He took a modest salary, being underpaid through 14 years of service, and piled up personal debts. Fortunately, his wife, Elizabeth Glover, kept a printing press in their home. It was the American colonies' first press, and its profits underwrote her husband's work. Dunster managed to turn the school around. Harvard's reputation soared, and students from throughout the colonies, the Caribbean, and the mother country flocked to newly built dorms.

Religious Schisms and a President's Heresies

Yet Dunster tripped up on one of the many religious disputes roiling the Puritan colony. In 1648, it was a criminal offense to engage in "Blasphemy, Heresie, open contempt of the Word preached, Profanation of the Lord's Day"; separation of church and state was unknown.

Baptism by Fire

A source of much of the controversy was infant baptism, which the Puritan fathers required by law. Drawing on his biblical knowledge, Dunster noted that John the Baptist had baptized the adult Jesus, but he could find no biblical examples of children being baptized.

In 1653, he refused to have his son Jonathan baptized. At Cambridge's Congregational Church, Dunster preached against "corruptions stealing into the Church, which every faithful Christian ought to [bear] witness against."

This put the Puritans of Boston and Cambridge in a quandary. Dunster's views made him a heretic, yet he was much liked for his work at the college. Early the next year, the colony's officers wrote that Dunster "hath by his practice and opinions rendered himself offensive to this government." They assembled a conference of 11 ministers and elders to interrogate him. Egged on by this assembly, in May 1654 the General Court forbade schools to employ those "that have manifested themselves unsound in the faith, or scandalous in their lives." Dunster resigned from Harvard.

The ex-president then petitioned the court to let him stay in the colony until he could repay the many debts he'd accumulated from his work. Court authorities coldly responded that "they did not know of [such] extraordinary labor or sacrifices. For the space of 14 years we know of none." Dunster, with Elizabeth and their youngest child ill, then beseeched the court to at least let his family stay the winter. The magistrates agreed grudgingly, but the following spring they banished the Dunster family to the backwater town of Scituate. Harvard's first president died there four years later, at age 47.

Elevating Invention to New Heights

When Elisha Graves Otis and his sons began their elevator business in the 1850s, the solid brick buildings of America's cities had four-story height limits. By the 1920s, with the widespread adoption of safe, power-driven lifts, skyscrapers had replaced church steeples as the hallmarks of urban design.

✳ ✳ ✳ ✳

ELEVATORS TO LIFT cargo have been around since the pyramidal ziggurats of ancient Iraq. In 236 B.C., the Greek scientist Archimedes used his knowledge of levers to deploy beast- and slave-drawn hoists. In 1743, technicians of French King Louis XV devised a "flying chair," with pulleys and weights running down the royal chimney, to carry his mistress, Madame de Pompadour, to and from the palace's upper floors.

An Uplifting Background

Elisha Otis was a descendant of American Revolutionary James Otis. Born in Vermont in 1811, Elisha Otis was Yankee ingenuity incarnate. In the 1840s, as a senior mechanic in a bedstead factory in Albany, New York, he patented a railroad safety brake, critical to quickly and safely hauling freight in and out of the factories of the Industrial Revolution.

By 1852, Otis was a master mechanic at another bedstead firm in Yonkers, New York. He began tinkering with a safety lift for its warehouse, but the company went belly-up. Otis was mulling a move to California's Gold Rush country when a furniture maker asked him to build two safety elevators. Fighting off chronically poor health, Otis established his own company and set to work.

All Safe

In 1854, Otis—looking quite distinguished in a full beard and top hat—took to a platform at the Crystal Palace exposition in

New York. A rope had pulled his newfangled "hoisting apparatus" high up a shaft, its side open to public view. With a flourish, he waved an ax toward the onlookers crowding the hall. Then, with a quick motion, Otis cleaved the rope with the ax. The onlookers gasped as the elevator began its downward plunge—only to suddenly stop after a three-inch fall. Elisha Otis tipped his hat and proclaimed: "All safe, gentlemen, all safe."

To ensure safety, Otis attached a wagon wheel's taut springs to the elevator ropes. "If the rope snapped," explained *Smithsonian* magazine, "the ends of the steel spring would flare out, forcing two large latches to lock into ratchets on either side of the platform."

Otis soon patented an elevator driven by a tiny steam engine, permitting retail stores and other small enterprises to purchase their own lifts. Despite the technical wizardry, Elisha Otis's commercial success and business sense were limited. Two years after his successful demonstration—despite a follow-up exhibit at P. T. Barnum's Traveling World's Fair—sales of Otis elevators totaled less than $14,000 a year. Even if proceeds picked up, wrote Otis's son Charles, "Father will manage in such a way [as] to lose it all," going "crazy over some wild fancy for the future." Five years later, in 1861, Otis died at age 49 of diphtheria, leaving his two sons a business that was $3,200 in the red.

Success

Charles and Norton Otis proved better businessmen and rivaled their father as technicians, making important improvements to their useful device. By 1873, Otis Brothers & Company, revenues soaring, had installed 2,000 elevators into buildings. Replacing steam-powered lifts, their hydraulic elevators sat on steel tubes sunk into shafts deep below the buildings. An influx of water pushed the platforms up. Reducing the water pressure lowered the elevators.

Where hotel guests previously had preferred the accessible first floor, they now opted to "make the transit with ease" (as an Otis catalog boasted), to the top floors, which offered "an exemption from noise, dust and exhalations of every kind."

Though taken for granted today, elevators were the height of opulence then. One elevator from that era in Saratoga Springs, New York, was outfitted with chandeliers and paneled in ebony and tulipwood.

Riding the skyscraper boom, the Otis firm went from one noted project to another. In 1889, the firm completed lifts for the bottom section of the Eiffel Tower. Around 1900, it bought the patents to a related invention, the escalator. In 1913, the Otis firm installed 26 electric elevators for the world's then-tallest structure, New York's Woolworth Building. In 1931, Otis installed 73 elevators and more than 120 miles of cables in another record-breaker, the 1,250-foot Empire State Building.

Setting the Ceiling

All the while, along with enhancements, such as push-button controls, came improvements in speed. Cities constantly changed their elevator "speed limits"—from a leisurely 40 feet per minute for Elisha Otis's original safety lifts, to a speedy 1,200 feet per minute in the 1930s, to today's 2,000 feet per minute. "That's probably as much vertical speed as most people can tolerate," says an Otis engineer.

Along the way, the elevator industry quashed early fears that speedy lifts were bad for people. In the 1890s, *Scientific American* wrote that the body parts of elevator passengers came to a halt at different rates, triggering mysterious ailments.

Like the earlier notion that fast trains would choke passengers by pushing oxygen away from their mouths, that theory has since been debunked.

There's No Place Like Home

Every now and then, conventional wisdom turns out to be dead wrong. Throughout history, humankind's big leaps forward have often come only when some bright thinker was willing to challenge generally accepted wisdom. At other times, long-cherished myths—such as "the world is flat"—simply wither and die over many years by mutual consent.

✳ ✳ ✳ ✳

SINCE ANCIENT TIMES, astronomers believed that Earth remained a fixed point in the cosmos around which all other bodies—the Sun, the Moon, other planets, and the stars—revolved in an orderly, predictable fashion. This arrangement, called the Aristotelian system, satisfied most everyone because it could be proven by simple observation; a farmer, for instance, could watch the Sun rise in the east and set in the west.

It was not until 1514 that Polish astronomer Nicolaus Copernicus began popularizing the theory of heliocentrism, which claims that Earth revolves around the Sun and not the other way around. The astronomer's theory was soundly criticized in his day (mostly by fellow scientists, and not so much by clergymen, as is often claimed). Subsequent studies showed Copernicus to be right, however, and the accepted wisdom of the previous 2,000 years went out the window.

That is, until 1905, when Albert Einstein concluded that one could never truly say whether the Sun revolved around Earth or vice versa; all you can say is that they move relative to each other. Beyond that, it's just a matter of perspective.

Don't Touch That Dial!
The Birth of Radio

At the turn of the 20th century, no one could have imagined today's world of shock-jocks, satellite radio, or streaming Internet audio. The idea of wireless communications was as foreign as the thought that humans would one day blast off into space.

✳ ✳ ✳ ✳

IN THE 1800S, discoveries by the German-born Heinrich Hertz and Scottish James Clerk Maxwell set the stage for Guglielmo Marconi's notable invention: the wireless telegraph. Because the Italian's home country offered no support for his work, Marconi sought and received aid from the British government. Soon the dots and dashes of Morse code were spanning the English Channel via radio signals. In 1897, Marconi founded the Wireless Telegraph & Signal Company Limited. A few years later, Morse code for the letter "S" was sent from the shores of England and received in Newfoundland, Canada. Marconi's radio signal had traveled across the Atlantic Ocean.

Enter Lee De Forest

Inventor Lee De Forest took wireless communications a step further. The brilliant De Forest labored with many types of wireless telegraphs in the 1900s, building some for Western Electric and the U.S. Navy. In 1906, he invented the Audion, a three-element electron tube that amplified audio signals (the Audion was an improvement of the two-element device patented by Sir John Ambrose Fleming in 1904). The Audion was capable of transmitting Morse code and—more importantly—voice farther than ever before.

Initially, wireless transmissions were used strictly as communication for business or military operations. However, De Forest thought the new medium had greater potential. From 1907 to 1912, he invited members of the press to listen at receiving sets during several demonstrations in which he broadcast opera performances. These "broadcasts," were done using arc radio-telephones, which were less sophisticated but more popular than the Audion at the time. Still, they showed that the wireless system could have much broader applications than its inventors had previously thought.

Moving Down the Dial

By 1913, De Forest had sold his patent for the Audion to AT&T, which used the device to boost voice signals across the continent. In 1916, the Audion tube became an essential part of commercial transmitters.

De Forest's work was not limited to radio. In 1920, he developed the first sound-on-film process (Phonofilm) for the motion-picture industry. He received Hollywood's highest award—an honorary Oscar—in 1959 for his "Pioneer Invention which brought sound to the Motion Picture." His process is still used today for analogue film audio.

---

* Some say the beginning of broadcasting was January 12, 1908. The USS *Ohio* had previously played music for its own troops, but on that date, the ship broadcast band tunes to nearby ships—and even took requests from their sailors.

* Live from New York: In 1916, Lee De Forest became the first person to broadcast election results to an audience. From the High Bridge in New York, he shared the results of the Hughes-Wilson presidential election.

"The wireless music box has no imaginable commercial value. Who would pay for a message sent to nobody in particular?"

—DAVID SARNOFF, AMERICAN RADIO PIONEER, 1921

The Story of Anesthesia

*In the middle of the 19th century, three intoxicating solvents
with bad reputations became the first crude "switches"
that could turn consciousness off and on—paving the
way for the revolution of painless surgical medicine.*

✳ ✳ ✳ ✳

O N MARCH 30, 1842, a doctor from rural Georgia laid
an ether-soaked towel across the mouth and nose of a
patient with two cysts on his neck. The physician, Crawford
Williamson Long, excised one of the growths while his patient
was under. In the process, he made medical and scientific history. Long was perhaps the first doctor to use "general anesthetic"—a substance that reduces or eliminates conscious
awareness in a patient, allowing a doctor to perform incisions,
sutures, and all other surgical procedures in between.

The "general"—which means complete or near-complete uncon-
sciousness—is different from the targeted "local" anesthetic, an
invention with origins shrouded in mystery. (Some ancient Inca
rituals involved drilling a hole in the patient's skull to allow evil
spirits to escape; to reduce the literally mind-numbing pain, the
Incan shaman chewed leaves of the narcotic coca plant and spat
the paste into the subject's wound.)

Unfortunately for Georgia's Dr. Long, the awards and acclaim
that should have accompanied his medical milestone went to a
dentist from Boston, who used ether four years later to knock
out a patient in order to remove a tooth. Because this procedure was performed at the world-renowned Massachusetts
General Hospital—and not at a backwoods country practice
in the Deep South—the fame of the Massachusetts innovator,
William T. G. Morton, was practically assured. Within two
months of Morton's tooth extraction, doctors across Europe
were toasting the Yankee who had invented pain-free surgery.

The story of the stolen spotlight, however, can't entirely be blamed on the prejudice of urban versus rural or North versus South. Long, who was known to enjoy the occasional "ether frolic," didn't publicize his use of ether as a general anesthetic until 1849, seven years after his initial use of it, and three years after Morton's world-acclaimed surgery.

Wake Up, Mr. Green. Mr. Green?

By 1849, a London physician, John Snow, had invented a specialized ether inhaler to better administer a safe but effective dose of the painless surgical gas. Snow was responding to the need for more scientific care in the fledgling field of anesthesiology. Lethal doses of ether had already been administered in some botched surgeries, and Snow eventually championed chloroform, which, he would later write, is "almost impossible . . . [to cause] a death . . . in the hands of a medical man who is applying it with ordinary intelligence and attention."

Chloroform and ether each had their downsides, though. Chloroform could damage the liver and occasionally even cause cardiac arrest, but ether required more time for the patient to both enter and exit the anesthetized state.

Nothing to Laugh About

Some American practitioners championed a third popular early anesthetic: nitrous oxide or "laughing gas," although its reputation suffered when not enough of it was administered in an early demonstration during a tooth extraction at Harvard Medical School. When the patient cried out in pain, the dentist, Horace Wells, was booed out of the room. In a turn of tragic irony, Wells became a chloroform addict and committed suicide in 1848, just three years after the Harvard fiasco.

By the 1860s and '70s, many surgeons had given up advocating one gas over another, preferring instead to use a mixture—either chloroform or nitrous oxide to induce anesthesia, followed by ether to keep the patient in an unconscious state.

The Opening of Tut's Tomb

There was a time when archaeology was commissioned privately by wealthy individuals. Some of these benefactors desired to advance historical knowledge, while others simply hoped to enhance their personal collections of antiquities. The much-heralded opening of the tomb of the Pharaoh Tutankhamun, better known today as "King Tut," represented one of the last hurrahs for these old days of archaeology.

✳ ✳ ✳ ✳

Who was King Tut, anyway?

King Tut was an ancient Egyptian ruler, or pharaoh. Tut ruled Egypt from 1333 B.C. to 1324 B.C., during what is referred to as the New Kingdom period. Sometimes called "The Boy King," he became pharaoh when he was 9 years old and died at age 19. Researchers believe Tut died after a leg injury became infected while his body was already fighting bone disease and malaria.

How was his tomb located?

Finding Tut's tomb required scholarship, persistence, patience, and lots of digging. A wealthy Englishman, Lord Carnarvon, sponsored Howard Carter, one of the day's brightest archaeologists. Carter poked around in Egypt between 1917 and 1922 with little luck. Then, in November 1922, just as Lord Carnarvon was ready to give up, Carter uncovered steps leading down to a tomb marked with Tut's royal seals. Carter dashed off a communiqué to Carnarvon, telling him to get to Egypt at once.

What happened next?

Carnarvon wasted no time, and once the sponsor reached the scene, Carter was ready to cut his way into the tomb. Workers soon exposed a sealed doorway bearing Tut's name. Those present would witness the unveiling of history as Carter peered into the tomb. However, thanks to the meticulous nature of archaeology, work on Tut's tomb could only happen at a slow pace. The entire process stretched across the next decade.

What was in there?

The contents of the tomb were incredible. It was clear that ancient plunderers had twice raided the tomb for some smaller items. Although they did leave the place a mess, many amazing treasures remained. Carter and company catalogued piles of priceless artifacts, including gold statues and everything from sandals to chariots. Tut's mummified body had been placed in an ornate coffin, and canopic jars held his internal organs. In addition, two mummified premature babies (thought to be Tut's children), were found. Tut was also buried with everything he would need to be stylish in the afterlife, including ornate bows and gloves fit for a pharaoh. Scholars would spend years preserving and studying the artifacts in the tomb.

King Tut's tomb was the archaeological find of the decade—perhaps even the find of the century.

❋ Approximately 130 walking sticks were found in Tut's tomb, leading researchers to believe that Tut was somewhat disabled as a result of his bone disease.

❋ Tut's famous mask actually covered the mummy's head. From the side, it looks like what could be an Egyptian deep-sea diver's helmet, contoured to fit the shoulders. This brilliant item made of gold and precious stones remains one of the best-known symbols of ancient Egyptian glory.

❋ Why wasn't everything of value in Tut's tomb ripped off by the ancient tomb raiders? The holes the raiders hacked through the mortar and rock weren't very big—nothing sizable could fit through them.

The Underground Railroad

The very mention of the Underground Railroad reaches deep into the American psyche, invoking images of secret tunnels and concealed doors, as well as the exploits of thousands of daring men and women.

✳   ✳   ✳   ✳

"...that all men are created equal"

THE STORY OF American slaves seeking escape from their masters long predates the invention of the railroad and its associated terms. The reasons for escape are easily understood and existed equally across slaves of all levels of privilege, from field hands to highly skilled laborers. Even before the Underground Railroad, escapees were often aided by individuals or organizations opposed to the institution of slavery. In fact, one prominent slaveholder—George Washington—complained in a letter that some of his fellow citizens were more concerned with helping one of his runaway slaves than in protecting his property rights as a slaveholder.

As the United States careened toward civil war, the arguments between supporters of slavery and those opposed to it became increasingly heated. Northern states began abolishing slavery on an individual basis—and became instant magnets for those fleeing servitude. In response, Congress passed Fugitive Slave Acts in 1793 and 1850, rendering escaped slaves fugitives for life, eligible for return to bondage on nothing more than the word of a white man. Any constable who refused to apprehend runaway slaves was fined. With the Northern states thus a less attractive final destination, runaways headed to Canada, where slavery had been outlawed in 1834. Meanwhile, abolitionist societies began to spring up, though a surprising number of them supported the return of escaped slaves to their masters, believing they could end the practice through moral persuasion rather than by violating the law.

All Aboard

Despite hesitation on the part of some abolitionist societies, however, there were always individuals and groups who were sympathetic to the cause of the runaway slave and willing to place themselves at risk to help slaves find freedom. These benefactors ranged from white citizens to free blacks to other slaves willing to risk being beaten or sold for giving aid to runaways. Often, these protectors acted alone with little more than a vague idea of where to send a fugitive slave other than in the general direction of north. When a sympathetic individual discovered a runaway, he or she would often simply do what seemed best at the moment, whether that meant providing food and clothing, throwing pursuers off the track, or giving the slave a wagon ride to the next town.

By the 1840s, the expansion of the railroad was having a major impact on American society, and abolitionist activists quickly adopted its terminology. Conductors were those people who helped their passengers—runaway slaves—on to the next station or town, where they made contact with a stationmaster—the person in charge of the local organization. The most famous conductor, Harriet Tubman, was herself an escaped slave who risked no less than 19 trips back into slave country to aid family members and others.

In some areas, small cells sprang up in which each person knew only about a contact on the next farm or in the next town, perhaps with the nebulous goal of somehow sending escapees into the care of well-known abolitionist societies in far-off Philadelphia or Boston. The image of one overriding national organization guiding the effort is largely a misleading one, but both abolitionists and slaveholders encouraged it. The abolitionists were not hesitant to play up the romantic railroad imagery in an effort to bolster their fund-raising efforts. Their descriptions were so vivid that Frederick Douglass himself suggested they cease talking about it, lest they reveal their methods to their enemies. Likewise, Southern plantation owners were quick to play up the reports as proof that there was a vast abolitionist conspiracy bent on robbing them of their legal investment in slaves. As a result, some slave owners in border states converted their slaves to cash—selling them to the Deep South rather than risking their escape—a fate many slaves considered nothing less than a death sentence.

Efforts at undermining the institution of slavery existed and were scarcely clandestine. Many abolitionists were quite open about their intentions.

"Devils and good people, walking in the road at the same time"

Despite the presence of Underground Railroad workers, the experience of a runaway slave was never anything other than harsh. On striking out for freedom, even successful escapees faced an ordeal that could last months. During their journey, they rarely had food, shelter, or appropriate clothing. Every white face was a potential enemy, as were some of their fellow black people, who were sometimes employed as decoys to help catch runaways. A false Underground Railroad even existed. Participants would take in a runaway and promise safe passage only to deliver the unfortunate individual up to the local slave market. Often the escapees had no idea where they were going or the distance to be covered.

Although estimates vary wildly, one widely reported figure is that approximately 100,000 slaves found freedom either through their own initiative or with the aid of the Underground Railroad before the rest of those in bondage were freed during and after the Civil War. The history of the Railroad was largely written decades after the fact, and it is occasionally hard to separate reliable facts from the aged recollections of those justifiably proud of their efforts at securing liberty for their neighbors.

The Super Weapon
That Fired Sound

One of the most important weapons of World War II never fired a shot and was helpless if attacked—but it brought down hundreds of enemy aircraft and saved thousands of lives.

✱　✱　✱　✱

RADAR WAS DEVELOPED independently by researchers in eight nations, beginning nearly four decades before World War II. The technology used sound waves to create an echo that would bounce off metal ships. When the echo returned to the sending unit, it could be analyzed to determine the distance and the size of the target.

Radar Developments

By the late 1930s, the major belligerents began crash programs to develop the technology for naval- and air-defense purposes. The U.S. Naval Research Laboratory, the British Meteorological Office, and the German *Kriegsmarine* had developed a series of workable sets by the time hostilities broke out in Europe.

As an island, Britain was protected by the sea and an impressive navy, but its vulnerability to air attacks meant it had much to gain from developing radar. In the late 1930s, it developed a rudimentary radar network called Chain Home. While the technology was merely adequate, the devices could be rushed into production in time to help defend the Home Isles against the *Luftwaffe* in the summer of 1940.

That same year, two British researchers at the University of Birmingham developed the cavity magnetron, a device that allowed radar operators to use higher-frequency sound waves that could be focused more tightly. Britain secretly shipped the prototype to the Massachusetts Institute of Technology, where researchers developed models for an improved radar system.

The Soviet Union had one ship-based radar device, the Redut-K system, in place by 1940. For its radar needs, the USSR relied heavily upon sets from the United States and Britain.

Neither Germany nor Japan kept pace with the Allies' radar development. Although Germany's Freya system was more sophisticated than the early Chain Home units fielded by Great Britain, Germany had only eight operational units in the field at the outbreak of the war. Further, Freya technology did not accurately determine altitude.

The *Kriegsmarine* received several Freya systems in 1937, and in 1942, the Third Reich established the Kammhuber Line, a chain of radar installations running from Denmark to central France. These stations helped the Germans defend against RAF attacks, but by 1942 British air planners could overwhelm the flak and air interception potential of the Kammhuber Line by concentrating bomber formations.

Japanese radar lagged well behind advances in the United States and Europe. Early in the war, the Japanese also created a small number of reasonably effective naval-radar sets. They relied on some captured devices, including a British model taken after the fall of Singapore and two American devices found when the army overran the Philippines.

Radar Evolves

Ships were equipped with radar to spot enemy craft (and periscopes) at night. De Havilland Mosquito fighter-bombers and Bristol Beaufighter fighters, among others, were fitted with miniature radar sets: These allowed the fighters to locate *Luftwaffe* bombers at night or in bad weather.

As radar became more sophisticated, air forces began using countermeasures, such as chaff (metal strips that reflected radar waves). On radar devices, chaff looked like an enemy formation. Raiders would drop the metal strips to divert interceptor resources from their planned targets and protect their planes.

The First Montessori Schools

You may have heard of Montessori schools, but what do you know about the woman behind them?

* * * *

WHEN MARIA MONTESSORI was a schoolgirl, a teacher asked if she'd like to become famous. "Oh, no," she answered, "I shall never be that. I care too much for the children of the future to add yet another biography to the list."

By any standard, Maria cared for the children. She was born on August 31, 1870, near Ancona, Italy. An excellent pupil, she went to technical school in 1886. After her graduation in 1890, she chose to study medicine—a strictly male field. At first, her father objected, and the medical school vetoed her desires— rather bluntly. Maria persisted, though, until they let her in.

As Montessori later explained, her movement really began on the street. She had just walked away from a dissection task, fed up with med school. As she moped down the street, a female beggar accosted Maria for money. The beggar woman's two-year-old sat on the sidewalk, her entire attention locked into play with a piece of colored paper. Seeing this child, oblivious to her poverty, sent Maria straight back to her grisly assignment with a new will. She soon earned a title then unique for an Italian woman: *La dottoressa* Montessori, of medicine.

In 1896, Montessori went to work with special-needs children. The status quo appalled her. Contemporary thinking classed them as "idiots" or "lunatics" and placed them in schools that were more jail than education. They were denied dignity, freedom, even anything to manipulate with their little hands. Montessori felt she knew what they needed. She believed she could help them through education.

Her chance came in 1899. Italy's educational bigwigs established Montessori in a small school composed of children rejected from mainstream schools. Most couldn't read. After two years, she sent her kids to take standardized tests. Not only did many pass, some did better than the mainstream students. It was nothing short of miraculous. Now Montessori had people's attention.

Task: Subdue the Hooligans

Montessori spent the next few years traveling, studying, thinking, experiencing, and doctoring. Then in 1906 Montessori was invited to take over a troubled preschool whose pupils were the rowdiest Rome had seen since Alaric the Visigoth. She was elated at the possibility: Given what happened with slower kids, what might children with typical intelligence manage?

Answer: Wonders. Montessori found that preschoolers had phenomenal powers of concentration. They loved repetition and preferred order to disorder. They responded very well to free choice of activity; work—not play—was their natural preference. They had a strong sense of personal dignity and flourished when that dignity was respected. They thrived on adult attention. And perhaps most shockingly: They taught themselves to write, a phenomenon called "explosion into writing." Reading soon followed. Unruliness gave way to great self-discipline and strong respect for others. They were now considered "great kids," which—of course—they always had been. Montessori had just found a way to let them show it.

From there, the Montessori movement gathered momentum. As she refined her methods, Montessori influenced educators all over the world, and her celebrity grew. By her death in 1952, a fair percentage of young adults in the child-development field were products of her approach. Fifty years and change since her passing, her methods remain popular.

Montessori didn't trademark her philosophy. You can use it without worrying about royalties, intellectual property lawyers, or cease-and-desist letters. Her life's work was her gift to children and to the future.

History's Great Escapes

Whether caught in the grip of wars hot and cold, palace intrigues, wilderness adventures gone wrong, or the consequences of their own misdeeds, men and women through the ages have risked great escapes to save their own lives and win their freedom.

✳ ✳ ✳ ✳

The Ballad of Mary

Though the throne of England would elude her, Mary, Queen of Scots, struggled most of her life to assume the crown she believed to be her birthright. Imprisoned in remote Lochleven Castle in 1567 during a rebellion of Scottish nobles, her pleas for help were ignored by Queen Elizabeth of England and Catherine de Medici, regent of France.

In March 1568, Mary attempted to escape by disguising herself as a laundress and fleeing by boat. Her plan was thwarted when the boatmen noticed her beautiful hands and face and suspected she was royalty. Mary managed to return to her cell without alerting her guards and tried again with the aid of an orphan she befriended in the castle.

On May 2, 1568, Mary escaped from the castle and rode to her freedom on a stolen horse—an exploit immortalized by Scottish poets, balladeers, and romantic novelist Sir Walter Scott. Her ultimate fate, however, was not as bright. She spent the last 19 years of her life imprisoned by her cousin, Queen Elizabeth I, and she was beheaded in 1587.

The World's Greatest Lover

Sentenced by a Venetian court to five years in prison in 1755 for Freemasonry, practicing magic, and numerous offenses of adultery, Giacomo Casanova was soon plotting his freedom.

Incarcerated in a Vienna prison called "the Leads" for the lead coating its walls and roof, escape at times seemed impossible to the young captive. He started work on a tunnel anyway, using an iron rod he found in the prison yard.

Several months into the project, Casanova was moved to another cell where he would be under close surveillance. He managed to slip his tool to a monk named Balbi who was imprisoned in an adjacent cell. Hiding messages in the spines of books they were allowed to trade, he convinced the monk to dig a tunnel joining their cells. After digging another tunnel from the monk's cell to the prison's roof, on the night of November 1, 1756, Casanova fled Venice in a stolen gondola—the only prisoner to that time to carry out a successful escape from the Leads.

Race with the Blackfoot

In 1808, John Colter, a member of the Lewis and Clark's expedition, and a hunter named Potts left the Corps of Discovery in the heart of Blackfoot Indian country to trap beaver on the Missouri River.

After a few weeks of trapping, Colter and Potts were paddling on a small creek when they found themselves surrounded by Blackfoot warriors. Potts killed a warrior who tried to take his rifle, and Potts was—in turn—shot full of arrows.

Colter was stripped naked, led to a nearby prairie, and given a head start of a few hundred yards to run for his life. With hundreds of warriors behind him, he ran six miles across a cactus-strewn plain, far outpacing the Indians except for one warrior. Colter eventually turned on his pursuer. The Indian collapsed from exhaustion, and Colter killed him with his own spear before diving into the river. The Blackfoot surrounded both banks looking for Colter, at one point climbing on a pile of floating driftwood under which he had ducked to hide. The Indians gave up after dark, and Colter swam downriver for miles before coming ashore, naked and alone.

Eleven days later, Colter walked into a trading post on the Yellowstone River more than a hundred miles away, sunburned and nearly starving—but alive.

On the Lam with Public Enemy No. 1

Among the gangsters whose bank robbery sprees riveted America at the height of the Great Depression, none was more notorious than John Dillinger. Imprisoned in the county jail in Lima, Ohio, on October 12, 1933, Dillinger was sprung by three members of his gang. Posing as lawmen, they shot the sheriff, set Dillinger free, and made their getaway. The group fled to Tucson, Arizona, where—months later—their cover was blown during a fire at their motel hideout.

Back in jail in Crown Point, Indiana, Dillinger bluffed his way out of his cell, reportedly using a homemade wooden gun. A few months later, Dillinger and his gang shot their way out of a bungled attempt by G-men to catch them at a remote resort in northern Wisconsin.

The FBI finally caught up with Dillinger on July 22, 1934, when he was gunned down as he left Chicago's Biograph movie theater.

Up, Up, and Away—Over the Iron Curtain

In September 1979, Peter Strelzyk, Günter Wetzel, their wives, and four children dropped from the night sky onto a field in West Germany in a homemade hot-air balloon.

Strelzyk and Wetzel had built the balloon's platform and burners in one of their basements. Their wives sewed random pieces of fabric together to make the 75-foot-high balloon. A bid to escape communist East Germany during the days of the Berlin Wall, their famous flight was two years in the making, spanned 15 miles, and took 28 minutes to complete. Unsure whether they had reached freedom, the two families spent the next morning hiding in a barn. When they saw an Audi traveling down a nearby road, they knew they had reached the West.

Hope Floats

It was a given: Boats made of metal would sink straight to the bottom of the ocean. And a heavier-than-air flying craft? Impossible!

✳   ✳   ✳   ✳

METAL SHIPS WERE such an obvious impossibility that no one made a serious effort to float steel until the end of the 18th century. Even after an enterprising shipbuilder crafted a canal barge in 1787 and Robert Dickenson patented a design for an iron ship in 1815, it was generally assumed that a sea-going vessel made of metal would sink.

Nine years passed between Dickenson's patent and the first attempt at building an iron passenger vessel (the Scottish vessel *Vulcan*), and no large navy dared field an iron-hulled fighting ship until Mexico bought one for its wars against Texas and Yucatán in the early 1840s.

At the other end of the transportation spectrum, the idea of a heavier-than-air flying machine was roundly ridiculed by the scientific establishment in the early 1900s. In 1902, the year before Wilbur and Orville Wright took their famous flight, the U.S. Navy's chief engineer declared the very idea "absurd." The following year, an eminent professor of mathematics and astronomy at Johns Hopkins University demonstrated to the world that a heavier-than-air craft was "scientifically impossible." Undeterred by this scientific pronouncement, the Wright brothers took their "flyer" to Kitty Hawk, North Carolina, a few weeks later and changed the world. Even after photographs circulated of the historic flight, the Wright brothers's hometown newspaper refused to print anything about their revolutionary contraption because, as the editor later admitted, "We didn't believe it."

Hollywood Versus History

You may not be surprised to learn that Hollywood doesn't always get history right.

✳ ✳ ✳ ✳

How about "bed-wetter"?
Alexander (2004)—Macedonian soldiers accuse Alexander of being a tyrant, which was no insult in Alexander's day.

Computer age-progression was so cool in the 18th century
The Man in the Iron Mask (1998)—Even though this film is about King Louis XVI as a young man, a portrait of an aged King Louis XVI is clearly visible at one point.

Everything sank but the schnitzel
Titanic (1943)—In this opulent Nazi version of the famed ship disaster, only one person aboard isn't a schemer and a braggart—a German national who serves on the ship's crew.

And the mayor is Latino
Chicago (2003)—A black prison matron oversees the Chicago women's jail—something highly unlikely in the ferociously segregated Chicago of the 1920s.

No, just horse flatulence
High Noon (1952)—In a shot where Gary Cooper stands in the middle of a street and the camera executes a graceful crane shot well above the ground, L.A. smog can be seen in the distance.

History is apparently willing to bend the rules
Guns Don't Argue (1957)—Everybody in this account of 1930s gangsters John Dillinger, "Ma" Barker, and others drives 1950s cars and sports 1950s wardrobes.

Oh, it could fly—it just couldn't *land*
GoodFellas (1990)—During a 1963 airport robbery, a 747 flies overhead. The 747 didn't fly until 1966.

The Story of Braille

How do you make up your own language? Louis Braille did it with equal parts perseverance and creativity.

✳ ✳ ✳ ✳

Ingredients

Take Louis Braille, an inquisitive, creative boy who lost his sight as the result of an accident he suffered at age three. Send him on scholarship to the National Institute for Blind Youth in Paris. Expose him to a cumbersome and slow method of reading. Now add a soldier from the French army by the name of Charles Barbier and his system, sonography, which used raised dots to represent sound. Barbier developed this language to help soldiers communicate in the field without drawing attention to their positions, but the army eventually nixed it for being too complex.

The Mixture

These ingredients laid the basis for Braille's work. Over time, Braille developed a system that could be recognized and understood by passing one's fingers over characters made up of an arrangement of one to six embossed points. Braille is a system made up of rectangles; each rectangle, or cell, has two columns and three rows. Each position has a particular number assigned to it—in the left column, moving down, the positions are numbered one, two, and three; in the right column, moving down, the positions are four, five, and six. Raised points at particular positions have specific meanings. For example, points raised at positions one, three, and four represent the letter *m*.

Because this system can be written with a stylus and a slate, the visually impaired have a means by which they can both read and write. Not only is that a recipe for further learning and efficient communication, but it's also a method by which they can increase their independence.

Barbed-Wire Revolution

In 1915, Robert Frost gave the world the line "Good fences make good neighbors." But fences have often meant much more than that; to the brave men and women of the Old West, fences meant nothing less than safety and survival. But what makes a "good" fence? In the American West, the answer was barbed wire—an invention that left its mark on an entire continent.

❊ ❊ ❊ ❊

As AMERICA'S SETTLERS spread out into its vast heartland, they tried to take their fences with them. However, in comparison with the rock-strewn fields of New England or the lush pine forests of the South from whence they came, the pioneers found their new environs to be lacking in suitable material with which to build barriers to protect their land. At the time, it was the responsibility of landowners to keep roving animals out of their fields (rather than it being incumbent upon the owner of the animals to keep them controlled). As a result, farmers were left to deal with the problem of how to protect their crops in conjunction with the impossibility of building their traditional fences. A new solution simply had to be found. The answer came from the state of Illinois, which was on the border between the civilized East and the wild West.

A Wayward Cow

In 1873, a farmer named Henry Rose was desperate to control a "breachy" cow. His original idea was to attach a board covered with metallic points directly to the head of his cow; when the cow ran into a fence, the points would prick the cow and cause it to retreat. It came as a surprise to Rose (though probably not to anyone else) that requiring his cow to wear a plank all the time proved impractical.

Rose then decided to attach the boards to his fence rather than to the cow. This solution seemed promising. Rose proudly showed off his invention at a county fair, where it caught the attention of a number of other inventors, including Joseph Glidden.

Glidden, working with a hand-cranked coffee mill in his kitchen, soon found that by twisting two lengths of wire together with a shorter piece in between to form a prickly barb, he could make a fence as effective as Rose's. He put up a test fence demonstrating his new invention, and word quickly spread. Isaac Ellwood, who had also seen Rose's display at the county fair and had been working on his own version, drove out to see Glidden's fence only to ride off in a rage when his wife commented that Glidden's barrier was superior to his. Ellwood was a shrewd businessman, however, and after he cooled down, he purchased an interest in Glidden's invention. The two went into business together making barbed-wire fencing. Joseph Haish, also inspired by the Rose invention, introduced a rival barbed-wire fence around the same time.

All that was left was to convince a doubtful public that a few strands of thin wire could hold back determined cattle. The innumerable herds of Texas would be the proving ground, as barbed-wire salesmen threw up enclosures and invited ranchers to bring their most ornery cattle. To the amazement of the onlookers, barbed wire proved equal to the task again and again. Sales skyrocketed.

Don't Fence Me In

Ironically, even though barbed wire's most obvious use was to protect farmers' fields, it wasn't until the cattle ranchers seized on barbed wire that it began to transform the West. After powerful ranchers realized they could effectively control the cattle industry by fencing off grazing land, miles of fencing sprang up across Texas and other territories. The fences weren't always well received; they injured cows and were sometimes put up without regard to traditional pasture or water rights. The winters of 1885 to 1887 were particularly brutal. Free-range cattle in northern ranges, accustomed to moving south in the face of impending blizzards, found their way blocked by the strange new fences. The cows froze to death by the thousands—carcasses stacked 400 yards deep against the fences in some places—in an event forever remembered as the Big Die-Up. Tempers naturally ran high, and there were open hostilities across the West, as armed factions cut down rival fences and put up new ones.

Despite the controversy, however, it proved impossible to reverse the trend to fence in land. Within about 25 years of the introduction of barbed wire, nearly all of what had previously been free-range land was fenced and under private ownership. The open land of the West, at one time considered an inexhaustible resource for all to use, was divided up and made off-limits to the general public. The new invention channeled people into fixed paths of transit centered around railroads and towns. These patterns evolved into the interstate highways and cities we know today. It's no exaggeration to say that barbed wire is responsible for the shape of the modern West—and it can all be traced back to one breachy cow.

"Where a new invention promises to be useful, it ought to be tried."

—THOMAS JEFFERSON

"An amazing invention—but who would ever want to use one?"

—RUTHERFORD B. HAYES, UPON MAKING A CALL FROM WASHINGTON TO PENNSYLVANIA WITH ALEXANDER GRAHAM BELL'S TELEPHONE, PATENTED ON MARCH 7, 1876

"Our inventions are wont to be pretty toys, which distract our attention from serious things. They are but improved means to an unimproved end."

—HENRY DAVID THOREAU

Brassieres: A *Bust*-ling Business

A simple strap of linen led to the padded, wired contraption that is the modern bra.

✳ ✳ ✳ ✳

IN ROMAN TIMES, women who had active jobs often wore straps of fabric around their busts to keep things stable. Thereafter, women vacillated wildly between incredibly restricting corsets and less restrictive support. In 1889, French *couturier* Herminie Cadolle created a two-piece undergarment that began to topple the reign of the corset. Cadolle's *soutien-gorge*, or "breast supporter" (the top half of the two-piecer), was an instant hit at the Great Exposition of 1900. Alas, it was still expensive to purchase, since it was made primarily of the same materials as the traditional corset.

In 1913, socialite Mary Phelps Jacob was dressing for her New York debut when she realized that the light, gauzy dress she'd selected would never go with her heavy corset. She enlisted the help of her maid, and the two of them stitched together two handkerchiefs with some ribbon. Jacob called her invention the "backless brassiere," and the name stuck.

Jacob was a society girl, not a businesswoman, and though she had the wherewithal to apply for a patent in 1914 for her new undergarment, she either didn't enjoy running the business or couldn't keep up with the demand. She eventually sold her patent to the Warner Brothers Corset Company for $1,500.

Perhaps if she'd been as creative with her product name as she had with the name she'd created to run the business—Caresse Crosby—she might have had better luck with the item. As it was, Jacob ended up becoming a fairly major literary influence, establishing two publishing imprints, and also founded the organization Women Against War.

"This . . . Is London!" Old-School Embedded Reporting

During World War II, CBS News broadcasters Edward R. Murrow and William Shirer assumed separate European beats and established the standard for live broadcast journalism.

✳ ✳ ✳ ✳

WHEN THE FIRST AM radio broadcast aired in 1906, enterprising listeners foresaw that the new medium would transform lives. By 1922, hundreds of radio stations were operating in the United States, and that number continued to increase as more households bought receivers. For the most part, radio shows were programmed, featuring music, sporting events, stories, news updates, and weather. The medium had seemed to reach a plateau in the 1930s, until a pioneer named Edward R. Murrow revolutionized radio journalism.

The New Voice of Radio

Murrow grew up in a small town and attended Washington State College, majoring in speech. He moved to New York after graduation and began planning radio broadcasts for CBS (Columbia Broadcasting System) in 1935.

In 1937, Murrow got a big break: CBS needed a new European director in London, and he landed the job. With tensions in Europe growing by the day, CBS would need a voice from the European continent to report on daily life and local culture. Hearing that seasoned European hand William Shirer was seeking work, Murrow made his pitch over dinner. While talking, the men arrived at the question, "Why report news after the fact? Why not report it from the scene?" Their thinking brought a whole new dimension to radio journalism.

In 1938, Murrow almost missed his chance for a momentous live broadcast. Just before Hitler's troops moved in to annex Austria, Murrow and Shirer were covering a series of children's choirs throughout eastern and central Europe. Murrow chartered a plane and arrived in Vienna to broadcast the Anschlüss.

Radio News Gets a New Format

Realizing the power of live broadcasts, CBS chief executive Bill Paley ordered his staff to broadcast live each night for a half hour. Murrow and Shirer were thrilled, and the news was fresh and authentic.

The new format, daily news broadcasts from multiple locations with analysis and commentary to follow, would outlast the war. As the situation across the world intensified, ears perked up. You couldn't easily get *The New York Times* on a Dakota wheat farm, but your whole family could hear history unfold on your farmhouse radio—and Ed Murrow's team would help you understand what you heard.

Murrow broadcasted from London rooftops during the Blitz with bomb explosions in the background: "This . . . is London!" One observer noted that although Blitz newsreel footage was in black and white, "Ed's radio reports were in color." He accompanied troops on bombing raids over Germany and recorded the events. The CBS news staff expanded to include many talented reporters, nicknamed "Murrow's Boys," all characterized by descriptive skill, intelligence, and daring.

Murrow chose his words carefully and revealed emotion in his broadcasts. One of his most powerful moments on the air came as the U.S. Army liberated the Buchenwald concentration camp:

"Murder had been done at Buchenwald. God alone knows how many men and boys have died there during the last 12 years. Thursday, I was told that there were more than 20,000 in the camp. There had been as many as 60,000. Where are they now?

"I pray you to believe what I have said about Buchenwald. I have reported what I saw and heard, but only part of it. For most of it, I have no words. If I have offended you by this rather mild account of Buchenwald, I'm not in the least sorry."

After the war, the partnership of Paley, Murrow, and Shirer would break up over various disputes, notably Paley's postwar commitment to television. Murrow left CBS in 1961 and died in 1965 of lung cancer. Paley remained a towering figure among media executives until his passing in 1990.

As for William Shirer, he gained particular fame for broadcasting from Berlin into autumn 1940, bringing Americans a powerfully honest perspective from Nazi Germany. Later he would write best-selling books based upon his experiences, notably *The Rise and Fall of the Third Reich*. Shirer died in 1993.

---

* Murrow didn't merely embellish his resumé to get hired at CBS; it was composed of out-and-out lies. He changed his major, added five years to his age, and awarded himself a master's degree from Stanford.

* The clincher for Murrow in hiring Shirer was that Paul White, Murrow's chief rival back at CBS New York, couldn't stand the sound of Shirer's voice. Deciding that anyone Paul White hated had to be all right, Murrow offered Shirer the job on the spot.

* One of "Murrow's Boys" was Mary Marvin Breckenridge, CBS's first female newscaster.

* During the early years of Hitler's rule, Murrow spent much of his time helping German scholars—Jewish and non-Jewish—escape persecution and find positions at U.S. universities.

* Hitler's original title for *Mein Kampf* (My struggle) was *Four Years of Struggle Against Lies, Stupidity, and Cowardice*.

Preston Tucker: Automobile Dreams

An old adage of invention is that if you build a better mousetrap, the world will beat a path to your door. In the case of Preston Tucker, he built a better car… but the resulting knock at his door came from the federal government.

✳ ✳ ✳ ✳

Preston Tucker couldn't leave things alone. In approximately 1919, at the young age of 16, he acquired an old car, fixed it up, and sold it. He was already demonstrating two of the skills that would occupy his life: building cars and selling them. These skills would lead Tucker to fame—if not quite to fortune.

Tucker briefly had a job on a Ford assembly line; he also worked as a police officer but was reprimanded for modifying his patrol car. He moved into car sales, tried his hand at modifying the engines of Indy race cars, and—after the onset of World War II—built vehicles for the military. His design for a combat car had an incredible top speed of around 120 miles an hour—well beyond the specifications provided by the military—and was rejected because it was *too* fast. However, the car's machine-gun turret was quickly adopted by the navy and eventually saw service on B-17 and B-29 bombers.

Following the war, America's automobile industry quickly returned to peacetime production. The easiest path for manufacturers was to recycle existing prewar designs with some cosmetic modification. In the booming postwar economy, demand was so high that cars essentially sold themselves.

Preston Tucker had other ideas. A wealth of knowledge related to aerodynamics, material science, and the craft of building high-performance engines had come out of the war. Tucker believed the American public would embrace a revolutionary automobile, and he set out to build "the car of the future."

"Where is my car?"

Tucker assembled a talented team of mechanics and other professionals, including designer Alex Tremulis, who had previously worked for automobile manufacturers Cord and Duesenberg. They went to work in the enormous Dodge Aircraft Engine Factory, a complex covering 475 acres in Cicero, Illinois, that had been used to build B-29 bombers during World War II. Tucker's car design was considerably advanced for the time: It would be powered by an engine designed for an aircraft and was to have four-wheel disc brakes, fuel injection, and magnesium wheels. Unfortunately, a number of the innovations were eventually cut in the interest of keeping the price of the car down. Still, their removal couldn't diminish the scope of Tucker's original vision.

The Tucker Torpedo, as it was called during design, was intended to be the safest car of the time: The dashboard was padded; the instrument panel was streamlined; a center front headlight would swivel to match the driver's steering; and the windshield was designed to harmlessly pop out in the event of a collision. The design also included seat belts, although—since no other car manufacturers were using them—some company officials were concerned that their presence would give the impression that the Tucker Torpedo was unsafe.

Tremulis had been given six days to design the car, and he succeeded. Two clay models were also built, but the 51 cars in the production run were largely constructed using only Tremulis's sketches as a reference. The Tucker 48s, as the final model of the car was called, were all hand-built—the factory never reached full production stage.

Tucker's Demise

The years 1947 to 1949 marked the end of the Tucker Corporation and its remarkable car. Concern over Tucker's fund-raising techniques—the company sold accessories and even licenses for dealerships before any cars actually existed—caused the Securities and Exchange Commission to launch an investigation that effectively put the company out of business. Investigators questioned whether Tucker ever really intended to mass-produce a car, and if he did, whether the company was capable of meeting production demands. Preston Tucker believed that the investigation was an attempt by rival auto-makers to crush his efforts so they wouldn't have to compete with the innovative Tucker 48 in the marketplace. In 1950, a jury acquitted Preston Tucker of wrongdoing, but by then it was too late—the company was already out of business.

After the trial, Preston Tucker continued with plans to produce a sports car in Brazil, but he died before his ideas could come to fruition. Of the Tucker 48s that were built, nearly all remain in existence, and they have become legendary in automotive circles. They regularly sell at auction in the $400,000 range, with one going for around $750,000—quite an increase over the original sticker price of $2,450. The vehicles themselves are proudly displayed in museums and at car shows around the world, and Preston Tucker's story was the subject of *Tucker: The Man and His Dream,* a 1988 Francis Ford Coppola movie starring Jeff Bridges as Tucker. While many of the features of the Tucker have found their way into the standard design of modern cars, none of these models can quite match the legend of the 1948 Tucker—an American original.

"That the automobile has practically reached the limit of its development is suggested by the fact that during the past year no improvements of a radical nature have been introduced."

—*Scientific American*, January 1909

America Goes to Kindergarten

Kindergarten—which literally means "children's garden" in German—is now considered a normal transition between home and full-time schooling for young children. But America was slow to warm to the idea.

✳ ✳ ✳ ✳

KINDERGARTEN WAS FIRST conceived in 1840 by German Frederich Froebel. He envisioned it as an introduction to art, mathematics, and natural history—a pre-education for children of all classes, as opposed to the custodial religious services that had been created for the offspring of the very poor. But after it became associated with radical feminist ideals, kindergarten was banned.

You Can't Keep a Good Idea Down

German liberals in exile, however, exported the idea to other countries: Bertha Ronge took it to England, and her sister Margarethe Meyer Schurz opened the first American kindergarten in Wisconsin in 1856. Elizabeth Palmer Peabody created the first English-speaking kindergarten, wrote many books about the topic, and edited a kindergarten-related newsletter. But it was Susan Elizabeth Blow who—in 1873—established the first public kindergarten, Des Peres School in St. Louis. By 1883, every St. Louis public school had a kindergarten, making the city a model for the nation.

The movement really garnered momentum after Commissioner of Education William Harris spoke to Congress on February 12, 1897, in support of public kindergartens: "The advantage to the community in utilizing the age from four to six in training the hand and eye; in developing the habits of cleanliness, politeness, self-control, urbanity, industry; in training the mind . . . will, I think, ultimately prevail in . . . the establishment of this beneficent institution in all the city school systems of our country."

Deceptively Soft

Silk is odd stuff. It's made out of cocoons, yet it looks and feels amazingly luxurious. This fabric has long connoted beauty, wealth, and power.

❋ ❋ ❋ ❋

❋ According to legend, Xi Ling-Shi, an emperor's wife, discovered silk more than 4,500 years ago. Xi was relaxing under a tree when a cocoon plopped into her teacup. Its fibers unraveled, revealing their strength and versatility.

❋ The Silk Road, named for its prized commodity, was a trade route between Asia and Europe that began around 200 B.C.

❋ China maintained a monopoly on silk until well after the fall of the Roman Empire.

❋ A strand of silk is significantly stronger than a strand of steel the same diameter.

❋ The silk fiber in a typical cocoon unrolls to a length of more than 3 football fields, or 360 yards.

❋ To produce a pound of silk, you need one-tenth of an ounce of silkworm eggs, which will hatch into 2,000 silkworms.

❋ The art of silk production is called sericulture. In proper sericulture, the sericin must be removed from the silk fiber. Sericin is a natural gum that protects the fiber but attracts and holds dirt and stains. It's great for the silkworm larva but not for a bridal gown.

❋ Silk's density is measured in mommes, abbreviated "mm." Weigh a bolt of silk 45 inches wide and 100 yards long. The bolt's weight in pounds is the mm rating of the silk.

❋ Raw silk begins at a density of about 40 mm. The lightest silks may weigh 5 mm or less.

* Wild-gathered silk cocoons are less economical to work with because the larva damages the fibers as it gnaws its way to hatching.

* Like many fabrics, silk has a back and a front. The properties of each side tell what sort of silk it is.

* As a woven fabric, silk has a warp and weft. The warp refers to the lengthwise threads; the weft describes the crosswise threads.

* That silky shimmer comes from the fibers' triangular shape. It's too small to see without magnification, but this prismatic quality bounces back incoming light at different angles.

Types of Silk

* **Raw silk** refers to any silk that contains sericin.

* **Charmeuse**—one of the most common kinds of silk—features a shimmering weave on the front and a flattened crepe on the back.

* **Dupioni** silk comes from cocoons spun by two worms "working" together, making the thread double strength.

* Some sericulturists use only wild and semi-wild silkworm cocoons to produce **ahimsa** silk. The silk is extracted from the cocoon after the silkworm has metamorphosed and left the cocoon, sparing the silkworm's life.

* **Tussah** silk comes from a wild silkworm that eats oak and juniper leaves and produces a large cocoon.

* Glossy **taffeta,** a plain-weave silk, can be made with different colors for the warp and weft, creating an interesting visual effect.

* **Organza** owes its crisp texture to the tight twist of its thread.

* **Chiffon**—the lightest silk—is airy and delicate.

A Discovery of Biblical Proportions

*While rounding up a stray animal in early 1947,
shepherd Mohammed el-Hamed stumbled across several
pottery jars containing scrolls written in Hebrew. It
turned out to be a find of immense consequence.*

✳   ✳   ✳   ✳

NEWS OF THE exciting discovery spurred archaeologists to
scour the area for additional material. Over a period of
nine years, the remains of approximately 900 documents were
recovered from 11 caves near the ruins of Qumran, a plateau
community on the northwest shore of the Dead Sea. The documents have come to be known as the Dead Sea Scrolls.

Tests indicate that all but one of the documents were created
between the middle of the 2nd century B.C. and the 1st century
A.D. Nearly all were written in one of three Hebrew dialects.
The majority of the documents were written on animal hide.

The scrolls are the earliest surviving copies of biblical documents. Approximately 30 percent of the material is from the
Hebrew Bible. Every book of the Old Testament is represented with the exception of Esther and Nehemiah. Another
30 percent of the scrolls contain essays on subjects including
blessings, war, and community rule. About 25 percent of the
material refers to Israelite religious texts not contained in the
Hebrew Bible, while 15 percent of the data has not been identified as of yet.

But What Does It All Mean?

Debate about the meaning of the scrolls has been intense.
One widely held theory subscribes to the belief that the scrolls
were created at the village of Qumran and then hidden by the
inhabitants. According to this theory, a Jewish sect known as
the Essenes wrote the scrolls. Those subscribing to this theory
have concluded that the Essenes hid the scrolls in nearby caves

during the Jewish Revolt in A.D. 66, shortly before they were massacred by Roman troops.

A second major theory, put forward by Norman Golb, professor of Jewish History at the University of Chicago, speculates that the scrolls were originally housed in various Jerusalem-area libraries and were spirited out of the city when the Romans besieged the capital in A.D. 68–70. Golb believes that the variety of conflicting ideas found in the scrolls indicates that the documents are facsimiles of literary texts.

The documents were catalogued according to which cave they were found in and have been categorized into biblical and nonbiblical works. Of the eleven caves, numbers 1 and 11 yielded the most intact documents, while number 4 held the most material—an astounding 15,000 fragments representing 40 percent of the total material found. Multiple copies of the Hebrew Bible have been identified, including 19 copies of the Book of Isaiah and 30 copies of Psalms. Also found were previously unknown psalms attributed to King David and stories about Abraham and Noah.

Getting the Word Out

Most of the fragments appeared in print between 1950 and 1965, with the exception of the material from Cave 4. Publication of the manuscripts was entrusted to an international group led by Father Roland de Vaux of the Dominican Order in Jerusalem. Access to the material was governed by a "secrecy rule"—only members of the international team were allowed to see them. Nearly 20 documents were published in late 1971, followed by the release of a complete set of images of all the Cave 4 material. The secrecy rule was eventually lifted, and copies of all documents were in print by 1995.

Many of the documents are now housed in the Shrine of the Book, a wing of the Israel Museum located in western Jerusalem. The scrolls on display are rotated every three to six months.

License to Drive

No one needed a license to ride a horse or drive a donkey cart. But then there's little chance of these animals slamming into one another at 30 miles per hour.

✳ ✳ ✳ ✳

WHY DID THE government stick its nose into driving? To understand this, it helps to consider the transition from animal to machine transportation. In the 1800s, roads were designed for horse, wagon, and foot traffic. While they were frequently dusty or muddy, they served their intended purpose well enough. Buildings weren't far from streets, so you couldn't make more room without knocking something down.

Now add an ever-increasing flow of noisy early automobiles trying to navigate the congestion without traffic control. The cars scared the horses, and spooked horses scared the pedestrians. Things were a mess.

Pressure for Change

By the late 1800s, any fool who could afford a motor vehicle was entitled to operate one. Even then, vehicles routinely achieved speeds that equaled that of a draft horse's gallop. But horseback riders didn't typically gallop their mounts through busy city streets, at least not any more than you would ride your mountain bike at full speed through a crowded mall.

As 1900 loomed, traffic had gone from being a mere annoyance to a growing public hazard. The new motorcars could be lethal (though on the positive side, they didn't void their bladders and bowels in the streets). One solution was to require drivers to obtain licenses, which could be revoked for bad driving.

Bringing Order

In the early 1900s, Germany and France became the first nations with mandatory licensing. The United States, which delegated the authority to individual states, proceeded slowly. In 1903, Massachusetts and Missouri became the first states to issue driver's licenses. Nearly 40 states had issued driver's licenses by 1935. Today all states do.

The driving test, which began in 1913 in New Jersey, gave the license meaning. Driver testing seeped into the system state by state, mainly between the 1930s and the 1950s. Of the first 48 states, South Dakota was the last to mandate licenses (1954) and driving tests (1959).

---

* America's modern interstate highway system was designed in the 1950s during the Eisenhower administration. Its primary purpose was not to enhance casual driving over long distances but to provide for efficient movement of military vehicles if and when necessary.

* Traffic lights were initially invented to control high horse-and-buggy traffic. The first, which only included red and green lights, was installed at a London intersection in 1868. Yellow was added in 1918.

* The first Ford automobiles featured engines made by Dodge. John and Horace Dodge built engines for the Ford Motor Company at their shop in Detroit.

* America's first federal gasoline tax, one cent per gallon, was instituted on June 6, 1932. By 2008, the rate was 18.4 cents per gallon.

The Brain of Roger Sperry

One of the most brilliant minds in recent history uncovered the truth behind how everyone else's mind really functions.

✳ ✳ ✳ ✳

Roger Sperry, the neurobiologist whose research helped redefine the common understanding of the human brain, was born in Hartford, Connecticut, in 1913. Sperry attended Oberlin College in Ohio on an academic scholarship. After receiving bachelor's and master's degrees from Oberlin, he performed doctoral work at the University of Chicago, receiving his degree in 1941. Following a stint at the National Institutes of Health, Sperry accepted a professorship at California Institute of Technology (Caltech), where his most famous and revolutionary work was to take place.

The "Dumb" Side of the Brain

When Sperry started his tenure at Caltech, mainstream scientific conclusions about the human brain were much different than they are today. Previous experiments had allegedly shown that the left hemisphere of the brain fueled human capacity for written and spoken language. This gave rise to the "classic" view of the brain, in which the left hemisphere was dominant and the seat of intellect, controlling all language mechanisms and higher functions. Under the classic theory, the right hemisphere was viewed as being inferior to the left, lacking higher cognitive functions.

The role of the corpus callosum, the fibrous tissue connecting the two hemispheres, was also poorly understood under this previous theory. In a cavalier display of ignorance, one neuroscience authority had even gone so far as to remark that it was there just to keep the two hemispheres from falling into each other. Most scientists believed that severing this tissue had no effect on the behavior and brain activity of the subject. Sperry's work at Caltech divulged the true role of the corpus callosum and turned conventional wisdom on its head.

Cutting Right to the Point

Sperry's studies on patients who'd undergone an operation severing the corpus callosum (as a treatment for epilepsy) found previous assumptions that the right hemisphere lacked all language skills were utterly wrong. Though unable to comprehend written language, the right hemisphere does understand spoken language and is the side that analyzes abstract meaning and physical space. Also, when tests were performed on the left brain to see if it had awareness about what was occurring in the right hemisphere during studies, it turned out to be completely unaware of them.

From these studies, called "Split-Brain" experiments, it was shown that brain functions are spread across the two hemispheres. While the left hemisphere is largely dedicated to sequential and verbal tasks such as reading and counting, the right hemisphere excels at spatial reasoning and contextual analysis of language. There is no "dumb" half and "super" half, just a delegation of duties. Pop culture latched onto this idea, but in his Nobel lecture, Sperry warned that talk of purely "left-brained" or "right-brained" individuals is a gross distortion of the true state of affairs. Under normal circumstances, a healthy corpus callosum transfers information between the left and right halves, allowing the hemispheres to work closely together as a functional unit, sharing duties.

* Scientists say that the average human brain can easily remember no more than seven numbers in random sequence at a time.

* Human thumbs have their very own "control room" in the brain, separate from the control area of the other digits on the hand.

* The average Neanderthal had a brain that was larger than yours.

Chapter 2

Momentous Events

"God Wills It!"

Pope Urban II's call to arms in 1095 set off a war for the Holy Land that would change the course of history.

✳ ✳ ✳ ✳

THE FIRST CRUSADE (1096–99) was born of a pope's desire to safeguard the holy sites of Palestine for Christian pilgrims and to assert papal influence over the kingdoms of Western Europe. One sermon, given in late 1095, did more to change the course of the second millennium than any other speech in history.

The Crusades Begin

The Crusades were born of a desire to roll back an Islamic empire that stretched from Afghanistan to northern Spain. In the 7th and 8th centuries, while many European nobles spent their time fighting one another, a wave of Arab-led, Islam-inspired armies thundered across North Africa, Central Asia, the southern Mediterranean, and the Iberian Peninsula, gobbling up huge chunks of territory—many of which were torn out of the predominantly Orthodox Christian Byzantine Empire.

It did not take a political genius to figure out that Western Europe could set aside brewing political and social differences by uniting against a dangerous enemy espousing a different religion. In 1074, Pope Gregory VII issued a call for Christian soldiers to rush to the aid of the Byzantine Empire; they may have been Orthodox Christians, but they were Christians nonetheless, and they were being threatened by the great imperial powers of the age, the Islamic Caliphates.

The publicity surrounding the pope's pleas attracted the attention of Christian pilgrims, who began visiting the Holy Land in record numbers. When priests began spreading tales of Muslims robbing Christian pilgrims on their way to Jerusalem, Europe was ripe for a battle over Palestine.

Urban's Call to Arms

Enter Pope Urban II. Elected in 1088, this savvy French priest carried out his diplomatic duties with finesse. When Emperor Alexius I of Byzantine called for help against the Muslim hordes, Urban was happy to oblige. He summoned bishops from all over Europe to Clermont, France. Once some 300 bishops had assembled in an open-air forum, Urban gave them a barn-burner of a sermon. He exhorted the Christians of Europe to take up arms to drive back the Muslim armies occupying the Holy Land.

Knowing his real audience was the kings, princes, and nobles who would be asked to send soldiers into battle, the cagy Urban was quick to point out the material benefits of a conquest of eastern lands. He proclaimed:

"This land which you inhabit, shut in on all sides by the seas and surrounded by the mountain peaks, is too narrow for your large population; nor does it abound in wealth; and it furnishes scarcely food enough for its cultivators ... Enter upon the road to the Holy Sepulcher; wrest that land from the wicked race, and subject it to yourselves."

The kicker, of course, was that the crusaders would have a spiritual carte blanche to kill and conquer. "God has conferred upon you above all nations great glory in arms. Accordingly undertake this journey for the remission of your sins, with the assurance of the imperishable glory of the kingdom of heaven," Pope Urban II said.

Urban's sermon wowed the bishops and nobles in attendance, who left the council chanting, "*Deus vult!*" ("God wills it!") European peasants, knights, and nobles answered Urban's call, and over the next year, a hodgepodge of crusaders (generally grouped into the unsuccessful "People's Crusade" and the more successful "Princes' Crusade") took up the Cross, looking for heavenly rewards, material treasure, and great victory.

Conquest of the Holy Land

The Crusades didn't get off to much of a start. The thousands of hungry, ill-supplied peasants who had joined the People's Crusade were neither trained nor organized, and they were quickly massacred once they set foot into Seljuk Turk territory. But the roughly 7,000 knights of the Princes' Crusade managed to capture Antioch, north of Jerusalem, in 1098. The following year, the crusading army—about 1,500 knights, supported by some 12,000 men-at-arms—reached Jerusalem, which it captured after a brief siege. The crusaders capped their victory by massacring men, women, and children of all faiths in all sections of the holy city. They set up the Kingdom of Jerusalem, which they ran as a Christian fiefdom until it fell to Saladin and his Arabian armies in 1187.

Echoes Through the Ages

The First Crusade set in motion a seesaw battle between the Christian west and the Islamic east that lasted another two centuries. As chunks of the Holy Land fell to one army or another, Urban's successor popes used the Crusades as a way to unite Europe. But the Crusades—and the orgies of blood they incited—left a bitter legacy. The rancor that the Crusades caused among both Christians and Muslims has persisted to this day, and even now the word "crusader" evokes very different feelings among Westerners and Middle Easterners.

A Short History of the Shortest War

*The British proved that it only takes 38 minutes to destroy
a palace, depose a king, sink a navy, and burn a harem.*

✳ ✳ ✳ ✳

No Friend of the Queen

O N THE MORNING of August 27, 1896, the new Sultan of
Zanzibar, Khalid bin Barghash, a 29-year-old who had
been sultan for a mere 48 hours, awoke to the sight of five
British warships anchored in the harbor just outside his palace.

Things were not going well for young Khalid. Although
he enjoyed the support of his people and had a legitimate
claim to the throne, the British were unhappy with him. In
a clearly worded communication to Queen Victoria, Khalid
had expressed his hope that friendly relations could continue
between his country and England but stated he could not
abandon the "house of his fathers." Meanwhile, the British felt
they could not tolerate the rule of a man they considered far
too traditional.

An Uneven Contest

To convince Khalid that he should abdicate the throne, the
British hastily assembled a fleet that, though small in number,
boasted the largest concentration of artillery ever deployed
in East Africa at the time. The Zanzibari navy consisted
of a showpiece called the *Glasgow*, a wooden steam vessel
equipped with ancient, muzzle-loading cannons. The crew
of the *Glasgow* affirmed their allegiance to Khalid—as did
almost 3,000 Zanzibari soldiers and loyalists who occupied
the palace—and prepared for a siege.

They didn't have to wait long. Just before the deadline hour of
9:00 A.M., the captain of the *Glasgow* was rowed to his ship,
which was anchored amongst the formidable British vessels.

The British took this as a sign that Khalid would not capitulate without a lesson.

A Short Lesson

At 9:05 A.M., the British warships opened fire. The *Glasgow* bravely returned fire but was soon sinking in the harbor's shallow water. The barrage on the palace was intense. By some estimates, more than a thousand shells were fired by the British ships that morning. Finally, the smoke obscuring the target and the complete cessation of return fire caused the British to stop their bombardment. The royal harem next to the palace was fiercely ablaze, and the palace itself had been reduced to ruins. The war was over less than 40 minutes after it had begun.

Aftermath

Khalid survived the bombardment and fled to the German embassy where he was given sanctuary for several weeks before escaping to Dar es Salaam. The royal palace was utterly destroyed and never rebuilt. The harem, however, was soon replaced. Khalid's British-supported successor, Hamoud bin Mohammed, made good on his promise to begin the modernization of his country. His first step was to outlaw slavery, and for this he was decorated by Queen Victoria.

* Zanzibari succession practices were once described as the crown falling to the eligible candidate with "the longest sword."

* Some believe that Zanzibar was originally a 1st-century outpost of the Queen of Sheba.

* After the destruction of the palace, Khalid never again set foot upon British soil. Instead he stepped directly from the German embassy, where he had sought sanctuary, onto a boat.

* The world's longest war is commonly considered to be that which existed between the Netherlands and Isles of Scilly off the Cornish Coast. War was declared by the Netherlands during the confusing years of the English Civil War (1642–51), and the proclamation was forgotten until 1985. Officially, the war lasted 335 years.

A Violent Run for the Roses

Power—not flowers—was at stake in the Wars of the Roses, a series of battles and skirmishes between two branches of England's royal family. The Lancaster clan had the throne, and the York clan wanted it. Then the tables turned and turned again.

✳ ✳ ✳ ✳

ONE DRAWBACK TO monarchies is that they often lead to quarrels over whose turn it is to sit on the throne. Brother turns against brother, son against father, and so on. More than 500 years ago, such a disagreement between noble cousins grew into a squabble that split England's ruling class into armed camps and repeatedly tore up the countryside.

The House of Lancaster and the House of York were branches of the royal Plantagenet family, descendents of King Edward III, who ruled from 1327 to 1377. The Wars of the Roses began in 1399, when Henry of Bolingbroke, a grandson of Edward III, ended the disastrous reign of his cousin, Richard II, and took the throne himself. Also known as the Duke of Lancaster, the new king, now Henry IV, founded the Lancastrian Dynasty. He passed his scepter down to son Henry V, who in turn passed it to his then nine-month-old son, Henry VI in 1422.

The Yorkist Claim

Lancastrian heirs might have continued this streak indefinitely, but pious Henry VI preferred the spiritual realm to his worldly kingdom, which sorely needed leadership. Worse, the king developed a mental disorder resulting in periodic breakdowns.

After Henry VI's 1453 breakdown, the powerful Earl of Warwick appointed the Duke of York to fill in as protector of the realm. York, an able leader, was also a descendent of Edward III and boasted a family tree that arguably made him a better claimant to the crown than the sitting king.

York earned the fierce enmity of the queen, Margaret of Anjou, who wielded more actual power than her husband did and who feared York would steal the throne. Battles ensued, beginning in 1455, with York defeating the royal forces more than once. In 1460, Lancastrian forces killed York in a sneak attack. The Yorkist cause passed to his 18-year-old son, Edward, who won a decisive battle, ran King Henry and Queen Margaret out of the country, and had himself crowned Edward IV in 1461.

The wars went on, however, as the new king clashed with his father's old supporter, the Earl of Warwick. For a time, Warwick got the upper hand and put addled King Henry back on the throne. Edward prevailed in 1471, however, and maintained order until his death in 1483.

The Fight Resumes and Ends

Edward IV's young son briefly succeeded him as Edward V, but the boy's uncle, brother of the late king, appears to have pulled a fast one. The uncle pushed little Eddie aside and became Richard III, one of England's most notorious monarchs. His notoriety is based on the widespread belief that Richard III murdered his two defenseless young nephews—Edward V and a younger brother.

For that reason and others, Richard lost the backing of many nobles, who flocked to support another royal claimant, Henry Tudor, the Earl of Richmond. A Welshman, this new contender also descended from Edward III on the Lancaster side.

Tudor famously killed Richard III in battle and became Henry VII, founder of England's Tudor Dynasty. He married the Yorkist heiress, the late Edward IV's daughter Elizabeth, in 1485, consolidating the family claim and ending, finally, the Wars of the Roses.

＊ These civil wars were called the Wars of the Roses because the symbol of the House of Lancaster was a red rose while the symbol of the House of York was a white rose.

The First World's Fair: A Smashing Success

England's hugely popular 19th-century exhibition set the standard by which all subsequent World's Fairs would be measured.

✳ ✳ ✳ ✳

I N HER DIARY on May 1, 1851, Queen Victoria could barely contain herself: "This day is one of the greatest and most glorious in our lives," she gushed. England's monarch wasn't referring to a glorious military triumph, but to the opening of the awkwardly named "Great Exhibition of the Works of Industry of all Nations," or, as it later came to be identified, the first World's Fair.

Who could blame Victoria for such lavish overstatement? Her husband, Prince Albert, was in charge of the great event. No doubt influenced by the successful French Industrial Exposition of 1844, the prince formed the Royal Commission for the Exhibition of 1851 to look into ways of bringing a similar event to England.

Held at the height of the Industrial Revolution, the Great Exhibition's objective was to demonstrate the leading manufacturing and engineering achievements of the day and to display the top arts and crafts that the world had to offer. Some contemporary cynics—including philosopher Karl Marx—sneered at the event, dismissing the inaugural Expo as a thinly disguised attempt for England to show off its economic, industrial, and military might.

And show off it did. On the premises of London's Hyde Park rose the event's centerpiece, the famous Crystal Palace, which would be imitated at subsequent World's Fairs. The structure, made of iron and glass and resembling a massive greenhouse, housed more than one million exhibits from England, its 15 colonies, and 25 other countries around the globe.

On opening day, 300,000 visitors paid their shilling entrance fee and eagerly made their way through the Expo, marveling at such displays as the world's largest organ, a knife with 80 blades, a prototype for a submarine, and the world's first life-size re-creations of dinosaurs.

The U.S. exhibits included such diverse offerings as furniture made out of coal, a Colt revolver, modern kitchen appliances, a model of Niagara Falls, and an astounding envelope machine that could process 60 pieces of mail per minute.

The event was popular right from the start and became an overwhelming success when organizers dropped the price to a penny to allow working families to take part in the festivities. Special train services were set up to run from all parts of England to London. When the doors finally closed in October 1851, more than six million people had filed through the Crystal Palace—almost a third of England's population.

Curiously, the contraption that drew the most attention and proved to have lasting value wasn't even an official exhibit. Public flush toilets made their debut at London's Expo: a brilliant innovation for which fair-goers ever since have been truly grateful.

---

* The immensely popular Crystal Palace was relocated after the fair so it could be made permanent. It was subsequently lost in a 1936 fire.

* Chicago's 1893 World's Fair introduced the Ferris wheel.

* The 1904 World's Fair in St. Louis, Missouri, marked the debut of iced tea.

* At the 1939 World's Fair in New York, Franklin Delano Roosevelt became the first president to appear on television.

* The Space Needle, located in Seattle, Washington, was built for the 1962 World's Fair.

Henry VIII Is Excommunicated

On April 20, 1534, a taut rope on the Tyburn gallows in Westminster, England, strangled the life out of a popular and charismatic 28-year-old nun. Elizabeth Barton, the "Holy Maid of Kent"—a veritable homegrown Joan of Arc—had become an unlikely public spokesperson against King Henry VIII. She claimed that God had told her (via a series of visions) that he would visit his vengeance upon the middle-aged king for defiling a divinely consecrated marriage. The king responded as he would to others who stood in his way (such as Sir Thomas More, author of Utopia, *the following year): Their opposition made them traitors, and therefore they had to die.*

✳ ✳ ✳ ✳

THE PREVIOUS YEAR, Henry had, in defiance of the pope, divorced his first wife Catherine of Aragon to marry one of Catherine's ladies-in-waiting, the charming and sophisticated (and pregnant!) Anne Boleyn. To marry Anne, Henry had not only to contravene the reigning Catholic Church's prohibition against divorce, he also had to face actual excommunication. The Church of England was the phoenix that ultimately rose from the ashes.

Although some accounts of Henry VIII's break with Rome portray the split as "King Marries Temptress, Starts Own Church," the historical reality is slightly more complex.

On one hand, Henry was undeniably enraptured with Anne. Seventeen of his love letters to her—nine of them in French, a language in which both were fluent but precious few other Englishmen were—can be perused today at the Vatican Library in Rome. Henry tells his mistress in one missive that "for more than a year, [I've been] struck with the dart of love." Elsewhere he implores her to give "body and heart to me, who will be, and has been, your most loyal servant."

On the other hand, Henry's extramarital love life wasn't happening in a historical vacuum either. In 1529, what historians now call "the Reformation Parliament" clapped economic and political shackles upon the operation of the Catholic Church in England—regulating excessive fees the church had levied for burials, reducing clergy's ability to make money on the side, and eliminating their de facto above-the-law status by subjecting church officials to the same secular courts as any English commoner.

The Church of England Is Born

What momentum Parliament had established was compounded by the rise of two reformist members of Henry's court in the early 1530s: Thomas Cranmer (made Archbishop of Canterbury, the highest ecclesiastical position in the nation, in 1533) and Thomas Cromwell (Henry VIII's chief advisor and principal minister). The two Thomases provided the political and theological muscle to establish an independent church body and, with it, put the squeeze on the Catholic Church in England. In 1533, Cranmer ensured swift approval by his bishops of the annulment of King Henry's first marriage, while at the same time Cromwell's Act in Restraint of Appeals effectively set forth the English monarch as ruler of the British Empire, rendering the papacy irrelevant by deriving a monarch's authority directly from God. The pope, thanks to Cromwell's legislative strong-arm, suddenly had no claim over true English subjects.

Naturally, Pope Clement VII did not take this news lightly. After three months of threats, Clement excommunicated Henry VIII in September 1533. Though true theological reform of the fledgling Anglican Church into a bona fide Protestant sect would have to wait for the brief but outsized reign of Henry's only son, Edward VI (reign 1547–53), there was no turning back. The Church of England had been born.

The Fallout

Both the inspiration and the instigators of the break with Rome eventually met with gruesome deaths: Boleyn lasted all of three years as her king's wife before Henry, in concert with Cromwell, rounded up four courtiers and servants to Boleyn who were all variously charged with luring Boleyn away from the marriage bed. Boleyn was swiftly tried for adultery and beheaded in May 1536. Cromwell lasted only four more years before he too became victim to the capricious whims of his monarch. For proposing a disastrous fourth marriage to Anne of Cleves, Cromwell faced a rigged jury, was found guilty of treason and, at the king's behest, faced the further brutality of an inexperienced executioner. Three unsuccessful ax blows drew out Cromwell's pain before a fourth severed his head, which was then boiled and placed on a pike on London Bridge.

Cranmer outlived his king and his king's son, only to face the furies of the brutally anti-Protestant queen "Bloody" Mary Tudor (reign 1553–58).

Yet perhaps it was Anne Boleyn herself who bequeathed the greatest legacy in the form of her daughter, who took the reins of power at Queen Mary's death. The frail young princess, not expected to survive any longer than her siblings, instead enjoyed a prosperous 45 years on the throne as perhaps England's greatest monarch, Queen Elizabeth I. Under Elizabeth, the Church of England established itself as the ecclesiastical force that underpinned the rise of a true global empire—on whose influence, to this day, the sun never sets.

✳ In total, Henry VIII married six times: Catherine of Aragon, Anne Boleyn, Jane Seymour, Anne of Cleves, Catherine Howard, and Catherine Parr.

✳ Henry had two of his six wives executed (Anne Boleyn and Catherine Howard). He divorced two (Catherine of Aragon and Anne of Cleves). Jane Seymour died and was the only one of Henry's wives to be buried with him. Catherine Parr was widowed after four years of marriage.

How Long Was the Hundred Years' War?

Although a monumental medieval-era struggle between England and France lasted more than 100 years, the actual fighting took only a fraction of that period. So how long did the war really last? It depends how you do the math.

❊   ❊   ❊   ❊

King of England, King of France

A LEGAL DISPUTE OVER the French crown turned violent in 1337, sparking the Hundred Years' War. English nobles believed that their king, Edward III, was next in line to rule France because his mother was sister to French King Charles IV, who had no direct male heir. French nobles, uneasy at the idea of an English king of France, disagreed. Their choice was nobleman Philip of Valois, who claimed that his own lineage from a 13th-century French king—through his father—gave him the more legitimate claim to the throne.

After Valois was crowned Philip VI, Philip attacked Edward's forces in Aquitaine, a region in France long ruled by England. Many English invasions of France followed, with the English—whose claims to French lands dated to 1066—repeatedly gaining ground and the French repeatedly striking back.

Peace Breaks Out

Although successive English kings steadfastly claimed the right to rule France, England lacked the resources to fight nonstop over many decades. It had other conflicts to deal with—military campaigns in Ireland, for example—and domestic strife such as the 1399 coup when Henry Bolingbroke stole the English crown from his cousin Richard II and became Henry IV.

France, meanwhile, fought other battles, too—including rebellious outbreaks by French nobles against the crown. Out of necessity, both sides agreed to long truces with one another. For example, peace was realized in 1360 and lasted nine years.

Sometimes the warring royal families cemented a truce with intermarriage. In 1396, England's Richard II married Princess Isabelle, the six-year-old daughter of French king Charles VI. Twenty-four years later, England's Henry V married Isabelle's younger sister Catherine as part of a treaty he imposed on the French after his crushing victory at the battle of Agincourt in 1415 and after another successful campaign in 1417–1419.

The Culmination

Although English invaders won major territorial concessions from the French over most of the war's duration, the tide turned in France's favor in 1429. That was when the peasant girl Joan of Arc rallied French forces and freed the city of Orléans from an English siege. The next 23 years saw the most intense fighting of the Hundred Years' War, culminating with a French victory at the Battle of Castillon in 1453. England lost all of its lands on the European continent except for the port city of Calais.

The English didn't give up their claim to France for centuries—but with the Wars of the Roses breaking out at home, they stopped attacking their continental neighbor. The Hundred Years' War ended after 116 years. It's correct to say that the war lasted well over a century, but it's just about impossible to subtract all the lulls and truces with accuracy. If you could, you would come out with fewer than 100 years of actual fighting.

"We make war that we may live in peace."

—ARISTOTLE

Francisco Pizarro and the Ransom of an Emperor

In 1532, Spanish explorer Francisco Pizarro—already a veteran of several expeditions to the New World—set out to conquer Peru. Through a combination of good luck and sheer hubris, Pizarro and his men met with astounding success. The most notable victim of their conquest was the Incan Emperor Atahualpa, who sought to bargain for his freedom by playing on Spanish greed.

✳ ✳ ✳ ✳

Fortune Favors the Bold

THE MORNING OF November 16, 1532, found Francisco Pizarro in a dodgy position. The would-be conqueror of Peru and his 150 men were camped in the village of Cajamarca awaiting the arrival of Atahualpa, emperor of the Inca. Atahualpa had agreed to meet with the strangers, and he was bringing his army with him. The approach of the Inca—80,000 strong— could be seen for miles, and the disparity in numbers caused no small amount of worry among the Spanish soldiers.

Pizarro, however, was made of sterner stuff. Hernán Cortés had conquered the Mexican Aztecs scarcely a dozen years earlier against similar odds, and Pizarro was determined to do no less. Regardless of the risks, Pizarro would go through with the meeting, promising to receive Atahualpa as a "friend and brother." If the emperor proved too strong, the ruse would be kept up; if not, the audacious plan was to demand political submission. If Atahualpa refused, he would be taken hostage.

The Conquistador Versus the Living God

The emperor entered town as the sun was setting, leaving most of his army to camp half a mile away. However, he was still personally accompanied by a retinue that numbered in the thousands. Atahualpa himself, bedecked in emeralds and wearing a crown and parrot feathers, rode ensconced on a gold-plated litter carried high by 80 finely dressed Incan nobles. When he momentarily halted, he was greeted by Vicente de Valverde, a Dominican friar accompanying the Spanish expedition. Valverde invited Atahualpa to dine with Pizarro—possibly a trick designed to separate the emperor from his men. When the invitation was declined, Valverde extended a crucifix and Bible, asking the Incan ruler to embrace the Christian faith and acknowledge himself a vassal of the Holy Roman Emperor. Predictably enough, Atahualpa did not look favorably on the friar's suggestion and slapped the book into the dirt. Atahualpa then demanded that the Spanish return all that they had stolen since arriving in his lands.

Tempers flared, and the Spanish opened fire. Concealed cannons tore into the massed Incan party, and Spanish horsemen cut through the crowd like a scythe. The sudden eruption of fire and noise, combined with the strange sight of mounted troops, threw the native force into a panic. After just minutes, the Incas were unable to mount an effective defense. They trampled each other underfoot, and many suffocated from the mass of their own numbers. The emperor's bearers continued to physically support him as long as they lived, some trying to carry him on their shoulders after their hands were severed by Spanish swords. Escape proved impossible, however, and the emperor was captured. Pizarro himself saved Atahualpa's life by parrying a blow from a Spanish soldier intent on killing the Incan leader. The clash was nothing less than a slaughter. Incan estimates put the number of local troops killed at 10,000 in less than two hours.

Business as Usual

After the bloody encounter, Atahualpa quickly adopted a pragmatic outlook. As he dined that night with Pizarro from seats overlooking a courtyard still littered with fallen men, Atahualpa dismissed the episode as "the fortune of war." The emperor blamed himself for the outcome; he had underestimated the Spaniards. Aware of the European thirst for treasure, Atahualpa sought to buy his freedom, promising to fill a room measuring 22 feet by 17 feet by 8 feet high with gold in exchange for his release. Pizarro agreed, and a cooperative Atahualpa continued to manage his empire from captivity. His top priority was to instruct his people to collect the ransom.

Pizarro was certainly interested in Atahualpa's gold, but he was in no particular hurry to see the process of collection finished. Atahualpa's word was the equivalent of divine law to the Incan people—a very useful resource for an outnumbered invader trying to control an entire country. However, as the treasure accumulated and Spanish reinforcements arrived, Atahualpa became progressively less important to the Spanish. The situation climaxed in August 1533, when Atahualpa was led forth to be executed by burning at the stake—a sentence that was reduced to death by garrote when the emperor requested baptism into the Christian faith at the last moment. After asking Pizarro to care for his children, Atahualpa was strangled to death as the assembled Spaniards offered prayers for his soul.

The Soldier Gets a Tongue-Lashing

The massacre of the Incas was largely seen as inconsequential at the time—a mere product of the way war was conducted. Indeed, the Incan leader himself said had their positions been reversed, he would have sacrificed some of the Spanish to the sun god while castrating the rest and using them to guard his concubines. However, many in Spain saw the execution of Atahualpa, a captive under Spanish protection, as murder and a scandal. Perhaps most notably, Holy Roman Emperor Charles V regarded the execution of a monarch by a common soldier as a bad precedent. Charles officially reprimanded Pizarro—another blow to the prestige of the fortune-hunting soldier.

European guilt notwithstanding, there is no record of the millions of pesos Pizarro sent back to Spain being anything but welcome.

Plight of the Pilgrims: Journey to the New World

When the Pilgrims began their voyage to the New World, they didn't expect to sail on the Mayflower, nor did they plan to land at Plymouth Rock.

✴ ✴ ✴ ✴

Destination: Holland

THE STORY OF the Pilgrims begins back in 1606—14 years before they set sail on the *Mayflower*.

A band of worshippers from Scrooby Manor, who belonged to the Church of England, decided that they would rather worship God according to the Bible than indulge in the extra prayers and hymns imposed by the church. However, separating from the church was easier said than done. In England, it was illegal to be a Separatist. Risking imprisonment, the worshippers escaped to Holland, a land of religious tolerance. But their time in Holland was a mixed blessing. Although they worshipped freely, they feared their children were becoming more Dutch than English.

Destination: Hudson River

Meanwhile, English noblemen were seeking brave, industrious people to sail to America and establish colonies in Virginia (which extended far beyond the Virginia we know today). They offered the Separatists a contract for land at the mouth of the Hudson River, near present-day New York City.

Led by William Brewster and William Bradford, the Separatists accepted the offer and began preparing for their voyage. They even bought their own boat: the *Speedwell*. In July 1620, they sailed to England to meet 52 more passengers who rode in their own ship, the *Mayflower*. The Separatists, who called themselves "Saints," referred to these new people as "Strangers."

Destination: Unknown

The *Speedwell* should have been called the *Leakwell*. After two disastrous starts, the Saints abandoned hope of her sailing again. On September 6, they joined the Strangers on the *Mayflower*.

The *Mayflower* was just 30 yards long—about the length of three school buses. The 50 Saints rode in the "tween" deck, an area between the two decks that was actually the gun deck. Its ceilings were only about five feet high.

Accommodations in the rest of the boat were hardly better. Cramped into close quarters were 52 Strangers, 30 crewmen (who laughed at the seasick landlubbers), 2 dogs (a spaniel and a mastiff), barley, oats, shovels, hammers, tools, beer, cheese, cooking pots, and chamber pots. There may have been pigs on board too.

As they journeyed across the Atlantic, storms and rough waters pushed them off course. After 65 days on the high seas, they realized they were nowhere near the Hudson River. Instead, they sighted the finger of Cape Cod—more than 220 miles away from their destination.

Though they were far from the land contracted for the English colony, the settlers saw their arrival in the New World as an opportunity to build a better life. In November 1620, more than 40 free men (Saints and Strangers alike) signed the Mayflower Compact. They agreed to work together for the good of the colony and to elect leaders to create a "civil body politic."

But What About Plymouth Rock?

After anchoring in a harbor (which is now Provincetown), the Saints formed three expeditions to locate a suitable place to live. One expedition ventured 30 miles west to a place called "Plimouth," which had been mapped several years earlier by explorer John Smith.

The settlers first noticed a giant rock, probably weighing 200 tons, near the shore. The land nearby had already been cleared. Likely, more than a thousand native people had lived there before being wiped out by an epidemic. Some remaining bones were still visible.

In December 1620, the group decided to make Plymouth its settlement. According to legend, each passenger stepped on Plymouth Rock upon landing. If this actually happened, leader William Bradford did not record it.

By springtime, half of the *Mayflower*'s passengers would be dead. Yet their accomplishments remain important. Helped by the native people, the Saints and Strangers would live and work together to form one of the first British settlements in North America.

---

* How do we know all of this? William Bradford kept a detailed journal, now known as *Of Plymouth Plantation.* In it, he detailed the history of the Plymouth colony between the years of 1630 and 1647.

* The "First Thanksgiving" was little more than a harvest feast. Thanksgiving was not an official holiday until 1863, when Abraham Lincoln proclaimed a national day for giving thanks.

* The journey to America left the pilgrims deeply in debt to English merchants who had financed the trip. The early fruits of pilgrim labor were used to repay the debt.

* Pieces of Plymouth Rock can be seen today at Pilgrim Hall Museum, as well as at the Smithsonian.

* According to estimates, Plymouth Rock is now only about one-third its original size. Over the years, the rock has been broken during attempts to move it, and people have chipped off pieces to take as souvenirs.

* The first historical references to "Plymouth Rock" appeared more than 100 years after the pilgrims landed.

The American Revolutionary War

How did the ramshackle colonists manage to win their independence from the mighty British?

❋ ❋ ❋ ❋

MANY AMERICANS CHALK it up to British stupidity and Yankee ingenuity. "The boneheaded British," they might say, "marched like scarlet practice targets while the colonials picked them off from behind rocks and trees." Hogwash.

In fact, the British massed volley system forced soldiers to do everything in unison. If you let every soldier fight his own way, your force is far less effective. Some would simply run away; others would stick around, crying and praying. More soldiers than you think would shoot blindly, even firing deliberately high so as not to kill. The remaining minority might actually harm the enemy.

In the poorly trained colonial forces, discipline was often that bad. In the European system, everyone loaded and fired together. An officer or sergeant directed that volley where it would do some good. The British followed a core principle of military science: Bash the key sector with all your might.

So where did we get this "from behind rocks and trees" notion? Small groups of colonials indeed sniped at British troops; harassing fire is annoying but doesn't in itself win a war.

The colonials won largely because of perseverance. But there were other factors that caused a major pain in His Majesty's Royal Posterior:

❋ The British accounts go on endlessly about humidity, heat, cold, wind, sleet, snowdrifts, cloudbursts, and other nasty weather conditions. Most British soldiers must have wondered, "What does my Sovereign want with this wretched hellhole? I notice he doesn't choose to live here."

* Being half-naked and short on food and ammo offers only one benefit: You travel light. The well-supplied, smartly uniformed British were slower.

* The attitude of the British domestic anti-war movement was this: "If those insane Yankees want to surrender all the benefits of membership in a great empire, good riddance! Why spend money and lives to keep them in our fold?"

* British leaders' constant indecision, infighting, and resigning undermined the cause. King George III must have wanted to crack their bewigged heads together. It wasn't always clear whose side they were on.

* The Royal Navy was (and is) the senior British service. By comparison, the army was a red-coated stepchild of sorts, often undermanned. It resorted to the help of German mercenaries (the famed "Hessian troops"), many of whom deserted. The British army lacked the means to field enough forces to pacify the colonies.

Revolutionary War Facts

* The Olive Branch Petition, written by John Dickenson of Pennsylvania, was approved by the Second Continental Congress in July 1775. The document attempted to assure King George III that the colonists were loyal to him, and it requested that he respond to their complaints. Instead, he quickly declared the colonists in rebellion.

* The first major battle of the Revolutionary War was the Battle of Bunker Hill, which took place in 1775. It followed the smaller opening battles at Lexington and Concord.

* The final major battle of the war was the Battle of Yorktown in October 1781. It ended with the surrender of the British.

Napoleon and the Sphinx

Itself a mystery, the Sphinx embodies another one: What happened to its nose? Despite evidence to the contrary, many people believe that Napoleon's soldiers used the Sphinx as target practice. Here's why that can't be true.

✳   ✳   ✳   ✳

WHEN NAPOLEON BONAPARTE conquered Egypt, he took along his artists, historians, civilian scholars, and a group of scientists known as savants. Although Napoleon was not an archaeologist, he is considered an early Egyptologist: He was one of the first world leaders to recognize the treasures of ancient Egypt and the need to preserve not only the artwork but also the culture itself.

The Battle of the Pyramids took place in July 1798 between the French army and the local Mamluk forces in Egypt. Six months before Napoleon entered Egypt, he sent ahead many of his savants, who contributed to the *Description de L'Egypte* (Description of Egypt)—a comprehensive report of ancient and modern Egypt. These chronicles and sketches clearly show that the damage to the Sphinx had been done well before Napoleon arrived. Even if there were no other proof to debunk the myth that Napoleon was responsible for defacing the Sphinx, his devotion to Egypt would be enough to dispute the idea.

So what happened to the famous statue? The most likely explanation is simple erosion from the sands of time. The Sphinx was carved from a solid piece of limestone, a material that is soft and wears easily. Besides the missing nose, there are several cracks in the face. If you observe statues of all sizes from ancient Egypt, you'll notice that the nose is the one common feature missing from most of them. This explanation is, perhaps, not as exciting as that of Napoleon's soldiers, but it's certainly more plausible.

The Donner Party Loses Its Way

Starting around 1845, thousands of Americans migrated west, believing that it was their "manifest destiny" to claim that territory. The story of the Donner party, however, is one of the most tragic tales in U.S. history.

❋ ❋ ❋ ❋

In 1846, farmers George and Jacob Donner and businessman James Reed succumbed to the land fever that was sweeping the country. Their families had plenty of land and money in Springfield, Illinois, but they were anxious to attain more wealth out west.

On April 16, 1846, the Donner party headed to Independence, Missouri. The group consisted of nine wagons (including the Reed family's luxurious, cumbersome wagon) carrying 87 people. The group left Independence on May 12, after the spring rains had subsided. The journey they were undertaking would take them 2,500 miles, across plains, deserts, the Great Basin, and three mountain ranges. It was necessary to arrive at Sutter's Fort in California ahead of the snows that blanketed the Sierra Nevada Mountains in winter.

A Tempting "Shortcut"

The group came upon the Little Sandy River (in present-day Wyoming) on July 20. Up to that point, the journey had been smooth, but here they made the fatal mistake of attempting a shortcut George Donner knew about from reading Lansford Hasting's *The Emigrant's Guide to Oregon and California.* Although Hastings described this shortcut in his publication, no one had ever actually tested it.

The first obstacle they encountered was dense brush, and it was a battle to get the wagons through. Next they faced a maze of canyons that took them a month to navigate. Finally they came across the Great Salt Lake Desert. The group struggled through five blistering days and freezing nights to make the 80-mile trek that *The Emigrant's Guide* had led them to believe would be only 40 miles.

Ominous Flurries

By the time the group made it out of the desert, it was early September. They soon began notic- ing snow flurries—the first sign of the coming winter. They were discouraged but trudged on, as there would be no point in turning back now. In early November, they became trapped in the snowy Sierra Nevada Mountains, 150 miles from their destination. All they could do was build rough cabins and settle in until the worst of the winter was over. They had little, if anything, left to eat.

Eventually, a small faction of the Donner party set out to find help. The rest of the group was too weak to travel, and conditions for them only worsened.

Shocking Discoveries

The rescue group finally found help in California. Accounts of what the first relief team saw when they arrived at the camp depict group members who were starving, freezing, and delirious. Those who were able to make the recovery trip were taken at that point; the rest were forced to wait for a second rescue team. As reported by the second group of rescuers, some of the remaining members of the pitiful Donner party had resorted to cannibalism in order to make it through the winter.

The survivors eventually reached Sutter's Fort more than a year after the party's departure from Independence and about six months after their expected arrival. Two-thirds of the men and one-third of the women and children had died on the journey.

❋ With the exception of the Donner party, all the groups that left Independence, Missouri, in 1846 arrived in California safely.

America's First Foreign War

Ever wonder why the U.S. Marines will fight their country's battles "to the shores of Tripoli"? Here's the answer.

✳ ✳ ✳ ✳

WILLIAM EATON, ACTING as an agent for the U.S. government, disembarked at Rosetta, Egypt, on November 26, 1804. His mission was to find Hamet Karamanli, the former ruler of Tripoli and leader of the Barbary pirates. A few years earlier, Hamet had been deposed in a coup and was replaced by his brother Yusuf Karamanli. Eaton wanted Hamet to become the ostensible leader of an expedition to overthrow Yusuf, whose pirates had captured the frigate USS *Philadelphia* and its crew.

Unsafe at Sea

For hundreds of years Britain, France, and Spain had been paying the Barbary pirates to leave their ships alone. The United States, now independent from Britain and no longer under its system of payments, became fair game. Captured sailors of all nations wound up in the dungeons of Tripoli, Tunis, and Algiers. In 1785, after the merchant ships *Maria* and *Dauphin* were captured, the significance of the problem was brought home to all Americans.

Secretary of State Thomas Jefferson thought the United States had but three choices: Pay tribute to the pirates like the European countries; forbid American vessels to sail in the Mediterranean; or go to war. Representative Robert Goodloe Harper made a stirring promise to spend "millions for defense, but not one cent for tribute."

Congress authorized $688,888.82 for the construction of six frigates, but an agreement on tribute was reached nonetheless. America would pay the pirates yearly tribute and a ransom of more than a million dollars. America had a merchant fleet to protect, and this arrangement was cheaper than full-scale war.

Never Enough

By 1797, John Adams had become president, and all of the American captives had either died in prison or been released. For four years there was relative peace. Then, near the end of Adams's term, Yusuf Karamanli decided that the Americans weren't paying enough and declared war on the United States. That was fine with most Americans, who were fed up with paying tribute.

Jefferson became president in 1801, and he saw America's fight with the Barbary pirates as a test of the young nation's mettle. He sent a six-ship squadron to the Mediterranean under Commodore Edward Preble.

Those six ships had to patrol more than 1,200 miles of coastline—a nearly impossible task. This was made more difficult when the frigate *Philadelphia* ran aground off Tripoli and was captured in October 1803. Something had to be done—such a warship could not be left in the hands of pirates.

On the night of February 16, 1804, Lieutenant Stephen Decatur led a raiding party into Tripoli harbor. He and his crew annihilated the Tripolitan prize crew and burned the *Philadelphia*—a feat Britain's Admiral Nelson called "the most daring act of the age."

The crew of the *Philadelphia* and Americans from other ships were still in the dungeons of Tripoli, however. The American captives couldn't just wait out the war. Those with exploitable talents were treated well, but most were tortured and forced to do hard labor. Men were dying, committing suicide, or converting to Islam and fighting for Yusuf.

Rescue Party

Back in Egypt, Eaton managed to scrape together 90 of Hamet's followers, joined by 50 Greek mercenaries, 20 Italian gunners, and a fire-eating Englishman named Farquhar. About 300 Bedouin Arab cavalry completed the local contingent.

Eaton wanted to include 100 U.S. Marines from the fleet, but Captain Samuel Barron refused. In the end, the only Americans who took part were Eaton, Lieutenant Presley O'Bannon of the marines with a sergeant and a few enlisted soldiers, and Midshipman Pascal Paoli Peck, U.S. Navy.

On March 5, 1805, the expedition set off across the desert. Lacking most necessary equipment, they stumbled into Bomba on April 15. They had been 25 days without meat and 15 days without bread; for two days, they'd eaten nothing at all. Smoke signals brought the USS Argus, which had ample provisions and one of two promised cannons.

The Battle of Derna

The group set off for Derna, arriving on April 26. When an attempt to negotiate with the governor of the town brought the response "your head or mine," Eaton attacked.

After his force took significant casualties and had its one cannon put out of action, Eaton decided on an all-out assault. Brandishing a sword and leading his force, Eaton swept through the barricades and took the town. Resistance collapsed, and the governor took refuge within his harem. It wasn't Tripoli, but it was close enough. Yusuf agreed to release American captives and leave American ships alone. The war was over.

✳ In addition to the "Shores of Tripoli" line in the Marine Corps Hymn, there is one other lasting legacy of the Tripolitan War. To this day, when a marine officer is commissioned, he proudly receives a Mameluke saber like the one presented to the valiant Lieutenant O'Bannon by Hamet Karamanli.

✳ Miguel de Cervantes, author of Don Quixote, spent five years as a Barbary captive in the late 16th century.

A License to Print Money

Faced with shortages of metal for coins, the Union decided that paper money was the way to keep the economy going.

✳ ✳ ✳ ✳

WHEN THE WAR began, the Union economy was far more robust and resilient than that of the Confederates, but that wasn't saying much. The shock of secession had severely affected the North as well. American citizens were hoarding gold and silver coins, the dominant currency of the day. For its part, the government was faced with a ballooning payroll packed with soldiers and other war expenditures. Bold action had to be taken to prevent bankruptcy. The U.S. government decided that the way to alleviate this pressure would be to introduce paper currency, which would allow it to have more control over the money supply.

Potential Paper Problems

There hadn't been a paper currency in the United States since colonial times, when the weak and easily faked "Continentals" were used to fund the Revolution. Furthermore, paper money has to be carefully regulated, because if too much of it is printed and put into use, it can cause inflation. If the inflation is bad enough, the paper money itself can become worthless. The Confederate economy fell into this trap, and the cost of goods skyrocketed. The Union was determined to avoid such a calamity, so the Treasury made a strong—and ultimately successful—effort to limit the amount of paper bills it would print.

The Color of Money

The first paper note to be issued for wide circulation in the North was the Demand Note. It was so named because it was redeemable for its worth in gold "on demand." This note was only issued for one year before it was replaced by another, the Legal Tender Note. The new notes were known as *fiat money*, which means that they weren't backed by anything other than the government's word. Naturally, these were not nearly as popular as the Demand Notes had been.

The design of these first paper notes was carefully considered to reduce the chance that they could easily be counterfeited. The familiar green color of American money was chosen for the first time during the Civil War. Photography was still in its early stages and could only create images in black, so the green color ensured that some clever person with a primitive camera couldn't create a convincing copy.

Although there was some green ink on the front of Demand Notes, the notes became known as greenbacks because the back was printed entirely in green. The patterns and designs on these notes were quite complicated. The greenback side displayed the value in large text on top of a field of smaller numbers. Alexander Hamilton was on the front of the five-dollar bill, and Abraham Lincoln was on the ten. The twenty featured a female representation of Liberty. The skilled engravers of Northern mints and print houses had created very fine and ornately constructed bills that would prove very difficult to replicate. When the Legal Tender Notes were released the following year, they had similar, but distinct, designs.

✳ In 1862, British Chancellor of the Exchequer William E. Gladstone predicted that secession would be successful: "There is no doubt that Jefferson Davis and other leaders of the South have made an army; they are making, it appears, a navy; and they have made what is more than either—they have made a nation . . . We may anticipate with certainty the success of the Southern States so far as regards their separation from the North."

✳ Abraham Lincoln's second secretary of war, Edwin M. Stanton, is believed to have originated Lincoln's nickname, "The Original Gorilla," although General McClellan adopted it and used it frequently in his correspondence with his wife.

Draft Riots Rock New York City

Angry draftees demonstrated just how much
they didn't want to join the army.

❋ ❋ ❋ ❋

THROUGHOUT ITS EARLY history, the United States survived with volunteer militias and armies; there had never been a draft. By 1863, however, not enough men were joining the Union army. President Lincoln signed a conscription bill into law. It assigned each congressional district a particular number of soldiers to recruit, and all men ages 20 to 45 were eligible, although various exemptions were available.

Much of the nation witnessed opposition to the draft, but New Yorkers seemed particularly resentful. The legislation had set the city's recruitment target at 26,000, and many felt this figure was too high. The Battle of Gettysburg had also just ended, and the gruesome descriptions of combat and long lists of casualties that appeared in New York papers likely rattled many prospective draftees.

Class Struggle

In addition, there were many loopholes in the draft legislation, one of which allowed able-bodied men to buy their way out of the obligation by paying $300. This obviously meant that rich people didn't have to fight if they didn't want to.

Further, because many poor whites in New York found themselves competing for jobs against blacks, they didn't want to fight a war that had the freedom of slaves as its root. Toss in the fact that Lincoln was strongly disliked by New York Democratic leaders, and the stage was set.

On Sunday, July 12, 1863, New York newspapers printed the names of those who had been drafted the day before. The next morning, groups of people gathered to protest, peaceably at first. Soon, however, the crowds started attacking people or places that symbolized the draft, such as police and the office of the Provost Marshall, where the draftees' names had been drawn. The targets of the violence continued to expand and ultimately included anything at all related to the draft, the Republican Party, or wealth.

A City Gone Wild

Crowds attacked jewelry stores, homes of business leaders, and the offices of the *New York Tribune*, a Republican newspaper. The armory at Second Avenue and 21st Street was burned to the ground.

Perhaps worst of all, the rioters began turning on black residents of the city. They looted the Colored Orphan Asylum, destroyed the homes of blacks as well as those of whites who tried to protect them, and lynched several blacks. By the end of the first day, it was clear that the draft had ignited a race riot.

As the second day of rioting began, city officials hotly debated how to quell the violence. One proposal was for the city to pay the federal government $2.5 million to cover the $300 fee to release each drafted New Yorker from his military obligation. But that didn't help. Even when the government announced that the draft would be delayed by a month, the rioters continued to wreck the city. Police proved ineffective in quashing the violence, as did troops from the National Guard. Not until soldiers fresh from the battlefields of Gettysburg marched into New York to keep the peace did the city begin to settle down.

At the end of five days of rioting, more than 70 people had been killed, and property damage totaled $1.5 million. Yet it still wasn't enough to stop the draft, which resumed in August with 10,000 federal troops stationed throughout the city. By then, however, New York Governor Horatio Seymour had convinced the federal government to reduce New York City's quota to 12,000 men. This time, the Democratic city leaders oversaw the lottery, which eased the anxiety in the working class about the fairness of the draft.

Brothers Killing Brothers

The ancient Greeks had two philosophies of war. A "blood war" was a nasty thing, with no good reason at its source. A "just war," however, was considered to be necessary and fair. The War Between the States might be considered the ultimate "just war," as it led the United States through its growing pains and into adulthood. The conflict, which raged between 1861 and 1865, brought carnage and death to levels seldom seen in the annals of world history.

✳ ✳ ✳ ✳

MORE THAN 623,000 Americans lost their lives in the Civil War. Yet only a third of that number actually died in battle. The rest succumbed to poor and ineffective medical care and massive outbreaks of contagious diseases, such as dysentery. Another 400,000 were wounded but survived.

New and more efficient weapons increased the death toll. Muskets with grooved bores, using a technique called "rifling" to give the bullet more spin, were much more accurate than the previously smooth-bored guns. Artillery shells delivered deadly payloads of 75 to 80 musket balls, and impact shells detonated with ten pounds of black powder upon landing. Canister shells exploded like giant shotgun shells, shooting 25 to 50 small iron balls in all directions. These munitions supported a revolutionary concept in war strategy: The main focus of weapons moved from destroying property to killing people.

The Deadliest of American Wars

The number of soldiers, both Union and Confederate, killed in the Civil War is higher than those of the American Revolutionary War, World War I, World War II, the Korean War, and the Vietnam War combined. The Battle of Antietam on September 17, 1862, was the single bloodiest day in American history—more than 23,000 soldiers were left dead or wounded in the aftermath.

Reconstruction

The war is over—but where to begin picking up the pieces?

✳   ✳   ✳   ✳

THE SOUTH WAS in shambles after the Civil War ended in 1865. Some 258,000 Southerners had died in the four-year conflict, and another 100,000 or so had been wounded. The surviving Confederate troops marched home through a devastated landscape past burned farms, shattered towns, and abandoned counties. What industry that had been established before the war was obliterated—infrastructure such as roads, bridges, and railways had been demolished, and anything like a normal economy was nonexistent.

For governing purposes, administrators divided the 11 states of the former Confederacy into 5 large military zones, each under the control of a U.S. Army general. Approximately 200,000 Union troops were deployed to the South to enforce the will of the federal government.

Finding Normalcy

As early as 1863, leaders in the North began to discuss how to "reconstruct" the South. Lincoln and his closest generals had favored a plan for Reconstruction that would have helped mend the rifts of the war. Had Lincoln survived, the country might have been put back together in a less painful manner.

Much of the clemency Lincoln desired died with him, however. Many of the measures Congress ultimately imposed under Reconstruction were intended as revenge and did little to help the country's healing process. Andrew Johnson, the Southerner who assumed the presidency after Lincoln's passing, did not have the popularity or political force to see Lincoln's plan through to completion. His attempts at a relatively lenient

"Restoration," rather than the harsh "Reconstruction" that was actually carried out, led to his impeachment.

Some Constitutional measures—such as the 13th, 14th, and 15th Amendments, which guaranteed social, political, and legal rights to the freed blacks—were designed to ensure civil rights and social justice. White Southerners seethed. One of the least popular institutions forced upon the former Confederacy was the Freedmen's Bureau, an agency established by Lincoln as part of the War Department in 1865 that helped newly freed slaves obtain their own land, become self-sufficient, and wield political power. The bureau quickly became rife with corruption and inefficiency.

Migrating South

During the period of Reconstruction, thousands of Northern civilians flooded into the devastated South. Some were opportunists, unscrupulous adventurers, and con artists seeking personal gain and political offices. Everyone who came from the North was dubbed a *carpetbagger* by Southerners, after a popular form of cheap luggage that many of them carried. Despite the widespread use of this derogatory term, however, many of these transplants were not self-seeking vagabonds at all—they emigrated to the South with the intent of rebuilding industry, restoring infrastructure, and educating blacks.

Some Southern politicians, including a number of former Confederate soldiers, joined the Northern-based Republican Party during this period and advocated working within the parameters of Reconstruction. Such men were widely hated by others in the South, and most were branded as unprincipled *scalawags* by those committed to resisting Union rule. Again, like the Northern carpetbaggers, some leeway has to be given: Certainly there were scoundrels active in Southern politics at this time, but some participants were sincere individuals who recognized that cooperating with the federal government was the quickest and most effective way to ensure the rapid withdrawal of federal troops and the return of some measure of autonomy to their states.

The Rise of Hate

These events and sentiments made Reconstruction a difficult and painful time for the South and nurtured long-term animosities. Many white Southerners resented the ability of newly enfranchised black voters to put hated Republican politicians in power. They formed organizations supporting white supremacy—secret societies opposed to blacks, the Republican Party, and the federal government. Most notable among these was the Ku Klux Klan (KKK), whose members were sworn to secrecy and hid their identities behind white robes and hooded masks.

Criminal paramilitary organizations such as the KKK conducted increasingly violent and horrifying terrorist activities against U.S. citizens and their government throughout the Reconstruction period and beyond. Some former Confederate soldiers carried on the war as "night riders," which had started as patrols of white men deputized specifically to look for runaway slaves, enforce slave curfews, and squash any possible black uprisings. One of the founding members of the KKK was former Confederate General Nathan Bedford Forrest, who served as the organization's first Grand Wizard.

Local Klan organizations, or "klaverns," touted the flaming cross as their symbol and were especially active during election campaigns, using intimidation, violence, rape, and murder to help sway votes and prevent Republican political victories in their states. Targets often included local Republican leaders and blacks who no longer conformed to antebellum standards of conduct.

In areas under Republican control, authorities were hardpressed to quell the violence and were loath to deploy their mostly black state militias against the KKK and other organizations for fear of provoking a full-blown race war. In areas under Democratic control, the authorities themselves were frequently members of the Klan or sympathizers. Even when local law enforcement authorities did take action, Klan members often sat on juries or judges' benches, ensuring little or no justice would be done.

Slowly Healing

By the early 1870s, most Americans—Northern and Southern alike—agreed that the KKK was out of control. Even Forrest publicly renounced its activities. In 1871, the Republican-led Congress authorized President Ulysses S. Grant to use federal troops to restore order in areas deemed the least under control. The troops had the power to arrest suspects and hold them indefinitely without trial.

By 1872, the Ku Klux Klan had been defeated, and it ceased to exist as an organization until it was revived more than four decades later in 1915. In the 1870s, Southerners opposed to the rule of the federal government ultimately regained influence over their towns, counties, and states through political and economic means. They then used that power to corrupt and undermine many of the changes the federal government had made. It would be another century before the rights won for blacks during the war would come to fruition.

Reconstruction lasted 12 years. Although the states that had seceded were readmitted to the Union by early 1870, violence, civil unrest, and military occupation continued until 1877. All of this contributed to a long-term bitterness that has survived far beyond the lives of those who fought in the bloodiest American conflict.

✳ Andrew Johnson's impeachment revolved around the Tenure of Office Act, which stated that the president could not remove a cabinet official without the consent of Congress. In 1868 Johnson moved to dismiss Secretary of War Edwin Stanton, who had been outspoken in his contempt for Johnson's lenient Reconstruction policies. After the dismissal, the House voted to impeach. Johnson was tried in the Senate and was acquitted. In 1926, the Supreme Court ruled that the Tenure of Office Act was unconstitutional.

Better Later Than Sooner

They trekked in by the tens of thousands to Oklahoma, by horse and by foot, under the blazing July sun. Hungry for land, they formed great lines, and thousands camped out in a single valley.

✳ ✳ ✳ ✳

ROM THE END of the Civil War, the Indian Territory, later known as Oklahoma, had come under irresistible pressure for land. In 1866, the federal government coaxed the local American Indian tribes into ceding two million acres. Soon, Anglo leaders such as William Couch were leading expeditions of "Boomers" (prospective settlers) into these "Unassigned Lands."

In 1889, a group of Creek Indians—in defiance of the opposition of the "Five Civilized Tribes"—sold the government three million more acres. That same year, the Indian Appropriations Act opened 160-acre blocks of Oklahoma land to homesteaders on a first-come, first-served basis.

A multitude—50,000 on the first day—swarmed into Kickapoo country. Many of the arrivals were former slaves. Thousands more—the Sooners—sneaked into the territories before the official start date. Gunfights broke out between Boomers and Sooners. Lawsuits between claimants dragged on for decades. Of every 14 Boomers, only one wound up with an irrefutable land claim. Four other land rushes through 1895 had similar woes. When the time came to redistribute the remainder of Okalahoma's turf, Washington resolved to find a better way.

The Land Lottery

On July 4, 1901, President McKinley proclaimed that 4,639 square miles of land from the Comanche, Apache, Wichita, and Kiowa reservations would be parceled out on the basis of a vast lottery.

Some groups were opposed to the giveaway. Ranchers wanted to continue grazing their stock on the lottery lands. Kiowa Chief Lone Wolf sued the Interior Department to keep the Indian Lands settler-free, but to no avail.

Large numbers came from across the nation to register to own a block of land. Crowds gathered at Fort Sill and in the town of El Reno between July 10 and 26. Tens of thousands of would-be settlers swarmed in from Texas, Kansas, and, most of all, from settled parts of Oklahoma.

Under the arrangement, 480,000 acres of pasture were reserved for the Indian tribes, though most of this was leased to ranchers for pennies an acre. Thousands of Indians did receive homesteads; many Native Americans leased most of their acreage to farmers for a yearly per-acre fee of $1.50. Off-limits to the land rush were the War Department's Fort Sill and the Wichita Mountain Forest Reserve.

At the registration offices, each applicant filled out a card with his or her name, birthdate, height, and other identifying information. The cards were placed in large, wheellike containers for mixing and selection. Land parcels were divided into two huge swaths of territory around Lawton and El Reno.

Tense Moments

As vast crowds waited to apply in heat over 100 degrees, trouble broke out. A Mexican was taken out and killed for trying to jump to the front of a registration line. People were required to notarize their applications: A mob almost lynched a fake notary, and lawmen arrested another notary who used an outdated seal. In the meantime, grifters and gamblers taking advantage of the bored multitudes waiting in line were banished from the streets. More welcome were painted Cheyenne Indians who offered spectators war dances for 25 cents.

Most registrants were farmers of limited income. No one owning more than 160 acres in another state was permitted to register. One registration card per person was the rule; hundreds trying to game the lottery with multiple applications were barred.

Single-day registration peaked at 16,700. In all, approximately 160,000 hopefuls signed up for a chance at 13,000 homesteads.

The Winners Are Announced

Drawings began on July 29 in El Reno in front of 50,000 witnesses, whose tents and booths packed the dusty streets. From a platform on the grounds of a school, officials pulled the lucky registrations out of twin containers, representing the El Reno and Lawton parcels.

At 1:30 P.M., to a great hurrah, Commissioner Colonel Dyer called out the first name from the El Reno bin—Stephen A. Holcomb of Pauls Valley in Indian Territory.

The first lottery winner for Lawton was James R. Wood, a hardware clerk. The second was Miss Mattie Beal, a telephone operator from Wichita. After Commissioner Dyer read out her description—5-foot-3, 23 years old—the crowd cried: "They must get married!"

On August 6, winners began filing claims for their new properties at a land district office. There they got to choose the shape of their new 160 acres: a narrow strip, a square, or even the shape of a Z. In an unlucky stroke, 1,362 winners who failed to show up for the filings forfeited their claims for good.

The land rush immediately led to the creation of new Oklahoma counties—Comanche, Caddo, and Kiowa. Lots in the county seats were sold to raise some $664,000 to build roads, bridges, and a courthouse.

In 1907, boosted by the growing number of settlers and the economic growth that followed the land lottery, Oklahoma became the 46th state.

Black Sunday Darkens a Nation

Sunday, April 14, 1935, began as a clear, pleasant day over much of the Midwest. But within hours, daytime would be transformed to night as a weather front with 60-mile-per-hour winds threw up a monstrous dust cloud from the barren fields of the Dust Bowl, burying homes in millions of tons of dirt.

✳ ✳ ✳ ✳

PEOPLE IN THE small towns and farms of Kansas, Oklahoma, Texas, and Colorado were used to dust storms and were ready to seal windows, doors, and every possible crack in their houses with sheets, blankets, and newspapers. But this particular storm, which came to be known as Black Sunday, was different. In Dodge City, Kansas, a strange nighttime fell for 40 minutes in the middle of the day, followed by three hours of near darkness. Inside their homes, men, women, and children huddled with handkerchiefs or wet sponges over their noses, struggling to breathe. Many believed the world was coming to an end. A few hours later in Chicago, the cloud dumped three pounds of soil for each person in the city. The next day, it blanketed New York and Washington, D.C., before sweeping out into the Atlantic Ocean.

Origin of a Disaster

The April 1935 storm was the worst of the Dust Bowl, an ecological disaster that lasted for years at the height of the Great Depression. Affecting 100 million acres of the Great Plains, it brought poverty and malnutrition to millions and spurred an exodus of poor farmers to the West Coast. For years, the Plains region had enjoyed high grain prices and phenomenal crops, but farmers had been overproducing for more than a generation. Overgrazing by cattle and sheep had further stripped the landscape. By 1930, more than 30 million acres of southern plains once held in place by native prairie grasses had been laid bare. The crisis began in 1931. Farmers

enjoyed another bumper crop of wheat, but the resulting surplus forced prices down. Many farmers went broke, and others abandoned their fields just at the start of a severe drought that would last much of the decade.

Stormy Weather

In 1932, more than a dozen dust storms—whipped skyward by strong, dry winds—ravaged the United States. The following year, the storms numbered 38, and a region centering on northern Texas, Oklahoma, and Kansas was dubbed the Dust Bowl. The first great storm occurred in May 1934, when high winds swirled 300,000 tons of soil from Montana and Wyoming skyward. By evening, the "black blizzard" began depositing dust like snow on the streets of Chicago. By dawn the next day, the cloud had rolled eastward over New York, Washington, D.C., and Atlanta, dimming the sun before moving out to sea and dusting ships 300 miles off shore. In the Midwest, summer temperature records were broken, and thousands of livestock starved and suffocated. Hundreds of people died from heat stroke, malnutrition, and dust pneumonia.

Black Sunday

In March 1935, another big storm again blew topsoil from the fields of Kansas, Colorado, Texas, and Oklahoma all the way to the East Coast, but it was only a prelude of what was to come.

Twenty huge dust storms tore through the region on April 14, 1935, converging in a single front headed east. Witnesses reported that at times they could not see five feet in front of them. A pilot who encountered a dust cloud at 20,000 feet assumed it was a thunderstorm. She tried to climb above it, but could not, and had to turn back. In Oklahoma and Texas, humble homesteads were literally buried beneath feet of dust.

When the dust settled, a drastic migration began that would culminate in 15 percent of Oklahomans leaving the state. Called "Okies" in California, the uprooted people searching for a new life actually came from all the states of the Midwest affected by the continuing disaster. Working for the Farm Security Administration, photographer Dorothea Lange documented their lives, while novelist John Steinbeck immortalized their plight with *The Grapes of Wrath*.

Aftermath

Black Sunday would be an impetus for change. With dirt from the storm still falling over Washington, D.C., Hugh Hammond Bennett—a soil surveyor from North Carolina who helped found the soil conservation movement—won the support of Congress, which declared soil erosion a national menace. Later that year, President Roosevelt signed into law the Soil Conservation Act of 1935, establishing Soil Conservation Service in the Department of Agriculture. Under Bennett's direction, an aggressive campaign to stabilize the region's soil began. Roosevelt also undertook banking reforms and agricultural policies to help rescue the Plains farmers. One of his programs led to the planting of more than 222,000 trees.

For the next year, however, the drought continued, as summer temperatures soared to 120 degrees. Sporadic rains and floods in 1937 and 1938 joined the continuing dust storms, and wintertime brought a new kind of storm called a "snuster"—a mixture of dirt and snow reaching blizzard proportions. The fall of 1939 finally brought the rains that ended the drought. With new farming methods and increased agricultural demand due to WWII, the Plains once again became golden with wheat.

The Phony Raid That Started the War

If one man could be said to have started World War II, some historians believe it would be Alfred Helmut Naujocks, an SS officer who led a fake attack on a German radio station outside the city of Gleiwitz on the Polish border.

✳ ✳ ✳ ✳

UNDER THE COMMAND of Nazi security chief Reinhard Heydrich, Alfred Naujocks served in the *Sicherheitsdienst* (SD), the intelligence service of the SS. He played a role in several Nazi espionage actions in the 1930s, including the smuggling of explosives to pro-German militants in Slovakia in March 1939. The explosives were used to create "incidents" in the days preceding Germany's occupation of Czechoslovakia.

Operation Himmler

The night before Germany invaded Poland, Germans staged numerous attacks along the Polish-German border. Part of Operation Himmler, the attack on a radio station near Gleiwitz, Poland, received the most attention.

On the night of August 31, 1939, Naujocks led a dozen SS troopers dressed in Polish uniforms to the Gleiwitz radio tower. There they waited for the delivery of the *Konserve*, or "canned goods," the Nazi code word for expendable prisoners. SS agents delivered 12 or 13 condemned criminals, including Franciszek Honiok, a German dissenter who had sympathized with the Poles. The prisoner had been given a lethal injection before reaching the site and was dressed in a Polish uniform. The SS troopers posed his body and shot several bullets into him.

Then, Naujocks and his team of SS men stormed the tower, surprising the staff, who knew nothing about the attack.

Speaking Polish, members of the assault team shouted anti-German statements on the air, broadcast a message calling on Poles to attack Germans, and fired several shots into the ceiling before leaving.

Radio stations across Germany announced that police were repelling an attack by Polish troops at Gleiwitz. The next morning, German authorities at Gleiwitz showed the inmates' bodies to journalists and foreign diplomats as proof of the incident. The German Army was already roaring into Poland as Hitler declared before the Reichstag in Berlin, "This night for the first time Polish regular soldiers fired on our own territory. Since 5:45 A.M. we have been returning fire, and from now on bombs will be met with bombs."

The Gleiwitz Incident Revealed

In October 1944, Naujocks deserted Germany and surrendered to American forces. Appearing as a witness at the Nuremberg trials after the war, he told the story of what happened at Gleiwitz. He later became a businessman in Hamburg. He is also alleged to have been one of the organizers of Odessa, a secret organization of Nazi veterans that helped former SS officers wanted for war crimes escape to South America. Naujocks is believed to have died, a free man, in 1960.

---

* The Nazis were not alone in using fake attacks to justify invasions. In 1931, the Mukden Incident occurred when Japanese officers blew up a section of a railroad, blaming Chinese dissidents and providing an excuse for the annexation of Northeast of China. In 1939, the Russian town of Mainila on the Finnish border was shelled by heavy artillery. The Soviets blamed Finland. Documents released after the fall of the Soviet Union proved that the Red Army had shelled the town to justify Stalin's invasion of Finland four days later.

* Italy went to great lengths to shield its antiquities from wartime damage: Statues were protected by sandbags; monuments were covered with masonry and sandbagged scaffolding.

Roosevelt's Road to War

From 1935 to 1941, America awoke from a decades-long spell of isolationism to the reality that it was part of the world, and the world was in flames.

✳   ✳   ✳   ✳

EVER SINCE THE Senate voted down the League of Nations Treaty in 1919, U.S. foreign policy was based on avoiding the kind of foreign entanglements that had cost America thousands of lives in World War I. For America, the 1920s were all about prosperity, Prohibition, and the creation of fabulous wealth, while the early '30s were consumed with a struggle against the Great Depression.

A Web of Isolation

As tensions mounted in Europe and Japan invaded Northeast of China, Congress began penning legislation that would keep America from another Great War entanglement. In 1935, Congress passed the first of its prewar Neutrality Acts, temporarily banning arms shipments to any nation at war.

When Mussolini's Fascist Italy announced plans to invade Ethiopia, President Franklin D. Roosevelt urged citizens to clamp a "moral embargo" upon Italy. Businesses refused to go along, though, and commercial exports to Italy increased as Italian tanks clattered through the African desert.

With the outbreak of civil war in Spain in 1936, Roosevelt urged U.S. arms manufacturers to impose a "moral embargo" of noninterference with Fascist and Nationalist factions, but again his pleas were ignored. One U.S. company managed to obtain an export license to sell bomber parts to the rebels—a sale that FDR opposed as unpatriotic.

In 1937, Congress passed legislation making the 1935 Neutrality Act permanent. The 1937 act also provided that, at the president's discretion, goods other than war matériel could be traded with belligerents so long as they were paid for in cash and carried on their own ships—to avoid the repayment mess the United States found itself in after World War I.

Although the public and Congress wanted no part in any European war, Roosevelt saw the rising empires of Germany and Japan as twin threats to U.S. interests.

Turning Points

Hitler's 1938 annexation of Czechoslovakia's Sudetenland and 1939 occupation of the rest of Czechoslovakia pushed Roosevelt even closer to the anti-German coalition. He began pressing for changes to the Neutrality Acts to allow aid to European democracies. By midyear, Congressional opposition persisted; FDR would have to await a further shift in public opinion before he could act.

It was not long before the Nazis handed Roosevelt the tools he needed to support Britain and France. On September 3, two days after Hitler's panzers rolled into Poland, German submarines sank the British liner *Athena*, killing 28 Americans. By the end of September, nearly two-thirds of Americans approved of matériel support to the Allies. On November 4, 1939, Roosevelt signed legislation allowing arms sales to belligerents on a "cash-and-carry" basis.

Lifeline to a Friend

In the spring of 1940, as Britain ran desperately short of war matériel, Prime Minister Winston Churchill appealed to FDR for help. In September, the Roosevelt administration entered into a swap agreement with Britain, trading more than 50 outdated destroyers for 99-year leases on territories that would be used as naval bases in the Caribbean and Newfoundland.

The War Department allocated large stocks of supplies to England and its allies, but the biggest obstacle was Britain's acute shortage of cash. On December 17, FDR proposed the Lend-Lease program, under which Britain would receive military aid in return for joint actions supporting creation of a liberalized postwar international economy. The president explained his policy in terms every voter could understand, likening England's anti-Nazi struggle to a neighbor whose house was on fire. "What do I do in such a crisis?" the president asked at a news conference. "I don't say, 'Neighbor, my garden hose cost me $15; you have to pay me $15 for it.' I don't want $15—I want my garden hose back after the fire is over." The following March, Congress passed the Lend-Lease Act, authorizing the president to sell, lease, lend, "or otherwise dispose of" military equipment the president deemed vital to the defense of the nation.

The Final Countdown

In early 1941, Hitler's invasion of Yugoslavia spurred Roosevelt to accelerate matériel aid to the Allies. In late March, Congress approved a $7 billion Lend-Lease appropriation, and on April 9, U.S. forces occupied Greenland to extend the security zone of convoys carrying supplies to England. A day later, the U.S. destroyer USS *Niblack* fired depth charges on a German U-boat, and by the summer of 1941, the United States was in a state of undeclared naval war against Germany.

After Germany's surprise invasion of the Soviet Union on June 22, FDR sent two emissaries to Moscow to negotiate Lend-Lease shipments. In August, FDR met with Churchill and his staff aboard the battleship Prince of Wales, where the two leaders reaffirmed their liberal war aims in what became known as the Atlantic Charter. Two months later, Congress approved $1 billion in Lend-Lease aid to Stalin, and before the war's end, the U.S. would send some $50 billion in matériel aid to Britain, the Soviet Union, and their allies.

Japan's surprise attack on Pearl Harbor on December 7 sealed the fates of many nations. The long journey from isolationism to war was over, and the world would never be the same.

The Death of Hitler's Dreadnought

From the time it set out on its first mission in May 1941, the German battleship Bismarck *inspired fear in the North Atlantic. Fortunately for the Allies, its reign was brief—albeit violent.*

✳   ✳   ✳   ✳

The Terror of the Seas

Realizing that Germany's *Kriegsmarine* could not hope to defeat Britain's Royal Navy in a ship-to-ship engagement, the Third Reich built the battleship *Bismarck* as a heavy commerce raider. It boasted eight 15-inch guns mounted on four massive turrets and could speed along at 32 knots in calm waters. Broad enough to ride out treacherous North Atlantic swells, *Bismarck* could outfight any ship that got in its way.

Commissioned in August 1940, *Bismarck* did not sail until May 19, 1941, when it weighed anchor in company with the heavy cruiser *Prinz Eugen*. The two ships were the core of Operation *Rheinübung* ("Rhine Exercise"), the Reich's plan to destroy Allied shipping, draw British battleships away from the Mediterranean, and temporarily cut Britain's lifeline to America.

Heading across the Norwegian Sea to the Denmark Strait, *Bismarck*'s commander, Admiral Günther Lütjens, hoped to break out into the open waters of the Atlantic and prey upon Allied convoys. Because the Royal Navy could eventually organize enough battleships to send him to the bottom, Lütjens knew that success would depend on evading the watchful eyes of British planes and vessels.

Sink the *Bismarck*!

From the time Britain's cryptologists got wind of *Bismarck*'s departure, the Royal Air Force (RAF) and Royal Navy worked overtime tracking the German threat. RAF bombers narrowly missed it at anchor, and two heavy cruisers patrolling the Denmark Strait, the *Suffolk* and *Norfolk*, were driven off by *Bismarck*'s massive, long-range guns.

On May 24, *Prinz Eugen* picked up the hydrophone signal of two large ships heading toward the Denmark Strait. Closing in, Admiral Lütjens engaged the British battleship *Prince of Wales* and its consort, the battle cruiser *Hood*. At about nine miles out, the British ships turned to bring their broadsides to bear against the Germans. But before they could range their targets, *Bismarck*'s gunners managed to drop a 15-inch shell onto the *Hood* from about nine miles away, plunging through its decks and setting fire to its magazines. *Hood* exploded amidships, broke in two, and sank within three minutes, taking all but three of its more than 1,420 crewmen to their deaths. *Prince of Wales*, hit seven or eight times during the 10- to 15-minute battle, pulled away under a smoke screen, all but one of its heavy guns out of action.

The Battle of the Denmark Strait was a resounding victory for the *Kriegsmarine*'s sailors, but they paid a price: *Bismarck*'s forward fuel tanks had been hit, the forward radar was smashed, and it had to reduce speed to 20 knots to conserve fuel. Worst of all, the Royal Navy knew exactly where the German squadron was; they would undoubtedly be back—and in greater numbers. Weighing his options, Admiral Lütjens decided to cross the Atlantic and head for St. Nazaire, a friendly French port in which he could safely repair his ship.

The Royal Navy gave top priority to sinking the *Bismarck*. With the ship still in their sights, a squadron of "Swordfish" torpedo bomber planes attacked the *Bismarck* shortly after the *Hood*'s sinking, but they did little damage. The savvy Admiral Lütjens managed to evade his pursuers for nearly two days, sailing to within 700 miles of the French coast. Then a reconnaissance plane spotted the flagship, and before long,

the aircraft carrier *Ark Royal*, the battle cruiser *Renown*, and the cruiser *Sheffield* managed to corner the wounded tiger before it could reach French waters.

Ark Royal launched a squadron of Swordfish against the German dreadnought, scoring one lucky hit that jammed *Bismarck*'s rudder, leaving it helpless. By May 27, the British battleships *King George V* and *Rodney* closed in for the kill. Lütjens knew what was to come. He radioed headquarters that his position was untenable but that he would fight to the last shell.

Bismarck's final battle began just before 9:00 A.M. on May 27, just nine days after leaving port. *Rodney, King George V*, and two heavy cruisers, *Norfolk* and *Dorsetshire*, fired some 2,876 shells at their prey, blowing apart *Bismarck*'s upper structure and killing most of its senior officers. About an hour later, the *Dorsetshire* ranged for attack. To avoid a mass drowning, the *Bismarck*'s executive officer ordered the crew to scuttle and abandon ship. Less than two hours from the initial salvos, *Bismarck* slipped beneath the waves, taking more than 2,100 sailors to the bottom of the Atlantic.

Hitler's Grey Ghost

The legend of the *Bismarck* persisted long after its death, through stories and films such as *Sink the Bismarck!* (1960) and a 2002 James Cameron documentary on its final resting place.

There was also a popular 1960 Johnny Horton tune that reminded radio listeners of the most dangerous battle cruiser to sail the oceans:

> The Bismarck *was the fastest ship that ever sailed the seas.*
> *On her decks were guns as big as steers and shells as big as trees...*

The tune ends with a musical tribute to the Royal Navy's gallant sailors and their bloody work:

> We found the mighty Bismarck
> And then we cut her down.

Words for the Ages

"God has a special providence for fools, drunks, and the United States of America."

—OTTO VON BISMARCK

"The likeness in features is striking, and the Character of the whole face is preserved & exhibited with wonderful Accuracy. It is more like Washington than any Portrait of him I have ever seen."

—CHIEF JUSTICE JOHN MARSHALL, ON REMBRANDT PEALE'S PORTRAIT OF GEORGE WASHINGTON (WHICH IS ON DISPLAY IN THE SENATE)

"[James] Monroe was so honest that if you turned his soul inside out there would not be a spot on it."

—THOMAS JEFFERSON

"We have met the enemy, and they are ours."

—COMMODORE OLIVER H. PERRY (TO GENERAL WILLIAM HENRY HARRISON AFTER THE BATTLE OF LAKE ERIE)

"If I see a murderous fellow sharpening a knife cleverly, I can borrow his way of sharpening the knife without borrowing his probable intention to commit murder with it."

—WOODROW WILSON, *THE STUDY OF ADMINISTRATION*, 1886

"There are two insults which no human being will endure: The assertion that he hasn't a sense of humor, and the doubly impertinent assertion that he has never known trouble."

—SINCLAIR LEWIS, AUTHOR

"If wishes were horses, beggars would ride."

—J. KELLY, *SCOTTISH PROVERBS*, 1721

"There is only one antidote to mental suffering, and that is physical pain."

—KARL MARX, *HERR VOGT*, 1860

"Censorship believes it has protected youth's soul, whereas it has, at one and the same time, done it violence and dulled it."

—JEAN DELANNOY

A Bodyguard of Lies

Germany had more than enough muscle behind the guns and forts of the Atlantic Wall to blast any seaborne invasion to pieces—but only if that muscle was all brought to bear swiftly in the right place. The main ingredient of this Allied mission, therefore, had to be trickery.

✳   ✳   ✳   ✳

"In wartime, truth is so precious that she should always be attended by a bodyguard of lies."

—Winston Churchill

THE GERMANS EXPECTED the Allies to attempt to invade France, but they weren't sure when or how. They knew the Allies would likely invade as near as possible to British ports to avoid aero-naval interception and remain in range of air cover. Royal Air Force fighters had enough range to cover Normandy and the Pas de Calais region just opposite Dover. As the Allies saw it, Calais was the quickest sail but also the Atlantic Wall's sharpest teeth. Instead, they planned to endure the longer ride to Normandy, where the defenses were less formidable.

Of course, any invasion could fail if the Germans guessed its location in advance. To throw them off, the Allies contrived Operation Bodyguard, a key part of which was Operation Fortitude, a deception plan divided into North and South. Fortitude North's goal was to tie German troops up in Norway with a phantom invasion. Fortitude South would try to mislead the Germans about the real invasion's location while disguising the fact that the Allies were planning multiple landings.

Fortitude North faked radio traffic to make the small northern UK garrison sound like a full army preparing to invade Norway. Thanks to achievements in broadcasting and recording, a single radio truck could simulate the chatter of a divisional headquarters; a signals battalion could simulate an army.

Fortitude South's first job was to convince the Germans that the blow would land near Calais, with possible feints elsewhere. After the troops landed in Normandy, the second phase of Fortitude South would be to maintain the impression that a second, heavier blow was still to come at the Pas de Calais. The planners invented a fictitious army under General Patton: the 1st U.S. Army Group (FUSAG), complete with nonexistent infantry divisions.

Germany depended upon its spies to confirm or contradict what the Allies were really planning. But its intelligence turned out to be unreliable—every German spy reporting from Britain was actually working for the British.

Prepared for Any Eventuality

General Dwight D. Eisenhower assumed that if at any point the Germans figured out the plans for the true D-Day invasion, Field Marshal Erwin Rommel would hurl every tank toward the Normandy beaches while the invasion was at sea—perhaps disobeying even Hitler—to prepare a lethal reception. Eisenhower took the possibility seriously enough to prepare two speeches before the invasion: one praising its success and one taking all blame if it failed.

As it was, D-Day achieved tactical surprise. The Germans had indeed expected the Allies to storm the Pas de Calais sector. Noting that "known" FUSAG elements had not yet been sent into battle, they committed only a portion of the panzer reserve to holding off the Allied forces at Normandy. The rest were withheld to oppose FUSAG's expected second invasion. This gave the Allies those few crucial days needed to reinforce and consolidate the Normandy beachhead. The second invasion came not in June at the Pas de Calais but on August 15, 1944, in southern France.

FUSAG never fired one rifle shot, yet it helped defeat Germany. The Allies' D-Day deception effort went down as one of the best-executed ruses in military history.

The Soviet Logistics Miracle

*With the German blitzkrieg hastily conquering Soviet
land, the Russians embarked on a bold evacuation
to salvage war production industries.*

✳ ✳ ✳ ✳

ON JUNE 22, 1941, three million German troops stormed
into Soviet territory across a 4,000-mile front, marking
the beginning of Operation Barbarossa. Riga and Minsk fell
within days as the Germans struck the center of Soviet industry. By the following day, Joseph Stalin had ordered the first
industrial evacuations of tank factories. By June 24, the Soviets
had formed a Council for Evacuation, and it began identifying
key factories that would head east to the Urals and even far-off
Siberia, out of reach of German air and ground forces.

There had been little planning for the massive undertaking. The
possibility of evacuation had been discussed before the war,
but there was no cohesive strategy. In contrast, the Germans
had extensive plans for such an eventuality despite their doubt
that they would ever be subject to invasion. Given this lack of
foresight on the Soviets' part, the entire operation became an
exercise in improvisation, and there were inevitable missteps
along the way. Some resources were captured by the enemy, and
a few factories had to be relocated twice because they had not
been moved far enough the first time.

Heading East

The Council made the necessary decisions, and Soviet industry
began to move. Entire factories were disassembled and sent
east at an average rate of 165,000 trailer loads per month. They
were then reassembled, and production began immediately.
Faced with the ridiculous edict to accomplish relocation and
yet not fall behind in production, Soviet workers performed
nothing short of miracles. Disassembled factories arrived in the
undeveloped regions of the interior and were reassembled in

the worst weather conditions. Workers at a munitions factory rebuilt a foundry in 28 days even though original construction had taken two years; another plant went from reassembly to operating at full capacity in two weeks. The Soviets adopted a scorched-earth policy toward factories that couldn't be moved in time, opting to raze them rather than let them fall into German hands.

At least 30 to 40 percent of factory laborers traveled with the machinery; the rest were called into the army. Many workers were given seeds and sent out to cultivate the land around the new factories after having worked a full shift in the plant. Women and adolescents often picked up the slack for missing employees. The displaced workers also had a disruptive impact on the areas they settled; Uzbekistan alone had to absorb two million additional people. The influx of people and technology produced miniature industrial revolutions in some of the less developed, more remote areas of the country.

The relocation succeeded in spectacular fashion. The Soviets moved 1,523 industrial concerns, including the bulk of the production facilities used for war-related industries such as chemistry and engineering. By 1943, overall production was four times what it had been in 1941.

The impact of the evacuation effort on the overall war would be hard to overestimate; after the war Soviet General Georgi Zhukov offered the opinion that the evacuation had been as significant as the battles fought by Soviet troops.

✳ The Soviets had great incentive for rebuilding quickly. For instance, in 1942 Stalin—showing his traditional gentle subtlety—told Soviet oil commissar and industrial planner Nikolai Konstantinovich Baibakov that he would be shot if the USSR lost the Caucasus oil fields to the Germans. He also threatened to shoot him if they did not produce immediately once safe from German hands.

Götterdämmerung in the East

In a war of titanic battles, Stalingrad stands out as a monument of a modern city turned into a vast killing ground. In a battle that ravaged the city, Soviet soldiers and civilians refused to yield to a mighty German Army.

✳ ✳ ✳ ✳

IN EARLY 1942, Germany's panzers were deep in Soviet territory, threatening Moscow and Leningrad to the north. But Hitler's attention was drawn to the south, toward the Caucasus Mountains and the rich oil fields that could keep his war machine driving across Asia Minor, the Suez Canal, and the Middle East. In April, he ordered his armies to move along the Don River. One field force, designated Army Group A, would push south into the Transcaucasus region, while another task force, Army Group B, would move east toward Stalingrad, an industrial city of 600,000 on the west bank of the Volga River.

The Drive to Stalingrad

On June 28, Hitler launched the summer-offensive phase of Operation *Blau* ("Blue"), sending the two army groups deep into Soviet territory. The Wehrmacht's initial advance was a smashing success, and the two army units gobbled up huge swaths of Soviet territory.

Confident that he could capture Stalingrad with just the 6th Army, under General Friedrich von Paulus, Hitler detached General Hermann Hoth's 4th Panzer Army from Army Group B and sent it south to join Army Group A. Before long, however, Hitler refocused on Stalingrad as his primary objective and sent a panzer corps and 4th Panzer's infantry back toward the city.

By the end of July, the 6th Army was a few dozen kilometers west of Stalingrad, with 4th Panzer's tanks advancing nearby. On August 23, the struggle for Stalingrad began.

Into the City

The battle opened with a massive *Luftwaffe* air bombardment that killed thousands of civilians and reduced huge sections of the city to rubble. Terrified civilians dug antitank ditches while workers' militias, antiaircraft teams, and the Red Army's defending force, General Vasili Chuikov's 62nd Army, began their slow, stubborn retreat into the city's neighborhoods.

By September 1, Army Group B had reached the Volga on the western side of Stalingrad, and the Red Army could reinforce the hard-pressed city only by sending supplies or men by boat across the broad, vulnerable river. The Germans pushed their way into the city, block by block, using tanks, artillery, and air power to support the advance. In response, local Soviet commanders began using "hugging" tactics, keeping their front lines so close to the German infantry that any *Luftwaffe* attacks or artillery fire called down upon the Red Army would endanger nearby Germans. The Germans referred to the hand-to-hand, house-to-house fighting as *Rattenkrieg*, or "rat war," joking bitterly about capturing an apartment's kitchen but having to fight for the living room.

Through the fall of 1942, Stalingrad consumed thousands of lives as foot soldiers, tanks, and artillery crews struggled through the wreckage of a dying city. Hiding beneath rubble and atop bombed-out apartments, snipers ruled entire neighborhoods; good snipers racked up hundreds of confirmed kills during the bloody siege. Battles raged around factories and buildings—the Red October steel mill, the Stalingrad Tractor Factory, and the Barrikady Gun Factory became the scenes of repeated, violent firefights that sometimes cut down thousands of men. On the ground, as panzers stalled in heaps of rubble, antitank crews descended upon the immobilized giants to knock them out by the score, killing the occupants as they scurried out of their burning armored vehicles.

As the year wore on, both Stalin and Hitler fed fresh troops into the inferno. Stalin shifted Moscow's strategic reserves from the capital area to the south, and General Chuikov obligingly threw these reinforcements into battle as soon as they arrived. Casualties mounted: In one three-day period, the Soviet 187th Rifle Division lost 90 percent of its men. By November, Paulus's 6th Army had taken about 90 percent of the city.

Counterattack and Encirclement

But during November, as Hitler's Wehrmacht reached its high-water mark, the weight of the Soviets' numbers began to shift the balance of power. On November 19, an army group under General Nikolai Vatutin, consisting of the 21st and 65th Armies and the 5th Tank Army, came crashing down upon the 3rd Romanian Army, which guarded the German 6th Army's northern flank. The offensive, known as Operation Uranus, shattered the 3rd Romanian after just one day. The following day, a two-army offensive from the south destroyed the Romanian 4th Army south of the Volga. Paulus's 6th Army, under orders from Hitler to maintain its position, was slowly being squeezed. Within four days, the two Soviet juggernauts linked up west of the city, encircling 250,000 Axis soldiers—most of the 6th Army, a corps from 4th Panzer, and some foreign Axis troops—in a ring of death.

The 6th Army's position was now desperate. It was in danger of starving or running out of ammunition and fuel—any of which would mean death. But Hitler had vowed that the German Army would never leave Stalingrad. When the high command pressed Hitler for permission to withdraw the 6th Army, *Reichsmarschall* Hermann Göring, chief of the *Luftwaffe*, glibly promised Hitler that the air force could supply the 6th Army's needs. With that, the fate of the 6th Army was sealed: Trapped along the Volga's banks, it would never leave Stalingrad.

Death of an Army

Göring's aerial supply effort failed almost from the start. Heavy Soviet antiaircraft emplacements, the Red Air Force, and miserable weather prevented most of the necessary food, fuel, and ammunition from reaching the beleaguered army.

The 6th Army was doomed, though its men did not yet know it. Officers pressed Paulus to defy Hitler and break out, but the ill-fated commander hesitated until his fuel stocks were too low to save himself.

On January 30, it was clear even to Hitler that the 6th Army was beyond hope. He ordered Paulus to fight to the last man—a glorious sacrifice to the heroic Third Reich's conquests. Hitler promoted Paulus to field marshal, noting cynically that no German field marshal had ever surrendered. The ploy did not work, and by February 2, 1943, *Generalfeldmarschall* Paulus led some 91,000 starving, disease-ridden soldiers into captivity. Only 5,000 of these prisoners would live to see their homes again.

The charnel house of Stalingrad cost Hitler and his allies over a quarter million soldiers (some estimates run as high as 850,000, including Axis troops near Stalingrad who were not part of the encirclement), while the Red Army lost close to 1.2 million on all fronts engaged around the city. With more than 40,000 civilians killed in the first week of bombardment, the total number of noncombatant deaths will never be known with precision. But the roughly two million casualty figure gives Stalingrad the sad honor of being the site of one of the bloodiest battles in history.

✳ At Stalingrad, Lieutenant General Vasily Chuikov insisted on having women operate communications posts, and they refused to bug out no matter how dangerous the situation.

Winter Shock

In the closing days of 1944, the Allies were anticipating a swift German fall. Instead, Hitler launched a surprise counteroffensive as a last-ditch measure to thwart the Allied advance.

✳ ✳ ✳ ✳

FOR WEEKS THE observation battalion of U.S. VIII Corps, the undermanned unit defending the strategic Ardennes Forest, knew something was afoot. Aiming sophisticated microphones at the *Schnee Eifel*, a wooded, German-occupied ridge near the Belgian-German border (and the spot from which the German Army had launched its invasions of France in 1914 and 1940), analysts picked up the telltale sounds of tracked vehicles and artillery moving into position.

The Allied high command, however, turned a deaf ear. Still elated from its swift liberation of France, top generals were convinced Germany had no punch left. Along 70 miles of Ardennes front, they'd placed just one armored division and four U.S. infantry divisions. To make matters worse, two of the infantry divisions were green, and the others were chewed up from previous battles.

Area commanders were focused on dealing with an outbreak of trench foot, which was triggered by the constant wetness and chill. They ordered a cutback in active reconnaissance by foot soldiers, which led to a sharp drop in prisoner grabs and local intelligence. Some VIII Corps intelligence officers employed their spotter planes for hunting wild boar. Most Allied craft were grounded by the bad weather.

Hitler's Bold Move

Under the cloak of late autumn's snow and mist, the Germans had secretly marshaled two panzer armies. Their forces bristled with 420 tanks and assault guns and 1,900 artillery pieces. Still, despite its ten panzer divisions, the German infantry was undermanned. *Volksgrenadier* units staffed with youths and overage men filled the gap.

Hitler slipped from his Wolf's Lair in East Prussia to the Eagle's Nest in Bavaria to direct the operation, code-named *Unternehmen Wacht am Rhein* (Operation Guard of the Rhine). His scheme foresaw the panzers rolling through the rugged Ardennes and, after seizing bridges over the River Meuse, driving north 60 miles to take Antwerp, the Allies' only close supply port. With the British and American armies cut off, the Wehrmacht could proceed east to deal with the Soviet Army nearing Germany's other frontier.

German General Alfred Jodl recalled the assault took place "in the West because the Russians had so many troops that, even if we had succeeded in destroying 30 divisions, it would have made no difference. On the other hand, if we destroyed 30 divisions in the West, [the Western Allies would be staggered]."

Unreasonable Expectations

Given Germany's weakened state, however, the ambitious operation was a huge gamble, and Hitler's commanders knew it. General Josef "Sepp" Dietrich, chief of the 6th SS Panzer Army, even noted sarcastically, "All Hitler wants me to do is to cross a river, capture Brussels, and then go on and take Antwerp. And all this...when the snow is waist deep."

A huge obstacle was petrol, in such scarce supply that horses hauled it to the front. Panzer crews were told to fill their tanks with captured stocks of American gasoline.

Yet playing to the Germans' advantage was the Allies' ULTRA intercepts of decrypted radio messages. In preparation for the offensive, the Wehrmacht imposed a strict wireless blackout. Further, it conducted a phantom buildup near Düsseldorf that gulled Allied intelligence. In occupied France, the German command had communicated by radio, which was open to interception. But it had now retreated to Germany, where messages were relayed by secure telephone and telegraph.

Attack!

At 0530 December 16, the artillery pieces slipped secretly into the Ardennes were unleashed on American troops. In the center, near the *Schnee Eifel*, the 5th Panzer Army cut off two regiments of the rookie 106th Division, forcing their surrender. At least 7,000 Americans were lost in the battle.

Confusion reigned for both sides in the heavy mists. Americans stranded in the woods tried to hook up with their units but bumped into German ones. Lieutenant Colonel Joachim Peiper's *Kampfgruppe* (armored battle group) was the spear point of the 6th Panzer Army. Troops in it came across an American truck column, mistook it for one of their own, and rode together unknowing before a firefight finally broke out.

German commandos disguised in American uniforms spread panic behind U.S. lines, causing traffic jams at hastily thrown-up checkpoints. Bad weather gridlocked the German columns, worsening their dire shortage of gas.

In Operation *Stösser* 1,200 *Fallschirmjägeren* parachuters were dropped at night in a snowstorm, with instructions to seize key crossroads. Blown by gusts over a wide area, the paratroops couldn't join up to take their objective. But the wide dispersal made the Americans think an entire division of elite troops had landed behind their lines.

Tied Up at the Bulge

After the initial shock, U.S. troops stiffened, spoiling the Nazi's timetable. In the north, the 1st and 3rd Battalions of the rookie 99th Infantry Division, with units from the battered 2nd Division, were outnumbered, but they were ordered to hold the vital Elsenborn Ridge for weeks against repeated attacks.

The German infantry bogged down trying to take critical roads. After failing to trap the U.S. divisions, Peiper's *Kampfgruppe* tried forcing its way to the Meuse. It was harried by teams of U.S. engineers, who torched gasoline dumps as they retreated. Then the *Kampfgruppe* was blocked on December 18 by a stout defense at the town of Stavelot. Peiper's 1st SS Panzer Regiment raced for a bridge on the river Amblève at Trois-Ponts, but American troops blew it up. On December 19, a U.S. counterthrust trapped the *Kampfgruppe*, forcing Peiper to retreat while abandoning his heavy equipment.

During these battles, a group of Reiper's 1st SS Panzer Regiment captured a U.S. artillery observation unit near the town of Malmédy. The *Waffen* (Fighting) SS men then massacred 84 of the captives. Enraged Allied troops began shooting SS prisoners in retaliation.

On December 19, Eisenhower and his generals huddled in a Verdun bunker. The press was reporting the 30-mile German salient as a dangerous bulge in the Allied lines. But Ike, aware his foe was more vulnerable outside his lair, was upbeat: "The present situation is to be regarded as one of opportunity and not of disaster," he pronounced. "There will be only cheerful faces at this table." Patton responded, "Hell, let's have the guts to let the bastards go all the way to Paris. Then, we'll really cut 'em off and chew 'em up." The head of the Third Army added he could have his troops counterattack in 40 hours. No one believed Patton, but he'd already issued orders to attack.

Defense of Bastogne

In the center of the Bulge, the towns of St. Vith and Bastogne straddled key crossroads. General Troy Houston Middleton, head of the VIII Corps, ordered a fighting retreat to slow the advancing juggernaut.

The Americans improvised, combining disparate units into coherent defenses. The terrain favored the defense, as the forests and ridges channeled the panzers onto narrow roads. Parts of two U.S armored and two infantry divisions held St. Vith until December 21—four days after the Germans had planned to take it. Under General Bruce Clarke, the Americans then fell back to prepared positions, slowed the 5th Panzer Army for two more days, and fell back to a river.

These events bought precious time for parts of the 9th and 10th Armored Divisions, and the 101st Division of paratroopers trucked in from Rheims to beat the Germans to Bastogne, setting up an epic defense. Still, by December 21, American forces at Bastogne were surrounded and badly outgunned by the 17th Panzer Corps. They had almost no medicine. Artillery teams were almost out of shells: Gunners were instructed to fire only at large groups of tanks.

An Ominous Ultimatum

The German commander had an ultimatum delivered to the 101st's acting chief, General Anthony McAuliffe. It read, in part, "There is only one possibility to save the encircled USA troops from total annihilation: that is the honorable surrender of the town.... German Artillery... are ready to annihilate USA troops... All the serious civilian losses caused by this would not correspond with the well-known American humanity."

McAuliffe scoffed ("Nuts," according to those present, but he may have used another four-letter word). In his formal written reply, he did employ "Nuts," which stumped the German commander as well as the French-speaking Belgians. The battle continued.

The panzer corps erred, however, by methodically attacking one point after another instead of using its superior numbers to rush the town. Assistant division commander Brigadier General Gerald Higgins, a veteran infantryman, shuttled about his best foot soldiers, the 327th Glider Regiment and the 502nd Parachute Regiment, to meet the assaults of the *Panzergrenadiers*. McAuliffe, the 101st's artillery commander, massed 130 cannons from 11 battalions against the mechanized attacks. The German's charges were repulsed, and they falsely concluded their enemy had plenty of ammunition.

It helped that the United States fielded elite troops, such as those in Easy Company of the 101st's 506th Parachute Regiment, depicted in the book and TV series *Band of Brothers*. With no armor and little morphine for the injured, the brethren dug out trenches in the frozen earth, withstood the terror of shells bursting in the forest canopy, and held their ground.

The Americans also helped themselves by obeying orders too slowly. Early on, the army group's headquarters ordered VIII Corps to evacuate Bastogne, but the paratroops hesitated after realizing they'd withdraw smack into the Panzer Lehr Division sweeping around the town.

Behind the scenes, Eisenhower acted decisively. Along with backing Patton's counterthrust, he had Field Marshal Bernhard Montgomery take command of the U.S. armies in the Bulge's north. Monty scraped together personnel to guard the Meuse bridges. Ike ordered up 250,000 reinforcements, many from England, and let 4,500 African American troops, previously barred from combat, volunteer for the infantry. In contrast, the German commander in the West, Field Marshal Gerd von Rundstedt, spent much of the battle drinking cognac and perusing novels. Certain the plan was doomed, he turned over the reins to Field Marshal Walther Model.

Clear Skies Turn the Tide of the Ardennes

Clear weather arrived on December 23. Waves of theretofore-grounded P-47 Thunderbolt fighters took off and strafed German columns and depots. Major General Frederic von Mellenthin of the 9th Panzer Division commented, "I witnessed the uninterrupted air attacks on our traffic routes and supply dumps. Not a single German plane was in the air, and innumerable vehicles were shot up and their blackened wrecks littered the roads."

At Bastogne, C-47s air-dropped 1,400 crates of supplies. The medical crisis eased when a team of doctors arrived suddenly by glider. The German units that had bypassed the town were gunned to a halt by the U.S. 2nd Armored Division and roving fighter-bombers.

In the north, Sepp Dietrich's fuel-starved panzers were stemmed well short of the Meuse. Manteuffel, chief of the other panzer army, recommended Hitler call off the offensive. Der Führer refused.

Improvisation

After swinging north, marching through snowstorms, Patton's men approached Bastogne. By Christmas his 4th Armored Division was within five miles of a linkup. The next day, the commander of its 37th Tank Battalion, Lieutenant Colonel Creighton Abrams, ignored orders to assault a stoutly defended town and raced through a lightly defended one, reaching Bastogne. After the war Abrams became Army Chief of Staff; the army's main battle tank is named for him.

Hitler desperately played a last card. On New Year's Day 1945, the *Luftwaffe* launched Operation Bodenplatte, a sneak attack by hundreds of aircraft on Allied airfields in Holland and Belgium. Four hundred sixty-five Allied planes were damaged or wrecked. But the secrecy of the attack proved a two-edged sword for the Germans. Its air force lost 277 precious craft— 171 to flak, and much of that from Nazi gunners. Kept in the dark about the raids, they downed many of their own bombers. The *Luftwaffe* was spent.

Patton's tanks advanced northeastward from Bastogne, while the more cautious Montgomery moved southeast, both pinching the center of the Bulge. On January 7 Hitler conceded to pull out his troops. They left, abandoning most of the irreplaceable panzers, fuel holds empty.

The human losses for the Allied victory and German debacle were similar. The official toll of U.S. casualties was 80,987; the German, 84,834.

The End of the Third Reich

With the Thousand-Year Reich collapsing, Hitler had no intention of facing Soviet justice. But did he escape after all?

❊   ❊   ❊   ❊

IN JANUARY 1945, Adolf Hitler moved into a 30-room underground complex. This *Führerbunker* was designed and built with spendthrift abandon. Along with Hitler, it sheltered Eva Braun, the Goebbels family, and various specialists and functionaries.

On March 13, 1945, Hitler left the Reich Chancellery alive for the last time to visit the nearby Oder front. His pasty, frail countenance was a shell of his once-animated manner. By then, few sights could shock Wehrmacht and SS officers, but this was one.

By April of that same year, what remained of Nazi Germany stretched from the Baltic Sea to Czechoslovakia, between the Elbe and Oder rivers. Its *Kriegsmarine* mostly rested on the ocean floor. Its *Luftwaffe* had few planes and little fuel. Its social systems were disintegrating. Once Nazi Germany had measured its strength in divisions and armies; now a "division" might mean a remnant *Waffen*-SS company or a platoon of clerks issued pistols. Germans in East Prussia were learning firsthand that Red Army occupation meant pillage and rape.

Hitler no longer broadcasted nor made public appearances. He limped, dragging his left leg. His left hand trembled so badly he had to clasp it in his right. Years of combined stress and paranoia, quack injections varying from vitamins to methamphetamine, and the 1944 assassin's bomb had eroded Adolf Hitler. Nearing 56, he looked, walked, and behaved as if suffering from Parkinson's disease. Sometimes he limped about, uncomprehending; other times he ordered nonexistent formations into battle or ranted about treason.

Hitler's Last Birthday

On April 20, Adolf Hitler celebrated his 56th birthday. Most remaining senior Nazis attended, as did Eva Braun and her brother-in-law Hermann Fegelein. The Americans and the British rattled the walls with a birthday spanking: their next-to-last massive bombing raid on Berlin. Zhukov's 3rd Shock Army gave Hitler "a pinch to grow an inch" with the first Soviet artillery shelling of Berlin's suburbs. In his last film appearance, Hitler went out to the Reich Chancellery garden to praise some Hitler Youth defenders.

The exodus began the next day. Hitler began to speak of suicide, weeping openly and screaming about betrayals. *Luftwaffe* commander Hermann Göring, oscillating between lucidity and drug-soaked apathy, entrained with his loot for Berchtesgaden. He then messaged the Führer asking to take over the Reich; Hitler ordered the presumptuous *Reichsmarschall* stripped of all titles and arrested. Heinrich Himmler, chief of the SS, went to north Germany and opened secret talks with the Allies. When this was reported by radio on April 28, Hitler sacked the *Reichsführer*-SS as he had Göring. Eva Braun maintained a sort of sad serenity through it all.

Once Soviet troops surrounded Berlin, entry and exit became problematic. General Ritter von Greim, heir apparent to *Luftwaffe* command, flew in with aviator Hanna Reitsch. They offered to remain with Hitler, but he ordered them to make sure Himmler did not become Führer. They flew north in a light plane dodging Soviet flak bursts. General Hermann Fegelein (Eva Braun's brother-in-law) was captured trying to sneak out of Berlin in civilian clothing; he was shot for desertion.

Wedding Bombs

On April 29, Adolf Hitler rewarded Eva Braun with the title no other woman ever held relative to him: *Frau* Hitler. Hitler wore his Nazi uniform; Eva wore black silk taffeta. Goebbels summoned civil servant Walter Wagner to perform the nuptials in Nazi uniform with *Volkssturm* armband. The ceremony was short, with Goebbels and *Reichsleiter* Martin Bormann signing as witnesses. Eva signed her new name to the marriage document: "Eva B Hitler, geb. [née] Braun." Hitler promptly went into a side room to dictate his will to Traudl Junge, one of the two remaining secretaries.

Hitlerdämmerung

The next day, Hitler obtained cyanide capsules from a *Reichskanzlei* doctor. He ordered one tested on his beloved German shepherd Blondi; her floppy-pawed puppies soon joined their dam in death. Hitler ordered Otto Günsche, his personal SS adjutant, to burn his and Eva's bodies after death. The *Führer* had a last lunch with his dietitian and secretaries, then traded farewells with Goebbels, Bormann, and the remaining generals.

Eva took cyanide around 3:00 P.M., and Hitler fired a Walther PPK semiautomatic pistol into his brain soon after. Günsche got help to carry the bodies up to a bomb crater and set them afire. The men buried the charred corpses beneath the abundant rubble.

Thereafter, the bunker's remnant population escaped, committed suicide, or surrendered to Soviet forces. On May 1, Goebbels insisted that his family must die; the children, he said, would be marked as the "children of Goebbels." A doctor helped Magda Goebbels inject her five daughters and one son with morphine, then poisoned them—adding six more innocent children to the war's toll. Next, husband and wife chewed cyanide capsules, with an SS officer firing two pistol shots to ensure the result. SS men cremated the Goebbels family near the Hitler burial crater.

Bormann died attempting to escape Berlin. Gestapo chief Heinrich Müller vanished; no one knows whether he survived—or where. Traudl Junge survived, as did Otto Günsche. *Grossadmiral* Karl Dönitz became *Führer,* in accordance with Hitler's wishes, and surrendered the Third Reich on May 8.

---

* By 1945 Hitler could not have read these words. His eyes had grown so bad that all his reports had to be prepared on special typewriters that used a typeface triple the normal size.

* Walter Wagner, who officiated at Adolf and Eva's wedding, was required by law to ask if both were Aryan, and if either had a family history of disease.

* Somehow, the *Führerbunker* was built without suitable military communications facilities. As the Red Army tightened the clamps on Berlin, German intelligence officers picked up the Berlin phone book and phoned random people in various suburbs, asking if they had seen any Russians. Sometimes the answer came in profane Russian phrases, which fairly well answered the question of the area's occupation.

* The NKVD and its intelligence/counterintelligence functions changed names and shifted responsibilities and whatnot during and immediately after the war. MVD, MGB, Smersh (*Smyert Shpionen,* "Death to Spies"), and the KGB are all part of the sea of names. To avoid confusion, the two best-known names—"NKVD" and "KGB"—are used here, though either may be technically inaccurate depending on the timing of a given event. Whatever the name, Russian intelligence was feared across Europe.

* Contrary to most accounts, Joseph Goebbels did not have a clubfoot. He had suffered from a bone marrow affliction as a child; surgery shortened and weakened his left leg. He wore orthopedic correctives most of his life, and witnesses brought by the NKVD to identify the Goebbels's corpses immediately spotted the brace and special shoe.

Was Hitler's Death a Hoax?

Rumors of Hitler's survival persisted for years: The charred corpse was a double; he had offspring; he was living in South America, keeping that old Nazi spirit alive. Some of the wilder tales were fueled by Soviet propaganda.

They were false. In 1993 the Russian government opened the old Soviet files. We now know beyond any reasonable doubt what happened.

The NKVD (Russian intelligence) investigation began the moment Soviet troops overran the *Führerbunker*. They exhumed the Hitler and Goebbels bodies, bringing in close acquaintances for positive I.D.; for example, Eva and Adolf's former dentist and his assistant both recognized their own professional handiwork. The original announcement had been correct: Adolf Hitler had died April 30, 1945. After sending Hitler's jaw back to Moscow for safekeeping, the NKVD secretly reburied the other remains at a military base near Magdeburg, German Democratic Republic (East Germany).

In 1970, the Soviet military prepared to transfer the Magdeburg base to East German control. The KGB (successor to the NKVD) dared not leave the Nazi remains. On April 4, 1970, the KGB exhumed the fragmentary remains of Adolf and Eva Hitler and the Goebbels family. Hitler's skull was identified, and the bullet-holed portion was sent to Moscow. The next day, the KGB incinerated the rest of the remains, crushed them to dust and dumped them in a nearby river.

Therefore, of Eva Braun and the Goebbels family nothing at all remains. Of Hitler, today only his jaw and a skull fragment exist in Russian custody.

Hard Times on Plum Pudding Island

John F. Kennedy proved his mettle
long before his days in the White House.

✳ ✳ ✳ ✳

IN AUGUST 1943, 26-year-old Lieutenant John F. Kennedy was serving as the skipper aboard PT-109, a high-speed boat assigned to patrol the Pacific and sabotage Japanese supply lines.

The nights were difficult out on the Pacific; with few lights in the area, it got about as dark as anyone could ever imagine. On the night of August 1, 1943, the moon was hidden by clouds, and the resulting complete darkness nearly did Kennedy in.

At one point that night, Kennedy looked up to see a Japanese destroyer pass by; he remembered it looking like a massive wall. Kennedy had little time to marvel at the sight, as the destroyer proceeded to slice Kennedy's boat in two.

After the collision, the surviving crew of PT-109 assembled on the wreckage of the boat's bow to discuss their options. They decided to set off for Plum Pudding Island, a tiny dot of land deemed too small to interest the Japanese. The crew swam for hours, Kennedy towing an immobile Patrick McMahon through the water by clenching the strap of the badly burned man's life jacket in his teeth. They stumbled to shore across the razor-sharp coral, and Kennedy, having swallowed copious amounts of seawater, vomited and collapsed on the beach.

After he recovered, Kennedy announced that he intended to swim the mile and a half into the sea to attempt to contact PT boats on patrol that evening. At about 6:30 P.M., he slipped back into the water.

No boats came that night. By 9:00 the next morning, the men on the island presumed the lieutenant dead. They were proved wrong around noon when Kennedy dragged himself back ashore. He ordered a skeptical Ensign Ross to make a similar attempt that night. Unfortunately, Ross's effort proved no more effective.

The men exhausted the resources on Plum Pudding by the second day. Driven by a need for more food and the desire to be closer to potential rescuers, Kennedy decided to move the group to another island, Olasana, covered with plenty of coconut trees and located closer to the PT patrol area.

Naru and Encounters with the Japanese

The next day, Kennedy and Ross decided to swim to the neighboring island of Naru. Searching the island, Kennedy and Ross found the wreckage of a small Japanese boat containing a crate filled with crackers and candy, as well as a small dugout canoe with a supply of water. Discussing their windfall, the two men made their way back down to the beach.

As Kennedy and Ross emerged onto the beach, they spotted two other men out on the reef. Convinced that the men were Japanese, Kennedy and Ross dived back into the bushes. The two strangers in question, Melanesian scouts Biuku Gasa and Eroni Kumana, were actually in the employ of the Australian military. Convinced that Kennedy and Ross were Japanese, the scouts leapt into their canoe and paddled away. Fortunately, they headed toward Olasana, where the remaining PT survivors were camped. Making contact with the crew, the scouts mentioned that Naru contained Japanese troops, which alarmed the PT crew. Little did they know that one of the "Japanese" the scouts referred to was actually their own skipper!

Coconuts and Rescue

Returning to Olasana in the canoe the next day, Kennedy found Ensign Leonard Thom chatting away with Biuku and Eroni. The scouts were sent off with two messages, one written with the stub of a pencil Thom had managed to keep throughout the entire ordeal; the other was carved into the side of a coconut by Kennedy. The coconut read, "NARU ISL / NATIVE KNOWS POSIT / HE CAN PILOT / 11 ALIVE / NEED SMALL BOAT / KENNEDY."

The news quickly made its way back to Lieutenant Arthur Reginald Evans, an Australian coast-watcher near Wana Wana, who had actually seen the wreckage of PT-109 and sent messages to the Americans inquiring about the possibility of survivors. Evans dispatched a larger canoe with supplies. Kennedy made his way back to Wana Wana in the larger canoe, hiding from Japanese air patrols under palm fronds in the bottom of the boat. He met Evans and rendezvoused with a PT-boat patrol bound to pick up his shipwrecked crew, who were rescued on August 8. Except for the two men lost in the initial collision, the crew of PT-109 survived.

Controversy erupted surrounding the loss of PT-109. General MacArthur thought Kennedy should face court-martial, but the official Navy report was much less critical. However, regardless of the circumstances of the loss, Kennedy's determined efforts to save his crew were beyond question. He was awarded the Navy and Marine Corps Medal for "extremely heroic conduct." Kennedy himself, however, felt as if he hadn't accomplished enough in the war and turned down an offer to return home, instead making a successful effort to obtain command of another boat.

John F. Kennedy kept the famous coconut on the desk in the Oval Office throughout his presidency. Despite all of his other successes, in 1963 he wrote, "Any man who may be asked in this century what he did to make his life worthwhile, I think can respond with a good deal of pride and satisfaction, 'I served in the United States Navy.'"

✱ Oceanographer Robert Ballard found pieces of PT-109 in 2002. Ballard has endeavored to keep the site a secret, though; it is a memorial to the boat's lost crew, and he wants it left in peace.

Hollywood Versus History

You may not be surprised to learn that Hollywood doesn't always get history right.

✳ ✳ ✳ ✳

Jack always appreciated a gal who could give a good back rub
PT 109 (1963)—This World War II adventure suggests that JFK's back problems began with a football injury and were aggravated when his PT boat was rammed by a Japanese destroyer. The truth, however, is that Kennedy had a bad back for most of his life; his father had to pull strings to even get him admitted into the service.

Would it be so hard to just stop at a gas station and pick up a new one?
Raiders of the Lost Ark (1981)—Indy studies a map that notes "Iran" when that country was still known as Persia. It also says "Thailand" when that nation was called Siam.

Are the drivers naked, too?
The Naked Prey (1966)—Although the film is set in 1915 Africa, modern cars are visible as they pass in the distance.

If not for this, the Best Picture award would have been in the bag
L.A. Confidential (1997)—The logo of *Hush-Hush* magazine is set in Helvetica Compressed, a typeface that wasn't created until the mid-1970s, some 20 years after the setting of this crime thriller.

I buy all my books on wormhole.com
Donnie Darko (2001)—A character in this story set in 1988 refers to Stephen Hawking's writings about wormholes—remarks that didn't appear until the 1998 tenth-anniversary reissue of Hawking's *A Brief History of Time*.

Shattering the Emperor's Sword

Across miles of rolling oceans, the world's two mightiest fleets were about to wage the greatest aircraft carrier battle of all time. At stake: command of the Pacific Ocean.

❊   ❊   ❊   ❊

THE EPIC CONTEST began as a battle over a tiny coral atoll called Midway, some 1,000 miles northwest of America's naval base at Pearl Harbor. Japanese naval commanders, stung by the carrier-based Doolittle Raid on Tokyo in April 1942, hoped to draw the American flattops out of the vast emptiness of the Pacific Ocean and into a decisive battle, where they could be destroyed once and for all. To force the Americans to battle, Admiral Yamamoto Isoroku, commander of the Japanese Combined Fleet, decided to attack the island of Midway. If successful, in one stroke Yamamoto would rid the Pacific of an irksome U.S. air outpost—the "unsinkable carrier," it was called—and pose a serious threat to the Hawaiian Islands.

Yamamoto's tactical plan was simple: A carrier force would blast the island's air defenses, a battleship fleet under his personal command would reduce the coastal defenses to rubble, and a landing force would capture the real estate. With luck, the attack would also draw the U.S. carrier fleet into the open, where Japan's superior forces would send it to the bottom.

Opposing Forces

In late May 1942, Japan ruled the seas. For his assault on Midway, Yamamoto would call upon four huge aircraft carriers under Vice Admiral Nagumo Chuichi: the *Kaga, Akagi, Soryu,* and *Hiryu.* Yamamoto would miss two other carriers damaged at the Battle of the Coral Sea that same month, but with a fighting force that included several battleships, 2 light carriers, 16 cruisers, and more than 70 destroyers, Yamamoto believed he had little to fear.

The U.S. Pacific Fleet, commanded by Admiral Chester W. Nimitz, could only muster two carriers, the *Enterprise* and the *Hornet*. A third carrier, the *Yorktown*, had been seriously damaged at the Battle of the Coral Sea. As Nimitz was planning his next moves, *Yorktown* was back at Pearl Harbor, where 1,300 dockyard workers labored around the clock to get her back into service.

But Japanese fleet strength, impressive as it was, was largely offset by America's super-secret trump card: American code breakers had cracked the naval ciphers that the Japanese government believed to be impregnable. From radio intercepts, Admiral Nimitz learned of Yamamoto's plans for Midway, and Nimitz was determined to ambush Yamamoto as he pounced on America's tiny outpost.

Nimitz combined the *Enterprise* and *Hornet* carrier group with Task Force 17, a cruiser group reinforced with the timely arrival of the *Yorktown*, which had managed to slip her cables at Pearl Harbor on May 30. He threw out a protective submarine screen around Midway, and his carriers kept search planes circling in all directions, looking for an enemy lurking in the dark Pacific waters.

Hammering the "Unsinkable Carrier"

The first contact with Nagumo's carrier fleet came around 5:30 A.M. on the morning of June 4, when a PBY reconnaissance plane based at Midway reported contact with a hostile carrier force. Base commanders at Midway scrambled their light bombers, and soon Nimitz knew the location of his foe. The contest for Midway was on.

Admiral Nagumo's four carriers launched 108 bombers and escorting fighters to devastate Midway's defenses, unaware of Nimitz's fleet just 215 miles away. U.S. Navy, Army, and Marine bombers from Midway took off to attack the Japanese fleet while fighters scrambled to take out the incoming Japanese bombers. The Marine warbirds waged a bitter fight against the agile A6M Zero fighters, but the attackers drove the Marines off with heavy losses, and soon bombs began falling on Midway. The Japanese effort was not wholly successful, however; circling over the island's air facilities, the Japanese attack commander radioed back  to his carrier group that another air strike would be needed to put the island's facilities out of commission. Admiral Nagumo accordingly ordered his second-wave squadrons to remove their torpedoes and refit with bombs to finish off Midway's defenses.

While Midway was being plastered, the plucky U.S. submarine *Nautilus* stuck up her periscope in the middle of the Japanese formation. She let loose a torpedo, missing her target. She attracted unwanted attention for the next hour or so by the destroyer *Arashii*, which circled the sub's last position while the carrier fleet steamed away. This seemingly inconsequential skirmish would make a huge difference later on.

As U.S. bombing runs from Midway were ending in disappointment for the Americans, a Japanese scout pilot spotted *Yorktown*'s flotilla and alerted his superiors. But his vague report did not fully communicate to Nagumo that a carrier group was heading his way. Nagumo had been in the middle of rearming his planes for a second bombing run against Midway, which he still considered the main threat, but after some delay he learned that the American surface ships included aircraft carriers. He ordered his planes to remove their bombs and again refitted his squadrons with torpedoes for an attack on the U.S. carrier force. Nagumo expected he was about to secure the eastern limits of the Empire of Japan.

Going for the Kill

While Midway's airmen were being cut apart by Japanese fighters, Nimitz's task force launched three squadrons of torpedo bombers and five squadrons of dive-bombers, with their usual cordon of escorting fighters. The first wave of TBD-1 Devastator torpedo bombers from the *Hornet* ran into a swarm of Zeros, and the entire U.S. squadron was shot down. Two more torpedo squadrons attempted to get through to the Japanese carriers, with similar results.

As the Devastators were being gunned down by the deadly accurate Zero pilots, three squadrons of SBD-3 Dauntless dive-bombers from the *Enterprise* and *Yorktown* arrived high overhead, having searched for enemy ships without luck until two squadrons from the *Enterprise* picked up the wake of the destroyer Arashii, which was speeding back to join her carrier group after her run-in with the submarine *Nautilus*. In a stroke of luck, the three American dive-bomber squadrons arrived high over the Japanese carrier group.

An Opportunity Seized

The Japanese carriers had just turned to launch their bombers when they saw dive-bombers screaming out of the sky. The Japanese carriers were at their most vulnerable—their fighter escorts were engaged at low altitude, their flight decks were stacked with bombs and fuel, their planes were aligned on deck wingtip to wingtip. Bombs rained down, setting fire to the decks and starting chain reactions as stored ordnance exploded and fuel burned out of control. Within minutes, the carriers *Kaga*, *Soryu*, and *Akagi*, Admiral Nagumo's flagship, were out of action with fires raging across their decks: All three would lie at the bottom of the Pacific by the next morning.

Nagumo's fourth carrier, *Hiryu*, steamed ahead of the other ships, striking back furiously at the American attackers. She managed to get 36 Type 99 Val dive-bombers and ten Kate torpedo planes off her decks around 11:00 A.M., sending them toward *Yorktown*. U.S. interceptors, Navy F4F Wildcats, shot down most of the Vals, but seven made their way to the *Yorktown* and three scored hits. A second wave of bombers put two torpedoes in her side, and she began to list. Her commander ordered the veteran ship abandoned, but she refused to die; the legendary carrier did not sink for another two days, and only then after a Japanese submarine put a third torpedo into her hull.

Although she had put *Yorktown* out of action, *Hiryu* would not live to see her victory. Dive-bombers from the *Enterprise* put four bombs along her flight deck, and fires soon gutted the hangar deck and engine rooms. The carrier's admiral and captain ordered the crew to abandon the doomed ship, and both commanders committed suicide. Japanese ships put a torpedo into her hull to keep her out of American hands, and she went down at 9:00 A.M. the next morning.

The Rising Sun Begins to Set

The Battle of Midway profoundly shifted the balance of power in the Pacific. Japan lost 3,400 sailors and experienced carrier pilots, an admiral, three carrier captains, and two heavy cruisers. Most critically, four of Japan's precious carriers had been sent to the bottom, giving the U.S. the edge in naval airpower.

The war's great carrier battle also enabled the United States to take the strategic initiative and shattered Japanese plans for a defensive perimeter close to United States territory. For the rest of the war, Japan would remain on the defensive, while the United States, with its huge industrial might, would dictate the tempo of the struggle.

✻ Japanese battleships' gun shells contained dye to help gunners adjust their fire by the colored splashes.

✻ Before the start of World War II, General Joseph Stilwell was nicknamed "Uncle Joe" for the concern he showed for average American GIs.

✻ Many of the U.S. aircraft that launched from Midway Island were outmoded F2A-3 Buffalos—chubby, alarmingly slow fighters that flyers dubbed "Flying Coffins."

The Plot to Assassinate Truman

Puerto Ricans have sought independence from the United States for decades. In 1950, two ardent nationalists took matters into their own hands.

✳ ✳ ✳ ✳

THE PUERTO RICAN Nationalist Party was spoiling for a fight. They had tried to reach independence through electoral participation, but by the 1930s, leader Dr. Pedro Albizu Campos began advocating a campaign of violent revolution.

In 1936, Albizu Campos was charged with conspiring to overthrow the government and was incarcerated. He spent the next six years in jail in New York. When he finally returned to Puerto Rico in 1947, the tinder of *nacionalismo puertorriqueño* was bone-dry and smoldering.

The Match Is Lit

On October 30, 1950, Nationalists seized the town of Jayuya. With air support, the Puerto Rico National Guard crushed the rebellion. Griselio Torresola and Oscar Collazo, two *nacionalistas*, decided to retaliate at the highest level: the president of the United States.

They had help from natural wastage. The White House, which looks majestic from the outside, has been quite the wretched dump at many points in its history. By 1948, it was physically unsound, so the Truman family moved to Blair House while the White House was being renovated. It would be a lot easier to whack a president at Blair House than it would have been at the White House.

The Attempt

At 2:20 P.M. on November 1, 1950, Torresola approached the Pennsylvania Avenue entrance from the west with a 9mm Luger pistol. Collazo came from the east carrying the Luger's cheaper successor, the Walther P38. White House police guarded the entrance. Truman was upstairs taking a nap.

Collazo approached the Blair House steps, facing the turned back of Officer Donald Birdzell, and fired, shattering Birdzell's knee. Nearby Officers Floyd Boring and Joseph Davidson fired at Collazo through a fence without immediate effect. Birdzell dragged himself after Collazo, firing his pistol. Bullets from Boring and Davidson grazed Collazo in the scalp and chest— seemingly minor wounds. Collazo sat down to reload.

Officer Leslie Coffelt staffed a guard booth at the west corner as Torresola took him unaware. Coffelt fell with a chest full of holes. Next, Torresola fired on Officer Joseph Downs, who had just stopped to chat with Coffelt. Downs took bullets to the hip, back, and neck. He staggered to the basement door and locked it, hoping to deny the assassins entry. Torresola advanced on Birdzell from behind as the officer engaged Collazo and fired, hitting his other knee. Birdzell lost consciousness as Torresola reloaded.

An Ounce of Luck

Weapon recharged, Oscar Collazo stood, then collapsed from his wounds. At that moment, a startled Truman came to the window. Torresola was 31 feet away. If he had looked up at precisely the right moment, the Puerto Rican nationalist would have achieved his mission.

Despite three chest wounds, Officer Coffelt forced himself to his feet, took careful aim, and fatally shot Griselio Torresola. Coffelt staggered back to the guard shack and crumpled.

Collazo survived and was sentenced to death. President Truman commuted Collazo's sentence to life imprisonment in 1952, shortly before he left office.

Officers Downs and Birdzell recovered. Officer Leslie Coffelt died four hours later. The Secret Service's day room at Blair House is now named the Leslie W. Coffelt Memorial Room.

Wisconsin's Federal Fearmonger

Wisconsin claims one very infamous senator, Joseph Raymond McCarthy, best known for his sensational communist witch hunt.

✳ ✳ ✳ ✳

ORN TO A farming family in rural Grand Chute on November 15, 1908, McCarthy dropped out of school after graduating from eighth grade and started his own chicken farm. Unfortunately, his birds fell victim to disease, and at the age of 20, McCarthy went back to school.

Somehow, he crammed an entire high school education into nine months, while also managing a grocery store in Manawa. He earned such stellar grades that Marquette University accepted him as a law student. At Marquette, he was known as "Smiling Joe" for his good humor and became a champion middleweight boxer, often felling larger opponents with his high-energy fighting style. McCarthy was so good that he even considered making a career in the ring, but a local boxing instructor talked him into getting his degree instead.

Throwing his energy into school, McCarthy dove into campus debate clubs where he proved he could be as much of a pit bull with his words as he was with boxing. After graduating in 1935, he became a lawyer in the small towns of Waupaca and Shawano and, by age 30, was elected judge in Wisconsin's Tenth Judicial Circuit.

Serving His Country

McCarthy put his legal practice on hold to join the Marines in 1942 and serve in World War II. He was an intelligence officer in the South Pacific and saw action as part of a bombing raid crew, which earned him a second nickname, "Tailgunner Joe."

McCarthy would later falsely say he carried ten pounds of shrapnel in his leg, but in truth, he returned to Wisconsin unscathed and determined to regain his circuit judgeship. In

1946, he dared to run for the Republican candidacy for the U.S. Senate against the popular 21-year incumbent, Robert M. LaFollette Jr. McCarthy barely squeaked through to win the nomination and became the youngest U.S. Senator at that time at age 38.

The Beginning of the End

The 1950 Senate election may have spurred McCarthy's monumental decline. Perhaps grasping for a campaign issue, McCarthy made the shocking claim that he had a list of 205 government officials who were communists. The government's House Un-American Activities Committee had already paved the way for such suspicion with its investigations of the Hollywood entertainment industry starting in 1947. The Senate opened hearings on McCarthy's allegations in March 1950, but McCarthy never proved his case. In 1952, the Senate turned the tables and began investigating McCarthy.

Although the committee found him guilty of unethical actions, his loyal base still reelected him in 1952. Ironically, McCarthy was made Chairman of the Committee on Government Operations and Investigations. "Tailgunner Joe" kept looking for communists, even going so far as to accuse the U.S. Army and the Eisenhower presidential administration. However, hearings broadcast via the new medium of television in 1954 helped discredit McCarthy. By December of that year, he was officially condemned by the Senate for abuse of power. He finished the two and a half years of his term, largely powerless and unpopular. At the same time, McCarthy began to drink heavily and suffered various physical ailments.

McCarthy succumbed to hepatitis on May 2, 1957. He left behind a wife, Jean, an adopted daughter, Tierney, and a new word that's still in use: "McCarthyism." Thanks to this term, Joseph McCarthy's name will forever be associated with the act of aggressively hunting for certain people based on unsubstantiated charges.

Our Long National Nightmare Is Over

Gerald R. Ford promised to bring closure to the era of unrest brought on by political corruption and the Vietnam War.

✳ ✳ ✳ ✳

BEFORE HE BECAME vice-president, Gerald Ford served in the U.S. House of Representatives for 25 years, playing the part of the consummate insider who enjoyed the clubby culture of Capitol Hill as much as its power over national affairs. He came to know Richard M. Nixon, who at that time was also a member of the House.

As Nixon's political career led him eventually to the presidency, Ford became House minority leader, remaining loyal to Nixon in nearly all his votes. Even as the Watergate conspiracy began to come to light, Ford remained convinced of Nixon's innocence. He was rewarded for his devotion in 1973, when Nixon's vice president Spiro Agnew resigned after pleading no contest to charges of tax evasion. Ford was chosen as Agnew's replacement, receiving strong support from his friends in Congress.

Ascending to the Presidency

Ford only had eight months as vice president before Nixon became the first American President to resign from office. Addressing a nation that was suffering both from the administration's disgrace and the uneasy conclusion to the Vietnam War, Ford tried in his acceptance speech to assure Americans that the troubled era was ending, saying, "Our long national nightmare is over."

For his first 30 days, Ford was wildly popular. But in his first major acts as President—pardoning both Nixon and Vietnam draft dodgers—he destroyed that goodwill. His administration accomplished little in the ensuing two years, and he lost the 1976 election to Jimmy Carter.

Red Quagmire

Americans cheered the early stages of modern Islamic extremism when it focused on the enemies of the United States. But the enemy of your enemy is not always your friend.

✳ ✳ ✳ ✳

IN FEBRUARY 1979, the Islamic Revolution in Iran ousted the U.S.-backed shah, setting the stage for the Hostage Crisis. On February 14, U.S. Ambassador to Afghanistan Adolph Dubs was abducted and killed by Islamists. In March, a peace treaty was signed between Egypt and Israel, which angered the Soviet Union. And Muslim Afghans were threatening the pro-Russian Afghan government. The situation was ripe for trouble.

Soviet Advances in Afghanistan

The Soviets had been sending arms and advisers to the Afghans for 60 years, and finally, an Afghan Communist government emerged. Neither the Soviets nor the new government was about to let a bunch of religious fanatics march in and take over.

Between April 1978 and December 1979, the government struck back, arresting Islamic mullahs and executing 27,000 people. The city of Herat rebelled, so the government and its Russian allies flattened the city, killing another 24,000. More than half of the 90,000 soldiers in the Afghan army deserted or joined the rebels. In no time, the United States and half a dozen Islamic states were supporting those rebels—called *mujahideen*. Near Christmas 1979, the Red Army stormed into Afghanistan.

Massive Power Can't Always Carry the Day

The 40th Army spread out across the country and began hunting insurgents. Soviet aircraft responded with air strikes, but 80 percent of the country remained outside their control.

The Afghan people have been mountain fighters since the time of Alexander the Great. They struck at the Russians and then melted away. Although the Russians won all of the major battles, they could never gain control of the countryside.

Building a Religious Resistance

The United States, Saudi Arabia, and Pakistan were busily supplying the rebels with weapons. The Muslim world actively recruited foreign fighters to wage war against the infidel Soviets. One was a young Saudi named Osama bin Laden.

The mujahideen paid great attention to sabotage, attacking power plants, pipelines, radio stations, public buildings, airports, hotels, and cinemas. They murdered anyone associated with the government and refused to back down.

Changes in the USSR

In 1982, hard-liner Leonid Brezhnev, general secretary of the Communist party of the Soviet Union died, and after two short-term successors, Mikhail Gorbachev took over. Gorbachev announced the Soviet withdrawal from Afghanistan. On February 15, 1989, the last soldiers left.

The Soviets had suffered hundreds of thousands killed and wounded. Material losses included hundreds of aircraft, helicopters, and tanks. Their army was wrecked, their economy ruined. The Soviet Union itself soon disappeared.

More than one million Afghans were killed, and five million fled to Pakistan. Cities were destroyed, and 10–16 million land mines were left scattered across the countryside. And worst of all, a civil war in Afghanistan still raged between the remnants of the Communist government and the mujahideen. The mujahideen took the upper hand in 1992, but when rural warlords continued to fight among themselves, a group of religious fundamentalist fighters called the Taliban rose up against them. By the end of 1996, the Taliban had taken control of the capital of Kabul and set up an Islamic state. The religious order it established evolved into a perfect breeding ground for the next holy war—led by Osama bin Laden and al-Qaeda.

Chapter 3

Lowlights

African Exploration

The meeting of Dr. David Livingstone and Henry Morton Stanley was a high point that would lead to a brutal colonial empire.

✳ ✳ ✳ ✳

IT HAD BEEN five years since Scottish missionary David Livingstone disappeared into central Africa to find the source of the Nile; young war correspondent Henry Morton Stanley saw potential for a great story, and he convinced newspaper magnate James Gordon Bennett Jr. to finance his search.

Dr. Livingstone, I Presume?

Stanley led a party of guards and porters into uncharted territory in March 1871. Within a few days, his stallion was dead from tsetse flies, and dozens of his carriers had deserted with valuable supplies. Over the months that followed, his party endured encounters with suspicious Africans.

Finally, on November 10, 1871, Stanley found the ailing Livingstone at a settlement on Lake Tanganyika in present-day Tanzania. Legend has it Stanley greeted the missionary with the words, "Dr. Livingstone, I presume?" Stanley's dispatches to the *New York Herald* were the media sensation of the age.

Fame and Misfortune

Upon his return to Great Britain, Stanley was met with public ridicule, as many scientists and journalists questioned the veracity of his accounts. Though his book, *How I Found Livingstone*, was a best seller, Stanley was deeply wounded by his detractors.

Indeed, Stanley was an unlikely hero. Born John Rowland, he was the illegitimate child of a disinterested mother. He left Britain at age 17 to work as a deckhand on a merchant vessel. He jumped ship in New Orleans and took the name of an English planter, whom he claimed had adopted him; historians doubt Stanley ever met the man.

Stanley's life was an improbable series of adventures. He served, unremarkably, on both sides during the Civil War and worked unsuccessfully at a variety of trades before trying his hand at journalism. He reported on the Indian wars in the West and on the Colorado gold rush. Before he embarked upon his search for Livingstone, Stanley accompanied a British military expedition into Abyssinia and became known for his colorful dispatches.

The Greatest African Explorer

Stanley may have found in Livingstone the father figure he never had. His accounts of the missionary created a portrait of a saintly doctor who, inspired by his opposition to Africa's brutal slave trade, had opened the continent to Western civilization and Christianity.

Livingstone died in 1873, and Stanley served as a pallbearer at his funeral. A year later, Stanley set out on another epic expedition to complete Livingstone's work. Over the next three years, Stanley established Lake Victoria as the source of the Nile and led his party down the uncharted Congo River—a 2,900-mile course that transversed the continent.

Though acclaimed as the greatest African explorer, Stanley's accounts of his methods—such as whipping porters and gunning down tribespeople—brought outrage in Britain. After examining his original notes, however, some historians believe that he often exaggerated his exploits to elevate his legend.

A Journey for Leopold

Unable to persuade the British government to employ him, Stanley undertook a third journey in 1879 under the sponsorship of Belgium's King Leopold II. He established trading posts along the Congo River, laying the foundation for a vast colonial empire that would exploit the rubber, copper, and ivory trades at the expense of millions of African lives.

This third expedition led to the scramble for Africa among European nations, culminating in the Berlin Conference of 1885, which divided the continent among colonial powers. Leopold II established his rights to the so-called Congo Free State, his private enterprise encompassing most of the Congo Basin. Historians estimate that millions of Congolese were murdered or died from disease or overwork under Leopold's regime.

A final African expedition between 1887 and 1889 further tarnished Stanley's name. Sent to rescue a dubious ally in southern Sudan, he left behind a rear column whose leaders—former British army officers and aristocrats—degenerated into sadism.

Finally marrying and adopting a son, Stanley retired from exploration to write books and conduct lecture tours. He won a seat in Parliament in 1895 and was knighted by Queen Victoria in 1899. He died in 1904 at age 63. Although he was considered a national hero, he was denied burial next to Livingstone at Westminster Abbey due to his mixed reputation.

✳ The Congo is rich in diamonds, gold, copper, cobalt, manganese, and zinc. Foreign speculators have taken notice and invested heavily in mining efforts. Despite this cash infusion, poverty remains rife and corruption runs rampant.

"We went into the heart of Africa self-invited; therein lies our fault."

—Henry Morton Stanley

The Ancient Pedigree of Biological and Chemical Warfare

Considered the pinnacle of military know-how, biological and chemical warfare has actually been around for millennia.

❊ ❊ ❊ ❊

China's Deadly Fog

INVENTORS OF GUNPOWDER and rockets, the Chinese were also among the first to use biological and chemical agents. Fumigation to purge homes of vermin in the 7th century B.C. likely inspired the employment of poisonous smoke during war. Ancient Chinese military writings contain hundreds of recipes for such things as "soul-hunting fog," containing arsenic, and "five-league fog," which was laced with wolf dung. When a besieging army burrowed under a city's walls, defenders struck back. They burned piles of mustard in ovens, then operated bellows to blow the noxious gas at the subterranean attackers. In the 2nd century A.D., authorities dispersed rebellious peasants with a kind of tear gas made from chopped bits of lime.

Ancient Greek Poisons

The ancient Greeks were also experienced with biological and chemical weapons. Herodotus wrote in the 5th century B.C. about the Scythian archers, who were barbarian warriors dwelling near Greek colonies along the Black Sea. By his account, Scythian bowmen could accurately fire an arrow 500 yards every three seconds. Their arrows were dipped in a mixture of dung, human blood, and the venom of adders. These ingredients were mixed and buried in jars until they reached the desired state of putrefaction. These poison arrows paralyzed the lungs, inducing asphyxiation.

A bioweapon figured prominently in the First Sacred War. Around 590 B.C., fighters from the city of Kirrha attacked travelers on their way to the Oracle of Delphi and seized Delphic territories. Enraged at the sacrilege, several Greek city-states formed the League of Delphi and laid siege to Kirrha. For a time, the town's stout defenses stymied the attackers. However, according to the ancient writer Thessalos, a horse stepped through a piece of a buried pipe that brought water into the city. A medicine man named Nebros convinced the Greeks to ply the water with the plant hellebore, a strong purgative. The defenders, devastated by diarrhea, were rendered too weak to fight, and the Greeks captured the town.

Flying Corpses Spread the Black Plague

In 1340, during the siege of a French town during the Hundred Years' War, it was reported that catapults "...cast in deed horses, and beestes stynking...the ayre was hote as in the myddes of somer: the stynke and ayre was so abominable." Vlad the Impaler, the 15th-century Romanian warlord and real-life model for Dracula, used a similar method against Turkish foes.

Scholars believe that this ghastly biological warfare tactic played a big role in spreading the worst plague in human history: the bubonic plague, better known as the Black Death. In 1346, merchants from Genoa set up a trading outpost in Crimea, which was attacked by Tartars, a warlike horde of Muslim Turks. However, during the siege, the attacking forces were decimated by the plague. To even the score, the Tartars catapulted the corpses of plague victims over the walls of the Genoan fortress.

Horrified, the Genoan merchants set sail for home. In October 1347, their galleys, carrying rats and fleas infested with the Black Death, pulled into Genoa's harbor. Within several years, the plague would spread from Italy to the rest of Europe, felling more than a third of its population.

A Pox on All Their Houses

In America, biological warfare darkened the French and Indian War. In 1763, during the vast rebellion of Native Americans under Chief Pontiac, the Delaware tribe allied with the French and attacked the British at Fort Pitt. Following the deaths of 400 soldiers and 2,000 settlers, the fort's defenders turned to desperate means.

William Trent, the commander of Fort Pitt's militia, knew that a smallpox epidemic had been ravaging the area, and he concocted a plan. He then made a sinister "peace offering" to the attackers. Trent wrote in his journal, "We gave them two Blankets and an Handkerchief out of the Small Pox Hospital. I hope it will have the desired effect." It did. Afflicted with the disease, the Delaware died in droves, and the fort held.

Trent's idea caught on. Soon after the Fort Pitt incident, Lord Jeffrey Amherst, the British military commander in North America, wrote to Colonel Henry Bouquet, "Could it not be contrived to send the Small Pox among those disaffected tribes of Indians? We must on this occasion use every stratagem in our power to reduce them." Amherst, for whom Amherst, Massachusetts, is named, added, "Try every other method that can serve to Extirpate this Execrable Race."

The Da Vinci Formula

Even Leonardo da Vinci—one of history's best and brightest minds—dabbled with chemical weapons. The artist, and sometime inventor of war machines, proposed to "throw poison in the form of powder upon galleys." He stated, "Chalk, fine sulfide of arsenic, and powdered verdigris [toxic copper acetate] may be thrown among enemy ships by means of small mangonels [single-arm catapults], and all those who, as they breathe, inhale the powder into their lungs will become asphyxiated." Ever ahead of his time, the inveterate inventor even sketched out a diagram for a simple gas mask.

"Some people are moulded by their admirations, others by their hostilities."

—ELIZABETH BOWEN

Miscalculated Insult: The British Burn the White House

On August 24, 1814, British forces brushed aside the Virginia militia and burned the White House. Why? To teach the upstart former colonists King George's lesson: "Don't mess with me." Unfortunately for the British, it only embarrassed and angered said colonists, who proceeded to mess with His Majesty anyway.

✳ ✳ ✳ ✳

COMING JUST A generation after the Revolutionary War, one might call the War of 1812 a grudge rematch—except this time King George had more than a colony to lose. From 1805 to 1815, crown forces were at full strain with Napoleon's France. Had the French fleet taken to the sea on a stormy day with a load of troops, England itself could have faced direct invasion.

This Means War!

One key British strategy was a blockade to deny France world trade, but the spunky Americans did business with Napoleon anyway. Britain seized such ships and cargos, which annoyed the Americans enough; worse still, the Royal Navy drafted the captured U.S. sailors into British service. Americans said: "This means war!" President James Madison asked Congress for a Declaration of War, and on June 18, 1812, Congress gave it to him.

James Madison

The Canadian border and the Atlantic seaboard were the natural battlefronts in a low-intensity conflict. The border battles went back and forth without decisive results for either side. U.S. privateers and navy warships harassed the British at sea but lacked the big ships-of-the-line necessary to challenge the world's dominant navy. Even so, in 1813, U.S. forces managed to burn York (now Toronto), including the Canadian Parliament. Now it was Britain's turn to take things personally, but retaliation could wait until Napoleon was exiled to a lonely Mediterranean island.

England Seeks Revenge

By 1814, Britain was ready to hit the yappy colonial terrier with a rolled-up newspaper. The man for the task was Admiral Sir George Cockburn, hater of all things American, who had taken great glee in raiding Chesapeake Bay the previous two years. On August 19, 1814, Cockburn landed General Robert Ross and a force of 4,700 British regulars at Benedict, Maryland—about 25 miles from the White House.

The D.C. militia was mustered in great haste. President Madison scrambled to organize the defense, such as it was; his wife, Dolley, rushed to pack up White House national treasures. The lightly armed minutemen prepared to make their stand at Bladensburg, Maryland, five miles from the White House. They were ready to teach King George how free men could fight. Just after noon, His Majesty knew the answer: "Very poorly." After a brief exchange of shots (now known as the Battle of Bladensburg), the militia panicked and fled, barely slowing Ross's redcoats in their march on D.C.

The capital's population focused on weighty matters: blaming everything on the president, looting, and running like hell. A small U.S. fleet scuttled itself in the Patuxent River to avoid capture.

The British waltzed into Washington, burning public buildings while sparing private structures. They set fire to the Washington Navy Yard, adding insult to the navy's self-inflicted injury. Redcoats heaped papers, desks, and chairs in the

Capitol's House and Senate chambers, then set the structure gloriously ablaze with a newfangled Congreve artillery rocket. They then headed up the road to the White House, where a hastily abandoned meal awaited them. The officers devoured the meal, overindulged in the fine wine, then left a fiery tip by putting the White House to the torch. Only its gutted stone skeleton survived.

Stars and Stripes

After a second day of organized arson, the British made for Baltimore. Here U.S. resistance held fast. The British attacked first by land, losing the battle and General Ross in the bargain. They tried next by sea, but the bombardment failed to reduce Fort McHenry. The next morning, a lyrical observer named Francis Scott Key wrote a poem honoring the defiance of the flapping Star-Spangled Banner, visible at night thanks to exploding British shells and the reddish light of Congreve rockets. Most Americans know this poem. However, they probably don't know that its tune comes from an old British drinking song, "To Anacreon in Heaven."

The rest of war was all United States. "Old Hickory" Andrew Jackson defeated the British-supported Creek Indians in Alabama in March 1814, then the British themselves at New Orleans in January 1815, before either force could learn that the war was over. The British agreed to leave U.S. shipping and seamen alone. No borders would change, but the young republic had asserted the right to avenge British slaps across its face. It had also gained a reality check. Reliance on a "people's army" of hastily raised militia sounded great but didn't work in practice. Many would not serve, and many—even when the stakes were the national capital—broke and ran as soon as they smelled gun smoke. The United States needed what the founding fathers had dreaded: a standing military.

The Great Hunger

When the Irish potato crop failed in 1845, it caused a tragedy that devastated the nation for generations.

✳ ✳ ✳ ✳

THE IRELAND OF 1845 was a British colony where many of the people labored as tenant farmers for English landlords, raising grain and grazing cattle for export. To feed themselves, the Irish cultivated potatoes on tiny plots of land. Some historians assert that by the 1840s, half of Ireland's population of eight million ate nothing but potatoes. Then an unwelcome visitor—a mold called *Phytophthora infestans*—arrived from America. This "potato blight" rotted the precious tubers in the fields. Between 1845 and 1849—a period that became known, in Gaelic, as *An Gorta Mór*, "The Great Hunger"—an estimated one million Irish died of outright starvation or from the diseases that stalked in famine's wake. Another 1–1.5 million left their homeland in desperation. Some went to England or to British colonies such as Australia. Many others chose to cut their ties to the British Empire and cross the Atlantic to settle in the United States, where they played a crucial role in building America. Seventy years after the famine ended, Ireland's population was only about half of what it had been in 1845.

The British government organized some relief efforts, but the effort was a classic case of too little, too late. Worse was the fact that even at the height of the famine, the Emerald Isle still teemed with food—for export to England! The fiercely independent, mostly Catholic Irish had long resented British domination of their island, but the timid British response to the famine fueled a new spirit of rebellion that culminated in Ireland's full independence in 1937.

Life in the Trenches

Trench warfare can be traced back to the Battle of the Trench in A.D. 627. It was also employed during the American Civil War, but it is most closely associated with World War I, when life in the trenches produced death in record numbers.

❋ ❋ ❋ ❋

BECAUSE THE ADVANCED weaponry of World War I rendered direct frontal warfare a dangerous—even suicidal—proposition, troops began employing trench warfare. Soldiers used earthen forts to defend their perimeters; soldiers could also be deployed from these forts to outflank the enemy. Everything in between the trenches was referred to as no-man's-land because any attempt to cross it was lethal. The distance between trenches was typically 100 to 300 yards, and the depth of the trenches was generally 8 to 16 feet.

Because armies often couldn't advance but refused to retreat, these fortifications were inhabited far longer than anyone expected. They literally became hellholes. At times temperatures hovered around 0°; other times, trenches filled with waist-deep water. Many soldiers contracted lice, which led to painful trench fever. A lack of dental hygiene led to gingivitis, which is still known as trench mouth today. Unrelenting artillery barrages caused even hardened veterans to suffer from shell shock (known today as post-traumatic stress disorder).

Overflowing latrines presented a continual health hazard—not to mention an ungodly stench—as did decaying corpses. This was before the time of antibiotics, and the slightest wound could result in death. The wounded often suffered agonizing pain for weeks before they could be taken to a hospital.

To this day, skeletal remains of World War I soldiers are still being uncovered at construction sites that were once part of the Western Front. Trench warfare was a true horror of war.

Ghosts of a Murdered Dynasty

The fate of Russia's imperial family remained
shrouded in mystery for nearly a century.

✳   ✳   ✳   ✳

In the wake of Russia's 1917 uprisings, Tsar Nicholas II abdicated his shaky throne. He was succeeded by a provisional government, which included Nicholas and his family—his wife, Tsarina Alexandra; his four daughters, Grand Duchesses Olga, Tatiana, Maria, and Anastasia; and his 13-year-old son, Tsarevich Alexei—under house arrest.

When the radical Bolshevik party took power in October 1917, its soldiers seized the royal family and eventually moved them to the Ural Mountain town of Yekaterinburg, where they were held prisoner in the House of Special Purpose. As civil war waged between the "White" and "Red" factions in Russia, the Bolsheviks worried that the White Army might try to free the royal family and use its members as a rallying point. When White troops neared Yekaterinburg in July 1918, the local executive committee decided to kill Nicholas II and his family.

The bedraggled imperial family was awakened by their captors in the middle of the night. The sounds of battle echoed not far from the home that had become their makeshift prison, and the prisoners were ordered to take shelter in the basement. Tsar Nicholas had to carry Alexei, who was gravely ill.

After a long wait, the head jailer reappeared, brandishing a pistol and backed by ten men armed with rifles and pistols. He declared, "Because your relatives in Europe carry on their war against Soviet Russia, the Executive Committee of the Ural has decided to execute you." Raising his revolver, he fired into Tsar Nicholas II's chest as his family watched in horror.

With that shot, the militia opened fire. Bullets ricocheted around the room as family members dove for cover. None made it. Those who clung to life after the firing stopped were dragged into the open and set upon with rifle butts and bayonets until no moaning could be heard.

A Bungled Disposal of Bodies

The bodies were taken into the Siberian forest, stripped, and thrown into an abandoned mine pit. The corpses were visible above the pit's shallow waterline. Fearing that the bodies would be discovered, the communist officials tried to burn them the following day. When that did not work, they decided to move the bodies to a deeper mine pit farther down the road. The truck got stuck in deep mud on the way to the mines, so the men dug a shallow grave in the mud, buried the bodies, and covered them with acid, lime, and wooden planks, where they remained untouched until their discovery in 1979.

In his official report, lead executioner Yakov Yurovsky stated that two of the bodies were buried and burned separately, giving rise to speculation that one or two of the Romanov children escaped the massacre. Several pretenders came forth claiming to be Tsarevich Alexei, heir to the Russian throne, and his sister Grand Duchess Maria. But the most famous of the "undead Romanovs" was young Anastasia.

Did Anastasia Survive?

Anastasia, the fourth daughter of Nicholas and Alexandra, was 17 at the time of the executions. At least ten women have stepped forward claiming to be the lost grand duchess. The most famous of these was Anna Tchaikovsky.

Two years after the murders, Ms. Tchaikovsky—who was hospitalized in Berlin after an attempted suicide—claimed to be Anastasia. She explained that she had been wounded but survived the slaughter with the help of a compassionate Red Army soldier, who smuggled her out of Russia.

Anna bore a striking physical resemblance to the missing Anastasia, enough to convince several relatives that she was indeed the last of the imperial family. She also revealed details that would be hard for an impostor to know—for instance, she knew of a secret meeting between Anastasia's uncle, the grand duke of Hesse, and Nicholas II in 1916.

Other relatives, however, rejected Anna's claim, noting, among other things, that Ms. Tchaikovsky refused to speak Russian (although she understood the language and would respond to Russian questions). A drawn-out German court case ended in 1970 with no firm conclusions.

Anna, later named Anna Anderson, died in 1984. It was not until DNA evidence became available in the 1990s that her claim to imperial lineage could finally be disproved.

The Romanov Ghosts

But what of the hidden remains?

After the location of the royal resting place was made public in 1979, nine skeletons were exhumed from the muddy pit. The bodies of the royal couple and three of their children—Olga, Tatiana, and Anastasia—were identified by DNA tests as Romanov family members. Their remains, as well as those of four servants who died with them, were interred in 1998 near Nicholas's imperial predecessors in St. Petersburg.

By all accounts, 11 people met their deaths that terrible night in July 1918. In late August 2007, two more sets of remains were found in a separate grave near Yekaterinburg. Based on results of DNA analysis that was completed in 2009, experts agree that the sets of remains were those of Tsarevich Alexei and Maria.

✳ The members of the firing squad were at first baffled as to why none of their bullets seemed to wound the Romanov women. The executioners resorted to beating the women to death with rifle butts and bayonets. When they went to dispose of the bodies, the killers realized the women's corsets were filled with jewels, which had deflected the bullets.

Mein Kampf

Dictated to Rudolph Hess in Landsberg Prison in 1924, Mein Kampf *gave the world a glimpse into the mind of Adolf Hitler.*

✳ ✳ ✳ ✳

THE FIRST EDITION of *Mein Kampf* (My struggle) was issued in 1925. It made Hitler a millionaire—and also a tax cheat, as he failed to report his income to the government. After he became chancellor, his debt was forgiven (imagine that!), and the government of Germany bought millions of copies to give as official presents to all couples getting married. In the book, Hitler goes on at length about a wide range of topics, but the core of the book revolves around his views on race and the German state.

The State and Racial Purity

Hitler describes the proper role of the state as existing to uphold the status of the race. He believes racial purity is the "center of all life," and the state must give its citizens the freedom to achieve it "based on the victorious sword of a master people, putting the world into the service of a higher culture." That culture, of course, is Aryan. The Aryan, in Hitler's view, rightly "subjected the lower beings" just as he made use of "various suitable beasts which he knew how to tame." The state should go on to defend the purity of the Aryan race by teaching the sickly that it is "a crime" to pass on their weakness, and even establishing racial commissions to monitor individual reproductive rights.

The People

Despite passages about the nobility of the German worker, average citizens are generally portrayed in a less-than-flattering light. Hitler reasons that speeches must be tailored to elicit an audience response, and "terror and force" should win out over logic. The truth should be avoided, since it "might bring out something favorable for the opponent." But avoidance of the truth is no matter, since the people "will more easily fall victim to a big lie than to a small one."

Once in charge, a leader's job is "consolidating the attention of the people against a single adversary" and "make different opponents appear as if they belonged to one category." For Hitler, the single adversary was obvious.

The Jews

Perhaps no topic is revisited as frequently in *Mein Kampf* as is the subject of the Jews. Jews are referred to as parasites, apes, or simply "the personification of the devil." Jews, Hitler writes, were "without any true culture," but rather wormed their way into and subverted other societies. Hitler associates the Jews with most major problems. He claims they control the press, the trade unions, and the banks. Syphilis is a "Jewish disease" which has spread to young Germans: The Jewish propensity to value the intellect leads to the "emergence of sexual ideas" at too young an age. The Jew represents "the counterpart to the Aryan"—in other words, the opposite of all that is good. He is a "force which always wants evil." In a passage near the end of the book, Hitler ominously foreshadows the policy that would ensure his future infamy as the murderer of millions. Speaking of Germany in World War I, he laments that if "twelve or fifteen thousand of these Hebrew corruptors of the people had been held under poison gas . . . the sacrifice of millions at the front would not have been in vain."

Hitler's rise to power and the subsequent events of the war place the book in an odd position. Its contents have value as a resource to document how one man could do so much harm; however, the danger also exists that the material could be used for inspiration to future generations of supremacists. As a result, *Mein Kampf* was banned in a number of countries following World War II. The copyright to the work is owned by the state of Bavaria, which even today restricts the publication of new editions.

The Firebombing of Dresden

The Allied raid on Dresden was well calculated to inflict as much damage and as many casualties as possible. This cultural center of Germany was demolished—a step many believe went too far.

✳ ✳ ✳ ✳

FOUR WAVES OF bombers hit Dresden, Germany, from February 13 to 15, 1945. The first wave used a greater proportion of higher explosives to damage buildings. Follow-up incendiaries stoked a firestorm, and high explosives hindered firefighters. The conflagration at Dresden reached temperatures of 2,700 degrees Fahrenheit, pushing a mass of superheated air above the town and causing gale-force winds to rush in, sucking people along with them.

Survivor Lothar Metzger recalled, "Burning people ran to and fro, [there were] burnt coaches filled with civilian refugees ... fire everywhere, and all the time the hot wind of the firestorm threw people back into the burning houses they were trying to escape." Some tried taking refuge in the Old Market's historic fountain, but were broiled alive when the heat boiled the water away. Said survivor Margaret Freyer, "I saw people one after the other simply seem to let themselves drop to the ground. Today I know that these unfortunate people were the victims of lack of oxygen. They fainted and then burnt to cinders."

A Dresden police report listed a toll of 5 cultural buildings, 39 schools, 29 hospitals, as well as 136 badly damaged factories and a ruined German Army headquarters. Based on German burial records and the number of bodies found after the war, approximately 25,000 were killed in the attack.

Why Dresden?

Plans for the attack originated from the highest levels. On January 15, 1945, General Eisenhower's Deputy Supreme Commander, Sir Arthur Tedder of the RAF, met with Stalin in

Moscow. The men discussed the danger of Germany's shifting hundreds of thousands of troops east to fight the Soviet armies. Tedder suggested using the Allied air effort to bomb strategic sites to hamper German communications.

On January 26, Chief of the Air Staff Sir Charles Portal noted "a severe blitz will [also] cause confusion in the evacuation" of German troops "from the East." That same day, Churchill asked whether "large cities in east Germany should not now be considered especially attractive targets." By January 31, Tedder prioritized bombing the rail centers of "Berlin, Leipzig, Dresden, and associated cities where heavy attack will...hamper movement of reinforcements from other fronts."

On February 4–11, Stalin met with Churchill and Roosevelt at Yalta. General Aleksei Antonov, Deputy Chief of the Russian General Staff, requested that Western "air action on communications hinder the enemy from carrying out the shifting of his troops to the East...In particular, to paralyze the junctions of Berlin and Leipzig." The Western Allies pointed out that "the structure of the Berlin-Leipzig-Dresden railway complex...required that Dresden, as well as Berlin and Leipzig, be bombed." Otherwise, the Germans could have rerouted rail traffic from the other cities through Dresden. The Allies and the Soviet Union were firmly in agreement to devastate Dresden.

Steeped in Controversy

Dresden was controversial from the start. Associated Press reporter Alan Cowan characterized the raid as a "terror bombing." The town harbored some 200,000 refugees, a fact that made some planners uneasy. British Labor Member of Parliament Richard Rapier Stokes condemned it in the House of Commons. Nazi Propaganda Minister Joseph Goebbels even elicited some sympathy in neutral countries with press coverage of the aftermath.

The bombings did not have the decisive effect on German output and morale that its chief advocates hoped. Some argue, however, that the bombings did help end the war. The raids diverted major resources of the German economy into antiaircraft production and greatly weakened the *Luftwaffe*, which lost masses of planes and pilots. Eventually the bombings also shut down German transportation and communication systems and destroyed many industrial plants.

A Manufacturer of Arms

Contrary to the assertions of sources eager to issue a blanket condemnation of the raid, the city of Dresden was an arms-manufacturing center. It contained the Zeiss-Ikon optical goods plant as well as factories for making radar parts, bomber engines, and fighter cockpits. However, by 1945, many of its factories had been moved outside the raid's target area.

On March 28, Churchill, who had strongly backed the raid, wrote: "It seems to me that the moment has come when the question of bombing of German cities simply for the sake of increasing the terror, though under other pretexts, should be reviewed. Otherwise we shall come into control of an utterly ruined land ... I feel the need for more precise concentration upon military objectives ..."

After the war, Dresden became part of East Germany, which claimed such bombings were meant to destroy the parts of Germany falling under Moscow's orbit. Some, like historian Jörg Friedrich, characterize the firebombing of Dresden as a war crime—an act of mass destruction taking place near the end of a conflict whose outcome was no longer in doubt.

Dresden has taken on a special importance, especially among intellectuals, partly because of its cultural cachet. It was, and is—due to painstaking postwar reconstruction—the home of such treasures as the Dresden State Opera House and the *Frauenkirche* cathedral. The tragedy of those killed has been commemorated in symphonies, films, and books, such as *Slaughterhouse Five* by Kurt Vonnegut, an American imprisoned in Dresden after his capture in the Battle of the Bulge.

Firebombing Tactics Put Into Perspective

The raid on Dresden occurred within a month of the Battle of the Bulge. To Allied war planners, that battle seemed to prove the war was still far from over, and called for the sternest actions against a still-dangerous foe.

The Dresden bombing was not without precedent; offensive air tactics had been evolving through the war. Japan shocked the world in the 1930s with its aerial attacks on Chinese cities. In Poland in September 1939 and Holland in May 1940, the *Luftwaffe* deliberately targeted civilian neighborhoods to force the surrender of those countries.

In autumn 1940, during the Blitz, the Germans tried to bomb Great Britain into submission, but ultimately failed. Once the British built up a large force of long-range bombers, they sought to turn the tables. The British and Americans were intent on area-wide attacks because the precision bombings attempted earlier had brought disappointing results.

Despite the attention since accorded Dresden, other saturation bombings caused far more fatalities and destruction. The firebombing of Hamburg in July 1943 killed some 50,000 and displaced a million people. Hit by continual raids, Berlin was turned to rubble. Just ten days after the Dresden bombing, a raid on the much smaller city of Pforzheim caused proportionally many more deaths. The Tokyo firebombing of March 9–10, less than a month after Dresden, killed some 100,000 and incinerated 16 square miles of a city built largely of paper and wood. The atomic bombing of Hiroshima in August 1945 killed more than 90,000 and destroyed 90 percent of the structures in the city.

Seen in this context, Dresden appears less of a unique event and more a part of its destructive time.

Who Betrayed Anne Frank?

*Anne Frank and her family thwarted the Nazis for
two years until someone blew their cover.*

✳ ✳ ✳ ✳

Annelies Marie Frank was born in Frankfurt am Main,
Germany, on June 12, 1929. Perhaps the most well known
victim of the Holocaust, she was one of approximately 1.5 million Jewish children killed by the Nazis. Her diary chronicling
her experience in Amsterdam was discovered in the Franks'
secret hiding place by friends of the family and first published
in 1947. Translated into more than 60 languages, *Anne Frank:
The Diary of a Young Girl* has sold 30 million copies and is one
of the most widely read books in the world.

The diary was given to Anne on her 13th birthday, just weeks
before she went into hiding. Her father, Otto Frank, moved
his family and four friends into a secret annex of rooms above
his office at 263 Prinsengracht on July 6, 1942. They relied on
friends and trustworthy business associates, who risked their
own lives to help them. Anne poignantly wrote her thoughts,
yearnings, and descriptions of life in the secret annex in her
diary, revealing a vibrant, intelligent young woman struggling to
retain her ideals in the most dire of circumstances.

On August 4, 1944, four or five Dutch Nazi collaborators
under the command of an Austrian Nazi police investigator
entered the building and arrested the Franks and their friends.
The family was deported to Auschwitz, where they were separated and sent to different camps. Anne and her sister, Margot,
were sent to Bergen-Belsen, where they both died of typhus in
March 1945. Anne was 15 years old. Otto Frank was the only
member of the group to survive the war.

Dutch police, Nazi hunters, and historians have attempted
to identify the person who betrayed the Franks. Searching

for clues, the Netherlands Institute for War Documentation (NIWD) has examined records on Dutch collaboration with the Nazis, the letters of Otto Frank, and police transcripts dating from the 1940s. The arresting Nazi officer was also questioned after the war by Nazi hunter Simon Wiesenthal, but he could not identify who informed on the Franks. For decades suspicion centered on Willem Van Maaren, who worked in the warehouse attached to the Franks' hiding place, but two police investigations found no evidence against him.

Two recent theories have been offered about who betrayed the Franks. British author Carol Anne Lee believes it was Anton Ahlers, a business associate of Otto's who was a petty thief and a member of the Dutch Nazi movement. Lee argues that Ahlers informed the Nazis to collect the bounty paid to Dutch civilians who exposed Jews. She suggests he may have split the reward with Maarten Kuiper, a friend of Ahlers who was one of the Dutch Nazi collaborators who raided the secret annex. Ahlers was jailed for collaboration with the Nazis after the war, and members of his own family—including his son—have said they believe he was guilty of informing on the Franks.

Austrian writer Melissa Müller believes that a cleaning lady, Lena Hartog, who also worked in the warehouse, reported the Franks because she feared that if they were discovered, her husband, an employee of Otto Frank, would be deported for aiding Jews.

The NIWD has studied the arguments of both writers and examined the evidence supporting their theories. Noting that all the principals involved in the case are no longer living, it concluded that neither theory could be proved.

✳ The house at 263 Prinsengracht and its secret annex were turned into a museum in 1960. Almost a million people visit the site each year.

Pulling the Wool over the Eyes of New York City

Throughout the 1860s and 1870s, a man named William "Boss" Tweed controlled New York City politics—and, subsequently, New York City itself. Graft, payoffs, cheating, and a healthy dose of high-quality corruption were the order of the day.

❋ ❋ ❋ ❋

It All Started with Tammany Hall

POLITICAL ORGANIZATIONS BEGAN to spring up across the East Coast following the American Revolution, as the United States struggled to stand on its own. The biggest and most influential of these organizations was the Tammany, named after Native American Chief Tamanend. Founded on May 12, 1789, it was first a social and political organization. Then, under the leadership of Aaron Burr, the group embraced the politics of Thomas Jefferson and began supporting candidates. It was no small coincidence that Burr was elected vice president in 1800.

Aaron Burr

The strength of Tammany continued to grow, aiding the presidential election of Andrew Jackson in 1828 and 1832. By then, the powerful Democratic faction ran all of New York City, based out of their huge headquarters called "Tammany Hall." The organization became known by the same name.

Tammany Hall soon became a tool of the Irish community, which had formed in New York City after the potato famine in Ireland drove its inhabitants to the shores of Manhattan in the mid-1840s. By the mid-1850s, Tammany Hall controlled the outcome of most political races. Skilled in the art of politics, the leaders of this political machine kept New York City running—and their pockets filled.

Who's the Boss?

In New York City, a young Scottish-Irish bookkeeper and volunteer firefighter named William Tweed used his municipal position to become elected a New York alderman in 1851. He soon became a member of Congress and, in 1857, the leader of Tammany Hall.

The next 14 years became a swirl of voting fraud, judge-buying, and contract kickbacks for "Boss" Tweed and his cronies. In one instance, a carpenter received more than $360,000 for work done in a building that had very little wood in it. A furniture dealer was paid nearly $180,000 for three conference tables and 40 chairs. A plasterer received more than $130,000 for a mere two days of work. Tweed orchestrated the construction of the New York County Courthouse—a task that took nearly 20 years (2 years past his death, in fact) and cost $13 million. It was estimated that the project's price tag should have been half that figure. When an investigation was conducted into the excessive amount, the resulting report cost nearly $8,000 to print. The owner of the printing company was William Tweed.

Getting Tweed Off

The "Tweed Ring," which included the mayor and city comptroller, profited to the tune of an estimated $100 million to $200 million by the time the illegal activities were exposed in 1871. New York newspapers and magazines, featuring unflattering political cartoons of Tweed by illustrator Thomas Nast, revealed the graft under the Tweed Ring, and the "Boss" was brought to trial in 1874. Found guilty of embezzlement, he was sentenced to 12 years in prison but served only a year on appeal.

Arrested the next year on a separate charge, Tweed escaped to Cuba but was found and held by Cuban officials. Before U.S. marshals could claim Tweed, however, he bolted to Spain. The Spanish government immediately grabbed him as he landed.

William Tweed was returned to a New York City jail, where he died two years later in April 1878. He was just 55 years old.

Tragedy at the Haymarket

What began as a campaign for an eight-hour workday ended with a bloody event that sent ripples far and wide.

✳ ✳ ✳ ✳

IT WAS THE mid-1880s, and Chicago was in a state of transition. Industry was growing more and more mechanized—good news for the corporations that were able to increase profits and lower wages, but bad news for workers who were putting in 12 to 14 grueling hours a day, 6 miserable days a week. In October 1884, the Federation of Organized Trade and Labor Unions set a goal to make the eight-hour workday standard, even if nationwide strikes were necessary to make that goal a reality. The stage was set.

The Calm Before the Storm

On May 1, 1886, hundreds of thousands of workers across the country took to the streets in support of an eight-hour workday. The first few days of the strike were relatively peaceful, but all hell broke loose on May 3, when police killed several unarmed strikers near Chicago's McCormick Reaper Works.

Workers gathered in a light rain in Haymarket Square on May 4. Mayor Carter Harrison Sr. stopped by as a show of support for the workers, then left early when it appeared that all was peaceful. The rest, as they say, is history—and a somewhat murky history at that, as many questions remain about what unfolded in the incident now known as the Haymarket Riot.

Once the mayor left, the police inspector sent the police in to disperse the crowd. Soon after, a bomb went off. The police opened fire; a few short minutes later, eight policemen were dead, and scores of workers had been injured.

The Fallout

Police immediately swept across the city in search of the bomber. They arrested eight known anarchists (August Spies,

Samuel Fielden, Oscar Neebe, Michael Schwab, Louis Lingg, George Engel, Adolph Fischer, and Albert Parsons) and charged them with the crime. After a well-publicized trial, the jury (which included a Marshall Field's sales rep and not a single industrial worker) returned guilty verdicts for all eight, even though only two of the men were even at the Haymarket the night of the incident. The men had clearly been tried for their incendiary speeches leading up to the Haymarket incident, not for anything they had actually done. Seven of the men were sentenced to death, and the show trial resulted in protests around the world.

Seriously, Who Threw the Bomb?

Spies, Fischer, Engel, and Parsons were hanged on November 11, 1887; Lingg had committed suicide in prison one day earlier. Governor Altgeld pardoned Schwab, Fielden, and Neebe in 1893. To the present day, no one is sure who threw the bomb, but historians believe it was one of two anarchists who were present at the protest that day: Rudolph Schnaubelt or George Meng—neither of whom was ever arrested for the crime.

Historians consider Haymarket one of the seminal events in the history of labor, and its legacy resonates to this day. The Haymarket defendants stand as icons of the American labor movement and are remembered with rallies, parades, and speeches around the world on the anniversary of the bombing.

Most important, however, is the spirit of assembly that can be traced back to Haymarket. Today, monuments stand at the corner of Des Plaines and Randolph streets (near the spot where the bomb was thrown) and in Forest Park, Illinois, at the grave of Spies, Fischer, Engel, Parsons, and Lingg. These symbols are poignant reminders of a critical time in labor history.

Only Death Is Surer: Creative Taxation Throughout History

They cursed it in ancient Mesopotamia just as we do today, but as a means of supporting public efforts, tax is as ancient as humanity. One may tax property, transactions, shipments ... anything humans do. This has led to some interesting ideas.

✳   ✳   ✳   ✳

Egypt

INCOME TAX VARIED based on your line of work. Lie and expect a whipping—or worse. They taxed cooking oil, with tax enforcers running around to make sure you bought new oil and didn't reuse the old gross stuff. By the Greek period, Egyptians had introduced "tax farming," a genteel term for organized crime: "In return for a lump sum of 100,000 drachmas, we'll grant you taxing rights." How often do you think tax farmers took a net loss?

Greece

Like the Egyptians, the Greeks used tax farming. They also imposed poll taxes on foreigners—twice as much for males as females, a reflection of ancient Greek views of women accepted everywhere except Sparta. One creative Greek taxation method was to insinuate the state into all phases of the olive oil industry. From cultivation to extraction to marketing, Uncle Samnos took his due.

India

India has had income taxes, business taxes, and so on, but where India set itself apart was foreign trade. India imported goods from several other countries, and foreign goods and their merchants got soaked in a big way. India also had progressive taxation, which is tax-speak for milking the rich.

Rome

Republican Rome also used tax farmers; the Bible referred to them as the hated publicans, from whom the poor took a major hosing. Augustus replaced this with a combination wealth tax and poll tax, in which the poor again took a hosing. Sense a trend? As the empire went on, though, taxes became more progressive. By Diocletian and Constantine's era (ca. A.D. 300), taxes on the wealthy began to strangle the economy. By A.D. 410, Alaric the Goth sacked Rome mainly because no one could be bothered to stop him from doing so.

Britain

Romans brought taxation to Britain, but in the Viking Age, the British had a special tax called Danegeld. The Vikings functioned like a seagoing street gang. If you paid the Dane his gold, the Dane went away for however long it took him to spend the gold. When he was broke, he'd come get more. This tax fell heavily on the wealthy, mainly because only the wealthy had anything worthwhile for Vikings to steal.

✳ One Sumerian clay tablet reads, "You can have a lord, you can have a king, but the man to fear is the tax collector."

✳ When the American colonies became the young United States, a hatred of British taxation led to strict rules about how the new republic could tax itself. Soon the founding fathers realized they'd have to get creative, so they taxed whiskey. That was a hot button in a relatively drunken nation, and it led to the Whiskey Rebellion.

Baseball's Darkest Hour

Baseball's Golden Age was preceded by its darkest hour: the 1919 World Series–fixing scandal.

❊　❊　❊　❊

THE YOUNG LAD who emerged from the crowd outside a Chicago courthouse on that September day in 1920 was described by the *Chicago Herald and Examiner* as "a little urchin." He was said to have grabbed Joe Jackson by the coat sleeve. The newspaper's report of the exchange went like this:

"It ain't true, is it?" the lad said.

"Yes, kid, I'm afraid it is," Jackson replied.

"Well, I'd never have thought it," the boy exclaimed.

Nowhere did the newspaper report that the boy demanded, "Say it ain't so, Joe," although this version of the story was passed down through the generations. A few years before his 1951 death, Jackson told *Sport Magazine* that the story was made up.

What *is* so is this: Members of the 1919 Chicago White Sox committed baseball's cardinal sin, deliberately losing the World Series to the Cincinnati Reds for pay.

The White Sox took the American League pennant, and the Sox were favored to defeat Cincinnati in the World Series— heavily favored, in some gambling circles. By all accounts, Sox infielder Chick Gandil made contact with known gamblers. He immediately involved 29-game-winner Eddie Cicotte, and others followed: Jackson, pitcher Claude Williams, infielders Buck Weaver and Swede Risberg, outfielder Oscar "Happy" Felsch, and utility man Fred McMullin. Some of the players would play lead parts in the fixing of games. Others—notably Weaver and some say Jackson—had knowledge of the plan but were not active participants.

When the Series began, the players were promised $100,000 to throw the games. By the time the Reds won the Series in eight games, the payout was considerably less, and whispers about what had taken place began swelling to a roar. Sportswriters speculated about a possible fix even before Cincinnati wrapped up the Series, but nobody wanted to believe it could be true.

Conspiracy to Defraud the Public

The 1920 season began with rumors about gambling in other big-league dugouts. In September a grand jury convened to examine instances of gambling in the game, and the jury soon looked at the 1919 World Series. Eight White Sox players were called to testify, and several admitted knowledge of the fix. All eight were indicted for conspiracy to defraud the public and injure "the business of Charles Comiskey and the American League." Although the group was acquitted due to lack of evidence, the damage had been done.

Judge Kenesaw Mountain Landis, baseball's newly appointed commissioner, suspended all eight players for life. It was a crushing blow for Chicago, and for Weaver and Jackson in particular. While Gandil had received $35,000 and Cicotte $10,000 for the fix, Weaver received nothing. Actually, it was proven that he had turned down an invitation to participate in the scam. And Jackson, considered one of the greatest outfielders and hitters in the history of the game, hit .375 with six RBI in the 1919 Series while playing errorless defense.

Many still clamor for Shoeless Joe to be enshrined in the Hall of Fame, arguing that his numbers support his claim that he did nothing to contribute to the fixing of the 1919 World Series. However, the $5,000 he accepted from the gamblers sealed his fate as a tragic figure in baseball's most infamous 20th-century scandal.

Say it ain't so, Joe.

Too bad it is.

A People Walled In

A symbol of suffocating Communist rule,
the Berlin Wall stood for more than 20 years.

✳   ✳   ✳   ✳

IN THE CLOSING days of World War II, conflict ensued over
the division of the defeated country of Germany. The four
Allied countries of France, Great Britain, the United States,
and the Soviet Union originally agreed to share the caretaking
of Germany equally. Plans were also made to split the capital of
Berlin into eastern and western halves.

East Versus West

The division of Berlin quickly led to cities with clearly different
economic and political structures. While West Berlin became
a free and democratic economy of "haves," East Berlin adopted
a planned financial system based on a Soviet-style government
that left them as "have nots."

Many East Berliners envied the wealth and success of West
Berliners. By 1961, thousands of East Germans had poured
across the border into West Berlin to work, visit, and live.
What's more, the open boundary provided access to a free
Europe and beyond.

Walter Ulbricht, the East German leader (along with Soviet
premier Nikita Khrushchev) was not happy with this coming
and going; soon a wall of barbed wire was proposed to restrict
free and easy travel. To the satisfaction of the East and the
concern of the West, nearly 28 miles of wire fence were erected
in August 1961. Eventually, chain-link fencing, booby traps,
and armed guards marked the entire border between East and
West Germany.

Within a year, a second fence of barbed wire was built nearly
300 feet from the first, creating a "no-man's-land" to discourage any attempts at defecting. Once the original fence went

up, the first successful escape was pulled off within two days—ironically, by an East German border guard.

Cementing the Hostilities

By 1965, the East Germans had replaced the barbed-wire fence with an enormous concrete barrier. By 1975, it stood 12 feet high and 4 feet thick and was topped with barbed wire and a rounded pipe to discourage any escapes. More than 300 watchtowers were spaced along the wall, offering armed East German guards a clear and unobstructed view of the "death strip" between the barriers.

The Berlin Wall kept East and West German citizens in their respective "backyards." Allied and Soviet personnel, however, could cross the border at certain passage areas called "checkpoints." The most famous Allied station was known as "Checkpoint Charlie," located halfway along the border, where Allied personnel and foreign travelers crossed between West and East Berlin. Today, it is part of the Allied Museum in western Berlin.

"Tear Down this Wall!"

In June 1987, President Ronald Reagan called for Soviet leader Mikhail Gorbachev to remove the long-standing icon of isolation. It took two and a half years for East German officials to announce that their citizens could openly cross the border. Drunk with freedom, many Germans attacked the wall with sledgehammers, breaking off pieces for posterity.

✳ More than 5,000 East Germans escaped into West Berlin during the Wall's existence.

✳ East German guards were allowed to shoot anyone who came anywhere near the eastern side of the Wall. One unfortunate would-be escapee, Peter Fechter, was shot scaling the Wall in 1962. Guards left him to bleed to death before coming forward to collect his body.

The Kent State Tragedy

Few know the full story of the tragic shootings at Kent State because of inaccurate media reports and the protracted legal proceedings against the National Guardsmen involved.

✳   ✳   ✳   ✳

DURING A DEMONSTRATION at Kent State University on May 4, 1970, members of the Ohio National Guard shot and killed four students and wounded nine others. To fully understand the reasons behind the tragedy, it is crucial to know the historical context.

Located in Northeast Ohio, Kent State was one of several universities organizing and protesting against President Richard Nixon's expansion of the Vietnam War. Nixon had been elected in 1968, partly on the promise that he would end the war.

In early 1969, Nixon took a few steps to decrease U.S. involvement, but on April 30, 1970, he approved a massive military operation in Cambodia. Antiwar protests were planned on many college campuses, and this angered Nixon, who referred to the protesters as "bums."

Unrest

On May 1, an antiwar rally was held at Kent State. Many young people created a disturbance in downtown Kent that night, committing acts of vandalism and frightening citizens. Business owners blamed students, but witnesses observed that outsiders—including a motorcycle gang and other nonstudents—were among those making trouble.

Police used tear gas to disperse the crowd, and Mayor Leroy Stanton declared a state of emergency. This allowed Governor James Rhodes to approve a request for the National Guard.

On May 2, the ROTC building went up in flames. Although the arsonists were never identified, the press and townspeople blamed the protesters. Demonstrators openly confronted police and slashed the hoses of the firefighters who came to extinguish the flames.

Guardsmen were stationed all over campus on May 3, and everything remained relatively quiet until Governor Rhodes held a press conference. He warned that he would use force to stop the demonstrators, comparing them to fascists, vigilantes, and communists. New clashes between the protesters and law enforcement broke the calm with more rocks and tear gas.

The Right to Dissent

On May 4, the university attempted to ban the rally, but by noon a crowd of 1,500 people had gathered. Students believed they had a right to hold a rally, and the presence of the guardsmen fostered resentment.

About 100 young, inexperienced National Guardsmen stood on the edge of the Commons. When General Robert Canterbury ordered the demonstrators to disperse, police and guardsmen drove across the Commons to push the crowd out of the way.

One particular group of National Guardsmen—their bayonets fixed—followed some students to the top of Blanket Hill, where those students dispersed. Then about a dozen guardsmen turned around and shot down the hill in the direction of the other demonstrators and students. Some fired in the air and at the ground, while others shot directly into the crowd.

More than 60 shots were fired, killing four students and wounding nine. Those killed were Allison Krause, Jeffrey Miller, Sandra Scheuer, and William Schroeder. Two of the dead were not even part of the protest: Sandra Scheuer was merely walking to class, and Schroeder—an ROTC student—was simply a bystander. The guardsmen retreated to the Commons, where angry students confronted them. A handful of faculty members and student leaders diffused the situation.

The school was closed, and students were ordered to leave campus. These shootings galvanized 4.3 million participants to protest the war on 500 college campuses around the country. State and federal investigations were launched, with criminal and civil charges brought against some of the guardsmen. In 1970, President Nixon's own Commission on Campus Unrest concluded that the "indiscriminate firing of rifles into a crowd of students and the deaths that followed were unnecessary, unwarranted, and inexcusable." However, none of the guards were convicted or punished, partly due to interference from Governor Rhodes.

Aftermath

Character assassinations of the dead and wounded students followed, which were spread to the press and circulated among top officials in Washington, with FBI Director J. Edgar Hoover calling one of the victims "nothing more than a whore." The jury in a 1975 civil trial ruled that none of the guardsmen were legally responsible for the deaths and injuries, but the judge ordered a new trial when it was discovered that one of the jurors had been threatened.

All legal action around the Kent State shootings ended in January 1979 with a $675,000 settlement for the victims. The National Guard signed a statement of regret but emphasized the fact that it was not an apology. The memory of the four students continues to endure, far beyond the Ohio border.

---

* In 1990, a granite May 4 Memorial was dedicated on the campus. It is surrounded by a field of daffodils—one for every American killed in Vietnam. Crowds gather at the spot every May 4 to remember the victims of the Kent State tragedy.

* In 2010, the site of the shootings was added to the National Register of Historic Places. A plan for a visitor center is currently under development.

The Big Bang?

In the late 1970s, the nuclear accident at Pennsylvania's Three Mile Island gripped the world.

✳   ✳   ✳   ✳

NUCLEAR POWER HAS always been controversial. Advocates see it as the answer to our energy needs, while opponents view it as a disaster waiting to happen. The latter group almost saw its nightmare come true on March 28, 1979, when a series of events led to a partial core meltdown at Three Mile Island's Unit Two nuclear reactor.

Many people still believe that the area around the power plant was blanketed with radioactive fallout. The Nuclear Regulatory Commission (NRC), however, maintains that the amount of radiation released was within safe levels.

According to an NRC report, which followed numerous studies of and investigations into the accident, the average dose of radiation to approximately 2 million people in the area was about 1 millirem. "To put that into context," the report explains, "exposure from a full set of chest X-rays is about 6 millirem."

Multiple Malfunctions

The cause of the accident was a combination of mechanical problems and human error. It started when the main feedwater pumps stopped running in a secondary section of the plant. This was caused either by a mechanical or an electrical failure, and it prevented the steam generators from removing heat. The reactor automatically shut down.

The pressure in the nuclear portion of the plant began to increase. To prevent that pressure from becoming excessive, a relief valve opened. The valve should have closed when the pressure decreased, but it failed to do so. Signals to the operator did not show that the valve was still open; water poured out of the valve and caused the core of the reactor to overheat.

Because the operators did not realize that the plant was experiencing a loss of coolant, they made conditions worse by further reducing the flow of coolant.

Days of chaos followed the accident. Specialists detected a hydrogen bubble inside the reactor, which caused widespread panic and confusion. It was a tense, delicate situation, but engineers were able to gradually bleed the hydrogen from the reactor into a containment room, where the hydrogen and oxygen were converted back into water. The reactor cooled and stabilized—and was permanently shut down.

The accident at Three Mile Island was serious; the plant was extremely fortunate to have avoided a catastrophic breach of the containment building and the release of massive amounts of radiation into the environment.

---

* Three Mile Island's Unit Two remains shut down, but Unit One is operational.

* Not a single nuclear reactor has been built in the United States since the Three Mile Island event. This may change in years to come; nuclear power does not produce carbon dioxide, which many believe causes climate change.

* France gets 80% of its electricity from nuclear power plants, and India and China have dozens of reactors in the works.

Chernobyl

The Three Mile Island event pales in comparison to the accident at Ukraine's Chernobyl nuclear power plant in April 1986. That event killed 31 people; produced a plume of radioactive debris that drifted over parts of the western Soviet Union, Eastern Europe, and Scandinavia; left huge areas dangerously contaminated; and forced the evacuation of more than 200,000 people. Chernobyl remains the largest nuclear power plant disaster in history.

The Tragic Tale of *The Conqueror*

Despite its marquee cast, The Conqueror *flopped like a beached garfish. As if that weren't bad enough, the cast learned a hard (and for some, fatal) lesson: You should never film a movie just downwind of a nuclear test site.*

✻ ✻ ✻ ✻

HOWARD HUGHES BOUGHT RKO, a Hollywood studio once known for classy black-and-white films starring the Katharine Hepburns and Cary Grants of cinema, in 1948. Soon, RKO was turning out money-losing, sensationalistic clunkers: *Vendetta* (1950, featuring Faith Domergue's breasts), *Underwater!* (1955, starring Jane Russell's breasts), and *Jet Pilot* (made 1949, released 1957 after eight years in cans, starring John Wayne) are examples. After *Underwater!* sank deep beneath the financial waves, Hughes—perhaps inspired by his own business style— decided that the time was ripe for a Genghis Khan movie.

Casting Call

Who would play the dreaded Mongol emperor? John Wayne, the most bankable actor of his day, stepped forward. No one had the spine to ask the Duke how his Western drawl was going to make for a convincing Asian warlord, nor was anyone going to turn away such a big name. Susan Hayward was cast as Khan's Tartar love interest/sexual assault victim, Bortai. Dick Powell would direct. Pedro Armendáriz, Agnes Moorehead, John Hoyt, and William Conrad were among the brighter lights in the cast.

St. George, and We're Draggin'

Filming began in 1955, near St. George, Utah. The location's inherent flaws surfaced immediately. With temperatures reaching 120°F, the faux-Asianizing makeup melted on the actors' faces. Hughes sent a number of exotic animals to Utah for use in the film; after the black panther tried to maul Hayward, producers rented a tame mountain lion and painted the poor creature black. The animal licked itself, liked the flavor, and began to slurp off most of the paint.

The dialogue and action were comically bad. Picture John Wayne, drawling in an imagined Mongol accent, sporting a German World War I spiked helmet with French Foreign Legion flaps. One horseback battle scene showed a series of repetitive, isolated flops by vanquished horsemen into the Utah dust. Women's rights lost a decade on the spot when Princess Bortai flailed feebly at the rapist Khan's back, then suffered Hollywood's old version of Stockholm Syndrome as her hatred turned to love.

By 1956 standards, Hughes spent a mint on *The Conqueror*, including $1.4 million pimping its supreme artistry to the great unwashed. He must have been chagrined when audiences viewed it as a comedy—a campy work that left them laughing (a better option than clawing out their eyes). *The Conqueror* was a multimillion-dollar clunker at the box office.

Howard Hughes

Tragedy

St. George, Utah, is near Yucca Flat, Nevada, where the U.S. government tested nuclear weapons in 1953. A lot of the fallout collected in Snow Canyon, a natural basin where most of the filming occurred. Everyone inhaled the windblown, radioactive dust throughout months of filming. Cast members played with Geiger counters and joked over the results.

In the end, it wasn't funny. Dick Powell died in 1963 of lymphoma at age 58. Pedro Armendáriz passed away later in 1963: suicide, inspired by terminal kidney cancer. Wayne survived lung cancer in 1964, succumbing to it in 1979 (though his heavy smoking muddied the causal waters). Others also died of cancer: Agnes Moorehead, uterine cancer in 1974; Susan Hayward, brain cancer in 1975; John Hoyt, lung cancer, 1991. A total of 220 Hollywood actors and crew worked on location. At last report, 91 have contracted cancer, and 46 have died.

Chapter 4

Sites and Structures

A True Pyramid Scheme

The Egyptians built three big pyramids at Giza, Egypt, to bury King Tut and so forth, right? There's actually much more to it.

※ ※ ※ ※

Mastabas

ONE MIGHT CALL mastabas proto-pyramids. The oldest examples date to 3500 B.C., and most resemble large pyramid bases of mud, brick, or stone. A typical mastaba contained artwork, images of the deceased, and—of course—mummified Uncle Kahotep (or whomever).

Throughout and after the pyramid era, mastabas remained the budget mausoleum alternative for moderately affluent Egyptians. Because builders clustered mastabas (as they would later do with pyramids), they are often found in groups.

Let's Stack These . . .

Our best information dates the earliest step pyramid to around 2630 B.C. at Saqqara, Egypt. The architect Imhotep built mastaba upon mastaba, fashioning a 200-foot-high pyramid as a mausoleum for Pharaoh Djoser. With its original white limestone facing, Djoser's tomb must have been quite a spectacle when struck by the light of the rising sun.

The new tomb style secured Imhotep's immortality—literally, for the Egyptians deified him, and the Greeks identified him with their healing-god Asklepios. Even today, some consider him a patron saint of civil engineers and architects.

I Want One Too!

Pyramid mania began. Over the next thousand years or so, Egyptian engineers built several pyramid complexes along the Nile's west bank. The most famous and popular today are those at Giza, but dozens survive. Some are majestic, but many are just mounds. We used to believe pyramids were built under the lash. Modern scholars doubt this, but pyramids were definitely huge projects. Some took decades to finish.

The foundation of each pyramid is carved into the bedrock, making the pyramid extremely stable. The Egyptians would do much of the construction work during the Nile's flood season. This way, huge limestone blocks could be floated from the quarries right to the building site. The blocks would then be transported up ramps using ropes made of papyrus twine.

Later, during Roman times, Egypt's neighbor Nubia had a pyramid-building phase. The workmanship and beauty of the Nubian pyramids impress visitors to this day.

What's Inside a Pyramid?

Stone, mostly. They aren't hollow. Long walkways angle down and up to burial chambers. Narrow shafts extend from these chambers and walkways to vent air out the upper exterior. Most contain painting and writing that has taught us much about Egyptian life; those that were not looted have yielded fabulous artifacts. The burial chambers housed the mummified deceased, of course, with his or her innards in jars nearby.

Why Build Them?

The Egyptians didn't have a separate word for religion; it touched all aspects of their daily lives. The Pharaoh was a semidivine figure, and a massive Pharaonic tomb represented immense faith and devotion. Egyptians believed that after a Pharaoh died, he would reach the heavens via sunbeams.

Egyptians also believed that the pyramid shape would help the Pharaoh on this journey.

Once the Pharaoh reached the heavens, he would become Osiris, the god of the dead. To adequately perform the duties of Osiris, the Pharaoh would need a well-preserved body and organs. The Egyptians feared that if they did not prepare the Pharaoh's body for the afterlife, disaster would fall upon Egypt.

The Egyptians carefully wrapped and mummified the Pharaoh's remains, which was a time-intensive process. They removed and placed the organs in canopic jars because they believed that a different god would watch over each organ. The heart was left in the Pharaoh's body because the Egyptians believed that—as the seat of intelligence and emotions—the Pharaoh would need his heart in the afterlife. The tomb itself was intended to protect the sacred remains and prized possessions.

Why Stop?

Well, building pyramids required a lot of resources. Worse yet, looters were a constant menace. All that expense and effort, and some jerk breaks in anyway? Some people have no respect!

After about 1800 B.C., the Egyptian art of pyramid construction declined in step with Egypt's own gradual eclipse.

✳ Excavators found a sarcophagus in the burial chamber of Menkaure's pyramid. They sent it to England aboard the ship *Beatrice* in 1838. Unfortunately, the ship sank during a storm on the Mediterranean en route. Wreckage of the *Beatrice* has never been located.

✳ The pyramid of Snefru is called the Red Pyramid because of the reddish limestone used to build it.

✳ Most of the precious white limestone used in the construction of the pyramids was later removed and used to build structures in Cairo.

Reward: One Lost Island

Did the legendary island of Atlantis ever really exist? Or did Plato make the whole thing up?

✳ ✳ ✳ ✳

IT'S HARD TO believe that Plato, an early Greek philosopher, was the type to start rumors. But in two of his dialogues, *Timaeus* and *Critias*, he refers to what has become one of the most famous legends of all time: the doomed island of Atlantis.

Plato

In *Timaeus*, Plato uses a story told by Critias to describe where Atlantis existed, explaining that it "came forth out of the Atlantic Ocean, for in those days the Atlantic was navigable; and there was an island situated in front of the straits which are by you called the Pillars of Heracles; the island was larger than Libya and Asia put together, and was the way to other islands..."

Plato also divulges the details of the island's fate: "afterwards there occurred violent earthquakes and floods; and in a single day and night of misfortune all your warlike men in a body sank into the earth, and the island of Atlantis in like manner disappeared in the depths of the sea. For which reason the sea in those parts is impassable and impenetrable, because there is a shoal of mud in the way; and this was caused by the subsidence of the island." In *Critias*, the story revolves around Poseidon, the mythical god of the sea, and how the kingdom of Atlantis attempted to conquer Athens.

Although many ascribe Plato's myth to his desire for a way to emphasize his own political theories, for centuries historians and writers perpetuated the idea of the mythical island. After the Middle Ages, the story of the doomed civilization was revisited by Francis Bacon, who published *The New Atlantis* in 1627. In 1870, Jules Verne published his classic *Twenty Thousand Leagues Under the Sea*, which includes a visit to sunken Atlantis aboard Captain Nemo's submarine *Nautilus*. And in 1882, *Atlantis: The Antediluvian World* by Ignatius Donnelly was written to prove that Atlantis did exist—initiating much of the Atlantis mania that has occurred since that time.

Santorini: A True Atlantis?

More recently, historians and geologists have attempted to link Atlantis to the island of Santorini (also called Thera) in the Aegean Sea. About 3,600 years ago, the Minoa (or Thera) eruption—one of the largest eruptions in history—occurred on Santorini. This eruption caused the volcano to collapse, creating a huge caldera or "hole" at the top of the mountain. Historians believe the eruption caused the end of the Minoan civilization on Thera and the nearby island of Crete, most likely because a tsunami resulted from the massive explosion. Since that time, most of the islands grew from subsequent volcanic eruptions around the caldera, creating what is now the volcanic archipelago of islands called the Cycladic group.

Could this tourist hot spot truly be the site of the mythological island Atlantis? Some say that Plato's description of the palace and surroundings at Atlantis were similar to those at Knossos, the ceremonial and cultural center of the Minoan civilization. On the scientific end, geologists know that eruptions such as the one at Santorini can pump huge volumes of material into the air and slump other parts of a volcanic island into the oceans. To the ancient peoples, such an event could literally be translated as an island quickly sinking into the ocean. But even after centuries of study, excavation, and speculation, the mystery of Atlantis remains unsolved.

Then And Now: Ancient Cities

In the ancient world, it took far fewer people to make a great city. Some didn't survive, but others have flourished. With the understanding that ancient population estimates are necessarily approximate, here are the fates of some great metropolises.

✳   ✳   ✳   ✳

Memphis (now the ruins of Memphis, Egypt): By 3100 B.C., this Pharaonic capital bustled with an estimated 30,000 people. Today it has none—but modern Cairo, 12 miles north, houses 7,786,640 people.

Ur (now the ruins of Ur, Iraq): Sumer's great ancient city once stood near the Euphrates with a peak population of 65,000 around 2030 B.C. The Euphrates has meandered about ten miles northeast, and Ur now has a population of zero.

Alexandria (now El-Iskandariya, Egypt): Built on an ancient Egyptian village site near the Nile Delta's west end, Alexander the Great's city once held a tremendous library. In its heyday, it may have held 250,000 people. Today more than 3,300,000 people call it home.

Babylon (now the ruins of Babylon, Iraq): Babylon may have twice been the largest city in the world, in about 1700 B.C. and 500 B.C.—perhaps with up to 200,000 people in the latter case. Now, it's windblown dust and faded splendor. Perhaps if the fighting ever ends in this area of the world, Babylon will be restored.

Athens (Greece): In classical times, this powerful city-state stood miles from the coast and was not a big place—something like 30,000 residents during the 300s B.C. It now reaches the sea with nearly 3,000,000 residents.

Rome (Italy): With the rise of its empire, ancient Rome grew into a city of more than 500,000 and the center of Western civilization. Though that mantle moved on to other cities, Rome now has 3,000,000 people.

Xi'an (China): This longtime dynastic capital, famed for its terracotta warriors but home to numerous other antiquities, reached 400,000 people by A.D. 637. Its nearly 8,000,000 people today make it as important a city now as then.

Constantinople (now Istanbul, Turkey): First colonized by Greeks in the 1200s B.C., this city of fame was made Emperor Constantine the Great's eastern imperial Roman capital with 300,000 people. As Byzantium, it bobbed and wove through the tides of faith and conquest. Today, it is Turkey's largest city with 10,000,000 people.

Baghdad (Iraq): Founded around A.D. 762, this center of Islamic culture and faith was perhaps the first city to house more than 1,000,000 people. It has sometimes faded but never fallen. Today it has a population of 4,500,000.

Tenochtitlán (now Mexico City, Mexico): Founded in A.D. 1325, this island-built Aztec capital had more than 200,000 inhabitants within a century. Most of the surrounding lake has been drained over the years. A staggering 19,000,000 souls call modern Mexico City home.

Carthage (now the ruins of Carthage, Tunisia): Phoenician seafarers from the Levant founded this great trade city in 814 B.C. Before the Romans obliterated it in 146 B.C., its population may have reached 700,000. Today, it sits in empty silence ten miles from modern Tunis—population 2,000,000.

❊ Memphis was something of an Egyptian New Orleans, with dikes built to keep out Nile floods. When the city declined, the dikes failed and the unwanted site silted up.

❊ Ur is famed for its great ziggurat, thought by many to be the biblical Tower of Babel. Only the lower base remains today.

Mythmaking in Early America

*The search for an improbable past—or how
to make a mountain out of a molehill.*

✳   ✳   ✳   ✳

IN THE EARLY 1840s, the fledgling United States was gripped
by a controversy that spilled from the parlors of the educated
men in Boston and Philadelphia—the core of the nation's
intellectual elite—onto the pages of the newspapers printed
for mass edification. In the tiny farming village of Grave Creek,
Virginia (now West Virginia), on the banks of the Ohio River,
stood one of the largest earthen mounds discovered during white man's progress westward. The existence of these
mounds, spread liberally throughout the Mississippi Valley,
Ohio River Valley, and much of the southeast, was commonly
known and had caused a great deal of speculative excitement
since Europeans had first arrived on the continent. Hernando
de Soto, for one, had mentioned the mounds of the Southeast
during his wandering in that region.

Money Well Spent

The colonists who settled the East Coast noticed that the
mounds, which came in a variety of sizes and shapes, were
typically placed near excellent sites for villages and farms.
The Grave Creek mound was among the first of the major
earthworks discovered by white men in their westward expansion. By 1838, the property was owned and farmed by the
Tomlinson family.

Abelard B. Tomlinson took an interest in the mound on his
family's land and decided to open a vertical shaft from its summit, 70 feet high, to the center. He discovered skeletal remains
at various levels and a timbered vault at the base containing the
remains of two individuals. More importantly, he discovered
a sandstone tablet inscribed with three lines of characters of
unknown origin.

Who Were the Builders?

Owing to the general belief that the aborigines were lazy and incapable of such large operations—and the fact that none of the tribes who dwelt near the mounds claimed any knowledge of who had built them—many 19th-century Americans believed that the mound builders could not have been the ancestors of the Native American tribes they encountered. By the early 19th century, the average American assumed that the mound builders had been a pre-Columbian expedition from the Old World—Vikings, Israelites, refugees from Atlantis—all these and more had their champions. Most agreed, however, that the New World had once hosted and given rise to a civilization as advanced as that of the Aztecs and Incas who had then fallen into disarray or been conquered by the savage barbarians that now inhabited the land. Speculation on the history of the mound builders led many, including Thomas Jefferson, to visit the mounds and conduct their own studies.

Mormons and the Mounds

Meanwhile, the Grave Creek tablet fanned the flames of a controversy that was roaring over the newly established—and widely despised—Church of Jesus Christ of Latter-day Saints. The Mormon religion is based upon the belief that the American continent was once inhabited by lost tribes of Israel who divided into warring factions and fought each other to near extinction. The last surviving prophet of these people, Mormon, inscribed his people's history upon gold tablets, which were interred in a mound near present-day Palmyra, New York, until they were revealed to fifteen-year-old Joseph Smith in 1823.

Though many Americans were ready to believe that the mounds represented the remains of a nonaboriginal culture, they were less ready to believe in Smith's new religion. Smith and his adherents were persecuted horribly, and Smith was killed by an angry mob while leading his followers west. Critics of the Saints (as the Mormons prefer to be called) point to the early 19th-century publication of several popular books purporting that the earthen mounds of North America were the remains of lost tribes of Israel. These texts claimed that evidence would eventually be discovered to support their author's assertions. That the young Smith should have his revelation so soon after these fanciful studies were published struck many observers as entirely too coincidental. Thus, Abelard Tomlinson's excavation of the sandstone tablet with its strange figures ignited the passions of both Smith's followers and his detractors.

Enter the Scholar

Into this theological, and ultimately anthropological, maelstrom strode Henry Rowe Schoolcraft, a mineralogist whose keen interest in Native American history had led to his appointment as head of Indian affairs. While working in Sault Ste. Marie, Michigan, Schoolcraft married a native woman and mastered the Ojibwa language. Schoolcraft traveled to Grave Creek to examine Tomlinson's tablet and concluded that the figures were indeed a language but deferred to more learned scholars to determine just which language they represented. The opinions were many and varied—from Celtic runes to early Greek; experts the world over weighed in with their opinions. Nevertheless, Schoolcraft was more concerned with physical evidence and close study of the mounds themselves, and he remained convinced that the mounds and the artifacts they carried were the products of ancestors of the Native Americans. Schoolcraft's theory flew in the face of both those who sought to defend and those who sought to debunk the Mormon belief, and it would be more than three decades until serious scholarship and the emergence of true archaeological techniques began to shift opinion on the subject.

Answers Proposed, but Questions Still Abound

History has vindicated Schoolcraft's careful and thoughtful study of the mounds. Today, we know that the mound builders were not descendents of Israel, nor were they the offspring of Vikings. They were simply the ancient and more numerous predecessors of the Native Americans, who constructed the mounds for protection from floods and as burial sites, temples, and defense strongholds. As for the Grave Creek tablet: Scholars today generally agree that the figures are not a written language but simply a fanciful design whose meaning, if ever there was one, has been lost to the ages. Though the Smithsonian Institution has several etchings of the tablet in its collection, the whereabouts of the actual tablet have been lost to the ages.

Mounds That Remain

The earth mounds are among the most studied features of primitive America. Many have been lost since Europeans first settled in North America, but some of the more prominent have been preserved for study and observation, including:

✳ **Cahokia Mounds State Historic Site (Collinsville, Illinois):** With an estimated population of 30,000, the city that once existed here was among the largest in the world in A.D. 1050. Then, suddenly, mysteriously, it ceased to exist. Today, visitors can walk among the 68 surviving mounds.

✳ **Serpent Mound State Memorial (near Cincinnati, Ohio):** Originally constructed in an area inhabited by the Adena people, the serpent-shape mound is more than 1,300 feet long and once inspired theories that it marked the original site of the biblical Garden of Eden. The notoriety generated by the mound led to the creation of Ohio's first state park to protect the grounds upon which it is situated.

✳ **Hopewell Culture National Historical Park (Hopewell, Illinois):** Also known as "Mound City," this collection of mounds was nearly annihilated by amateur archaeologists. The Hopewell culture flourished between 200 B.C. and A.D. 500, with an extensive trading network that allowed them to acquire copper, which they fashioned into jewelry. By the time Europeans arrived in the New World, none of the tribes retained the practice, and the presence of copper in burial mounds convinced many early archaeologists that the mound builders could not have been Native Americans.

The Seven Wonders of the Ancient World

It was the ultimate destination guide—seven of the most spectacular hand-built wonders of the world. In fact, the Greek referred to these wonders as theamati, *which translates roughly to "must-sees."*

✳ ✳ ✳ ✳

THE FIRST COMPREHENSIVE listing of the Seven Wonders has been attributed to Herodotus, a Greek historian dating back to the 5th century B.C. Other versions soon followed—each reflecting the writer's opinion of what was worth mentioning and often naming many more than seven sights.

THE SEVEN WONDERS OF THE ANCIENT WORLD

Most of the earliest lists were lost; the oldest existing version known today was compiled by Antipater of Sidon in 140 B.C. The items on his list, with a few revisions, are the ones that came to forever be known as the Seven Wonders of the Ancient World. Unfortunately, only one of the seven still exists today; all that remains of the other six are descriptions from writers over the centuries.

So What's the Big Deal?

What makes the seven wonders so wonderful? It's a combination of factors: the intricacies of the architecture, the scale of engineering, and the beauty of each project—not to mention the construction technology and materials available for use at the time.

Religion often played a big role in the significance of these structures. Some were built to honor certain gods. Others were built to showcase important rulers, a number of whom had achieved a godlike following.

And the Seven Wonders Are...

1. **The Great Pyramid of Giza:** Located on the west bank of the Nile river near Cairo, Egypt, this is the largest of ten pyramids built between 2600 and 2500 B.C. Built for King Khufu, the Great Pyramid was constructed by thousands of workers toiling for nearly a quarter of a century (2609 B.C.–2584 B.C.).

   The structure consists of more than two million 2.5-ton stones. If the stones were piled on top of each other, the resulting tower would be close to 50 stories high. The base covers an astonishing 13 acres. It's not known exactly how the blocks were lifted. Theories include mud- and water-coated ramps or an intricate system of levers. Not only did the blocks have to be lifted, but they also had to be transported from the quarries. Even the experts can't say exactly how that was done. The mystery is part of the fascination.

   The pyramid originally stood 481 feet high but has been weathered down to about 450 feet. It was considered the tallest structure on the planet for 43 centuries. The Great Pyramid is the only Wonder of the Ancient World still standing—a testament to one of the mightiest civilizations in history.

2. **The Hanging Gardens of Babylon:** Legend has it that King Nebuchadnezzar II, ruler of Babylon (near modern Baghdad, Iraq), built the gardens around 600 B.C. as a present for his wife, Amytis of Media. The gardens consisted of a series of terraces holding trees, exotic plants, and shady pools—all fed by water piped in from the Euphrates River and rising about 60 feet high. References to the Gardens appear as late as the first century B.C., after which they disappear from contemporary accounts. There has been some

speculation over whether or not the Gardens ever even actually existed.

3. The Temple of Artemis at Ephesus: Constructed around 550 B.C. in what is now Turkey, the Temple was built in honor of Artemis (Diana), goddess of hunting and nature. The marble temple measured 377 by 180 feet and had a tile-covered roof held up by at least 106 columns between 40 and 60 feet high. The temple held priceless art and also functioned as the treasury of the city. It stood until 356 B.C. when it was purposely destroyed by an artist, known in infamy as Herostratus, who burned the Temple merely so his name would be remembered for ages. The outraged Ephesians rebuilt the temple, this time entirely of stone, but the new building was destroyed by invading Goths in A.D. 262. A few surviving sculptures are displayed at the British Museum.

4. The Statue of Zeus at Olympia: Even contemporary historians and archaeologists consider the Statue of Zeus at Olympia to be one of the best-known statues in the ancient world. The image, standing 40 feet high with a 20-foot base, was constructed by Phidias around 435 B.C. to honor Zeus, king of the gods. The statue depicted a seated Zeus (made of ivory, though his robes and sandals were made of gold) holding a golden figure of the goddess of victory in one hand and a staff topped with an eagle in the other. Atop his head was a wreath of olive branches.

In the flickering lamplight of the temple, the statue seemed almost alive and attracted pilgrims from all over Greece for eight centuries. After the old gods were outlawed by Christian emperor Theodosius, the statue was taken as a prize to Constantinople, where it was destroyed in a fire around A.D. 462.

5. The Mausoleum of Maussollos: This white marble tomb, built in what is today southwestern Turkey, was built around 353 B.C. for Maussollos, a Persian king. Around 45 stories tall, the building was covered in relief sculpture depicting scenes from mythology; gaps were filled in with bigger-than-life statues of famous heroes and gods. The very top was capped with a marble statue of Maussollos, pulled in a chariot by four horses. The structure was so impressive that the king's name has been lent to the present-day word *mausoleum*, now used to refer to an impressive burial place.

The tomb remained largely intact until the 13th century, when it was severely damaged by a series of earthquakes. In 1494, the Knights of Saint John raided its stonework to use as building materials for a castle being constructed nearby, and thus the Mausoleum was lost to history.

6. **The Colossus of Rhodes:** Standing nearly 110 feet tall—rivaling the modern Statue of Liberty, which tops out at 151 feet—the Colossus of Rhodes was a sight to behold. The bronze statue was built near the harbor of Rhodes in the Aegean Sea in honor of the sun god Helios. Construction took 12 years—from approximately 292 B.C. to 280 B.C. The exact pose of the statue is a matter of debate; records say that one arm was raised but are maddeningly silent on other details. The statue stood for only 56 years before it was toppled by an earthquake. It lay on the ground for another 800 years, still a tourist attraction. Accounts say a popular tourist game was to see if a person could encircle one of the fallen statue's thumbs with their arms. Finally, in A.D. 654, Rhodes was captured by Arab invaders who broke up the statue and melted it down for its bronze.

7. **The Lighthouse of Alexandria:** The youngest of the ancient wonders was a building with a civic, rather than a spiritual, purpose. The famed lighthouse of Alexandria was built around 250 B.C. to aid ships making the journey

into that city's harbor. At 380 feet tall, it was a marvel of ancient engineering. Overshadowed only by the two tallest Egyptian pyramids, a tower of greater height wouldn't be constructed for centuries. An interior ramp led up to a platform supporting a series of polished bronze mirrors, which would reflect sunlight during the day and firelight at night. The fuel source is uncertain but may have been oil or even animal dung. Some accounts claim the lighthouse could be seen 300 miles from the shore; this is almost certainly exaggerated, but more reasonable claims of 35 miles are impressive enough. The lighthouse was destroyed by an earthquake in the 1300s.

Legacy

It is a tribute to our ancestors that they were able to create works of architecture that capture our imagination even thousands of years after the structures themselves were destroyed. Several efforts are under way to name a definitive list of modern wonders, with such candidates as the Eiffel Tower and the Golden Gate Bridge. One such effort elicited votes from people all over the world via the Internet. The resulting list of the "New 7 Wonders of the World" was released in July 2007. The finalists, in no particular order, are: Petra, Jordan; the Great Wall of China; the Christ Redeemer, Brazil; the Taj Majal, India; Chichén Itzá, Mexico; the Colosseum, Italy; and Machu Picchu, Peru.

---

* Proof that the famed Hanging Gardens may be mythical: Herodotus, a very cosmopolitan fellow, visited Babylon but never mentioned them. Indeed, no archaeological evidence of the Gardens has ever been found.

* In addition to the Seven Ancient Wonders of the World and the New 7 Wonders of the World, there is also a list of natural world wonders: Mount Everest, Ayers Rock, the Matterhorn, the Grand Canyon, the Meteor Crater, the Great Barrier Reef, and Victoria Falls.

Ghost Towns of the Ancients

It's hard to think of great cities like New York or London ever becoming the ghost towns of future centuries. But many New Yorks and Londons of the ancient world did just that—then kept archaeologists and scientists busy studying them for hundreds of years.

✳   ✳   ✳   ✳

A Wall, a Horse, and a Mystery

Homer

MOST PEOPLE HAVE heard of the siege of Troy, that epic battle over a stolen princess that the blind poet Homer immortalized in the *Iliad*. The image of a "Trojan Horse" has made its way into film (and even computer) lingo. But the city that gave us the famed wooden horse faded into legend around 700 B.C. For the next 25 centuries, the city of Troy was dismissed as a fable—an elusive ghost for archaeologists and historians.

Details of the real Troy are fragmentary, handed down mostly through Greek myths and Homer's poetry. The city—which was located on the Aegean coast of modern-day Turkey—lay along major trade routes from the Mediterranean to the Black Sea, and it steadily prospered after its Bronze Age founding around 3000 B.C.

As Troy grew wealthy and powerful, its inhabitants protected themselves with massive stone walls. Homer's Troy boasted towers nearly 30 feet high and probably contained around 10,000 inhabitants at the time of the Trojan War. The city rose and fell several times (the last around the end of the 8th century B.C.), and it was rebuilt as a Roman outpost around the time of Christ. The "Roman Troy" remained an important trading center until Constantinople became the capital of the Eastern Roman Empire.

Troy then began its final journey into decline and ruin. By the time Europe emerged from the Dark Ages, the city had ceased to exist.

In the 1870s, an eccentric German businessman named Heinrich Schliemann, who had been schooled on the *Iliad* as a boy, built a small fortune and began searching for the lost city. Over a 19-year period, Schliemann completed several amateur digs around a city that, in due course, yielded nine sites to bear the name "Troy." The seventh "Troy," a city from around 1200–1000 B.C., appears to have been destroyed by fire and is the most likely candidate for the Troy of Homer's epic.

Go Tell the Whom?

Today we think of the ancient Greek city of Sparta as the "Spartan" (austere, militant, and culturally empty) counterpart to the more enlightened Athenian society. But in ancient times, Sparta lay at the cutting edge of political and military arts.

Sparta, the capital of the Lacedaemon kingdom on Greece's Ionic coast, inaugurated many idealistic traditions for which the Greek world became famous. It established a democratic assembly years before the Athenians adopted the practice; it allowed women broad educational and property rights; and it took its religion and art seriously.

After the Greek city-states combined to defeat the Persian invasion of 480 B.C., a rivalry between Sparta and Athens led to the bitter Peloponnesian War (431–403 B.C.). The war ended in Spartan victory, but Sparta's defeat by Thebes 30 years later sent the city into a period of decline. It ultimately vanished into ruin before A.D. 400.

In a passage from Thucydides's ancient work *The History of the Peloponnesian War*, the old chronicler muses: "Suppose the city of Sparta to be deserted, and nothing left but the temples and the ground-plan, distant ages would be very unwilling to believe that the power of the Lacodaemonians was at all equal to their fame."

Sure enough, the city left little of its original grandeur for later generations. It was not until some 1,500 years later that serious efforts were made to recover the home of the Spartans. In 1906, the British School at Athens did significant archaeological work and opened the world's eyes to the magnificent culture that was Sparta.

Rome: Total War

One of the ancient world's greatest cities had the misfortune of bumping up against the most powerful military force of its time. Set on the North African coast near modern Tunisia's capital city, Tunis, the great city of Carthage was the hub of a Mediterranean trading empire that rivaled that of the later Italian upstarts. This rivalry with Rome produced three great wars of antiquity, called the Punic Wars.

By virtue of its location—south of Sicily on Africa's Mediterranean coast—Carthage, a trading empire founded by the seagoing Phoenician people around 814 B.C., held a dominant position in Mediterranean trade from the 3rd and 2nd centuries B.C. In 264 B.C., Rome and Carthage were dragged into a war over Sicily. Round One went to the Romans. Two decades later, the Carthaginian general Hannibal led his elephants over the Alps into Italy on a legendary campaign of destruction, but the Romans eventually won that one as well.

A half century later, Rome goaded the Carthaginians into a third war. This time, the Roman general Scipio Africanus led a three-year siege of Carthage. He burned the metropolis to the ground and sold the populace into slavery.

In the 1st century A.D., the Romans rebuilt the city, and the "new" Carthage became a major food supplier. It remained a center of Roman Christianity until the end of the 7th century, when Arab invaders replicated Scipio's "complete destruction" formula. The city was supplanted by nearby Tunis, and today the ancient capital is a series of ruins in Tunis's suburbs.

Red City of the Nabataeans

*In the wilds of southern Jordan lies one of
antiquity's most beautifully preserved sights.*

* * * *

Where exactly is Petra?

Petra is a city within the Hashemite Kingdom of Jordan,
perhaps 80 miles south of Amman in the Naqab Desert, about
15 miles east of the Israeli border. It is a World Heritage Site
and a Jordanian national treasure, cared for accordingly.

Why settle out in the desert?

Petra was a key link in the trade chain connecting Egypt,
Babylon, Arabia, and the Mediterranean. It had water (if you
knew how to look) and was quite defensible.

When was it founded?

In 600 B.C., the narrow red sandstone canyon of Petra housed a
settlement of Edomites: seminomadic Semites said to descend
from the biblical Esau. Egypt was still rich but declining. Rome
was a young farming community dominated by its Etruscan
kings. The rise of classical Athens was decades away. Brutal
Assyria had fallen to Babylonian conquerors. With the rise of
the incense trade, Arab traders began pitching tents at what
would become Petra. We know them as the Nabataeans.

Did they speak Arabic?

Nabataean history spanned a millennium. They showed up
speaking early Arabic in a region where Aramaic was the
business-speak. The newcomers thus first wrote their Arabic
in a variant of the Aramaic script. But Petra's trade focus meant
a need to adopt Aramaic as well, so Nabataeans did. By the end
(about 250 years before the rise of Islam), Nabataean "Arabaic"
had evolved into classical (Koranic) Arabic.

What were these Nabataeans like?

The Swiss or Swedes of the biblical world. They weren't expansionists, but defended their homeland with shrewd diplomacy and obstinate vigor. Despite great wealth, they had few slaves. Despite monarchical government, Petra's Nabataeans showed a pronounced democratic streak. Empires rose and fell around them; business was business.

The trade must have been lucrative indeed.

Vastly. The core commodity was incense from Arabia, but many raw materials and luxuries of antiquity also passed through Petra—notably bitumen (natural asphalt), useful in waterproofing and possibly in embalming.

Speaking of religion, were they religious?

Religious, yes; fanatical, no. Most Nabataeans were pagan, worshipping benevolent fertility and sun deities. Jews were welcome at Petra, as were Christians in its later days.

What of Nabataean women's roles?

Nabataean women held a respected position in society, including property and inheritance rights. While no major ancient Near Eastern culture was truly egalitarian, the women of Petra participated in its luxuriant prosperity.

Take me to Petra in its heyday. What do I experience?

It is 70 B.C., and you walk the streets of Petra, home to about 20,000 people. Ornate homes and public buildings rivaling Athenian and Roman artistry are carved into the high red sandstone walls of the canyon. A camel caravan arrives from Arabia loaded with goods; white-robed traders dismount with elegant gifts for their buying contacts. The wealthy aroma of frankincense constantly reminds your nostrils why Petra exists. Most people wear robes and cloaks, often colored by exotic dyes. Petra is luxurious without being licentious.

You overhear conversations in Aramaic and Arabic: A new cistern is under construction. Workers are shoring up a building damaged by a recent earth tremor. Old-timers grouse that reigning King Aretas III wishes he were Greek. A modestly robed vendor walks past with dates for sale; you fish out a thick silver coin to offer her. Along with your bronze change and the delicious dates, she wishes you the favor of al-Uzza, the Nabataean goddess identified with Aphrodite and Venus.

You ask a passing water-bearer: Who's that guy in the outlandish robe draped over one shoulder, followed by servants? A man of faraway Rome, says she. You've heard of this Rome, a dynamic market for Petra's goods, with domains beginning to rival Alexander the Great's once-mighty empire. Only time will tell how Petra will reckon with this next tide of power.

No one lives at Petra now. When and why did it decline?

Petra's last king, Rabbel II, willed his realm to Rome. When he died in A.D. 106, Nabataea became the Roman province of Arabia Petraea. Again the Nabataeans adjusted—and kept up the trade. In the 2nd and 3rd centuries A.D., the caravans began using Palmyra (in modern Syria) as an alternate route, starting a slow decline at Petra. An earthquake in 363 delivered the knockout punch: damage to the intricate water system sustaining the city. By about 400, Petra was an Arabian ghost town.

How might I see this for myself?

Thousands do it daily. If you can travel to Jordan, you can travel to Petra—either with an organized tour booked through a travel agent or on your own if that's your style. Nearby hotels and restaurants offer modern accommodations. The site charges a daily entrance fee.

✳ Scientists are currently studying frankincense because there seems to be a substance within it that inhibits the growth of cancerous cells.

Built to Defend,
The Great Wall Now Beckons

The Great Wall of China was built and rebuilt over a span of 2,000 years by millions of laborers. Each year, sections of the wall draw crowds of tourists, who marvel at the world's largest artificial structure.

✳ ✳ ✳ ✳

FOR CURIOUS EXTRATER-RESTRIALS who swing their spacecraft close to Earth, the Great Wall of China provides a particularly dramatic notion of what human beings are all about: cleverness, grandeur, self-preservation, even paranoia.

Portions of the Wall stretch from Gansu Province in the west to Shanhai Pass near the Bohai Sea in the east, but the combined length of the various walls that comprise the Great Wall has never been accurately calculated. The most common estimate is a staggering 4,000 miles.

The Wall's oldest portions date back more than 2,000 years. In 221 B.C., First Emperor Qin Shi Huangdi unified several feudal Chinese states. At the same time, he transformed the many walls that once separated the warring nations into a single defensive barrier meant to repel barbarian invaders. Due to the organic nature of the construction material, most of this first "Great Wall" has eroded and is no longer visible.

Rulers of the Ming Dynasty (A.D. 1368–1644) used brick and stone to transform the wall into the structure we know today. Upper-floor watchtowers were rebuilt with lookouts, and lower floors were fitted with cannons.

Some sections of the Wall were built in desolate areas, where they acted as signaling outposts. Towers along the wall alerted other stations with smoke signals during the day and bonfires at night, calling reinforcements to the area under attack.

Popular wisdom claims the Great Wall is the only artificial object visible to the naked eye from the moon. That's a neat claim but, alas, it's false. While the Wall can be seen by astronauts in low Earth orbit, the structure cannot be seen outside of Earth's orbit and certainly not from the moon—from there even the continents are barely visible.

The Wall's magnificence, however, has never been disputed. Today, this Wall that was designed to repel barbarian invaders is swarmed by wide-eyed tourists. Despite years of restoration work, many sections of the Wall lie in ruins, destroyed by the elements and by locals who steal brick and stone.

Significant sections of the Great Wall are located near the Chinese capital of Beijing. When you visit, make time for:

Badaling

Built in 1571, Badaling was the first area of the Wall to be opened to tourists. In 1987, it was declared a United Nations Educational, Scientific, and Cultural Organization (UNESCO) World Heritage Site. It is now heavily visited and has become an unabashed tourist draw, with hundreds of booths that sell souvenir kitsch.

Juyong Guan

An attack in A.D. 1213 by Mongol warrior Genghis Khan was repulsed along this section when defenders poured molten iron on the fortress gates. However, a Mongol emissary in the Chinese capital told a Khan general, Tsabar, about a little-known path through Juyong Pass. Tsabar quickly bypassed the Wall and pounced on the defenders from the rear, causing some disruption. When the Mongols retreated in 1368, Ming General Xuda built five defensive walls in and around the pass.

Mutianyu

Tourists have been invited to this portion since 1986. For those unable to climb the Wall, Mutianyu sports a cable car that whisks visitors to the top.

Simatai

Stretches of this portion have crumbled into disrepair. Nevertheless, a trek up to Wangjinglou Tower gives an impressive view of distant Beijing. To reach this summit, however, visitors must climb a 70-degree slope nicknamed the "Stairway to Heaven." Even hardy visitors find the climb challenging.

Jinshanling

Starting in A.D. 1386, and for nearly 200 years thereafter, this section of the Wall was built and subsequently reconstructed. Jinshanling has 150 battle platforms and obstacle walls with peepholes and shooting holes incorporated into the design. Despite a lack of recent repairs, this is the Wall's second most complete section, after Badaling.

Huanghuacheng

The builder of this portion, Ming General Kai, was so methodical that construction took many years. Emperor Wanli became impatient and believed deceitful ministers who told him that General Kai was spending too much money on a subpar job. The emperor had Kai beheaded but later sent inspectors to the site, who reported that Kai had actually done an amazing job. A devastated Wanli had *Jin Tang* (solid and firm) carved in stone near this section to honor the builder he had wronged.

Gubeikou

This rugged location in the Yanshan Mountain Range was breached in 1549 by Mongol leader Altan Khan, who pillaged Beijing's suburbs before returning home. During World War II, parts of Gubeikou were hit by Japanese artillery fire.

The Mystery of Easter Island

On Easter Sunday in 1722, a Dutch ship landed on a small island 2,300 miles from the coast of South America. Polynesian explorers had preceded them by a thousand years or more, and the Europeans found the descendants of those early visitors still living on the island. They also found a strange collection of almost 900 enormous stone heads, or moai, *standing with their backs to the sea, gazing across the island with eyes hewn out of coral. The image of those faces haunts visitors to this day.*

✳ ✳ ✳ ✳

Ancestors at the End of the Land

EASTER ISLAND LEGEND tells of the great Chief Hotu Matu'a, the Great Parent, striking out from Polynesia in a canoe, taking his family on a voyage across the trackless ocean in search of a new home. He made landfall on Te-Pito-te-Henua, the End of the Land, sometime between A.D. 400 and 700. Finding the island well-suited to habitation, his descendants spread out to cover much of it, living off the natural bounty of the land and sea. With their survival assured, they built *ahu*—ceremonial sites featuring a large stone mound—and on them erected *moai*, which were representations of notable chieftains who led the island over the centuries. The *moai* weren't literal depictions of their ancestors, but rather embodied their spirit, or *mana*, and conferred blessings and protection on the islanders.

The construction of these *moai* was quite a project. A hereditary class of sculptors oversaw the main quarry, located near one of the volcanic mountains on the island. Groups of people would request a *moai* for their local *ahu*, and the sculptors would go to work, their efforts supported by gifts of food and other goods. Over time, they created 887 of the stone *moai*, averaging just over 13 feet tall and weighing around 14 tons, but ranging from one extreme of just under four feet tall to a behemoth that towered 71 feet. The moai were then transported across the island by a mechanism that still remains in doubt, but that may have involved rolling them on the trunks of palm trees felled for that purpose—a technique that was to have terrible repercussions for the islanders.

When Europeans first made landfall on Easter Island, they found an island full of standing *moai*. Fifty-two years later, James Cook reported that many of the statues had been toppled, and by the 1830s none were left standing. What's more, the statues hadn't just been knocked over; many of them had boulders placed at strategic locations, with the intention of decapitating the *moai* when they were pulled down. What happened?

A Culture on the Brink

The original Dutch explorers had encountered a culture on the rebound. At the time of their arrival, they found two or three thousand living on the island, but some estimates put the population as high as fifteen thousand a century before. The story of the islanders' decline is one in which many authors find a cautionary tale: The people simply consumed natural resources to the point where their land could no longer support them.

By the 1600s, life had changed: The last forests on the island disappeared, and the islanders' traditional foodstuffs vanished from the archaeological record. Local tradition tells of a time of famine and even rumored cannibalism, and it is from this time that island history reveals the appearance of the spear. Tellingly, the Polynesian words for "wood" begin to take on a connotation of wealth, a meaning found nowhere else that shares the language.

Perhaps worst of all, with their forests gone, the islanders had no material to make the canoes that would have allowed them to leave their island in search of resources. They were trapped, and they turned on one another.

The Europeans found a reduced society that had just emerged from this time of terror. The respite was short-lived, however. The arrival of the foreigners seems to have come at a critical moment in the history of Easter Island.

Either coincidentally or spurred on by the strangers, a warrior class seized power across the island, and different groups vied for power. Villages were burned, their resources taken by the victors, and the defeated left to starve. The warfare also led to the toppling of an enemy's *moai*—whether to capture their *mana* or simply prevent it from being used against the opposing faction. In the end, none of the *moai* remained standing.

Downfall and Rebound

The troubles of Easter Island weren't limited to self-inflicted chaos. The arrival of the white man also introduced smallpox and syphilis; the islanders, with little natural immunity to the exotic diseases, fared no better than native populations elsewhere on the planet.

As if that weren't enough, other ships arrived, collecting slaves for work in South America. The internal fighting and external pressure combined to reduce the number of native islanders to little more than a hundred by 1877—the last survivors of a people who once enjoyed a tropical paradise.

Easter Island, or Rapa Nui, was annexed by Chile in 1888. Currently, there are around 2,200 Rapanui living on the island, all descended from the 111 remaining in 1877. There are projects under way to raise the fallen *moai*. As of today, approximately 50 have been returned to their former glory.

---

* The largest *moai* weighs between 145 and 165 tons.
* Easter Island's nearest neighbor is Pitcairn Island, which is 1,400 miles away.
* The size of Easter Island is only 64 square miles.

Horace Greeley's Gripe

Did this 1800s news mogul and presidential hopeful coin the phrase "Go West, young man"? He was—at the very least—the most prominent person to say it in a memorable way.

✳   ✳   ✳   ✳

HORACE GREELEY WAS a self-made journalist who built the influential *New York Tribune* into a mighty voice for change. He opposed monopolies, the death penalty, and slavery, and he advocated egalitarianism. In a *Tribune* editorial dated July 13, 1865, Greeley wrote, "Washington is not a place to live in. The rents are high, the food is bad, the dust is disgusting and the morals are deplorable. Go West, young man, go West and grow up with the country."

Although he was a solid advocate for Western settlement, Greeley was speaking to a different issue. He was addressing civil servants in D.C. who were unhappy about low pay and high living costs. What Greeley meant was, "If you don't like it here, go somewhere else."

A number of historians credit the phrase to John B. Soule, writing in the *Terre Haute Express* in 1851. That credit lacks one key component: a specific date. If we're sure someone said or wrote something, we usually know exactly when. With Soule, we do not, so a firm credit becomes problematic. He probably did say it, but just as likely, so did others before and after. In the 1800s, many thousands sought their fortunes out West. "Go West" was the era's equivalent of saying, "Apply to college."

Greeley's own story ended less optimistically. He ran against Ulysses S. Grant for president, was soundly defeated, lost his mind and his newspaper, and died insane. His assessment of Washington, D.C., however, has in many ways endured the test of time.

10 Structures That Define America

There are numerous structures that represent the American dream. Here are a few of those defining monuments.

✳ ✳ ✳ ✳

1. **White House:** The history of the White House began when President George Washington and city planner Pierre-Charles L'Enfant chose the site for the presidential residence. Irish-born architect James Hoban's design was chosen in a competition to find a builder of the "President's House." Construction began in October 1792. Although Washington oversaw the building of the house, he never lived in it. When the White House was completed in 1800, President John Adams and his wife, Abigail, moved in as the first residents. Since then, many presidents have made changes and additions. The White House survived a fire at the hands of the British during the War of 1812 and another blaze in the West Wing in 1929. President Harry Truman gutted and renovated the building during his time there. Encompassing approximately 55,000 square feet, the White House has 6 levels and 132 rooms, including 35 bathrooms. It is the world's only private residence of a head of state that is open to the public.

2. **Brooklyn Bridge:** Every day, thousands of commuters cross the East River via the Brooklyn Bridge, and they have John A. Roebling and his son, Washington, to thank. In 1867, the elder Roebling was hired as chief engineer to build "the greatest bridge in existence"; he died before construction began, however. Washington stepped in, and construction began in January 1870. The 85-foot-wide bridge was the first steel wire suspension bridge and the largest suspension bridge in the world at the time. On May 24, 1883, the bridge opened to the public, carrying pedestrians, livestock, and trolley cars between Manhattan and

Brooklyn. The pedestrian toll that day was a penny but was raised to three cents the next morning. Today, the bridge carries upwards of 144,000 vehicles a day in six lanes of traffic. About 2,000 pedestrians and hundreds of bicyclists also cross the bridge's 1.14 miles each workday.

3. **Washington Monument:** The Washington Monument, a 555-foot-high white obelisk situated at the west end of the National Mall in Washington, D.C., honors George Washington, Revolutionary War hero and the first president of the United States. Comprised of 36,491 marble, granite, and sandstone blocks, the structure was designed by Robert Mills. Construction began in 1848, but due to the outbreak of the Civil War and lack of funding, it took nearly 40 years to complete. It is clearly visible where work resumed in 1876 by the difference in the marble's shading, about 150 feet up the obelisk. The monument was dedicated in 1885 but did not officially open to the public until October 9, 1888, after the internal construction was complete. At the time it was the world's tallest structure.

4. **Lincoln Memorial:** "In this temple, as in the hearts of the people for whom he saved the Union, the memory of Abraham Lincoln is enshrined forever." These words are inscribed at the top of the Lincoln Memorial. Designed by architect Henry Bacon, sculptor Daniel Chester French, and artist Jules Guerin, the structure was completed in 1922. The monument is ringed by 36 columns, one for each state in the Union (at the time of Lincoln's death). Seated within the monument is a sculpture of Lincoln, and inscriptions from both the Gettysburg Address and his second inaugural address adorn the walls.

5. **Empire State Building:** The Empire State Building is the crown jewel of the New York City skyline. Designed by William Lamb, the structure was the world's tallest building when it opened in 1931. More than 3,000 workers

took fewer than 14 months to build the structure, with the framework erected at a pace of 4.5 stories per week. On a clear day the observatory offers glimpses of the five surrounding states.

6. **Golden Gate Bridge:** San Francisco's Golden Gate Bridge was the vision of chief engineer Joseph B. Strauss, whose contemporaries maintained that such a bridge could not be built. Nevertheless, construction began on January 5, 1933. Nearly four and a half years, $35 million, and 11 worker fatalities later, the bridge was opened to an estimated 200,000 pedestrians on May 27, 1937, and to vehicles the next day. The bridge is 1.7 miles long and 90 feet wide. The bridge has two principal cables passing over the tops of the two main towers. If laid end to end, the total length of wire in both main cables would total 80,000 miles. The Golden Gate Bridge is painted "International Orange," making it more visible to ships and the 38 million vehicles that cross it annually in the lingering and persistent fog.

7. **St. Louis Arch:** The St. Louis Arch on the bank of the Mississippi River marks the city as the "Gateway to the West." Thomas Jefferson's vision of freedom and democracy spreading from "sea to shining sea" inspired architect Eero Saarinen's contemporary design for a 630-foot stainless steel memorial. Construction began in 1963 and was completed on October 28, 1965. The Arch's foundation is set 60 feet into the ground and is built to withstand earthquakes and high winds. A 40-passenger train takes sightseers from the lobby to the observation platform, where on a clear day the view stretches for 30 miles.

8. **Sears Tower:** In 1969, retail giant Sears, Roebuck & Co. wanted to consolidate its employees working in offices around the Chicago area. Designed by chief architect Bruce Graham and structural engineer Fazlur Khan of Skidmore, Owings & Merrill, construction on Chicago's Sears Tower

began in 1970. The colossal structure—the world's tallest building at the time—opened in 1973. It remains the tallest building in the United States, though it has a new name: Willis Tower. The structure now features an area called the Ledge, where visitors can stand in retractable enclosed glass boxes that jut out four feet from the building. If you look down at your feet, the view is either thrilling or vertigo-inducing.

9. **Vietnam Veterans Memorial:** This memorial in Washington, D.C., honors the men and women who served in one of America's most divisive wars. The memorial was intended to heal the nation's emotional wounds and was designed to be neutral about the war itself. Three components comprise the memorial: the Wall of Names, the Three Servicemen Statue and Flagpole, and the Vietnam Women's Memorial. The Wall was built in 1982 and designed by Maya Lin. Visitors descend a path along two walls of black granite with one wing pointing at the Washington Monument a mile away and the other at the Lincoln Memorial about 600 feet away. The names of 59,000 soldiers killed or missing in action dominate the Vietnam Veterans Memorial.

10. **World Trade Center:** A list of some of the nation's iconic structures would be incomplete without mentioning the 110-story Twin Towers and five smaller buildings of the World Trade Center in New York City, which were destroyed on September 11, 2001. Of the approximately 50,000 people who worked in the complex, 3,000 died on that tragic day.

Sandstone Gateway to Heaven

For hundreds of years, rumors of the lost city of Angkor spread among Cambodian peasants. On a stifling day in 1860, Henri Mahout and his porters discovered that the ancient city was more than mere legend.

❋   ❋   ❋   ❋

FRENCH BOTANIST AND explorer Henri Mahout wiped his spectacles as he pushed into a Cambodian jungle clearing. Gasping for breath in the thick mists, he gazed down weed-ridden avenues at massive towers and stone temples wreathed with carvings of gods, kings, and battles. The ruins before him were none other than the temples of Angkor Wat.

Although often credited with the discovery of Angkor Wat, Mahout was not the first Westerner to encounter the site. He did, however, bring the "lost" city to the attention of the European public when his travel journals were published in 1868. He wrote: "One of these temples—a rival to that of Solomon, and erected by some ancient Michelangelo—might take an honorable place beside our most beautiful buildings."

Mahout's descriptions of this massive unexplored Hindu temple sent a jolt of lightning through academic circles. Explorers combed the jungles of northern Cambodia in an attempt to explain the meaning and origin of the mysterious lost shrine.

The Rise of the Khmer

Scholars first theorized that Angkor Wat and other ancient temples in present-day Cambodia were about 2,000 years old. However, as they began to decipher the Sanskrit inscriptions, they found that the temples had been erected during the 9th through 12th centuries. While Europe languished in the Dark Ages, the Khmer Empire of Indochina was reaching its zenith.

The earliest records of the Khmer people date to the middle of the 6th century. They migrated from southern China and other locations and settled in what is now Cambodia. The early Khmer retained many Indian influences—they were Hindus, and their architecture evolved from Indian building methods.

In the early 9th century, King Jayavarman II laid claim to an independent kingdom called Kambuja. He established his capital some 190 miles north of Phnom Penh, the modern Cambodian capital. Jayavarman II also introduced the cult of *devaraja*, which claimed that the Khmer king was a representative of Shiva, the Hindu god of destruction and rebirth. As such, in addition to the temples built to honor the Hindu gods, temples were also constructed to serve as tombs for kings.

The Khmer built more than 100 stone temples spread out over about 40 miles. The temples were made from laterite (a material similar to clay that forms in tropical climates) and sandstone. The sandstone provided an open canvas for the statues and reliefs celebrating the Hindu gods.

Home of the Gods

During the first half of the 12th century, Kambuja's King Suryavarman II decided to raise an enormous temple dedicated to the Hindu god Vishnu, a religious monument that would subdue the surrounding jungle and illustrate the power of the Khmer king. His masterpiece—the largest temple complex in the world—would be known to history by its Sanskrit name, "Angkor Wat," or "City of Temple."

Pilgrims visiting Angkor Wat in the 12th century would enter the temple complex by crossing a square, 600-foot-wide moat that ran some four miles in perimeter around the temple grounds. Approaching from the west, visitors would tread the moat's causeway to the main gateway. From there, they would follow a spiritual journey representing the path from the outside world through the Hindu universe and into Mount Meru, the home of the gods. They would pass a giant statue of an eight-armed Vishnu as they entered the western *gopura*, or gatehouse, known as the "Entrance of the Elephants."

They would then follow a stone walkway decorated with *nagas* (mythical serpents) past sunken pools and column-studded buildings once believed to house sacred temple documents.

At the end of the stone walkway, a pilgrim would step up to a platform surrounded with galleries featuring six-foot-high bas-reliefs of gods and kings. One depicts the Churning of the Ocean of Milk, a Hindu story in which gods and demons churn a serpent in an ocean of milk to extract the elixir of life. Another illustrates the epic battle of monkey warriors against demons whose sovereign had kidnapped Sita, the beautiful wife of Rama (the Hindu deity of chivalry and virtue). Others depict the gruesome fates awaiting the wicked in the afterlife.

A visitor to King Suryavarman's kingdom would next ascend the dangerously steep steps to the temple's second level, an enclosed area boasting a courtyard decorated with hundreds of dancing *apsaras*, female images ornamented with jewelry and elaborately dressed hair.

For kings and high priests, the journey would continue with a climb up more steep steps to a 126-foot-high central temple, the pinnacle of Khmer society. Spreading out some 145 feet on each side, the square temple includes a courtyard cornered by four high conical towers shaped to look like lotus buds. The center of the temple is dominated by a fifth conical tower soaring 180 feet above the main causeway; inside it holds a golden statue of the Khmer patron, Vishnu, riding a half-man, half-bird creature in the image of King Suryavarman.

Disuse and Destruction

With the decline of the Khmer Empire and the resurgence of Buddhism, Angkor Wat was occupied by Buddhist monks for many years. A cruciform gallery leading to the temple's second level was decorated with 1,000 Buddhas; the Vishnu statue in the central tower was replaced by an image of Buddha. The temple fell into various states of disrepair over the centuries and is now the focus of international restoration efforts.

Treasures of an Empire

A product of the Age of Enlightenment, London's British Museum carved a new path in the diffusion of human knowledge when it opened to the public in 1759.

✳   ✳   ✳   ✳

IT TOOK THE death of an obscure British physician, Sir Hans Sloane, to launch the world's first public museum. In his will, Sloane left a collection of some 71,000 natural and historical objects to the United Kingdom in return for a £20,000 payment to his heirs.

Britain's King George II expressed little interest in the purchase of oddities and miscellanea, but far-sighted members of Parliament were moved to accept Sloane's posthumous deal. An Act of Parliament dated June 7, 1753, accepted the bequest and established a lottery to raise funds for the purchase and maintenance of the Sloane collection, as well as other items left to the king and country by wealthy collectors.

The collection originally consisted of three groups: Printed Books, Manuscripts (including medals), and "Natural and Artificial Productions," which included everything else. It slowly grew as George II contributed the Old Royal Library—rare works owned by Britannia's sovereigns. But the British Museum's place in world history was secured on January 15, 1759, when the museum opened its doors to "all studious and curious Persons" free of charge. Great Britain had founded the world's first public museum.

As the sun rose over the British Empire, the museum naturally benefited from exotic artifacts acquired from other lands by explorers, merchants, and generals. Classical sculptures from long-gone civilizations became a central feature of the growing museum, and before long, the 17th-century mansion in which the collection was housed had to make way for a larger building.

Between 1823 and 1857, the space around the old museum was rebuilt to accommodate a growing collection, as well as the throngs of ordinary citizens who came to see what the empire had collected.

Reaching Out to the Masses

In the early 19th century, the British Museum's curators embarked on a project that today would be called "community outreach." They scheduled public lectures, improved displays for visitors, and published a *Synopsis*, or museum guidebook, that ran to 60 editions before the end of the century. The museum also sponsored excavation projects abroad, and many treasures uncovered in these digs were sent to the museum.

The August 1939 Nazi-Soviet pact shook up British authorities, who decided to disperse much of the museum's collection amongst safer locations. Their precautions were warranted, as the museum was damaged by German incendiary bombs during the Blitz. Fortunately, Britain's most important treasures remained untouched and were repatriated when the war ended.

The postwar years marked a renewed effort to make the museum's holdings enjoyable and accessible. The 1972 exhibition "Treasures of Tutankhamun" drew more than 1.6 million visitors to the museum and became the museum's most successful exhibit of all time. Since then, the museum has promoted temporary exhibits, as well as traveling exhibitions spanning the globe.

Today, some five million visitors tour the astonishingly varied collection of art and artifacts annually, which totals some 13 million objects. At the British Museum, tourists can find highlights of the collection, such as the Rosetta Stone; the Elgin Marbles, ancient statues that graced the pediments of the Athenian Parthenon; Michelangelo's sketch *The Fall of Phaeton*; the earliest surviving copy of *Beowulf*; and a colossal bust of Egyptian Pharaoh Ramses II. The world's first public museum is a fitting capstone to the empire that built it.

The Best of the Rest

Any list of the world's greatest museums is necessarily subjective. But beyond the British Museum (see p. 230), the Louvre (p. 467), and the Smithsonian (p. 236), one could round out a list of the world's top museums with the following:

1. Vatican Museums (Vatican City): The world's smallest independent state boasts one of the world's largest collections of art. Founded in 1503 by Pope Julius II, the Vatican Museums showcase a huge collection of sculpture, tapestry, and literature. Moreover, the architecture of the buildings housing these treasures are themselves works of art; frescoes such as Rafael's *School of Athens* and the ceiling of the 15th-century Sistine Chapel provide a dramatic backdrop to one of the world's greatest assemblies of masterpieces. Little wonder that some three million visitors annually tour the museum's splendid halls.

2. The Hermitage (St. Petersburg): Built in a city that symbolized the emerging Russian empire of the 1700s, the Romanov dynasty's Winter Palace and its associated buildings house more than three million works of art. Ranging from a 7th-century B.C. Scythian gold statue to one of the world's greatest collections of impressionist art, the Hermitage has become one of Europe's most popular tourist attractions, drawing some two and a half million visitors annually. Taken together with its Moscow counterpart, the Kremlin Armory (home to the tsarist crown jewels and a magnificent collection of diamonds), the Hermitage ranks high on the list for any connoisseur of art.

3. Metropolitan Museum of Art (New York City): Founded in 1870, the Met boasts a permanent collection of more than two million works of art covering some 5,000 years of human expression. Highlights of its American art collection include Emmanuel Leutz's *Washington Crossing the Delaware*. The museum boasts an equally impressive collection of Asian and Islamic art. The

Met now draws about 4.5 million visitors annually, making it one of the world's most-visited museums.

4. National Museum of China (Beijing): China's ancient culture is on display at Beijing's National Museum. Some 610,000 pieces of archaeological and artistic works are housed at this gem of a museum, which gives the public a glimpse into China's 5,000-year history.

5. Egyptian Museum (Cairo): Although the museum's 120,000-piece collection runs from prehistoric times to the Greco-Roman period, the highlights are naturally found in its vast collection of Egyptian artifacts. Since its founding in 1835, the Egyptian Museum has grown to encompass the great works of the Pharonic eras, from ornate sarcophagus lids to golden statues of Egyptian gods.

6. J. Paul Getty Museum (Los Angeles): Financed by oil magnate J. Paul Getty, the museum complex spreads out over some 750 acres in the foothills of the Santa Monica Mountains. Its highlights include Greco-Roman statues, illuminated monastic manuscripts, and some 450 European paintings dating from 1300 to the impressionist period. The Getty Museum arguably holds the world's finest private art collection.

7. Museo Nacional del Prado (Madrid): Situated in downtown Madrid, the Prado Museum has bragging rights to more than just Spanish masters such as Goya, Velázquez, El Greco, and Picasso. Like the Hermitage, the Louvre, and the Vatican, the Prado benefits from the global reach of Spain's pre-Renaissance empire. In 1868, the collection, which was the property of the Spanish crown, was nationalized for the benefit of its citizens, and each year some 2.5 million visitors view its collection of 7,600 paintings (plus another 11,700 drawings, prints, and sculptures), which includes works by famed French, Italian, Flemish, Dutch, and German artists.

The Maginot Line: Winning the Previous War

France built the Maginot Line in order to win another World War I. Unfortunately for the French, Germany did not plan to refight World War I.

✳ ✳ ✳ ✳

WHICH ILLUSTRIOUS GENERAL said, "The side which stays within its fortifications is beaten"?

Answer: Napoleon Bonaparte, Emperor of France

To understand why France built the Maginot Line, review the French World War I experience: France hosted nearly the entire Western Front, with six million soldiers killed, wounded, or captured. French generals concluded that modern defense was stronger than modern offense. "Next time," reasoned French generals, "we will inflict rather than suffer those losses."

From 1930 on, France spent vast sums blanketing its German and Luxembourg frontiers with a network of steel and concrete fortifications. A much lesser version extended along the Belgian frontier to the English Channel. People named it the Maginot Line for the French Minister of Defense who spearheaded it, André Maginot.

A Defensive Masterpiece

The Line was no modern Great Wall, but a series of mutually supportive fortifications. Let's tour a section to get a clear image.

Picture a verdant hill topped by an armored observation post, studded with concrete bunkers and steel turrets, flanked by lesser forts and pillboxes. Interlocking fields of fire take excellent defensive advantage of all terrain. In places the concrete is ten feet thick. Out front are tank traps and wire. In the distance to each side you can see another hill with similar defenses;

interval casemates lie between. Indoors, several stories of tunnels connect the various bastions like the roots of a gigantic tree. Ammunition elevators and railways move ammo to the guns and the wounded to a modern sickbay.

One thousand men defend this clean, modern fort complex, called an *ouvrage*. No more gas attacks; no more muddy, filthy trenches. Artillery can (and would, in one case) shell it all day without effect. The Maginot Line contained 44 large *ouvrages*, 58 small *ouvrages*, and 360 interval casemates.

A Huge Blow to France

German generals saw no reason to assail the Line: A quick and violent strike through the Netherlands and Belgium would enable Germany's mobile advance guard to bite deep into France north of the *ouvrages*, aided by close air support. The infantry, using standard tactics, would follow to occupy, consolidate, and control.

The strategy worked to perfection. On May 10, 1940, Germany tore into the Low Countries, quickly breaking into France well north of the *ouvrages* at Sedan. A minor German covering force tied down the 36 divisions defending the Line. Forty-six days later France surrendered.

All the Maginot Line did was encourage the Germans to find an easier place to invade.

---

* Perhaps it was a mercy that Maginot himself did not live to see what became of his defensive line and his nation. He died in 1932, of typhoid caused by contaminated oysters.

* Germany did attack the Maginot Line during the French Campaign, but only halfheartedly, to make sure significant forces stayed holed up in the *ouvrages*.

* Mushroom farms now occupy portions of the line.

A Nation's Inheritance

Perhaps no American museum is as well known—and as beloved—as the Smithsonian Institution's complex of art, science, history, and zoological museums in Washington, D.C.

✳ ✳ ✳ ✳

IN 1835, AN unknown Englishman named James Smithson died, childless but not penniless. He had inherited a substantial estate from his parents—one of royal blood and the other a duke. In death he left the world a magnificent gift: an endowment for an American institution "for the increase and diffusion of knowledge among men"—the Smithsonian Institution.

James Smithson

Smithson's motives behind his unusual bequest remain a mystery. He never visited the United States, and there is little evidence that he ever even wrote to any American. Illegitimate son of the Duke of Northumberland, he may have felt slighted by a British society that deprived him of the privileges of a "legitimate" ducal heir. Or he may have taken a far-off interest in the bustling new democracy in which ideas and industry appeared to rule the day.

Whatever his motives, Smithson's offer of 100,000 gold sovereigns was too enticing for the young republic to refuse. President Andrew Jackson urged Congress to accept Smithson's gift, and upon congressional approval, the British gold was recast into 508,318 Yankee dollars.

Now What?

Having accepted the money, the nation faced an important question: "What do we do with it?"

Initially, Congress leaned toward using Smithson's gold to establish a national university. Plans for an institution specializing in the classics, science, or teaching skills were all proposed and rejected in turn. Other ideas—a national observatory, a laboratory, a museum, or a library—drew both support and opposition from the divided legislature. So the deadlocked Congress settled the matter by avoiding the issue entirely, leaving it to the Smithsonian's board of directors to determine the direction of the new institution.

America's Attic

The first proceeds were used for a building that would house the many tasks assigned to the new institution—teaching, experimenting, exhibiting to the public. The building, located on the National Mall and now known as "the Castle," was designed in the medieval revival style, reminiscent of the ancient universities of Smithson's homeland.

While the research and scientific functions of the Smithsonian grew steadily after the 1855 completion of the Castle, it was the national collection of odds and ends that captured the public's mind and earned the Smithsonian its reputation as "America's attic." Fueled by the great American explorations of the Arctic, Antarctic, and interior regions of the United States, the Smithsonian's holdings grew from a small collection of pressed flora and preserved animal specimens to an assemblage that required the construction of a new building, the United States National Museum, in 1881.

Today, more than 170 years after Smithson died, the institution that bears his name comprises 19 museums, 4 research centers, a zoo, and a library research system and is the largest single museum complex on the globe. From the fabled Hope Diamond to the historic Wright Flyer, from George Washington's dress sword to the original Kermit the Frog, the Smithsonian Institution pulls together the best of America's history and many relics of the world in which we live. Its collection (an astounding 136.9 million objects) and its museums are graced by 23 million visitors per year. With assets worth $2.2 billion today, James Smithson's bequest has grown into the world's biggest museum.

Words for the Ages

"It isn't hard to love a town for its greater and lesser towers, its pleasant parks or its flashing ballet. Or for its broad and bending boulevards ... But you never really love it till you can love its alleys too."

—NELSON ALGREN

"I was ordered to take a height, which I did,
under the most withering fire I have ever known ..."

—GENERAL GEORGE PICKETT, IN A LETTER TO HIS WIFE AFTER HIS ILL-FATED CHARGE

"You're looking for a fight and now you can have it."

—WYATT EARP, TO THE CLANTONS AND MCLAURYS

"Not of any commercial value."

—THOMAS EDISON, ON THE PHONOGRAPH, 1880

"Stocks have reached what looks like a permanently high plateau."

—IRVING FISHER, PROFESSOR OF ECONOMICS, YALE UNIVERSITY, 1929

"A severe depression like that of 1920–1921 is outside
the range of probability."

—THE HARVARD ECONOMIC SOCIETY, 1929

"[There is] a world market for maybe five computers at most."

—THOMAS J. WATSON, CHAIRMAN OF IBM, 1943

"Computers in the future may have only 1,000 vacuum tubes
and weigh no more than 1.5 tons."

—POPULAR MECHANICS MAGAZINE, 1949

"Louis Pasteur's theory of germs is ridiculous fiction."

—PIERRE PACHET, PROFESSOR OF PHYSIOLOGY AT TOULOUSE, 1872

"It is hard to fail; but it is worse never to have tried to succeed."

—THEODORE ROOSEVELT

"The people are responsible for the character of their Congress.
If that body be ignorant, reckless, and corrupt, it is because
the people tolerate ignorance, recklessness, and corruption."

—JAMES A. GARFIELD

Underground Cities: What's Going on Down There?

Most of us give little thought to what is going on beneath our feet. Under many cities, however, there exists another city that contains other people—or did at one time.

❊ ❊ ❊ ❊

Edinburgh, Scotland

IN THE 1700S, space was at a premium in Edinburgh. Hemmed in by hills and surrounded by protective walls, Edinburgh had no more clear land to build upon within the city limits. Arched bridges, such as South Bridge, were built to connect hilltop to hilltop, and, in a marvel of architectural design, small honeycombed chambers and tunnels were built into the vaults. At first, fashionable shops used these rooms for storage and workspace areas. But their underground nature attracted the seedier members of society, and the areas quickly became a breeding ground for crime and disease. Although the vaults were closed in the mid-1800s, they were rediscovered and excavated in 1995. Today, a few restaurants, nightclubs, and ghost tours operate in the vaults.

Seattle, Washington

In 1889, the Great Seattle Fire destroyed more than 25 city blocks near the waterfront. In rebuilding the Pioneer Square area, city leaders decided to raise the street level to avoid flooding. With street level now a full story higher, merchants moved most of their businesses to their second (now ground) floors. Sidewalks built at the new street level created underground tunnels connecting the taverns and businesses that remained open. In 1907, fear of crime and disease caused the underground to be condemned, but a few of these abandoned tunnels and rooms have been restored and are currently open to the public.

Cappadocia, Turkey

It is believed that hundreds of underground cities exist underneath the Cappadocia rock, although only 40 have been found and a mere six are open to visitors. These cities first appeared in literature around 400 B.C. and were used for storage and protection. Carved out of soft volcanic rock, the largest of these cities could hold as many as 30,000 people and has 600 doors leading to the surface, as well as connecting rooms that tunneled underground eight excavated stories (and possibly as many as 12 unexcavated levels below those).

Paris, France

Built upon a network of 12th-century quarries, Paris sits atop 170 miles of tunnels. From 1785 until the 1880s, these tunnels received the bones of nearly six million people from condemned or overcrowded cemeteries around the city. During World War II, the tunnels were used to hide Resistance fighters. Today, a portion of the catacombs is open as a museum to visitors, but the rest is left to foolhardy explorers, illegal partiers, and the dead.

Montreal, Quebec, Canada

Montreal is sometimes called two cities in one due to its subterranean counterpart. The underground city was started in 1962 as a shopping center, and it eventually grew to connect important buildings and house more shopping space. Now, 60 percent of offices in Montreal are linked to the underground city, and there are more than 200 entrances. The underground city's 22 miles of corridors are used by more than 500,000 people every day to go to work, school, or any of the bus terminals, metro stations, 1,700 shops, 1,615 apartments, 200 restaurants, 40 banks, 40 cinemas and entertainment venues, 8 hotels, or other places that are part of the network.

13 Vintage Businesses on Historic Route 66

Route 66 opened in 1927, although the entire road wasn't paved until 1938. The Federal Highway Act of 1956 led to its demise with the creation of several new interstates, but most of Route 66 can still be traveled today. Ready for a road trip? Here are some places you may want to stop.

✳ ✳ ✳ ✳

1. **Buckingham Fountain (Chicago, Illinois):** Located in Chicago's Grant Park, Buckingham Fountain is where Route 66 began. The fountain, which represents Lake Michigan, is adorned with sculptures of four sea horses that symbolize the states bordering the lake—Illinois, Indiana, Michigan, and Wisconsin. The fountain's 134 jets shoot 14,000 gallons of water (per minute) 150 feet into the air for a magnificent display, which incorporates music and a light show in the evening.

2. **The Cozy Dog Drive In (Springfield, Illinois):** While working at an army base in the early 1940s, Illinois native Ed Waldmire was toying with the idea of wrapping hot dogs in corn bread. Following the advice of a friend that the key was frying the meat in the batter, Waldmire started experimenting at the USO in Amarillo, Texas. Originally called crusty curs, Waldmire changed the name to cozy dogs and opened his first stand in Springfield in 1946, after being discharged from the army. The Cozy Dog Drive In continues to be a popular family-run business.

3. **Ted Drewe's Frozen Custard (St. Louis, Missouri):**
Ted Drewe started selling frozen custard in Florida in
1929. The ever-busy entrepreneur split his time between
midwestern carnivals during the summer and Florida
beaches in the winter, finally opening a permanent stand
in St. Louis in 1931. In 1941, he opened another store in
St. Louis along Route 66. Despite offers to franchise, the
business has remained family-owned and operated.

4. **66 Drive-In Theater (Carthage, Missouri):** In 1949,
the 66 Drive-In Theater was a new attraction. It fell into
disrepair until the Goodman family bought it and set out
to return it to its former glory; they finished renovations in
1998. Feature films are still shown under the stars during
the summer months.

5. **Ed Galloway's Totem Pole Park (Foyil, Oklahoma):** What
better place to stretch your legs on a road trip than at the
park that boasts the world's largest totem pole? It's 90 feet
tall, made of 200 carved pictures, and was sculpted by Ed
Galloway between 1937 and 1948. He used 28 tons of
cement, 6 tons of steel, and 100 tons of sand and rock to
form his tribute to Native American culture.

6. **Lucille's (Hydro, Oklahoma):** Lucille's is currently one
of only two porch-style gas stations still operating on
Oklahoma's portion of Route 66. Lucille Hamons and her
husband bought the structure (originally built in 1927 and
called the Provine Station) in 1941, and she operated it
herself until she died in 2000. Lucille was known as "the
Mother of the Mother Road" because of her many stories
of the people who stopped by for a tank of gas or a snack.

7. **Cadillac Ranch (Amarillo, Texas):** Artists and auto enthu-
siasts alike will appreciate the beauty of ten Cadillacs,
buried halfway into the ground, nose first. Passersby are
encouraged to add a personal touch by wildly decorating

the vehicles, which span the model years 1949 to 1963. Created in 1974 by the Ant Farm, a San Francisco art collective, Cadillac Ranch has become part of the nation's kitschy culture.

8. **Haunted Natatorium (Amarillo, Texas):** This indoor swimming pool opened in 1922, but by 1926 it had been purchased by J. D. Tucker, who covered the pool with a wooden dance floor and hosted flappers during the Roaring Twenties. Musical legends Tommy Dorsey, Louis Armstrong, and Buddy Holly came to play, and, at one time, it took a staff of 52 to serve the crowds. The Natatorium has been meticulously restored to reflect the whimsical roadway architecture of Route 66. It still hosts musical acts and is a popular entertainment venue, attracting artists such as the Dixie Chicks. It is said that several apparitions, including a ghostly couple, can be spotted among today's dancers.

9. **Tee Pee Curios Trading Post (Tucumcari, New Mexico):** Tucumcari has a five-mile stretch of pure Route 66 nostalgia in the form of motels, diners, and curiosity shops. One of the famed shops is Tee Pee Curios Trading Post, which was built in the early 1940s as a gas station that sold groceries and novelty items. When the road was widened in the 1950s, Tee Pee got rid of its gas pumps and focused solely on the fun stuff.

10. **The Wigwam Village Motels (Holbrook, Arizona, and Rialto, California):** Frank Redford built the first of several Wigwam Village motels in 1934 near Kentucky's Mammoth Cave. Two more opened out west by the mid-1950s—one in Holbrook, Arizona, and one in Rialto, California. Each wigwam featured a guest room that was naturally suited to the southwestern stretch of Route 66. The Arizona, California, and Kentucky locations are still in business, with the marquee in front of

the Holbrook location posing the question: "Have you slept in a wigwam lately?"

11. **Jackrabbit Trading Post (Joseph City, Arizona):** In 1949, James Taylor (not the folksinger) converted a simple shack into one of the most popular souvenir shops along the Mother Road. To attract the growing throngs of tourists passing through town, Taylor painted dancing American Indians on the facade and lined the rooftop with 30 jackrabbits that appear to hop along the top of the building. To ensure that the road weary noticed his shop, he and another local retailer traveled from Arizona to Springfield, Missouri, and dotted more than 1,000 miles of roadside with billboards of jackrabbits and dancing cowgirls!

12. **Roy's (Amboy, California):** During the 1930s, Roy and Velma Crowl owned the café, motel, and service station that comprised most of Amboy, a tiny town on a desolate stretch of Route 66. Years later, Roy's daughter Betty and her husband, Buster Burris, took over the business and continued the tradition of caring for road-weary travelers. Today, the entire 690-acre town and all of its contents are owned by the Route 66 Museum in San Bernardino, California. The owners plan to restore the gas station, diner, and motel to their 1950s-era charm.

13. **Georgian Hotel (Santa Monica, California):** The Santa Monica Pier is literally the end of the road for Route 66. Within walking distance is the Georgian Hotel, steeped in history since opening its doors in 1933. The hotel, which served as a speakeasy during Prohibition, has also been a hideaway for the famous and infamous. Clark Gable and Carole Lombard hid from the press at the Georgian, and you might find today's Hollywood royalty doing the same.

"Ship to Shore! Ship to Shore! Oh S—t!"

The Bermuda Triangle—an infamous stretch of the Atlantic Ocean bordered by Florida, Bermuda, and Puerto Rico—has been the location of strange disappearances throughout history. The Coast Guard does not recognize the Bermuda Triangle or the supernatural explanations for the mysterious disappearances in its midst. There are some probable explanations for the missing vessels, including hurricanes, undersea earthquakes, and magnetic fields that interfere with positioning devices. But it's tempting to wonder if the following vessels got sucked into another dimension, abducted by aliens, or simply vanished into thin air.

✱　✱　✱　✱

1. **Flight 19:** On December 5, 1945, five Avenger torpedo bombers left the Naval Air Station at Fort Lauderdale, Florida, with Lieutenant Charles Taylor in command of a crew of 13 student pilots. About an hour and a half into the flight, Taylor radioed the base to say that his compasses weren't working, but he figured he was somewhere over the Florida Keys. The lieutenant who received the signal told Taylor to fly north toward Miami. Although he was an experienced pilot, Taylor got horribly turned around; the more he tried to get out of the Keys, the further out to sea he and his crew traveled. As night fell, radio signals worsened, until, finally, there was nothing at all from Flight 19. A U.S. Navy investigation reported that Taylor's confusion caused the disaster, but his mother convinced them to change the official report to read that the planes went down for "causes unknown." The planes have never been recovered.

2. **Flight 201:** This Cessna left Fort Lauderdale on March 31, 1984, en route for Bimini Island in the Bahamas, but it never

made it. Not quite midway to its destination, the plane slowed its airspeed significantly, but no radio signals were made from the plane to indicate distress. Suddenly, the plane dropped from the air into the water, completely vanishing from the radar. A woman on Bimini Island swore she saw a plane plunge into the sea about a mile offshore, but no wreckage has ever been found.

3. **USS *Cyclops*:** As World War I heated up, America went to battle. The *Cyclops*, commanded by Lieutenant G. W. Worley, stayed mostly on the East Coast of the United States until 1918, when it was sent to Brazil to refuel Allied ships. With 309 people onboard, the ship left Rio de Janeiro in February and reached Barbados in March. After that, the *Cyclops* was never heard from again. The Navy says in its official statement, "The disappearance of this ship has been one of the most baffling mysteries in the annals of the Navy, all attempts to locate her having proved unsuccessful. There were no enemy submarines in the western Atlantic at that time, and in December 1918 every effort was made to obtain from German sources information regarding the disappearance of the vessel."

4. **Star *Tiger*:** Captain B. W. McMillan commanded the *Star Tiger*, which was flying from England to Bermuda in January 1948. On January 30, McMillan said he expected to arrive in Bermuda at 5:00 A.M., but neither he nor any of the 31 people onboard the *Star Tiger* were ever heard from again. When the Civil Air Ministry launched a search and investigation, they learned that the SS *Troubadour* had reported seeing a low-flying aircraft halfway between Bermuda and the entrance to Delaware Bay. If that aircraft was the *Star Tiger*, it was drastically off course. The fate of the *Star Tiger* remains an unsolved mystery.

5. **Star *Ariel*:** A Tudor IV aircraft like the *Star Tiger* left Bermuda on January 17, 1949, with 7 crew members and

13 passengers en route to Jamaica. That morning, Captain J. C. McPhee reported that the flight was going smoothly. Shortly afterward, another more cryptic message came from the captain, when he reported that he was changing his frequency; then nothing more was heard, ever. More than 60 aircraft and 13,000 men were deployed to look for the *Star Ariel,* but not a hint of wreckage was ever found.

6. **The *Spray:*** Joshua Slocum, the first man to sail solo around the world, would be an unlikely candidate for getting lost at sea, but it appears that's exactly what happened. In 1909, the *Spray* left the East Coast of the United States for Venezuela via the Caribbean Sea. Slocum was never heard from or seen again and was declared dead in 1924. The ship was solid and Slocum was a pro, so nobody knows what happened. Perhaps he was felled by a larger ship or maybe he was taken down by pirates. No one knows for sure that Slocum disappeared within Triangle waters, but Bermuda buffs claim Slocum's story as part of the legacy of the Devil's Triangle.

7. ***Teignmouth Electron:*** Who said that the Bermuda Triangle only swallows up ships and planes? Who's to say it can't make a man go mad too? Perhaps that's what happened on the *Teignmouth Electron* in 1969. The 1968 *Sunday Times* Golden Globe Race left England on October 31 and required each contestant to sail his ship solo. Donald Crowhurst was one of the entrants, but he never made it to the finish line. The *Electron* was found abandoned in the middle of the Bermuda Triangle in July 1969. Logbooks recovered from the ship reveal that Crowhurst was deceiving organizers about his position in the race and going a little nutty out there in the big blue ocean. The last entry of his log was dated June 29—it is believed that Crowhurst jumped overboard and drowned himself in the Triangle.

Peace for Amityville?

The famous haunting that inspired books, movies, sequels, and remakes seems to have been nothing more than a famous fraud.

✳ ✳ ✳ ✳

ON NOVEMBER 13, 1974, a drug-crazed Ronald DeFeo shot and killed his parents and four siblings as they slept in their Amityville, New York, home. DeFeo was sentenced to 25 years to life and remains in a New York prison to this day.

A year after the murders, George and Kathy Lutz, along with their three children, moved into the DeFeo house. They stayed only 28 days, alleging the residence was possessed by demons.

A New York TV station employed the services of a team of psychics and ghost hunters who duly confirmed the Lutzes' claims: The house was haunted. *The Amityville Horror: A True Story*, written by Jay Anson, was published in 1977 and became a national best seller; the movie was released in 1979.

Eventually, the story came under scrutiny. Anson confessed that his book was based on recollections of the Lutzes and that he hadn't verified any facts. The Lutzes had never contacted the Amityville police department about mysterious activity. Weather records show that there was no snowfall on the day the family claimed to have discovered cloven hoofprints. Most damning of all was Butch DeFeo's attorney, who claimed that he and the Lutzes, inspired in part by the popular movie *The Exorcist*, had concocted the stories over several bottles of wine.

✳ George Lutz is still living, and he insists that the stories he related about the Amityville house are true.

✳ Investigators at the DeFeo crime scene were baffled by the fact that all of the victims seemed to have been shot in their sleep (there were no signs of struggle) even though the murder weapon did not have a silencer attached.

Chapter 5

Towering Figures

The First Renaissance Man?

Anaximander was one of the greatest thinkers of all time.

※ ※ ※ ※

Anaximander was the first philosopher in history to write down his work—perhaps that is why he's also known as such a groundbreaker. Unfortunately, even though he produced and recorded the work, for the most part it has not survived. We mostly know of Anaximander through Aristotle and Plato.

Born in ancient Greece in the seventh century B.C., Anaximander came from Miletus, a city in Ionia, which is now the western coast of Turkey. This area was a cultural enclave known for its progressive views on philosophy and art. It paved the way for the brilliant artistic development of Athens in the fifth century B.C.

A true rationalist, Anaximander boldly questioned the myths, the heavens, and the existence of the gods themselves. He wanted to devise natural explanations for phenomena that had previously been assumed to be supernatural. As founder of the science of astronomy, he was credited with building the first *gnomon*, or perpendicular sundial, which he based on the early work of the Babylonians and their divisions of the days.

Breaking new ground in geography as well, Anaximander is credited as the first cartographer to draw the entire inhabited world known to the Greeks. The map was likely circular, and a river called Ocean surrounded the land. The Mediterranean Sea appeared in the middle of the map, and the land was divided into two halves, one called Europe and the other, Southern Asia. What  was assumed to be the habitable world consisted of two small strips of land to the north and south of the Mediterranean Sea.

This map is far more significant than it appears at first glance. Firstly, it could be used to improve navigation and trade. But secondly—and perhaps more importantly—Anaximander thought that by displaying the lay of the land and demonstrating which nations and people were where, he might be able to convince the Ionic city-states to form a federation to push away outside threats.

Earth Is a Tabletop

Watching the horizon, Anaximander concluded that Earth was cylindrical, its diameter being three times its height, with man living on the top. He thought that Earth floated free in the center of the universe, unsupported by pillars or water, as was commonly believed at the time. "Earth didn't fall," Aristotle recounted, "because it was at equal distances from the extremes and needed not move in any particular direction since it is impossible to move in opposite directions at the same time."

These were amazing ideas for one simple reason: They were not based on things that Anaximander could have observed but, instead, were the result of conclusions he reached through rational thought. These are the first known examples of arguments based on sufficient reason, rather than myth.

By boldly speculating about the universe, Anaximander molded the direction of science, physics, and philosophy.

Are You Related to Genghis Khan?

Your DNA may carry the stuff that will conquer the world.

❋ ❋ ❋ ❋

From Riches to Rags to Riches

GENGHIS KHAN WAS one of the first self-made men in history. He was born to a tribal chief in 1162, probably at Dadal Sum, in the Hentii region of what is now Mongolia. At age 9, Genghis was sent packing after a rival tribe poisoned his father. For three years, Genghis and the remainder of his family wandered the land living from hand to mouth.

Genghis was down, but not out. After convincing some of his tribesmen to follow him, he eventually became one of the most successful political and military leaders in history, uniting the nomadic Mongol tribes into a vast sphere of influence. The Mongol Empire lasted from 1206 to 1368 and was the largest contiguous dominion in world history, stretching from the Caspian Sea to the Sea of Japan. At the empire's peak, it encompassed more than 700 tribes and cities.

A Uniter

Genghis gave his people more than just land. He introduced a writing system that is still in use today, wrote the first laws to govern all Mongols, regulated hunting to make sure everybody had food, and created a judicial system that guaranteed fair trials. His determination to create unity swept old tribal rivalries aside and made everyone feel like a single people, the "Mongols."

Today, Genghis Khan is seen as one of the founding fathers of Mongolia. However, he is not so fondly remembered in Asia, the Middle East, and Europe, where he is regarded as a ruthless and bloodthirsty conqueror.

Who's Your Daddy?

It seems that Genghis was father of more than the Mongol nation. Recently, an international team of geneticists determined that one in every 200 men now living is a relative of the great Mongol ruler. More than 16 million men in central Asia have been identified as carrying the same Y chromosome as Genghis Khan.

A key reason is this: Genghis's sons and other male descendants had many children by many women; one son, Tushi, may have had 40 sons of his own, and one of Genghis's grandsons, Chinese dynastic ruler Kubilai Khan, fathered 22 sons with recognized wives and an unknown number with the scores of women he kept as concubines.

Genetically speaking, Genghis continues to "live on" because the male chromosome is passed directly from father to son, with no change other than random mutations (which are typically insignificant). When geneticists identify those mutations, called "markers," they can chart the course of male descendants through centuries.

Is the world large enough for 16 million personal empires? Time—and genetics—will reveal the answer.

＊ Kubilai Khan is said to have added as many as 30 virgins to his harem each year.

"I am the punishment of God . . . If you had not committed great sins, God would not have sent a punishment like me upon you."

"The greatest happiness is to vanquish your enemies, to chase them before you, to rob them of their wealth, to see those dear bathed in tears, to clasp to your bosom their wives and daughters."

—QUOTES FROM GENGHIS KHAN

Awesome Ottoman

Süleyman the Magnificent was a warrior-scholar who lived up to his billing. A Turkish Sultan who reigned from 1520 to 1566, Süleyman led the Ottoman Empire to its greatest heights.

✳ ✳ ✳ ✳

Not only was Süleyman a brilliant military strategist, he was also a great legislator, a fair ruler, and a devotee of the arts. During his rule, he expanded the country's military empire and brought cultural and architectural projects to new heights. For all this and more, Süleyman is considered one of the finest leaders of 16th-century Europe.

Under Süleyman's leadership, his forces conquered Iraq and successfully occupied it until the First World War. Süleyman annexed or made allies of the Barbary States of North Africa, which remained a thorn in Europe's underbelly until the 1800s. He also led an army that went deep into Europe itself, crushing the Hungarian King Louis II at the great Battle of Mohács in 1526, which led to the Siege of Vienna.

An accomplished poet, Süleyman was gracious in victory, saying of the young Louis: "It was not my wish that he should be thus cut off while he scarcely tasted the sweets of life and royalty." To his favorite wife Hurrem, a harem woman and daughter of a Ukrainian Orthodox priest, he wrote: "My springtime, my merry faced love, my daytime, my sweetheart, laughing leaf... My woman of the beautiful hair, my love of the slanted brow, my love of eyes full of mischief..."

While Shari'ah, or sacred law, ruled his farflung land's religious life, Süleyman reformed the Ottomans' civil law code. In fact, the Ottomans called him Kanuni, or "The Lawgiver." The final form of Süleyman's legal code would remain in place for more than 300 years.

Bluebeard Versus Blackbeard

Bluebeard often gets confused with the infamous English pirate Blackbeard. Turns out, the two were equally vicious, but in different ways.

✳ ✳ ✳ ✳

Bluebeard

BLUEBEARD WAS IN fact the title character of a fairy tale written by Charles Perrault about a violent nobleman who murdered his wives. The tale was first published in 1698, a few years before Blackbeard the pirate came to prominence. In the story, the character was a man "so unlucky as to have a blue beard, which made him so frightfully ugly that all the women and girls ran away from him." When Bluebeard finally persuaded a woman to marry him, she was driven by curiosity to discover the contents of a room in his home that he always kept locked. When she entered the room, she was greeted by the sight of blood-stained floors and the bodies of her husband's former wives hanging from the walls. Before Bluebeard could add his new wife to the collection, she was rescued by her brothers, who slew the murderous nobleman. The tale of Bluebeard was used as the basic plot for Kurt Vonnegut's 1988 novel of the same name.

Blackbeard

Blackbeard, on the other hand, was the ferocious pirate Edward Teach, who terrorized the waters of the Caribbean. He's usually depicted armed to the teeth, often lighting matches off the hemp woven into his mangy black beard. His most audacious act came in 1718, when his pirate fleet blockaded the harbor of Charleston, South Carolina. Without having to fire a shot, Blackbeard plundered merchant ships trapped in the harbor and terrorized the town. He was later accused of deliberately grounding two of his own vessels so he had fewer crew members with whom to share his loot.

Founding Father with Odd Habits

Benjamin Franklin was an unsurpassed diplomat, writer, and inventor. He may also have been the most eccentric—and funniest—of the founding fathers.

✳ ✳ ✳ ✳

IN THE EARLY 1760s, early-rising Londoners passing the apartment of the noted representative from the American colonies would get quite a surprise. Each morning, stout Benjamin Franklin would step naked through his rooms, opening up the windows to let in the fresh air he found so invigorating. If the weather was mild, Franklin would step outside and peruse the morning's newspaper outside his digs, a gentle breeze lapping at his bare body.

The famous printer and scientist urged others to try his scanty approach to apparel, but he was less encouraging to strangers who crowded around his property. Interlopers pressing against the iron fence of one domicile were shocked, literally, by an electric charge sent coursing through the metal by the discoverer of electricity.

Franklin on the Human Body

As his displays of nudity might attest, Franklin was very comfortable with his body. He was evidently also proud of his bodily functions. He penned an essay dubbed "Fart Proudly," in which he proposed to:

"Discover some Drug wholesome & not disagreeable, to be mixed with our common Food, or Sauces, that shall render the natural Discharges of Wind from our Bodies, not only inoffensive, but agreeable as Perfumes."

With regard to another key physical function, Franklin urged a friend, who was having trouble landing a young wife, to take an elderly woman as his mistress. He counseled:

"Because in every animal that walks upright, the Deficiency of the Fluids that fill the Muscles appears first in the highest Part: the Face first grows lank and wrinkled; then the Neck; then the Breast and Arms; the lower Parts continuing to the last as plump as ever: So that covering all above with a Basket, and regarding only what is below the Girdle, it is impossible of two Women to know an old from a young one.

And as in the dark all Cats are grey, the Pleasure of corporal Enjoyment with an Old Woman is at least equal, and frequently superior."

Franklin on Religion

Franklin also had distinctive religious views—often skeptical, sometimes more traditional. He anonymously copublished an *Abridgment of the Book of Common Prayer*, which shortened funeral services to six minutes to better "preserve the health and lives of the living."

In the run-up to the American Revolution, Franklin's Committee of Safety—a sort of state provisional government—was deadlocked over whether Episcopal priests should pray for King George. Franklin told the committee:

"The Episcopal clergy, to my certain knowledge, have been constantly praying, these twenty years, that 'God would give the King and his Council wisdom,' and we all know that not the least notice has ever been taken of that prayer."

The prayers were canceled.

Yet, Franklin believed religion had a salutary effect on society and men's morals. In a letter to pamphleteer Thomas Paine, a decided agnostic, he wrote: "If men are so wicked with religion, what would they be if without it?" Asked to design the Great Seal of the United States, Franklin submitted a sketch of Moses and the Israelites drowning the Pharaoh's army in the Red Sea, with the motto: "Rebellion Against Tyrants is Obedience to God."

On ultimate questions of faith—
the afterlife, the nature of God—
Franklin was sometimes droll:

"As to Jesus of Nazareth ... I
think the System of Morals and
his Religion ... the best the world
ever saw or is likely to see; but I
apprehend it has received various
corrupt changes, and I have, with
most of the present Dissenters in
England, some Doubts as to his divinity; tho' it is a question I
do not dogmatize upon ... when I expect soon an Opportunity
of knowing the Truth with less Trouble."

The End

In 1785, a Frenchman wrote a satire of Franklin's famous
literary character Poor Richard in which the notoriously
frugal Richard bequeathed a small amount of money, whose
accumulating interest was not to be touched for 500 years.
Franklin wrote the satirist, thanking him for a "great idea," and
proceeded to bequeath 1,000 pounds each to his home and
adopted towns, Philadelphia and Boston, to be placed in trust
for 200 years. By 1990, the amount in the Philadelphia fund
had reached $2 million and was dispensed as loans to towns-
people and scholarships for students. The other trust tallied
close to $5 million, paying for a trade school that blossomed
into the Franklin Institute of Boston.

Lastly, the eccentric, sharp-witted founder composed his own
epitaph. It read:

"The Body of B. Franklin Printer; Like the Cover of an old
Book, Its Contents torn out, And stript of its Lettering and
Gilding, Lies here, Food for Worms. But the Work shall not
be wholly lost: For it will, as he believ'd, appear once more,
In a new & more perfect Edition, Corrected and Amended By
the Author."

Kamehameha I, Hawaiian King

Kamehameha was a strong peacetime leader and an outstanding general. One might even call him Hawaii's George Washington.

✳ ✳ ✳ ✳

✳ His given name was Pai'ea. It is said that Pai'ea was born on Hawaii's Big Island shortly after an appearance of Halley's Comet, which occurred in 1758. Legend had it that a bright light in the skies would herald the birth of a great unifier. Depictions of him in later life support this time frame. A portrait from 1810 shows a hearty, gray-haired individual, which seems about right for a man with a proud warrior youth.

✳ As he got older, Pai'ea earned the name "Kamehameha" (meaning "lonely one") because of his solitary, stern disposition.

✳ In 1779, he met his first Europeans when Captain Cook and his men arrived in Hawaii. At first, the Hawaiians thought Cook was a representative of Lono, the harvest god. However, they grew skeptical when Cook's ship sustained storm damage. The battered ship hardly seemed like a godly vessel anymore. Some speculate that Cook's arrival prompted Kamehameha to believe that Hawaii's islands should be strengthened through unification.

✳ Kamehameha gained a reputation as a feared warrior. During a raid in 1782, his foot became stuck in a crevice, and while he was trapped, a couple of fishermen broke a paddle over his head. Fortunately for Hawaii, they didn't cut Kamehameha's throat before fleeing. Their small show of mercy would later inspire a crucial policy decision from Kamehameha.

✳ Kamehameha worked his way up the royal chain of command of the Big Island. By 1790, he was well on his way to consolidating the Big Island under his rule as *ali'i nui*, or supreme chief.

* In 1794, Kamehameha remembered the fishermen who had knocked him on the head and ordered that they be brought before him. Instead of punishing them, though, Kamehameha put the blame on himself for having assaulted noncombatants. In a gesture of apology, he granted them land and set them free. Also, a new *kapu*, or law, was enacted that forbade harming civilians. It was called *mamalahoe kanawai*, "the law of the splintered paddle," and it decreed, "Leave the elderly, women, and children in peace." This law has remained in force since it was enacted; even today it is part of Hawaii's state constitution.

* By 1795, with the Big Island firmly under control, Kamehameha assembled a large army and thousands of war canoes to invade the rest of the Hawaiian islands. He overtook Maui and Molokai without much trouble. Soon his forces landed on Oahu's beaches. Oahu's defenders had European cannons, which held up Kamehameha until he sent a couple of battalions to flank the artillery. Soon, Oahu fell to Kamehameha as well.

* After the capture of Oahu, Kamehameha ran into some snags. He was getting ready to invade Kauai and Niihau when a rebellion on the Big Island forced him to return and shore up his power base. In 1803, he attempted another invasion, which was cut short by an epidemic among his troops. Kamehameha also became ill but managed to survive.

* When he finally came for Kauai in 1810, Kamehameha had European schooners equipped with cannons to supplement his war canoes. The ali'i nui of Kauai took one look at that armada and surrendered. Kamehameha was now king of all of the Hawaiian islands.

* The great king ended the tradition of human sacrifice but remained a devout follower of traditional Hawaiian religion. Christianity didn't impress him, though he let its followers live in peace.

* A figure closely associated with Kamehameha I is his favorite wife, Queen Ka'ahumanu. Traditional kapu was fairly harsh for women. Ka'ahumanu could be called an early feminist. She used her strong influence to end most of the kapu that treated women unfairly.

* In 1816, Kamehameha introduced another lasting tradition: Hawaii's flag. Kamehameha's banner, with the Union Jack in the upper left corner and one horizontal stripe for each of the eight major islands, is now the state flag.

* The king loved to fish. When he didn't have more important things to do, he could be found angling off the Kailua coast. He even scheduled affairs of state around the prime fishing seasons.

* King Kamehameha I died in 1819. During his illness, tradition dictated that human sacrifice was necessary to save the king, but Kamehameha refused to bend his kapu, even to save his own life. After he died, a close friend hid his body, and his burial site remains unknown to this day. This was done intentionally, as the body of a king was believed to contain *mana*, or spiritual force. This mana could be stolen if someone were to possess the king's remains.

* Kamehameha's dynasty lasted through eight rulers between 1810 and 1893. Unfortunately for Hawaii, this was also an unhappy time of exploitation and loss of independence. The dynasty ended in 1893, when Americans overthrew Queen Lili'uokalani and took the first steps toward creating the Republic of Hawaii. In 1898, Hawaii was incorporated as a U.S. territory, and in 1959, Hawaii became the 50th state.

* Every year in Hawaii on June 11, people celebrate King Kamehameha Day in honor of the visionary leader and hero.

Oppressor or Enlightened Leader?

Julius Caesar is one of the most recognized figures in all of human history. However, most people don't know as much about him as they think.

✳ ✳ ✳ ✳

CAESAR WAS NOT the first Roman emperor; indeed, he was never an emperor at all. He was a dictator, but in his time that word had a reasonable and legitimate political connotation. As history suggests, Caesar was capable in many areas. He led men into battle with courage and skill and was also a brilliant administrator and politician who instituted reforms that benefited most Romans.

Rising Out of Chaos

Caesar's birth in 100 B.C. coincided with great civil strife in Rome. Although his parents' status as nobles gave him advantages, Caesar's childhood was volatile. As an adult, he learned to be wary in his dealings with others. By the time Caesar was 20, a patrician named Sulla had been the Roman dictator for about 20 years. Although Caesar and Sulla were friends, Sulla later became enraged when Caesar refused to divorce his wife, Cornelia, who was the daughter of Cinna, a man Sulla loathed. To save his neck, Caesar promptly left for Asia.

When Sulla died in 78 B.C., Caesar returned to Rome and took up the practice of law. Caesar had everything necessary for success: He had received the best possible education, developed impressive oratorical skills, and was an outstanding writer. He also spent huge sums of money, most of which he had to borrow. The money went to bribes and sumptuous parties and bought Caesar access to power. Leading politicians looked on him favorably and rewarded him with a series of increasingly important political positions in Spain and Rome. Caesar's time in Spain was especially useful, as he used his position there to become very wealthy.

Coming Out on Top

In 59 B.C., Caesar, who was by now a general, made a successful bid for power in concert with Marcus Licinius Crassus, the richest man in Rome; and Pompey, another ambitious general who was known, to his immodest pleasure, as Pompey the Great. These three Type-A personalities ruled Rome as the First Triumvirate, with Caesar becoming first among equals as consul. Caesar had always been popular among the common people and with Rome's soldiers, and he aimed to cement that loyalty with reforms that would benefit them. Soon, Caesar was made governor of Gaul and spent the next 11 years conquering all of what is now France, with a couple of profitable trips to Britain for good measure. While on campaign, he wrote an account of his actions, called *Commentaries*, which is among the finest of all military literature.

Old Friends and New

To leave Rome, even for military glory, was always risky for any of the empire's leaders. While Caesar was abroad, Crassus was killed in battle. This void encouraged Pompey, who made it clear that Caesar was no longer welcome in Rome. Caesar and his army responded by crossing the Rubicon River in 49 B.C. to seize control of the city. Within a year of the civil war that followed, Caesar defeated Pompey. He also began a torrid affair with Egypt's Queen Cleopatra. After a few other actions against Rome's enemies, Caesar was acclaimed by all of Rome as a great hero. In turn, he pardoned all who had opposed him.

Hail, Caesar

Mindful of the fleeting nature of popularity, Caesar continued to promote a series of important reforms:

✳ Some of the land that had been held by wealthy families was distributed to common people desperate to make a living. As one might expect, this didn't go over well with the wealthy.

* Tax reforms insisted upon by Caesar forced the rich to pay their fair share. This innovation didn't win Caesar many new friends among the powerful.

* Retired soldiers were settled on land provided by the government. Because this land was in Rome's outlying territories, it became populated with a happy, well-trained cadre of veterans meant to be Rome's first line of defense, if needed. Unemployed citizens were also given the opportunity to settle in these areas, where jobs were much more plentiful. This reduced the number of poor people in Rome and decreased the crime rate.

* As he had done earlier, Caesar made residents of the provinces, such as people living in Spain, citizens of Rome. This idea proved quite popular. Many years later, some of the Roman emperors actually came from Spain.

* Working people are happy people (so it's said). In a clever move, Caesar instituted a massive public works program that provided both jobs and a sense of pride among the citizens of Rome.

Beware the Ides of March

All these reforms notwithstanding, Caesar's enemies feared he would leverage his great popularity to destroy the Roman Republic and institute in its place an empire ruled by one man. So, in one of those moments of violence that turns the wheel of history, Caesar was assassinated on March 15, 44 B.C.— the Ides of March, for those of you who remember your Shakespeare. The civil war that followed was ultimately won by Caesar's nephew, Octavian, who changed his name to Caesar Augustus ... and who replaced the republic and instituted in its place an empire ruled by one man! Augustus was the first of a long succession of emperors who ruled virtually independent of the Roman Senate. It was the rulers who followed Caesar, then, and not Caesar himself, who proved the undoing of the system so cherished by Caesar's enemies.

Hollywood Versus History

You may not be surprised to learn that Hollywood doesn't always get history right.

❋　❋　❋　❋

How much did you pay for that sundial wristwatch?
Julius Caesar (1953)—Cassius casually makes mention of a striking clock, many centuries before there were such things.

So long, suckers
Bonnie and Clyde (1967)—This biopic suggests depthless empathy, but Bonnie and Clyde didn't care one iota about the Depression-era poor.

For those long-distance ship-to-shore calls
Midway (1976)—During a long tracking shot of the Japanese carrier *Agaki* in the middle of the Pacific, the camera pans up to reveal power lines.

Hippies raus!
Victory (1981)—In the climax to this soccer movie set inside a German-run World War II POW camp, the playing field is overrun by people wearing flare pants.

No wonder Jackie's always a step ahead of everybody else
Jackie Brown (1997)—Although the story is set in 1995, the calendar in Jackie's kitchen is for 1997.

Know whut I'm sayin'?
Bobby (2006)—Telephone operators in this biopic set in 1968 tell callers to "Have a nice day"—a phrase that wouldn't become annoyingly popular for another 20 years.

Blunderoso
Apocalypto (2006)—Mayan villages seen in this historical thriller set in the 16th century date from the 9th century.

Important People You've Probably Never Heard Of

✳ ✳ ✳ ✳

"Ötzi the Iceman" (ca. 3300 B.C.) was a natural mummy found on the border between Austria and Italy in 1991. This spectacularly preserved specimen of a middle-aged Chalcolithic (Copper Age) European male was popularly named after the Otztal Alps where he was discovered in a glacier. He stood about five feet four inches, weighed about 84 pounds, and boasted 57 tattoos—mostly small lines. Ötzi was amazingly well-equipped for his journey across the mountains: He carried a copper axe with a yew handle, a flint knife, a quiver full of arrows, and an unfinished yew longbow. The pouch on his belt was a combined fire-starting and medicinal kit that contained flint, pyrite, tinder fungus, birch fungus (known to have antibacterial properties), two bark baskets (one containing charcoal), berries, and more than a dozen different plants. His wardrobe consisted of a cloak made of woven grass; a loincloth, leggings, vest, and belt made of leather; a bearskin hat; and waterproof shoes made of bearskin, deer hide, and tree bark, stuffed with grass for warmth. Petr Hlavacek, a Czech footwear expert from Tomas Bata University, re-created Ötzi's shoes using a prehistoric tanning process that involved boiling the liver and brains of pigs. The result, he writes, was "like going barefoot, only better."

Aristarchus of Samos (310 B.C.–230 B.C.) was a Greek astronomer and mathematician who first proposed a heliocentric model of the solar system, placing the Sun instead of Earth at the center of the system and arranging the other planets in correct order from the Sun. His argument for this bold theory hinged on his calculations of the relative sizes of the Sun and Earth—he found the Sun to be about 300 times larger—and a suspicion that the Sun was really a star positioned close to Earth. Aristarchus was criticized by laypeople for impiety and by astronomers for proposing a theory that did not account for the observable retrograde motion of the planets—periods when planets seemed to switch direction and begin to move backward in the sky over the course of several weeks or months. Thus soundly trampled, Aristarchus's theory languished until Copernicus authored his revolutionary tract *Of the Revolutions of the Heavenly Spheres* in 1543. Although he briefly mentioned Aristarchus in an early draft, Copernicus decided to cross his name out of the book before publication.

Athanasius Kircher (1602–80) was a German Jesuit scholar and philosopher. Nicknamed "the master of a hundred arts" and sometimes called the last Renaissance man, Kircher taught mathematics, physics, and several languages at Collegio Romano, the first Jesuit university in the world. He also pioneered the study of Egyptian hieroglyphics and was the first to put forth the idea that the plague was caused by microorganisms. Kircher produced more than 40 weighty tomes on a bewildering variety of subjects, from China to musical theory to fossils to magnetism. In his spare time, Kircher terrorized the superstitious peasants of the countryside around his villa by sending up hot air balloons in the shape of dragons with the words "Flee the Wrath of God" blazoned on their bellies. He also constructed a great number of mechanical devices, such as speaking statues, megaphones, clocks, and musical instruments. The strangest by far was the cat piano: Caged cats with differently pitched voices were arranged side by side inside a conventional piano. When a piano key was depressed, a mechanism drove a spike into the appropriate cat's tail. "The result," wrote Kircher, "was a melody of meows that became more vigorous as the cats became more desperate. Who could not help but laugh at such music?" Who, indeed.

Eugène François Vidocq (1775–1857) was a French convict-turned-detective, reformer of the civil police force, and inventor of the criminal-fiction genre. After a misspent youth that left him wanted for manslaughter, forgery, robbery, and numerous prison escapes, Vidocq boldy presented himself to the prefect of police in Paris, offering his services as an insider to the criminal world in exchange for his freedom. Within a few years, Vidocq and several ex-convicts surpassed the police in the number of arrests made. This brigade de Surete ("security brigade") was the beginning of a civil police occupied with the active pursuit of criminals; before Vidocq's intervention, the activities of the police in large cities were mostly limited to political espionage and directing traffic. After resigning from the newly revolution-ized police force, Vidocq published his memoirs, which were a big success and formed a lasting testimonial to Vidocq's charac-ter; today they are considered the first work of criminal fiction.

Nadezhda Andreyevna Durova (1783–1866) was a woman who joined the Russian army around the time of the Napoleonic wars. Reviled by her mother, who had wanted a boy, Durova was raised primarily by her father, a cavalry officer. Brash, fearless, and accustomed to horse-riding and sabre-swinging, Durova was in for a rude shock when her father gave her away in marriage at the age of 18 to a local court official. The marriage eventually ended, and Durova returned to her parents' house, leaving her ex-husband with an infant son. In 1807, she fled home dressed as a man and enlisted under a false name in a cavalry regiment. Several years later, she was discovered and brought before Czar Alexander I; Durova pleaded with him not to make her return to her intolerable life and begged to continue serving her country as a warrior. Moved by her plea, the czar gave his permission for her to remain in the army, decorated her with St. George's Cross for saving a fellow officer's life in battle, and raised her in rank. Durova retired in 1816 and wore masculine attire for the rest of her life. In her later years, she wrote of her army adventures in her widely read memoirs, *The Notes of a Cavalryman-Maiden*.

Ada Lovelace (1815–52) was the only legitimate daughter of the poet Lord Byron and the author of the first-ever computer program. Lord Byron and his wife, Annabella Milbanke, had a tumultuous relationship. To prevent their daughter from following in his professional footsteps, Annabella gave her a rigorously mathematical education—rather unorthodox in the days when upper-class women were educated mostly in music, art, and languages. In her youth and adulthood, Ada was in close correspondence with mathematician Charles Babbage, who was highly impressed with her intellect. In 1841, Babbage gave a seminar at the University of Turin about the possibility of an "analytical engine": a mechanical calculating device capable of interpreting human instructions—in other words, a computer. After a young Italian engineer transcribed and published the lecture in French, Babbage asked Ada to translate it back into English and add her own notes to it. The notes took Ada about a year to complete and ultimately were more extensive than the paper itself; the last and longest of the seven sections describes an algorithm for the analytical engine to compute Bernoulli numbers. Because they contain the first set of instructions specifically intended for a computer, Ada Lovelace's notes are widely considered the world's first computer program, predating the first computer by about a century.

Sir Francis Galton (1822–1911) was a child prodigy and cousin of Charles Darwin. Among his accomplishments are extensive exploration of the African continent; the creation of the first weather map; coining the terms "eugenics" and "nature versus nurture"; the statistical concepts of correlation and regression to the mean; the first implementation of the survey as a method of data collection; Differential Psychology, also known as the London School of Experimental Psychology; the first scientific investigation into human fingerprints; and the biometric approach to genetics. On these and many other topics, Galton produced more than 340 papers and books throughout his lifetime. He received every major award the Victorian scientific community bestowed, and he was knighted in 1909.

William James Sidis (1898–1944) was possibly the smartest man who has ever lived. Sidis is believed to have had an IQ between 250 and 300. He was accepted to Harvard at the age of 11 after completing all of his primary and secondary schooling in seven months; he was also able to learn a new language a day and actually invented his own. However, constant media attention took its toll, and Sidis left the public eye soon after reaching adulthood, holding only menial jobs until his death from a stroke at the age of 46. The only topic to which he applied himself studiously and on which he produced a definitive text was streetcar transfers.

Norman Ernest Borlaug (1914–2009) was an American microbiologist and agricultural scientist who was instrumental in developing high-yield, disease-resistant wheat varieties in Latin America, Africa, and Asia. Borlaug effectively saved billions of people from starvation and was awarded the Nobel Peace Prize in 1970. According to the Congressional Tribute to Dr. Norman E. Borlaug Act of 2006, "Dr. Borlaug has saved more lives than any other person who has ever lived."

Vladimir Vysotsky (1938–80) was a Russian stage and film actor, writer, poet, and singer of immense talent and productivity. In the course of his relatively brief life, Vysotsky wrote between 600 and 800 songs about every aspect of Soviet living, from labor camps to popular TV shows. When not engaged in theater performances, concerts, or movie shoots, he wrote novels, novellas, short stories, and screenplays. Although the government refused to allow him to make records, fans defiantly taped his countless live concerts and distributed the recordings all over the country. Despite Vysotsky's ruthless satirizing of the poor living conditions in the U.S.S.R., he was all but immune from political prosecution by virtue of his stardom. Vysotsky died of heart failure in 1980, when the summer Olympics were in full swing in Moscow; to avoid rioting, the state-controlled media made no mention of the star's untimely demise. But the news quickly leaked out, and huge crowds began gathering at Taganka Theatre, where Vysotsky had played Hamlet until a week before his death. It's reported that close to a million people attended his funeral.

Charlemagne: Illiterate Reader

Charlemagne created a major Frankish Empire that unified most of what we now call western and central Europe, helped establish the dominance of the Roman Catholic Church in that area, began the Middle Ages, and brought about a revival of arts and literature that helped preserve the works of ancient Greek and Roman writers. Not bad for a fellow whose name isn't even known for certain!

✳ ✳ ✳ ✳

THE FIRST MENTION of his name is the Latin *Carolus Magnus*, which translates as Charles the Great. The French, who claim him as one of their kings, call him Charlemagne (which translates more or less the same), while the Germans (who also claim him as their own) call him Karl der Grosse. The English-speaking world generally knows him by his French name, Charlemagne. We're not even entirely sure when he was born, though 742 is the commonly accepted date.

Of Popes and Kings

Charlemagne came from two lines of Frankish kings. His grandfather was the great Charles "The Hammer" Martel. Charles's tribe was known as the Merovingians, and Charles had largely unified modern-day France and had defeated the Arabian invaders at the Battle of Tours in 732. His son, Pepin the Short, was eventually made king and established a new line known as the Carolingians. The pope stated his approval for this, starting a tradition of kings seeking the pope's approval, a situation that often led to religious wars and other difficulties. When Pepin died, his two sons, Charles and Carloman, ruled together until Carloman died in 771, leaving Charles to rule the kingdom. Charles went on to gain historic renown.

Like so many great people in history, Charlemagne earned much of his reputation through military conquest. Over the years, he fought in Italy, Saxony, Spain, Bavaria, and pretty much anywhere else he was threatened. His campaign in Spain was immortalized by the epic poem "Song of Roland." A devout Christian, Charlemagne went to the aid of the pope several times. On Christmas Day 800, Pope Leo III crowned Charlemagne holy roman emperor. There is some dispute as to whether or not Charlemagne was really aware that this was going to happen, but he is said to have remarked later that allowing it to happen had been a mistake. Kings and emperors wanted to rule as the top dog, and having a pope approve or—worse yet—actually crown you as king meant that even in temporal matters the pope was above the emperor. It wasn't until Napoleon crowned himself in 1804 that this conflict was finally resolved in favor of the power of the state.

Savior of Western Civilization

One might think, given all this fighting, that Charlemagne didn't have much time for anything else. To the contrary, Charlemagne's biggest contributions to history may well be what he did off the battlefield. Here are just a few of the major cultural contributions made by Charlemagne:

* After the fall of the Roman Empire, education in Europe had gone into a steep decline. Charlemagne reversed that trend by increasing the number of schools. His palace school in the capital of Aachen featured Alcuin of York, perhaps the top scholar of his day. The school, and the nearby court, were crowded with other leading minds of that age, and Charlemagne and his sons attended classes from time to time. Not bad for a fellow who couldn't write. On the other hand, he could read, and most kings in those days were completely illiterate. Oh yes, one thing more: Education was normally reserved for the nobility, but Charlemagne made sure that really deserving commoners also had a chance to be educated. He understood that the more educated people there were, the more people there would be to help run things. Charlemagne also encouraged the education of women and established empire-wide curriculum standards.

* The script of the period was difficult to read. Scholars and scribes under Charlemagne eventually came up with a new system that used both upper- and lowercase letters. This script is called Carolingian Minuscule and is one of the foundations of modern Western script.

* The works of the ancients were in danger of being lost. Many ancient documents had been destroyed by Christian clergy who were determined that people should only have Christian materials to read. Since they were all handwritten, there were obviously not many copies available. So, when one was lost, that was likely all she wrote (so to speak). Charlemagne established writing centers where scribes spent all day making copies of these works. He sent other people all over the countryside, peeking into musty old monastic libraries, trying to find copies of ancient texts that could then be copied. Many, if not most, of the ancient works that we still have were saved due to this effort.

* Given all of this, it may not surprise you to hear that Charlemagne was a great fan of books. He would give and receive books, often bound in sumptuous ivory and jewels. Those that survive today are wonders to behold.

These educational and literary accomplishments, along with some other reforms, have led historians to give Charlemagne credit for starting the Carolingian Renaissance, or a rebirth of learning and of interest in the ancient texts. Some historians even feel that he was largely responsible for saving Western civilization. When he died in 814, his empire began a decline, and within a generation had broken into a feudal system that would last through much of the Middle Ages. Emphasis on learning and literature would decline as well, but thanks to Charlemagne, it never completely died out. When the Italian Renaissance began several centuries later, scholars had a base upon which to begin their march to the modern era; a base that was created by Charlemagne, one of history's greatest figures.

Quirky Inventor's Explosive Career Leads to Noble Testament

He created the Nobel Peace Prize. He also invented dynamite. When Alfred Nobel wrote his legendary will, was it to atone for his devastating invention?

✳ ✳ ✳ ✳

Protecting a Secret Prize

IN DECEMBER 1896, Ragnar Sohlman rode nervously in a carriage through Paris, sitting atop a box containing one of the world's great fortunes. Sohlman was the main executor for the will of Alfred Nobel, the Swedish-born industrialist—and inventor of dynamite—who had just died at an Italian villa, after years of residing in the French capital.

Sohlman had his hands full. Nobel's will consisted of one long, vague paragraph, directing that the then-huge amount of $4.2 million be awarded to those "who during the preceding year shall have conferred the greatest benefit to mankind" in the fields of medicine, chemistry, physics, literature, and peace.

Nobel had named the organizations he wanted to dispense the awards but hadn't bothered to tell them. Nor had he set up a foundation.

Nobel had lived in Italy, Russia, Germany, the United States, and other lands. Thus, many different nations could claim his wealth.

Setting Up a Famous Award

After secreting the treasure with Swedish authorities, Sohlman undertook drawn-out negotiations with the awarding bodies Nobel had chosen. These were the Swedish Academy of Sciences (for chemistry and physics), the Stockholm-based Caroline Institute (medicine), the Swedish Academy (literature), and the Norwegian Parliament (peace). The first Nobel prizes were finally granted on December 10, 1901—the fifth anniversary of Nobel's death.

A Polymath's Polyglot Interests

Born in 1833, Alfred Nobel had science and technology in his blood. He was a descendant of medical professor Olof Rudbeck the Elder, who discovered the lymphatic system. Alfred's father Immanuel, an architect and engineer, was the inventor of plywood. His brothers founded Russia's oil industry.

Apart from ancestry, Nobel's interest in medicine derived from his chronically bad health. He endured awful migraines and black depression. He said of himself: "Alfred Nobel—a pitiful half-life which ought to have been extinguished by some compassionate doctor as the infant yelled its way into the world." He also suffered from angina. The popularizer of the explosive as well as the medicine known as nitroglycerin wrote: "Isn't it the irony of fate that I have been prescribed nitroglycerin to be taken internally?" He became an amateur authority on blood transfusions. He even underwrote early experiments in physiology, funding the work of Ivan Pavlov.

As for literature, Nobel was a poet and authored the play *Nemesis*. It concerned a terrified family who bludgeoned a violent father to death. His family had 97 of the 100 copies destroyed because the play was considered blasphemous.

One subject Nobel wasn't interested in was law. He wrote: "Lawyers have to make a living, and can only do so by inducing people to believe that a straight line is crooked." It's little wonder he penned his own will.

It's often thought that Nobel's interest in peace was due to guilt over his invention of dynamite. An 1888 French obituary that mistakenly reported his death called him the "merchant of death." It read, "Dr. Alfred Nobel, who became rich by finding ways to kill more people faster than ever before, died yesterday."

However, evidence regarding his feelings of guilt (or lack thereof) is mixed. Recently revealed correspondence with his mistress Sophie, an Austrian flower clerk half his age, indicates he did harbor doubts about his work. However, since he lived in a time of relative peace, almost none of his inventions were used in battle. Indeed, he long believed the destructive power of creations such as dynamite would deter war. Anticipating atomic weapons, he once told a peace activist, "When two armies of equal strength can annihilate each other in an instant, then all civilized nations will retreat and disband their troops."

Devising a Double-Edged Sword

Nobel's family was among the leading explosives and armaments manufacturers of the time. His father established a factory in Russia to build naval mines. During the Crimean War, the family business prospered but went belly-up when peace arrived in 1856.

This spurred Alfred into a rabid search for new products. He and his brothers experimented with volatile nitroglycerin, invented by Ascanio Sobrero decades before. In 1864, his youngest brother Emil died when the Nobel nitro factory near Stockholm blew up. Two years later, another accident destroyed a Nobel nitro plant outside Hamburg, Germany.

Undeterred, that same year Alfred tested the substance in a safer place—a raft on the German river Elbe. Finally, at a demonstration in Manhattan, he proved nitro could be used safely.

His famous breakthrough came the next year. He added an inert substance, silicon-laden soil, to nitro, which yielded dynamite, a material that could be handled and transported safely.

Next came blasting caps, patents for 355 inventions, and profitable businesses in many lands. Most of Nobel's explosives were employed for construction purposes.

It seems Nobel's quirky idealism may have been behind his eventual interest in peace: "I've got a mass of screws loose and am a superidealist who can digest philosophy better than food."

Aaron Burr: Hero or Villain?

Mention the name Aaron Burr and the thing most people think of is his famous duel with Alexander Hamilton. That may have been the high point of his life, because by the time Burr passed away in 1836, he was considered one of the most mistrusted public figures of his era.

✳ ✳ ✳ ✳

How to Make Friends...

BURR SEEMED TO have a knack for making enemies out of important people. George Washington disliked him so much from their time together during the Revolutionary War that as president, he had Burr banned from the National Archives, didn't appoint him as minister to France, and refused to make him a brigadier general.

After the war, Burr became a lawyer in New York, frequently opposing his future dueling partner Alexander Hamilton. But it wasn't until Burr beat Hamilton's father-in-law in the race for a Senate seat that the problems between them really started.

In 1800, Burr ran for president against Thomas Jefferson. Back then, the candidate with the most votes got to be president; whoever came in second became vice president—even if they were from different parties. When the election ended in a tie in the Electoral College, it was thrown to the House of Representatives to decide. After 35 straight tie votes, Jefferson was elected president, and Burr became vice president.

Like Washington, Jefferson didn't hold Burr in high regard. In 1804, Burr decided to run for governor of New York. When he lost, he blamed the slandering of the press in general and the almost constant criticism from Hamilton in particular.

Hamilton later shot off at the mouth at a dinner party, and Burr decided he'd had enough. After giving Hamilton a chance to take his comments back (Hamilton refused), Burr challenged him to the famous duel.

Shots Discharged

Burr and Hamilton met on July 11, 1804, at Weehawken, New Jersey. Some say that Hamilton fired first, discharging his pistol into the air; others say that he just missed. Burr, on the other hand, shot Hamilton, who died the next day.

Aaron Burr

After the duel, Burr fled to his daughter's home in South Carolina until things cooled down. He was indicted for murder in both New York and New Jersey, but nothing ever came of it. He eventually returned to Washington to finish his term as vice president, but his political career was over.

King Burr?

After his term as vice president, Burr decided to head west, to what was then considered Ohio and the new lands of the Louisiana Purchase. It seemed that Burr had things on his mind other than the scenery, however. According to some (mostly his rivals), Burr intended to create a new empire with himself as king. As the story goes, he planned to conquer a portion of Texas still held by Mexico, then convince some of the existing western states to join his new confederacy. Called the Burr Conspiracy, it got the attention of President Jefferson, who issued arrest orders for treason. Eventually, Burr was captured, and he was brought to trial in 1807.

But Burr caught a break. The judge was Chief Justice John Marshall. Marshall and Jefferson didn't get along, and rather than give his enemy an easy victory, Marshall demanded that the prosecution produce two witnesses that specifically heard Burr commit treason. The prosecution failed to come up with anybody, and Burr was set free.

Burr then left the United States to live in Europe. Returning to New York in 1812, he quietly practiced law until his death in 1836.

Pioneer Tree Planter

What kind of person would run around planting trees? Didn't he need a job? For once the folktale is less impressive than the reality.

✳ ✳ ✳ ✳

✳ Jonathan Chapman (who would become known as Johnny Appleseed) was born in 1775. His father, a farmer, was a Revolutionary officer and veteran of Bunker Hill; Johnny was just seven years old when Lord Cornwallis hung it up at Yorktown. His mother died young, and Johnny was raised by relatives. Perhaps with his father away at war and in the care of family members, he grew up not really thinking of any place as a permanent home. He was a natural roamer.

✳ Johnny went west in 1792. By the end of the 1790s, he was a nurseryman: He picked the seeds out of apples, planted them, grew saplings, and sold them to new settlers. Because many Continental veterans received land grants in the Ohio Valley, lots of people in Pennsylvania and Ohio wanted fruit trees.

✳ Johnny may have been the closest thing to a Jainist monk in U.S. frontier history. He tried hard to avoid killing any insect, much less any animal.

✳ He didn't just wander around tossing seeds at random. Johnny Appleseed was a smart businessperson, though he usually wore cast-off clothing and went barefoot. He would get the seeds for free from cider mills, plant a nursery, fence it, and then leave it in a neighbor's charge. Johnny would show up every so often to check on the orchards. If the neighbor had collected any payment for saplings, Johnny would pick that up.

✳ Chapman was a Swedenborgian. That's a religion, members of which are still around today (and they sure revere Chapman). Emmanuel Swedenborg was an 18th-century Swedish genius and Christian mystic whose church could best be described as non-mainstream Protestantism with an occult streak.

* Johnny never married and apparently had no children. When anyone asked him why he wasn't married, he told them he believed he would have two great wives in heaven, provided he didn't marry on Earth.

* Why didn't someone else plant more trees and push him out of business? Johnny had a knack for showing up just before major population waves. Ask any skilled businessperson: It is partly about marketing, partly about finance, and all about timing and location. By the time most people arrived, Johnny's trees were ready for sale and transplant.

* As much money as Chapman earned through his business skill, he left most of it on the table. If people couldn't pay him cash, he took goods in barter or sold on credit. He tended to forgive bad debt. During his life, he tried very hard to give his wealth away.

* Along with apples, Johnny planted many and varied medicinal herbs wherever he went. Fennel, a licorice-smelling perennial often used as a spice, was referred to as "Johnny Weed" back in those days.

* In areas where relations with Native Americans could at times be tense, Johnny Appleseed walked in complete safety. Not only did the tribes respect him, some thought him touched by the Great Spirit. He seemed to be a man without an enemy.

* If you lived in the Ohio Valley and liked a drink now and then, you'd have had good reason to toast John's health. Most of his apples were made into cider. And Johnny definitely enjoyed a drink and a pinch of snuff, relaxing for an evening with a traveling or settled family, or any stranger who happened to be around.

* An early animal rescuer, Johnny would buy neglected horses and find them good homes or put them out to graze and see if they got well. If they did, he would foster them, extracting a promise of good treatment.

* Chapman was also a Swedenborgian missionary. He donated a considerable portion of his assets to the church, spent a lot of his money on Swedenborgian literature, and tried his best to spread his faith as he traveled.

* As if all that weren't enough, John Chapman was a deeply patriotic man whose oratory would have served him well in politics, had he cared for such things. He loved Fourth of July festivals and always found time to participate.

* Johnny "Appleseed" Chapman passed away on March 18, 1845, near Fort Wayne, Indiana.

---

* Apples are a member of the rose family.

* Apple trees produce fruit four to five years after they're planted. There are approximately 7,500 varieties of apples grown around the world.

* Apples ripen six times faster if you leave them at room temperature rather than refrigerate them.

* When the colonists arrived in North America, they found just crab apples, the only apples native to the United States.

* Early apple orchards produced very few apples because there were no honeybees. Historical records indicate that colonies of honeybees were first shipped from England and landed in the colony of Virginia early in 1622.

* None of Johnny Appleseed's trees are still standing, but it is possible to purchase a sapling of his favorite type of apple tree—the Rambo—from historictrees.org.

Orator, Author, Abolitionist—and Slave

One of the most influential American writers and lecturers of the 19th century was a man who was not sure what day he had been born and had to change his name to keep from being returned to slavery.

* * * *

FREDERICK BAILEY, WHO later became internationally renowned as Frederick Douglass, was born the son of a black slave mother and an unknown white father in Maryland. Although he once thought his date of birth lay somewhere in February 1818, he was never certain of the year, and his calculations later in life led him to believe he had been born in 1816. Douglass grew up surrounded by the brutality of slavery.

Escape from Shackles

Trained as a shipwright (and having secretly learned how to read), young Frederick Bailey made a daring escape to freedom in 1838 and eventually ended up in Massachusetts. He took the name Douglass to reduce his chances of being identified as an escaped slave. Soon after, he met abolitionist William Lloyd Garrison, who hired him to lecture for his Anti-Slavery Society. Like his new friend and mentor, Douglass attacked the institution of slavery in the most vehement terms: "I assert most unhesitatingly that the religion of the South is a mere covering for the most horrid crimes—a justifier of the most appalling barbarity, a sanctifier of the most hateful frauds, and a dark shelter under which the darkest, foulest, grossest, and most infernal deeds of slaveholders find the strongest protection."

Achieving Success

Douglass achieved national prominence with the 1845 publication of his first book, *Narrative of the Life of Frederick*

Douglass, an American Slave. Immediately fearing arrest and reenslavement, he went to Great Britain for two years, traveling throughout England, Ireland, and Scotland. He gave human rights lectures in many locales (mostly Protestant churches) and became a very popular figure. Befriending Irish Nationalist Daniel O'Connell and feeling treated not "as a color, but as a man," these were important years for Douglass. As a testament to his influence in the British Isles, there remains to this day a colorful mural dedicated to him in Belfast. During the time he was in Britain, friends purchased his freedom from his Maryland owner, and he was able to return triumphantly to New England. Soon after, Douglass launched the abolitionist newspaper *North Star*, which in 1851 merged with the *Liberty Party Paper* and officially became *Frederick Douglass's Paper*.

Becoming a Man of Influence

As might be expected, the fiery Douglass exerted some of his greatest influence on the struggle against slavery during the war, urging abolition no longer simply on moral grounds but as a means of taking a critical strategic asset from the rebellious South. He also campaigned for the federal government to allow blacks to serve as soldiers. In both of these efforts, he was ultimately successful.

President Lincoln respected Douglass's opinions on emancipation, and the two conferred on a number of occasions. Douglass repeatedly urged the President to proclaim that the emancipation of slaves was the supreme purpose of the war, but Lincoln was frank in explaining that he couldn't do that until it would actually benefit the war effort. Looking for an opportunity, he finally found one after a Confederate advance into the North was stopped at Antietam, and Lincoln announced the Emancipation Proclamation. That new policy went into effect on New Year's Day 1863, to tremendous celebration by Douglass and other abolitionists.

Bringing Black Troops to the Fight

As a great orator and respected member of the black community, Douglass also recruited regiments of U.S. Colored Troops. "Fly to arms," he urged, "and smite with death the power that would bury the government and your liberty in the same hopeless grave." These regiments included the famous 54th Massachusetts, in which two of his sons served, and the 55th Massachusetts. Douglass was disappointed however, with how poorly these units were treated and with the fact that they were paid less than their white counterparts, so he continued to work tirelessly on their behalf.

Public Service

After the war, Douglass did not cease his activism but in fact added the duties of a public official. Throughout the years, he served as U.S. marshal to the District of Columbia, recorder of deeds for the District of Columbia, U.S. minister to Haiti, and chargé d'affaires to Saint Domingue. He published two more books and several essays.

Douglass's first wife, Anna Douglass, died in 1882, and Douglass married Helen Pitts in 1884. Pitts was a white feminist 20 years his junior, which caused quite the scandal at the time. Douglass also began aligning himself with feminist causes and spent his later days traveling extensively throughout Europe. He finally retired to his home in Washington, D.C., where he died at age 77—or 79, depending on how you count it.

"What, to the American slave, is your 4th of July? I answer: a day that reveals to him, more than all other days in the year, the gross injustice and cruelty to which he is the constant victim. To him, your celebration is a sham; ... your sermons and thanksgivings, with all your religious parade and solemnity, are, to Him, mere bombast, fraud, deception, impiety, and hypocrisy—a thin veil to cover up crimes which would disgrace a nation of savages."

—FREDERICK DOUGLASS, "THE MEANING OF JULY FOURTH FOR THE NEGRO"

It's About Time

*Baseball's color line is finally history as
Jackie Robinson takes the field.*

✳   ✳   ✳   ✳

OF ALL THE moments in baseball, this is one that tran-
scended sports history and became American history.
When Jackie Robinson stepped onto Ebbets Field in April 1947,
the game was forever changed. Yet Robinson's appearance as the
first African American in the professional leagues received little
fanfare the day it happened. The crowd didn't roar, and most
major newspapers did not highlight the story on their front
pages. Many treated this as any other opening day.

While Robinson had the support of some teammates, others had
actively campaigned against him. But Dodgers general manager
Branch Rickey, baseball commissioner Happy Chandler, and
Dodgers manager Leo Durocher had all worked to ensure that
this milestone event would take place.

Robinson went 0–3 that day and hit into a rally-killing double
play, but he also scored the winning run when his speed forced
an error. (The Dodgers won 5–3.) It wasn't nerves that kept him
hitless, he said—it was the talent of pitcher Johnny Sain.

Robinson went on to hit .297, steal 29 bases, and score 125 runs
that season. He helped his team make it to the World Series, and
he was named Rookie of the Year.

It didn't take long for Robinson to make his mark and for baseball to throw off the stigma of segregation, helping it to truly
become "America's game."

---

*"I don't care if half the league strikes. This is the United States of
America and one citizen has as much right to play as another."*

—NATIONAL LEAGUE PRESIDENT FORD FRICK TO CARDINALS PLAYERS, WHO HAD BEEN
PLANNING TO STRIKE WHEN THE DODGERS CAME TO ST. LOUIS IN 1947

Emiliano Zapata

Most people know Emiliano Zapata as the revolutionary leader of southern Mexico who, along with Poncho Villa in the North, fought in the Mexican Revolution. Some also know him as the subject of the film Viva Zapata!, *starring Marlon Brando, for which John Steinbeck wrote a masterful screenplay. Few, however, know him as the spiritual and intellectual father of Mexico's land reform movement. But Emiliano Zapata, who loved nothing more than the lifestyle of the agrarian village in which he was raised, was a passionate proponent of land-use rights for Mexican farmers.*

✳ ✳ ✳ ✳

Land and Liberty

A T THE START of the 20th century, Mexico's small farmers were becoming increasingly disenfranchised by the powerful *hacienda* owners who sought to supplant the native corn crop with the more internationally valuable sugarcane plant. Through intimidation, violence, and indentured servitude, the *hacienda* owners—and the government that backed them—steadily encroached upon land that had been farmed by peasant families for generations.

In 1909, the village of Anenecuilco, in the small central-Mexico state of Morelos, elected Emiliano Zapata to the traditional post of defender of the village's interests. The orphaned son of a prosperous but humble local mestizo family whose ancestors had fought against the Spanish and the French, Zapata was a perfect fit for the position. He worked to establish land rights for farmers through ancient title deeds and petitioned the government to recognize the farmers' rightful ownership of their lands. Sometimes he was able to settle land disputes through diplomacy, but the lack of government support increasingly frustrated him.

In 1910, just a year after Zapata's election, the Mexican Revolution began. Zapata, who counseled the villagers to farm with rifles over their shoulders, joined the forces of Francisco Madero, a revolutionary who planned to overthrow Mexican President Porfirio Díaz. Zapata became a general of the Liberation Army of the South and aided Madero to success. Díaz was overthrown, and Francisco Madero became the new president of Mexico. Unfortunately, Zapata was soon disappointed by the slow pace of land reform under Madero, and relations between the two former allies broke down.

By this time, Zapata had become a popular leader. His soft-spoken but passionate dedication to the peasants' cause attracted thousands of people willing to fight for the right to farm their own land as they pleased. Through a succession of corrupt leaders and broken promises, Zapata maintained his agrarian ideals and his rallying slogan of *Tierra y Libertad* (Land and Liberty).

The "Liberal-Bourgeois" Revolutionary

Zapata's ideology found its fruition in the Plan de Ayala, a radical document that outlined a plan for land reform that Zapata wrote with his former teacher and mentor, Otilio Montaño Sanchez, in 1911. Though awkwardly worded, full of misspellings, and rife with redundancies, the land reform proposed by the Plan de Ayala was incendiary and galvanized support around Zapata's movement. Though Zapata admired Communist ideas, he considered Marxism impractical and instead simply sought to return the land to those from whom it had been taken.

When the Plan de Ayala was first printed, the intellectual elite in Mexico City scoffed at the poorly written work. Zapata's old enemy, President Francisco Madero, gave the editor of the *Diario del Hogar* permission to reprint the Plan de Ayala, reportedly saying, "Publish it so that everybody will know how crazy Zapata is." The plan backfired, and the Plan de Ayala received enthusiastic support that eventually led to Madero's ousting.

In the Plan de Ayala, Zapata did not seek to destroy the *hacienda* system, but rather to place legal checks upon its powers to seize and hold land. Under the Plan de Ayala, *ejidas*, or communally held lands, would be re-established in the villages that chose such a system. Alternately, the farmers could elect to establish individual plots. Zapata's ideology has since been labeled "liberal-bourgeois" or "bourgeois democratic," as it was truly an inclusionary, practical system that maintained as its primary goal peasant enfranchisement without recourse to completely subverting the existing capitalistic system.

Life After Death

The corrupt revolutionary leader Venustiano Carranza (who took over the reins of power from President Madero) consolidated his power by ordering his followers to assassinate Zapata in 1919. After Zapata was killed, the government forces took pictures of his face while shining a flashlight upon it to prove he was dead.

The agrarian leader's ideas were not so easily dispatched, however. Soon after Zapata's murder, men who had been sympathetic to Zapata's philosophy ousted Carranza and began to institute the land reform policies championed by their fallen leader. Today's Zapatistas, the spiritual descendents of Emiliano, have departed markedly from the specifics of the Plan de Ayala, but they retain the goal of uplifting the peasant class by striving against social injustice and government interference.

"I am determined to fight against anything and anyone with nothing more than the confidence and support of my people."

"It is better to die on your feet than to live on your knees."

—Quotes from Emiliano Zapata

The Original Demolition Man

*With a single spark from his torch, Guy Fawkes could have
killed dozens and changed the course of British history.*

✳   ✳   ✳   ✳

IT HAPPENS EACH year after nightfall on November 5 in
England and in former British colonies such as Australia:
Rowdy groups of people gather around blazing bonfires to
dance, chant, and set off fireworks. At a climactic moment, a
straw effigy of a man—the "Guy"—is tossed into the flames,
while the revelers shout a poem that begins, "Remember,
remember the fifth of November/The gunpowder treason and
plot/I know of no reason why the gunpowder treason/Should
ever be forgot."

Today, "Bonfire Night" is a lighthearted social event. It's likely
that many of the revelers who are bathed in firelight and swept
up in the noise of celebration have only the vaguest idea of the
origins of this uniquely British tradition. But Bonfire Night
grew out of one of the most dramatic episodes in English history—the Gunpowder Plot of 1605.

A Church Under Fire

In 1534, King Henry VIII broke with the Roman Catholic
Church to set up the Church of England, touching off decades
of religious and political strife. Most of the common folk
ultimately accepted the "New Faith" (Protestantism). A minority remained loyal to Rome, although English Catholics faced
discrimination and repression—especially after King James I
ascended the throne in 1603. For years, some English
Catholics had hoped that Spain would conquer England and
restore the nation to Rome. By the turn of the 17th century
that prospect looked unlikely, as Spain was preoccupied with
fighting various wars on continental Europe. So a small group
of Catholic plotters, led by the wealthy Robert Catesby, turned
to terrorism. Catesby and his fellow conspirators decided to

attempt what modern military commanders would call a "Decapitation Strike": They intended to take out all of England's leadership by blowing up London's House of Lords during the state opening of Parliament on November 5, 1605—an event that would be attended by the king, most of his family, and the leading nobles of the land. But they needed an expert with explosives, which in those days meant gunpowder. So they turned to Guy Fawkes.

"A Penny for the Old Guy..."

Fawkes was born in York, England, in 1570. Raised a Protestant, he converted to Catholicism in his teens and later went off to fight for Spain in its war against Protestant rebels in the Netherlands. Guy—or Guido, as he now styled himself—gained a reputation for coolness in combat and skill with explosives. In the spring of 1604, Robert Catesby sent an agent to the Netherlands to recruit Fawkes, who agreed to help the plotters, though he probably didn't learn the details of the plan until he arrived back in England.

At first the plotters intended to reach the House of Lords from below, via a tunnel, but when the task of disposing the dirt proved too troublesome, they simply rented cellar storage space and, under Fawkes's direction, packed it with 36 barrels of gunpowder—about a ton of the stuff. However, one of the plotters sent a warning to one of his co-religionists after he realized that some Catholic aristocrats would also be in the building on November 5. Despite the fact that the scheme had been compromised, the plotters went ahead. Word of the plan reached the government via an anonymous letter, and in a scene reminiscent of a Hollywood thriller, the authorities raided the cellar just in time to pounce on Fawkes as he was lowering a torch to set off the fuse. (Or so some official accounts have it—the real circumstances may never be known.)

Furious at the assassination attempt "not only... [on] my person, nor of my wife and posterity also, but of the whole body of the State in general," King James authorized the use of torture in Fawkes's interrogation. Fawkes grimly held out for several days and didn't name names until he was subjected to the rack—a vicious instrument that stretched a victim's limbs until they popped from their sockets. Even then, Fawkes only gave up the names of plotters who'd already been arrested.

A brief trial in January 1606 ended with guilty verdicts for Fawkes and the others. He was sentenced to the traditional punishment for treason—to be "hung, drawn, and quartered." This meant he was to be hanged until not quite dead, then taken down from the gallows so that his organs could be torn from his body. After that (!), he'd be beheaded and his body would be chopped into four parts. Fawkes managed to escape this awful fate by jumping from the gallows and breaking his neck.

Protestant England rejoiced at the country's "deliverance" from the plot and developed the Bonfire Night tradition over the next few years. Included among the participants were children who begged for "a penny for the Old Guy." (The penny was to buy fireworks.) And eventually "guy" entered the English language as a slang term for any male.

---

* The heads of Guy Fawkes and the other plotters were placed on stakes as a warning to others.

* In January 1606, Parliament met to pass the Thanksgiving Act, which marked November 5 as a day of remembrance for the foiled plot. Early celebrations included sermons, ringing church bells, and fireworks displays.

* In early celebrations of Guy Fawkes Day, revellers would burn effigies of the pope and the devil, rather than of Guy Fawkes.

Nutty Nietzsche

A brilliant philosophical career was cut short when one of the world's greatest thinkers began to spiral into madness.

✳ ✳ ✳ ✳

THERE WERE THOSE who thought Friedrich Wilhelm Nietzsche was crazy before he actually went mad. Nietzsche's work formed the basis of existentialism, a controversial postmodern philosophical movement that formed while religious focus was petering out in intellectual circles. His writing has influenced scores of artists, teachers, and leaders.

The basic idea of Nietzsche's philosophy is quite simple: Human beings are responsible for the creation and meaning of their own lives. When Nietzsche proclaimed his infamous tenet "God is dead," what he meant was that people have the right to believe or not believe in the concept of God because they are responsible for the daily makeup of their own lives and minds. Although Nietzsche's life may have ended in the depths of mental depravity, this fact does not weaken the philosophies he unleashed upon the world in the areas of culture, science, morality, and religion.

Finding His Way in the World

Nietzsche was born October 15, 1844, in the Prussian province of Saxony. He was the oldest of three children. Tragically, his father and younger brother died within a year of each other before Nietzsche was seven. For a time it appeared the young boy was destined for a theological career, much to the approval of his mother. At the university in Bonn, he studied theology and philology (the study of how language changes over time), but after one semester Nietzsche rejected his faith and abandoned his theological studies. Needless to say, his mother was not pleased. Nietzsche continued his studies in philology and became one of the youngest professors ever to teach the discipline at the University of Basel.

Despite being quite sickly for most of his adult life, Nietzsche was able to serve as a medical orderly during the Franco-Prussian War of 1870. During this time, he contracted dysentery, diphtheria, and syphilis, the latter of which may have been a cause of his eventual mental illness. Because of these various health woes, Nietzsche had to take a number of sabbaticals, which marked the end of his career as a philologist. Some suggest that these sabbaticals also led to his emergence as a philosopher. There's nothing like being alone in a miserable physical state to make one consider the human condition.

In his immodest, candid, and at times humorous autobiography, *Ecce Homo*, Nietzsche relates in no uncertain terms that he saw in himself how the rest of humanity should be. It's possible that Nietzsche really did see himself as *Übermensch*, or superman, a philosophical idea he created in *Thus Spoke Zarathustra*.

Breakdown

Nietzsche's first symptoms of serious mental illness surfaced in 1889, when he experienced an episode of delirium on a street in Turin, Italy. Nietzsche caused a public disturbance before being restrained by two police officers. After Franz Overbeck, Nietzsche's closest friend, received a brief, puzzling, almost incoherent letter from Nietzsche, Overbeck traveled to Turin and brought Nietzsche home to Basel, Switzerland. Overbeck placed Nietzsche in the care of a psychiatric clinic. Although Nietzsche was displaying many of the signs of mental illness caused by syphilis, he also exhibited conflicting behavior. The true cause of his madness is still a matter of conjecture: Did the great thinker's brain blow a fuse from an overload of mental stress, or did his short military stint, turn of patriotism, and possible indiscretion have dire consequences? Whatever the reason, the man who gave the world pause to think was, at the end, himself completely uncommunicative. Friedrich Wilhelm Nietzsche died of pneumonia on August 25, 1900, proving yet another of his philosophical theories: We are indeed *Human, All Too Human*.

The Harlem Cat

Known for his catchphrase "Keep the faith, baby," this flashy and enigmatic politician helped usher in the civil rights era.

✳ ✳ ✳ ✳

BORN IN CONNECTICUT in 1908 and raised in Harlem, Adam Clayton Powell Jr. spent his youth reconciling the teachings of his minister father with the messages he received in speakeasies and from jazz music. After Powell flunked out of New York's City College, his father pressured him into attending Colgate University in upstate New York, where he earned his bachelor's degree. That was quickly followed up with a master's in religious education from Columbia University.

While at Columbia, Powell began to take notice of the plight of fellow African Americans. Operating a food bank and organizing literacy classes, he built a reputation throughout Harlem for his generosity and commitment to fighting the racism that was so rampant in New York City.

Frustrated by the persistent refusal of businesses to hire African American workers, Powell started to encourage people to use their money as a force for change. His "Don't buy where you can't work" campaign rocked the status quo.

Powell's reputation for activism and community service led to a stint on the New York City Council. It didn't take long, however, before he was flummoxed by what he perceived as a lack of power to effect real change. Powell decided to run for a seat in the U.S. Congress, and on January 3, 1945, he began a 22-year career in the House of Representatives. The people of the district of Harlem now had a tireless advocate for equal rights.

In an era in which public use of racial slurs was common even on the floor of the Capitol, Powell was unlike anything the House of Representatives had ever seen. He was confident and eager to make the country a better place. One of only two African Americans in the House, he stormed into Washington determined to rock the boat. He railed against Congress for not doing more to eliminate the horrible practice of lynching African Americans, which was still pervasive in the Deep South and Midwest. When he felt his colleagues in Congress were dragging their feet or snubbing his efforts, he publicly took them to task.

Ushering in Civil Rights

Powell learned early about the power of the dollar, and he continued to leverage that power in Congress. He frequently used what came to be known as the "Powell Amendment," a rider attached to federal legislation requiring all recipients of federal funding to stop discriminatory practices. This paved the way for racial integration in public schools and helped spark the broader civil rights movement. Powell continued to gain power and influence in Congress as chairman of the House Education and Labor Committee, a position he was elected to in 1961. He helped enact the major social programs of the time, including antipoverty initiatives and federal minimum wage laws.

Powell's relentless agitation in Congress frustrated and outraged many of his colleagues. Despite his dedication to the worthy causes of civil rights and the eradication of poverty, Powell was hardly a man without flaws. He had extravagant tastes, and his reckless ways eventually caught up with him. In 1967, he was expelled from the House for questionable behavior with female staffers and controversy surrounding his wife's congressional paychecks. However, he regained his seat in the House in 1969 after taking his case to the Supreme Court. Unfortunately for Powell, the people of Harlem had had enough, and he lost his bid for reelection the next year.

Through success and failure, Powell never ceased to be a thorn in the side of those who would tolerate racism. He succumbed to prostate cancer on April 4, 1972.

Sinclair's EPIC Proposal

It was 1934, and the Depression that had started in 1929 was still dragging on despite President Franklin Roosevelt's programs to bring economic relief. Author Upton Sinclair proposed a remedy that could make all the difference.

✳ ✳ ✳ ✳

UPTON SINCLAIR KNEW a little something about wealth and poverty. Born in 1878 into an extremely poor family, he spent periods of time living with his wealthy grandparents. He would later say that witnessing these two extremes turned him into a socialist.

Sinclair funded his college education by selling stories and articles, and he was soon supplying his parents with regular income. After reading such authors as Jack London and Frank Norris, he formed the Intercollegiate Socialist Society along with London, Clarence Darrow, and Florence Kelley. In 1904, Fred Warren, editor of *Appeal to Reason*, commissioned Sinclair to write *The Jungle*, a novel about the Chicago meat-packing industry.

After President Theodore Roosevelt read *The Jungle*, he ordered an investigation of industry practices. He told Sinclair that, while he disapproved of his advocacy of socialism, "radical action must be taken to do away with the efforts of arrogant and selfish greed on the part of the capitalist."

A Failed Political Career

Sinclair split with the Socialist party over American involvement in World War I, but in 1926, he rejoined the party to run for governor of California. He was trounced. He ran again in 1934—this time as a Democrat—touting a program called End Poverty In California (EPIC).

"The meaning of our movement to End Poverty In California and its polling the largest vote ever cast in a California primary," he wrote, "is that our people have reached the saturation point as regards suffering... We have one-and-a-quarter million persons dependent upon public charity, and probably as many more who are able to get only one or two days' work a week or who are dependent on relatives and friends. That is too heavy a burden of suffering for any civilized community to carry."

EPIC was a cooperative program. Through it, Sinclair planned to put the unemployed to work in the numerous empty factories. He believed his plan would relieve taxpayers and lead to a better standard of living for everyone. Sinclair planned to fund EPIC through a tax on property assessed above $100,000. This, of course, raised the ire of businesspeople, and they closed ranks behind Republican Frank Merriam, who painted Sinclair as a radical. Sinclair lost the race, but he did manage to win 879,537 votes against Merriam's 1,138,620.

✳ Chicago's notorious Union Stockyards were the nation's largest cattle processing and meatpacking operation. An area along the South Fork of the Chicago River's South Branch that was once at the very center of the stockyards is still referred to as "Bubbly Creek." When the stockyards were in operation, the creek received so much blood and offal that it began to bubble methane and hydrogen sulfide as the various waste pieces were decomposing. The creek would churn violently at times, with some bubbles as large as basketballs.

✳ Eugene Victor Debs (1855–1926) ran for president four times as the Socialist Party candidate.

✳ Only two members of the U.S. Congress have been elected under the banner of the Socialist Party: Meyer London from New York, who served from 1915 to 1919 and from 1921 to 1923; and Wisconsin representative Victor Berger, who served from 1911 to 1913 and from 1923 to 1929.

Stetson Kennedy:
An Unsung Hero for Civil Rights

"Stetson was deeply involved in ways few, if any, white people were, and he did it in ways that are inspirational to us folks that grew up surrounded by a bunch of conformist racists."
— Hodding Carter III, professor of public policy,
University of North Carolina, Chapel Hill

✳ ✳ ✳ ✳

STETSON KENNEDY RISKED his life to infiltrate the Ku Klux Klan during the 1940s, a time when the Klan was extremely popular. The Ku Klux Klan, also known as the KKK, consists of members who deem anyone of anything other than white descent to be a threat to the United States. During that time, one important Klan duty was to "protect" white heritage by any means necessary, including murder, rape, burning crosses, and other vile activities.

An Activist Lifestyle

Born in Florida in 1916, Kennedy was a passionate writer with an interest in Southern and African American folklore. In 1937, at age 21, he left university to manage folklore, oral histories, and ethnic studies at the Works Progress Administration (WPA) Florida Writers' Project. Kennedy was always a human rights activist, and as a member of the NAACP, he believed in a live-and-let-live policy—so much so that he even ran for a spot in the Senate with that phrase as his platform.

After World War II, in response to what Kennedy saw as unchecked racism, he decided to infiltrate the Klan as John Perkins, an encyclopedia salesman, eventually working his way up to become a hit man in the organization. With the help of another Klan informant, he penned *I Rode with the Ku Klux Klan*, a gripping book that detailed murders, initiations, and other rituals. The work was published in 1954, and needless to say, the Klan was furious, even going so far as to put a price on Kennedy's life, offering $1,000 for every pound of his dead flesh.

Local law enforcement and the FBI were hardly moved by the book, but thankfully, the media couldn't get enough. Various newspapers published Kennedy's articles detailing his KKK activities. Minutes from KKK meetings were read on the radio, and the *Superman* radio program aired several episodes in which the Man of Steel fought the Klan and revealed their code words to thousands of listeners. This exposure cost the Klan a measure of the mystique that had surrounded it, and it is believed that membership began to decline as a result.

Questions and Controversy

In the 1990s, *I Rode with the Ku Klux Klan* was rereleased as *The Klan Unmasked*. This time, however, it came under closer scrutiny, and Kennedy faced accusations of fabricating parts of his nonfiction book, claims that were renewed in the 21st century. Some writers argued that Kennedy had fictionalized part of the material and reported on the activities of a second infiltrator and informant as if he had experienced the events himself.

In his 90s, Kennedy claimed that he couldn't remember every detail but insists that he did, in fact, infiltrate the Klan. His friends and defenders, including Studs Terkel and other scholarly and noted names, have argued that what Kennedy's work has accomplished is far more important than the specifics of how he compiled it and whether or not he should have given more acknowledgment to other sources, especially considering that it happened more than 60 years ago.

"With half a dozen Stetson Kennedys, we can transform our society into one of truth, grace and beauty."

—Studs Terkel

The Inscrutable Sigmund Freud

*As it turns out, the "Father of Psychoanalysis"
was a case study of neurotic behavior.*

✳ ✳ ✳ ✳

A NEUROLOGIST AND PSYCHIATRIST, Sigmund Freud conducted research on human behavior that
had a lasting impact on the field of psychology.

Freud himself was not without issues. He was a
heavy smoker—smoking as many as 20 cigars a
day for most of his life—and as a result, endured
more than 30 operations for mouth cancer. In
the 1880s, he conducted extensive research on
cocaine, advocating use of the drug as a cure for a number of ills,
including depression. Reports indicate that Freud was probably
addicted to cocaine for several years during this time period. And
a friend for whom he prescribed cocaine was later diagnosed
with "cocaine psychosis" and subsequently died in what is referred
to by biographers as the "cocaine incident."

Freud suffered psychosomatic disorders and phobias, including agoraphobia (a fear of crowded spaces) and a fear of dying.
Though his Theory of Sexuality was being widely denounced as a
threat to morality, he decided that sexual activity was incompatible
with accomplishing great work and stopped having sexual relations with his wife. Yet he is thought to have had a long affair with
his wife's sister, Minna Bernays, who lived with the couple. Freud
denied these persistent rumors, but in 2006, a German researcher
uncovered a century-old guest book at a Swiss hotel in which
Freud registered himself and Minna as "Dr. Freud and wife."

Freud fled his native Austria after the Nazi Anschluss in
1938 and spent his last year of life in London. In September
1939, Freud—who was dying of mouth cancer—convinced his
doctor to help him commit suicide with injections of morphine.

Dorie Miller: An Unlikely Hero

Doris "Dorie" Miller—so named because his mom's midwife had expected a girl—stood that infamous December 1941 morning on the deck of the USS West Virginia. *Trained as a cook, Miller seemed unlikely to emerge from Pearl Harbor a hero.*

✳ ✳ ✳ ✳

TWENTY-YEAR-OLD DORIE MILLER joined the navy in September 1939. He enrolled at the recruiting post in his hometown of Waco, Texas, after taking a ride in the back of the bus with a group of other black recruits. Blacks in the navy were then restricted to kitchen duty, and Miller became a mess attendant. He eventually worked his way up to ship's cook.

On an otherwise sleepy Sunday, Miller watched as an array of aircraft drew near. Two sections of the squadron dove toward the harbor and the airfield at adjacent Ford Island. Alongside his ship, the *West Virginia*, was the battleship *Tenneesee*. Along the quays forward were the *Maryland* and the *Oklahoma*, and to the stern was the *Arizona*. Unlike most of the crew, Miller was on duty that Sunday morning, collecting officers' laundry. Although barred from a combat post because of his race, he had proved himself a fighter: He was the *West Virginia's* heavy-weight champ.

It was odd, Miller thought, that aircraft were training so close to a naval and air base. Then four of the planes dove *toward* Ford Island. Suddenly, the airport's hangar and a clutch of Devastor dive bombers on the runways exploded.

Miller watched another group of planes, rising suns on their wings, veer down toward the *West Virginia* and drop five 18-inch-wide torpedoes into the waves. Within seconds, the ship shuddered and heaved from massive explosions. Soon after, Japanese planes dropped two armor-piercing bombs into the battleship, sparking massive fires.

Pressed into Action

The ship's communications officer directed Miller to help him move the captain, who was bleeding badly. Miller and the officer made a nightmarish journey through the dark, smoke-filled corridors of the vessel. En route, Miller felt a gigantic explosion—not from the *West Virginia*, as it turned out, but from the nearby USS *Arizona*, which had blown up, taking the lives of 1,177 men. Employing his strength as a boxer and an ex-high-school fullback, Miller helped hoist the gravely injured captain to the forecastle.

Back on deck, Miller saw the ship was listing; water poured over the side. Just ahead, Miller could see the now-capsized hull of the *Oklahoma*. He pulled wounded sailors on the main deck to the relative safety of the quarterdeck. Miller and Lieutenant Commander Frederic White then turned to a half-dozen survivors bobbing in the fiery, oily waters alongside their battleship. He and White tossed out ropes, hauled the sailors aboard, and then collapsed from exhaustion. The Japanese aircraft continued their bombing and strafing runs.

Miller and White rushed to a pair of Browning .50-caliber antiaircraft machine guns. Miller had been trained for combat, though not specifically in the use of antiaircraft guns. He put his training to use. "The sky seemed filled with diving planes and the black bursts of exploding antiaircraft shells," he remembered. He tracked a swooping Japanese plane through the gun sight, his thumbs squeezing the firing levers. Smoke billowed out of the aircraft. Seconds later, it crashed, throwing up a great plume of water from the embattled harbor.

"It wasn't hard," Miller stated. "I just pulled the trigger and she worked fine. I had watched the others with these guns." As the attackers tried to finish off the U.S. Pacific Fleet, Miller and a few others battled back. Finally, the *West Virginia* settled into the harbor, with 130 of its 1,541-man crew killed. Miller and other survivors swung over by rope to the waiting *Tennessee*.

Word spread back to the mainland about Miller's Pearl Harbor heroism. The *Pittsburgh Courier*, a prominent black newspaper, campaigned to have the sailor decorated. In May 1942, Admiral Chester W. Nimitz, commander of the Pacific Fleet, stood on the aircraft carrier USS *Enterprise* and personally awarded Miller the Navy Cross, the service's third-highest decoration. Said Nimitz: "This marks the first time in this conflict that such high tribute has been made in the Pacific Fleet to a member of his race and I'm sure that the future will see others similarly honored for brave acts." Capitalizing on Miller's fame, the navy sent him stateside on a war-bonds tour, with stops in his hometown of Waco and in Dallas, and at Chicago's Great Lakes Naval Training Center, which had begun training blacks for positions other than mess attendant.

A Return to Service

One more mission awaited Miller. He was onboard the escort carrier USS *Liscome Bay*, whose planes supported the bloody November 1943 Tarawa invasion. As the invasion fleet was readying to leave the area, the Japanese submarine I-175 struck the carrier. Its torpedo ignited the magazine and practically tore off the vessel's stern where Miller was manning an antiaircraft gun. He was most likely killed instantly (though not officially presumed dead until a year and a day later). Three hundred seventy-three of his fellow 646 crewmen were also killed.

Miller's courage against the enemy and against the racial codes of the day had great effect. In February 1944, the Navy commissioned its first black officers, and in 1948 President Truman formally integrated all branches of the U.S. armed services. A final legacy of Miller's was the commissioning in 1973 of the Knox-class frigate the USS *Miller*, which saw service in the Persian Gulf, the Black Sea, and elsewhere.

✳ **Actor Cuba Gooding Jr. played the part of Dorie Miller in the 2001 film *Pearl Harbor*.**

Words for the Ages

"The final reward of the dead—to die no more."

—FRIEDRICH NIETZSCHE

"Capital punishment is as fundamentally wrong as a cure for crime as charity is wrong as a cure for poverty."

—HENRY FORD

"Our scientific power has outrun our spiritual power. We have guided missles and misguided men."

—MARTIN LUTHER KING JR.

"My grandfather once told me that there were two kinds of people: Those who do the work, and those who take the credit. He told me to try to be in the first group; there was much less competition."

—INDIRA GANDHI

"We are what we repeatedly do. Excellence, then, is not an act but a habit."

—ARISTOTLE

"Happiness in intelligent people is the rarest thing I know."

—ERNEST HEMINGWAY

"I can run either the country or Alice—not both."

—THEODORE ROOSEVELT, WHEN QUESTIONED
ABOUT THE ANTICS OF HIS DAUGHTER, ALICE LEE ROOSEVELT

"I am oppressed with a dread of living forever. That is the only disadvantage of vegetarianism."

—GEORGE BERNARD SHAW

"The art of procreation and the members employed therein are so repulsive, that if it were not for the beauty of the faces and the adornments of the actors and the pent-up impulse, nature would lose the human species."

—LEONARDO DA VINCI

Going Under the Covers

Proper folks never mentioned it. If there was a problem, it was never solved. "It" was sex.

✳ ✳ ✳ ✳

IN THE 20TH century, American society's view on sex was the same as it had been in the 19th century—and the 18th century, as well. The common belief was heavily influenced by religious conventions and held that sex was for procreation. It was dirty and something about which civilized people never spoke. Then along came Alfred Kinsey.

Kinsey was born in Hoboken, New Jersey, in 1894. His devout Methodist parents forbade any discussion of sex. This, combined with a sickly childhood, may have contributed to Kinsey's interest in his future profession. He joined the Boy Scouts and became an Eagle Scout. This exposure to the outdoors eventually led to his fascination with gall wasps, which became the subject of his doctoral thesis.

Kinsey graduated magna cum laude from Bowdoin College in Maine with degrees in biology and psychology. Continuing at Harvard University, he earned his doctorate in 1919 and joined the faculty of Indiana University as an assistant professor of zoology. He wrote a textbook on the subject, which was widely adopted by high schools across the country.

Clara "Mac" McMillen was a recent graduate of Indiana University when she met Dr. Kinsey. They were married within a year, although the start of their relationship was anything but ideal. Honeymooning by hiking and camping through the White Mountains of New Hampshire led to an unconsummated beginning. There is some question as to the cause— some suggest the less-than-romantic environment, while others point to some physical issues that made the act inherently difficult. Many believe that this experience was only one of the many factors that led to Kinsey's ultimate research.

The professor quickly realized that many people shared the same difficulties and frustrations about sex as he faced with Mac. What's more, Kinsey was angered at the total lack of scientific information that could explain the phenomenon of sex and all its variations. No one had ever made a serious study of human sexuality—until Kinsey.

By the late 1930s, Kinsey offered a course on marriage at the university. Working without notes, Kinsey addressed the mechanics of sex, the acts of love and self-satisfaction, and the resulting pleasure from the natural biological activities of humans. The reaction was overwhelmingly positive, yet Kinsey still had a few questions.

Doing the Deed

Kinsey and his staff began a systematic process of interviewing men—more than 5,000 of them. Using codes to ensure confidentiality, the surveys were clinical and to the point. They began with 12 basic demographic questions to identify the respondent: age, race, education level, occupation, and the like. The interview then moved to 350 queries based on sexual data—specific questions concerning likes, dislikes, techniques, partners, variety, and frequency.

Respondents spoke freely, discussing sex with wives, lovers, themselves. Kinsey also broke ground concerning the most unpleasant subjects (pedophilia, sex with animals, bodily functions). The mass of information he compiled was beyond anything previously attempted.

Kinsey's research also took on the subject of homosexuality. Until 1973, the American Psychiatric Association classified homosexuality as a mental disorder. Kinsey's inquests refuted that notion, showing that more than a third of males had taken part in a homosexual experience at least once and that 8 percent were "exclusively homosexual" for at least three years at some point in their lives. He even pointed out that, biologically speaking, almost every animal species exhibited some sort of homosexual behavior. Kinsey's interest in the subject may have been due to his own bisexuality.

Climax

Kinsey founded the Institute for Sex Research at Indiana University in 1948. The next year he published his findings in a landmark book, *Sexual Behavior in the Human Male*. Within six months, more than 150,000 copies had been sold, and the book was translated into French and Italian. If people didn't want to hear about such things, they certainly seemed ready to read about them. Known as the Kinsey Report, the book ruffled the feathers of more than a few: Kinsey found himself accused of being party to a Communist plot on one end of the spectrum and chastised for largely ignoring the emotional elements of sex on the other. Kinsey contributed profits from book sales to the institute for further research.

By 1953, Kinsey and his team had interviewed nearly 6,000 females and issued *Sexual Behavior in the Human Female*. A Gallup poll reported that people, by a two-to-one margin, believed the Kinsey Reports were "a good thing" to have available. Of course, church groups responded with rage: Billy Graham denounced the book, saying it was "impossible to estimate the damage . . . to the deteriorating morals of America."

Much of this criticism was deserved, as Kinsey's samples didn't accurately reflect the makeup of the country. Yet his work clearly changed society's views of human sexuality, laying the foundation for the sexual revolution of the '60s.

❋ One assumption that Kinsey's team of interviewers made was that "everyone had done everything." Questions never asked, "Have you ever . . . ?" Rather, they began, "When did you first . . . ?"

Pancho Villa: The Man with Two Faces

Hero or criminal? You decide.

✳ ✳ ✳ ✳

THE MAN THE world knew as Pancho Villa led a contradictory life that caused some to venerate him as a saint and others to loathe him as a fiend. Certainly, Pancho Villa was a man of bold action with an uncanny sense of destiny whose exploits—whether actual or mythical, inherently good or evil—have become the stuff of legend. Even in his own time, he was celebrated as a living folk hero by Mexicans and Americans alike. In fact, film companies sent crews to revolutionary Mexico to chronicle his exploits—a circumstance that pleased the wily Villa, if for no other reason than the gold the directors brought with them. Journalists, novelists, friends, and enemies all conspired to create the image of a man whose true nature remained elusive. To the present day, the name of Francisco "Pancho" Villa continues to inspire both admiration and scorn with equal fervor... depending on whom you ask.

Hero of the People

Pancho Villa was born Doroteo Arango in Durango, Mexico, in either 1877 or 1879. As the son of a peasant family working for a hacienda owner, he realized that he would eventually inherit his father's debt and work the land until the day he died. At age 16, however, Doroteo returned home to find his sister fending off the lecherous advances of a local don. Unable to countenance the dishonoring of his beloved sister, Villa obtained a pistol, shot and killed the offending "gentleman," and escaped to the hills. For nearly ten years, he lived as a bandit, robbing from the rich and giving to the poor men who joined him. With the start of the Mexican Revolution, Villa came down from the mountains to form an army in support of the populist platform espoused by Francisco Madero.

As a general, Villa staged bold cavalry charges that overwhelmed his opponents even at great risk to his own life. General Villa was very popular with the ladies (purportedly marrying 26 times) and loved to dance. However, he did not drink and once famously choked on a dram of brandy offered him by fellow revolutionary General Emiliano Zapata. As the Mexican Revolution ground through a series of corrupt leaders, Villa remained true to his populist ideology.

When his political rival, Venustiano Carranza, came to power, Villa became a wanted man again, this time in both Mexico and the United States. As in his youth, he took to the mountains, evading capture for several years until, weary of life on the run, he surrendered in 1920. Villa purchased a former hacienda known as La Purísima Concepción de El Canutillo and moved there with about 400 of his soldiers and their families. Rather than become like the wealthy landowners he despised, however, Villa used the hacienda to form an agricultural community that soon swelled to approximately 2,000 men, women, and children who received an education and shared in the profits.

Murderous Thug

When American President Woodrow Wilson chose to support the presidency of Villa's rival Venustiano Carranza, Villa retaliated. On January 11, 1916, Villa and a group of his men stopped a train in Santa Ysabel, Mexico, and brutally killed 18 Texas businessmen. Murder and banditry were nothing new to Villa; as a young man he had made his living stealing cattle and was a murderer before he reached 20. As a revolutionary general, he ordered executions for specious reasons, robbed herds of cattle to sell north of the border, and shot merchants who refused to take the money he had printed for his army. His cattle thieving incensed powerful newspaper magnate William

Randolph Hearst, who conducted a long-term smear campaign against the bandit. This campaign was one factor that led to the criminalization of marijuana in the United States.

Pancho Villa's greatest moment of infamy, however, came at 2:30 A.M. on March 9, 1916, when he led a band of 500 horse-mounted followers against the 13th U.S. Cavalry and then into Columbus, New Mexico, where the bandits killed indiscriminately and destroyed property. When the Villistas departed at 7:00 A.M., 14 American soldiers, 10 civilians, and scores of bandits lay dead. President Wilson ordered Brigadier General John J. Pershing to lead a punitive cavalry expedition into Mexico to capture Villa. Multiple costly attempts to corner the cunning outlaw proved fruitless. Soon, the nuisance of Pancho Villa was replaced in the national consciousness by the United States' entry into the war raging in Europe.

The End of the Man, the Start of the Legend

Pancho Villa was assassinated by unknown persons while visiting the village of Parral in 1923. After Villa's death, one of his officers allegedly opened his tomb in Parral and removed his head to sell to a Chicago millionaire who collected skulls. Villa's body was later moved to Mexico City and interred in the Tomb of the Illustrious. Many believe, however, that it was simply a headless decoy and his true resting place is still in Northern Mexico. Thus, even the final resting place of Villa's body has become obscured by speculation and doubt.

✳ Pershing's pursuit of Villa in Northern Mexico marks the last time that the U.S. Cavalry was deployed for military purposes.

✳ *División del Norte*—Soldier of fortune Captain Tracy Richardson, legendary journalist John Reed, a Californian bank robber called the "Dynamite Devil," and Sam "the Fighting Jew" Drebben, as well as a quartet of barnstorming pilots with their primitive aircraft, all served under Pancho Villa at one time or another.

Guts and Glory

Profane. Pious. Aggressive. Poetic. More than 60 years after his death, General George S. Patton Jr. fascinates like no other American general of the last century.

❋ ❋ ❋ ❋

Born in Southern California in 1880, George Smith Patton was raised on stories of his ancestors' exploits in the Scottish wars, the American Revolution, and the Civil War. He did not learn to read until he was 11 years old—and he may have been an undiagnosed dyslexic—yet his early love of military history laid the foundation for an understanding of war that few other people have attained.

Patton graduated from West Point in 1909, having repeated his first year after failing mathematics. He married into one of Boston's wealthiest families and spent the next seven years learning the basics of cavalry command.

Patton worked to establish himself in the eyes of his superiors. He represented the army on the U.S. Olympic team in 1912 (Patton finished fifth in the pentathlon), he redesigned the cavalry saber in 1913, and he rewrote army swordsmanship doctrine. In 1916, Second Lieutenant Patton persuaded General John J. Pershing to bring him to Mexico during Pershing's expedition against Pancho Villa. Patton's gun battles there made him an instant hero, and the next year he followed Pershing to France as America entered the Great War.

Patton commanded a unit of light tanks in the newly formed Tank Corps. He spent months drafting the light tank doctrine. Patton set forth the tanker's credo:

If you are left alone in the midst of the enemy, keep shooting. . . . As long as one tank is able to move it must go forward. Its presence will save the lives of hundreds of infantry and kill many Germans . . .

Practicing what he preached, Patton led his battalion in Pershing's St. Mihiel offensive of 1918. In September of that year, Patton (now a temporary lieutenant colonel) took a serious bullet wound through the thigh while leading his tankers in the Meuse-Argonne offensive.

The end of the war threw Patton and the rest of the army into an aimless two-decade drift of boredom, rank reductions, and personnel cuts. The War Department folded his beloved Tank Corps into the infantry, and Patton returned to the cavalry, where he earned a reputation as an ultra-competitive polo player, a prolific writer on military topics, a tough taskmaster, and the army's most aggressive combat commander.

World War II Comes Calling

As war clouds formed on the European horizon, the awakening army made changes that would put Patton's years of training to use. Patton again left the cavalry to take charge of the 2nd Armored Division of the newly reconstituted Armored Force (nicknamed "Hell on Wheels"). Before long, Patton (now a major general) had established the army's desert training center in California, where tankers began preparing for war in North Africa.

World War II provided an outlet for Patton's martial genius. Serving under the command of his old prewar friend, Lieutenant General Dwight D. Eisenhower, Patton led a large landing force in the November 1942 invasion of North Africa. When fighting in the Axis stronghold of Tunisia bogged down after the American defeat at Kasserine Pass, Eisenhower ordered Patton to take charge of the U.S. II Corps, the only all-American combat formation in North Africa. Patton soon led the Americans to an impressive victory at El Guettar before turning over command to his deputy, Major General Omar N. Bradley.

Patton left the North African fighting to plan America's participation in the invasion of Sicily. Commanding the U.S.

7th Army alongside the British Army of General Bernard L. Montgomery, Patton's men fought their way ashore. When Eisenhower's ground commander ordered Montgomery to follow the main highways to Messina, the main Axis base, Patton swept around Montgomery and fought his way along Sicily's north coast in a brilliant series of land and amphibious hops. He became a national hero for his leadership.

A Hot Temper and Sharp Tongue

Patton's simple yet eloquently profane approach appealed to his enlisted men. "Hold 'em by the nose and kick 'em in the pants," which meant pinning the enemy with heavy fire along its front and enveloping it with mobile forces from the flank and rear, was his way of explaining his method of fighting. He once declared:

When I want my men to remember something important, to really make it stick, I give it to them double dirty. It may not sound nice to some bunch of little old ladies at an afternoon tea party, but it helps my soldiers to remember. You can't run an army without profanity; and it has to be eloquent profanity. An army without profanity couldn't fight its way out of a piss-soaked paper bag.

In August 1943, as his military reputation reached its zenith, Patton encountered two battle-fatigued soldiers whom he suspected of cowardice. Working himself into a violent, cursing rage, he slapped the enlisted men, violating army regulations and putting Eisenhower under intense pressure to send him home. Eisenhower, however—who was aware that the Germans feared Patton—retained Patton on the condition that he apologize to the men he had offended.

As Allied attention drew toward the French coast, Patton's mouth again got him into trouble. An ill-advised public comment that predicted Anglo-American world domination—at the expense of the Soviet allies—landed him back in the political doghouse. Instead of participating in the major D-Day operations, he led a dummy army to hold German attention near Calais. When he returned to France, he would be working under his old deputy, General Bradley.

Leading His Men to Victory

In France, Patton led the U.S. 3rd Army across central France in a dash to the Rhine. As he was about to push through Germany's Siegfried Line, he received word of Hitler's Ardennes Offensive, which had smashed through the U.S. 1st Army to the north. In a legendary feat of arms, Patton pulled three divisions out of a hostile line and led a six-division counterattack against the German flank, smashing Hitler's panzers and destroying Germany's last chance of knocking the western Allies out of the war.

After the German surrender in May 1945, Patton, now a four-star general, spent the next few months as military governor of Bavaria. As a man who was happiest during wartime, he pressed the War Department to continue the fight—correctly predicting that the Soviet Union would become America's deadly postwar foe—and got his superiors into political hot water over his opposition to some elements of the Allied de-Nazification policy. (For instance, Patton wanted to push the Soviets back to their pre-war borders.) Because it appeared that Patton had outlived his usefulness as a war leader, his old friend Eisenhower reluctantly relieved him as commander of the 3rd Army.

On December 9, 1945, seven months after the war in Europe ended, Patton was paralyzed in a serious automobile accident near Mannheim, Germany. He died of complications 12 days later and was buried with full military honors in Luxembourg, among the men he had led.

"Courage is fear holding on a minute longer."

—GEORGE S. PATTON

Tale of a Fateful Trip

Robinson Crusoe, Daniel Defoe's classic tale of survival on a deserted island, is widely thought to be purely fictional. In fact, the story is based on the real-life adventures of Alexander Selkirk.

❋ ❋ ❋ ❋

ROBINSON CRUSOE REMAINS one of the most enduring adventure stories, having spawned TV shows and movies that include *Gilligan's Island* and *The Swiss Family Robinson*. The book is a fictional autobiography of an Englishman who is stranded on a remote tropical island for 28 years. The real-life Scottish sailor who inspired the classic tale was born in 1676 as Alexander Selcraig, later to become Alexander Selkirk.

In 1704, Selkirk was part of a pirate expedition that set out to plunder Spanish vessels in the Pacific Ocean. Selkirk quarreled with his captain, insisting that the ship be repaired before they attempted to sail around the treacherous Cape Horn. When the captain refused, Selkirk deserted the ship and wound up marooned on the most western of the Juan Fernandez Islands, approximately 400 miles off the coast of Chile.

It turns out that Selkirk's desertion was wise—the ship soon sank, and most of those onboard died. At the time, though, he had no way of knowing this, as he had been stranded on the island for nearly four and a half years before being picked up by a passing ship captained by English privateer Woodes Rogers.

Some claim that Defoe actually met Selkirk in person and even gained access to his personal papers. Others believe that Defoe simply read Rogers's published account of Selkirk's adventures. Either way, the link between the two was cemented in 1966 when the Chilean government changed the name of Selkirk's island home to "Robinson Crusoe Island."

Socrates

Socrates was born in Athens circa 470 BCE. We know about him largely through the writings of his students, including Plato and Xenophon. His method of testing philosophical ideas—the Socratic Method—laid the foundation for Western philosophy and logic.

SOCRATES WAS BORN in Athens circa 470 BCE. It's thought that he worked as a mason before devoting himself to philosophy, and he also briefly served in the Athenian army. He had three sons with his wife Xanthippe, but was not much of a family man, devoting himself to educating Athens' youth.

Socrates taught that philosophy should advance the greater wellbeing of society. He was perhaps the first philosopher to propose a system of ethics based on human reason instead of theological dogma. Because human choices are motivated by the desire to be happy, and because wisdom is couched in knowing oneself, he argued, the more a person knows the better they will be able to reason and make choices that bring true happiness. Socrates thought that this logically meant government worked best when it was ruled by knowledgeable, virtuous, and completely self-aware individuals, or what he called philosopher kings.

Socrates strolled the streets of Athens, asking questions of nobles and commoners alike in an effort to find truths, rather than lecture about what he did know. The Socratic Method of questioning fellow Athenians was designed to force them to think through a problem and realize the conclusion themselves.

Athens was undergoing a period of political turmoil during his life, and Socrates publicly attacked what he considered the backwards thinking. As a result, he was arrested, tried for heresy and "corrupting the minds" of Athenian youth. Found guilty, he was sentenced to death by drinking a mixture containing poison hemlock in 399 BCE.

Indestructible Fidel

American intelligence agencies were very active during the cold war. But how come no one could kill the leader of Cuba?

✳ ✳ ✳ ✳

PERHAPS NO HUMAN being in history has survived more assassination attempts than Fidel Castro. A popular leader who overthrew the hated Cuban dictator Fulgencio Batista in 1959, Castro first attempted to organize the people of Cuba directly into revolution, but he was thrown into prison in 1953. He had his first brush with assassination there: Batista ordered the guards to poison Castro, but none of them would do it.

In 1955, after Batista made an election promise to free political prisoners, he ordered Castro's release. But the dictator was not about to let bygones be bygones. He sent an assassin named Eutimio Guerra to get close to Castro, but the revolutionary leader gave Guerra the slip. Castro seemed to lead a charmed life, and his revolutionary army moved from town to town fighting for Cuba until it was free of Batista.

After overthrowing the dictator and liberating Cuba, Castro was wildly popular with the majority of Cubans, although he was looked on with suspicion by almost everyone else. Because he received limited support from Cuba's traditional allies, including the United States, Castro had little or no choice but to ally Cuba with the Soviet Union.

Before the Bay of Pigs

Most people think that the halfhearted backing of the Bay of Pigs invasion was the starting gun for hostility between Castro and John F. Kennedy, but it was Dwight Eisenhower who set the "Kill Fidel Contest" in motion in 1960 with what ultimately became Operation Mongoose—400 CIA agents working full-time to remove the Cuban dictator. At first, they decided to train paramilitary guerrillas to eliminate Castro in a traditional commando operation, but his immense popularity among the Cuban people made that impossible. The CIA did all the preliminary work on the Bay of Pigs. Then Eisenhower left office, and Kennedy came upon the scene.

The Bay of Pigs invasion turned out to be a fiasco, and a year and a half later the Cuban Missile Crisis almost triggered full-scale nuclear war. America's only answer seemed to be to get rid of Fidel and try to turn Cuba back into a pliant banana republic (or in this case, sugarcane republic). But who would do it—and how?

Who *Didn't* Want Him Dead?

The problem was that everyone wanted to get in on the act. The U.S. government hated having a Soviet base 90 miles from Florida. Cubans who had lost their businesses during the Batista and Castro regimes wanted their old lives back. Anticommunists such as FBI boss J. Edgar Hoover viewed a plot to assassinate Castro as a struggle against elemental evil. American businesses that relied on sugar felt the loss of their cheap supply. The Mafia, which had owned lucrative casinos and brothels in Havana, wanted revenge. As it turned out, the Mafia had the best shot—and they had help.

The CIA, not being able to handle the job themselves, hired Mafia members to terminate Castro with extreme prejudice. In exchange, the CIA pressured the FBI to offer the Mafia a certain amount of immunity in the United States. But the Mafia got used to the new leniency, which they feared would end once Castro was actually killed, so they strung the Agency along with false promises to kill Castro if the CIA would continue to protect them from the FBI. Meanwhile, President Kennedy grew impatient. Changing the name of Operation Mongoose to Operation Freedom, he sent the American intelligence community in to whack Fidel. The attempts became more strange after the Bay of Pigs because intelligence planners believed that conventional measures wouldn't work:

* During a United Nations meeting at which Castro was present, an agent working for the CIA managed to slip a poisoned cigar into Fidel's cigar case. Someone figured it out before Castro could light up, however.

* Another idea was to send Castro on an acid trip by dosing his cigars with LSD. He would appear psychotic, and his sanity would be questioned. When this story finally came out, it merely gave a lot of old hippies a few laughs.

* Castro was an avid scuba diver, so the CIA sprayed the inside of a wet suit with tuberculosis germs and a fungal skin disease called Madura foot. Then they gave it to a lawyer heading to Havana to negotiate the release of Bay of Pigs prisoners. He was supposed to give the suit to Castro, but at the last minute the lawyer decided that the plot was too obvious and was an embarrassment to the United States, so he didn't take the suit with him.

* Perhaps the most famous dumb idea of all was to find out where Fidel's favorite diving spot was and prepare an exploding conch shell to kill him. This plan was dropped as being unfeasible.

* Traditional assassination methods were also tried. Cuban exiles were sent to Havana with high-powered rifles and telescopic sights to take care of the problem with good old-fashioned lead, but none of them could get close enough to shoot Castro.

* One of Castro's guards was given a poison pen that worked like a hypodermic needle, but he was discovered before he could get close enough to inject the leader.

Starting in the 1970s, the CIA seemed to lose interest in these plans, and thereafter most attempts to kill the leader were carried out by Cuban exiles (with CIA funding, of course). Fabian Escalante, Castro's head of security, claimed that there have been 638 plots to kill Castro.

Chapter 6

Notable Groups

Coming to America

This land is your land, this land is my land... But who was here "first"? Although the Vikings (A.D. 1000) and 15th- and 16th-century Europeans claimed to be among the first to inhabit North America, this legacy actually belongs to the Native Americans. But where did THEY come from?

※ ※ ※ ※

NATIVE AMERICANS AND Eastern Asians have several strong similarities—hair and skin color, little or no facial and body hair, and distinctive dental shapes. Even DNA studies show links between the two groups. This evidence lends credence to the theory that a migration from Eastern Asia into North America occurred via a land bridge.

At the time of the last Ice Age—about 10,000 to 12,000 years ago—a large glacier formed across much of North America. The ice drew from the waters between Siberia and Alaska. The result was a dry ocean bed nearly 1,000 miles wide called Beringia. Hunter-gatherers from Eastern Asia began moving across Beringia in a constant search for food, such as small game animals, nuts, berries, and roots. Seasonal changes continued to push these visitors down the Pacific Coast and inland to what are now the Rocky Mountain states. As the ice melted, Beringia began to shrink, returning to its watery origins within about 4,000 years.

According to anthropologist Paul Martin, the migration across the Americas continued at a rate of about eight miles per year. It took nearly 1,000 years to reach the southern tip of South America.

Dizzying Possibilities

Another theory of migration suggests that a small group of Japanese fishermen or sailors were caught in a mighty sea current some 3,000 to 4,000 years ago. They followed the tides from mainland Japan to the western coast of Ecuador in South America called Valdivia. Sound impossible? Consider the anthropological evidence: Ecuadorian pottery was found to be identical to the Jomon styles that existed in Japan at the very same time. Yet many experts suggest it is merely coincidence.

The famous finds of arrowheads near Clovis, New Mexico, in the 1930s showed that these Americans may have lived nearly 14,000 years ago—2,000 years earlier than those who crossed Beringia. More recent finds show that the early inhabitants from that area (and south, all the way to Brazil) resemble ancient Australian Aborigines. Other skeletal finds in contemporary times point to possible origins in Polynesia. What's more, the Topper archaeological site in South Carolina offered artifacts that predate Clovis by as much as 35,000 years!

Though little hard evidence exists to suggest the origin of the Topper inhabitants, many doubt any connection to Asia or South America—leaving Europe and/or Africa as the possible homes of these early travelers to the New World.

"The American Indian is of the soil, whether it be the region of forests, plains, pueblos, or mesas. He fits into the landscape, for the hand that fashioned the continent also fashioned the man for his surroundings. He once grew as naturally as the wild sunflowers, he belongs just as the buffalo belonged..."

— LUTHER STANDING BEAR, OGLALA SIOUX CHIEF

The Earliest Civilizations

The fame of the ancient Egyptians—pyramids, pharaohs,
eye makeup!—has led to the common misconception
that ancient Egypt was the world's first civilization.

※　※　※　※

The Contestants

1 Ancient Sumer. The first civilization is believed to have begun around 4000 B.C. The great city of Ur, associated with Sumer, is possibly the world's first city. Archaeological evidence suggests that "pre-civilized" cultures lived in the Tigris and Euphrates river valleys long before the emergence of Sumer.

2 The Harappan. Next in line are the ancient Indus Valley civilizations, located in the Indus and Ghaggar-Hakra river valleys in modern-day Pakistan and western India. The first mature civilization associated with this area is called the Harappan, generally cited as beginning around 3500 B.C., thus placing it in time after Sumer. However, some agricultural communities are believed to have inhabited the area as early as 9000 B.C.

3 Ancient Egypt. Located in Africa's Nile Valley, Egypt is generally cited as beginning in 3200 B.C. But as with the Indus Valley civilizations, it is difficult to establish a firm beginning date because some evidence points to agricultural societies settling in the Nile River Valley as early as the tenth millennium B.C.

4 and 5 Ancient China and Elam. The final two, and least known, contestants (from the Western perspective) are the ancient Chinese civilizations and the Elam civilization of modern-day Iran. The ancient Chinese civilizations located in the Yangtze and Yellow river valleys are said to have begun around 2200 B.C. The Elamite kingdom, meanwhile, began around 2700 B.C. (though recent evidence suggests that a city existed in this area at a far earlier date—perhaps early enough to rival Sumer).

The Criteria

The most salient feature of a civilization is a city, which, unlike a village, has large religious and government buildings, evidence of social stratification (mansions for the rich and more primitive dwellings for the poor), and complex infrastructure such as roads and irrigation. Civilizations are also defined by elaborate social systems, organized trade relations with outside groups, and the development of writing.

Marking a "civilization" is difficult because in all five possible cradles of civilization described above, complex societies lived in the same areas long before true civilization emerged. In fact, this is surely why civilizations first developed in these regions—human groups lived in the areas before the development of agriculture. Human populations have roamed the sprawling Eurasian continent for at least 100,000 years.

The emergence of civilization can be seen as the result of culture after culture living in one geographic area for countless generations until something happened that set these seminomadic groups on the path to civilization.

That Certain Something

Historians agree that the development of agriculture around 10,000 B.C. was the "something" that led to civilization. There is a strong correlation between agriculture, population size and density, and social complexity. Once agriculture began, human populations were increasingly tied to the land. They could no longer be nomadic, moving around at different times of the year and setting up temporary villages. As people continued to stay in one place and social relationships became more hierarchical, permanent villages developed into cities.

The First Monotheistic Faiths

Judaism is often thought to be the first monotheistic religion—that is, faith in a single, all-powerful God. But the idea of one all-knowing deity may have come along about the same time as another monotheistic creed—Zoroastrianism.

✳ ✳ ✳ ✳

Zoroastrianism is named after its founding prophet, Zoroaster, a Median, or ancient Persian, who is believed to have lived around 1000 B.C. Roughly the same time that Hebrew tribes were beginning to worship a sole deity named Yahweh (or Jehovah), the followers of Zoroaster were taking up a faith with remarkable similarities to the Jewish creed.

The Faith of the Magi

Zoroastrians, of whom there are perhaps 200,000 today, believe in a universal God, Ahura Mazda (Wise Lord). He is seen as the opposite of evil, which Zoroastrians believe is embodied in Angra Mainyu (Enemy Soul), the destructive energy that opposes Ahura Mazda's creative energy. Zoroastrians battle evil with good deeds, words, and thoughts. They see the choices they face each day as opportunities to be either a helper of Ahura Mazda or a helper of Angra Mainyu.

Zoroastrians believe that after they die, their souls leave their bodies, dwell in an intermediate world, and then are reunited at the end of time with Ahura Mazda, who judges them for their behavior on Earth. In another parallel with Judeo-Christian tradition, each person has a protecting *fravashi*, or guardian angel. Zoroastrianism was the preeminent religion of the Persian Empire, and Zoroastrian priests, known as Magi, were renowned for their knowledge. In the New Testament, the wise men who journeyed to Bethlehem with gifts for the newborn Jesus were Magi.

According to scholar Hannah Shapero, the people and the cultures of the ancient Hebrews and Zoroastrians interacted during and after the Babylonian Captivity—the exile of the Jews from Palestine to Babylon in 586 B.C., which ensued after the Assyrian conquest of the Kingdom of Judah. In 539 B.C., the Jews returned to the land of Zion after King Cyrus of Persia conquered the Assyrians.

The trauma of their defeat by the Assyrians, and their exposure to the ideas of Zoroaster, may have bolstered the Jews' sometimes wayward monotheism (remember the golden calf?). Indeed, there are hints of Zoroastrian influence in Jewish thought. Their notion of a *saoshyant*, or savior, influenced the prophet Isaiah, who spoke of a coming messiah. And the biblical word *paradise* comes from the Persian term *pairidaeza*, or enclosed garden.

Shapero suggests that the Jews' time in an alien land made their faith more universal and their view of God less tribal, laying the ground for the universal faiths of Christianity and Islam. After its return from Babylon to Palestine, Judaism was firmly monotheistic, and it has been ever since. Perhaps Jews and Zoroastrians can take dual credit for devising the belief in a single God.

✳ Most Zoroastrians live in India and Iran.

✳ Some observers wrongly see the Zoroastrians as fire worshippers. Zoroastrians simply revere fire as a symbol of God's wisdom and holiness.

✳ Zoroastrians believe that natural disasters, aging, sickness, and death are the results of Angra Mainyu attacking God's pure world.

The Druids and the Picts

What do you know about the Druids? How about the Picts?
Chances are, what you know (or think you know) is wrong.

✳   ✳   ✳   ✳

MOST CONTEMPORARY PERCEPTIONS of the Druids and Picts are derived from legend and lore. As such, our conceptions of these peoples range from erroneous and unlikely to just plain foolish.

Let's start with the Druids. They are often credited with the building of Stonehenge, the great stone megalith believed to be their sacred temple as well as their arena for savage human sacrifice rituals. True or False?

False. First of all, Stonehenge was built around 2000 B.C.— 1,400 years before the Druids emerged. Second, though we know admittedly little of Druidic practice, it seemed to be traditional and conservative. It is not known whether the Druids actually carried out human sacrifices.

What about the Picts? Although often reduced to a mythical race of magical fairies, the Picts actually ruled Scotland before the Scots.

So who were the Druids and the Picts?

The Druids—The Priestly Class

As the priestly class of Celtic society, the Druids were the Celts' spiritual leaders—repositories of knowledge about the world and the universe, as well as authorities on Celtic history, law, and religion. They were the preservers of Celtic culture.

The Druids preached of the power and authority of the deities and taught the immortality of the soul and reincarnation. They had an innate connection to all things living and preferred holding great rituals among natural shrines—the forests, springs, and groves.

To become a Druid, one had to devote as many as 20 years to study and preparation.

More Powerful than Celtic Chieftains

In terms of power, the Druids took a backseat to no one. Even the Celtic chieftains, well-versed in power politics, recognized the overarching authority of the Druids. Celtic society had well-defined power and social structures and territories and property rights. The Druids were deemed the ultimate arbiters in all matters relating to such. If there was a legal or financial dispute between two parties, it was unequivocally settled in special Druid-presided courts. Armed conflicts were immediately ended by Druid rulings. Their word was final.

In the end, however, there were two forces to which even the Druids had to succumb—the Romans and Christianity. With the Roman invasion of Britain in A.D. 43, Emperor Claudius decreed that Druidism was to be outlawed throughout the Roman Empire. The Romans destroyed the last vestiges of official Druidism in Britain with the annihilation of the Druid stronghold of Anglesey in A.D. 61. Surviving Druids fled to unconquered Ireland and Scotland, only to become completely marginalized within a few centuries.

Stripped of power and status, the Druids of ancient Celtic society disappeared. They morphed into wandering poets and storytellers with no connection to their once illustrious past.

The Picts—The Painted People

The Picts were, in simplest terms, the people who inhabited ancient Scotland before the Scots. Their origins are unknown, but some scholars believe that the Picts were descendents of the Caledonians or other Iron Age tribes who invaded Britain.

No one knows what the Picts called themselves; the origin of their name comes from other sources and probably derives from the Pictish custom of tattooing or painting their bodies. The Irish called them *Cruithni*, meaning "the people of the designs." The Romans called them *Picti*, which is Latin for "painted people"; however, the Romans probably used the term as a general moniker for all the untamed peoples living north of Hadrian's Wall.

A Secondhand History

The Picts themselves left no written records. All descriptions of their history and culture come from secondhand accounts. The earliest of these is a Roman account from A.D. 297 stating that the Picti and the Hiberni (Irish) were already well-established enemies of the Britons to the south.

The Picts were also well-established enemies of each other. Before the arrival of the Romans, the Picts spent most of their time fighting amongst themselves. The threat posed by the Roman conquest of Britain forced the squabbling Pict kingdoms to come together and eventually evolve into the nation-state of Pictland. The united Picts were strong enough not only to resist conquest by the Romans, but also to launch periodic raids on Roman-occupied Britain.

Having defied the Romans, the Picts later succumbed to a more benevolent invasion launched by Irish Christian missionaries. Arriving in Pictland in the late 6th century, they succeeded in converting the polytheistic Pict elite within two decades. Much of the written history of the Picts comes from the Irish Christian annals. If not for the writings of the Romans and the Irish missionaries, we might not have knowledge of the Picts at all.

Despite the existence of an established Pict state, Pictland disappeared with the changing of its name to the Kingdom of Alba in A.D. 843, a move signifying the rise of the Gaels as the dominant people in Scotland. By the 11th century, virtually all vestiges of the Picts had vanished.

World's Oldest Parliament

*Contrary to popular belief, the world's
oldest parliament is not in Britain.*

✳   ✳   ✳   ✳

A PARLIAMENT IS A representative assembly with the power to pass legislation. It most commonly consists of two chambers, or houses, in which a majority is required to create and amend laws. Congress became the supreme legislative body of the United States in 1789. The roots of the British Parliament date back to the 12th century. It wasn't until 1689, however, that the Bill of Rights established Parliament's authority over the British monarch and gave it the responsibility of creating, amending, and repealing laws.

The title of Oldest Functioning Legislature in the World belongs to the Parliament of Iceland, known as Althing, which is Icelandic for "general assembly." Althing was established in A.D. 930 during the Viking age. The legislative assembly met at Thingvellir (about 30 miles outside of what is now the country's capital, Reykjavik) and heralded the start of the Icelandic Commonwealth, which lasted until 1262. Althing convened annually and served as both a court and a legislature.

Even after Iceland lost its independence to Norway in 1262, Althing continued to hold sessions (albeit with reduced powers) until it was dissolved in 1799. In 1844, Althing was restored as an advisory body, and in 1874 it became a legislative body again, a function it performs to this day. The parliament is now located in Reykjavik.

✳ One of Althing's earliest pieces of legislation was to ban the Viking explorer Erik the Red from Iceland in 980 after he was found guilty of murder.

The Rise and Fall of the Knights Templar

The Crusades, Christendom's quest to recover and hold the Holy Land, saw the rise of several influential military orders. Of these, the Knights Templar had perhaps the greatest lasting influence—and took the hardest fall.

✳ ✳ ✳ ✳

JULY 15, 1099: On that day, the First Crusade stormed Jerusalem and slaughtered everyone in sight—Jews, Muslims, Christians—it didn't matter. This unleashed a wave of pilgrimage, as European Christians flocked to now-accessible Palestine and its holy sites. Though Jerusalem's loss was a blow to Islam, it was a bonanza for the region's thieves, as it brought a steady stream of naive pilgrims to rob.

Defending the Faithful

French knight Hugues de Payen, with eight chivalrous comrades, swore to guard the travelers. In 1119, they gathered at the Church of the Holy Sepulchre and pledged their lives to poverty, chastity, and obedience before King Baldwin II of Jerusalem. The Order of Poor Knights of the Temple of Solomon took up headquarters in said Temple.

The Templars did their work well, and in 1127 Baldwin sent a Templar embassy to Europe to secure a marriage that would ensure the royal succession in Jerusalem. Not only did they succeed, they became rock stars of sorts. Influential nobles showered the Order with money and real estate. With this growth came a formal code of rules. Some highlights include:

✳ Templars could not desert the battlefield or leave a castle by stealth.

✳ They had to wear white habits—except for sergeants and squires, who could wear black.

* Templars had to tonsure (shave) their crowns and wear beards.

* They were required to dine in communal silence, broken only by Scriptural readings.

* Templars had to be chaste, except for married men joining with their wives' consent.

A Law unto Themselves

Now with offices in Europe to manage the Order's growing assets, the Templars returned to Palestine to join in the Kingdom's ongoing defense. In 1139, Pope Innocent II decreed the Order answerable only to the Holy See. Now the Order was entitled to accept tithes! The Knights Templar had come far.

By the mid-1100s, the Templars had become a church within a church, a nation within a nation, and a major banking concern. Templar keeps were well-defended depositories, and the Order became financiers to the crowned heads of Europe—even to the Papacy. Their reputation for meticulous bookkeeping and secure transactions underpinned Europe's financial markets, even as their soldiers kept fighting for the faith in the Holy Land.

Downfall

The Crusaders couldn't hold the Holy Land. In 1187, Saladin the Kurd retook Jerusalem, martyring 230 captured Templars. Factional fighting between Christians sped the collapse. In 1291, the last Crusader outpost fell to the Mamelukes of Egypt. The Templars' troubles had just begun.

King Philip IV of France owed the Order a lot of money, and in 1307, Philip ordered all Templars arrested. They stood accused of devil worship, sodomy, and greed. Hideous torture produced piles of confessions. The Order was looted and officially dissolved. In March 1314, Jacques de Molay, the last Grand Master of the Knights Templar, was burned at the stake.

Many Templar assets passed to the Knights Hospitallers. The Order survived in Portugal as the Order of Christ, where it exists to this day in form similar to British knightly orders. A Templar fleet escaped from La Rochelle and vanished; it may have reached Scotland. Swiss folktales suggest that some Templars took their loot and expertise to Switzerland, possibly laying the groundwork for what would one day become the Swiss banking industry.

Shroud of Turin: Real or Fake?

Measuring roughly 14 feet long by 3 feet wide, the Shroud of Turin features the front and back image of a man who was 5 feet, 9 inches tall. The man was bearded and had shoulder-length hair parted down the middle. Dark stains on the shroud are consistent with blood from a crucifixion.

First publicly displayed in 1357, the Shroud of Turin has ties to the Knights Templar. At the time of its first showing, the shroud was in the hands of of the family of Geoffrey de Charney, a Templar who had been burned at the stake in 1314 along with Jacques de Molay. Some accounts say it was the Knights who removed the cloth from Constantinople, where it was kept in the 13th century.

Some believe the Shroud of Turin is the cloth that Jesus was wrapped in after his death. All four gospels mention that the body of Jesus was covered in a linen cloth prior to the resurrection.

Others assert that the cloth shrouded Jacques de Molay after he was tortured by being nailed to a door.

Still others contend that the shroud was the early photographic experiments of Leonardo da Vinci. He mentioned working with "optics" in some of his diaries and wrote his notes in a sort of mirrored handwriting style, some say, to keep his experiments secret from the church.

Is the Shroud of Turin authentic? In 1988, scientists using carbon-dating concluded that the material in the shroud was from around A.D. 1260 to 1390, which seems to exclude the possibility that the shroud bears the image of Jesus.

Sealed with a Kiss

In the times when nations were led by families, a great way to improve diplomatic relations with a neighboring state was to marry into its ruling house.

✳   ✳   ✳   ✳

"I Now Pronounce You Ally and Vassal"

THE IDEA OF using marriage to seal a deal or shore up shaky diplomatic relations dates back well before the time of Israel's King Solomon, who picked up 700 wives in his pursuit of alliances with neighboring kingdoms. Rome's Pompey the Great married the daughter of archrival Julius Caesar to seal their power-sharing agreement in 59 B.C., and Eastern kingdoms such as China regularly doled out daughters to vassal states as a matter of diplomatic protocol. But it was during the Middle Ages that political marriages became as much a finely honed tool of foreign policy as poison, coded messages, and trade agreements.

The marital record of the Duchess of Aquitaine, a beautiful, intelligent lass named Eleanor, is a case in point. Heir to the largest and wealthiest French province, Eleanor was first married to Prince Louis, the son of King Louis VI of France, in 1137. After Eleanor failed to produce a male heir, the couple had the marriage annulled, and she quickly married Henry, the count of Anjou, duke of Normandy, and—within two years—king of England. The couple had a stormy relationship (Henry even had Eleanor locked up in a castle for 15 years at one point). The marriage was so dysfunctional that it inspired an award-winning play and movie, both titled *The Lion in Winter*. The couple managed to sire five sons, however, and most of their royal offspring were wedded to cement alliances with other noble families. In 1199, one of Eleanor's last duties was to select a Castilian niece of her son, King John, to marry off to Prince Louis, the heir to the French throne.

Though most political marriages provided a veneer of protection for participating states, they usually flopped in the romance department. In 1328, King Afonso VI of Portugal married off daughter Maria to King Alfonso XI of Castile. Although their marriage was not a happy one (the Castilian king was enamored with his mistress, who bore him ten children), Alfonso offered his niece Constanza to Afonso's son, Prince Pedro. That relationship soured when Pedro fell madly in love with Constanza's lady-in-waiting; the prince and servant conducted a not-so-secret affair until Constanza's death in 1345. (Even that romantic link was ill-fated, as King Afonso—worried that his son would be too heavily influenced by the Castilian throne—had assassins murder Pedro's lover in 1355, inciting a revolt and a family rift that took a year to patch up.)

Not-So-Jolly Old England

England has long been a fertile land for disastrous political marriages. Take the Tudors, whose love lives were as tangled as the ivy that graced their castles. In 1509, England's King Henry VII arranged the marriage of his son Henry (later King Henry VIII) to Catherine of Aragon, the daughter of King Ferdinand and Queen Isabella of Spain. Catherine was the widow of Henry's older brother, Arthur, who had died unexpectedly, and young Henry was offered up to take his brother's place. The idea was to shore up relations with the most powerful Continental power, but the marriage was allegedly never legal, and Henry VIII divorced Catherine to take up with the second of his six wives.

Henry VIII's eldest daughter, Queen "Bloody Mary" Tudor, married Spain's Prince Philip strictly to produce a Catholic heir, which the queen hoped would keep her Protestant half-sister Elizabeth off the English throne. But that effort failed too. Mary's love for Prince (later King) Philip went sadly unrequited—they had not met until two days before their wedding—and she died childless in 1558, whereupon the unconcerned Philip proposed marriage to the incoming queen, Elizabeth I. For diplomatic reasons, Queen Elizabeth entertained marriage proposals from nobles of Spain, France, Austria, Sweden, Saxony, and Denmark, among others. None of the would-be royal consorts ever made the cut.

Weaving Tangled Webs

The practice of sealing relationships through marriage continued through the early 19th century, when Napoleon I of France negotiated with Tsar Alexander I of Russia for a marriage to Alexander's daughter to strengthen the 1807 Treaty of Tilsit between the two countries. Negotiations broke down (Napoleon's influential foreign minister, Charles Tallyrand, opposed the prospective nuptials), and the French emperor instead married the daughter of Emperor Francis I of Austria. Like most other political marriages, this one didn't last; when Napoleon was sent into exile on a South Atlantic island in 1815, his Austrian wife returned to Vienna and took up with an Austrian count two years later.

The entwined family trees that took root in Europe's early centuries left the royal houses in such an incestuous mess that by the time World War I broke out, three of the five chief belligerents—Kaiser Wilhelm II of Germany, Tsar Nicholas II of Russia, and King George V of England—were relatives. Nicholas and George were first cousins (both were grandsons of the King of Denmark), and George and Wilhelm were also cousins (both were grandsons of Queen Victoria); Nicholas and Wilhelm were more distantly related (both were descendants of the King of Prussia). Virtually all established royal houses, from the Thames to the Danube, could boast family ties to every other ruling house.

✳ Napoleon's love for Josephine, his first wife, ran very deep. She died during his exile on Elba; after hearing of her death, he stayed locked in his room for two days. Upon his return to France, he visited her former home and plucked some of her beloved violets. He kept the violets in a locket on his person until his own death.

Lords of the Rising Sun

For nearly 800 years, they held the power of life and death in the Heavenly Kingdom. The supreme lords of the samurai, they were called shogun.

✳ ✳ ✳ ✳

SINCE ANCIENT TIMES, the title *sei-i taishogun,* or "great general who subdues barbarians," had been awarded to the highest military officers recognized by Japan's imperial court at Kyoto. But in A.D. 1184, the title took on a new, more powerful meaning. That year, General Minamoto Yoritomo wrested power from the emperor during a brutal civil war. Thus was born the *shogunate,* a period in which the emperor retained formal power—as mandated by heaven—but where the real power lay with the shogun (the short form of *sei-i taishogun*) and his administrators.

Two great houses nominally ruled a patchwork of warring feudal provinces from 1192 to 1600, when one climactic battle settled Japan's affairs for the next two and a half centuries. At the Battle of Sekigahara, nearly 150,000 samurai, retainers, musketeers, and men-at-arms viciously fought against one another in two rival factions. General Tokugawa Ieyasu destroyed his rivals and emerged as master of Japan.

Tokugawa established the Tokugawa shogunate at Edo (now called Tokyo) and began his reign by redistributing lands and political power among his most loyal vassals. Two years after taking office, he abdicated, putting into practice the Japanese custom of officially retiring but sharing the governing of the country with his son, Hidetada. Hidetada and his successors consolidated the shogun's authority, and the Tokugawa dynasty survived as the dominant Japanese government until 1868.

The Tokugawa ruled Japan with an iron fist. Its early governors banned Christianity and other Western influences. They established a formal caste system that placed *samurai*, the warrior class akin to Western knights, at the top of the hierarchy, followed by farmers, artisans, and merchants. The great *han*, or provinces (akin to European duchies), were ruled by the *daimyo*, powerful nobles who were required to live at the Edo court every other year and keep their family members in Edo when they spent their alternating years at home.

In the late 1630s to early 1640s, the Tokugawa imposed sharp limitations on foreign business and immigration that created an insular kingdom little known to the outside world until the turbulent 19th century. As a result of this strict control, Japan grew up in isolation, creating new forms of philosophy, poetry, and literature within its borders and promoting trade almost exclusively within the kingdom.

The shogunate system was efficient but inflexible and fostered a groundswell of local dissent that percolated under the surface during its 264-year reign. Lower classes chafed at the impossibility of advancement, while the business class became frustrated by the shogun's monopoly on foreign trade.

Breaking the Sword

In the mid-1800s, foreign powers pushed Japan into accepting the outside world. In 1853, Commodore Matthew Perry led a U.S. naval squadron into Tokyo Bay in a dramatic display of American military might, and the following year coerced the shogun into opening diplomatic relations with the United States. As foreign powers forced the shogunate to open its borders, Japanese liberals began pressing for a restoration of the emperor's powers. The last Tokugawa shogun abdicated his throne in November 1867, and civil war broke out between forces backing Emperor Meiji and those of the former shogun. The Boshin War, or "War of the Year of the Dragon," ended in early 1869 with the destruction of the emperor's foes, many of whom met their ends in the ancient suicide ritual of *seppuku*.

The age of the mighty shogun had ended.

They Built Castles in the Air

Employing the fearless Mohawk Indians as ironworkers, the Dominion Bridge Company set into motion a constructive force that—six generations later—has built up the entire New York City skyline.

✳ ✳ ✳ ✳

IN 1886, DOMINION crews were building a cantilevered bridge for the Canadian Pacific railway to cross the St. Lawrence river, near Montreal. The path skirted an island reservation of the Mohawk nation Kahnawake and, to ease any qualms that the bridge's new neighbors might raise, Dominion agreed to hire day-laborers from the reservation.

Spanning New Heights

A Dominion official, consulting internal company documents and memoranda, told *The New Yorker* in 1949 that the Mohawks hired for the job were given menial tasks like unloading materials for the actual steelworkers to use. However, the official noted, "They were dissatisfied with this arrangement and would come out on the bridge itself every chance they got. It was quite impossible to keep them off. As the work progressed, it became apparent to all concerned that these Indians were very odd in that they did not have any fear of heights. If not watched, they would climb up into the spans and walk around up there as cool and collected as the toughest of our riveters, most of whom at that period were old sailing ship men especially picked for the experience in working aloft."

And so a legend was born. Sprouting cities across the American and Canadian northeast had no shortage of jobs for skywalkers who could wield a rivet gun. Kahnawake residents soon found work as actual riveters at the Soo Bridge, spanning Sault Ste. Marie, Ontario, and Michigan—a job that served as vocational college for these previously unskilled tradespeople. By 1907,

Kahnawake was home to some 70 bridgemen, who would hop as an ensemble from one project to the next.

Disaster

But 1907 was also when disaster transformed this would-be trade union. Construction was under way on the Québec Bridge, which was to span the St. Lawrence from Québec City to Lévis, Québec. On August 29, minutes after a foreman ended the workday with the sound of his whistle, the bridge collapsed due to defective parts in the anchor arm near the main pier. More than 70 men were sent to a watery grave. In Kahnawake, which lost 33 bridgemen, this tragedy is known to this day simply as "The Disaster." The men left behind 24 widows and dozens of children.

After The Disaster, the village women gathered in this matriarchal society and decided that to avoid another widespread tragedy, their ironworking husbands, fathers, and brothers would never again work en masse. The practical upshot of this policy decision was to scatter Mohawk ironworkers to the winds, which led many of them to New York at a moment in history when buildings were pushing up like rows of sunflowers. From the 1920s onward, Mohawks from Kahnawake (and Akwesasne, near Québec City) riveted their way across patches of sky that became the Empire State Building, the Chrysler Building, Rockefeller Center, the Triborough Bridge, and of course, the World Trade Center.

On the morning of September 11, 2001, skywalkers from Kahnawake raced down to New York to be some of the first construction crews to dismantle what uncles, fathers, and cousins had assembled three decades ago.

Today, Mohawks from Kahnawake and Akwesasne are members of ironworkers' union locals in Montreal and New York, as well as New Jersey, Boston, Detroit, and Kentucky.

Peace Churches

The Protestant Reformation of the 1500s sent Christians flying in all directions. The Anabaptists (Mennonites, Amish, Brethren, and Hutterites) and Friends (Quakers) represented some of the more radical trends in late medieval Christian thought.

✳ ✳ ✳ ✳

Anabaptists

THE WORD *ANABAPTIST* means "rebaptizer." In early 1525, a group of young Swiss Christians agreed that Christian faith should be an informed adult decision, not something imposed upon an infant. Anabaptists baptized one another and planned to put off baptizing their children until they were of age.

Anabaptism spread swiftly throughout German-speaking Europe and the Netherlands. Many of its adherents paid the ultimate price for their "heresy," however. Amid gruesome persecution and martyrdom, they began to scatter, forming the sects described as follows.

Mennonites

Father Menno Simons, a Dutch Catholic priest, became an Anabaptist in 1536. Soon, his followers began to call themselves Mennonites, and most eventually moved to Prussia and Russia. In the 1870s, they joined the great waves of immigration to the United States. Today, there are some 350,000 Mennonites in the world, two-thirds of them in the United States. They range from communal groups (who practice with varying degrees of strictness) to mainstream urban dwellers who simply attend Mennonite services.

Amish

By 1693, some Mennonites in Alsace (modern France) felt the movement had lost its way. Under the leadership of Jakob Ammann, they separated to form their own communities removed from worldly influence and corruption. During the following century, Amish groups started migrating to the Americas. Nearly all of today's approximately 100,000 Amish live in the United States. Their strict communities are the most conservative of all Anabaptist groups.

Brethren

The story of the German Baptist Brethren begins (not surprisingly) in Germany in 1708 with Alexander Mack. Mack's congregants embraced many Anabaptist beliefs and found themselves mockingly called "Dunkers" by the general public for their pratice of baptism by immersion. By 1740, nearly all had moved to what would soon become the United States. Today, there are some 215,000 North American Brethren, mostly in the United States. Some Brethren subgroups are very conservative, others less so.

Hutterites

In 1528, one group of Anabaptists fled to Moravia, taking their name from leader Jakob Hutter. Their efforts to live in communal peace came to naught in Moravia; Hutter himself was burned alive in 1535.

In 1770, the small Hutterite remnant fled to Russia. One hundred years after that, the group began a migration to Canada. Today, they number approximately 24,000. About 70 percent live in Canada's western provinces, pursuing a communal farming lifestyle. Dedicated pacifists, they refuse to fight in any war.

Anabaptist diversity is nearly as great as the general diversity of Christianity itself. Less conservative Anabaptists accept government benefits and serve in the military; members of stricter groups do neither (though all pay taxes). Although some use technology in business and agriculture, the conservative Swartzentruber Amish have gone to jail rather than affix reflectors to their buggies.

Friends

In the early 1650s, some 60 independent-thinking English Puritans reached a radical conclusion for the day: direct experience of the light of Christ was universally possible regardless of clergy, sacrament, or church. Founded by George Fox, they soon organized as the Religious Society of Friends. Their worship was centered on the Meeting (congregation), where silent prayer was combined with preaching and testimony. Outsiders began calling them Quakers due to their emotional way of trembling when giving their testimony of faith. They believed in pacifism and refused to take part in warlike actions.

While the Friends were originally mocked as "Quakers," most today have embraced the term. Oliver Cromwell's Puritans, not known for their warm tolerance or rollicking sense of fun, threw many Friends in jail. From that prison experience stems the longtime Quaker sympathy with inhumane jail conditions—a tradition of social activism that would become, after worship, a second raison d'être of the Quaker faith.

By 1656, Friends had begun moving to North America. Unfortunately for them, the Massachusetts Bay Colony, like England, was in Puritan hands. Many Friends were jailed and abused. Most moved to less hostile Colonial areas: Rhode Island, New Jersey, Delaware, Maryland, and especially Pennsylvania. It didn't take long for the plight of the slaves to trouble the collective Quaker conscience, and Friends were early rejectors of the "peculiar institution." They wouldn't have countenanced war to free slaves, but from the Quaker standpoint, if ever a wrong spawned a right, it was the Civil War, since it led to the abolition of slavery.

Most of today's 350,000 Quakers live in the United States and England. Unlike many Anabaptists, Quakers don't live apart from society. You'll find them active in all professions and volunteering in numerous organizations that promote peace and human rights.

Culture and History of the Cherokee

When 16th-century European explorers first began surveying what would later be called the United States, they found a land already inhabited by a variety of groups. Among these were a people living in the southeast corner of the continent who referred to themselves as the Aniyunwiya, *or "the principal people." Their Creek Indian neighbors, however, called them the* Tsalagi, *and the white tongue morphed that word into Cherokee, the name generally used today.*

✳ ✳ ✳ ✳

THE ORIGIN OF the Cherokee is uncertain. Tribal legend speaks of an ancient time of migration, which some historians have projected as far back as the time of a land bridge linking North America to Asia. Linguists report that the Cherokee language is linked to the Iroquois, who lived far to the north; others point out that traditional Cherokee crafts bear a resemblance to those of the people of the Amazon basin in South America. Regardless of their origin, the Cherokee held sway over a great deal of land when Spaniard Hernando de Soto made contact with the tribe in the 1540s.

De Soto did not find the gold he was looking for in Cherokee territory. What he did find was a people who had heard of his treatment of other tribes and did everything they could to hasten his exit from their land. They quickly traded him some food and other supplies—including two buffalo skins, the first European contact with the animal, which at the time ranged as far east as the Atlantic coast—and suggested that he might be better off looking to the west. With that, de Soto headed off. The total number de Soto found living in their traditional lands is a matter of speculation; the oldest reliable count dates from 130 years later, long after the smallpox the Spaniard left behind had wreaked havoc on the tribe. The disease left somewhere between 25,000 to 50,000 people alive after killing an estimated 75 percent of the native population.

Culture Shock

The Cherokee soon realized that the white intruders were there to stay, and they did what they could to adapt to the changing world. On the arrival of the British, they became active trading partners, seeking to improve their situation through the acquisition of European goods and guns. They also became military allies—by many accounts, a trade at which they excelled—fighting with the British against the French and later against the Colonists in the American Revolution.

The British, however, always viewed their Cherokee allies with suspicion, the effects of which ranged from the occasional massacre to the imposition of treaties demanding that the British be allowed to construct forts in Cherokee territory. This ceding of property was only the beginning of one of the biggest land-grabs in history, culminating in the 1838 Trail of Tears, in which 17,000 Cherokee were forcibly sent west. Thousands died during their forlorn trek.

Part of the difficulty with the early treaties was that the Europeans were in the habit of making them with anyone who claimed they represented the tribe; in reality, nobody could speak for all of the Cherokee. Their system was one of local autonomous government, with each village being responsible for its own affairs. The individual villages even had two chiefs: a White Chief in charge of domestic decisions and a Red Chief in charge of war and general relations with outsiders. The society was matrilineal and focused on a spiritual balance that the Cherokee believed existed between lower and higher worlds, with the earth caught in the middle. Europeans were ill-suited to understanding such a culture.

The Times, They Are A-Changin'

Cherokee society proved up to the challenge, however. Part of the advance was because of Sequoyah. Sequoyah was a silversmith who devised the first syllabary for the Cherokee language in 1821. Although he was illiterate, he had observed the white man's system of written communication. His Talking Leaves system, consisting of more than 80 symbols that each represented a syllable of Cherokee speech, was rapidly adopted; soon the Cherokee had a higher literacy rate than most of their white neighbors. One immediate result was the publication of a newspaper, *The Cherokee Phoenix*, in 1828; it was soon renamed the *Cherokee Phoenix and Indian Advocate* to indicate that its pages addressed issues faced by all Native Americans.

The 1820s proved a time of change for Cherokee society as a whole. The Cherokee unified their autonomous tribes by the close of the decade. They adopted a constitution that provided for a formal judiciary and elected legislature, electing John Ross as principal chief and declaring themselves to be an independent nation. They took the nearly unheard-of step of sending Indian representatives to Washington, D.C., to persuade Congress and the Supreme Court that the United States ought to be held to both the spirit as well as the letter of various treaties that were signed over the years. Despite impressing many with the quality of their arguments, their efforts proved fruitless. The Cherokee were treated as second-class citizens for decades to come.

The repercussions from the almost unimaginable changes imposed on the Cherokee as European settlers came to dominate the continent echo to the current day. However, Cherokee society has proved itself equal to the task, and today its people are the most numerous of any Native American population. The leadership of various parts of the tribe continues to actively work to remedy past inequities.

"It is but a little spot of ground that you ask, and I am willing that your people should live upon it."

— CHEROKEE CHIEF ATTAKULLAKULLA, WRITING TO JOHN STUART, BRITISH AGENT

Cracked Despots

They say it's lonely at the top—perhaps that's why certain world leaders have wandered over the fine line separating genius from insanity.

✳ ✳ ✳ ✳

Nero

LEGEND HAS IT this Roman ruler fiddled while Rome burned. While technically incorrect (the violin hadn't been invented yet), figuratively speaking Nero may have somehow fiddled with the great fire of A.D. 64. Although he was out of town when the blaze began, it was widely rumored that Nero wanted to raze Rome's slums and rebuild the city into a shiny-new Neropolis.

Whether he ordered the arson or his enemies did in an attempt to frame him, Nero turned the situation to his advantage by blaming an obscure new sect called the Christians. Nero had their leader Peter crucified upside down on Vatican Hill and had Paul beheaded. He turned the persecution of Christians into public entertainment by throwing them in with wild beasts at his circus. Some he used as human torches to light his gardens, smearing their bodies with pitch and setting them ablaze.

Nero certainly was no hero, and his immoral activities shocked even the most liberated Romans. He took his own mother for a mistress and then had her murdered. He also trumped up charges of adultery against his wife Octavia, then later had her killed so he could marry his mistress Poppaea Sabina, who also happened to be his friend's wife.

When not indulging his lusts, Nero entertained himself by entertaining others—whether they wanted to be entertained or not. Performing before captive audiences, Nero sang songs, recited poetry, and played the lyre. No one was allowed to leave the building while the Emperor was on stage. It is rumored that some men feined death in order to escape.

As Nero's popularity waned, his enemies grew stronger. When his imperial guard refused to serve him, Nero realized the writing was on the wall. He stabbed himself and died on June 9, A.D. 68—the anniversary of his wife's murder.

Turkmenbashi

Born Saparmurat Niyazov, the Turkmenistan head of state adopted the name of Turkmenbashi, meaning "Leader of All Ethnic Turkmen." In 1999, he became ruler for life of this former Soviet republic situated north of Iran and Afghanistan.

Turkmenbashi rebuilt Turkmenistan in his own image—literally. His face was everywhere and could be found on posters, statues, currency, and vodka bottles. Streets and airports were named after him, and in 1998, a meteorite found in Turkmenistan was named Turkmenbashi. The head of state even renamed the calendar months to honor himself and his family. Turkmenbashi also ordered government officials and students to devotedly study the Ruhnama, a book he wrote combining poetry, philosophy, and revisionist history to guide his citizens to a higher life.

In addition to his megalomania, Turkmenbashi was also a control freak. He controlled the media, the universities, and the country's borders. He controlled the appearance and habits of his people by banning beards, long hair, and gold teeth. When he quit smoking, the rest of the nation had to as well. He also prohibited circuses, opera, and ballet, as well as the playing of music at public events, on television, and on car radios.

Although Turkmenistan is rich in gas reserves, its people are poor and its infrastructure is failing. Turkmenbashi spent more money on his pet projects than his people, even building a lake in the desert and an ice palace in the country's capital. After his death in December 2006, Turkomans elected a new president to a five-year term limit.

Suetonius's Subjects

Not only is Suetonius one of the most interesting Roman writers, but much of what he says is likely true! Here are some facts about the emperors he wrote about.

Tiberius sent the "first citizen" concept out to sea, preferring to goof off on the Isle of Capri and have underlings and bureaucrats keep the empire humming.

"Caligula" was an army-brat nickname ("Little Army Boots") that stuck, though no one would call him that when he was emperor. He did some of the psychopathic things you've heard about, and some worse; he also did good things, but those make boring history.

Claudius actually looked like a clod: He drooled, stammered, and had some sort of head twitch, likely the result of a nervous condition. What most people don't realize is how well he ran the empire (though Caligula was an easy act to follow).

Galba ushered in the Year of Four Emperors, a revolving-door era when the new guy barely had the new drapes measured before dying. Galba ruled for just six greedy months before the army butchered him.

Otho managed to stick around for three months, which is about how long it took the next guy's legions to reach Italy. He wasn't in charge long enough to do anything too crazy and might have made a decent emperor had he not stabbed himself.

Vitellius was a repugnant person, both physically and in his vulgar, loutish manner. Always eating, he'd gobble sacrificial food right off the gods' altar. He lasted eight months.

Vespasian straightened out Rome handily. Popular with the Roman military and the bane of the senatorial staff, he groomed his son Titus as a worthy successor. If you go to Rome and admire the Colosseum, thank Vespasian for having it built.

The Other Secessionists

Until 1851, Mormons had their very own state called Deseret. But the dream of Mormon autonomy was not ultimately achieved.

✳   ✳   ✳   ✳

THE CHURCH OF Jesus Christ of Latter-day Saints values purity and hard work. Certainly, the Mormons who fled persecution in the early 19th century, moving westward across North America, were a resilient lot determined to maintain their faith in the face of increasingly hostile gentiles.

When their leader Joseph Smith was killed by a mob in Illinois, the Mormons fled to a sparsely inhabited region in the Great Basin. Under Brigham Young's leadership, pioneer settlements of Mormons prospered as far north as the Oregon territory and as far west as the Pacific Ocean. When the United States annexed this land following its war with Mexico, the Latter-day Saints saw an opportunity to achieve statehood. To some, it seemed that the promised Zion (the place where the church elders could maintain the people's virtue until the prophesied fall of the U.S. government) was prepared.

Deseret Becomes Utah

Meeting in Salt Lake City in early 1849, the Latter-day Saints established the state of Deseret—the name taken from the Book of Mormon in reference to the industrious, communal honeybee. Brigham Young, the nominal head of the new state, sent representatives to the U.S. Congress with a proposed state constitution borrowed hastily from that of Illinois. The Saints proposed that their new state encompass all the territory from Mexico to Oregon and from the Green River to the Sierra Madre.

The House of Representatives denied the claim and opted instead to create the Utah Territory, with Brigham Young as provisional governor. The Mormon representatives considered the choice of an Indian name for their perceived Zion particularly offensive.

Territorial status was not what the Deseret General Assembly had envisioned when they sent their request for statehood to Congress. Only with statehood, on their own terms, could they set the agenda for their land. Moreover, while its representatives were being dismissed by the federal government, the Deseret General Assembly had truly been industrious. In a short time, it had appointed judges, formed a militia, enacted taxes, outlawed gambling, and incorporated the Church of Latter-day Saints.

Whatever the federal government chose to call it, the new territory was fiercely loyal to the Church of Latter-day Saints, and its inhabitants were determined to defend it from encroachment. Mormon zealots began to lash out at gentiles who traveled through their land. The federal government became increasingly frustrated. Several non-Mormon, territorial governors were sent to the area with the intention of replacing Young, who ceded his title but did not relinquish his power.

The Utah War

The situation reached a boiling point in 1857 after a band of church zealots massacred a group of pioneers traveling through the territory. President Buchanan dispatched Colonel A. S. Johnston with a federal army to assert authority over the territory and quell its inhabitants. Disdainful of the federal troops, yet incapable of mounting an effective defense, the Mormon settlers fled from their villages ahead of Johnston's army. Hundreds of men, women, and children laden with supplies trekked across the barren land toward Salt Lake City. With troops approaching, Brigham Young threatened to burn the city rather than allow a "foreign army" to enter it.

Contrary to Buchanan's expectations, the war was immensely unpopular with the American public, who considered the entire expedition unnecessary and expensive. Therefore, Buchanan was happy to end it peacefully in 1858 after the Mormons allowed federally appointed Governor Alfred Cumming to take office. Aside from destroyed property, the Utah War, or "Buchanan's Blunder" as it was called, ended without a single pitched battle.

Ghost Government

Officially, the State of Deseret was dissolved in 1851 when the U.S. government established the Utah Territory. Unofficially, however, it continued to exist, as the Utah General Assembly disregarded the protests of a succession of federal governors and continued to meet and pass resolutions for the State of Deseret.

In 1862, Brigham Young officially reconvened the Deseret General Assembly, which drew up a new resolution for statehood. This and subsequent efforts, including one in 1872 that dropped the demand for the name "Deseret" from the text, failed to meet federal approval. When the Eastern and Western railroads joined with the ceremonial driving of the golden spike at Promontory Point, Utah, in 1869, the dream of Deseret ended with the promised flood of new arrivals that would soon dilute the Mormon population.

❋ The Utah stone at the Washington Monument contains two references to "Deseret."

❋ The hard-working Deseret honeybee survives today in the beehive on the Utah flag.

❋ Coins were minted for use in Utah by the Church of Latter-day Saints in 1849, 1850, and 1860.

❋ Approximately 30,000 people were evacuated from their homes during the Utah War.

Words for the Ages

"I hold that no man should ever put away a wife except for adultery—not always even for that . . . I do not say that wives have never been put away in our Church, but that I do not approve of the practice."

    —Brigham Young, interviewed in the *New York Tribune,* July 13, 1859

"History is more or less bunk. It's tradition. We don't want tradition. We want to live in the present and the only history that is worth a tinker's damn is the history we make today."

    —Henry Ford

"History is a set of lies agreed upon."

    —Napoleon Bonaparte

"If one morning I walked on top of the water across the Potomac River, the headline that afternoon would read: 'President Can't Swim.'"

    —Lyndon B. Johnson

"You can tell the size of a man by the size of the thing that makes him mad."

    —Adlai Stevenson

"No man has a good enough memory to be a successful liar."

    —Abraham Lincoln

"'On with the dance, let the joy be unconfined!' is my motto, whether there's any dance to dance or any joy to unconfine."

    —Mark Twain

"Everything comes gradually and at its appointed hour."

    —Ovid

"A people that values its privileges above its principles soon loses both."

    —Dwight D. Eisenhower

"The U.S. Constitution doesn't guarantee happiness, only the pursuit of it. You have to catch up with it yourself."

    —Benjamin Franklin

9 Noteworthy Native Americans

America's history is not exactly neat and tidy. When white settlers arrived in America, they realized they had a big problem: There were people already living there! The following figures represent the hundreds of tribal leaders who did everything they could to preserve the history and culture of their threatened people.

✳ ✳ ✳ ✳

1. **Tatanka-Iyotanka, aka Sitting Bull:** The principal chief of the Dakota Sioux was less than forgiving of the white miners who tried to take over the Black Hills in the late 1870s. Sitting Bull was born in 1831, and his big moment came in 1876. Trying to protect their land, Sitting Bull and his men defeated Custer's troops at the Battle of the Little Bighorn. Sitting Bull then escaped to Canada. In 1881, he returned to America on the promise of a pardon, which he received. The legendary warrior then joined Buffalo Bill's Wild West Show, exhibiting his riding skills and hunting prowess. When he died in a gunfight with federal troops at age 69, Sitting Bull was still advising his people to hold on to their heritage.

2. **Tecumseh:** While Tecumseh, a Shawnee chief, was no stranger to battle, he is more often recognized for his diplomatic efforts. Born in Ohio in the late 1760s, Tecumseh was an impressive and charismatic orator. In 1809, when the Treaty of Fort Wayne signed over 2.5 million acres to the United States, Tecumseh was outraged. He tried to get all the Native American nations to join together, claiming that the land belonged to the people who were there first, and no one tribe could buy or sell any part of it. Tecumseh's idea came too late. Tecumseh

eventually joined forces with the British and was killed in battle in 1813.

3. Sequoyah: If it weren't for Sequoyah, a huge piece of Native American culture might be missing. Thanks to this Cherokee born around 1766, the Cherokee language is not a mystery. Sequoyah created the syllabary, or syllable alphabet, for his people and taught the Cherokee how to read and write. The ability to communicate via the written word helped make the Cherokee Nation a leader among tribes everywhere. The giant sequoia tree is named after the man who felt that the pen would outlast the sword.

4. Pontiac: Not much is known about Pontiac's early life, but it is believed that he was born in the Detroit or Maumee River region to Ottawan parents. By age 30, he was a prominent figure within his tribe. After the French and Indian War, Pontiac was none too pleased with the British and their trading policies. In 1763, he responded with widespread attacks against British forts and settlements in the Ohio region; these skirmishes came to be called Pontiac's Rebellion. However, neighboring tribes and other Native American leaders didn't like the way Pontiac conducted himself. Some felt he used a fake title of "chief" given to him by the white man to exert influence and enjoy undue power. Pontiac was killed by a member of the Peoria tribe in 1769.

5. John Ross: Though only one-eighth Cherokee, John Ross was a chief in the Cherokee Nation from 1828 until his death in 1866. Over the years, Ross owned a farm (and slaves) in North Carolina and served as a translator for missionaries and a liaison between the Cherokee people and Washington politicians. By the early 1820s, things did not look good for the Cherokee people. Ross took legal action to prevent the forced exile of the tribe. He was president of the Cherokee Constitutional Convention of

1827 and, for the next ten years, worked with the U.S. government to seek assistance and justice for the Cherokee. Even though several court rulings found the Cherokee to be the rightful owners of land, they weren't enforced, and Ross's efforts went largely unrewarded. Ross is known for leading the Cherokee to Oklahoma on what is commonly referred to as the "Trail of Tears."

6. **Geronimo:** Historical figures are often described with embellishment, but rarely are they mythologized to Geronimo's levels. Geronimo's wife, children, and mother were killed by Mexicans in 1858. He led many attacks on both Mexican and American settlers and was known for his legendary war skills—some even said he was impervious to bullets. But later in life, this fearless leader of the Chiricahua tribe of the North American Apache was forced to settle on a reservation, his group having dwindled to just a few people. He died a prisoner of war in 1909.

7. **Tashunca-uitco, aka Crazy Horse:** At the tender age of 13, this legendary warrior was stealing horses from neighboring tribes. By the time he was 20, Crazy Horse was leading his first war party under the instruction of Chief Red Cloud. The Lakota warrior spent his life fighting for the preservation of his people's way of life. He amassed more than 1,200 warriors to help Sitting Bull defeat General Crook in 1876. After that, Sitting Bull and Crazy Horse joined forces, eventually defeating Custer at Little Bighorn. Crazy Horse continued to tirelessly defend his people's rights, but by 1877, there was little fight left in him. After Crazy Horse left the reservation without authorization in an attempt to get his sick wife to her parents, Crazy Horse was killed during a struggle with officers sent to arrest him.

8. **Hin-mah-too-yah-lat-kekt, aka Chief Joseph:** Born in 1840 in what is now Oregon, Joseph the Younger (also called Chief Joseph) had some big shoes to fill. His father,

Joseph the Elder, had converted to Christianity in 1838 in an attempt to make peace with white settlers. His father's efforts seemed to work, for his Nez Percé people were given land in Idaho. But in 1863, the U.S. government took the land back, and Joseph the Elder burned his Bible and his flag and refused to sign any new treaties. After Joseph succeeded his father as tribal chief in 1871, he agreed to move his people to the now smaller reservation in Idaho but never made it. They came under attack by white soldiers, fought back, and then dealt with the wrath of the government. In an impressive battle, 700 Native Americans fought 2,000 U.S. soldiers successfully until Joseph surrendered in 1877. Joseph died in 1904.

9. **Makhpiya-Luta, aka Red Cloud:** For most of his life, Red Cloud was fighting. At first, it was to defend his Oglala people against the Pawnee and Crow tribes; by the time he reached his forties, Red Cloud was fighting the white man. His efforts led to the defeat of Fort Phil Kearny in Wyoming in 1867 and kept soldiers at bay for the rest of the winter. In the two years that followed, the government signed the Fort Laramie Treaty and gave the Native Americans land in Wyoming, Montana, and South Dakota. Soon after, the Black Hills were invaded, and Red Cloud's people lost their land. Until his death in 1909, Red Cloud worked with government officials and agents in an attempt to preserve the culture of his people.

"I am tired of fighting. . . . It is cold, and we have no blankets. The little children are freezing to death. My people, some of them, have run away to the hills, and have no blankets, no food. No one knows where they are—perhaps freezing to death. I want to have time to look for my children, and see how many of them I can find. Maybe I shall find them among the dead. Hear me, my chiefs! I am tired. My heart is sick and sad. From where the sun now stands I will fight no more forever."

— FROM CHIEF JOSEPH'S SURRENDER SPEECH

Civil War–Era Presidents

Six Civil War soldiers went on to lead the country.

✳   ✳   ✳   ✳

FOUGHT PRIMARILY BY young people, wars exert great influence in shaping a person's character and sometimes even his or her life path. The Civil War was no exception, serving as a proving ground for no fewer than six U.S. presidents.

Ulysses S. Grant

Grant rose to prominence during the war and was elected president in 1868 based on his service. He ran as a Republican in the first presidential election to follow his victory at Appomattox.

Rutherford B. Hayes

Almost 40 when the war broke out, Hayes volunteered and nearly lost his left arm to a musket ball in 1861. Following a miraculous recovery, he saw action in the Shenandoah Valley and ended the war as a major general. In 1877, he became president.

James Garfield

Garfield served under General Don Carlos Buell in Kentucky and at the Battle of Shiloh. In early 1862, he personally led a charge that drove Confederate troops out of the eastern part of the state. He left the army after the Battle of Chickamauga to take a seat in Congress in 1863, and he was elected president in 1880. Shortly after he took office, however, he was assassinated.

Chester A. Arthur

Although Arthur served the Union cause, he was nowhere near the front lines. He served as quartermaster general for the state of New York and was thus responsible for obtaining and delivering supplies to New York soldiers. He was ultimately awarded the rank of brigadier general. Elected vice president in 1880, he became president upon James Garfield's death.

Benjamin Harrison

Harrison raised a unit of volunteers in the Indiana Infantry and served as their colonel, later receiving a brevet promotion to general. Harrison was elected president in 1888, interrupting Grover Cleveland's two nonconsecutive terms.

William McKinley

The bloodiest single day of the war occurred at Antietam in 1862. Serving as a wagon driver under heavy enemy fire was one Sergeant William McKinley from Ohio. In the heat of the battle, he coolly drove two mule teams into the field at considerable personal peril to disperse food rations to hungry troops. His bravery that day won him a promotion to second lieutenant by his commanding officer—Rutherford B. Hayes. McKinley was elected president in 1896 and 1900.

Grover Cleveland

The one Civil War–era president who didn't serve in the military was Grover Cleveland. His widowed mother's sole support, Cleveland hired a substitute to serve in his place. Although perfectly legal, this didn't endear him to Grand Army of the Republic veterans who were quite politically influential during Cleveland's burgeoning political career. Nevertheless, he won election in 1884 and 1892.

❊ Ten of the first twelve U.S. presidents owned or had owned slaves. George Washington, Thomas Jefferson, James Madison, James Monroe, and John Tyler each came from Virginia plantation aristocracy. William Henry Harrison did too, although he moved to the free-soil Northwest Territories and changed his slaves' status to indentured servants. Andrew Jackson and James K. Polk became wealthy as Tennessee lawyers; Jackson was even a slave trader for a time. Zachary Taylor owned a Mississippi plantation. The one Northerner among these Southerners, Martin Van Buren of New York, owned one slave before the practice was outlawed in his state. Of the early presidents, only John Adams and his son John Quincy Adams never owned slaves.

Too Good to Be Sidelined

A legendary aura surrounds the great Negro Leaguers.

✳ ✳ ✳ ✳

Most of the numbers can't be found in record books, leaving many of the best stories to be passed on by word of mouth. This is both the curse and the blessing of the Negro Leagues. While it's a shame the records and statistics don't hold up to encyclopedic accuracy, there's a certain charm and reverence in the way these stories have been retold.

The Black Babe Ruth

Josh Gibson would undoubtedly have challenged major-league home run records had he been given the chance to swing his mighty bat against white contemporaries. The "Black Babe Ruth" is said to have hit as many as 962 home runs in his career, though some came against semipro competition.

In Negro League games, the number is in the vicinity of 800— nearly 40 more than Barry Bonds's major-league record of 762. In 1936, one year before he traded his Pittsburgh Crawfords jersey for the Homestead Grays, Gibson is said to have hit 84 round-trippers, 11 more than Bonds's big-league record.

It was not only the frequency of Gibson's home runs that stood out, but also the power. One story holds that he once hit a ball right out of Yankee Stadium. A taller tale has him hitting a ball so far in Pittsburgh that it dropped into an outfielder's glove in Philadelphia the next day. The umpire declared, "You're out— yesterday in Pittsburgh!"

Speaking of Home Runs . . .

Dale Long, Don Mattingly, and Ken Griffey Jr. share the major-league record of belting home runs in eight consecutive games. Had any of them extended their streaks by three more games, they would merit mention with John Miles's feat of 1948. Stated Negro League historian Dean Lollis, "You can take the greatest home-run hitters in baseball history—Babe Ruth, Hank Aaron, Willie Mays, Mark McGwire, Sammy Sosa, Barry Bonds—and even in their greatest years, they never came close to that streak."

Miles, a tall man with long arms and big, strong wrists, could not recall the locations of those 11 consecutive games. Because his team, the Chicago American Giants, played almost all of their games in major-league parks, the legitimacy of the accomplishment is seldom questioned.

Super Speedy

By his own count, James "Cool Papa" Bell once stole 175 bases in a 200-game season. The dazzling leadoff man, baserunner, and center fielder hit .400 or better several times. He once forfeited a Negro League batting title to Monte Irvin to increase Irvin's chances of being allowed to play in the majors.

Two tall tales were Bell's most lasting legacies. Fellow Negro Leaguers liked to say that he was so fast, he could turn out the light and be tucked in bed before the room got dark. They also said that he once hit a ball up the middle and was called out because it hit him as he was sliding into second.

Tales from the Mound

Satchel Paige is widely considered to be the greatest pitcher of the Negro League era. He dominated major-league hitters in exhibition games, fared well against them when he finally got his big-league chance at age 42, and made a career out of entertaining fans—not only with his deep repertoire of first-rate "stuff" and crazy trick pitches, but also as a showman.

Bell once said Paige "made his living by throwing the ball to a spot over the plate the size of a matchbook." Satch, as he was called, threw so many no-hitters in his 1,500 (or more)-game career that somewhere along the line the count was lost. He is said to have tossed more than 300 shutouts, but that, too, is a number that will never be verified.

"Smokey" Joe

Paige was hardly the only Negro League pitcher with an amazing tale. Smokey Joe Williams, pitching for the Homestead Grays at age 44 in 1930, struck out 27 Kansas City Monarchs in a 12-inning, 1–0 victory. He is said to have pitched dozens of no-hitters himself. "If you have ever witnessed the speed of a pebble in a storm," Leland Giants owner Frank Leland once said of Williams, "you have not seen the equal of the speed possessed by this wonderful Texan."

Iron Glove

One of the Negro Leagues' most amazing accomplishments came from a man who stood only five feet eight inches tall and weighed 160 pounds. Larry Brown arrived from Pratt City, Alabama, as a 17-year-old catcher for the Birmingham Black Barons and gained acclaim as one of the greatest defensive backstops of all time.

If Lou Gehrig was the "Iron Horse" and Cal Ripken Jr. was baseball's record-setting "Iron Man," Brown deserves a metallic nickname as well. In 1930, he reportedly caught 234 games in one season. No one knows how many consecutive games he played during a career that spanned more than four decades and ten teams, but it would likely compare with the well-documented streaks of Gehrig (2,130) and Ripken (2,632).

And, like his durable white counterparts, it was not only the number of games played by Brown that was impressive but also the quality of his performance. He led his clubs to three championships and played in six East-West All-Star Classics while calling games for the likes of Paige, Willie Foster, and Ted "Double Duty" Radcliffe. "He was strong as an ox and could throw bullets to catch stealing baserunners," Radcliffe said of Brown.

Although we'll never know the exact numbers racked up by these legends of the Negro Leagues, their talent can never be disputed.

Lieutenant Vernon Baker and the Buffalo Soldiers

Of the almost one million African Americans who were either drafted or voluntarily enlisted in the U.S. Army during World War II, only one all-black Army division experienced infantry combat in Europe—the 92nd Infantry Division.

* * * *

URING THE WAR, most African American soldiers were relegated to duty as cooks, clerks, and other positions in rear-echelon units. The military, like much of American society at the time, was segregated. But in 1941—after years of pressure from civil rights advocates—the U.S. federal government rescinded official policy that had excluded African Americans from combat duty.

Bring Back the Buffalo Soldiers

Under the new policy, the 92nd Infantry Division was reactivated in October 1942. (The original 92nd Infantry Division was activated in October 1917. The all-black unit was sent overseas in July 1918 and saw action in the Meuse-Argonne Offensive, one of the last big military battles of World War I.)

The 92nd Infantry Division of World War II was a segregated unit composed of mostly Southern black enlisted men and junior officers under the exclusive command of white senior officers. Most of the enlisted men in the unit could neither read nor write.

The men of the 92nd maintained a proud tradition started by members of their World War I unit—they retained the buffalo as their divisional insignia. (Native Americans originated the "buffalo soldiers" term in 1866, in reference to the 9th and 10th black U.S. cavalry regiments.) The design featured a black buffalo in silhouette against an olive background.

The 92nd kept a buffalo as its mascot and even named its newsletter after the animal.

The unit was sent overseas, disembarking in Naples, Italy, on July 30, 1944. Shortly after coming ashore, members of the 92nd first experienced combat when they faced off against German Field Marshal Albert Kesselring's troops at the infamous Gothic Line—a series of fortifications across the northern part of the Italian peninsula. One component of the 92nd, the 370th Regimental Combat Team, had its first taste of combat in September 1944 near the Arno River. By midmonth, the all-black regiment had managed to drive the defenders to the base of the Apennines mountain range.

Valor in Action: Lieutenant Vernon Baker

Vernon Joseph Baker was born in Cheyenne, Wyoming, on December 17, 1919. Tired of being what he called a "servant," Baker quit his job as a railroad porter and enlisted in the Army on June 26, 1941. He was later assigned to the 370th Regimental Combat Team.

On April 5 and 6, 1945, Lieutenant Baker led his weapons platoon, as well as three rifle platoons, in an attack on a German stronghold at Castle Aghinolfi near Viareggio, Italy. During the patrol, Baker managed to kill nine Germans single-handedly and destroy three machine-gun positions, an observation post, and a dugout. The following evening Baker led an advance patrol through minefields.

During the engagement, Baker claimed his white company

commander abandoned him. When he returned to regimental headquarters to deliver the dogtags of the 19 men killed during the patrol, Baker later recounted being "chewed out by the regimental commander Colonel Sherman himself, because I wasn't wearing a steel helmet."

Lieutenant Vernon Baker was originally passed over for a Medal of Honor. He was awarded the Distinguished Service Cross for his actions. However, a 1992 study commissioned by the U.S. Army discovered "systematic racial discrimination in the criteria for awarding medals" during the war. The study recommended several African American recipients of the Distinguished Service Cross, including Baker, be upgraded to the Medal of Honor. He received the highest military award from President Bill Clinton in a ceremony held at the White House on January 13, 1997. Of the seven African Americans so honored at the ceremony, Baker was the only living recipient.

Recognition for Service

The 370th fought German and Italian units throughout the Serchio River Valley in Tuscany and finished the war in the Ligurian city of Genoa. During the Italian campaign, 2,848 soldiers of the Buffalo Division lost their lives. These gallant African American soldiers captured or helped capture some 24,000 enemy soldiers and, in return for their gallant conduct on the battlefield, received more than 12,000 decorations and citations.

Segregation in the military ended officially on July 26, 1948, when President Harry Truman issued Executive Order 9981. The order declared that "there shall be equality of treatment and opportunity for all persons in the armed services without regard to race, color, religion, or national origin."

The "Tuskegee Airmen" Take to the Skies

One of the first groups of African Americans to see action in World War II were the "Tuskegee Airmen." In June 1943, pilots from the 332nd Fighter Group conducted a dive-bombing mission against German units on the Italian island of Pantelleria. Battling the *Luftwaffe* throughout the war, the 332nd racked up an impressive record. They flew more than 15,000 sorties, often escorting bombers to their targets. In all, they downed 109 *Luftwaffe* planes.

The Rise and Fall of the *Luftwaffe*

*It screamed out of the Polish sky, rained destruction
upon London, and smashed tanks along the
Russian steppes. But by the last year of the war,
Reichmarschall Hermann Göring's dreaded* Luftwaffe
*had become a beast in its death throes, slain by
the overwhelming industrial might of the United
States, Great Britain, and the Soviet Union.*

✳ ✳ ✳ ✳

THE ARM THAT gave the *Blitzkrieg* its devastating reach
began as a covert project before Hitler came to power.
The Treaty of Versailles forbade Germany from fielding an air
force. To evade the Versailles restrictions, the Weimar Republic
developed training programs for ostensibly civilian pilots, often
at Dutch or Soviet bases. As Germany's land power grew and
the Third Reich no longer feared the threat of an invasion to
enforce Versailles restrictions, the German government began
contracting with manufacturing concerns such as Junkers,
Bayerische Flugzeugwerke (Bavarian Aircraft), and Heinkel to
build a new generation of warplanes.

By 1936, when the Spanish Civil War broke out, the Nazi
government sent pilots to Spain to undergo real combat testing under the name "Condor Legion," fighting on the side of
General Francisco Franco's Fascists. Hitler's smuggled crews
put the famous Messerschmitt Bf-109 fighter and the Junkers
JU-87 Stuka bomber through their paces. They flew terror-
bombing raids on Republican strongholds such as Guernica,
which later became the subject of Pablo Picasso's famous painting of the same name.

By September 1939, when World War II broke out, Göring's
Luftwaffe ruled the skies. The Stuka became the symbol of the
Blitzkrieg, while the Bf-109 fighter dominated the air from the
English Channel to the Soviet border. Consistent with the

Blitzkrieg nature of German fighting, heavy, long-range strategic bomber development was given a backseat to medium bombers such as the Heinkel HE-111 and the JU-88, which carried payloads of about 2,500 pounds of bombs.

Target: Britain

In the summer of 1940, Hitler assigned the *Luftwaffe* its most ambitious operation to date—the destruction of the British will to resist. Göring assured his master that the *Luftwaffe* was up to the task, but the Battle of Britain handed his beloved air service its first major defeat. By asking vulnerable dive-bombers and slow medium bombers to enter skies swarming with hostile Spitfire and Hurricane fighters (and tipped off by radar installations), Hitler's eagles found a task beyond their ability.

After Hitler's invasion of Russia in 1941, the Eastern Front demonstrated the limits of German airpower. Horrendous weather grounded much of the *Wehrmacht*'s vaunted close air support, and the vast scale of fighting in the East—1,280 combat planes were committed to the invasion effort—drained the *Luftwaffe* of its most talented fliers.

By the end of 1942, Allied bombing had begun to affect supplies of fuel, engine oil, and parts needed for aircraft manufacture, and plants producing warplanes came under attack. British and American bombers began penetrating Göring's protective fighter screen, and the balance of airpower decisively turned against the men flying the swastika.

To make up for the disparity in numbers, Göring's engineers upgraded existing airframes with improvements such as heavier armament. The Stuka was fitted with a 37-mm under-wing cannon to combat tanks, the JU-88 fighter-bomber was accessorized with night-fighting radar, and the Bf-109 fighter was upgraded with a more powerful engine and heavier guns. From 1941 on, German designers mass-produced a few superior new models, such as the Focke-Wulf 190 ground attack plane. With increasing numbers of Allied P-38 Lightning and Yak-9 fighters appearing on both fronts after 1943, however, Germany's obsolete engines and airframes could not keep up.

To remedy the imbalance, the Reich looked for technological innovations. In mid-1944, it developed the first operational jet fighter, the Messerschmitt-262 (Me-262), which could outrun anything in the Allied inventory. But by then German factories could not produce the fast, high-flying Me-262 in the numbers needed to overcome their opponents in the air war. An even swifter rocket plane, the *Komet*, barely progressed beyond prototypes.

The Allies responded with improved models, such as the upgraded Spitfire and Soviet La-7 fighters. When American P-51 Mustangs were able to escort bombers into the Reich's heartland, the *Luftwaffe* was doomed. One by one, aircraft engine plants, parts factories, and fuel refineries were shut down.

By early 1945, the *Luftwaffe* was a small (though still dangerous) shell of its former self. Antiaircraft crews knocked down four times as many Allied planes as the once-proud airmen, who could do little more than protect the skies above Prussia to buy time for their comrades to surrender to the west. Many pilots flew into captivity, their planes impounded. After the war, Göring, the once-cocky *Luftwaffe* chief, committed suicide in a Nuremberg jail cell, his swastika-emblazoned eagles grounded for all time.

* *Reichsmarschall* Hermann Göring had also been appointed Reich Hunt Master and Chief Forester; he took pains to preserve endangered raptors.

* Germany placed dozens of "rescue floats" in the English Channel to help *Luftwaffe* pilots who'd bailed from their aircraft. Each station provided food, shelter, and a first aid kit to tide the airmen over until rescue.

Efforts to Save a Threatened People

During World War II, many individuals worked to save their Jewish neighbors, risking their own freedom or lives in the process. Here are four individuals whose courage and moral fortitude saved thousands.

✳ ✳ ✳ ✳

Raoul Wallenberg

WALLENBERG WAS A Swedish diplomat stationed in Budapest who saved more than 100,000 Hungarian Jews from July to December 1944. He designed and personally distributed some 4,500 "protective passports" that gave Jewish holders perceived safe passage to Sweden under the protection of the Swedish Crown. Wallenberg issued at least another 12,000 passports. When acting personally, he often handed the passports to Jews aboard trains awaiting deportation and convinced authorities they were to be released under his protection. He also established havens for Jews in Budapest homes, which were dubbed "Swedish houses" because they flew the Swedish flag and were declared Swedish territory. Finally, he used diplomatic and moral pressure to prevent the liquidation of the Jewish ghettos in Budapest. On January 17, 1945, Wallenberg was arrested by Soviet agents and never seen again. In 2000, the Russians admitted his wrongful imprisonment and reported that he died in captivity in 1947—a claim that many still doubt.

Yvonne Nèvejean

Nèvejean headed the Oeuvre Nationale de l'Enfance (ONE), a Belgian agency supervising children's homes. Funded by underground Jewish organizations and the Belgian government-in-exile, Nèvejean rescued more than 4,000 Jewish children by providing them with new identities and places of permanent refuge in private homes and institutions. She also arranged for the release of a group of children taken by the Gestapo to an internment camp to be readied for deportation. Children rescued by Nèvejean became known as "Yvonne's children."

Sugihara (Sempo) Chiune

Sugihara was the Japanese consul general in Kovno at the time of the Soviet invasion of Lithuania. When the Soviets ordered all foreign delegations out of Kovno in July 1940, Sugihara asked for a 20-day extension and, in defiance of explicit orders from the Japanese Foreign Ministry, issued transit visas to Polish and Lithuanian Jews seeking to escape both the Nazis and the Soviets. Through August 1940, he and his wife, Yukiko, worked day and night signing papers for Jews waiting in long lines around the Japanese consulate building. In a race against time, he provided lifesaving documents for more than 6,000 "Sugihara Survivors," signing papers and shoving them through the train window even as he was leaving Kovno.

Oskar Schindler

Immortalized in the film *Schindler's List*, Schindler was a German businessman and Nazi Party member who entertained and bribed German Army and SS officials in Poland to obtain contracts and Jewish labor for an enamel kitchenware factory in Kraków. After his Jewish accountant informed him that work in his factory meant survival for Jews, Schindler hired more Jews than he needed, convincing SS officials that he needed their "essential" skills. In all, he saved more than 1,300 "Schindlerjuden" by employing them in his various factories. When Nazis who elected to ignore Schindler's "arrangement" put scores of Schindler workers onto a train headed for Auschwitz, Oskar came up with bribes and had the workers released into his custody.

"If you saw a dog going to be crushed under a car, wouldn't you help him?"

—Oskar Schindler

Philosophy of Peace

Followers of one ancient religion wouldn't hurt a fly—literally.

✳ ✳ ✳ ✳

JAINISM IS ONE of India's three ancient religions, along with Buddhism and Hinduism. To Jainists, the world is divided into the living (or the soul) and the nonliving. They believe that the soul is invaded by karmic matter, or negative passions, that can dominate people's lives. These include self-indulgence, greed, anger, and violence. This karma bonds to the soul and impedes the search for perfect understanding and peace. To reach the heavenly stage, Jainists must stop the inflow of bad karma and shed the karmic matter that has already bonded to their souls. Once this has been accomplished, they reach *moksha*—a level of pure understanding where the soul is liberated from all earthly matter.

Achieving this heavenly stage is not easy. An individual must spend 12 years as a Jainist monk and go through 8 reincarnations in order to get there. Along the way, each must also adhere to the "Three Jewels": Right Faith, Right Knowledge, and Right Conduct. More extreme worshippers deny themselves even the most basic of life's pleasures by fasting and wearing only the simplest clothing.

Jainism's most famous principle is that all life—whether plant, animal, or human—is sacred. For this reason, Jainist followers go to great lengths to refrain from harming any living creature. Besides practicing strict vegetarianism, white-robed Jainist monks often carry a broom to sweep insects out of the way of their footsteps to avoid inadvertently taking a life.

✳ **Some Jainists refuse to brush away mosquitoes, even if it means being bitten.**

Striving for International Order

Countries from around the world come together to try to work out their differences at the United Nations in New York.

✳ ✳ ✳ ✳

THE UNITED NATIONS was officially born October 24, 1945, but it wasn't a new idea. Actually, an international peace-keeping organization was established after World War I. The 1919 Treaty of Versailles that ended that conflict created the League of Nations. American President Woodrow Wilson was one of the main backers of the League; he couldn't win support for it from Congress, however, so the United States never joined its membership. When the League was unable to prevent World War II, it fell apart.

In January 1942, midway through the war, representatives from 26 nations fighting the Axis powers pledged to hold together until victory was achieved. President Franklin Roosevelt first coined the phrase *United Nations* to describe the group. The name became official when it was used in the title of *The Declaration by the United Nations*.

Months earlier, Roosevelt and British Prime Minister Winston Churchill had secretly negotiated the Atlantic Charter, which set up principles for a postwar world. In the declaration, the Allies committed to follow those ideas. It also officially referred to the alliance as the United Nations Fighting Force, a rather odd name for a group meant to abolish war and promote peace.

Organizing the War's Aftermath

Various configurations of Allies met in Tehran, Moscow, and Cairo throughout the war. In summer and fall 1944, representatives of four key Allied nations—the United States, the Republic of China, Great Britain, and the Soviet Union—gathered in Washington, D.C., to formulate the ground rules for an organization that would strive to maintain international peace. On April 25, 1945, San Francisco hosted representatives from 50 nations to draft a charter to that effect. On October 24, the charter was ratified by the five permanent Security Council members—those nations represented at the conference in Washington, D.C., with the addition of France—and endorsed by most of the additional signatories. Poland, which was invited but did not attend the conference, later signed the charter and brought the initial membership to 51 nations.

Continuing to Work Together

As of this writing, 192 member states represent virtually all recognized independent nations. The first session of the general assembly convened January 10, 1946, in the Westminster Central Hall in London under the auspices of acting Secretary-General Gladwyn Jebb, a prominent British diplomat. On February 1, Norway's Trygve Lie was chosen to be the United Nations' first secretary general. The secretary general is appointed for a renewable five-year term; to date no secretary general has served more than two terms.

Today the United Nations is headquartered at an 18-acre Manhattan site. The land was purchased in 1946 through a donation from John D. Rockefeller Jr.; even though it's physically located in New York City, it is considered international territory. It recognizes six official languages—English, Arabic, Chinese, French, Russian, and Spanish—and is comprised of six principle operating organs: the General Assembly, the Security Council, the Economic and Social Council, the Secretariat, the International Court of Justice, and the Trusteeship Council. The General Assembly operates on a one-state-one-vote system, and a two-thirds majority is required to pass many resolutions. The organization has twice been honored with the Nobel Peace Prize.

✳ Despite the best intentions of its delegates, the UN is not a perfect entity. For instance, the UN was roundly criticized for its inaction during the 1993 Rwandan genocide.

All Things Presidential

* When he was elected, **George Washington** (1789–1797) had only one tooth and wore dentures made from hippopotamus and elephant ivory, not wood as commonly thought.

* After a long feud, **John Adams** (1797–1801) and **Thomas Jefferson** (1801–1809) finally called a truce and developed a friendship that lasted the rest of their lives. Both men died on July 4, 1826—the 50th anniversary of the adoption of the Declaration of Independence.

* **William Henry Harrison** (1841) was the first president to die in office. During his lengthy inaugural speech, which was more than two hours long, he contracted a cold that quickly developed into pneumonia.

* Two decades after leaving the White House, **John Tyler** (1841–1845) joined the Confederacy and became the only president named a sworn enemy of the United States.

* **Abraham Lincoln** (1861–1865) was the only president to receive a patent; it was for a device designed to lift boats over shoals.

* **Andrew Johnson** (1865–1869) never received any formal schooling; he credited his wife with teaching him to read and write.

* **Ulysses S. Grant** (1869–1877) was cast in the role of Desdemona in an all-soldier production of *Othello* during the Mexican-American War.

* After his election, **Chester A. Arthur** (1881–1885) sold more than two dozen wagons full of White House furniture. Arthur commissioned Louis Comfort Tiffany as designer for his White House makeover.

* Early in his career, **Grover Cleveland** (1885–1889 and 1893–1897) served as a New York sheriff and carried out at least two hangings, refusing to delegate the unpleasant task to others. After being diagnosed with mouth cancer in 1893, he had a secret operation on a yacht to remove part of his upper jaw.

* **Benjamin Harrison** (1889–1893) was the first president to use electricity in the White House. After getting an electrical shock, he refused to touch light switches.

* **William H. Taft** (1909–1913) was the first president to own a car while in office. In 1930, his funeral was also the first presidential funeral to be broadcast on the radio.

* **Woodrow Wilson** (1913–1921) played golf as a source of exercise, even in winter. He had his golf balls painted red so he could see them in the snow.

* **Warren G. Harding** (1921–1923) suffered his first nervous breakdown at age 24 and spent time in a sanitarium run by J. H. Kellogg of breakfast cereal fame.

* Having never held an elected office before becoming president, **Herbert Hoover** (1929–1933) was the first self-made millionaire to reside in the White House. He had earned his fortune in the mining industry.

* **Harry Truman** (1945–1953) suffered from bad eyesight, which kept him from attending West Point. When World War I broke out, he passed his vision test by memorizing the eye chart beforehand.

* The first Catholic president, **John F. Kennedy** (1961–1963) was also the first president to have been a Boy Scout.

* **Lyndon B. Johnson** (1963–1969) and his wife, Lady Bird, were married with a $2.50 wedding ring bought at Sears the day after he proposed to her.

* **Richard M. Nixon** (1969–1974) wanted to be an FBI agent. He applied to the Bureau but wasn't accepted.

* **Gerald R. Ford** (1974–1977) played football for the University of Michigan from 1931 to 1934, and was offered tryouts by both the Detroit Lions and Green Bay Packers.

* Actor **Ronald Reagan** (1981–1989) became increasingly interested in politics while serving as president of the Screen Actors Guild. He was elected governor of California in 1966 and was soon viewed as a contender for the presidency.

* **George H. W. Bush** (1989–1993) At age 19, Bush became the youngest pilot in U.S. Navy history. He went on to fly 58 combat missions during World War II and was shot down in 1944 (he was rescued after four hours on a life raft).

* **Barack Obama** (2009–2017) cut his political teeth as a communty organizer on Chicago's South Side. In 2008, the former senator defeated John McCain to become the first African American president of the United States.

Fighting Words

The 1828 presidential campaign was a nasty one, mostly because of resentments that remained after the last election, which was between the same individuals. Each opponent hurled incendiary insults at the other. Andrew Jackson's supporters claimed that John Quincy Adams—during his years as a diplomat stationed in Russia—procured an American girl to service the needs of the Russian czar (this charge was completely false). Adams's supporters accused Jackson of adultery and accused Jackson's wife, Rachel, of bigamy because there was some confusion over the timing of her divorce from her first husband. When Rachel suffered a heart attack and died before she could attend his inauguration, a bitter, heartbroken Jackson blamed Adams and his supporters.

Chapter 7

Let's Hear It for the Ladies!

The Maid of Orléans

The Hundred Years' War was a disaster for the French. They had not won a major battle in a generation. England controlled most of northern France. The French needed a savior, and they found one in a 17-year-old peasant named Joan.

✳   ✳   ✳   ✳

JOAN WAS BORN on January 6, 1412, in the eastern French village of Domrémy. She led a normal life until around 1424, when she started having visions of St. Michael (commander of the armies of heaven) as well as St. Catherine and St. Margaret (both early Christian martyrs). God had taken pity on the French people, they told Joan, and she was chosen to drive the English out of France and ensure the coronation of Charles VII.

From Serf to Savior

In March 1429, Joan managed to get an audience with Charles, the leader of the French army (the other side of the royal family had taken sides with the English). She got his attention by repeating for him a private prayer he had made the previous November. Charles sent her to be evaluated by a group of theologians, and when they gave their approval, he placed her in titular (or ceremonial) command of the French army.

Charles's first mission for Joan was to break the siege on the city of Orléans. When Joan joined the army, she restored discipline by running off the prostitutes and requiring all soldiers to go to church. She led the army into battle at Orléans, giving encouragement to the troops by sharing the same dangers they did. Within nine days, she had lifted the siege and had the English army on the run. The victory and Joan's leadership had raised the morale of the army and attracted many more volunteers, who wanted to fight for the "Maid of Orléans."

Fulfilling her vision, Joan led Charles and 12,000 men through English-controlled territory to Reims where, on July 17, 1429, he was crowned Charles VII.

From Savior to Heretic

Joan continued to lead men into battle after Charles's coronation, but court politics and a wound she had suffered restricted her command to only minor companies. Just as the saints told of her future, they also foretold her end. Around Easter 1430, Joan revealed that she would be captured "before St. John's day" (June 24). The saints were true to their word: On May 23, 1430, during a skirmish with the Burgundians (the rival faction of the French royal family), Joan was taken prisoner.

Charles's defenders claim he offered a ransom for Joan and tried to rescue her. His critics contend that he did nothing. Whatever the case, after four months the French sold her to the English for 10,000 francs.

The English put her on trial from February 21 to March 17, 1431. Convicted of heresy, she was burned at the stake on May 30, 1431, and her ashes were thrown into the Seine.

From Heretic to Saint

The Hundred Years' War continued for another 22 years after Joan's death, but her efforts had turned the tide in France's favor. After the war, Pope Callixtus II reopened her case and—declaring her a martyr—found her innocent of heresy. Joan of Arc was beatified in 1902 and canonized in 1920.

Cleopatra: Stranger Than Fiction

In his work Antony and Cleopatra, *the immortal William Shakespeare gave the Egyptian queen the following line: "Be it known that we, the greatest, are misthought." These "misthoughts" could be the myths, untruths, and fallacies that seem to surround Cleopatra. Though movies and the media tend to focus on these misconceptions, the true stories are equally fascinating.*

✳ ✳ ✳ ✳

MYTH: Cleopatra was Egyptian.

FACT: Cleopatra may have been the queen of Egypt, but she was actually Greek. Though her family had called Egypt home for hundreds of years, their lineage was linked to a general in Alexander the Great's army named Ptolemy who had come from Macedonia, an area in present-day Greece.

MYTH: Cleopatra was a vision of beauty.

FACT: Beauty, of course, is in the eye of the beholder. In ancient times, there were no cameras, but a person of Cleopatra's stature and wealth could have their likeness sculpted. If the image on an ancient Roman coin is believed to be accurate, then Cleopatra was endowed with a large, hooked nose and was as cheeky as a chipmunk.

MYTH: Cleopatra dissolved a pearl earring in a glass of vinegar and drank it. As the story goes, upon meeting Marc Antony, Cleopatra held a series of lavish feasts. On the eve of the final gala, Cleopatra bet Antony that she could arrange for the costliest meal in the world. As the banquet came to a close, she supposedly removed an enormous pearl from her ear, dropped it into a goblet of wine vinegar, then drank it down, with Antony admitting defeat.

FACT: Scientifically speaking, calcium carbonate—the mineral of which pearls are composed—will dissolve in an acid such as vinegar. However, based on the description of the pearl in question, it is likely that the short dip in vinegar resulted in nothing more than a soggy gem, as it would have taken a very long time for that amount of calcium carbonate to dissolve.

MYTH: Julius Caesar allowed Cleopatra to remain queen of Egypt because he loved her.

FACT: Cleopatra did bear Caesar a son, Caesarion. However, that was hardly reason enough to hand over an entire country to her. Most likely, Caesar felt that any male ruler would pose a formidable threat to his empire, whereas Cleopatra was a safer alternative to rule Egypt.

MYTH: Cleopatra died from the bite of an asp after learning of Marc Antony's death.

FACT: It's unknown exactly how or why Cleopatra committed suicide. According to legend, after hearing of the death of her lover, she had two poisonous asps brought to her in a basket of figs. The person who found the expired Cleopatra noted two small marks on her arm, but the snakes in question were never located. Cleopatra may very well have been distraught about her lover's demise, but it is more likely that rumors she was about to be captured, chained, and exhibited in the streets of Rome drove her to suicide.

❋ Before marrying Marc Antony, Cleopatra was married to two of her brothers. But not at the same time! She married one brother, Ptolemy XIII, when he was 11. When he died, she married her other brother, Ptolemy XIV. He died not long after they were married.

Demonized by Mythology

In public perception, she rates alongside Jezebel for conniving promiscuity. But who was the real Lucrezia Borgia?

✳ ✳ ✳ ✳

Lᴜᴄʀᴇᴢɪᴀ Bᴏʀɢɪᴀ'ѕ ʟɪꜰᴇ was orchestrated by the intense political competition of the Renaissance. Italy was a gaggle of city-states and noble families, all jostling for advantage in a sleazy chess game of shifting alliances, political marriages, and warfare. Lucrezia was an unfortunate pawn.

Lucrezia's father was Cardinal Rodrigo Borgia, later Pope Alexander VI. His Holiness fathered Lucrezia and her three brothers with a mistress. Lucrezia's most prominent brother, Cesare, was ruthless even by Renaissance standards. Lucrezia was born into a family whose name evoked fear and loathing.

When Lucrezia reached age 13 in 1493, her father married her off to Giovanni Sforza to cement an alliance with Sforza's powerful Milanese clan, thus boosting Cesare's fortunes. When Alexander no longer needed to make nice with the Sforzas, he claimed Giovanni was impotent and had the marriage annulled.

Months later, Lucrezia gave birth to a son. The father was Pedro Calderon, a Spanish page. To preserve the reputation of the Borgia family (such as it was!), Alexander stated that Giovanni was Cesare's child by his mistress.

In 1498, Lucrezia entered an arranged marriage to Alfonso of Bisceglie to ingratiate Cesare with the king of Naples. When that notion soured, "unknown assailants" (probably Cesare's henchmen) assassinated Alfonso. Lucrezia had grown to love her husband, and she went into a deep depression.

In 1501, Alexander brokered Lucrezia's marital hand to Alfonso d'Este, Prince of Ferrara. The new bride's sister-in-law, Isabella, delighted in snubs, but Lucrezia now knew the game.

While keeping up appearances, she carried on with Isabella's husband.

After the deaths of Alexander (1503) and then Cesare (1507), Lucrezia could finally settle down. She died on June 24, 1519, at age 39, of complications from childbirth.

Detractors love to paint Lucrezia as a Renaissance floozy who had incestuous relations with her father and brother. It makes lurid reading, but the truth is rather dull and tame. She did have lovers, as did many in her time. Living as a political pawn, can anyone really blame her for having flings?

There's no evidence supporting the incest slander—but there are good reasons to reject it. The rumor likely started with her first husband, who probably spread it because he was angry that the Borgias had alleged that he was impotent. Lucrezia remained fond of her father and brother unto their deaths and mourned both; would she have lamented those who'd traumatized her? Her later life is inconsistent with childhood molestation: She had a healthy love life and was never self-destructive.

Some aspersions were bandied during her life, mainly as weapons against the Borgias. In 1833, Victor Hugo wrote *Lucrèce Borgia,* a play that painted Lucrezia as a princess of poison, reveling in each toxic takedown. This—in addition to the popular Donizetti opera based on Hugo's play—has adhered to the public perception. These works libel a loving woman whose fortunes were dictated by men of limitless greed.

✳ In 2008, Australia's National Gallery of Victoria announced that it believed it had in its collection a painting by Dosso Dossi— and the sitter in the painting was none other than Lucrezia Borgia. The painting had been in the museum's collection for decades but was something of a mystery. Years of careful study have left museum officials confident of their findings. If the museum's claims are backed up by other scholars, this would be the only portrait of Lucrezia Borgia in the world.

Man-Eaters of the Ancient World

*They were the ultimate feminists—powerful, independent
women who formed female-only societies that had no use
for men beyond procreation. They were the epitome of girl
power, fierce mounted warriors who often emasculated
the best male fighters from other societies. They were
the Amazons—man-eaters of the ancient world.*

✳ ✳ ✳ ✳

THE ANCIENT GREEKS were enthralled by the Amazons.
Greek writers, like today's Hollywood gossip columnists,
relished lurid tales of love affairs between Amazon queens and
their Greek boy toys. Others wrote of epic battles between
Amazon warriors and the greatest heroes of Greek mythology.

Given their prominent place in Greek lore, the story of the
Amazons has generally been considered the stuff of legend. But
recent archaeological finds suggest that a race of these warrior
über-women actually did exist.

The Amazons According to the Greeks

History's first mention of the Amazons is found in Homer's
Iliad, written in the 7th or 8th century B.C. Homer told of a
group of women he called Antianeira ("those who fight like
men"), who fought on the side of Troy against the Greeks. They
were led by Penthesilea, who was slain by Achilles. According
to some accounts, Achilles fell in love with her immediately
afterward. Achilles was highly skilled in the art of warfare, but
it seems he was sorely lacking in the intricacies of courtship.

From then on, the Amazons became forever linked with the
ancient Greeks. Their very name is believed to derive from the
Greek *a-mazos*, meaning "without a breast." This referred to the
Amazon practice of removing the right breast of their young
girls so that they would be unencumbered in the use of the bow
and spear. This may have made Greek, Roman, and European

artists a bit squeamish—their depictions of Amazons showed them with two breasts, though the right breast was often covered or hidden.

According to Greek mythology, the Amazons were the offspring of Ares, god of war, who was the son of the mightiest of the Greek gods, Zeus. Though the Amazons may have had Greek roots, they didn't want anything to do with them. Like young adults eager to move from their parents' homes, the Amazons established their realm in a land called Pontus in modern-day northeastern Turkey, where they founded several important cities, including Smyrna.

The Greeks paint a picture of the Amazons as a female-dominated society of man-haters that banned men from living among them. In an odd dichotomy between chastity and promiscuity, sexual encounters with men were taboo except for once a year when the Amazons would choose male partners from the neighboring Gargareans strictly for the purposes of procreation. Female babies were kept; males were killed or sent back with their fathers. Females were raised to do everything a man could do—and to do it better.

Soap Opera Encounters with Greek Heroes

The Greeks and the Amazons interacted in a love-hate relationship. As one of his labors, Hercules had to obtain the girdle of the Amazon queen Hippolyte. He was accompanied in his task by Theseus, who stole Hippolyte's sister Antiope. This led to on-going warfare between the Greeks and Amazons as well as several trysts between members of the two societies. One account has Theseus and Antiope falling in love, with her dying by his side during a battle against the Amazons. Another account has Theseus and Hippolyte becoming lovers. Stories of Hercules have him alternately wooing and warring with various Amazonian women.

Jason and the Argonauts met the Amazons on the island of Lemnos. Completely unaware of the true nature of the island's inhabitants, Jason queried the Amazons as to the whereabouts of their men. They told him their men were all killed in an earlier invasion. What the Argonauts didn't realize was that the Amazons themselves were the killers! The Amazons invited the Argonauts to stay and become their husbands. But Jason and the boys, perhaps intimidated by the appearance of the Amazons in full battle dress, graciously declined and hightailed it off the island.

More than Myth?

The Greek historian Herodotus provides perhaps the best connection of the Greeks to what may be the true race of Amazons. Writing in the 5th century B.C., Herodotus chronicles a group of warrior women who were defeated in battle by the Greeks. These Androktones ("killers of men"), as he called them, were put on a prison ship, where they went about killing the all-male Greek crew. The women then drifted to the north shores of the Black Sea to the land of the Scythians, a nomadic people of Iranian descent.

Here, says Herodotus, they intermarried with the Scythian men on the condition that they be allowed to keep their traditional warrior customs. They added a heartwarming social tenet that no woman could wed until she had killed a man in battle. Together, they migrated northeast across the Russian steppes, eventually evolving into the Sarmatian culture, which featured a prominent role for women hunting and fighting by the sides of their husbands. The men may have given their wives the loving pet name *ha-mazan*, the Iranian word for "warrior."

Though the Amazons are still mostly perceived as myth, recent archaeological discoveries lend credence to Herodotus's account and help elevate the Amazons from the pages of Greek legend to historical fact. Excavations of Sarmatian burial grounds found the majority of those interred there were heavily armed women, all of whom got the very best spots in the site.

The Reich's Favorite Aviatrix

"My parents had shown me as a child the storks in their quiet and steady flight, the buzzards, circling ever higher in the summer air... when I, too, expressed a longing to fly, they took it for a childish fancy... but, the longing... grew with every bird I saw go flying across the azure summer sky, with every cloud that sailed past me on the wind, till it turned to... a yearning that went with me everywhere."

—Hanna Reitsch, The Sky My Kingdom

✳   ✳   ✳   ✳

Hanna Reitsch was born on March 29, 1912, in Hirschberg, a small town in Lower Silesia that was conceded to Poland after World War II. Reitsch's father was an ophthalmologist, her mother a devout Catholic. When she was just a teenager, Reitsch declared that she wanted to become a flying missionary doctor in Africa. Having been obsessed with flying from an early age, the decision marked her ascent as one of the world's most accomplished pilots.

After completing secondary school, Reitsch enrolled in the Grunau School of Gliding. She quickly outpaced her male rivals and became the first member of her class to pass the introductory flying course. Shocked by her rapid progress, school officials forced Reitsch to retake the exam, which she passed again. Reitsch then completed the next two levels of flight courses before beginning medical studies at the University of Berlin.

During the 1930s, Reitsch set many records as a glider pilot; these accomplishments further enhanced her love of flight. In 1931 Reitsch set the women's world record for nonstop glider flying when she remained aloft for 5.5 hours. She extended this record to 11.5 hours in 1933. In 1934 Reitsch set the women's world altitude record when she soared to 2,800 meters.

In the mid-1930s, Reitsch traveled to South America, where she participated in an international study of thermal conditions during flight. She quit medical school after returning to Germany and became a glider test pilot at the German Institute for Glider Research. While at the institute, Reitsch tested the first glider seaplane and naval glider catapults.

Reitsch continued her record-breaking feats throughout the 1930s. In 1936, she set the world record in nonstop distance flight. In 1937, she became the first German to cross the Alps in a glider. She set another world record two years later, this time for the longest point-to-point flight.

Service in the *Luftwaffe*

Reitsch's reputation landed her at the forefront of German aviation development. In 1936 she was introduced to Ernst Udet, head of the Technical Branch of the German Ministry of Aviation. Impressed with her work on the development of air brakes in gliders, Udet appointed Reitsch to the position of civilian test pilot in the *Luftwaffe* the following year.

In February 1938, Reitsch became the first person to fly a helicopter inside a building when she piloted the Focke-Achgelis FW-61 in a demonstration inside the *Deutschlandhalle* during the Berlin Motor Show. In the fall of that year, she traveled overseas to the International Air Races at Cleveland, Ohio, where she demonstrated the Habicht aerobatic glider.

Back in Germany, Reitsch participated in the Messerschmitt Me-361 *Gigant* glider program, which sought to develop a glider capable of carrying cargo, troops, and fuel. But tragedy befell the program: A catastrophic crash resulted in the deaths of the glider's tow-plane pilots, the *Gigant*'s crew, and more than 100 troops aboard. Reitsch was not aboard when the glider crashed, but the project ceased following the accident.

Despite the *Gigant* incident, the *Luftwaffe*'s research branch far outpaced its rivals during the war. In 1942, pilots began testing one of the first single-seat rocket-powered interceptors—the Messerschmitt Me-163 *Komet*. Through her contacts, Reitsch managed to test fly the Me-163A prototype and the Me-163B production model. During a test flight in the 163B, the plane's fall-away wheel carriage did not disengage from the airplane after takeoff. After several attempts to dislodge the dolly, Reitsch was forced to land the plane with the carriage still attached. As she brought the jet fighter down, the plane stalled and crashed. Reitsch suffered severe injuries, including several skull fractures.

Reitsch needed five months to recover from her injuries. The Nazi leadership was sufficiently impressed with her devotion to award her a diamond-encrusted Gold Medal for Military Flying and later, the Iron Cross First Class.

In 1943 Reitsch participated in Operation *Selbstopfer* ("self-sacrifice"). She test flew a cockpit-added V-1 rocket bomb, which was uncoupled in flight from a Heinkel He 111 bomber. The data Reitsch collected helped the project's engineers develop a stabilization system for the V-1 bombs. The Germans planned to eventually send pilots on suicide missions, steering the bombs toward Allied production and communication centers, but that idea was abandoned.

A Final Attempt to Save the *Führer*

On April 25, 1945, Reitsch's longtime friend Field Marshal Robert Ritter von Greim asked Reitsch to accompany him on a flight to see Hitler in Berlin. Hitler had just dismissed *Luftwaffe* head Herman Göring after Göring's attempt to take control of Germany in the war's closing days. The Nazi dictator wanted to appoint Greim as the new commander in chief of the *Luftwaffe*.

The two pilots managed to land a small Fieseler Fi-156C *Storch* on a boulevard near the Brandenburg Gate. In the process, their plane was hit by Russian antiaircraft fire and Greim was seriously wounded in the foot. Reitsch and Greim stayed in the *Führerbunker* for several days, intent on dying alongside Hitler when he refused to fly with them to safety. The Nazi dictator ordered the two to leave the bunker and had an Arado 96 lightweight aircraft delivered from an underground hangar for their use. The two pilots managed to escape. On May 9, Reitsch brought Greim to a hospital in Kitsbuhel, where she was promptly arrested.

Reitsch was interrogated by military-intelligence personnel, who were convinced she had flown Hitler out of Berlin. Reitsch was cleared of war crimes but spent 15 months in prison.

New Records

Following the war, German citizens were forbidden to fly. A few years later, gliding was permitted, and Reitsch resumed her prewar record-setting ways by taking third place in a Spanish gliding championship and later breaking the women's altitude record (6,848 meters). In 1959, she opened a gliding center in India, and in 1961 she was invited to the White House. In 1962, she opened a glider school in Ghana, Africa, where she lived for four years.

As one of the Third Reich's only female test pilots, Reitsch flew everything the Nazis had in their inventory, from the first functional helicopter to the first jet-powered fighter. She set more than 40 flight records, many of them while flying a glider. A devout follower of National Socialism, Reitsch often wore her Nazi medals after the war. She died of a heart attack in Frankfurt in 1979.

✳ Hanna Reitsch test-flew the astonishing Messerschmitt Me-163 *Komet*, a swept-wing rocket plane with a top speed of 596 mph. A one-seat fighter, the *Komet* had an impractically brief flight time of just 7.5 minutes; pilots had to glide back to base. Limited production of the *Komet* began in 1944, but Germany's diminishing resources prevented the plane from becoming a factor in the war.

Killer Queens

When playwright William Congreve wrote,
"Hell hath no fury like a woman scorned,"
he may have had these warrior queens in mind.

✳ ✳ ✳ ✳

Boudicca (A.D. 61)—Nemesis of Nero

S HE STOOD SIX feet tall, sported a hip-length mane of fiery red hair, and had a vengeful streak a mile wide. She was Boudicca, queen of the Celtic Iceni people of eastern Britain. In A.D. 61, she led a furious uprising against the occupying Romans that nearly chased Nero's legions from the island.

Boudicca didn't always hate the Romans. The Iceni kingdom, led by her husband, Prasutagus, was once a Roman ally. But Prasutagus lived a life of conspicuous wealth on borrowed Roman money, and when it came time to pay the piper, he was forced to bequeath half his kingdom to the Romans; the other half was left for his daughters.

The Romans, however, got greedy; on Prasutagus's death, they moved to seize all Iceni lands as payment for the dead king's debt. When the widow Boudicca challenged the Romans, they publicly flogged her and raped her daughters. While most of the Roman army in Britain was busy annihilating the Druids in the west, the scorned Boudicca led the Iceni and other aggrieved Celtic peoples on a bloody rebellion that reverberated all the way back to Rome.

Boudicca's warriors annihilated the vaunted Roman Ninth Legion and laid waste to the Roman cities of Camulodunum (Colchester), Londinium (London), and Verulamium (St. Albans). Boudicca's vengeance knew no bounds and was exacted on both Romans and fellow Britons who supported them. Upwards of 80,000 people fell victim to her wrath.

The Romans were floored by the ferocity of Boudicca's attack, and Nero actually considered withdrawing his army from

Britain. But the Romans regrouped, and later a seasoned force of 1,200 legionnaires trounced Boudicca's 100,000-strong rebel army in a decisive battle. The defeated Boudicca chose suicide by poison over capture.

Today, a statue of the great Boudicca can be found near Westminster Pier in London, testament to the veneration the British still hold for Boudicca as their first heroine.

Empress Jingo (A.D. 169–269)—Persuader of Gods and Men

She led the Japanese in the conquest of Korea in the early 3rd century. In 1881, she became the first woman to be featured on a Japanese banknote—no small feat given the chauvinism of imperial Japan. More than 1,700 years after her rule, Empress Jingo is still revered in Japan.

Perhaps Jingo's success as a warrior queen can be attributed to the irresistible sway she held over both the ancient deities and mortal men. As regent ruler of imperial Japan following the death of her emperor husband, Chuai, Jingo was determined to make Korea her own. According to Japanese lore, she beguiled Ryujin, the Japanese dragon god of the sea, to lend her his magical Tide Jewels, which she used to create favorable tides that destroyed the Korean fleet and safely guided the Japanese fleet to the Korean peninsula. From there, she commanded and cajoled her armies to an illustrious campaign of conquest that secured her exalted status in Japanese history.

Jingo purportedly had amazing powers of persuasion over the human reproductive cycle as well. Pregnant with Chuai's son at the time of the invasion, Jingo remained in Korea for the duration of the campaign, which by all accounts lasted well beyond the length of a normal pregnancy term. Legend has it, however, that she delayed giving birth until after the conquest so that her son and heir, Ojin, could be born in Japan.

Once home, Jingo cemented her power by using brute force to convince several rivals to the throne to concede to her rule, which would last for more than 60 years.

Zenobia (A.D. 274)—
Mistress of the Middle East

Like Boudicca before her, the warrior queen Zenobia made her name by leading an army against the mighty Romans. Unlike the Celtic queen, however, Zenobia would experience a much different fate.

Zenobia and her husband, Odenathus, ruled the prosperous Syrian city of Palmyra. Though technically subordinate to Odenathus, she certainly didn't take a backseat to him. She established herself as a warrior queen by riding at her husband's side into battle against the Persians—often overshadowing her more reserved mate by shouting loud battle cries, walking for miles within the ranks of the foot soldiers, and drinking the boys under the table in victory celebrations.

Zenobia became the undisputed ruler of Palmyra in 267 following the assassination of Odenathus (which some attribute to Zenobia herself). As an ostensible ally of Rome, Zenobia launched a campaign of conquest in the Middle East, leading, walking, and drinking with her men as always. Within three years she expanded her realm to Syria, Egypt, and much of Asia Minor.

Flushed with success, Zenobia declared Palmyra's independence from Rome. But in 272, the Romans struck back. Zenobia was up for the fight, but her forces were overextended. The Romans easily recaptured Zenobia's outlying territories before laying siege to Palmyra itself.

After its fall, Palmyra was destroyed, and Zenobia was captured. She was taken to Rome and paraded in golden chains before Emperor Aurelian. But even in defeat, Zenobia triumphed. The striking beauty with the defiant stride struck a chord with Aurelian, who later pardoned her and allowed her to live a life of luxury on an estate outside Rome.

Aethelflaed (A.D. 869–918)—"Noble Beauty" of the Anglo-Saxons

In England at the beginning of the 10th century, the Anglo kingdom of Wessex and the Saxon kingdom of Mercia were both under siege by the Danish Vikings. The cocksure Vikings were confident of victory, but they hadn't counted on the rise of the Mercian queen, Aethelflaed (her name means "noble beauty"), who would earn her warrior reputation by leading her armies in victory over the Vikings and emerging as one of Britain's most powerful rulers.

Aethelflaed's father, Alfred the Great, was king of Wessex. Aethelflaed, at age 15, married the Mercian nobleman Ethelred, thus forming a strategic alliance of the two kingdoms against the Vikings. Her first fight against the Vikings occurred on her wedding day, when the Norsemen tried to kill her to prevent the nuptial and political union. Aethelflaed took up the sword and fought alongside her guards while holed up in an old trench, eventually driving the Vikings away.

From then on, battling Vikings became old hat for Aethelflaed. When her husband died in 911, she assumed sole rule of Mercia and began taking the fight to the Vikings. Perhaps remembering her wedding-day experience in the trench, she built formidable fortifications to defend Mercia. She also used exceptional diplomatic skills to form alliances against the Vikings. By the time of her death in 918, she had led her armies in several victories over the Vikings, had them begging for peace, and had extended her power in Britain.

Aethelflaed made her name as a Viking killer, but her most important legacy was her success in sustaining the union of the Angles and the Saxons, which would later germinate into the English nation.

Jezebel—Pagan Priestess or Manipulative Minx?

There are more seductresses, fallen women, temptresses, adulteresses, and manipulative minxes in the Old Testament than in the steamiest television soap opera yet written. None, however, suffered so cruel a fate nor are still so reviled as Jezebel.

✳   ✳   ✳   ✳

JEZEBEL MAKES HER first appearance in the Bible in the First Book of Kings, Chapter 16, Verse 31, when Ahab, king of Israel "also took to wife Jezebel, daughter of Ethbaal, king of the Sidonians." One of Jezebel's first acts as queen was to convince her husband to "rear up an altar for Ba'al," the god of her people, and to join her in worshipping him. In so doing, as the Bible says, "Ahab did more to provoke the Lord God of Israel to anger than all the kings of Israel that were before him."

That is no small accomplishment, considering the sins of Ahab's predecessors and the short temper of the frequently wrathful God they served. Jezebel, of course, gets the blame for her husband's fall from grace, even though initially all she was guilty of was convincing the king to come along with her to the ancient equivalent of Sunday services.

A Phoenician people from what is now southern Lebanon, the inhabitants of Sidon had worshipped the god Ba'al for at least a thousand years before the Israelites wandered into the land of Canaan. Assyrians, Babylonians, and Egyptians had each in turn conquered Sidon (which still exists and lies just 25 miles south of Beirut). While other gods came and went with the occupying armies, Ba'al remained in the hearts and devotions of the Sidonians.

Jezebel brought that devotion with her, which in hindsight was not a particularly wise or politically correct thing to do in the land of the Chosen People. Damned and challenged by the holy men of Israel for what they saw as her idolatry, she responded by convincing her husband to cut off their heads. As "Jezebel slew the prophets of Israel," so the Bible reports, she also imported some 450 priests of Ba'al—along with another 400 "prophets of the groves," caretakers of outdoor arboreal shrines where pagans gathered to dance, sing, party, and participate in lewd rituals.

Making an Enemy of a Prophet

This attempt to suborn the faith of the nation of Israel, turn their king away from God, and undermine the power of the religious elite brought Jezebel into direct confrontation with Elijah, arguably the "most valuable player" to ever carry a staff in the league of prophets.

Elijah and Jezebel battled for the soul and purse of Israel for some 20 years, their fight marked by tornadoes, earthquakes, and fires that the Lord God of Hosts brought down upon pagan sites. Even so, at first, things went Jezebel's way, thanks to her ability to get the king to do as she wished. As is written in 1 Kings 25: "There was none like unto Ahab, which did sell himself to work wickedness in the sight of the Lord, whom Jezebel his wife stirred up."

Ahab, however, began to repent, and for a time "put sackcloth upon his flesh and fasted." Soon after that, he died in battle. Jezebel continued to fight on through Ahab's son and heir Ahaziah, who as king of Israel, the Bible says "walked in the way of his father, and in the way of his mother." Ahaziah "made Israel to sin," notes the Book of Kings, "served Ba'al, and worshipped him, and provoked to anger the Lord God of Israel."

That anger was made manifest in the hero, Jehu. As the country devolved into revolt and civil war, Jehu arose, and in an epic chariot-to-chariot duel was able to "smite" the idolatrous king. The victorious Jehu then rode into Jerusalem, came to the palace as Jezebel was painting her face, and ordered the queen's servants to "throw her down." They dutifully tossed her out the window, makeup and all. Her "blood was sprinkled on the wall and on the horses" as she fell, or so the Bible records. Trampled by Jehu's chariot horses for good measure, her body was then consumed by dogs—which left "no more of her than the skull and the feet, and the palms of her hands."

Ever since her bloody demise, the pagan queen who was devoured by dogs in the street has been held up as a cautionary figure to warn men and women alike of the danger and eventual fate of femme fatales who use their sexual power to seduce the righteous and lead them astray. The lesson and legend of Jezebel has been and continues to be reinforced and perpetuated by literature, religious tracts, film, and music. The very name Jezebel has become a powerful marketing tool and literary device used to conjure up the image of the coquette, the seductress, the insatiable demonic spirit made supple flesh to sow discord among men. An impressive, if unflattering, legacy for a Phoenician princess from south Lebanon.

"For most of history, Anonymous was a woman."

—VIRGINIA WOOLF

"The very ink with which history is written is merely fluid prejudice."

—MARK TWAIN

"Historians are gossips who tease the dead."

—VOLTAIRE

Ms. President?

When Victoria Woodhull ran for president in 1872, some called her a witch, others said she was a prostitute. The idea of a woman even casting a vote for president was considered scandalous—which may explain why Woodhull spent election night in jail.

✳ ✳ ✳ ✳

KNOWN FOR HER passionate speeches and fearless attitude, Victoria Woodhull became a trailblazer for women's rights. Woodhull advocated revolutionary ideas, including gender equality and women's voting rights. "Women are the equals of men before the law and are equal in all their rights," she said. America, however, wasn't ready to accept her "radical" ideas.

Woodhull was born in 1838 in Homer, Ohio, the seventh child of Annie and Buck Claflin. Her deeply spiritual mother often took little Victoria along to revival camps where people would speak in tongues. Her mother also dabbled in clairvoyance, and Victoria and her younger sister Tennessee believed they had a gift for it as well. With so many chores to do at home (washing, ironing, chipping wood, and cooking), Victoria only attended school sporadically and was primarily self-educated.

Soon after the family left Homer, a 28-year-old doctor named Canning Woodhull asked the 15-year-old Victoria for her hand in marriage. The marriage was no paradise for Victoria, who soon realized her husband was an alcoholic. She experienced more heartbreak when her son, Byron, was born with a mental disability. While she remained married to Canning, Victoria spent the next few years touring as a clairvoyant with her sister Tennessee. At that time, it was difficult for a woman to pursue divorce, but Victoria finally divorced her husband in 1864. Two years later she married Colonel James Blood, a Civil War veteran who believed in free love.

In 1866, Victoria and James moved to New York City. Spiritualism was then in vogue, and Victoria and Tennessee established a salon where they acted as clairvoyants and engaged in political discussions with their clientele. Among their first customers was Cornelius Vanderbilt, the wealthiest man in America.

A close relationship sprang up between Vanderbilt and the two attractive and intelligent young women. He advised them on business matters and gave them stock tips. When the stock market crashed in September 1869, Woodhull made a bundle buying instead of selling during the ensuing panic. That winter, she and Tennessee opened their own brokerage business. They were the first female stockbrokers in American history.

Aiming High

Woodhull had more far-reaching ambitions, however. On April 2, 1870, she announced that she was running for president. In conjunction with her presidential bid, Woodhull and her sister started a newspaper, *Woodhull & Claflin's Weekly*, which highlighted women's issues. It was another breakthrough for the two since they were the first women to ever publish a weekly newspaper.

That was followed by another milestone: On January 11, 1871, Woodhull became the first woman ever to speak before a congressional committee. As she spoke before the House Judiciary Committee, she asked that Congress change its stance on whether women could vote. Woodhull's reasoning was elegant in its simplicity. She was not advocating a new constitutional amendment granting women the right to vote. Instead, she reasoned, women already had that right. The Fourteenth Amendment says that, "All persons born or naturalized in the United States ... are citizens of the Unites States." Since voting is part of the definition of being a citizen, Woodhull argued, women, in fact, already possessed the right to vote. Woodhull, a persuasive speaker, actually swayed some congressmen to her point of view; the committee chairman, however, remained hostile to the idea of women's rights and made sure the issue never came to a floor vote.

Woodhull had better luck with the suffragists. In May 1872, before 668 delegates from 22 states, Woodhull was chosen as the presidential candidate of the Equal Rights Party; she was the first woman ever chosen by a political party to run for president. But her presidential bid soon foundered. Woodhull was on record as an advocate of free love, which opponents argued was an attack on the institution of marriage.

That year, Woodhull caused an uproar when her newspaper ran an exposé about the infidelities of Reverend Henry Ward Beecher. Woodhull and her sister were thrown in jail and accused of publishing libel and promoting obscenity. They would spend election night of 1872 behind bars as Ulysses Grant defeated Horace Greeley for the presidency.

Woodhull was eventually cleared of the charges against her (the claims against Beecher were proven true), but hefty legal bills and a downturn in the stock market left her impoverished and embittered. She moved to England in 1877, shortly after divorcing Colonel Blood. By the turn of the century she had become wealthy once more, this time by marriage to a British banker. Fascinated by technology, she joined the Ladies Automobile Club, where her passion for automobiles led Woodhull to one last milestone: In her sixties, she and her daughter Zula became the first women to drive through the English countryside.

✳ The Equal Rights Party was also the first to nominate a black man for vice president. They selected Frederick Douglass, but he declined the offer.

Words for the Ages

"It will be years—not in my time—before a woman will become Prime Minister."

—MARGARET THATCHER

"Would the world ever have been made if its maker had been afraid of making trouble? Making life means making trouble."

—GEORGE BERNARD SHAW

"Bear in mind this sacred principle, that though the will of the majority is in all cases to prevail . . . the minority possess their equal rights, which equal law must protect, and to violate would be oppression."

—FROM THOMAS JEFFERSON'S 1801 INAUGURAL ADDRESS

"No one can make you feel inferior without your consent."

—ELEANOR ROOSEVELT

"Ours has been the first, and doubtless to be the last, to visit this profitless locality."

—LIEUTENANT JOSEPH IVES, AFTER VISITING THE GRAND CANYON, 1861

"No matter what happens, the U.S. Navy is not going to be caught napping."

—SECRETARY OF THE NAVY FRANK KNOX, DECEMBER 4, 1941

"Aeroplanes are interesting toys but of no military value."

—MARSHAL FERDINAND FOCH, FRENCH MILITARY STRATEGIST, 1911

"With over 50 foreign cars already on sale here, the Japanese auto industry isn't likely to carve out a big slice of the U.S. market."

—BUSINESS WEEK MAGAZINE, 1968

"A few decades hence, energy may be free, just like unmetered air."

—JOHN VON NEUMANN, PHYSICIST, TOP MEMBER OF THE MANHATTAN PROJECT, 1956

"Grief can take care of itself, but to get the full value of joy you must have somebody to divide it with."

—MARK TWAIN

Catherine de' Medici

Speculation still swirls around the life of this memorable queen.

✳ ✳ ✳ ✳

✳ The daughter of Lorenzo the "Magnificent" and a French princess, Catherine was orphaned as an infant. Her mother died 15 days after Catherine's birth, and her father died six days later.

✳ The Medicis were overthrown in Florence when Catherine was eight years old, and she was taken hostage and moved from convent to convent around the city. She was often threatened with death or with life in a brothel to ruin her value as a bride.

✳ As was common at the time, Catherine was only 14 when she married. The match was arranged by her uncle, Pope Clement VII, and Henri's father, François I, king of France.

✳ Catherine spent her married life overlooked in favor of Henri's lifelong mistress, Diane de Poiters, the Duchesse de Valentinois. Even at Catherine's coronation, Diane was publicly honored as well.

✳ Henri and Catherine didn't have children for the first ten years of their union, but at the insistence of Diane, the couple finally consummated their marriage. They eventually had ten children.

✳ Catherine supposedly saw a vision of Henri's death days before it happened. She begged him not to joust at the tournament held in celebration of their daughter Elisabeth's marriage to Philip II of Spain. He did so anyway and died from an eye infection caused by a splinter from a broken lance.

✳ After Henri died, Catherine wore mourning clothes for the rest of her life. She also took a broken lance as her emblem, bearing the motto "From this come my tears and my pain."

* Once out from under Henri's and Diane's influence, Catherine spread her wings and began to exercise control over her children—in fact, she dominated them. She ruled France as regent during the minority of Charles IX (and continued to rule during his adulthood, though as the king's "advisor" rather than regent), and Henri III relied heavily on her throughout his reign.

* The Medici family, though very wealthy, was a merchant family rather than nobility. Catherine was reviled by many of the French because she was thought to be a commoner and, therefore, in their eyes, unfit to be queen of France.

* Despite her reputation as a persecutor of Protestants, Catherine actually tried to compromise between the Catholic and Protestant factions. She made concessions to Protestants, allowing them to worship their own way in private, but war broke out nonetheless.

* Though she is often blamed for the St. Bartholomew's Day Massacre, it is not known what role Catherine played in the disaster. Some historians believe she intended it only to be a culling of Protestant nobles who had been leaders against her in the religious wars, but the situation got out of control.

* Among Catherine's ten children were three kings of France (François II, Charles IX, and Henri III, respectively) and two queens: Margaret, called Margot, married Henri of Navarre, and Elisabeth became Queen of Spain.

* François II, Catherine's eldest son, was married to Mary, Queen of Scots.

* Tragically, Catherine's large brood turned out to be sickly, and she outlived all but two of her ten children. Three had died in infancy, and only Henri and Margot were still alive when Catherine died.

Witches to the Gallows

In 1692, the quiet little town of Salem Village, Massachusetts, convulsed in the grip of witchcraft.

✳ ✳ ✳ ✳

IN THE EARLY 1690s, Salem Village, a small Massachusetts town on the Danvers River, was experiencing growing pains: It was making the transition from farming community to mercantile center; a violent Indian war raged less than 100 miles away; and poor harvests and disease frequently threatened the Puritans who lived there. The community weathered a rough winter in early 1692, and as spring approached, odd behavior among some local children began to frighten the adults.

In February 1692, nine-year-old Betty Parris, the daughter of a preacher brought in from Boston, began acting wildly. She ran about screaming, dove under furniture, contorted in pain, and complained of fever. There was no obvious explanation for Betty's condition, but a local minister named Cotton Mather thought he had found one: Betty was a victim of witchcraft. When two of Betty's playmates showed similar symptoms and local medicines failed to cure them, the townspeople drew the only logical conclusion: There was a witch in their midst.

Suspicion first fell on a Caribbean slave named Tituba, who worked in Betty's home. Tituba had been known to tell the children stories of voodoo, and when Tituba was caught trying to cure Betty by feeding a "devil cake" to a dog (dogs being common forms of demons), Tituba's guilt seemed certain.

The hunt for Salem's witches took a new turn when the afflicted girls, now seven in all, began accusing other local women of sending evil spirits against them. Tituba and two others were hauled into Ingersoll's Tavern on March 1 and examined by local magistrates. Thoroughly frightened, Tituba confessed to being a witch.

Tituba's confession lit a powder keg that would claim the lives of 19 men and women before it was over. Four more women, along with the four-year-old daughter of one of the accused, were collectively charged with sending spirits to torment their accusers. The young accusers grew more theatrical in their stories, and during the next several months, they and other witnesses identified some 200 townspeople as witches, all of whom were thrown into jail.

Wild Accusations

Panic spread. To get a handle on the growing alarm, Governor William Phips commissioned a seven-judge court to try those accused of witchcraft, a capital offense under Massachusetts law. At Reverend Mather's urging, the court admitted "spectral evidence"—testimony that an accuser had seen the ghostly specter of a witch—as well as evidence of "witch's teats," moles on a defendant's body on which a familiar spirit, such as a black cat, might suckle. The judges found the evidence persuasive.

Armed with this compelling evidence, the court had no choice but to execute the newly discovered witches. Between June 10 and September 22, nearly 20 individuals (one of whom was the village's ex-minister) were carted off to Gallows Hill and hanged. One 80-year-old man who refused to participate in his trial was punished by pressing, a gruesome execution method in which the sheriff placed large stones on the man's chest until he expired. Four others died in prison, and two dogs were executed as accomplices to witchcraft.

By August, the town's mania began to subside. Cooler-headed villagers questioned the fantastic evidence against the accused, and in May 1693, Governor Phips shut down the proceedings and freed all the remaining defendants. One judge made a public apology for sentencing so many to death, and several jurors admitted that they had been horribly misled by juvenile actors, hysterical townspeople, and fanatical judges.

High Priestess of the Cult of Peronismo

Long before cinema and media drama brought her back into North American eyes, the woman many called "Santa Evita" was a legend in her native land. Her memory now casts a shadow larger than life, which makes it hard to believe that she held influence for less than ten years and didn't live to be 35.

✳ ✳ ✳ ✳

Is it "Eva" or "Evita"?

Eva liked the familiar version, which translates roughly to "Evie." It's like calling Lady Diana "Di."

What do we know about Evita's origin?

Eva María Ibarguren breathed her first on May 7, 1919, in Los Toldos, Argentina. Her mother, Juana, was involved with married estate manager Juan Duarte. Juana adopted Juan's last name for herself and her kids, but he soon went back to his wife in another town. When he died, Juana insisted on attending his funeral—scandalous, but the move hints at the origin of Evita's own strength and bravery. Juana's family endured small-town whispers, breeding in young Eva much contempt for the stratified Argentine social order.

How did Evita find her way to greater things?

Early on, Evita was a thin, quiet, often truant girl. Acting in a school play convinced her she wanted a career in show business, so she headed to Buenos Aires. She was a hit at theater, movies, and radio acting, making herself one of Argentina's best-paid actresses by 1943. Her stage presence and sense of public opinion would come in handy later in life.

Then came Juan Perón.

Argentina, theoretically democratic, was ruled by a series of oligarchies. Some were better, some worse, some in between. El coronel and widower Juan Domingo Perón was an influential soldier involved in politics, normal for the Argentine military of the day. In 1944, with Perón serving in the military government, an Andean earthquake devastated San Juan. Perón organized a benefit performance, and there he met Evita Duarte.

Fireworks?

For both. She soon moved in with him; their mutual love shows in all they did.

And that brought her into politics?

Evita left acting to lend her influential voice to peronismo, a cultlike mix of populism, nationalism, and authoritarianism. In effect, she became its high priestess.

So, Perón vaulted her into power?

Or perhaps Evita vaulted Perón into a position of power. Evita Duarte was influential independent of and before Juan Perón; he didn't make her. They were a mutually complementary political dream team.

When did Evita become Señora Dictator?

Perón's government enemies arrested him in October 1945. The peronista masses rallied, and the ruling junta yielded in time to save itself. Reunited with his jubilant partner, Juan planned to run for president. One problem: They were still living in sin. Evita became Señora Eva Duarte de Perón in a private civil ceremony. On June 4, 1946, Perón was elected president of Argentina.

Good deal for Evita?

Yes—but it also polarized perceptions of her. Argentina knew her well from Juan's campaign trail. To peronistas, Evita was the caring face of the movement. For anti-peronistas (now keeping low profiles), she was the upstart soap opera harlot, living high on the hog.

Which is more accurate?

The space between the extremes called her a "strong, smart woman." She did live far better than the impoverished descamisados ("shirtless") she championed. Monastic heads of state, or spouses of same, are rare anywhere. But she was wealthy and popular before peronismo, and her affinity for the downtrodden rings genuine given her upbringing. By building her husband's personality cult, she built her own. She held a political religion in the palm of her hand, and she learned to wield it with gutsy skill.

What else did she do?

Argentine women got the vote in 1947. ¿Coincidencia o Evita?

In 1947, she also toured Europe, beginning with Franco's Spain. When the British didn't treat her visit as equal to one by Eleanor Roosevelt, Evita snubbed the U.K. Peronistas swelled with patriotism to see their defiant heroine on the world stage. Evita also founded a charity and a women's political party. By 1951, however, uterine cancer had begun to sap her strength.

Could the disease have been arrested if caught sooner?

Only Evita herself could tell us when she first felt something was wrong, but the physical impact is documented as early as 1950. By the time she underwent chemo and a radical hysterectomy, it was far too late. On July 26, 1952, Eva María Duarte de Perón, now anointed "Spiritual Leader of the Nation," passed from life to legend. Argentina wept bitter tears for her.

I heard that it didn't end with her death—some ghoulish story about embalming and a lost corpse. What really occurred?

Soon after she died, an embalmer did an outstanding job preserving Evita. She was supposed to be exhibited under glass in perpetuity, like Lenin. However, in 1955, a military coup booted Juan out of office—and out of Argentina. Peronismo was proscribed. Evita's body vanished.

Turns out she was interred in Milan, Italy, under an assumed name. In 1971, Evita was exhumed and sent to Juan's Spanish exile house, which in itself is a little macabre: "Excuse me, *Señor*, but that is my wife, not a coffee table." In 1973, Perón returned to Argentina to fan the *peronista* coals into a presidency. After his death in 1974, Evita Perón was reinterred in the securest possible crypt.

The heroine lay at last in the only true place that could give her rest: Argentina.

More on Evita

* Perón's first wife also died of uterine cancer.

* So far as we know, Evita never said, "Don't cry for me, Argentina." Hollywood put the words in her mouth. Since Evita began as an actress and camouflaged her own history, it's fitting that Hollywood embossed her on American pop culture with a mythical line.

* Interesting linguistic twist: *evitar* can mean "to avoid," "to prevent," or "to shun." Evita could thus be read "she avoids." We see it in the English word "inevitable." It's amusing because the only thing Evita definitely avoided was letting the truth come out about her childhood. She even had her birth certificate removed from the official files.

* Hollywood got it wrong; Evita didn't orchestrate the massive demonstrations for Perón's 1945 release. However, the swiftness and energy of the peronista demonstrations in Juan's favor owed plenty to Evita's past contributions to his image.

* In 1947, *TIME* magazine alleged (correctly) that Evita was illegitimate. This act of lèse-majesté got *TIME* banned from Argentina for months.

Her Maligned Majesty, Marie

"Let them eat cake." Most people recognize this dismissive remark as a slight uttered by the supremely snooty Marie Antoinette. As it turns out, she didn't say it.

✳ ✳ ✳ ✳

I T'S 1789, AND the French Revolution is under way. Peasants are rioting in the streets, protesting a shortage of bread. Their queen, Marie Antoinette, not only ignores their hungry cries but flippantly feeds them a wisecrack. If there's no bread to be found, her haughtiness reasons, "Let them eat cake."

In French, the original quote is *"Qu'ils mangent de la brioche,"* in reference to a type of bread characterized by a sweet flavor and flaky texture. Perhaps the queen was simply suggesting that her subjects not limit themselves to their usual staple and that they consider other forms of sustenance—like, well, *fancy* bread.

In fact, historians maintain that the line had nothing to do with the queen. Records show that it had been used in print to highlight aristocratic abuses since at least 1760. Philosopher Jean-Jacques Rousseau (who died more than a decade before the French Revolution began) claimed to have heard it as early as 1740.

Even if such evidence didn't exist, the utterance of such a remark seems out of character for Marie Antoinette. According to biographer Lady Antonia Fraser, the queen had faults, but she wasn't tactless. "It was a callous and ignorant statement," explains Fraser, "and she [Marie Antoinette] was neither." Fraser believes the remark was actually made by Queen Marie Thérèse (wife of Louis XIV) nearly a century before the revolution.

So why is the remark attributed to Marie Antoinette? Most historians blame propaganda. During the revolution, turning people against the queen was almost sport, and Marie endured plenty of scorn in the days leading up to her beheading in 1793.

From Cotton Field to Magnificent Mansion

Born to former slaves and hit hard by fate, this ambitious woman became a cosmetics queen and devoted herself to African American affairs.

❋ ❋ ❋ ❋

DECADES BEFORE A woman named Oprah Winfrey arrived on the scene, an African American woman built a highly impressive business empire. Like Oprah, she used much of that wealth in the service of good causes. But Madam C. J. Walker did this at a time when segregation was the law of much of the land, and economic opportunities for African Americans—let alone African American women—were practically nonexistent.

A Louisiana native, Madam was born to former slaves in 1867 and named Sarah Breedlove. She had a crushingly hard early life, picking cotton as a little girl and finding herself orphaned by the time she was seven. Sarah married at 14, and by 20 she was a widow with a young daughter.

Sarah moved to St. Louis, where she labored as a laundress and cook. A mysterious scalp ailment that left her bald inspired her to develop a restorative compound she dubbed "Madam Walker's Wonderful Hair Grower" (she'd taken the name "Madam C. J. Walker" after marrying a man named Charles Walker). A carefully recruited network of African American saleswomen distributed the product door-to-door and helped make Madam's enterprise a huge success.

In 1910, Walker established a factory in Indianapolis to manufacture the hair grower and other cosmetics. By 1917, Walker's company had assets of a million dollars—a huge sum at the time and an unprecedented achievement for someone of her background.

Philanthropist

Walker built a townhouse in New York City's Harlem neighborhood and a magnificent estate, Villa Lewaro, in suburban Westchester County. But Madam Walker was a philanthropist as well as an entrepreneur. She gave generous financial support to organizations devoted to improving the lives of her fellow African Americans—including the newly founded National Association for the Advancement of Colored People (NAACP).

Her influence went beyond just giving money: She traveled to the White House as part of a delegation protesting lynching in the South, and she regularly hosted the leading African American intellectuals and activists of the day.

Madam Walker died on May 25, 1919. In her words, "There is no royal, flower-strewn road to success, and what success I have obtained is the result of many sleepless nights and real hard work."

"I am a woman who came from the cotton fields of the South. From there I was promoted to the washtub. From there I was promoted to the cook kitchen. And from there I promoted myself into the business of manufacturing hair goods and preparations . . . I have built my own factory on my own ground."

—Madam Walker, National Negro Business
League Convention, July 1912

Sarah Emma Edmonds (aka Frank Thompson)

This patriotic and devoted woman was determined to fight for her country—even if it meant posing as a man.

✳   ✳   ✳   ✳

URING THE CIVIL War, women, their hearts full of worry and sorrow, watched their husbands, brothers, and sons march away to the battlefield. While such emotional partings were difficult, some women also felt deep regret that they couldn't suit up to defend their country as well. The life of the average woman in the 1860s was one of restrictions and clearly defined gender roles: They were to maintain the home and raise the children. Joining the military certainly was not an option. Still, as many as 400 women snuck into brigades from both North and South by posing as male soldiers. Some successfully maintained their disguise, while others were discovered and discharged for "sexual incompatibility." These female soldiers were trailblazers who put their lives on the line for their beliefs.

Sarah Emma Edmonds, born in 1841, believed that everyone should have the chance to fight for freedom and liberty—no matter what their gender. By age 17, she had already proven herself bold and willing to buck convention, fleeing her home in New Brunswick, Canada, to escape her overbearing father. She stole away in the night to create a new, unencumbered life for herself in the United States, settling in Flint, Michigan.

Starting Over

Edmonds knew that if she was going to experience the world in the way she wished, she'd have to reinvent herself entirely. As a woman, she could never fulfill her dreams of adventure—too many doors were closed to her on the basis of gender. But she believed those doors would open if she could become a man. Discarding the identity of Sarah Emma Edmonds, she became

Franklin Thompson, a book salesman. Dressed as a man and acting with assertiveness and confidence, she was soon able to support herself independently. Edmonds saw America as a land of unlimited potential, and she was determined to make the most of it.

When war broke out, Edmonds saw another opportunity to prove her mettle and joined up with a Michigan infantry as a male nurse and courier. "I am naturally fond of adventure," she later explained, "a little ambitious and a good deal romantic and this together with my devotion to the Federal cause and determination to assist to the utmost of my ability in crushing the rebellion, made me forget the unpleasant items."

Upping the Ante

Posing as Franklin Thompson, Edmonds blended in with the men of her unit, served admirably, and aroused no suspicions during her tour of duty. Since her disguise seemed to be working so well, she volunteered to spy for General George McClellan at the start of the Peninsula Campaign. Edmonds continued to be effective in her use of disguises. She infiltrated the Confederates at Yorktown as a black slave by darkening her skin with silver nitrate and wearing a wig. After several days there, she returned to McClellan and shared the information she had gained. Edmonds's next assignment found her portraying a heavyset Irish woman named Bridget O'Shea. As O'Shea, she crossed enemy lines, peddled her wares, and returned with an earful of Confederate secrets. In August 1862, Edmonds assumed the guise of a black laundress in a Confederate camp. One day, while washing an officer's jacket, she found a large packet of official papers. After giving the jacket a thorough "dry cleaning," Edmonds returned to Union camp with the packet.

The Game's Up

All this time, army officials continued to believe Edmonds was Franklin Thompson. In the spring of 1863, she contracted malaria. She knew that she couldn't visit an army hospital for fear of being found out as a woman. She reluctantly slipped away to Cairo, Illinois, and checked into a private hospital. Although Edmonds had planned to return to her previous duty after her recovery, she discovered that during her sickness her alias, Private Thompson, had been pegged as a deserter. Edmonds couldn't reassume that identity without facing the consequences, and so she remained dressed as a woman and served as a nurse to soldiers in Washington, D.C.

After the Fighting Stopped

Two years after the Civil War ended, she married Linus Seelye, a fellow Canadian expatriate. The couple eventually settled down in Cleveland, Ohio. Determined that the world know her story and see that a woman could fight just as well as a man, she wrote the best-selling *Nurse and Spy in the Union Army*, which exposed her gender-bending ways. She also fought hard for her alter ego, petitioning the War Department to expunge Frank Thompson's listing as a deserter. Following a War Department review of the case, Congress granted her service credit and a veteran's pension of $12 a month in 1884. She died five years later and was buried in the military section of a Houston cemetery.

---

* Military unit patches were not authorized by the U.S. Army for general use until 1918, but in 1862 General Philip Kearney ordered badges made of square pieces of cloth be worn on caps. General Joseph Hooker took it further by assigning different colors to the divisions within each corps. The 24th Corps wore heart-shape patches similar to what the unit wears today.

* Lincoln had Congressman Clement Vallandigham, a leading Copperhead, arrested, tried for treason, and thrown into a military prison for his antiwar activities, which included encouraging soldiers to desert and to avoid conscription. He was arrested during his campaign for the Ohio governorship. Lincoln changed the prison sentence to banishment behind Confederate lines after other politicians protested on Vallandigham's behalf.

Oh the Calamity!

You probably know her from the HBO series Deadwood. *But what's the real story behind Wild Bill Hickok's gal pal? And how did she get that nickname?*

✳ ✳ ✳ ✳

S HE SWORE. SHE drank. She was an expert rider and handy with a gun. She scouted for the army. She mined for gold. She wore pants. She did just about everything that 19th-century American women weren't supposed to do. But Calamity Jane got away with it—and became a Wild West legend.

As with most of the legendary figures of the Wild West, it's hard to separate fact from fiction when it comes to Calamity Jane. We don't even know her real birth date. What we *do* know is that she was born Martha Jane Canary in Missouri, probably in 1852. Orphaned not long after her family left Missouri for the Montana Territory, teenage Martha turned to prostitution—a trade she'd ply occasionally throughout her life.

Over the next decade or so, Martha drifted through the mining camps and army posts of the West, where she earned the respect of her masculine peers by showing that she could do anything a man could do—and in some cases, do it better. A heavy drinker, Calamity was thrown into various frontier jails for disturbing the peace.

She first started wearing men's clothes while scouting and carrying messages for the army during the Indian campaigns of the early 1870s. She won the name "Calamity Jane" when she rode to the rescue of an officer caught in an ambush—he declared that she'd saved him from "a calamity." (Though some say her moniker came from her threat that if any man messed with her, "it would be a calamity" for him.)

Welcome to Deadwood

Around 1876, Calamity landed in Deadwood, South Dakota, where she developed a serious crush on the handsome gun-slinger Wild Bill Hickok. Later in life, she claimed they'd been married and had a child together, but they were probably just "friends." She stayed in Deadwood after Hickok caught a bullet during a poker game. A couple of years later, tough Calamity showed her tender side by nursing victims of a smallpox epidemic that swept the town.

By then, word of this crossdressing hell-raiser had reached the publishers back East who were busy churning out dime novels to satisfy the public's taste for tales of Western derring-do. Calamity Jane quickly became a recurring character in these outlandish fictions. She was usually described as a beautiful woman; in illustrations, her baggy trousers mysteriously turned into skin-tight leggings. Photographs of Calamity don't exactly bear out this image.

It was all downhill from there for Calamity. She resumed drifting around the West, married briefly, and in the 1890s she toured the country with Buffalo Bill's famous Wild West Show. She got fired for drinking and ultimately died in poverty in 1903. But she gets to spend eternity with Wild Bill; as per her deathbed request, she's buried next to him in Deadwood's cemetery.

※ During her brief stint as a married woman, Calamity Jane is said to have given birth to a daughter, who was given up for adoption.

※ Calamity Jane allegedly penned an autobiography, *The Life and Adventures of Calamity Jane,* in 1896. Some sources speculate that the book was actually written by a ghostwriter.

11 Renowned Women of the Wild West

Perhaps no other time in America's history is as steeped in myth, legend, and adventure as the pioneering age of the "Wild West." Outlaws, lawmen, cowboys, American Indians, miners, ranchers, and more than a few "ladies of ill repute" emerged in this era, from 1865 to 1900. Any female settler in the West was a heroine in her own right, but listed here are a few of the more famous (and infamous) women of this intriguing period.

✳ ✳ ✳ ✳

1. **Annie Oakley:** Probably the best-known woman of the Wild West, Annie Oakley was born Phoebe Ann Oakley Moses in Dark County, Ohio, in 1860, and she was shooting like a pro by age 12. Germany's Kaiser Wilhelm II trusted her with a gun so much that he let her shoot the ash off his cigarette while he smoked it. Oakley is the only woman of the Wild West to have a Broadway musical loosely based on her life (*Annie Get Your Gun*), which depicts her stint in Buffalo Bill's famous traveling show. When she joined the show, Bill touted her as "Champion Markswoman." When she died in 1926, it was discovered that her entire fortune had been spent on various charities, including women's rights and children's services.

2. **Belle Starr:** Myra Maybelle Shirley was born in Carthage, Missouri, in 1848. Frank and Jesse James's gang hid out at her family's farm when she was a kid, and from then on she was hooked on the outlaw life. Later, when her husband Jim Reed shot a man, the two went on the run, robbing

banks and counterfeiting. Reed was killed in 1874, and Belle married Sam Starr in 1880. Belle, who was known to wear feathers in her hair, buckskins, and a pistol on each hip, was shot in the back while riding her horse in 1889. It's still unclear whether her death was an accident or murder.

3. **Charley Parkhurst:** Times were rough for ladies in the Wild West, so this crackerjack stagecoach driver decided to live most of her life as a man. Born Charlotte Darkey Parkhurst in 1812, she lived well into her sixties, in spite of being a hard-drinking, tobacco-chewing, fearless, one-eyed brute. She drove stages (not an easy or particularly safe career) for Wells Fargo and the California Stage Company. Using her secret identity, Parkhurst was a registered voter and may have been the first American woman to cast a ballot. She lived out her later years raising cattle and chickens. After she died in 1879, her true identity was revealed, much to the surprise of her friends.

4. **Josephine Sarah Marcus:** A smolderingly good-looking actor born in 1861, Marcus came to Tombstone, Arizona, while touring with a theater group performing Gilbert & Sullivan's *HMS Pinafore*. She stuck around as mistress to Sheriff John Behan, but when Wyatt Earp showed up, her relationship with Behan went cold, and she and Earp reportedly fell in love. Josephine passed away in 1944 and claimed until her dying day that Wyatt Earp was her one and only true love.

5. **Laura Bullion:** More commonly referred to as "Rose of the Wild Bunch," this outlaw was born around 1876 in Knickerbocker, Texas, and learned the outlaw trade by observing her bank-robbing father. Eventually hooking up with Butch Cassidy and his Wild Bunch, Bullion fenced money for the group and became romantically involved with several members. Most of those men died by the gun, but "The Thorny Rose" gave up her life of crime after

serving time in prison. She died a respectable seamstress in Memphis, Tennessee, in 1961.

6. **Etta Place:** Like many women of the Wild West, Etta Place's life is shrouded in mystery and legend. Was she a schoolteacher who left her quiet life for the drama of the outlaw life? Was she Butch Cassidy's girlfriend? Was she in love with the Sundance Kid, or were they just friendly cousins? Evidence seems to indicate that Place was born around 1878 and became a prostitute at Fanny Porter's bordello in San Antonio, Texas. When the Wild Bunch came through, Place went with them to rob banks. She wasn't with the boys when they were killed in South America in 1909; some believe she became a cattle rustler, but no one really knows for sure.

7. **Lillian Smith:** Before Britney and Christina, even before Tonya Harding and Nancy Kerrigan, there was the rivalry between this sharpshooter and her nemesis, Annie Oakley. Born in 1871, Smith joined Buffalo Bill's show at age 15 and was notorious for wearing flashy clothes, cursing like a sailor, and bragging about her superior skills. When the show went to England in 1887, Smith shot poorly and was ridiculed, while Oakley rose to the occasion. This crushing blow put Smith behind Oakley in the history books, and she died in 1930, a relatively obscure relic of the Old West.

8. **Pearl de Vere:** One of the most famous madams in history, this red-haired siren was born in Indiana around 1860 and made her way to Colorado during the Silver Panic of 1893. De Vere told her family she was a dress designer, but in fact rose to fame as the head of the Old Homestead, a luxurious brothel in Cripple Creek, Colorado. The price of a night's stay could cost patrons more than $200—at a time when most hotels charged around $3 a night! The building was reportedly equipped with an intercom system and boasted fine carpets and chandeliers. De Vere died in

1897 after a huge party at the Old Homestead. An overdose of morphine killed her, but it is unclear whether it was accidental or not.

9. **Ellen Liddy Watson:** Also known as "Cattle Kate," this lady of the West made a name for herself in the late 1800s when she was in her mid-twenties. Watson worked as a cook in the Rawlins House hotel, and there she met her true love, James Averell. The two were hanged in 1889 by vigilantes who claimed Averell and Watson were cattle rustlers. It is now believed that their murder was unjustified, however—the result of an abuse of power by land and cattle owners.

10. **Pearl Hart:** Pearl Hart was born in Canada around 1870, but by the time she was 17, she was married to a gambler and on a train to America. She especially liked life in the West, and, at 22, she tried to leave her husband to pursue opportunities there. Her husband followed her and won her back, but Hart was already living it up with cigarettes, liquor, and even morphine. After her husband left to fight in the Spanish-American War, Hart met a man named Joe Boot, and they robbed stagecoaches for awhile before she was caught and jailed. Hart is famous for saying, "I shall not consent to be tried under a law in which my sex had no voice in making." She was eventually released, but the rest of her life is unknown.

11. **Rose Dunn:** In a family of outlaws, it was only a matter of time before "The Rose of Cimarron" was working in the business, too. Dunn met Doolin Gang member George Newcomb and joined him as he and his crew robbed stagecoaches and banks. During a particularly nasty gunfight, Dunn risked her life to supply Newcomb with a gun and bullets. She then helped him escape after he was wounded in battle. Dunn died around 1950 in her mid-seventies, a respectable citizen married to a local politician.

Don't Mess with This Mary

There were hundreds, if not thousands, of typhoid carriers in New York at the turn of the 20th century. Only one of them, however, was labeled a menace to society and banished to an island for life.

* * * *

THE POPULAR IMAGE of Typhoid Mary in the early 1900s—an image enthusiastically promoted by the tabloids of the day—was of a woman stalking the streets of New York, infecting and killing hundreds of hapless victims. Mary Mallon, the woman who came to be recognized as Typhoid Mary, is known to have infected 47 people, 3 of whom died.

Mary Mallon immigrated to the United States from Ireland in 1883 at age 15. For a time, she lived with an aunt in New York City. She soon began working as a domestic servant, one of the few avenues of gainful employment open to a poor young woman of the day. Sometime before the turn of the century, she must have contracted and then recovered from a mild case of typhoid. Since a mild case of typhoid can mimic the symptoms of the flu, it is quite possible that she never even knew she had contracted the disease.

Mallon, an excellent cook, was working in the kitchens of the city's wealthiest families. In August 1906, she was hired by banker Charles Warren to cook for his family at their rented summer home on Long Island. After 6 of the 11 people in the house fell ill with typhoid, George Soper, a sanitary engineer, was hired by Charles Warren's landlord to pinpoint the source of the outbreak. Soper's attention eventually focused on the cook. After months of tracing Mary Mallon's job history, Soper discovered that typhoid had struck seven of the eight families for whom she'd cooked!

In March 1907, Mallon was working at a home on Park Avenue when George Soper paid a visit. Soper told Mary that she was a possible typhoid carrier and requested samples of her blood, urine, and feces for testing.

The idea that a healthy person could pass a disease on to others was barely understood by the general public at the time. For someone like Mary Mallon, who prided herself on never being sick, Soper's requests seemed outrageous. Believing herself falsely accused, she picked up a carving fork and angrily forced Soper out of the house.

Because Mallon refused to submit voluntarily to testing, the New York Health Department called in the police. Officers dragged her into an ambulance and took her to Willard Parker Hospital. Tests revealed high concentrations of typhoid bacilli in her blood.

Quarantine

Declaring her a public menace, the health department moved Mallon to an isolation cottage on the grounds of Riverside Hospital on North Brother Island in the East River. She had broken no laws and had not been given a trial, but she remained in quarantine for nearly three years.

In 1909, Mallon sued the health department, insisting that her banishment was illegal and unjustified. The judge ruled against Mallon. In 1910, a new health department inspector freed her on the condition that she never work as a cook again. Mallon kept her promise for a time, but eventually returned to the only profession she knew that could offer her a decent income.

A 1915 typhoid outbreak at Sloane Maternity Hospital in New York City killed 2 people and infected 25 others. An investigation revealed that a recently hired cook named "Mary Brown" was in fact Mary Mallon. Mallon was immediately returned to her lonely cottage on Brother Island, where she remained quarantined until her death in 1938.

Historians have debated why Mallon was treated so differently than hundreds of other typhoid carriers. At the time of her first arrest, there were 3,000–4,500 new cases of typhoid each year in New York City. Approximately three percent of typhoid fever victims became carriers, which translated to roughly 100 new carriers per year. The city would have gone bankrupt had it tried to quarantine even a handful of them as it did Mallon.

Why Mary?

Typhoid Mary was not even the deadliest carrier. A man named Tony Labella was responsible for 122 cases and 5 deaths in the 1920s. Despite the fact that he handled food and was uncooperative with authorities, he was isolated for only two weeks and then released. A bakery and restaurant owner named Alphonse Cotils was also a carrier. In 1924, Cotils was arrested after officials discovered him inside his restaurant after being warned to stay away from food. Cotils was released after promising to conduct his business by phone.

So why was Mary Mallon forced into a life of quarantine when others were not? For one thing, Mallon was the first discovered healthy carrier of typhoid. Also, Mallon's use of an assumed name in the Sloane Maternity Hospital case was seen by the public as a deliberate act, maliciously designed to put others at risk.

Some historians suspect that Mallon's fate was tied to the fact that she was a single female and an Irish immigrant. Prejudice against the Irish still ran high at the time, and it was considered unnatural—if not immoral—for a woman to remain single all her life. Another strike against Mary Mallon was her work as a domestic servant. Diseases like typhoid fever were associated with the unclean habits of the "lower classes." These factors combined to transform Mary Mallon from a simple woman into the menacing, legendary Typhoid Mary—a threat that had to be contained.

America's First Female President

President Woodrow Wilson suffered a stroke on October 2, 1919. The White House became shrouded in secrecy, and his wife, Edith, controlled all access to the president. Many wondered whether she actually controlled the White House as well.

✳ ✳ ✳ ✳

BORN ON OCTOBER 15, 1872, Edith Bolling was a direct descendent of Pocahontas and John Rolfe. She was raised in Wytheville, Virginia, and married Norman Galt, a Washington jeweler. They lived happily until Norman died of influenza in 1908, leaving Edith a widow at age 35.

One of Edith's close friends, Helen Bones, was a cousin of Woodrow Wilson. In March 1915, Edith and Helen stepped out of a White House elevator, both of them muddy from a walk. By chance, they met the recently widowed President Wilson and his friend and physician, Dr. Cary Grayson. On that soggy afternoon, Edith joined President Wilson for tea. Almost immediately, Wilson was drawn to Edith's charm and intellect, and by the end of April, she was dining at the White House on a nightly basis, enjoying intimate conversations about politics and world concerns. On May 4, 1915—a shocking two months after they met—Wilson proposed.

Marriage and War

Following their marriage on December 18, 1915, Edith's political partnership with Wilson continued—perhaps beyond the lines of propriety. In fact, as the United States became involved in the Great War, Edith coded and decoded confidential messages, enjoying direct access to classified information.

After World War I ended on November 11, 1918, Edith shared Wilson's enthusiasm for the Treaty of Versailles and his proposed

League of Nations to maintain world peace. However, the Senate refused to ratify the Treaty without several changes.

Wilson refused to compromise. In September 1919, he embarked on a 10,000-mile whistle-stop tour of the country to promote the League, but extreme exhaustion debilitated him between Pueblo, Colorado, and Wichita, Kansas. Edith (along with Doctor Grayson and secretary Joseph Tumulty) canceled the rest of the tour and rushed Wilson back to Washington.

On October 2, Edith found Wilson on the White House bathroom floor. He'd suffered a debilitating stroke that rendered the left side of his body paralyzed.

The Shroud of Secrecy

Late that afternoon, Wilson lay nearly lifeless. But according to Edith's memoir, the words of Dr. Francis Dercum offered assurance. Although Wilson's body was maimed, his mind was "clear as crystal." While Dercum recommended that Wilson not resign from office, he warned Edith that Wilson must be guarded from stress and unnecessary decisions.

So, Edith became Wilson's gatekeeper and spokesperson. Very few people besides Grayson or Tumulty were allowed in Wilson's room. Meanwhile, Grayson told the public that the president was suffering from "nervous exhaustion."

Rumors began to fly as the public demanded answers. Had the president become a drooling, babbling infant? Was he actually suffering from venereal disease? Political enemies accused Edith of running a "petticoat government"; other critics called her the "Presidentress."

Running the Nation?

While Edith took over many routine duties of government, she maintained that Wilson was in control of major decisions. She defined herself as a steward. In *My Memoir*, she stated: "I, myself, never made a single decision regarding the disposition of public affairs. The only decision that was mine was what was important and what was not, and the very important decision of when to present matters to my husband."

According to some, this was equivalent to running the country, but there is no evidence that she contradicted Wilson. Even when the Treaty was heading for defeat in November 1919, she obeyed her husband's emphatic murmurs that compromise would be dishonorable.

In December 1919, the shroud was lifted: Edith allowed Albert Fall (a Republican senator and political foe) to enter Wilson's room to discuss a crisis in Mexico. Carefully covering his weakened left side, Edith helped present the bedridden Wilson in his best form. Wilson's appearance, intelligence, and wit convinced the senator and other leaders that he was still capable of leading the nation.

Wilson finished his term in 1921 and retired in Washington, D.C. He died on February 3, 1924. During her long widowhood, Edith promoted the legacy of her husband by publishing *My Memoir* (1939) and releasing *Wilson* (1944), a film biography in which she held full control of the script. Edith died on December 28, 1961, the 105th anniversary of her husband's birthday.

What Really Happened?

The truth of Edith Wilson's finely crafted memoir was questioned when documents revealed that Doctors Dercum and Grayson were fully aware of the severity of Wilson's stroke and his immediate mental impairment. Furthermore, Grayson's private correspondence indicated that Edith would not allow those details to be released to the nation. If Wilson's true condition had been revealed in the weeks following the stroke, Wilson likely would have been replaced by Vice President Thomas Marshall. Edith's harshest critics believe her secrecy may have changed the course of history, speculating that if Marshall had become president, he may have chosen to negotiate a modified version of the League of Nations that included the United States.

American Women Get the Vote

Between 1818 and 1820, Fanny Wright lectured throughout the United States on women's issues. Little did she know that it would take another 100 years for American women to achieve the right to vote.

❋   ❋   ❋   ❋

MARGARET BRENT, a landowner in Maryland, was the very first woman in the United States to call for voting rights. In 1647, Brent insisted on two votes in the colonial assembly— one for herself and one for the man for whom she held power of attorney. The governor rejected her request.

Then there was Abigail Adams. In 1776, she wrote to her husband, John, asking him to remember the ladies in the new laws he was drafting. Her husband did not take her request seriously, however.

Almost half a century later, Fanny Wright showed up from Scotland. Although she recognized the gender inequities in the United States, she nonetheless fell in love with the country and became a naturalized citizen in 1825.

It wasn't until the 1840s that the feminist ball really got rolling. Because progress was achieved in fits and spurts, women's suffrage took the better part of a century to come to fruition.

Progress

Before the Civil War, the women's suffrage movement and abolition organizations focused on many of the same issues. The two movements were closely linked, specifically at the World Anti-Slavery Convention in London in 1840. However, female delegates to the convention, among them Lucretia Mott and Elizabeth Cady Stanton, were not allowed to participate because of their gender. London is a long way to travel to sit in the back of a room and be silent; Stanton and Mott resolved to organize a convention to discuss the rights of women.

The convention was finally held in 1848 in Seneca Falls, New York. Stanton presented her *Declaration of Sentiments*, the first formal action by women in the United States to advocate civil rights and suffrage.

Two groups formed at the end of the 1860s: the National Woman Suffrage Association (NWSA) and the American Woman Suffrage Association (AWSA). The NWSA, led by Susan B. Anthony and Stanton, worked to change voting laws on the federal level by way of an amendment to the U.S. Constitution. The AWSA, led by Lucy Stone and Julia Ward Howe, worked to change the laws on the state level. The two groups were united in 1890 and renamed the National American Woman Suffrage Association.

Fulfillment

In 1916, Alice Paul formed the National Woman's Party (NWP). Based on the idea that action, not words, would achieve the suffragists' mission, the NWP staged Silent Sentinels outside the White House during which NWP members held signs that goaded the president.

When World War I came along, many assumed the Silent Sentinels would end. Instead, the protesters incorporated the current events into their messages. Once the public got wind that some protestors had been imprisoned and were experiencing horrendous treatment, the tide turned in their favor.

In 1917, President Woodrow Wilson announced his support for a suffrage amendment. In the summer of 1920, Tennessee ratified the 19th Amendment—the 36th state to do so. In August of that year, women gained the right to vote. It had certainly been a long time coming.

✳ **Lucretia Mott was one of many suffragists who were also abolitionists. Mott refused to use cotton cloth, cane sugar, and other goods produced through slave labor, and she often sheltered runaway slaves in her home.**

She Struck Out DiMaggio

Babe Didrikson Zaharias left her mark on the sporting world.

✳ ✳ ✳ ✳

I**T WAS THE** most unusual of baseball showdowns. Two of the 20th century's greatest sports icons stared each other down across a distance of 60 feet, 6 inches. At the plate: Yankee legend Joe DiMaggio. On the mound: a woman.

But this was no ordinary woman. She was, perhaps, the greatest female athlete of all time. Babe Didrikson Zaharias had been throwing harder and running faster than the boys since she was a girl in Port Arthur, Texas. On this day, she was pitching for the barnstorming House of David men's team.

The details of this legendary face-off between DiMaggio and Zaharias have become cloudy with the passage of time. However, DiMaggio once described it to writer Bert Sugar. "Struck him out on three pitches," Sugar said.

Born Mildred Ella Didrikson, Babe earned her nickname after a Ruthian feat: smashing five home runs during a childhood game. Baseball was not even her best sport. She set Olympic records at the 1932 Games, winning the javelin and breaking a world record in the 80-meter hurdles. She was also a basketball star, a world-class swimmer, and—above all else—a brilliant golfer whose titles included the 1948, 1950, and 1954 United States Women's Opens.

In 1934, Zaharias pitched in two major-league spring training games in Florida. She threw the first inning of a Philadelphia Athletics match against Brooklyn, walking one batter but not allowing a hit. Two days later, she pitched an inning for the Cardinals against the Red Sox, yielding her first runs. She did not bat in either game, but in warm-ups she reportedly chucked a baseball from center field to home plate—a distance of 313 feet.

Queen of Curves

Bettie Page had a sunny smile that would melt butter. Whatever happened to this pinup who disappeared at the height of her fame?

✳ ✳ ✳ ✳

BETTIE PAGE, THE sexy queen of pinups, easily transitioned from sweet to sultry to dark. The 2005 movie *The Notorious Bettie Page*, starring indie darling Gretchen Mol, only begins to skim the surface of her complex life. Page disappeared from the limelight at her peak, leaving many fans, fanzines, and products behind.

Many young women have tried to copy those signature bangs, but a body like hers is less appreciated in the modern day. A waist that small with hips that shapely? Most of today's stars seem more intent on achieving the "waif" look.

From 1950 to 1957, Bettie Page ruled everything from girl-next-door swimsuit spreads to bondage films. In his book, *The Real Bettie Page*, Richard Foster calls her "a swinging fifties chick who looks like the girl next door, yet tells you she knows the score. She winks, tosses back her famous gleaming black bangs, and flashes you her killer come-hither smile. Her curves entice, entrance, and devastate. She's a leggy, torpedo-chested weapon aimed at your heart . . . She's bikinis and lace. She's cotton candy and a ride on the Tilt-a-Whirl at Coney Island."

But Foster's love for the Dark Angel, as Bettie Page is sometimes called, led him to the awful truth—that after her Queen-of-Curves years, Page's life spiraled downward. She ended up in a mental institution after being convicted of attempted murder.

Humble Beginnings

Betty Mae Page, born in Tennessee in 1923, was the second of Edna and Roy Page's six children. Roy, a mechanic, couldn't find work during the Great Depression. The combination of Roy's criminal tendencies (he sexually abused all of his daughters and impregnated a 15-year-old neighbor) and Edna's cold shoulder toward her children created a perfectly dysfunctional family pie.

Page was a good student, but she wasn't involved with boys—her devout, God-fearing mother didn't allow her to date. She escaped her oppressive upbringing by envisioning herself as a movie star. A few years after graduating from college, Page moved to New York.

Page met Jerry Tibbs at Coney Island in October 1950. Tibbs, a Harlem police officer with a passion for photography, immediately asked Page if she'd ever thought about modeling. She agreed to let him shoot her.

Tibbs showed Page tricks of the trade, doing her makeup and giving her tissues to stuff her bra. Eventually, he realized that her hairstyle—a simple part down the middle—was taking away from her beauty on camera. With a quick snip, the Bettie Page bangs arrived.

In Front of the Camera

Tibbs introduced Page to photographer Cass Carr, and her modeling career began to take off. In 1952, Page met Irving Klaw, the man who would turn the Queen of Curves into the Dark Angel. Klaw ran a successful business selling movie stills, but bondage photos were his bread and butter. Klaw shot photographs of girls being spanked, tied up, and wearing six-inch heels with black lingerie. Today, you'll see racier displays in a Victoria's Secret ad, but this was the 1950s. Page's carefree photos inspired countless sexually repressed Americans.

Klaw, along with his business partner and sister, Paula, took Page in like family. She enjoyed modeling but never gave up on her dream of being an actress; she spent her $75-per-day modeling payments on acting classes.

By 1955, Page was at her peak, gracing the pages of the January issue of *Playboy* in her most famous pose: wearing only a Santa hat and a naughty smile. But by 1957, Page was burned out on show business. She moved to Florida, rekindled a relationship with an old flame, and got married.

A Slow Slide

By New Year's Eve of that same year, the new relationship had fizzled. Frustrated, financially unstable, and brokenhearted, Page spent the night crying along the roads of Key West. She felt hopeless—and that's when she spotted a church. Page spun into religious fervor. She spent the next few years in various Bible camps and schools. She wanted to be a missionary, but Page was a bit too fanatical, even for Baptist ministers. Her classmates and instructors began to see that Page wasn't well.

During the next few years, Page committed several violent acts. She pulled a gun on a missionary at a Bible camp, and she attacked and stabbed her elderly landlords. Page was diagnosed with paranoid schizophrenia and confined to a mental hospital.

Page was released early because of good behavior. Through a roommate service, she moved into the home of Leonie Haddad. After a few months of living together, Page heard Haddad on the phone with the agency asking for a new roommate. Page snapped, stabbing Haddad 12 times.

Page went on trial for attempted murder in 1983 and spent seven years in a mental institution before being released (again, for good behavior). Older, heavier, and with no money, Page became a recluse.

During her later years, powerful individuals such as Hugh Hefner reached out to Page. Through the efforts of such people, Page began to receive proceeds from the use of her likeness. Although she passed away in 2008, her likeness appears to be immortal.

The Mission That Never Went

In 1961, a group of highly qualified women were selected for astronaut flight training. They passed every test and endured every poke, prod, and simulation. In some cases, they actually fared better than their male counterparts. But was America really ready to send women into space? Apparently not.

✳ ✳ ✳ ✳

THE SOVIETS FIRED the starter's gun in the space race by launching the *Sputnik* satellite on October 4, 1957. Threatened by the Soviets' ability to beat them to the punch, the United States accelerated their own space initiatives, including the formation of the National Aeronautics and Space Administration (NASA). Next time, the United States would be first.

There was much yet to learn about space. What could humans tolerate? Jet pilots required pressure suits; what of weightless space? What of the confinement? Military test pilots—fit, brave, and calm during crises—seemed logical candidates. Of course, since women weren't allowed to be military test pilots, they weren't considered for astronaut training. At least, not at first.

Secret Experiments

Freethinking researcher Dr. Randy Lovelace II helped screen the first seven male astronauts as part of the Mercury 7 program. Then Lovelace had a flash of inspiration, thinking: *A space rocket needs every joule of energy. Every gram of weight counts. Women are lighter; they use less oxygen and food. We know for sure they can fly; heck, Jackie Cochran helped me start my research foundation. Maybe they're actually better suited! Let's explore this!*

Cochran herself was well over the age limit of 35, but Oklahoman Geraldyn "Jerrie" Cobb wasn't. A record-setting aviator, Cobb had earned her private pilot's license when she was just 17 years old. Between 1957 and 1960, she set four aviation world records for speed, distance, and absolute altitude.

When Jerrie received an invitation from Dr. Lovelace to train for space flight, she dropped everything for what seemed like the opportunity of a lifetime. She arrived in Albuquerque in 1960 and began the torture tests. She underwent barium enemas and had all her body fluids sampled. Supercooled water was squirted into her ear canal to test her reaction to vertigo. She endured the infamous "Vomit Comet" spin simulator.

Frenzy Over a Celebrated "Astronette"

Cobb breezed through the trials. When Lovelace announced this to the media, they fawned over the "astronette." Cobb was the first of 25 women tested for astronaut potential. Only some of the women met one another in person, but Cobb was involved in their recruitment and knew them all. Thirteen passed all the tests to become FLATs: Fellow Lady Astronaut Trainees, an acronym taken from Cobb's written salutation to them.

During this phase, Soviet cosmonaut Yuri Gagarin orbited the planet, lapping NASA once again in the space race.

The women's next planned step was testing at navy facilities in Pensacola. Each went home to wait. But when Lovelace asked to use Pensacola, the navy said they could not allow it without an official request from NASA, and NASA declined to submit a request.

In September 1961, each FLAT got a telegram: *Sorry, program cancelled. You may now resume your normal lives.*

The women couldn't have been more dismayed. All that work—for nothing! They didn't give up, but they didn't coordinate their lobbying either. Cobb, the FLATs' self-appointed spokesperson, didn't get along well with Cochran—who in turn had her own ideas. Cobb's appeals up the national chain of command were honest, impassioned, and naive. Cochran, with personal contacts ranging from Chuck Yeager to VP Lyndon

Johnson, preferred to work gradually within the sexist system rather than have an open challenge slapped down. One FLAT, Jane Hart, was the wife of a U.S. senator and was arguably the savviest political spokesperson available. Hart fumed as Cochran testified to Congress that she was against a "special program for women."

Did It Ever Stand a Chance?

What if all the Mercury 13 women and Cochran had spoken to the country in a unified voice? We can guess the outcome based on LBJ's reaction to the memo across his desk concerning the female astronauts. He scrawled: "LET'S STOP THIS NOW!" If President Kennedy's space tsar had that attitude, there had never been any real hope. The men leading the nation weren't ready to send women into space. Period.

Was Lovelace deluded? Give him credit for trying, but he also didn't clue NASA in until news of the Pensacola plans blindsided them, resulting in a reflex "no way." On the other hand, had he sought advance permission, odds of NASA giving it were unlikely.

On June 16, 1963, about a year after Cobb, Hart, and Cochran spoke before Congress, cosmonaut Valentina Tereshkova of the Soviet Union flew in space. She was not a test pilot but a parachute hobbyist. It would be 20 more years before the first American woman, Sally Ride, made it into space.

❋ Techs took 100 X-rays of each bone in Jerrie Cobb's body.

❋ For Jerrie Cobb, perhaps the worst part was the initial media barrage. She had to field important technical questions: Was she scared; could she cook; what were her measurements?

❋ As unfortunate an acronym as FLATs may be, posterity has tried to filch it from Jerrie Cobb's purse. Most chroniclers spell it out as "First Lady Astronaut Trainees," as though it were an official term conferred by NASA. The women themselves have never embraced it, preferring Mercury 13.

Ancient Egypt—
A Woman's World

When today's feminists talk about women's rights and equality with men, they may do well to look to the good old days of ancient Egypt for inspiration.

✻ ✻ ✻ ✻

ALTHOUGH THE WOMEN of ancient Greece could not leave their homes without a spouse or male relative, ancient Egyptian women enjoyed equal privileges with men on many fronts, including property, marriage, and occupational rights. In fact, ancient Egyptian women had more rights than many women do today!

How do we know this? As they did with everything else, the Egyptians recorded their legal and economic lives in art and historical inscriptions. And it seems that legal rights and social privileges were different between social classes rather than between genders. In other words, women and men in the same social class enjoyed fairly equal rights.

An Egyptian girl became universally acknowledged as a wife after she physically left the protection of her father's house and entered her new home. Before the marital home was established, the couple would hire the services of a scribe, who would record their individual assets.

The ancient Egyptian woman had full control of property, including the right to buy and sell land, goods, livestock, and servants, and she could free slaves. A woman could, without the guidance of a man, manage her own property. She could appear in court on her own behalf and sue a party who wronged her—all without a male representative. In fact, there are many recorded instances of women winning lawsuits, particularly in land disputes.

When an ancient Egyptian woman acquired property on her own—through inheritance, gifts, or with money she earned through employment—it was hers to keep before, during, and after her marriage, whether that marriage ended through widowhood or divorce. If her husband requested, she could grant him rights to use or borrow the property.

One of the best examples of women's rights is in the area of wills and estates. An ancient Egyptian woman could inherit one-third of all the property she acquired through marriage (the remaining estate was divided among the children and siblings of the deceased), and she was free to bequeath property from her husband to her children.

Employment Opportunities

In terms of careers, the work of the upper-class woman was often limited to the home because of her customary role as mother. But ancient art and texts show women as middle-class housekeepers, skilled laborers in household workshops, paid priestesses, and entertainers (dancers, musicians, and acrobats). All professions were open to educated women and men, including clergy, administrators (there was a woman named Nebet during the Sixth Dynasty who was titled vizier, judge, and magistrate), business owners, and doctors. Records mention Lady Peseshet, who is considered the first female physician in Africa—perhaps even in world history.

Some of Egypt's greatest rulers and heroes were women. Queen Ahhotep, of the early Eighteenth Dynasty, was granted Egypt's highest military decoration—the Order of the Fly—at least three times for saving Egypt during the wars of liberation against the Hyksos invaders from the north. The best example, however, is Hatshepsut (also of the Eighteenth Dynasty), who reigned as pharaoh of Egypt rather than as queen. Ancient reports during a military campaign in Nubia tell of the homage she received from rebels defeated on the battlefield.

Chapter 8

Health and Medicine

Going for the Jugular

The human body has always been fertile ground for misconceptions.

✳ ✳ ✳ ✳

T HE CELEBRATED GREEK doctor Hippocrates postulated that all human emotions flowed from four bodily fluids, or humors: blood (which makes you cheerful and passionate), yellow bile (which makes you hot-tempered), black bile (which makes you depressed), and phlegm (which makes you sluggish or stoic). Though the good doctor's humors have given behavioral scientists a nice structure for examining personality types (sanguine, choleric, melancholic, and phlegmatic), the idea that our bodily fluids make us angry, depressed, or elated died out in the 1800s.

The withering of the Hippocratic belief in humors proved to be good news for patients who were not thrilled with the practice of bloodletting, a process of opening a patient's veins to lower blood levels in an attempt to bring the humors into balance and cure all manner of mental and physical ills. Bloodletting, with a knife or with leeches, was an accepted medical practice from the time of the Greeks, Mayans, and Mesopotamians, and it was still going strong at the end of the 18th century, when George Washington had almost two liters of blood let out to "cure" a throat infection. (He died shortly afterward.)

Dance of the Black Death

The Black Death, the epidemic best known for devastating Europe between 1347 and 1350, was as deadly in the east as it was in the west. By the time the plague reached the outskirts of Europe, it had already killed an estimated 25 million people. Within three years, approximately 25 million more victims would follow in the first wave of a cycle of plagues that continued to hound Europe for three centuries.

✳ ✳ ✳ ✳

THE PLAGUE ISN'T pretty. Whether primarily in the lymph nodes (bubonic), blood (septicemic), or lungs (pneumonic), the plague is caused by the bacterium *Yersinia pestis*, which lives in the digestive tract of fleas. It primarily transmits from animals to humans through flea bites, though humans in close contact can transmit pneumonic plague to each other. The bacteria was discovered by Japanese and European researchers in the late 19th century. Patients manifest symptoms such as swollen and tender lymph nodes (buboes) in the area of the bite, fever, bloody sputum and blotching, rapidly worsening pneumonia, and—as the bacteria overwhelms the nervous system—neurological and psychological disorders. Untreated, plague has a morbidity rate of 50–60 percent; the rate is even higher for pneumonic plague. Between 1,000 and 3,000 cases are reported each year worldwide.

Origins of a Disease

The Black Death originated in Asia in the 1340s. Making its way along the Silk Road, the epidemic ravaged India, Egypt, the Middle East, and Constantinople before spreading rapidly through trading ports to Europe. Even Greenland and Iceland were struck. From 1347 to 1350, a third of Europe's population died an agonizing, dramatic, mysterious—and sudden—death. In cities such as Florence, the death toll reached 75 percent, and many rural villages were wiped out completely. Nearly annual outbreaks of the plague continued, culminating in the great 1665 plague of London, in which perhaps 100,000 Londoners died. Overall, some estimates of the combined death toll reach 200 million people.

It would be hard to underestimate the pervasive effects of the plagues on Europe. All aspects of society and culture suffered intense disruption and experienced profound change as the plagues brought on economic stress, social dissolution, religious extremism, and skepticism. The trauma on the European psyche as a result of living in circumstances where, as the 14th-century Italian writer Boccaccio put it, people could "eat lunch with their friends and dinner with their ancestors in paradise," can be seen in the pervasive use of skeletons in art and drama. They act as grim and often ironic reminders of *memento mori* ("Remember, you die"), illustrations of *quod es fui, quod sum eris* ("what you are I was; what I am you will be"), and participants in the "Dance of Death" (*Danse Macabre, Totentanz*) throughout this period.

Was That the Last Dance?

Although the Black Death and its subsequent outbreaks ended in the 17th century, its rapid spread and descriptions, as well as the patterns of outbreaks do not—in some cases—correspond well to *Y. pestis*, nor to the complex conditions required for the bacteria to find its way into fleas that can then infect humans. This has recently led some researchers in Britain and the United States to advance the theory that the plague was actually caused by a human-borne virus that lies dormant in the earth until it is introduced into the population. If so, another round of "Black Death"—especially in an age of continuous global travel and trade—remains a frightening possibility.

✳ **The plague wiped out nearly half of all medieval Europeans.**

Early Contraception

Ever since humans realized how babies were made,
they have tried to control the process.

✳ ✳ ✳ ✳

A N ANCIENT GREEK gynecologist told women not wishing to have a child to jump backward seven times after intercourse. Ancient Roman women tried to avoid pregnancy by tying a pouch containing a cat's liver to their left foot or by spitting into the mouth of a frog.

Barrier methods of contraception have included pebbles, half a lemon, and dried elephant or crocodile dung. In 1550 B.C., a suggested concoction of ground dates, acacia tree bark, and honey applied locally was probably fairly effective, since acacia ferments into lactic acid, which disrupts a normal pH balance. In eastern Canada, one aboriginal group believed in the efficacy of women drinking a tea brewed with beaver testicles.

As early as the seventh century B.C., a member of the fennel family called silphium was discovered to be an extremely effective "morning-after pill." But since it only grew in a small area on the Libyan mountainside and attempts to cultivate it elsewhere failed, silphium was extinct by the second century.

Men have almost always used some sort of sheath, dating back to at least 1000 B.C. The ancient Romans and the 17th-century British employed animal intestine, while the Egyptians and Italians preferred fabric, which they sometimes soaked in a spermicidal solution. Vulcanized rubber appeared around 1844.

The main responsibility for contraception still lies with women, many of whom alter their body's hormonal balance with "the pill," which was introduced in 1960. Meanwhile, due to lack of male interest, research into male contraceptive injections, pills and/or nasal sprays has stalled, and "the sheath" remains the primary resource for men.

Rasputin: Gifted Healer or Depraved Freak?

We know this much: Rasputin, a barely literate Russian peasant, grew close to the last tsaritsa—close enough to cost him his life. Incredibly lurid stories ricocheted off the walls of the Winter Palace: drunken satyr, faith healer, master manipulator. What's true? And why does Rasputin continue to fascinate us to this very day?

✳ ✳ ✳ ✳

ON JANUARY 22, 1869, Grigory Yefimovich Rasputin was born in the peasant village of Pokrovskoe, Russia. Baby Rasputin entered the world on the day of the Orthodox saint Grigory and was named after him. There wasn't much to distinguish little Grigory from tens of millions of Russian peasant kids, and he grew into a rowdy drunk. He married a fellow peasant named Praskovia, who hung back in Pokrovskoe raising their three kids in Rasputin's general absence.

At 28, Rasputin was born again, rural Russian style. He sobered up and wandered between monasteries seeking knowledge. Evidently, he fell in with the *khlysti*—a secretive, heretical Eastern Orthodox sect swirling with rumors of orgies, flagellation, and the like. Rasputin gained a mystical aura during this time.

In 1903, he wandered to the capital, St. Petersburg, where he impressed the local Orthodox clergy. Word spread. The ruling Romanov family soon heard of Rasputin.

The Romanovs held a powerful yet precarious position. Ethnically, they were more German than Russian, a hot-button topic for the Slavs they ruled over. Greedy flatterers and brutal infighters made the corridors of power a steep slope with weak rock and loose mud: As you climbed, your prestige and influence grew—but woe to you if you slipped (or were pushed). In that event, the rest would step aside and let you fall—caring only to get out of your way. This was no safe place for a naive peasant, however spiritually inclined. Even the Romanovs lived in fear, for tsars tended to die violent deaths. They ruled a dirt-poor population seething with resentment. Tsaryevich ("tsar's son") Alexei, the heir apparent, was a fragile hemophiliac who could bleed out from a skinned knee, aptly symbolic of the blood in the political water in St. Petersburg in those final days of the last tsar, Nicholas II.

Rasputin Finds a Friend in the Tsaritsa

As the tsaritsa worried over gravely ill Alexei in 1906, she thought of Rasputin and his healing reputation. He answered her summons in person, blessed Alexei with an Orthodox *ikon*, and left. Alexei improved, and Tsaritsa Alexandra was hooked on Rasputin. She consulted him often, introduced him to her friends, and pulled him onto that treacherous slope of imperial favor. Rasputin became a polarizing figure as he grew more influential. His small covey of upper-crust supporters (who were mostly female) hung on his every word, even as a growing legion of nobles, peasants, and clergy saw Rasputin as emblematic of all that was wrong with the monarchy.

What few ask now is: What was Rasputin thinking? What was he feeling? His swift rise from muddy fields to the royal palace gave him an understandable ego trip. He was not an idiot; he surely realized his rise would earn him jealous enemies. The sheer fury of their hatred seems to have surprised, frightened, and saddened him, for he wasn't a hateful man. He certainly felt duty-bound to the tsaritsa, whose unwavering favor deflected most of his enemies' blows. Rasputin's internal spiritual struggle between sinfulness and holiness registers authentic, though it is an established fact that he made regular visits to prostitutes. Defenders claim that he was only steeling himself against sexual temptation; one can imagine what his enemies said.

Life worsened for Rasputin in 1914, when he was stabbed by a former prostitute. After recuperating, he abandoned any restraint he'd ever exercised. Rasputin began drinking again and had many and varied sexual encounters; perhaps he expected death and gave in to his desires. After Russia went to war with Germany, cartoons portrayed Rasputin as a cancer infecting the monarchy. Military setbacks left Russians with much to mourn and resent. A wave of mandatory patriotism swept Russia, focusing discontent upon the royal family's Germanic ties.

In the end, clergy and nobility agreed with the media: down with Rasputin.

A Violent Demise

Led by a fabulously rich libertine named Felix Yusupov, Rasputin's enemies lured him to a meeting on December 29, 1916. The popular story is that he scarfed a bunch of poisoned food and wine, somehow didn't die, was shot, got up, was beaten and shot some more, then was finally tied up and thrown into an icy river. What is sure: Rasputin was shot, bound, and dumped into freezing water to die.

The tsaritsa buried her advisor on royal property. After the Romanovs fell, a mob dug up Rasputin and burned his corpse. Nothing remains of him.

Rasputin had predicted that if he were slain by the nobility, the Russian monarchy wouldn't long survive him. His prophecy came true: Less than a year after his death, the Russian Revolution deposed the tsar. The Bolsheviks would soon murder the entire royal family; had they captured Rasputin, it's hard to imagine him being spared. For the "Mad Monk" who was neither mad nor monastic, the muddy road of life had dead-ended in the treacherous forest of imperial favor.

Grim Places of Quarantine

Life has never been easy for lepers.

❋ ❋ ❋ ❋

Leprosy has affected humanity since at least 600 B.C. This condition, which is now called Hansen's disease, attacks the nervous system primarily in the hands, feet, and face. It causes disfiguring skin sores, nerve damage, and progressive debilitation. Medical science had no understanding of the condition until the late 1800s and no effective treatment for it until the 1940s. Prior to that point, patients faced a slow, painful, and certain demise.

Misinterpretations of the Bible passage Leviticus 13:45–46, which labeled lepers as "unclean" and dictated that sufferers must "dwell apart . . . outside the camp," didn't help matters. (The "leprosy" cited in Leviticus referred to several skin conditions, but Hansen's disease was not one of them.) It's really no surprise that society's less-than-compassionate response to the disease was the leper colony.

The first leper colonies were isolated spots in the wilderness where the afflicted were driven, forgotten, and left to die.

The practice of exiling lepers continued well into the 20th century. In Crete, for instance, lepers were banished to mountainside caves, where they survived by eating scraps left by wolves. More humane measures were adopted in 1903, when lepers were corralled into the Spinalonga Island leper colony and given food and shelter and cared for by priests and nuns. However, once you entered, you never left, and it remained that way until the colony's last resident died in 1957.

Still, joining a leper colony sometimes beat living among the healthy. It wasn't much fun wandering from town to town while wearing signs or ringing bells to warn of one's affliction. And you were always susceptible to violence from townsfolk gripped by irrational fear—as when lepers were blamed for epidemic outbreaks and thrown into bonfires as punishment.

Life in the American Colony

American attitudes toward lepers weren't any more enlightened. One of modernity's most notorious leper colonies was on the Hawaiian island of Molokai. It was established in 1866.

Hawaiian kings and American officials banished sufferers to this remote peninsula ringed by jagged lava rock and towering sea cliffs. Molokai became one of the world's largest leper colonies—its population peaked in 1890 at 1,174—and more than 8,000 people were forcibly confined there before the practice was finally ended in 1969.

The early days of Molokai were horrible. The banished were abandoned in a lawless place where they received minimal care and had to fight with others for food, water, blankets, and shelter. Public condemnation and the efforts of such caring individuals as Father Damien de Veuster led to improved conditions on Molokai. The practice of sending the afflicted to Molokai ended in 1969; some individuals remain, however, because it is where they feel most at home.

A Leper Haven in Louisiana

While sufferers of leprosy were being humiliated in Hawaii, they were being helped in Louisiana.

In 1894, the Louisiana Leper House, which billed itself as "a place of treatment and research, not detention," opened in Carville. In 1920, it was transferred to federal authority and renamed the National Leprosarium of the United States. Known today as the National Hansen's Disease (leprosy) Program (NHDP), the facility became a leading research and rehabilitation center, pioneering treatments that form the basis of multidrug therapies currently prescribed by the World Health Organization (WHO) for the treatment of Hansen's disease.

It was here that researchers enlisted a common Louisiana critter—the armadillo—in the fight against the disease. It had always been difficult to study Hansen's disease. Human nerves are seldom biopsied, so direct data on nerve damage from Hansen's was minimal. But in the 1960s, NHDP researchers theorized that armadillos might be susceptible to the germ because of their low body temperature. They began inoculating armadillos with it and discovered that the animals could develop the disease systemically. Now the armadillo is used to develop infected nerves for research worldwide.

A Thing of the Past?

In 1985, Hansen's disease was still considered a public health problem in 122 countries. In fact, the last remaining leper colony, located in Croatia, didn't close until 2002. However, WHO has made great strides toward eradicating the disease; by 2000, the rate of infection had dropped by 90 percent. The multidrug therapies currently prescribed for the treatment of Hansen's are available to all patients for free via WHO. Approximately four million patients have been cured since 2000.

"One of the worst things about this illness is what was done to me as a young boy. First, I was sent away from my family. That was hard. . . . They told me right out that I would die here; that I would never see my family again. I heard them say this phrase, something I will never forget. They said, 'This is your last place. This is where you are going to stay, and die.' That's what they told me. I was a thirteen-year-old kid."

—MALE PATIENT AT MOLOKAI COLONY, CIRCA 1977–78

✳ Approximately 95 percent of humans are not susceptible to the bacteria that causes Hansen's.

✳ Hansen's disease is quite treatable today (though it is often misdiagnosed). It is only contagious over prolonged periods of close contact, and within three days of the start of antibiotic treatment, the patient is no longer contagious.

Bathing Is Bad for You—Huh?

As late as 1920, barely one out of a hundred American homes had bathtubs. The lack of bathing facilities wasn't due to inferior technology or inadequate sanitation, but to prevailing attitudes. From the time of the Renaissance, most Europeans were wary of bathing—deeming it unhealthy.

✳   ✳   ✳   ✳

THE TERRIBLE PLAGUES of the late Middle Ages may have contributed to hydrophobia. Diseases such as cholera and typhoid were spread by filthy water. The people of the time didn't know about germs but may have intuited the link between bad water and ill health. The phrase "catch your death of cold" arose during an era when there was no hot running water.

By the time of America's colonization, the fear of water had taken firm root. When John Smith and his fellow settlers moved to Jamestown, Virginia, the native Powhatans, who bathed every day, literally held their noses when downwind of the colonists.

But it wasn't always so.

Light in Darkness

Contrary to myth, folks in the "Dark Ages" were relatively enlightened about cleanliness. According to the book *A History of Private Life*, medieval *fabliaux*—tall tales like those of Chaucer—are replete with lovers taking hot baths before lovemaking. Ladies and lords of the manor soaked on stools placed in wooden vats filled with hot water. They also scrubbed their hands and faces before meals and washed their mouths out after, according to the etiquette guides of the time. The more common folk soaked in urban public baths called "stews," the opening of which were heralded by the sound of trumpet and drum each morning. Doughty burghers marched to the stews naked to stop thieves from picking their pockets. Inside, the two sexes bathed together, sometimes clothed.

The Catholic Church frowned on the mixed-gender aspect. Some orders of monks prescribed bathing only for Christmas and Easter, with the private parts covered during these sacred ablutions. But the clergy wasn't totally doctrinaire. The founder of the modern papacy, Pope Gregory I, advised taking a bath each Sunday. And monasteries featured *lavabos*, fountains for hand washing.

Hildegard of Bingen (1098–1179), a noted early scientist, offered these prescriptions for good health: "If a person's head has an ailment, it should be washed frequently in this water and it will be healed . . . If your lord wishes to bathe and wash his body clean . . . have a basin full of hot fresh herbs and wash his body with a soft sponge." Along with roses, herbs added to bath water included hollyhock, brown fennel, danewort, chamomile, and green oats. (At times, the Middle Ages sound positively New Age.)

Hildegard also offered advice for overly randy fellows: "A man who has an overabundance in his loins should cook wild lettuce in water and pour that water over himself in a sauna bath."

Bathing's Bad Rap

By the 1400s, however, public opinion had swung the other way. Fires were common in the public baths, where water was heated by the burning of wood. Wood itself was hard to find as growing prosperity led to the leveling of forests. Moreover, peasants often fell ill from the custom of the entire family washing from the same barrel of water.

Furthermore, it was believed that disease spread by way of vapors that passed into the skin through pores that opened during bathing. (This is where the term *malaria*, which means "bad air," comes from.) No less an authority than English philosopher Francis Bacon advised: "After Bathing, wrap the

Body in a seare-cloth made of Masticke, Myrrh, Pomander, and Saffron, for staying the perspiration or breathing of the pores." If body odor lingered, courtiers—male and female—cloaked their smell with copious applications of cologne.

Yet, attitudes were never monolithic. In the spring of 1511, the diary of one Lucas Rem of Germany reports that he took 127 baths. Thinking was slowly turning back in the direction of sanitary health.

Back to Cleanliness

In the mid-19th century, bathing bounced back in the United States. Millions of the "unwashed masses" were forsaking farms for crowded, filthy cities, and millions more were arriving on immigrant ships. In response, the healthier, better-educated natives crusaded for better health. Healthy living—physical and spiritual—became all the rage.

One fad among the wealthy was "taking the waters" at spas such as Saratoga Springs, New York, which was frequented by Edgar Allan Poe and Franklin Roosevelt.

In the 1880s, the Standard Sanitary Manufacturing Company made cast-iron bathtubs available to the public. These were actually advertised as horse troughs/bathtubs; few thought anyone would buy a tub only for bathing.

During the Roaring Twenties, middle-class folk, envious of mansions trendily outfitted with indoor plumbing, began putting sinks, toilets, and tubs into separate rooms called bathrooms.

Today, Americans are famous the world over for their frequent showering. Sir John Harington, inventor of the water closet, would be pleased.

"Everything is a miracle. It is a miracle that one does not dissolve in one's bath like a lump of sugar."

—PABLO PICASSO

Paleolithic Children Did Not Have to Brush Their Teeth Before Bed

If modern dentistry's mandate to brush three times a day seems excessive, it becomes even more so compared to zero times a day. The origins of toothbrushing lie with the Neolithic Revolution, when humans switched from hunting and gathering to agriculture.

✻ ✻ ✻ ✻

A WORLD WITHOUT TOOTHPASTE, toothbrushes, and biannual visits to the dentist may be difficult for the contemporary mind to grasp, but there was a time when modern exercises in dental hygiene were simply not necessary. The primary purpose of toothbrushing is to rub abrasive substances against the teeth so as to dislodge food and scratch away plaque. Before agriculture, the hunter-gatherer diet included harder, uncooked foods that worked as natural abrasives. This diet was also low in the types of carbohydrates and sugars that lead to cavities. Hunter-gatherer groups dislodged food from their mouths with sharpened sticks—and they chewed on substances with antiseptic properties to reduce oral infection—but toothbrushing as we know it wasn't done.

Junk Food Gets the Brush-Off

And then came the Neolithic Revolution, with its carbohydrate-rich staple crops and an abundance of soft, cooked foods. As dental cavities became a widespread problem, innovations in toothbrush and toothpaste developed. Since the very beginnings of the written word, references to dental cavities and the multifarious ways to get rid of them can be found. The ancient Egyptians probably used their fingers in lieu of a toothbrush and made abrasive tooth powders from myrrh, pumice, the ashes of ox hooves, and burnt and powdered eggshells. The ancient Greeks and Romans were fond of toothpaste that included crushed bones and oyster shells. Ancient Persian records indicate the use of, among other things, the burnt shells of snails. Meanwhile, in China, the ingenious use of the chew stick became popular around 1600 B.C. One end of a stick was chewed down into a frayed brush, while the other end was sharpened into a toothpick: brushing and flossing in one tool.

China also appears to be one early source of the bristled toothbrush. The bristles were made of the hairs of wild boar, which were placed into a carved bone or bamboo handle. Early toothbrushes—no matter where in the world they popped up—were usually made from bone and animal hair. By the early 1800s, bristled toothbrushes were widespread in Europe and Japan. Yet even at this time, it was still popular to simply use a toothpick and homemade toothpaste. Toothbrushing as it is known today began with the mass manufacture and commercialization of toothbrushes and toothpaste.

Uncle Sam Wants YOU to Brush Your Teeth!

It was William Addis of late 18th-century England who first developed a toothbrush that was meant for mass manufacture. The toothbrush was patented in the United States in 1857, and in 1939, the first electric toothbrush was developed in Switzerland. Synthetic materials (particularly nylon) came to replace animal hair as bristles, and bone handles were replaced with plastic handles. Yet even with all these innovations, toothbrushing was not pervasive in the United States until after World War II, when GIs were mandated to brush their teeth daily. Since then, advances in toothbrush and toothpaste technology have powered ahead at incredible speed, as companies compete to create the perfect product of oral hygiene— plaque control, fresh mint, whitening, you name it. Meanwhile, organizations such as the American Dental Association and the National Institute of Dental and Craniofacial Research keep busy to ensure best practices in oral hygiene are followed nationwide. Thus, children in the United States don't garner much sympathy when they refuse to brush their teeth before going to bed—even if their Paleolithic peers got away with it.

Chapter 9

The Art of It All

Was the Fantastic Fabler a Fable Himself?

Aesop's tales of talking animals have been a staple of traditional folklore for centuries. But as it turns out, Aesop himself may have been as much a fable as his famous tales.

✳   ✳   ✳   ✳

IT'S FUN TO tell Aesop's tales—especially since many of them take the air out of someone else's inflated ego or show the comic consequences of someone else's bad behavior. And with talking animals to boot! What's not to love?

By various traditions, Aesop (620–560? B.C.) was a slave from Phrygia (central Turkey), Thrace (northern Greece), Sardis (western Turkey), or Ethiopia (horn of Africa). He was brought to the Greek island of Samos in the early 6th century B.C. and was eventually set free because of his wit and wisdom.

What we actually know of Aesop's life may be as fictional as his stories. His first official biography wasn't composed until the 14th century, and it was written for entertainment—not history. In it, Aesop appears as an unsightly, ungainly, yet clever rogue who is always undermining and outwitting his master with his clever use of language. In one instance, after his master Xanthus gives precise directions for fixing "a lentil soup" for a special dinner party, Aesop fixes one boiled lentil and then avoids punishment by forcing the embarrassed Xanthus to admit that Aesop was only following his directions. In this version, Aesop the fabler is a subversive figure who turns the tables on the powerful—a trickster as common to folklore around the world as animal stories.

Later biographies frame Aesop as a serious moral teacher and take most of the fun out of him. He becomes, after meritoriously winning freedom, a famous personality in the court of the Lydian King Croesus in Sardis (modern Sart, Turkey). Besides amazing the king and the wisest men of the day, Aesop traveled about Greece instructing the powerful with his fables.

Even Aesop's death became a tale with as pointed a moral as any of his fables. He was framed and executed by dishonest men at Delphi (a famous Greek shrine) when he refused to distribute some of Croesus's gold (which the king had sent as a gift) because of the men's greed. However, ensuing disasters forced the guilty to fess up, and so the "the blood of Aesop" became a proverb that refers to dishonest deeds that eventually come home to roost.

So, Was There an Aesop?

Well, perhaps. The Greeks and Romans certainly thought there was. But, as with Homer—the famous bard who traditionally composed the *Iliad* and *Odyssey*—the question of whether the author created the works or the works created the author is open for debate. Just as Demodocus, the blind bard who appears in Book Eight of the *Odyssey*, may have suggested the tradition that Homer was blind, the sly and satirical characters of the fables may have helped to create the character that became Aesop. In any case, both Aesop's fables and Aesop's life make for "fabulous" reading.

"Every truth has two sides; it is as well to look at both, before we commit ourselves to either."

—Aesop

7 Notorious Art Thefts

Some people just can't keep their hands off other people's things.

※ ※ ※ ※

1. **Boston, March 1990; $300 million:** Two men dressed as police officers entered the Isabella Stewart Gardner Museum in the wee hours of the morning. After overpowering two guards and grabbing the surveillance tape, they collected Rembrandt's only seascape, *Storm on the Sea of Galilee,* as well as several other works. Authorities have yet to find the criminals despite investigating everyone from the Irish Republican Army to a Boston mob boss.

2. **Oslo, August 2004; $120 million:** Two armed and masked thieves threatened workers at the Munch Museum during a daring daylight theft. They stole *The Scream* and *Madonna.* In May 2006, authorities convicted three men, who each received between four and eight years in jail. The paintings were recovered three months later.

3. **Paris, August 1911; $100 million:** In the world's most notorious art theft to date, Vincenzo Peruggia—a Louvre employee—stole Leonardo da Vinci's *Mona Lisa.* Peruggia simply hid in a closet, grabbed the painting once alone in the room, hid it under his long smock, and walked out of the museum after it had closed. Police found Peruggia (and the *Mona Lisa*) two years later when the thief tried to sell the work to an art dealer in Florence.

4. **Oslo, February 1994; $60–75 million:** *The Scream* has been a popular target for thieves. Another version of Munch's famous work (he painted four) was taken from Oslo's National Art Museum. In less than one minute, the crooks came in through a window, cut the wires holding up the painting, and left through the same window. They left a piece of the frame at a bus stop, and this clue helped

authorities recover the painting. Four men were convicted of the crime in January 1996.

5. **Scotland, August 2003; $65 million:** Two men joined a tour of Scotland's Drumlanrig Castle, subdued a guard, and made off with Leonardo da Vinci's *Madonna with the Yarnwinder*. Alarms around the art were not set during the day, and the thieves dissuaded tourists from intervening, reportedly telling them, "Don't worry...we're the police. This is just practice." Escaping in a white Volkswagen Golf, the perpetrators have never been identified—and the painting remains missing.

6. **Stockholm, December 2000; $30 million:** Eight criminals each got up to six and half years behind bars for conspiring to take a Rembrandt and two Renoirs—all of which were eventually recovered—from Stockholm's National Museum. You have to give the three masked men who actually grabbed the paintings credit for a dramatic exit: They fled the scene by motorboat. Police unraveled the plot after recovering one of the paintings during an unrelated drug investigation.

7. **Amsterdam, December 2002: $30 million:** Robbers used a ladder to get onto the roof of the Van Gogh Museum, then broke in and stole two of the Dutch master's paintings—*View of the Sea at Scheveningen* and *Congregation Leaving the Reformed Church in Nuenen*. Police told the press that the thieves worked so quickly that despite setting off the museum's alarms, they had disappeared before police could get there. Authorities in the Netherlands arrested two men in 2003 based on DNA from hair inside two hats left at the scene, but they have been unable to recover the paintings, which the men deny taking.

✳ Vincenzo Peruggia stole the *Mona Lisa* because he believed it belonged in Italy.

The Beguiling *Mona Lisa*

Researchers may have finally uncovered the secrets of Leonardo da Vinci's masterpiece.

✳   ✳   ✳   ✳

THE RENAISSANCE GENIUS began his portrait of Lisa del Giocondo, a Florentine gentlewoman, in 1503 and is believed to have finished the painting just before his death in 1519. Using a process of brushwork he called "sfumato" (from the Italian *fumo*, meaning smoke), Leonardo created a painting that he said was composed "without lines or borders, in the manner of smoke or beyond the focus plane." Although he left many notes on his other projects, Leonardo never explained how he created the subtle effects of light and shadow that give his masterwork its realistic, three-dimensional quality.

Although the painting has been studied extensively over the centuries, even the most modern scientific instruments have been unable to uncover all of its secrets.

French artist and art historian Jacques Franck, however, believes he has discovered Leonardo's methods through his own trial and error. According to Franck, after completing a conventional sketch of his subject, Leonardo applied a base coat of pale yellow imprimatura—a diluted semiopaque wash—then began one of history's greatest creative marathons. Using minute crosshatching techniques, Leonardo spent more than 15 years brushing on 30 successive layers of paint. Apparently requiring a magnifying glass, the process took 30 to 40 small dots of oil paint smaller than the head of a pin to cover one square millimeter of canvas. Franck believes Leonardo applied additional layers of imprimatura between each layer of paint to further soften lines and blend colors, creating successively finer layers of shading and tones.

Although Franck's conclusions have been disputed by some art historians, he has convincingly reproduced the effects with his own copies of small sections of the painting. An exhibit at the Uffizi Gallery in Florence displayed six panels by Franck that re-create one of the eyes from the *Mona Lisa* and illustrate the step-by-step process of how Leonardo may have worked.

Though his artistic sleuthing remains controversial, Franck points out that the use of minute dots of paint—similar to the pointillism developed by modern artists—is an artistic technique that has been used since Roman times and is clearly evident in some of Leonardo's earlier paintings. With the *Mona Lisa*, Leonardo apparently took the technique to an unmatched level.

Other research has used a noninvasive technique called x-ray fluorescence spectroscopy to study the layers and chemical compositions of Leonardo's works. These studies have revealed that he was constantly testing new methods. He did not always use glaze, for example, and while working on the *Mona Lisa*, he mixed manganese oxide in with his paint. Ongoing studies are sure to reveal even more of da Vinci's masterful techniques.

"Art is never finished, only abandoned."

"A picture or representation of human figures, ought to be done in such a way as that the spectator may easily recognise, by means of their attitudes, the purpose in their minds."

"Life is pretty simple: You do some stuff. Most fails. Some works. You do more of what works. If it works big, others quickly copy it. Then you do something else. The trick is the doing something else."

—QUOTES FROM LEONARDO DA VINCI

Illustrious Thinkers

Most of our knowledge and thinking have been shaped by philosophers, who spend their lives searching for truth. Here's a very brief overview of the great Western philosophers.

❋ ❋ ❋ ❋

Socrates: 470–399 B.C.

Major works: Socrates's philosophy was not written down until after his death.

In a nutshell: Devised the Socratic method of argument. Believed people have souls that lead us to virtue, which is synonymous with truth. Once we find truth, we must order our lives by it.

Quote:

"In every one of us there are two ruling and directing principles, whose guidance we follow wherever they may lead; the one being an innate desire of pleasure; the other, an acquired judgment which aspires after excellence."

Fact: Socrates was tried for corrupting youth and was executed with a drink poisoned by hemlock.

Plato: 427–347 B.C.

Major works: *Republic, Phaedo, Symposium*

In a nutshell: Devised an idea of Forms, which are the perfect representations of everything, assuring a constant thread of truth in an ever-changing universe. Plato also discussed ideal forms of government and determined that philosophers make the best leaders.

Quotes:

"Ignorance is the root and stem of every evil."

"The rulers of the state are the only persons who ought to have the privilege of lying, either at home or abroad; they may be allowed to lie for the good of the state."

"The people always have some champion whom they set over them and nurse into greatness ... This and no other is the root from which a tyrant springs; when he first appears he is a protector."

Fact: As a student of Socrates, Plato recorded his teacher's wisdom and expounded on it further.

René Descartes: 1596–1650

Major works: *Discourse on Method, Rules for the Direction of the Mind, Meditations on First Philosophy*

In a nutshell: Descartes believed that the only thing we really know is that we are thinking beings: "I think, therefore I am." By casting everything else into doubt, Descartes attempted to arrive at fundamental truths—such as the existence of God.

Quotes:

"If you would be a real seeker after truth, it is necessary that at least once in your life you doubt, as far as possible, all things."

"All that is very clearly and distinctly conceived is true."

Fact: Descartes was also a trailblazing mathematician. He invented the Cartesian coordinate system, which led to great advances in algebra and geometry.

Blaise Pascal: 1623–1662

Major work: *Thoughts: An Apology for Christianity*

In a nutshell: Pascal felt that reason and thought weren't enough to solve problems; rather, people need to believe in God. He came up with a formula to measure the odds of the existence of God.

Quote:

"If I wager for and God is—infinite gain;
If I wager for and God is not—no loss.
If I wager against and God is—infinite loss;
If I wager against and God is not—neither loss nor gain."

Fact: At age 19, Pascal invented a calculating machine.

John Locke: 1632–1704

Major works: *Essay Concerning Human Understanding, Two Treatises on Civil Government*

In a nutshell: Locke delved into the process through which the mind understands the world. He founded the school of

Empiricism, which maintains that everything people know is derived through experience. His political philosophy centered on a citizen's right to property and the right to revolution.

Quotes:

"New opinions are always suspected, and usually opposed, without any other reason but because they are not already common."

"Consciousness is the perception of what passes in a man's own mind. Can another man perceive that I am conscious of any thing, when I perceive it not myself? No man's knowledge here can go beyond his experience."

Fact: Locke's political writings were so controversial at the time that he was forced to publish them anonymously. He had a tremendous influence on the writers of the U.S. Constitution.

Immanuel Kant: 1724–1804

Major works: *Critique of Pure Reason, Foundations of the Metaphysics of Morals*

In a nutshell: Kant believed that morality and justice were governed by universal laws, just as nature is. Kant's Categorical Imperative meant that even though God's existence can't be proven, everyone has a duty to act as if there is a God.

Quotes:

"Act only according to that maxim by which you can at the same time will that it should become a universal law."

"But although all our knowledge begins with experience, it does not follow that it arises from experience."

Fact: Generally regarded to be the greatest modern philosopher, Kant has had significant influence on those who have followed.

Friedrich Nietzsche: 1844–1900

Major works: *The Birth of Tragedy, Twilight of the Idols, Thus Spake Zarathustra*

In a nutshell: Nietzsche is famous for his criticism of culture: science, history, philosophy, art, and religion. He argued that one can't rely on the abstract—religion or philosophy—to find truth. Only superior individuals can rise above traditional concepts of good and evil to achieve a truly worthy human life.

Quotes:

"God is dead...and we have killed him."

"In the mountains of truth, you never climb in vain. Either you already reach a higher point today, or you exercise your strength in order to be able to climb higher tomorrow."

Fact: In 1889, Nietzsche saw a horse being whipped by a coachman. He threw his arms around the horse, and it is said that he never regained his sanity. Nietzsche died eleven years later.

Martin Heidegger: 1889–1976

Major works: *Being and Time, The Basic Problems of Phenomenology*

In a nutshell: Heidegger investigated the nature of human existence, which he defined as active participation in the world, or "Being There." He also looked at existence in relation to the pressures of modern society and acknowledgment of human mortality.

Quote:

"Man acts as though he were the shaper and master of language, while in fact language remains the master of man."

Fact: Although he rejected the title, Heidegger is often credited with being the founder of Existentialism.

"Be as you wish to seem."

—SOCRATES

"I attribute the little I know to my not having been ashamed to ask for information, and to my rule of conversing with all descriptions of men on those topics that form their own peculiar professions and pursuits."

—JOHN LOCKE

"Even philosophers will praise war as enabling mankind, forgetting the Greek who said, 'War is bad in that it begets more evil than it kills.'"

—IMMANUEL KANT

The Library of the Muses

*The most famous library in history, the Library of
Alexandria held an untold number of ancient works.
Its fiery destruction meant the irrecoverable loss of a
substantial part of the world's intellectual history.*

✳ ✳ ✳ ✳

THE CITIES OF ancient Mesopotamia (e.g., Uruk, Nineveh,
Babylon) and Egypt (e.g., Thebes, Memphis) had cultivated archives and libraries since the Bronze Age. The idea
for a library as grand as the one at Alexandria, however, did
not occur in Greek culture until the Hellenistic Age, when
Alexander the Great's conquests brought both Greece and
these civilizations under Macedonian rule. Previous Greek
libraries were owned by individuals; the largest belonged to
Aristotle (384–322 B.C.), whose work and school (the Lyceum)
in Athens were supported by Alexander.

When Alexander died suddenly in 323 B.C., his generals carved
his empire into regional dynasties. These Hellenistic dynasties
competed with each other for three centuries (until each was
in turn conquered by either Rome or Parthia). Each desired
cultural dominance, so they invited famous artists, authors, and
intellectuals to live and work in their capital cities.

Alexander's general Ptolemy, who controlled Egypt, developed
a collection of the world's learning (the Library) and a research
center (the Mouseion, or Museum, which was also called the
"Temple of the Muses"), where scholars on subsidy could
study and add their research to the collection. This idea may
well have come from Demetrius of Phaleron (350–280 B.C.),
Ptolemy's advisor and the former governor of Athens (who had
been a pupil at the Lyceum), but the grand project became one
of the hallmarks of the Ptolemaic dynasty. Under the first three
Ptolemies, the Museum, a royal library, and a smaller "daughter" library at the Temple of Serapis (the Serapeum) were built

and grew as Alexandria became the intellectual capital of the Hellenistic world.

Egypt and Alexandria offered the Ptolemies distinct advantages for accomplishing their goals. Egypt was not only immensely rich, which gave it the wealth to purchase materials and to bring scholars to Alexandria, but it was a major producer of papyrus. Alexandria was also the commercial hub of the Mediterranean, so goods and information from all over the world passed through its port.

Bibliomania: So Many Scrolls, So Little Time

Acquiring materials for the libraries and museum became something of an obsession for the Ptolemies. Although primarily focused on Greek and Egyptian works, their interests included translating other traditions into Greek. Among the most important of these efforts was the production of the *Septuagint*, a Greek version of the Jewish scriptures.

Besides employing agents to scour book markets to search out works not yet in the library, the rulers of Alexandria required boats coming into port to declare any scrolls on board. If they were of interest, the scrolls were confiscated and copied, and the owners were given the copies and some compensation. Ptolemy III (285–222 B.C.) may have acquired Athens' official state collection of the plays of Aeschylus, Sophocles, and Euripides in a similar way—putting up 15 talents of silver as a guarantee while he had the plays copied, then giving up the treasure in favor of keeping the originals. Whether or not this is true, it speaks to the value he placed on obtaining important works and the resources he had at his disposal to do so.

The Ptolemies' efforts were fueled by competition with the Hellenistic kingdom of Pergamum (modern Bergamo, Turkey), which had created its own library. Each sought to claim new finds and produce new editions, which led at times to the acquisitions of forgeries and occasional embarrassment. Alexandria finally tried to undercut its rival by cutting off papyrus exports, but Pergamum perfected a method for making writing material out of animal skins and continued to build its holdings. Eventually, however, Alexandria gained the upper hand when the Roman general Marcus Antonius (Marc Antony) conquered Pergamum and made a present of its library to his Egyptian lover Cleopatra.

Estimates as to the number of volumes in the Alexandrian library ranged wildly even in antiquity, generally falling between 200,000 and 700,000. These assessments are complicated by the fact that it isn't clear whether the numbers originate from works or scrolls: Some scrolls contained one work, some multiple works, and long works like the *Iliad* took multiple scrolls. Over time, a complex cataloguing system evolved, which culminated in a bibliographic survey of the library's holdings called the Pinakes. It was assembled by the great Hellenistic scholar and poet Callimachus of Cyrene (305–240 B.C.). Unfortunately, only fragments of this important work remain.

Burning Down the House

The Royal Library and its holdings were accidentally set aflame in 48 B.C. when Julius Caesar (who had taken Cleopatra's side in her claim to the throne against her brother) tried to burn his way out of being trapped in the port by opposing forces. Further losses probably occurred in A.D. 271 when Emperor Aurelian destroyed part of the Museum while recapturing Alexandria from the forces of Queen Zenobia of Palmyra.

The Serapeum—the "daughter" library—was finally destroyed by Christians under Emperor Theodosius near the end of the 4th century. But by then, much of the contents (like the contents of other great civic libraries of antiquity) had decayed or found their ways into other hands, leaving the classical heritage scattered and fragmented for centuries. Much later, Christians dramatically blamed Muslim conquerors for the burning of the library. Although this made for a good story, the legendary contents of the library were already long gone.

The Mysterious Voynich Manuscript

Dubbed the "World's Most Mysterious Book," the Voynich manuscript contains more than 200 vellum pages of vivid, colorful illustrations and handwritten prose. There's only one small problem: No one knows what any of it means—or whether it means anything at all.

✳ ✳ ✳ ✳

I T WAS "DISCOVERED" in 1912 after being hidden from the world for almost 250 years. An American antique book dealer named Wilfried Voynich came across the medieval manuscript at an Italian Jesuit College. Approximately nine inches by six inches in size, the manuscript bore a soft, light-brown vellum cover, which was unmarked, untitled, and gave no indication as to when it had been written or by whom.

Bound inside were approximately 230 yellow parchment pages, most of which contained richly colored drawings of strange plants, celestial bodies, and other scientific matter. Many of the pages were adorned by naked nymphs bathing in personal-size washtubs. Handwritten text written in flowing script accompanied the illustrations.

Although Voynich was an expert antiquarian, he was baffled by the book's contents. And today—nearly a century later—the manuscript that came to bear his name remains a mystery.

Weird Science

The mystery surrounding the Voynich manuscript begins with its content, which reads (so to speak) like a work of weird science presented in six identifiable "sections":

✳ a botanical section, containing drawings of plants that no botanist has ever been able to identify

✳ an astronomical section, with illustrations of the sun, moon, stars, and zodiac symbols surrounded by the ever-present bathing nymphs

* a "biological" section, showing perplexing anatomical drawings of chambers or organs connected by tubes—and which also features more nymphs swimming in their inner liquids

* a cosmological section, consisting mostly of unexplained circular drawings

* a pharmaceutical section, depicting drawings of plant parts (leaves, roots) placed next to containers

* a recipe section, featuring short paragraphs "bulleted" by stars in the margin

Weirder still are the ubiquitous nymphs—a nice touch perhaps, but how they relate to the subject matter is anyone's guess.

Many Mysteries, Still No Answers

And then there's the enigmatic text. The world's greatest cryptologists have failed to unravel its meaning. Even the American and British code breakers who cracked the Japanese and German codes in World War II were stumped. To this day, not a single word of the Voynich manuscript has been deciphered.

This, of course, has led to key unsolved questions, namely:

* Who wrote it? A letter found with the manuscript, dated 1666, credits Roger Bacon, a Franciscan friar who lived from 1214 to 1294. This has since been discredited because the manuscript's date of origin is generally considered to be between 1450 and 1500. There are as many theories about who wrote it as there are nymphs among its pages. In fact, some believe Voynich forged the whole thing.

* What is it? It was first thought to be a coded description of Bacon's early scientific discoveries. Since then, other theories ranging from an ancient prayer book written in a pidgin Germanic language to one big, elaborate hoax (aside from that supposedly perpetrated by Voynich) have been posited.

* Is it real writing? Is the script composed in a variation of a known language, a lost language, an encrypted language, an artificial language? Or is it just plain gibberish?

What Do We Know?

Despite the aura of mystery surrounding the manuscript, it has been possible to trace its travels over the past 400 years. The earliest known owner was Holy Roman Emperor Rudolph II, who purchased it in 1586. By 1666, the manuscript had passed through a series of owners to Athanasius Kircher, a Jesuit scholar who hid it in the college where Voynich found it 250 years later.

After being passed down to various members of Voynich's estate, the manuscript was sold in 1961 to a rare-book collector who sought to resell it for a fortune. After failing to find a buyer, he donated it to Yale University, where it currently resides—still shrouded in mystery—in the Beinecke Rare Book and Manuscript Library.

The Search for Meaning Continues...

To this day, efforts to translate the Voynich manuscript continue. And still, the manuscript refuses to yield its secrets, leading experts to conclude that it's either an ingenious hoax or the ultimate unbreakable code.

The hoax theory gained some ground in 2004 when Dr. Gordon Rugg, a computer-science lecturer at Keele University, announced that he had replicated the Voynich manuscript using a low-tech device called a Cardan grille. According to Rugg, this proved that the manuscript was likely a fraud—a volume of jibberish created, perhaps, by the infamous Edward Kelley in an attempt to con money out of Emperor Rudolph II.

Mystery solved? Well, it's not quite that simple. Many researchers remain unconvinced. Sure, Rugg demonstrated that the manuscript might be a hoax. But the possibility that it is not a hoax remains. And thus, the search for meaning continues...

Gift of the Revolution

Built by French kings over six centuries, the famed Louvre found its true calling with the bloody end of the dynasty that built it.

✳ ✳ ✳ ✳

THE ART COLLECTION known throughout the world as the Louvre began as a moated, medieval arsenal erected to protect the city's inhabitants against the Anglo-Norman threat. Built by King Philippe Auguste in the late 12th century, the fortress lost much of its military value as the city expanded far beyond the castle walls over the next 150 years. In 1364, King Charles V had the Louvre redesigned as a royal residence.

During the next three centuries, French kings and queens remodeled and redesigned portions of the Louvre, connecting it with the nearby Tuileries palace. Apartments and galleries were added, and remnants of the medieval fortress were demolished.

During the reign of King Louis XIV, the palace came into its own, as classical paintings and sculptures by the great artists of the day graced the palace's walls and ceilings. Work halted briefly in 1672, when Louis moved the French court to his fantastic palace at Versailles, but in 1692 Louis sent a set of antique sculptures back to the Louvre's Salle de Caryatides, inaugurating the first of the Louvre's many antique accessions. Academies of arts and sciences took up residence at the palace, and in 1699, the Académie Royale de Peinture et de Sculpture held its first exhibition in the Louvre's Grand Galerie.

The artistic treasures housed by the French monarchs were, of course, the property of the king and off-limits to the masses. But in 1791, in the wake of the French Revolution, the French Assemblée Nationale declared all Bourbon property to be held by the state for the people of France. The government established a public art and science museum at the Louvre and Tuileries, and in 1793, the year King Louis XVI and his queen,

Marie Antoinette, were sent to the guillotine, the Museum Central des Arts opened its doors to the public.

As Napoleon's armies marched through Italy, Austria, and Egypt in the late 1790s, the museum's collections grew with the spoils of war. Napoleon and Empress Josephine inaugurated an antiquities gallery at the Louvre in 1800, and three years later, the museum was briefly renamed the Musée Napoléon. With the emperor's fall in 1815, however, the Louvre's status diminished as many of its artifacts were returned to their rightful owners.

A Representative Collection

In the mid-19th century, the Louvre opened additional galleries to showcase Spanish, Algerian, and Egyptian art. As the Louvre soldiered on into the 20th century, its more exotic holdings— particularly Islamic and Middle Eastern art—expanded, and the museum was progressively remodeled to accommodate its growing collection.

At the outbreak of World War II, French officials fretted that the Louvre's holdings would become a target for Nazi pillage, so they dispersed most of the treasures among the Loire valley chateaus. The Nazis had the museum reopened in September 1940, though there was little left for the cowed Parisians to view until the country was liberated four years later.

In 1945, the restored French government reorganized its national art collections, and in 1983 the government announced a sweeping reorganization and remodeling plan under the direction of the famed Chinese American architect I. M. Pei. Impressionist and other late 19th-century works were moved to the Musée d'Orsay, while Pei's famous glass pyramid, which towers over the Cour Napoleon, signaled a new stage in the Louvre's life. Further renovations from 1993 to the present have given the Louvre its distinctive look, as well as its status as one of the world's premier museums.

Quotes on Creativity

"Creativity is allowing yourself to make mistakes. Art is knowing which ones to keep."

—SCOTT ADAMS, CARTOONIST

"The chief enemy of creativity is good taste."

—PABLO PICASSO

"The art of creation is older than the art of killing."

—ANDREI VOZNESENSKY, POET

"My place in society was at the bottom. Here life offered nothing but sordidness and wretchedness, both of the flesh and the spirit; for here flesh and spirit were alike starved and tormented."

—JACK LONDON, "WHAT LIFE MEANS TO ME," FROM *REVOLUTION AND OTHER ESSAYS* (1910)

"Necessity is the mother of invention, it is true, but its father is creativity, and knowledge is the midwife."

—JONATHAN SCHATTKE, SCIENTIST

"Creative minds always have been known to survive any kind of bad training."

—ANNA FREUD, FOUNDER OF CHILD PSYCHOANALYSIS

"The whole difference between construction and creation is this: that a thing constructed can only be loved after it is constructed; but a thing created is loved before it exists."

—CHARLES DICKENS

"True creativity often starts where language ends."

—ARTHUR KOESTLER, WRITER

"A hunch is creativity trying to tell you something."

—FRANK KAPRA

"There is a correlation between the creative and the screwball. So we must suffer the screwball gladly."

—KINGMAN BREWSTER, AMERICAN DIPLOMAT AND FORMER PRESIDENT OF YALE UNIVERSITY

Going Under the Knife to Hit the High Notes

"Mutilated for their art" is how one period writer praised the castrati, male sopranos and alto-sopranos whose manhood was intentionally removed before puberty to keep their voices "sweet."

✳ ✳ ✳ ✳

PUTTING YOUNG BOYS under the knife to create a corps of eunuchs had been done since antiquity. While the practice was applied by the Byzantine, Ottoman, and Chinese to create castes of priests, civil servants, and harem guards, the Italians of the 16th century used it to populate their church choirs.

Young boys can hit high notes for only so long before hormones kick in and thicken the vocal cords. Late Renaissance Italians, with the blessing of a Papal Bull from 1589, pre-empted this progression of nature. Priests and choirmasters recruited boys, and parents sold or volunteered their sons (often as young as eight years old) to undergo castration. The removal of their testicles ensured that the boys would keep their sweet, angelic voices—voices that, as they grew into men, would become stronger and louder and more powerful without dropping in tone and timbre. Castrati had the "chest of man and the voice of a woman," as one enthusiastic supporter of the practice observed.

The Italians were not the first to introduce prepubescent emasculation in the name of art. Byzantine Empress Eudoxia first sanctioned this practice in A.D. 400 at the urging of her choirmaster, Brison, but the practice soon fell out of favor. Even so, as the Renaissance and the golden age of church music dawned, the castration of young boys began to occur with regularity throughout Europe, particularly in Germany. It was in Italy, however, where it became something of a mania and where it continued for the longest amount of time.

By the late 18th century, as many as 4,000 boys a year were inducted into the ranks of the castrati in Italy alone—an especially staggering statistic considering the crude medical practices and almost complete lack of anesthesia of the era. (Some patients were given drink and opium before the procedure, however.)

Taking to the Stage

Castrati also appeared in plays, taking female roles at a time when women were still banned from performing in public. Although most castrati never left the choir, the popularization and proliferation of opera in the 17th, 18th, and 19th centuries gave them a new stage on which to showcase their talents. Opera castrati were the superstars of their era; noted composers wrote lead roles for them. Prized for the power and pitch of their angelic voices, the best of them were the toast of Europe, courted by kings, praised by artists, and sought after by women.

The revolutions that rocked Europe eventually turned public opinion against the practice. At first only frowned upon, it was soon banned by law. Italy, in 1870, was the last of the European countries to enact such legislation. The Catholic Church, however, continued to welcome castrati into church choirs until 1902, and it was not until the following year that Pope Leo XIII revoked the Papal Bull of 1589.

Even as their ranks thinned, cries of *eviva il coltello* or "long live the knife" continued to resound for these aging stars when they performed. Castrati hit the high notes right up until the eve of the First World War. Alessandro Moreschi, who retired in 1913, was the last of the castrati. His angelic falsetto has been preserved in a rare recording made in 1902.

﹡ King Philip V of Spain suffered from severe depression. The castrato Farinelli was summoned to sing for the king in an attempt to soothe him, and it did the trick. Farinelli stayed on and served in the king's court for two decades.

The Makings of a Rock Star

Although the musical form had yet to be invented, Niccolò Paganini was perhaps the first rock star in history.

✳   ✳   ✳   ✳

A MERE MORTAL SIMPLY couldn't play the way Niccolò Paganini did—that was the popular opinion, at least; the rumor was that the Italian virtuoso had sold his soul to the devil in exchange for his extraordinary talent. According to reports, at least one audience member had seen a mysterious goatlike creature standing behind the violinist on stage, guiding his hands as he played. Another account told of a mysterious black coach, pulled by horses whose eyes were made of fire, disappearing into the night after a concert. Indeed, Paganini's very name translated to "the little pagan." And, to top it all off, he refused the Last Rites on his death bed. Could there be any doubt that he was in league with Satan? The fact that these outlandish claims found support during the great Age of Enlightenment only reinforces the legend that was Paganini.

There is, of course, a more prosaic explanation for Paganini's skill: mere genius. And it was fortunate for young Niccolò that he was just that. His father, Antonio Paganini, an 18th-century version of a show-business parent, saw a business opportunity in his son. He constantly reminded the boy that Mozart had composed his first works at the age of five and allegedly forced Niccolò to practice the violin for hours a day, locking him in a room and withholding food—but not withholding the strap.

Niccolò composed his first sonata when he was 8 and was performing for aristocracy by age 11. He was sent to study under the renowned teachers of the day and undertook a tour of Italy at 15 years old. The young musician caused something of a sensation, but the money from the concerts went to his father. Niccolò took full advantage of his growing fame, going to parties, drinking, spending time in the company of a succession of young ladies, and gambling—even, at times, wagering his violin. Eventually tiring of the lifestyle, he left home and kept company with a Tuscan woman whose identity is still a mystery. During Niccolò's three-year absence, he enjoyed her companionship and focused on the guitar rather than the violin.

Back in the Spotlight

When Paganini appeared in public again, he took a job in Lucca as composer for Napoleon's sister Elise; according to rumor, he was also her lover and had similar relationships with other ladies of the court. While in her employ, he was charged with playing two concerts a week; he would often put them together in as little as two hours, writing out an accompanying piece and leaving it to himself to improvise his own performance. Improvisation would always be Paganini's favored element. When touring, he would rehearse his accompanying orchestra, requiring the professional musicians to demonstrate mastery of their parts. When his turn came, he would scrape a few notes on his Guarnerius violin before waving his hand and dismissing the orchestra with an "Et cetera, Signori"—much to their frustration. His time with Elise also produced one of Paganini's famous tricks: She challenged him to play an entire performance on one string of his violin; he complied, sometimes walking out on stage and breaking the other strings in full view of his audience.

Paganini undertook tours of Europe to great initial success. Wherever he went, crowds reached out to touch him; portraits of him went on sale; and ladies abandoned their embroidery and other crafts to take up the violin. Other musicians would attend concert after concert in hopes of learning his technique; one even followed him on tour, renting adjacent hotel rooms and peeking through the keyhole in Paganini's door. He was not rewarded, however. People rarely saw Paganini practice; in his view, he had practiced enough for one lifetime. Always nervous before a performance, he was rumored to lie motionless across his bed for hours—whether sleeping or mentally running though his music—perhaps occasionally rising to silently try a fingering on his violin before springing up at the last minute and racing out to his concert.

Two Thumbs Down?

Paganini's career was not without controversy. His love for improvisation was such that other musicians accused him (incorrectly) of being unable to play anything else. In fact, he was quite familiar with Beethoven and other masters and would play them in private, but for public performances he preferred his own compositions. Some critics saw his stage antics—playing on one string, drawing forth animal noises from his instrument, and even at one point playing on a wooden shoe that had been strung—as mere parlor tricks hiding a serious musician. Others complained that he was a money-grubber due to the enormous increase in ticket prices his appearances were able to command. For his part, Paganini did not go out of his way to appease his critics. At one point, he told a royal patron who had complained about Paganini's requested fee that he ought to pay for admission to a public concert instead.

Still, when all was said and done, Paganini's reputation overcame all criticism. While most of his music was never written down, he did leave behind six concertos, an equal number of sonatas, and a variety of other works that continue to challenge the top virtuosos of today. Paganini died on May 27, 1840. Those present say that in his final days, he found the strength to play one last improvisational piece that lasted for hours; listeners claim it was the finest the master had ever played. Following that performance, he retired to his bed and died three days later, clutching his violin.

"Where our reason ends, there Paganini begins."

—Giacomo Meyerbeer, opera composer

Blooming Bust in the Dutch Republic

One of the most unlikely of all dramas began in 17th-century Holland, when a French botanist planted a Turkish bulb in a university garden. The resulting flower mesmerized a nation and eventually became a major export and mainstay of the Dutch economy.

✳ ✳ ✳ ✳

C AN A MERE flower incite great nationalist passion? Well, if it's a tulip, it can. What might be dubbed "Tulipmania" swept what is now Holland in 1636 and 1637. The flowers' popularity turned the pretty plants into serious money spinners and encouraged a competitive fad among the nouveau riche. Suddenly, the tulip was a coveted status symbol.

The instigator of all this was a French-born botanist named Carolus Clusius, who lived and died before the craze hit. Born in 1526 and originally educated as a lawyer, Clusius was encouraged by a professor to switch his studies to botany. He subsequently traveled the world gathering plant specimens and became one of Europe's leading botanists. His reputation was so sterling that Austrian Emperor Maximilian II appointed him court physician and overseer of the royal medicinal garden.

In 1593, Clusius settled in the Netherlands, where he was appointed prefect for the newly established horticulture academy at the University of Leiden. That fall, Clusius planted a teaching garden and a private plot that showcased hundreds of varieties of plants, including several hundred tulip bulbs given to him by his friend, Ogier Ghiselin de Busbecq, Austrian Ambassador to the Ottoman Empire.

Prior to Clusius, no Dutch person had ever seen a tulip bulb or blossom. The rarity and beauty of the new flower caused a national sensation. Members of the aristocracy clamored to add tulips to their private gardens. When Clusius declined to sell any of his private stock, many were stolen from his garden. One nighttime raid netted thieves more than 100 bulbs.

Big Money in the Dutch Republic

Carolus Clusius died in 1609, but the engine he had set in motion continued to chug without him. In the 1620s, the Dutch Republic began its ascent to global power, gaining a trade monopoly with the East Indies and Japan. Sound government monetary policy demanded that national currency be backed 10 percent by gold and silver deposits, held by the Bank of Amsterdam. The republic was flush with cash.

Money supply in the Dutch Republic was increased further by an influx of precious metals, which were traded for paper currency, as well as by the Dutch East India Company's seizure of Portuguese ships laden with gold, silver, and jewels. At the height of Tulipmania, the Bank of Amsterdam's deposits increased by more than 40 percent. People had more money to spend than ever before, and they became bold in an atmosphere that was ripe for speculation.

My Kingdom for a Tulip

The tulip quickly became a status symbol. Members of the upper class spent huge amounts of money to acquire rare bulbs. Some sums were utterly ridiculous. Consider that during the 1600s, the average Dutch worker earned 150 florins per year. In 1623, one particularly rare tulip bulb sold for 1,000 florins. In another famous sale, an extraordinary *Semper Augustus* bulb sold for 6,000 florins. The price per pound of some bulbs reached the equivalent price of a modest house.

By 1636, a structured, but unregulated, futures market had developed for the tulip trade. Most of the trading occurred in local taverns, where bulbs were bought and resold many times before actual delivery. The Dutch referred to this practice as *windhandel*, or *wind trade*, because payment for the bulbs occurred only when they were dug from the ground in the summer, after the plant had bloomed and died back. Local-government legislation designed to curtail speculation did little to affect the trade.

The Flower Economy Crashes

In February 1637, the Dutch guild of florists, which had been marginalized by the wildcat trading, decreed that all futures contracts were now mere options contracts. With a futures contract, both parties must fulfill the contract's terms. With an options contract, the holder has the right, but is not obligated, to exercise the contract. The florist guild's decision allowed buyers to break their contracts for a fraction of actual value.

On April 27, 1637, the Dutch government canceled all tulip contracts with a decree stating that tulips were a product, not an investment. Between this and an oversupply of bulbs, the value of tulips plummeted and the market crashed. Buyers refused to honor their contracts and simply walked away from their deals. Growers were not only unable to sell their stock, they suddenly had no hope of collecting any of the money owed to them.

Between 1635 and 1637, the number of bankruptcies in Amsterdam doubled. Prices for bulbs stabilized at reasonable levels shortly after the collapse, but many Dutch were so discouraged they never entered the tulip market again.

✳ The breathtaking *Semper Augustus* tulip was red with white striations, which were actually the result of a virus. Because of the virus, this bulb was rather weak, and *Semper Augustus* tulips no longer exist. Many heirloom varieties do, however. Go to oldhousegarden.com to explore the possibilities.

Muse of the Nursery

There was an old lady,
With the name Mother Goose.
She told children stories,
Could she just be a ruse?

Did she really exist?
That legend of old.
The elderly storyteller,
Of whom we were told.

You'll have to read on,
To discover the truth.
To tell you right here,
Would be rather uncouth.

✳ ✳ ✳ ✳

WHETHER IT'S THE muffin man, the farmer in the dell, or Humpty Dumpty, Mother Goose has rhymes for them all. While collections of these nursery rhymes bear the name Mother Goose and the illustration of an old peasant woman, most of the so-called Mother Goose tales originated centuries ago as folktales and legends handed down from generation to generation. Mothers would comfort their young children by singing rhyming verses to the tunes of ballads and folk songs.

Many have tried to track down the identity of the real Mother Goose, but she is mythical. The earliest written reference to Mother Goose appeared in a poem titled *La Muse Historique* in a 1660s issue of French critic Jean Loret's monthly periodical. Loret wrote, "...*comme un conte de la Mère Oye*," which translated means "...like a Mother Goose story."

Charles Perrault, who served on the staff of King Louis XIV, was the first author to use the name Mother Goose in the title of a book. In 1697, Perrault published a collection of children's stories titled *Histoires ou Contes du temps passe* ("Histories or Tales from the Past with Morals"). The frontispiece carried the subtitle, *Contes de ma mère l'Oye* ("Tales from My Mother Goose"). On the book's cover was an illustration of an old woman telling stories to a group of children. The book contained a compilation of eight folktales, including Sleeping Beauty, Cinderella, Little Red Riding Hood, and Puss in Boots.

It took more than 30 years for Mother Goose to make her debut in English. In 1729, writer Robert Samber translated Perrault's book under the title, *Histories or Tales of Past Times, Told by Mother Goose.*

London bookseller John Newbery had published a collection of nursery rhymes in 1744. In 1765, he incorporated the name Mother Goose when he published *Mother Goose's Melody, or Sonnets for the Cradle.* Newbery's book contained more than 50 rhymes and songs and marked a shift in the subject of children's books from fairy tales to nursery rhymes.

Claiming a Spot in the Hearts of Americans

Mother Goose made her first appearance in America in 1786, when Massachusetts printer Isaiah Thomas reprinted Robert Samber's book using the same title. It was in America that Mother Goose would take hold as the keeper of nursery rhymes. In the early 19th century, she became even more popular when Boston-based Munroe & Francis began printing inexpensive and lavish Mother Goose editions.

Regardless of whether the original Mother Goose was an actual person, she is real in the minds of many young children. The rhythms, alliteration, and silly stories found in the Mother Goose tales have entranced children for centuries, and as long as there are babies to sing to, they will no doubt continue to do so.

The Vanishing Treasure Room

In the Age of Enlightenment, kings and emperors built immense palaces to outdo one another—each one bigger and more gilded and bejeweled than the last. But one of Russia's greatest 18th century treasures became one of the 20th century's greatest unsolved mysteries.

✳ ✳ ✳ ✳

THE STORIED HISTORY of the Amber Room begins in 1701, when it was commissioned by Frederick I of Prussia. Considered by admirers and artists alike to be the "Eighth Wonder of the World," the sparkling, honey-gold room consisted of wall panels inlaid with prehistoric amber, finely carved and illuminated by candles and mirrors. In 1716, Prussian King Freidrich Wilhelm I gifted the panels to then-ally Russian Tsar Peter the Great to ornament the imperial palace at his new capital, St. Petersburg.

After sitting at the Winter Palace for four decades, the Amber Room was moved to Tsarskoye Selo, the Romanov palace just south of St. Petersburg. During the mid-18th century, Prussia's King Frederick the Great sent Russia's Empress Elizabeth more of the amber material from his Baltic holdings, and Elizabeth ordered her court's great Italian architect, Bartolomeo Rastrelli, to expand the Amber Room into an 11-foot-square masterpiece.

The golden room was not finished until 1770, under the reign of Catherine the Great. Incorporating more than six tons of amber and accented with semiprecious stones, the fabled room became not only a prized jewel of the Russian empire, but a symbol of the long-standing alliance between Prussia and Russia.

Two centuries after the Amber Room was removed to the Tsarskoye Selo, the world was a much darker place. Prussia and Russia, formerly faithful allies, were locked in a deadly struggle that would bring down both imperial houses. By 1941, the former dominions of Frederick and Peter were ruled by Adolf Hitler and Joseph Stalin.

In a surprise attack, Hitler's armies drove across the Soviet border in June 1941. German panzers drove from the Polish frontier to the gates of Moscow in an epic six-month campaign, devouring some of the most fertile, productive territory in Eastern Europe.

An Attempt to Cover

One of the unfortunate cities in the path of the Nazi onslaught was St. Petersburg, renamed Leningrad by its communist masters. Frantic palace curators desperately tried to remove the Amber Room's antique panels, but the brittle prehistoric resin began to crumble as the panels were detached. Faced with probable destruction of one of Russia's greatest treasures or its abandonment to the Nazis, the curators attempted to hide the room's precious panels by covering them with gauze and wallpaper.

Although Leningrad withstood a long, bloody siege, German troops swept through the city's suburbs, capturing Tsarskoye Selo intact in October 1941. Soldiers discovered the treasure hidden behind the wallpaper, and German troops disassembled the room's panels over a 36-hour period, packed them in 27 crates, and shipped them back to Königsberg, in East Prussia.

The fabled Amber Room panels were put on display in Königsberg's castle museum. They remained there for two years—until the Third Reich began to crumble before the weight of Soviet and Anglo-American military forces. Sometime in 1944, the room's valuable panels were allegedly dismantled and packed into crates, to prevent damage by British and Soviet bombers. In January 1945, Hitler permitted the westward movement of cultural treasures, including the Italo-Russo-German masterpiece.

And from there, the Amber Room was lost to history.

The Great Treasure Hunt

The world was left to speculate about the fate of the famous imperial room, and dozens of theories have been spawned about the room's whereabouts. Some claim the Amber Room was lost—sunk aboard a submarine, bombed to pieces, or perhaps burned in Königsberg. This last conclusion was accepted by Alexander Brusov, a Soviet investigator sent to find the Amber Room shortly after war's end. Referring to the destruction of Königsberg Castle by Red Army forces on April 9, 1945, he concluded: "Summarizing all the facts, we can say that the Amber Room was destroyed between 9 and 11 April 1945." An in-depth hunt by two British investigative journalists pieced together the last days of the Amber Room and concluded that its fate was sealed when Soviet troops accidentally set fire to the castle compound during the last month of combat, destroying the brittle jewels and obscuring their location.

Other treasure hunters, however, claim the room still sits in an abandoned mine shaft or some long-forgotten Nazi bunker beneath the outskirts of Königsberg. One German investigator claimed former SS officers told him the room's panels were packed up and hidden in an abandoned silver mine near Berlin; a Lithuanian official claimed witnesses saw SS troops hiding the panels in a local swamp. Neither has been able to prove his claims.

The Trail Goes Cold

The hunt for the Amber Room has been made more difficult because its last witnesses are gone—several under mysterious circumstances. General Gusev, a Soviet intelligence officer who spoke to a journalist about the room's whereabouts, died in a car crash the day after their conversation. In 1987, Georg Stein, a former German soldier who had devoted his life to searching for the Amber Room, was found murdered in a forest, his stomach slit open by a scalpel.

In 1997, the world got a tantalizing glimpse of the long-lost treasure when German police raided the office of a Bremen lawyer who was attempting to sell an amber mosaic worth $2.5 million on behalf of one of his clients, the son of a former German lieutenant. The small mosaic—inlaid with jade and onyx as well as amber—had been stolen from the Amber Room by a German officer and was separated from the main panels. After its seizure, this last true remnant of the legendary tsarist treasure made its way back to Russia in April 2000.

Decades of searches by German and Soviet investigators have come up empty. The fate of the fabled room—worth an estimated $142 million to $250 million in today's currency—has remained an elusive ghost for treasure seekers, mystery writers, and investigators looking for the Holy Grail of Russian baroque artwork.

In 1979, the Soviet government, with help from a donation made by a German gas firm in 1999, began amassing old photographs of the Amber Room and pieces of the rare amber to create a reconstructed room worthy of its predecessor. Carefully rebuilt at a cost exceeding $7 million, the reconstructed room was dedicated by the Russian president and German chancellor at a ceremony in 2003, marking the tricentennial of St. Petersburg's founding. The dazzling Amber Room is now on display for the thousands of tourists who come to Tsarskoye Selo to view the playground of one of Europe's great dynasties.

---

* **Amber comes from the dried resin of prehistoric trees.**
* **Of all gems, amber is the lightest.**
* **When rubbed, amber can acquire an electric charge.**

Plato's Academy

Many people may refer to the ancient philosopher Plato in only one context: As the inspiration for the term platonic love, *he unwittingly loaned his name to a description of love* sans carnality. *But his other gifts to humanity are infinitely more precious.*

✳ ✳ ✳ ✳

PLATO (C. 428–347 B.C.) had been a student of Socrates, a philosopher who wandered Athens. Plato adopted Socrates' philosophy concerning virtuousness and the formation of a noble character, but after Socrates' death, he abandoned his original plans to become a politician. The older philosopher had angered the powerful rulers of the day with calls for virtuous behavior, so they sentenced him to execution via a poisonous drink of hemlock.

After Socrates was dead, Plato traveled for more than a decade, studying geometry, geology, astronomy, and religion in Italy and Egypt. Plato's writing picked up considerably after 400 B.C. He may be best known today for *The Republic*, which is written in a question-and-answer format. It is one of the most influential works of philosophy ever written, touching upon the great issues of life: wisdom, courage, justice, how an individual relates to him- or herself as well as society as a whole, what it means to live a "good life." Plato had a threefold theory of the structure of society, which he saw as divided into governing class, warriors, and workers. He held a similar theory about the soul, which he believed consisted of reason, spirit, and appetite. In Plato's view, an ideal government would have only philosophers as rulers.

Plato created his Academy around 387 B.C. on a site that was related to a mythological Athenian hero called *Akademos*. This became the basis for the word *academia*. Located just outside the city walls of Athens, the area contained a sacred grove of olive trees that may have been dedicated to Athena, the goddess of wisdom. Festivals, athletic events, and even funerals were held there.

Plato's Academy is considered to have been the first European university—it offered subjects including biology, mathematics, political theory, and, of course, philosophy. Perhaps most important, it sometimes advocated skeptical thinking and denied the possibility of ever attaining an absolute truth: Since people perceive everything through subjective senses, all they can strive for is a high degree of probability. The manner in which Plato ran the Academy and his ideas of what an educated citizen should be still exert a major influence on educational theory, logic, and legal philosophy today.

The Academy's Downfall

Plato remained associated with the Academy until his death, and the Academy flourished until it came into direct conflict with the Byzantine Emperor Justinian (c. A.D. 481–565). Justinian oversaw many positive accomplishments, such as the rewriting of Roman law, *Corpus Juris Civilis*, which still remains the basis for much contemporary civil law. But he was also devoted to the restoration of the Byzantine Empire, and he didn't mind using despotic force (such as the compulsory conversion of everyone to his form of Catholicism) to achieve his goals.

Anyone who didn't subscribe to Justinian's faith was either converted or hideously tortured to death. Justinian ordered Plato's Academy closed down (on the grounds that it was pagan in nature) and its property confiscated, beginning a surge of religiously justified seizures and destruction. Further, the emperor demanded the total erasure of Hellenism, which had given the world its first democratic constitutional reforms, dramatic tragedies about individual human dignities and rights (the Greeks were the first people on record to question the morality of slavery), and the Olympic Games—in all, the very concept of humanism.

Stealing History

The theft of priceless artifacts has been going on for centuries.

❋   ❋   ❋   ❋

IT'S LIKE SOMETHING out of a James Bond movie: An international collector pays big bucks to organized criminals to steal priceless antiquities and smuggle them over international borders. National treasures have been purloined for centuries—taken to distant lands to bring prestige and value to museums and private collections.

Sometimes, looters go straight to the source. Since the days of the earliest pharaohs, Egyptian rulers lived in fear of tomb robbers and went to great lengths to protect the possessions they intended to take into the hereafter.

But thieves were not always cloaked peasants who dug into pyramids in the dark of night; sometimes even Egyptian kings entered the graves of their predecessors to "borrow" goodies. King Tutankhamen's tomb included a second inner coffin, four miniature coffins, and some gold bands that had been removed from the tomb of Smenkhkare. The tomb of Pharaoh Pinudjem I included "recycled" sarcophagi from the tomb of Thothmosis I, Egypt's ruler from three dynasties earlier. (Perhaps this sort of grave robbing was simply considered "borrowing from Peter to pay Peter," since every Egyptian king was believed to be a reincarnation of the falcon god Horus.)

More recently, archaeological sites in the western United States have suffered a rash of thefts by shovel-toting bandits intent on digging up Native and Central American artifacts to sell in thriving legitimate and gray-market art and collectibles markets. In 2003, for instance, one Vanderbilt University professor worked with Guatemalan police, villagers, and even local drug lords to track down a stolen 1,200-year-old monument to a Mayan king.

Museums Robbed and Looted

Museum robberies have become a huge problem, especially for institutions that cannot afford state-of-the-art security systems. In 2001, Russia's Culture Ministry stated that, on average, one Russian museum was victimized by theft each month. In Iraq in April 2003, during the chaos of the U.S.-led invasion, some 170,000 Iraqi National Museum items were looted or destroyed; many of these artifacts subsequently made their way into private hands.

Authorities are slowly stirring themselves to crack down on a burgeoning traffic in stolen artifacts. In 2005, an Italian court sentenced a Roman antiquities dealer to ten years in prison for receiving and exporting stolen artifacts. The dealer's company sold 110 items through the prestigious auction house Sotheby's and sold another 96 artifacts to ten museums around the world before the operation was shut down.

Government Theft

Conquest has provided other sources for collections. The Israelite temple in Jerusalem was looted at least twice: by Babylonian King Nebuchadnezzar around 586 B.C. and by Roman Emperor Vespasian in A.D. 70. In 480 B.C., when the Persian army sacked Athens, artifacts in the wooden Acropolis temple were carted off to Persepolis, and during his 1798–99 expedition to Egypt, Napoleon's army uncovered one of the most famous spoils of war, the Rosetta Stone—which was in turn captured by Britain in 1801. Equally famous are the "Elgin Marbles," relief statues from Greece's Parthenon that were brought to London's British Museum in 1816.

During World War II, the Nazi regime took the pastime of art collecting to a new level. Thousands of priceless paintings, drawings, and sculptures were removed from museums in France and Russia. After Europe was liberated in 1945, many works of art were recovered, but others, such as Russia's fabled Amber Room panels, were not.

Art on Trial

The publication of Gustave Flaubert's Madame Bovary *shocked national sensibility and caused Flaubert to be charged with offending morality and religion.*

✳ ✳ ✳ ✳

The Case

WHEN MADAME BOVARY was first published serially in the *Revue de Paris* in 1851, the *Revue's* editor, Leon Laurent-Pichat; the work's author, Gustave Flaubert; and the publisher, Auguste-Alexis Pillet, were charged with "offenses to public morality and religion" by the conservative Restoration Government of Napoleon III. Many, including Flaubert, believed that his work was being singled out because of the regime's distaste for the notoriously liberal *Revue*.

Prosecutor Ernest Pinard based his case upon the premise that adultery must always be condemned as an affront to the sanctity of marriage and society at large. In this, Pinard had a point. The novel conspicuously lacks any voice reminding the reader that adultery is reprehensible and simply tells the tale of Emma Bovary's gradual but inevitable acceptance of her need for sexual satisfaction outside the confines of a provincial marriage. Other works of the period, notably the popular plays of Alexandre Dumas, commonly featured adulterous characters. But in these, there was a voice of reason reminding the audience that the character's actions were wrong. That *Madame Bovary* lacked such perspective was certainly unprecedented and—according to the government—worthy of censure.

The Defense

Defense attorney Jules Sénard (a close friend of Flaubert's and one of the people to whom the work was dedicated) argued that literature must always be considered art for art's sake and that Flaubert was a consummate artist whose intentions had nothing to do with affecting society at large.

Whether or not Flaubert intended to undermine any aspect of French society is debatable. The son in a wealthy family, he could afford to sit in his ivory tower and decry what he perceived as the petty hypocrisies of the emerging middle class. Certainly, Gustave Flaubert was a perfectionist who spent weeks reworking single pages of prose. In *Madame Bovary*, he sought to create a novel that was stylistically beautiful. To test his craft, Flaubert would shout passages out loud to test their rhythm. It took the author five years of solitary toil to complete the work. The literary elite, notably Sainte-Beuve, Victor Hugo, and Charles-Pierre Baudelaire, immediately recognized the novel's genius, but the general public largely ignored the work when it was first published.

The Verdict

In the end, the judges agreed with Sénard and acquitted all of the accused—but not before the sensational trial had sparked public interest in a work that might otherwise have gone unnoticed by the very society (the emerging middle class of France's provinces) the trial was meant to protect.

∗ *Madame Bovary* was Flaubert's first published novel, and when it appeared in full, the author received a commensurate fee: 800 francs. The morality trial, however, boosted sales, and Flaubert estimated that he missed out on some 40,000 francs worth of income.

∗ Although it survived the trial, the influential *Revue de Paris* finally capitulated to political and financial pressure and stopped publication a year later.

∗ *Madame Bovary* was first published in book form in 1857.

The Bard Versus Bacon

"What's in a name? That which we call a rose, by any other name, would smell as sweet." But would that which we call prose, by any other name, read as neat?

✳   ✳   ✳   ✳

THE QUOTE ABOVE was penned by William Shakespeare— or was it? Many scholars have raised doubts as to whether he really wrote some of the finest words in Western literature. Did other writers actually do the deed? Both sides believe they have the evidence to prove their point.

William Shakespeare was born in Stratford-upon-Avon, England, in April 1564. The exact date is unknown; this and many other details of his life are vague, which has fueled the rampant speculation about authorship. It is generally accepted that he was the first in his family to read and write, although the extent of his education has been widely questioned. His father was involved in local politics, so it is likely that Shakespeare attended school until his early teens to study Latin and literature. At age 18, Shakespeare married Anne Hathaway, who was eight years older than he was and three months pregnant with their first child, Susanna. Twins Hamnet and Judith were born two years later.

The Bard's life story seems to disappear for more than seven years at this point, resurfacing in 1592, when he became involved in London theater. As a playwright and actor, he founded a performing troupe that was soon part of the court of King James I. Shakespeare retired in 1613, returning to his hometown with some wealth. He died in 1616 and was laid to rest in the Holy Trinity Church of Stratford-upon-Avon.

While Shakespeare's plays were performed during his lifetime, they were not collected and published in book form until seven years after his death; *The First Folio* contained 36 of his theatrical works. Editors John Heminge and Henry Condell categorized the plays as tragedies, comedies, and histories. Many of Shakespeare's works, such as *Hamlet* and *King Lear*, were based on writings of former playwrights or even of Shakespeare's contemporaries—a common practice of the time. He also penned more than 150 sonnets, which often focused on love or beauty.

The diversity of this amazing body of work is what leads many to wonder whether Shakespeare had the education or ability to write it all. Certainly, they insist, others with better academic credentials were more likely to have written such timeless works of literature.

Furthermore, many of the plays displayed the acumen of a well-traveled writer—someone who had a great knowledge of foreign languages, geography, and local customs. This does not seem to jibe with Shakespeare's known experiences. Who could have written such worldly plays?

Bringing Home the Bacon

Francis Bacon was born into a royal London family in 1561. Fragile as a young child, Bacon was schooled at home. He spent three years at Trinity College at Cambridge and traveled to Paris at age 15. Bacon became a lawyer and a member of the British Parliament in 1584. He soon joined the court of Queen Elizabeth and was knighted by King James I in 1603. Bacon eventually ascended to the position of solicitor general of the British government. He died of bronchitis in 1626.

Bacon is best remembered for his part in developing the scientific method. This standard prescribes defining a question, performing diligent research about the subject, forming a hypothesis, experimenting and collecting data, analyzing the results, and developing a conclusion. The progression has become commonplace in all types of scientific work, from grade school projects to research labs, and is still used today. But the multitalented Bacon was also a writer and essayist. His works include *Novum Organum*, *Astrologia Sana*, and *Meditationes Sacrae*. But could the man who penned these works be diverse and capable enough to also write *Much Ado About Nothing* and *Romeo and Juliet?*

Something Is Rotten in the State of...Authorship

Speculation about the origin of Shakespeare's work began in the mid-1800s, as writers and scholars sought to demystify the works of the Bard. By the early 1900s, even the great American humorist Mark Twain had weighed in and questioned the authenticity of Shakespeare's plays and sonnets, albeit in his own way. In *Is Shakespeare Dead?*, Twain parodied those intellectuals who tried to discredit the man from Stratford-upon-Avon. The satiric piece questioned how biographers could write such detailed stories about their subject when so little solid information existed in the first place. But Twain also raised the question of whether Shakespeare could even write.

Similarities between the writings of Shakespeare and Bacon are abundant, and perhaps a bit too coincidental. For example, Shakespeare's Hamlet offers, "To thine own self be true, ... Thou canst not then be false to any man." In *Essay of Wisdom*, Bacon wrote, "Be so true to thyself as thou be not false to others." Plagiarism? Who can really say? The Bard wrote, "Tomorrow, and tomorrow, and tomorrow/Creeps in this petty pace from day to day" in *Macbeth*. Bacon observed in *Religious Meditations*, "The Spanish have a proverb, 'To-morrow, to-morrow; and when to-morrow comes, tomorrow.'" Is it possible that Shakespeare knew the same Spanish proverb? Certainly, but enough disbelief and lack of concrete evidence remain to thrill the world's doubting Thomases.

✳ Amid the swirl of controversy, most academics believe Shakespeare himself wrote the plays and sonnets that made him famous.

The First American Novel

Steeped in controversy, the plot of the first American novel—with its themes of seduction, incest, and suicide—would be more readily accepted in today's culture than it was in late 18th-century America.

✳ ✳ ✳ ✳

WILLIAM HILL BROWN wrote *The Power of Sympathy*, the first American novel, in 1789. Printer Isaiah Thomas was contracted to publish a limited run of the book and to sell it through his two bookshops. In an ironic twist— given the historical significance the book later assumed— *The Power of Sympathy* was presented as the work of an anonymous author.

Even if the book had been properly credited at the outset, few readers outside of upper-crust Boston would have been familiar with the author. When *The Power of Sympathy* appeared, William Hill Brown was a reasonably prolific but little-known playwright; he later wrote a comic opera, poetry, essays, and two more novels.

The son of a respected clockmaker, Brown was born in Boston in November 1765. He attended the Boston Boy's School, where he pursued creative writing, a craft encouraged by his step-aunt. Brown spent his formative years in an upper-class Boston neighborhood, living across the street from a married, politically active lawyer named Perez Morton.

In 1788, rumors of a romantic scandal involving Morton and his sister-in-law, Frances Apthorp, circulated among Boston's elite. The rumor turned out to be true, and rather than face public ridicule, the mortified Frances committed suicide. Perez, on the other hand, continued with his life as though nothing had happened. The public apparently went along with this tactic; Morton was later elected speaker of the lower house in the General Court of Massachusetts in 1806 and was named attorney general in 1810.

Writer (and former neighbor) William Brown was naturally well aware of the Morton-Apthorp scandal and published his book just a year later.

Following a novelistic style popular during the period, *The Power of Sympathy* unfolds via letters exchanged by central and secondary characters. The stinger is that the protagonists, Thomas Harrington and Harriot Fawcett, are about to unknowingly embark on an incestuous relationship.

In the novel, Harriot is Thomas's half-sister, born out of wedlock to a mistress of Thomas's father. For obvious reasons of propriety, the pregnancy and birth had been kept secret from the community and the rest of the family. When Harriot discovers the truth, she commits suicide. The facts soon become clear to Thomas as well, and he elects to follow his half-sister in suicide.

Credit Where Credit Is Due

Pressure from the Morton and Apthorp families, as well as from other prominent citizens, forced Brown to remove his book from circulation. Many copies were subsequently destroyed, and few exist today. In an odd twist, when the novel was reissued in the 19th century—nearly 100 years later—it was attributed to a deceased, once-popular Boston poet named Sarah Apthorp Morton, who happened to be the wife of Perez Morton—the man whose indiscretion helped inspire the novel in the first place! A correction issued by William Brown's aged niece not long after the book's republication led to proper attribution at last. Brown would finally be recognized as the author of the first novel written and published in America.

"Love is more pleasant than marriage for the same reason that novels are more amusing than history."

—SÉBASTIEN-ROCH-NICOLAS CHAMFORT, FRENCH PLAYWRIGHT, 1741–94

The Profound Effect of
Uncle Tom's Cabin

A first-time novelist dramatized the
problem of slavery for all to see.

✳   ✳   ✳   ✳

WHEN HARRIET BEECHER Stowe was introduced to President Abraham Lincoln, as the story goes, he said, "So, you're the little woman who wrote the book that started this great war." There's no question that few elements fueled the flames of hate across the country as much as *Uncle Tom's Cabin*. Stowe's story of Tom, a saintly black slave, earned both praise and condemnation. Abolitionists across the North thought it was brilliant and oh, so true. Southern critics, however, complained that it was completely inaccurate in the way it portrayed plantation life.

Borrowing from Real Life

Stowe was a dedicated abolitionist who was more concerned about illustrating the evils of slavery than creating an accurate view of life on the plantation. Although she lived in Cincinnati, Ohio (just across the river from the slave state of Kentucky), she had little actual experience with Southern plantations. The information in most of her book was taken either from abolitionist literature or her own imagination.

Stowe was researching a series of articles she intended to write when she heard about a slave woman who escaped from her masters in Kentucky across a frozen Ohio River. Stowe immediately realized that she could use such a scene in a book. One of the most exciting parts of *Uncle Tom's Cabin* features Eliza, the slave heroine, escaping across the ice.

A Publishing Sensation

Uncle Tom's Cabin first appeared in 1851, serialized in the abolitionist newspaper *National Era*. Its popularity led to the book's publication as a complete work the next year. It was an instant success, selling 10,000 copies in the first week and more than 300,000 by the end of its first year. *Uncle Tom's Cabin* had even greater popularity in Britain, where more than one million copies sold within a year. Stowe exposed the general public to an issue that most knew very little about. But the book didn't simply educate its readers—it also provoked heated debates in state and federal legislatures.

Interestingly, given today's negative meaning of the term *Uncle Tom*, the character in Stowe's book demonstrated strength and traits that were quite heroic. In one instance, when ordered to whip a sickly female slave, Tom refuses and suffers the lash himself. He is ultimately killed by his wicked master, Simon Legree, because he will not betray two runaway slaves. When Legree tries to have the information beaten out of him, Tom goes to his death without revealing a thing.

Not Controversial Enough?

As shocking as a lot of people found *Uncle Tom's Cabin*, many—particularly radical abolitionists—didn't think the book went far enough in denouncing slavery. Others, usually those who lived in the South, condemned the book as grossly exaggerated. One of Stowe's admirers was William Lloyd Garrison, the editor of an abolitionist newspaper called *The Liberator*. "I estimate the value of antislavery writing by the abuse it brings," he wrote to tell her. "Now all the defenders of slavery have let me alone and are abusing you."

"It was God's will that this nation—the North as well as the South—should deeply and terribly suffer for the sin of consenting to and encouraging the great oppressions of the South."

—HARRIET BEECHER STOWE, AFTER THE CIVIL WAR BROKE OUT

God's Architect

More than 80 years after his death, Antoni Gaudí's greatest work is still under construction.

✳ ✳ ✳ ✳

ANTONI GAUDÍ WAS born in Catalan, Spain, in 1852. As a boy, he was fascinated by the shapes peculiar to the natural environment of his boyhood home—a lifelong inspiration that would later take form in the fantastical designs of his buildings.

After studying architecture in Barcelona in the 1870s, he began work on a series of commissions for private homes and commercial buildings, some of which stand as the most innovative architecture ever built.

In 1883, Gaudí accepted a commission to build a new church in the heart of Barcelona. Inspired by the strange mountains at nearby Montserrat, his design for La Sagrada Família (Holy Family Church) called for 18 towers more than 300 feet tall, with a 580-foot-tall central tower representing Jesus Christ.

As the years went on and backers balked at escalating expenses, Gaudí sank all of his own savings into continuing the cathedral project. Work nearly ceased as Barcelona's economy collapsed and Gaudí suffered the deep personal losses of a beloved niece and his longtime companion. He grew more reclusive, and his appearance became increasingly eccentric. In fact, Gaudí may have been deep in thought about his epic construction when he walked into the path of a tram in 1926. Thousands attended his interment at La Sagrada Família.

Work resumed on the church in the 1950s and continues today, funded by private donations and admission fares. During his life, Antoni Gaudí was often ridiculed by his peers, but in death he became known as "God's Architect."

Church of Churches

Sprawling across nearly six acres in the Vatican,
the Basilica of Saint Peter was the world's largest
Christian church for almost four centuries.

✳ ✳ ✳ ✳

St. Peter's is not the "official" church of the pope: That
honor goes to St. John Lateran. But St. Peter's is the edifice
most closely identified with the papacy because its enormous
size (together with St. Peter's Square out front) can accommodate tens of thousands of worshippers and pilgrims. (The term
basilica comes from a Latinized Greek word that describes a
church built to a pattern dating back to the late Roman Empire,
or a church accorded special ceremonial privileges by the pope.)
The structure is built on the site on which, according to tradition, the first bishop of Rome—St. Peter, the apostle whom
Jesus chose to lead the Church after his death—was crucified
in the 1st century A.D.

Storehouse of Masterpieces

Pope Julius II laid the cornerstone for the basilica in 1506,
but the structure wasn't completed until 1615, during the
reign of Pope Paul V. Donato Bramante provided the original
design, but after his death in 1514, a succession of architects
and artists—including such great figures as Raphael and
Michelangelo—worked on the project. St. Peter's eventually
included Michelangelo's great sculpture the *Pietà*, as well as
other important Baroque artworks, including the baldacchino
(altar canopy) by Lorenzo Bernini. Within St. Peter's is the
Vatican Grotto, the burial place of 91 popes (most recently
Pope John Paul II in 2005) and other notables.

✳ Michelangelo is often credited with designing St. Peter's magnificent dome, but it was in fact modified from Michelangelo's
original plans.

Statue of Liberty Facts

*She is a thrill to behold, but how much
do we really know about her?*

✳ ✳ ✳ ✳

1. Her real name is "Liberty Enlightening the World."

2. Construction of the statue began in France in 1875.

3. Lady Liberty was sculpted by Frédéric-Auguste Bartholdi. Alexandre-Gustave Eiffel was the structural engineer.

4. The statue was completed in Paris in June 1884, given to the American people on July 4, 1884, and reassembled and dedicated in the United States on October 28, 1886.

5. The model for the face of the statue is reputed to be the sculptor's mother, Charlotte Bartholdi.

6. A bronze replica of Lady Liberty was erected in Paris in 1889 as a gift from Americans living in the city. The statue stands about 35 feet tall and is located on a small island in the River Seine, about a mile south of the Eiffel Tower.

7. There are 25 windows and 7 spikes in Lady Liberty's crown. The spikes symbolize the seven seas.

8. The statue's tablet is inscribed with the date July 4, 1776 (in Roman numerals).

9. More than four million people visit the Statue of Liberty each year.

10. Lady Liberty is 152 feet 2 inches tall from base to torch and 305 feet 1 inch tall from the ground to the tip of her torch.

11. The statue's hand is 16 feet 5 inches long and her index finger is 8 feet long. Her fingernails are 13 inches long by 10 inches wide.

12. Lady Liberty weighs about 450,000 pounds (225 tons).

13. Her sandals are 25 feet long, making her shoe size 879.

14. The statue functioned as an actual lighthouse from 1886 to 1902. There was an electric plant on the island to generate power for the light, which could be seen 24 miles away.

15. Visitors can choose to climb either to the top of the pedestal or up a winding staircase to the top of her crown for a spectacular view of New York Harbor. However, only 240 visitors are allowed up to the crown each day, so tickets must be ordered months in advance.

16. There are 192 steps from the ground to the top of the pedestal and 354 steps from the pedestal to the crown.

17. Visitors who cannot climb to the crown can view the interior framework through the pedestal's glass ceiling.

18. The Statue of Liberty underwent a multimillion dollar renovation in the mid-1980s before being rededicated on July 4, 1986. During this process, she received a new torch because the old one was corroded beyond repair. The original torch is now on display at the monument's museum.

19. Visitors used to be allowed to climb into the torch, but this practice was discontinued after an explosion on nearby Black Tom Island in 1916. German agents orchestrated the incident to sabotage American aid to the Allied powers during World War I.

"Give me your tired, your poor,
Your huddled masses yearning to breathe free,
The wretched refuse of your teeming shore.
Send these, the homeless, tempest-tost to me,
I lift my lamp beside the golden door!"

—EMMA LAZARUS, *THE NEW COLOSSUS*

The Group of Seven

*Seven Canadian landscape painters formed the
appropriately named Group of Seven in 1919.*

✳   ✳   ✳   ✳

MEMBERS OF THE Group of Seven met in 1912 and
1913 as regular patrons of the Toronto Arts and Letters
Club. They were landscape painters who shared the sentiment
that Canadian landscape art should be distinct from the popular European Impressionist landscapes. The Seven's art was
strongly influenced by Impressionism, but there were several
departures from it, such as the use of bold, vivid color; strong
symbolism; and an altogether sharper and more potent feel.

The group went on excursions to nearby hubs of pristine
wilderness. One of their favorite destinations was Algonquin
Park, where one of the painters, Tom Thomson, died mysteriously in a canoeing accident in 1917. Were it not for his
untimely death, the painters would surely have been known as
the Group of Eight (they were not officially named until 1919,
two years after Thomson's death). The Group of Seven consisted of Franklin Carmichael, Lawren Harris, A. Y. Jackson,
Frank Johnston, Arthur Lismer, J.E.H. MacDonald, and
Frederick Varley.

The group's first exhibition was held in 1920 at the Toronto
Art Gallery. During the next decade, they traveled throughout
Canada, painting landscapes and promoting their art. Two
members of the group, Jackson and Harris, made trips to the
Arctic. Over the years, the group lost and gained members;
their name became obsolete. In 1931, they officially disbanded,
and the Canadian Group of Painters was formed.

The Group of Seven was successful in instituting a uniquely
Canadian school of art. Many of the group's members went on
to teach at various institutions, and they all enjoyed prestige

throughout their careers. They served as mentors and inspirations for subsequent generations of artists.

The McMichael Canadian Art Collection

The most salient display of the group's legacy is the McMichael Canadian Art Collection, which is located just north of Toronto. The wealthy McMichael family amassed the group's work, and in the 1960s they donated the entirety of their collection to the Province of Ontario, along with a large rural property. The McMichaels mandated that the museum must hold only works by the original Group of Seven or their contemporaries. Six members of the Group of Seven are buried in a small graveyard on the museum grounds.

A series of legal battles was waged after the museum hosted modern artists whose work did not reflect the artistic tradition established by the Seven. The museum has changed hands a few times, but in 2004, a court ordered that the museum's original mandate be upheld. It is now home to works by the Seven, their followers, and Canadian aborigines.

Complications Arise

The Group of Seven has sparked much controversy among art historians. The Seven thought that Canada needed to have its own landscape art because, well, Canada has its own landscape: The often rough and jagged features of the land don't mesh well with Impressionism, which was founded in the more pastoral landscapes of Northern Europe. The criticism is that the Seven's landscapes symbolically robbed Canadian aborigines of their proper claim to the land. The Seven wanted Canadian artists to paint their land with a sense of ownership and pride, yet their works never included images of the indigenous structures that are found throughout the Canadian wild. This criticism is given more weight by the famed Seven idea that "the great purpose of landscape art is to make us at home in our own country." A tenuous compromise to this debate is found in the McMichael Canadian Art Collection's display of aboriginal art.

Ludwig II: King of Castles

His desire to build fantastic castles and his patronage of (and infatuation with) famed composer Richard Wagner led many to refer to Bavarian King Ludwig II as the Dream King, the Swan King, the Fairytale King—even the Mad King.

❋　❋　❋　❋

SOME SAY AN insular childhood shaped Ludwig II into the eccentric he became. Peculiarities surrounded him from the moment he was born on April 24, 1845—his birth announcement was delayed so its date would coincide with his grandfather's birthdate.

Ludwig was crowned king at age 18. That same year, he held his first meeting with composer Richard Wagner. Ludwig's infatuation with Wagner eventually led him to pay the composer a stipend and fund construction of a theater dedicated to performances of Wagner's operas.

After Bavaria's absorption into the new German Empire, Ludwig retreated into seclusion. From his mountain retreat in the Bavarian Alps, the king launched several grand construction projects that became trademarks of his reign.

Fantasies in Stone

Ludwig's bizarre building projects included an underground lake—complete with electrical lights—at Linderhof Castle. Ludwig often rowed about the lake in a shell-shape boat while singers performed operas on shore. The castle's architecture was influenced by French King Louis XIV. It was the king's only castle project to be completed.

The most famous of Ludwig's castles is New Castle Hohenschwangau. Several swan motifs were incorporated into the castle's design, which led the edifice to be renamed Neuschwanstein, or "New Swan Stone," after his death. Built high above Pollat Gorge, Neuschwanstein is a mix of Byzantine and Gothic design elements. It is one of the most recognized castles in the world. In fact, Disney used it as inspiration when designing the Sleeping Beauty castle that is featured at Disneyland.

Despite 22 years of construction, only 14 rooms of Neuschwanstein were ever completed. The castle's interior features several wall paintings that depict scenes from Wagner's operas. Never one to forgo contemporary conveniences, Ludwig built this castle with several state-of-the-art features, including a forced-air heating system and a flush toilet.

Ludwig's third castle, Herrenchiemsee, was located on an island in Lake Chiemsee. It was modeled after the central section of the Palace of Versailles and contained a reproduction of its ambassador's staircase. Unfortunately, Ludwig died during its construction, and Herrenchiemsee was never completed.

A World of Dreams

On June 8, 1886, Ludwig was declared "mentally disordered" by a psychiatrist who hadn't even examined him. On June 10, the king was deposed by his uncle. Two days later, Ludwig was arrested and taken to Castle Berg, south of Munich.

After taking a walk along Lake Starnberg with the doctor who had declared him unfit to rule, Ludwig was discovered floating in the shallow water; the doctor's body was found in the water as well. The king's death was ruled a suicide despite the fact that an autopsy showed no water in Ludwig's lungs. This finding has led some to speculate that the king was murdered.

On June 19, Ludwig's remains were interred in the crypt of Saint Michael's in Munich. In accordance with tradition, his heart was placed in a silver urn and interred in the Chapel of the Miraculous Image in Altötting.

Hollywood Versus History

You may not be surprised to learn that Hollywood doesn't always get history right.

✳ ✳ ✳ ✳

Today the place is a Motel 6
Interview with the Vampire (1994)—When Brad Pitt and Kirsten Dunst tour Bavaria in the 1790s, they visit the castle of King Ludwig, which wasn't built until about 90 years later.

And this is supposed to make the Bronx feel better?
Operation Crossbow (1965)—The Nazi "New York rocket" that's investigated by Allied agent George Peppard wasn't an intercontinental ballistic missile, as shown in the film, but a two-stage rocket with a winged second stage.

Leave it alone—it's magic
Houdini (1953)—Houdini performs a Halloween stunt from inside a locked trunk after it's dumped into the frozen Detroit River. The problem? The river is never frozen in October.

They said "Spaniel"
Gladiator (2000)—Maximus's nickname is "Spaniard." Never mind that Spain did not yet exist.

And leave the trail-driving to us
The Comancheros (1966)—A Greyhound bus is briefly visible behind a hill in this Western set in the 19th century.

Grisly executions are so-o boring
Braveheart (1995)—As a crowd gathers to watch a disemboweling, a female extra loses mental focus and shoots glances at the camera.

Those subscriber-only perks are amazing
The Green Mile (1999)—Actor Michael Jeter relaxes with the November 1937 issue of *Weird Tales* in this story set in 1935.

Hermann Göring's Karinhall

Adolf Hitler had the Berghof, his luxurious chalet located in the Bavarian Alps, and Hermann Göring had Karinhall.

✳ ✳ ✳ ✳

IN OCTOBER 1933, the Prussian Department of State granted to Hermann Göring, as a gift for his personal use, an old hunting lodge located in the Schorfheide forest approximately 65 kilometers northeast of Berlin. Almost immediately, Göring embarked on a reconstruction, expansion, and renovation plan that would transform the modest lodge into the opulent Karinhall, a 120-hectare country estate and hunting retreat. Reflecting the pompous and extravagant manner of the Third Reich's No. 2 man, Göring spared no expense in creating a sumptuous mansion, which was built to satisfy his particular senses of taste and self-importance.

Karinhall was built by Göring as a tribute to his first wife, Swedish noblewoman Karin von Kantzow, who died in 1931. One of the first new structures built at the site was a large mausoleum that served as a hallowed resting place for Karin. Her remains were interred at the estate in 1934 after her gravesite in Sweden was vandalized.

Wanting only the best for the place dedicated to Karin's memory, Göring commissioned renowned German architect Werner March to design Karinhall. March was best known for his design of Berlin Olympic Stadium, the showpiece edifice of the 1936 Olympic Games.

Karinhall was large and lavish. It featured a great main hall with four long wings and built-in stages that extended beside and behind it. The estate also had a large inner courtyard adorned with statues and lush gardens, as well as several ancillary buildings. Other amenities included two casinos, a tennis court, and a shooting range.

The main hall was a testimony to Göring's personal ego. Its 50-meter corridor displayed paintings, tapestries, and other treasures stolen from museums throughout occupied Europe. It also had a heavy oak bar with an inscribed plaque proclaiming: "To his Prussian Prime Minster Hermann Göring, who leads the fate of Prussia with strong hand."

The hall's numerous showrooms were decked out with more stolen art and hunting trophies, including one that featured dozens of mounted antlers surrounding a framed photo of Göring wearing the uniform of Reich Master of the Hunt.

It is not known exactly how much money Göring spent on Karinhall, although Prussian state tax records show a 1944 insured value of 15 million Reichsmarks (about $6 million). What is known is that Göring had even grander designs for the place. In 1944, plans were drawn for the construction of a new wing featuring a luxurious art museum, which would offer the public a glimpse of Göring's looted art treasures.

VIP Grounds

Göring firmly believed that problems could be more easily solved and deals better made in the realm of the hunt and the comfort of the fireplace than at the cold negotiating table. As such, Karinhall hosted many meetings of Nazi party and government bigwigs. High-level political, economic, and military planning—including Germany's 1940 air assault against Britain—occurred there as well.

Göring also entertained foreign dignitaries at Karinhall, often taking his guests on hunting trips in the Schorfheide. Benito Mussolini and his foreign minister Count Ciano, British foreign minister Lord Halifax, British ambassador Neville Henderson, and U.S. undersecretary of state Sumner Welles all visited the elite estate.

As the war went on and the fortunes of Germany began to turn, Göring retreated more frequently to the tranquility of Karinhall. Although he felt comfortable there, it was evident that he never felt completely secure. Fearful of Allied air attack, Göring had camouflage nets erected around the property to thwart air reconnaissance. Searchlight towers and flak guns were also installed nearby.

Most telling, however, was the presence of deep underground bomb shelters at the estate; they were allegedly built a year before Göring's fateful boast that no enemy plane would ever penetrate German airspace. Allied bombers did take a toll on Germany, of course, and Karinhall was a potential target.

A Ruined Retreat

As the war neared its end, Göring moved to ensure that neither Karinhall nor the art treasures within it fell into enemy hands. In January 1945, his art collection was relocated by train to Berchtesgaden for storage and hiding. In April, as the Red Army approached Berlin, Göring ordered Karinhall to be completely destroyed. Most of the art was eventually recovered.

Today, little is left of Karinhall, although there are a few relics at the site that testify to its existence. A granite road marker bearing the estate's name still sits near the former front entrance along with two large stone gateposts. Beyond that are a few crumbling foundation walls, broken cellars, and remnants of the swimming pool.

In the end, Karinhall's ruin, like that of its pompous owner, was inglorious and complete.

✳ One reason the swastika became so universal a symbol may lie in a basket. Many natural basketweaving patterns result in swastikas, and it's hard to find a culture without some heritage of this useful craft.

A Display of Plundered Art

Nazi leaders engaged in a systematic plunder of Europe's great works of art. A postwar Allied inventory showed Göring to possess more than 1,375 paintings, 250 sculptures, and 108 tapestries—a collection estimated in 1950 to be worth about $162 million.

Much of Göring's collection was displayed or kept at Karinhall. Ironically, the Karinhall collection revealed Göring's personal taste to be very much in contrast with the official preferences espoused by the Nazi government.

Here is a look at some of the more notable pieces once available for view at Karinhall.

* *Portrait of the Artist's Sister*—Rembrandt, c.1632. One of five works by Rembrandt displayed in Karinhall.

* *Sunflowers*—Vincent Van Gogh, c.1888. Displayed along with other works by the Dutch master.

* *Mary Magdalene*—Gregor Erhart, c.1500. Limewood sculpture taken from the Louvre.

* Nine Flemish tapestries depicting hunting scenes. Six were woven by Daniel Eggermans in the mid-17th century. The other three were woven by Frans van der Borght and date to the mid-18th century. All were "lent" to Karinhall by the Museum of Art History in Vienna and remain missing.

* *Venus and Amor*—Lucas Cranach the Elder, 1531. This is but one of 19 works by the German Renaissance artist that Göring owned.

* *Pretty Polish Girl*—Jean Antoine Watteau, early 18th century. Stolen from Poland.

* *Young Girl with Chinese Figure*—Jean-Honoré Fragonard, 18th century. Confiscated from the private Rothschild collection in France.

* *Infanta Margarita*—Diego Velázquez, ca.1656. Purchased in the Netherlands.

Memories of Home

Why did Hollywood celebrities leave their comfortable lifestyles to face deprivation, disease, enemy bombing—and sometimes death?

✳ ✳ ✳ ✳

D URING WORLD WAR II, approximately 7,000 entertainers joined the United Service Organization (USO), which was established in 1941 to boost the morale of the young men and women serving at home and abroad during World War II. The USO provided centers, clubs, and live entertainment, which sometimes included Hollywood celebrities. Many stars traveled to Europe and the Pacific islands to perform for the troops. Their experiences during the war were forever etched in their minds.

Bob Hope: "No Tears, Please"

The toughest part of the job for many USO entertainers was visiting wounded GIs. It took willpower to keep from shedding tears when seeing the broken bodies of the young men. Bob Hope resolved to remain strong—he didn't want the soldiers to see him or his troupe crying. He wanted the soldiers to forget their pain and to enjoy life, if even for just a little while. He would remind his fellow entertainers, "No tears, please, you can't have tears. You can cry later, but you can't cry in front of them."

For Frances Langford, A Visit Touched Her Life Forever

During a visit to a military hospital, singer Frances Langford was asked to meet a severely wounded soldier. She readily agreed and went to see the young man. While holding her hand and listening to the beautiful starlet sing softly, the soldier looked up, smiled, and then died. The incident was heartbreaking for Langford, who held her tears until after she left the room.

Patty Thomas: "Don't They Love Tap Dancing?"

During a tour of the Pacific, a USO troupe's PBY Catalina seaplane lost engine power over New Guinea and had to make a forced landing. Patty Thomas worried that her tap shoes would be lost and decided to tie them around her neck. It is likely, though, that most of the soldiers, sailors, and airmen loved her for reasons besides her dancing skills. "I was a 21-year-old with a 34–24–34 figure with long legs. The tap dancing wasn't exactly what they wanted to hear and see."

Carole Lombard: Tragedy of the Profane Angel

Film actress Carole Lombard earned the nickname the "Profane Angel" because of the bawdy language she used. She joined the USO shortly after the United States entered the war and went on a bond rally tour. After a rally in her hometown of Fort Wayne, Indiana, she, her mother, and 20 others boarded a TWA DC-3 Skysleeper that was headed to California. As Lombard boarded the plane, she exhorted her fans to "cheer—'V' for Victory!" Her plane crashed into a mountain outside of Las Vegas, leaving no survivors. A widowed Clark Gable was devastated by the tragic loss of his wife.

Glenn Miller and His Army Air Force Band

Big Band legend Glenn Miller recorded such numbers as "Chattanooga Choo-Choo," "In the Mood," "Moonlight Serenade," and "Tuxedo Junction." In 1942, at the peak of his fame, he joined the U.S. Army. The army placed him in command of the service's band, which he named the Glenn Miller Army Air Force Band.

His band toured with the USO in the United States during 1942 and 1943 and went to the United Kingdom a year later. After a show on December 15, 1944, he boarded a plane that was headed for Paris. Somewhere over the English Channel, the plane mysteriously disappeared. Miller, along with two passengers and the pilot, was never seen again.

The Teenager
Who Invented Television

*Responsible for what may have been the most
influential invention of the 20th century, this farm
boy never received the recognition he was due.*

✳ ✳ ✳ ✳

PHILO T. FARNSWORTH's brilliance was obvious from an
early age. In 1919, when he was only 12, he amazed his
parents and older siblings by fixing a balky electrical generator
on their Idaho farm. By age 14, he had built an electrical laboratory in the family attic and was setting his alarm for 4 A.M.
so he could get up and read science journals for an hour before
starting his chores.

Farnsworth hated the drudgery of farming. He often day-
dreamed solutions to scientific problems as he worked.
During the summer of 1921, he was particularly preoccupied
with the possibility of transmitting moving pictures through
the air.

At around the same time, big corporations like RCA were
spending millions of research dollars trying to find a practical way to do just that. As it turned out, most of their work
was focused on a theoretical dead-end. Back in 1884, German
scientist Paul Nipkow had patented a device called the Nipkow
disc. By rotating the disc rapidly while passing light through
tiny holes, an illusion of movement could be created. In
essence, the Nipkow disc was a primitive way to scan images.
Farnsworth doubted that this mechanical method of scanning
could ever work fast enough to send images worth watching.
He was determined to find a better way.

His "Eureka!" moment came as he cultivated a field with a team
of horses. Swinging the horses around to plow another row,

Farnsworth glanced back at the furrows behind him. Suddenly, he realized that scanning could be done electronically, line by line. Light could be converted into streams of electrons and back again with such rapidity that the eye would be fooled. He immediately set about designing what would one day be called the cathode-ray tube. Seven years would pass, however, before he was able to display a working model of his breakthrough.

Upon graduating from high school, Farnsworth enrolled at the University of Utah but dropped out after a year because he could no longer afford the tuition. Almost immediately, though, he found financial backers and moved to San Francisco to continue his research. The cathode-ray tube he developed there became the basis for television.

In 1930, a researcher from RCA named Vladimir Zworykin visited Farnsworth's California laboratory and copied his invention. When Farnsworth refused to sell his patent to RCA for $100,000, the company sued him. The legal wrangling continued for many years, and though Farnsworth eventually earned royalties from his invention, he never did get wealthy from it.

By the time Farnsworth died in 1971, there were more homes on Earth with televisions than with indoor plumbing. Ironically, the man most responsible for television appeared on the small screen only once—a 1957 guest spot on the game show *I've Got a Secret*. Farnsworth's secret was that "I invented electric television at the age of 15." None of the panelists guessed Farnsworth's secret, and he left the studio with his winnings—$80 and a carton of Winston cigarettes.

✳ Philo T. Farnsworth grew to regret his contributions to television. He viewed TVs as machines through which people wasted unfathomable amounts of time.

The Story of Kong

Long before Godzilla terrorized audiences, a gorilla by the name of Kong served up king-size quivers to the moviegoing masses.

❋ ❋ ❋ ❋

MONKEYS ARE A mainstay of zoos today, but in the early 20th century, when Merian C. Cooper's *King Kong* was released, few zoos displayed the entertaining and excitable creatures. Capitalizing on that void and incorporating his own anthropological background, Cooper conspired with fellow filmmaker and friend Ernest B. Schoedsack to transform their nature documentary into a feature film. Little did they know at the time how their "creature feature epic," the first of its kind, would change the landscape of cinema and pop culture.

Cooper lived an exciting life before creating one of the most adventurous films of all time. As a U.S. Army officer and bomber pilot in World War I, he traveled the globe and was a prisoner of war. His early filmmaking career was devoted to creating nature documentaries for Paramount Pictures. As such, much of his time was spent exploring exotic locales. Always the innovator, even with these documentaries, he incorporated techniques to ensure that action-packed sequences were the main features of his works. Unlike the typical nature documentary, Cooper's films always included stage-set action sequences that accompanied the nature footage to ensure just the right feel of excitement.

Schoedsack, too, was an ardent fan of technological advancements in filmmaking. Schoedsack and Cooper met while both were serving in the military during World War I. Upon their return to the United States, they forged a working relationship that combined their mutual interests in nature, adventure, and film. Their initial collaborations continued their work in the documentary genre, but their efforts on *King Kong* put Cooper and Schoedsack on the cinematic map.

It's All in the Script

From the start, the filming of *King Kong* was riddled with odd and unexpected roadblocks. The original scriptwriter commissioned by Cooper fell ill and died before producing a workable text. Even though scriptwriter Edgar Wallace is credited as a writer on the film, Cooper, Ruth Rose (Schoedsack's wife), and James Ashmore Creelman were forced to quickly rework the entire script to get it done in time for production.

King Kong also went through several name changes before its release. The movie went by *The Beast, The Ape,* and *The Eighth Wonder* before finally being released as *King Kong.* In fact, even as press packets were being sent out in anticipation of the release, the film was referred to as *The Eighth Wonder.* Only one known pamphlet—which brought $11,000 at auction in 2005—exists with this designation.

Pushing Film Technique Forward

Several technologically innovative methods were employed in *King Kong's* production. One technique, stop-motion, was a new trick in which objects were filmed in different positions in many frames to mimic movement. This animation method was utilized to create special effects involving the film's creatures— dinosaurs and the ape himself. By today's standards, the choppiness of the animation might appear hokey, but at the time, stop-motion was a cutting-edge means to meet the movie's needs.

Another method, rear-projection, was combined with the magic of stop-motion to create the illusion that Kong was tromping alongside the live actors. To achieve rear-projection, a camera projects a previously recorded background onto the scene's backdrop while live action takes place in front of it. This technique was not a first choice—in fact, multiple alternatives were explored fully. However, just as filming was scheduled to start, an advanced version of rear-projection was introduced, and Cooper jumped on it.

Although some have suggested that Kong was, at times, portrayed by a man in an ape suit, all scenes with the beast were in fact made by utilizing stop-motion, rear-projection, and other special effects with one of the four Kong models that were crafted in various sizes. The differing dimensions could not produce a consistently accurate Kong, however.

Boffo Box Office

King Kong, which was released in 1933, had the biggest opening weekend of its time. It became the highest-grossing film of the year and the fifth-highest-grossing of the entire decade. (Not bad considering that 1933 was the lowest point of the Great Depression.) The film's great success brought RKO, the production company that financed it, back from the brink of bankruptcy.

Critics and the public fell in love with the mammoth gorilla. In fact, the film was so popular that it was rereleased three times in the next 20 years. But with each new release, the strong arm of censorship took its toll. Through the years, various images deemed too horrifying were cut out. Thankfully, the original film was pieced back together in 1971 and rereleased.

Since *King Kong* popped into pop culture, countless monster movies have been created. But it was the great Kong and the technological ambitiousness of its creators that set the stage for the special effects and terrifying monsters that scare audiences out of their seats today.

---

* One scene that censors found objectionable saw Kong knocking several sailors from a bridge to the ground, where they were eaten by giant spiders. This scene never made it back into the film, but it is hinted at in Peter Jackson's 2005 remake. Jackson also tried his hand at the scene for the DVD version of the 1933 classic.

* Kong's roar was created by combining the roars of a tiger and a lion, then running the new roar in reverse.

Chapter 10

Pastimes

The Game of Kings

Protecting the king is key in chess.

※   ※   ※   ※

CHESS MESHES SIMPLICITY with complexity. One of the world's most popular games, it is played by friends, in clubs, and even in international championships. Now played on the Internet as well, thoughtful games can last years.

Chess has its roots in India and dates to the sixth century A.D. It arrived in Europe in the tenth century. Modern gamepieces include a king, a queen, and other medieval ranks: eight pawns, a pair of knights, a pair of bishops, and a pair of rooks.

The game is played on an 8-by-8 board of 64 squares. Players take turns, and the game continues until one player is able to "checkmate" the opponent's king, a strategic move that prevents the king from escaping an attack on the next turn. Each piece moves according to specific rules that dictate how many squares it can traverse and in what direction. The queen is generally considered the most powerful piece.

Computer programmers have developed game strategy using artificial intelligence, and for years there were attempts to create a computer that could defeat the best human players. This finally happened in 1997 when a computer defeated world champion Garry Kasparov.

Football

The game of football today bears little resemblance to the disorganized brawls of the late 1800s.

✳ ✳ ✳ ✳

1861: The first documented football game (essentially rugby) is played at the University of Toronto.

1869: An era begins as Princeton travels to Rutgers for a game of "soccer football." The field is 120 yards long by 75 yards wide (about 25 percent longer and wider than the modern field). It plays more like soccer than modern football, and with 25 players on a side, the field is a crowded place. Rutgers prevails 6–4.

1874: McGill University (of Montreal) and Harvard play a hybrid version of rugby. The rule changes soon affect the U.S. version of the game.

1875: The game ball officially becomes an egg-shape rugby ball. Henceforth the field is supposed to be 100 yards long by 53.5 yards wide (though this won't be fully standard for some years), so teams are cut to 15 players per side. Referees are added.

1876: A crossbar is added to goal posts, resulting in an H shape.

1880–85: The modern game's fundamentals are introduced. A downs system goes into use (five yards in three downs equals a first down), along with the scrimmage line and yard lines. Teams are now 11 on a side. A field goal is worth five points, a touchdown and conversion count four points each, and a safety is two points. The first play-calling signals and planned plays come about.

1892: Desperate to beat the Pittsburgh Athletic Club team, Allegheny Athletic Association (AAA) leaders create the professional football player by hiring Pudge Heffelfinger to play for their team. Heffelfinger plays a pivotal role in AAA's 4–0 victory.

1894: The officiating crew is increased to three: a referee and two bodyguards (also known as the umpire and linesman).

1896: Only one backfielder may now be in motion before the snap, and he can't be moving forward.

1897: A touchdown now counts as five points.

1902: College football is getting a little unbalanced, as Michigan outscores its regular schedule 501–0. Also, the first African American professional football player takes the field: Charles Follis of the Shelby (Ohio) Athletic Club.

1905: Teddy Roosevelt tells the Ivy League schools: "Fix this blood sport, or I'll ban it." Rules Committee (forerunner of the NCAA) comes into being and legalizes the forward pass, bans mass plays responsible for brutish pileups (even deaths), establishes the neutral zone along the line of scrimmage, and prohibits players from locking arms.

1909: A field goal is now worth three points. This rule will stand, but the distances, hash marks, and goal posts will change many more times.

1910: Seven players must now be on the line of scrimmage when the ball is snapped, establishing the basic offensive formation concept. The forward pass becomes commonplace in college football games.

1912: Rules Committee determines that a touchdown is worth six points, and it adds a fourth down. It is now practical to punt.

1921: Fans hear the first commercially sponsored radio broadcast of a game, with University of Pittsburgh beating West Virginia 21–13.

1922: The American Professional Football Association becomes the National Football League (NFL).

1932: The NFL begins keeping statistics. Collegiate football doesn't see the benefits of official stat keeping until 1937.

1933: There is a major NFL rule change: The passer can throw from anywhere behind scrimmage (prior to this, he had to be five yards behind scrimmage.)

1934: The football takes its current shape.

1937: College football players must now have numbers on the fronts and backs of their jerseys.

1939: The Brooklyn Dodgers–Philadelphia Eagles game is the first to be beamed into the few New York homes that can afford TV sets in this late-Depression year. Helmets become mandatory in college football, and the pros follow within a decade.

1941: It's the end of the drop-kick score. Ray McLean boots a conversion off the turf in the NFL championship game. (Actually, it wasn't the last one kicked: In 2005, Doug Flutie created a sensation by doing it again.)

1946: The NFL's first major rival league, the All-America Football Conference (AAFC), begins play. It lasts four seasons, with the Cleveland Browns winning all four titles.

1950: NFL rules now permit unlimited free substitution, opening a hole for platoon football (exclusive offensive or defensive squads).

1951: First coast-to-coast TV broadcast of an NFL game occurs as the Los Angeles Rams face the Cleveland Browns in the league championship game. Face masks show up in the college game.

1956: The NFL penalizes face masking (except for the ball carrier, who can be slammed to the turf by the face cage for another four years).

1958: In college football, a run or pass for conversion now counts two points.

1960: The American Football League (AFL), the NFL's new rival, begins play. Everyone derides it as inferior.

1967: The NFL offsets goal posts with a recessed curved pole in a "slingshot" shape. Super Bowl I is played: The Green Bay Packers beat the Kansas City Chiefs 35–10.

1970: The AFL wins the Super Bowl, then merges into the NFL, creating the biggest sports-marketing titan of all time. Ten modern NFL teams trace heritage to the AFL.

1974: The NFL adds sudden-death overtime for regular-season games, moves the goal posts to the back of the end zone, moves kickoffs back from the 40- to the 35-yard line, and spots the ball at the line of scrimmage for missed field goals beyond the 20. Pass defense rules now restrict defenders, opening up the air game.

1975: Kicker/quarterback George Blanda of the Oakland Raiders finally hangs up his cleats at age 48.

1979–80: No more blocking below the waist on kicks, refs are to whistle a play dead when a player has the quarterback in a death grip but has not yet slammed him to the turf, and personal-foul rules tighten up.

1987: Arena Football League season starts with four teams: the Chicago Bruisers, Denver Dynamite, Pittsburgh Gladiators, and Washington Commandos.

1988: The NFL increases the play clock to 45 seconds between plays. Eventually this is shortened to 40 seconds. College still uses the 25-second play clock.

1991: The World League of American Football (WLAF)—history's first league outside of North America—begins in Europe as a sort of NFL minor league.

1994: Professional football institutes the two-point conversion.

1999: The NFL begins using an instant replay challenge system.

2007: The NFL Europa, successor to the WLAF, finally shuts down; Europeans still prefer soccer.

Hot-rodding Heats Up

Victorious American GIs returned from World War II ready to kick up their heels. They had fought hard, and they wanted to play hard. For many, the mechanical skills they had honed during the conflict prepared them for the perfect pastime—hot-rodding.

✳ ✳ ✳ ✳

Excess cash, combined with the first automobiles to be manufactured in the country in five years, created a boom in new car sales across the United States. But instead of merely junking their old sedans, people began to tinker under the hood and chop the bodies of these beaters.

The term *hot rod* most likely derived from *hot roadster*, and that's exactly what these cars were. These supercharged flying flivvers cropped up from coast to coast. But the center of this new diversion was Southern California, where warm weather and open land combined to make the perfect spot for racing.

The area north of Los Angeles, near the towns of Glendale, Pasadena, and Burbank, was covered with dry lake beds. The miles of barren land became the meeting place for gearheads. Abandoned military airport runways were also natural racetrack straightaways, giving hot rods the chance to flex their metallic muscles in exciting drag races.

The phenomenon was not lost on people such as Wally Parks, who founded the National Hot Rod Association (NHRA) in 1951; the organization focused on safety and innovation. Magazines such as *Hot Rod* (which premiered in 1948) also supported action that was based on quality and care.

Unable to contain the growing craze, Southern California gave up its hold on hot-rodding as it spread across the country. But areas such as the Midwest and New England were short on dry lake beds, so hot rods took to the streets of America, forcing police officers to chase down these speedsters.

Sports Terminology

✻ ✻ ✻ ✻

Hail Mary: Dallas Cowboys quarterback Roger Staubach coined the term when his desperation pass in the waning moments of the Cowboys-Vikings 1975 playoff game was caught by receiver Drew Pearson for the winning touchdown. After the game, Staubach told reporters that he "closed his eyes, threw the ball as hard as he could, and said a Hail Mary prayer."

Bullpen: In the early days of baseball, relief pitchers warmed up behind the outfield fence because the fence and the signs around it provided shade from the sun. The outfield fences in those days often featured advertisements for Bull Durham chewing tobacco. Thus, the area became known as the bullpen.

Southpaw: A southpaw is a left-handed pitcher. In the early days of the game, baseball diamonds were designed so that most batters were facing east to prevent the sun from shining in their eyes. In this configuration, left-handed pitchers were throwing from the south.

Hat Trick: This hockey term was borrowed from cricket. *The Oxford English Dictionary* explains that a hat trick is "the feat of a bowler who takes three wickets by three successive balls: originally considered to entitle him to be presented by his club with a new hat or some equivalent." In the 1940s, a Toronto haberdasher would award a free hat to Maple Leaf hockey players who connected for three goals in a game. Today, any player who scores three goals in a game is credited with a hat trick. His reward is the parade of hats that cascade down to the ice.

Dump and Chase: The "art" of shooting the puck into the corner and sending in a group of skaters to fight for possession of the disc was originated by Red Wings coach Jack Adams during the 1942 Stanley Cup finals. The strategic ploy was meant to take advantage of the slow Toronto Maple Leaf defensemen.

Hollywood Drops the Ball

It's hard not to like a sports movie, even if you're not into sports. However, sometimes the filmmakers take dramatic license. Here are some all-star sports movies that stand out for fumbling a few details.

✳ ✳ ✳ ✳

Knute Rockne All American (1940): Remembered for Ronald Reagan's portrayal of George "The Gipper" Gipp and Pat O'Brien's performance as Knute Rockne, this one has plenty of heart. Some of the facts are a bit clouded, however—such as Rockne's role in developing the forward pass. Although he may have *popularized* it, it had been used before Knute hit the gridiron. Likewise, Gipp's famous deathbed speech was most likely an inspiring fabrication.

Pride of the Yankees (1942): This film went to great lengths to get the facts straight, including having right-handed Gary Cooper wear a uniform with the letters reversed to depict the lefty slugger Gehrig and then reversing the film during processing. However, there were notable departures, including the fact that the "luckiest man" speech was heavily rearranged for dramatic effect. In reality, Gehrig ended with the famous line rather than beginning with it.

Chariots of Fire (1981): This film took the Oscar for Best Picture for its portrayal of the 1924 Summer Olympics in Paris, but it also took liberties with the accuracy of events. In real life, Eric Liddell knew months in advance that the preliminary heats in his main event would be held on a Sunday, and teammate Harold Abrahams competed and *lost* in the 1920 Olympics. Also, the two were not rivals as the film depicts. Instead, the experiences of these two athletes, whose religions defined them (Liddell was Christian and Abrahams was Jewish), are used to weave a timeless story of tolerance and the power of faith.

Eight Men Out (1988): This film recounts the story of the 1919 World Series between the Chicago White Sox and the Cincinnati Reds, after which eight White Sox players were accused of accepting bribes to lose the series. The players were accurately depicted as victims caught between organized gambling syndicates and team owners, but the film takes liberties with some facts. For example, Chick Gandil's pro career did not end because of the scandal. He had already retired before the scandal was exposed because Sox owner Charles Comiskey would not give him a $1,000 raise.

Rudy (1993): The true story of Daniel "Rudy" Ruettiger was the first film given permission to shoot on the campus of the University of Notre Dame since *Knute Rockne All American*. And while this true story is proof that dreams do come true in the world of sports, the film's low budget did allow for some inaccuracies to creep in. Cars in street scenes were of later models than those of the era in which the film was set, and a New York City scene set in the late 1960s included the World Trade Center towers, which were not completed until the early 1970s. The film also portrays Ruettiger's high school as coed years before it was in real life. One scene has a player set his shirt on Coach Dan Devine's desk to sacrifice his place on the "dress list." It never happened. In fact, Devine had planned to put Ruettiger in the game all along. But for the sake of a dramatic story line, Devine agreed to be painted as the villain in the film.

Invincible (2006): It's a fantasy that every Monday morning quarterback dreams about—playing for his favorite professional football team. This film starring Mark Wahlberg captured the look and feel of the 1970s authentically enough, but it fumbled on a few key points. The most notable error was the implication that Vince Papale was a complete unknown when he tried out for the Philadelphia Eagles in 1976. In fact, Papale had played for the World Football League's Philadelphia Bell for two seasons before trying out for the Eagles.

Lacrosse

Along with basketball, lacrosse is arguably the most North American game there is—First Peoples/Native Americans invented it.

✳   ✳   ✳   ✳

ALGONQUIANS CALLED LACROSSE *baggataway* and the Iroquois called it *tewaarathon*. Natives played the game to honor the Great Spirit or revered elders, or to celebrate. Lacrosse also served a diplomatic role. Suppose you were a Mohawk elder and you learned that the Oneidas were fishing on your side of the lake (violating your long-standing agreement). Rather than sending your warriors to fight the Oneida, you'd send an emissary to challenge them to settle the dispute with a tewaarathon match. These early games, which could be quite violent, took place on fields that were miles long and involved as many as 1,000 participants. We can thank French Canadians for its name: *La crosse* means "the bishop's staff," and that's what the stick looked like.

Europeans' first record of a lacrosse match dates to the 1630s in southern Ontario, when missionary Jean de Brébeuf watched the Hurons play. By the 1800s, the game was popular with French Canadian settlers. In 1867, the same year Canada became a dominion, Canadian dentist W. George Beers standardized the rules of lacrosse. By 1900, the Canadian game had spread into the United States, with men's and women's versions.

There are two primary forms of lacrosse today: box (indoor) and field (outdoor). Box lacrosse is largely a Canadian sport, but Canadians also compete well in men's and women's field lacrosse. The game values speed and agility above brawn. The crosse (stick) takes skill to manipulate as players move the ball around. Play flow is similar to hockey or soccer; a team tries to control the ball and send it past a goaltender into the net. Fouls are similar to those in hockey, as is the penalty box. Lacrosse is a physical, speedy, demanding game that requires the toughness of rugby and the stamina of soccer.

First Nations in the Game

Only one First Nations team is sanctioned for international sport competition: the Iroquois Nationals, in field lacrosse. They're even sponsored by Nike!

Positions in Men's Lacrosse

Attack: There are three attackers on the field at one time. The attackers use "short-sticks" and must demonstrate good stick-handling with both hands; they must know where their teammates are at all times and be able to handle the pressure of opposing defense. Attackers score most of the goals.

Defense: Three defensive players with "long-poles" and one long-stick midfielder are allowed on the field at a time, using their sticks to throw checks and try to dislodge the ball. One of the "long-poles" may also play midfield as a strategic defender, aka a long-stick middie. Teams usually use this to anticipate losing the face-off and to be stronger on defense.

Midfield: Three "middies" are allowed on the field at once. There are two types of midfielders, defensive and offensive. The two can rotate by running off the sidelines. Midfielders are allowed to use short-sticks and up to one long-pole. While on offense, three short-sticks are generally used for their superior stick-handling. While on defense, two short-sticks are used with one long-pole. Some teams have a designated face-off middie who takes the majority of face-offs and is usually quickly substituted after the face-off is complete.

Goalkeeper: Goalies try to prevent the ball from getting into the goal, and they also direct the team defense. A goalkeeper needs to be tough both physically and mentally, and he has to be loud enough to call the position of the ball at all times so the defense can concentrate on where the players are.

Good Ol' Boys Make Good

"Heck, I had faster bootleg cars than race cars."
—*NASCAR pioneer Robert Glen Johnson Jr. (aka Junior Johnson)*

✳ ✳ ✳ ✳

THE 1930S AND 1940s saw a new breed of driver tearing up the back roads of the American South. Young, highly skilled, and full of brass, these road rebels spent their nights outwitting and outrunning federal agents as they hauled 60-gallon payloads of illegal moonshine liquor from the mountains to their eager customers in the cities below. In this dangerous game, speed and control made all the difference. The bootleggers spent as much time tinkering under their hoods as they did prowling the roads. A typical bootleg car might be a Ford Coupe with a 454 Cadillac engine, heavy-duty suspension, and any number of other modifications meant to keep the driver and his illicit cargo ahead of John Law.

With all that testosterone and horsepower bundled together, it was inevitable that these wild hares would compete to see who had the fastest car and the steeliest nerve. A dozen or more of them would get together on weekends in an open field and spend the afternoon testing each other's skills, often passing a hat among the spectators who came to watch. Promoters saw the potential in these events, and before long organized races were being held all across the South. As often as not, though, the promoters lit out with the receipts halfway through the race, and the drivers saw nothing for their efforts.

Seeking to bring legitimacy and profitability to the sport, driver and promoter William "Bill" Henry Getty France Sr. organized a meeting of his colleagues at the Ebony Bar in Daytona Beach, Florida, on December 14, 1947. Four days of haggling and backslapping led to the formation of the National Association for Stock Car Auto Racing (NASCAR), with France named as its first president. The group held its inaugural race in 1948, on the well-known half-sand, half-asphalt track at Daytona.

Over the next two decades, the organization built a name for itself on the strength of its charismatic drivers. Junior Johnson, Red Byron, Curtis Turner, Lee Petty, and the Flock Brothers (Bob, Fonty, and Tim) held regular jobs and raced the circuit in their spare time. And these legendary pioneers were some colorful characters: For example, Tim Flock occasionally raced with a pet monkey named Jocko Flocko, who sported a crash helmet and was strapped into the passenger seat.

Dawn of a New Era

During these early years, NASCAR was viewed as a distinctly Southern enterprise. In the early 1970s, however, Bill France Jr. took control of the organization from his father, and things began to change. The younger France negotiated network television deals that brought the racetrack into the living rooms of Middle America. In 1979, CBS presented the first flag-to-flag coverage of a NASCAR event, and it was a doozy. Race leaders Cale Yarborough and Donnie Allison entered a bumping duel on the last lap that ended with both cars crashing on the third turn. As Richard Petty moved up from third to take the checkered flag, a fight broke out between Yarborough and Allison's brother Bobby. America was hooked.

France also expanded the sport's sponsorship beyond automakers and parts manufacturers. Tobacco giant R. J. Reynolds bought its way in, as did countless other purveyors of everyday household items, including Tide, Lowe's Hardware, Kellogg's Cereal, the Cartoon Network, Nextel, and Coca-Cola. Today, NASCAR vehicles and their beloved drivers are virtually moving billboards. Plastered with the logos of their sponsors as they speed around the track, Jeff Gordon, Dale Earnhardt Jr., Tony Stewart, Bobby Labonte, and their fellow daredevils draw the eyes of some 75 million regular fans and support a multibillion-dollar industry that outearns professional baseball, basketball, and hockey combined.

The Early Days of Video Games

Today's die-hard gamers might chuckle at the concept of playing a simple game of table tennis on a TV screen. But without Pong, *there might not be* Grand Theft Auto: Vice City. *Read on to marvel at how far the industry has come.*

✳ ✳ ✳ ✳

Spacewar: At MIT in 1962, Steve Russell programmed the world's first video game on a bulky computer known as the DEC PDP-1. *Spacewar* featured spaceships fighting amid an astronomically correct screen full of stars. The technological fever spread quickly, and by the end of the decade, nearly every research computer in the United States was equipped with a copy of *Spacewar*.

Pong: Nolan Bushnell founded Atari in 1972, taking the company's name from the Japanese word for the chess term "check." Atari released the coin-operated *Pong* later that year, and its simple, addictive action of bouncing a pixel ball between two paddles became an instant arcade hit. In 1975, the TV-console version of *Pong* was released. It was received with great enthusiasm by people who could play hours of the tennislike game in the comfort of their homes.

Tetris: After runaway success in the Soviet Union in 1985 (and in spite of the Cold War), *Tetris* jumped the Bering Strait and took over the U.S. market the next year. Invented by Soviet mathematician Alexi Pajitnov, the game features simple play—turning and dropping geometric shapes into tightly packed rows—that drew in avid fans in both countries. Many gamers call *Tetris* the most addictive game of all time.

Space Invaders: Released in 1978, Midway's *Space Invaders* was the arcade equivalent of *Star Wars*: a ubiquitous hit that generated a lot of money. It also presented the "high score" concept. A year later, Atari released *Asteroids* and outdid *Space*

Invaders by enabling the high scorer to enter his or her initials for posterity.

Pac Man: The 1980 Midway classic is the world's most successful arcade game, selling some 99,000 units. Featuring the yellow maw of the title character, a maze of dots, and four colorful ghosts, the game inspired rap songs, Saturday morning cartoons, and a slew of sequels.

Donkey Kong: In 1980, Nintendo's first game marked the debut of Mario, soon to become one of the most recognizable fictional characters in the world. Originally dubbed Jumpman, Mario was named for Mario Segali, the onetime owner of Nintendo's Seattle warehouse.

Q*bert: Released by Gottlieb in 1982, this game featured the title character jumping around on a pyramid of cubes, squashing and dodging enemies. Designers originally wanted Q*bert to shoot slime from his nose, but it was deemed too gross.

✳ From 1988 to 1990, Nintendo sold roughly 50 million home-entertainment systems. In 1996, the company sold its billionth video game cartridge for home systems.

✳ In 1981, 15-year-old Steve Juraszek set a world record on Williams Electronics' *Defender*. His score of 15,963,100 got his picture in *TIME* magazine—and it also got him suspended from school. He played part of his 16-hour game when he should have been attending class.

✳ Atari opened the first pizzeria/arcade establishment known as Chuck E. Cheese in San Jose in 1977. Atari's Nolan Bushnell bought the rights to the pizza business when he parted ways with his company in 1978, and he turned it into a nationwide phenomenon. It was later acquired by its primary competitor, ShowBiz Pizza.

Chapter 11

Pop Culture

Life in the Iroquois League

Long before English settlers swarmed over the eastern coast of the "New World," Native Americans occupied the land around Lake Ontario now known as New York, as well as parts of New England and Canada.

※ ※ ※ ※

FIVE OF THESE tribes experienced much intertribal fighting. According to legend, a wise sachem (chief) named Deganiwidah sought to make peace and foster goodwill among the nations through the efforts of another sachem named Hiawatha (no, not *the* Hiawatha). These five tribes—Seneca, Cayuga, Onondaga, Oneida, and Mohawk—sent 50 chiefs as a council and formed an alliance between 1500 and 1650 that came to be known as the "Five Nations of the Iroquois League." (A sixth nation, Tuscarora, joined in 1722.)

Each tribe in the League was unique. The Seneca tribe— "People of the Great Hills"—was the largest, while the Cayuga, called the "Pipe People," was the smallest. The Onondaga were relatively peaceful and known as the "People of the Mountain." The Oneida—"People of the Standing Stone"—were violent. The Mohawk, known as the "People of the Flint," were the fiercest of all. Yet the League had four moral principles on which they all agreed: a love of peace, respect for their laws, a sense of brotherhood, and a reverence for their ancestors.

A Longhouse Is a Home

Life in an Iroquois village was based on farming, even though the tribes did not have animals to help cultivate their fields. As such, many settlements were situated along rivers, where a spiral wooden fence surrounded the main buildings. These structures, known as "longhouses," could be anywhere from 30 to 350 feet long and were home for many, many families in individual living quarters under one roof (a somewhat primitive form of tenement housing). Several longhouses in an Iroquois village could house as few as 100 to as many as 3,000 people. A number of fires were kept burning in the middle of the longhouse to provide heat in the winter months and allow cooking and baking year-round.

So strong was the concept of the longhouse in the Iroquois League, the tribes actually regarded their occupied land as one enormous longhouse. The Seneca considered themselves the "Keepers of the Western Door," and the Mohawk were the "Keepers of the Eastern Door" on the other end at the Atlantic Ocean. In between, the Onondaga were the "Keepers of the Fire," the Cayuga were the "Younger Brothers of Seneca," and the Oneida were the "Younger Brothers of Mohawk."

The Role of Women

The social order of the League was matrilineal—women owned the longhouse, as well as garden plots and farming tools. They also set and maintained rules in the village and could appoint religious leaders. Women in the village were wholly responsible for daily life, as the men were seldom in camp. Their jobs— warfare, trading, trapping, and hunting—kept them away from the longhouse for months at a time.

Though the League claimed to have a "love of peace," they engaged in warlike activities. The Huron and Algonquian tribes were natural enemies of the League, and tribal warfare was a component of Iroquois society. The Mohawk were known for wielding heavy tomahawk axes to kill their enemies and pillage their goods. But the League avoided large-scale war, remaining satisfied with small skirmishes.

The League lacked the social economics and organization to maintain standing armies and stage war. Europeans landed in America in the mid-1600s and joined the list of foes. The Iroquois were forced to move out into other territories for their prey, and their aggressive attacks increased.

The Iroquois were masters of psychological warfare. They intimidated their foes through kidnapping and torture. Many captives were used as slaves. Hideous instances of cannibalism were also common among the Iroquois.

The Iroquois League held many religious beliefs, including the power of medicine men. One group, known as the "False Face Society," donned fearsome carved wooden masks. They danced, shook turtle shells, and sprinkled ashes to bring about a cure for illness. A similar curing group, called the "Huskface Society," wore cornhusks as masks.

Working with the White Man

The Iroquois had much to offer in the way of operating a complex government body. The council of 50 sachems required that all decisions of the village had to be unanimous. If a sachem caused problems in the council, he was given three warnings; after that, he was ousted.

Some historians believe that portions of the U.S. Constitution were based on the Iroquois Confederacy. Benjamin Franklin observed many of the council meetings. The Presidential Seal of America features an eagle holding 13 arrows—one for each original colony. Similarly, the Iroquois seal showed an eagle with five arrows in its talon—one for each nation. The Iroquois nations signed a treaty with the United States in 1794. Terms of the agreement endure to this day; some members receive calico cloth as annual payment, while other tribes receive $1,800 a year.

The Oldest Family Businesses

Many people prefer companies with long, sturdy family histories.

✳ ✳ ✳ ✳

Kongo Gumi (Osaka, Japan; contractors, founded 578): After nearly 1,400 years of general contracting, this business is still going strong. Flexibility may be its key—during World War II, the company switched its focus to coffin construction.

Château de Goulaine (Haute Goulaine, France; vintners and museum-keepers, founded 1000): The Goulaines have cared for this castle for a thousand years. The highlight of the museum is its butterfly collection, but its Loire Valley wines are also prized.

Fonderia Pontificia Marinelli (Agnone, Italy; bell founders, founded around 1000): The Marinellis are still casting bronze bells using techniques employed by bell masters in the Middle Ages and the Renaissance. Today, bells crafted by the Marinellis ring in prestigious churches throughout the world.

Barovier & Toso (Murano Venezia, Italy; glassmakers, founded 1295): The world's oldest continuous maker of fine crystal, this business originally operated in Venice but moved to the nearby island of Murano, ostensibly to guard its glassblowing secrets.

Hotel Pilgrim Haus (Soest, Germany; hoteliers, founded 1304): The Andernach family has operated this inn through every wave of conflict that has washed over the Ruhr. Its survival could be attributed to its stone walls, which are three feet thick.

Richard de Bas (Ambert d'Auvergne, France; papermakers, founded 1326): When your family has supplied paper for art by Braque and Picasso, you strive to keep up the tradition.

Camuffo (Portogruaro, Italy; shipbuilders, founded 1438): This company, relocated from Crete, has supplied ships to many navies over the centuries, including Napoleon's. A Camuffo is to boats what a Stradivarius is to violins.

Domaine de Coussergues (Beziers, France; vintners, founded 1495): This gold-medal-draped winemaker is noted for Sauvignon Blanc, Chardonnay, Syrah, Grenache, Pinot Noir, Cabernet Franc, and Merlot. The winery was started through a land grant from King Charles VIII.

Grazia Deruta (Turin, Italy; ceramicists, founded 1500): The Grazias make majolica, a tin-glazed pottery with a surface that takes paint exceptionally well. Their customers include Neiman Marcus and Tiffany.

William Prym GmbH (Stolberg, Germany; clothing industry, founded 1530): If it's made of metal and it's used in clothing, Prym likely started making it well before the Pilgrims landed. The company specializes in needles, fasteners, and now microelectronics.

John Brooke & Sons Holdings (Huddersfield, UK; formerly clothiers, now real estate, founded 1541): Brooke used to make naval and military uniforms but has recently gotten out of manufacturing. It now manages office and retail space on the site of the firm's former mill buildings.

von Poschinger Manufaktur (Frauenau, Germany; glaziers, 1568): Though glassmaking is still the priority at von Poschinger, the family has diversified into farming and forestry on its ancient lands near the Czech border. The subtle colors and artistic beauty of their glassware make von Poschinger crystal a prized collectible.

Hacienda Los Lingues (San Fernando, Chile; diversified, founded about 1575): These prestigious stables once bred fine cavalry horses. The firm also sponsors a line of well-regarded wines and operates an elegant hotel.

"High technology leads us to products that are repetitive."

—PASQUALE MARINELLI

With This Ring, I Thee Wed

A wedding ring, traditionally a simple gold band, is a powerful symbol. The circle represents eternity and is an emblem of lasting love in many of the world's cultures. But the history of the wedding ring also includes less spiritual associations.

✳   ✳   ✳   ✳

H ISTORIANS SUGGEST THAT wedding rings are a modern version of the ropes with which primitive men bound women they had captured. This suggests that the phrase "old ball and chain" may have referred more to the passage of a bride from person to prisoner than to the husband's matrimonial outlook.

Our current perceptions of the wedding ring evolved over time and are rooted in a variety of ancient practices. In Egypt, a man placed a piece of ring-money—metal rings used to purchase things—on his bride's hand to show that he had endowed her with his wealth. In ancient Rome, rings made of various metals communicated a variety of political and social messages. In marriage, the ring holding the household keys was presented to the wife after the ceremony when she crossed the threshold of her new home. Later, this key ring dwindled in size to a symbolic ring placed on the woman's finger during the wedding. Among Celtic tribes, a ring may have indicated sexual availability. A woman might have given a man a ring to show her desire; putting her finger through the ring may have symbolized the sexual act.

Wedding rings were not always made of gold. They could be made of any metal as well as leather or rushes. In fact, in the 13th century, a bishop of Salisbury in England warned young men against seducing gullible virgins by braiding rings out of rushes and placing them on their fingers. In the 17th century,

Puritans decried the use of a wedding ring due to its pagan associations and ostentatious value, calling it "a relique of popery and a diabolical circle for the devil to dance in."

The Ring Finger of Choice

Why is the ring placed on the fourth finger of the left hand? According to fourth-century A.D. Roman grammarian and philosopher Ambrosius Theodosius Macrobius, the fourth finger is the one most appropriate to that function. Macrobius described the thumb as "too busy to be set apart" and said "the forefinger and little finger are only half-protected." The middle finger, or *medicusm*, is commonly used for offensive communications and so could not be used for this purpose. This leaves only the fourth finger for the wedding ring.

It was once believed that a vein ran directly from that finger to the heart, the so-called *vena amoris*, or vein of love. Since the right hand is commonly the dominant hand, some scholars suggest that wearing a ring on the left, or "submissive," hand symbolizes a wife's obedience to her husband. The importance of the Trinity in Christian theology provides another explanation for the identification of the fourth finger on the left hand as the "wedding ring finger." In the early Catholic Church, the groom touched the thumb and first two fingers of his bride as he said, "In the name of the Father, Son, and Holy Ghost." He then slipped the ring all the way onto the next, or fourth, finger as he said, "Amen." This four-step placement of the ring was a common custom in England until the end of the 16th century, and it remained a tradition among Roman Catholics for many more years.

"For years [my wedding ring] has done its job. It has led me not into temptation. It has reminded my husband numerous times at parties that it's time to go home. It has been a source of relief to a dinner companion. It has been a status symbol in the maternity ward."

—AMERICAN HUMORIST ERMA BOMBECK

Rural 1920s America

The mechanization of American agriculture during the Roaring Twenties created a good news–bad news scenario for small farmers. The following account explores what "a day in the life" might have been like.

✳　✳　✳　✳

IT'S SHORTLY AFTER sunrise on a July day in Nebraska. Hollis stands by the roadside watching a billowing dust cloud rumble its way toward his 30-acre family farm. It's 1925, and the cloud is bringing another dose of modernity to Hollis's farm in the form of a big, noisy, steam-driven threshing machine.

Modernity first arrived last year, when Hollis partnered with four fellow farmers to buy a gasoline-powered tractor. The tractor was a godsend. It plows an acre three times faster than his five horses did. The ten acres of land he previously used to grow horse feed now yield cash crops. The tractor pulls the seeder, manure spreader, and binder (which cuts and bundles wheat stalks)—other machines that have reduced Hollis's dependence on paid labor.

Today, the thresher will separate wheat kernels from their stalks in a fraction of the time it takes a gang of workers to do it by hand. Threshing season is as much a social gathering as it is work. Area farmers band together to work each farm using the same thresher. Meanwhile, the women prepare home-cooked feasts.

Hollis and the men gravitate to the thresher as it chugs into the field. Clad in ubiquitous denim overalls, short-sleeved shirts, and wide-brimmed hats, they feed bundles of dried wheat into the thresher. The machine spits out straw to be used for livestock bedding and shoots grain through a spout into a wagon hitched to Hollis's tractor.

Meanwhile, the women butcher chickens, cook, and set up tables and chairs. Kids tote sandwiches and cold well water to the men.

The women will lay out gigantic spreads at mid-morning, noon, and late afternoon. Platters of fried chicken, ham, homemade bread and biscuits, butter, jams, mashed potatoes, vegetables, pies, cakes, iced tea, and lemonade are gobbled up.

At 7 P.M. the works stops, and everyone heads home. The pattern will be repeated on Hollis's farm over the next several days.

More Signs of the Times

Exhausted, Hollis leans against another machine transforming American rural life: his 1920 Ford Model T pickup. The vehicle enables his family to make daily visits to town, whether it's to sell produce at the market, visit friends, attend a baseball game or church social, or see a movie. The car has ended their isolation from the outside world.

Tonight, however, Hollis is too tired for any of that, choosing to stay home and listen to his radio. Sandwiched between music programs is a broadcast from the U.S. Department of Agriculture offering weather and market reports. Hollis grimaces as the crackling radio voice warns of lower wheat, oat, and corn prices this fall.

Although technology is helping Hollis produce more than ever, he's finding this is not necessarily a good thing. Food production in the United States is now outpacing demand, causing steadily declining commodity prices. Hollis is producing more but earning less. He's swimming in debt from buying new machines. He's hoping to eke out a profit this year—hoping.

Many small farmers have already succumbed to this cruel irony and have sold their farms, joining the exodus of people leaving rural America for the cities during the 1920s. But Hollis doesn't want to leave. As upbeat ragtime music blares from the radio, he somberly wonders how much longer he can hold out.

A Brief History of Underwear

From fig leaves to bloomers to thongs, people have covered themselves a little or a lot, depending on social preferences and mores. Here is a brief history of the undergarment.

✳   ✳   ✳   ✳

✳ The earliest and most simple undergarment was the loin-cloth—a strip of material passed between the legs and around the waist. King Tutankhamen was buried with 145 of them, but the style didn't go out with the Egyptians. Loincloths are still worn in Asia and Africa.

✳ Men in the Middle Ages wore trouserlike undergarments called braies, which one stepped into and tied around the waist and legs about mid-calf. To facilitate urination, braies had a codpiece, a flap that buttoned or tied closed.

✳ Medieval women wore a close-fitting undergarment called a chemise, and corsets began to appear in the 18th century. Early versions of the corset were designed to flatten a woman's bustline, but by the late 1800s, corsets were reconstructed to give women an exaggerated hourglass shape.

✳ Bras were invented in 1913 when American socialite Mary Phelps-Jacob tied two handkerchiefs together with ribbon. Maidenform introduced modern cup sizes in 1928.

✳ Around 1920, as women became more involved in sports such as tennis and bicycling, loose, comfortable bloomers replaced corsets as the undergarment of choice. The constricting corset soon fell out of favor altogether.

✳ The thong made its first public U.S. appearance at the 1939 World's Fair, when New York Mayor Fiorello La Guardia required nude dancers to cover themselves. Thongs gained popularity as swimwear in Brazil in the 1970s and are now fashionable in many parts of the world.

Life Amid the Falling Bombs

Nighttime air raids. Crowded bomb shelters.
Burned-out houses. Loved ones killed. That was
everyday life for Britons during the Blitz.

✳ ✳ ✳ ✳

Tʜᴇ Bʟɪᴛᴢ, Gᴇʀᴍᴀɴʏ's terror-bombing campaign against
Britain in 1940–41, was a horrifying experience. More
than 43,000 civilians died during the bombing, and one million
homes were destroyed or damaged.

The Blitz shook Britons to their very core. They were scared
and depressed; their homes and neighborhoods lay in ruins.
But their spirit was never broken. Somehow, they found a way
to get through it all and show Hitler that the best he could
throw at them wasn't good enough.

To mark the 60th anniversary of the end of World War II, the
BBC invited Britons to relive their wartime experiences for
a unique online archive titled WW2 People's War. Included
among the archive's 47,000 recollections are thousands of firsthand accounts from those who survived the Blitz. They depict
both perilously close calls and the indomitable fortitude that
enabled the British people to persevere. Here are some excerpts.

Denis Gardner, Peckham, Southeast London
BBC article ID A4104343

[I was] not quite 14 when the Blitz started … [The woman
who owned the paper shop] did not have an Anderson shelter in the back garden, but the hallway of the house had been
reinforced to make a shelter. She had said if a raid started
during the time I was delivering the papers I was to make my
way back to the shop and take shelter. On the morning of 15th
October the siren sounded, so I finished the deliveries in the
street I was in, and then I started to make my way back to the
shop. On the way I could see German aircraft in the sky and

see bombs leaving the planes. It was fascinating. There were other people around all staring at the sky. I carried on cycling [to] the shop... The next thing I remember was being put in an ambulance and being taken to St. Giles Hospital, Camberwell.

A bomb had hit a house as I was cycling past. I had cuts on the forehead and back of the head. Also my wrist was cut and my arm was injured. They told me afterwards that my greatest concern was whether my bike was O.K... I did not go back to delivering papers any more. I was now the local hero...

Peter Addis, Portsmouth
BBC article ID A2097236

In the summer of 1940 I was 16... At school we all cheered when the Air Raid Siren [sounded], it meant we could play around in a very interesting shelter and skip the lesson. Our teacher said that one day we might stop praying for air raids... Then came the time when silly boys stopped praying for air raids. It was a January night 1941. The bombing started at dusk and the first bombs put out all the lights. Continuous incendiary bombs set whole streets alight... I was not thrilled anymore, I was scared... Daylight came and the raid finished... Then we went home. But it was gone. All that was left was a small square of rubble... It was a bitter blow to my parents, not only was it their home but also their shop and means of livelihood... We walked out of town, carrying a small bag [that] held all the important family documents... We travelled up to Maidenhead to relatives... our arrival was a complete surprise [but] we were given a great welcome... The next night we went over to Marlow and met more family, all evacuated from London, they took us to the local pub, where there was an impromptu dance. My mum and dad were dancing less than 48 hours after losing everything.

Doris Fisher, Ilford, Essex

BBC article ID A2124316

I was 24 years old when overnight my life changed forever. A so-called Doodlebug [V-1 flying bomb] landed on my home, destroying everything that I owned and uprooting the Anderson Shelter in which I had taken refuge with my dog, Trixie. Blind, deaf and with multiple injuries I was taken to the nearest emergency centre. Trixie was dead, mercifully still curled around as though asleep. At the emergency centre I was transferred to a plastic surgery unit in Hill End Hospital, St Albans where a medical team not only saved my life but my very reason for I had horrific facial injuries . . . Plastic surgery cannot be hurried and as the weeks in that ward turned into months, it became my second home and the other patients around me a surragate [sic] family. There was Kitty in the next bed to me who had been in a bus when a bomb exploded nearby and shattered the glass causing her to lose an eye amongst other injuries. There was the young housewife who had been blinded but cared only that the baby she carried inside her still stirred. We all shared each others' joys and sorrows, forming a bond of sympathy when a husband or boyfriend failed to turn up at visiting time, unable to cope with the altered appearance of their partner. [But] there was laughter when I threatened to shoot the first cow I saw when leaving hospital. Having had my fractured jaw in clamps . . . and been on a daily diet of milk, Horlicks or Ovaltine through a straw.

Eric Bowker, Salford, Lancashire

BBC article ID A2066933

December 1940, nine years old . . . We had a lovely time with Uncle Bill, Auntie Elsie and their three daughters, time for going home. [Auntie Maggie and I] got on the bus just as it was going dusk . . . Then the sirens sounded . . . we proceeded at snails pace until we eventually arrived at Trafford Bar . . .

Maggie took my hand, the night sky was alive and loud with shell burst and the distinctive drone of German aeroplanes.

We got to a street shelter an air raid warden...popped out from behind the blast wall "You can't come in here its [sic] full" then he popped back in. Maggie found our way to Trafford Bridge, a policeman, stationed in the middle of the road, "Sorry love I can't let you cross here, there's an unexploded bomb on the other side." My brave courageous Auntie Maggie, all four foot four of her, was not beaten yet...Passing the coal yard we crossed Robert Hall Street, then just a few doors down and knocking on the front door we were admitted by Gladys, Maggie's younger sister...Moments after our arrival a great explosion rent the air...A parachute bomb...obliterated the coal yard that we had walked by not more than five minutes ago. With the cold grey dawn came the wail of the all clear. Maggie and I began our long walk home...Then at the start of Mulgrave Street [we saw] devastation, piles of rubble, the heavy rescue squad digging for survivors, blanket covered stretchers. Told that we could not pass, Maggie explained "We live at the end of this street on the corner of Montague and Edith Street"...[There was] a great gaping hole in the roof of our house, windows and frames blown out, a blackened remnant of curtain hanging forlornly from a downstairs window...Our front door hung open, the acrid rotten smell of burning was everywhere. Mam, Dad and Vera were in, what was left, of the living room, "Are you all right," from everybody. Bone tired, blackened, our home a shambles. We were alive. Thank God.

I think lots of ordinary civilian folk deserved medals in that war. Including my Auntie Maggie.

✳ **Nearly 180 Londoners died during a raid on March 3, 1943— but not from bombs. A woman tripped entering an underground station; the crowd rushing for cover crushed her and many others, suffocating them.**

Baby Ruth's Truth?

Many people believe that the Baby Ruth candy bar was named for baseball great Babe Ruth. Others contend that the honor belongs to President Grover Cleveland's daughter Ruth.

✳   ✳   ✳   ✳

GERMAN IMMIGRANT OTTO Schnering founded the Curtiss Candy Company in Chicago in 1916. With World War I raging in Europe, Schnering decided to avoid using his Germanic surname and chose his mother's maiden name for the business. His first product was a snack called Kandy Kake, a pastry center covered with peanuts and chocolate. But the candy bar was only a marginal success, and to boost sales, it was renamed Baby Ruth in 1921. Five years later the company was selling millions of dollars' worth of the bars every day. Whenever pressed for details on the confection's name, Curtiss claimed the appellation honored Ruth Cleveland, the late and beloved daughter of President Grover Cleveland. But the company may have been trying to sneak a fastball past everybody.

Cleveland's daughter had died of diphtheria in 1904—a dozen years before the candy company was even started. The gesture may have been appropriate for a president, but a president's relatively unknown daughter?

The more plausible origin of the name might be tied to the biggest sports star in the world at the time—George Herman "Babe" Ruth. Originally a star pitcher for the Boston Red Sox, Ruth became a fearsome hitter for the New York Yankees, slamming 59 home runs in the same year the candy bar was renamed Baby Ruth. Curtiss may have found a way to cash in on the slugger's fame—and name—without paying a dime in royalties. In fact, when Ruth gave the okay to use his name on a competitor's candy—the Babe Ruth Home Run Bar—Curtiss successfully blocked it, claiming infringement on his own "baby."

Before Barbie

The Barbie doll is considered by most people to be an American original. But before her, there was Bild Lilli, the German fashion doll that became the prototype for Barbie and friends.

✳ ✳ ✳ ✳

THE WORLD'S MOST successful toy doll (with more than a billion sold in over 150 countries), Barbie is an 11¹/₂-inch plastic fashion figure with unachievable body structure and an inexhaustible wardrobe. Introduced in 1959 at the American International Toy Fair by Mattel Inc., Barbie has staked her place in American pop culture. She's been parodied countless times by the media (notably as the vacuous Malibu Stacy doll on *The Simpsons*) and honored with a section of Times Square renamed Barbie Boulevard. Her unrealistic body image and prissy persona have riled feminists for 50 years, yet her iconic status earned Barbie 43rd place on the list *101 Most Influential People Who Never Lived*, published in 2006.

A German Predecessor

Barbie's indelible mark on the national psyche leads most people to assume that she's a purely American creation. But Barbie had a predecessor whose name was Bild Lilli. This German fashion doll was based on a popular comic-strip character who sassily used men to get what she wanted. The adult-figured Lilli doll was originally sold as a sexy novelty item for men, but it spawned an idea in the mind of Ruth Handler, an American who discovered Lilli while visiting Europe in 1956. Handler set about designing a more wholesome version of Lilli geared toward girls. She named her creation Barbie, after her daughter, Barbara, and pitched the idea to her husband, who was a cofounder of Mattel.

Whatever became of Lilli? Mattel bought the rights to the doll in 1964 and promptly stopped its production—effectively removing the skeleton from Barbie's cavernous closet.

Fashion Comes to the Fore

Today, it seems like everything that can be done with fashion has pretty much been done. But imagine what it must have been like before all those doors were opened.

✳ ✳ ✳ ✳

IN THE 1950S, modern fashion and classic looks were just beginning to take shape. Surely it was exciting, after the rationing of everything from butter to stockings during World War II, for women to wear a beautiful, billowing dress, soft to the touch and conjuring images of a fashionable beauty the world had never seen before.

One might think that women everywhere would've tripped over themselves to make this look their own, but many were indignant: How dare an unknown designer waste luxurious fabrics creating elaborate dresses and suits while everyone else was mending old items and rationing?

The designer, of course, was Christian Dior, who never compromised fashion for responsibility.

Born in Granville in the Normandy region of France in 1905, Dior was an unassuming man who wouldn't even compromise with his beloved family. His father, a fertilizer manufacturer, hoped that Christian would go into the family business, but the young man had no desire for that line of work. Instead, Dior pursued a career in the arts, and in 1938 he landed a job as an assistant to designer Robert Piquet. But World War II loomed, and just one year later, Dior was off to fight.

Surviving the war, Dior returned home. The fighting had ravaged France, but the economy was slowly rebuilding; Dior knew he'd have to act soon to make his mark. He approached fabric magnate Marcel Broussac with an idea that would reinvent fashion—good-bye to the fabric shortage and stiff textiles, hello to accentuated curves and attention to detail.

Celebrating Women

On February 12, 1947, with backing from Broussac, Dior debuted his Corelle line, a refreshing, uplifting look. Shoulder pads were gone, waists were slimmed, and dresses flowed. Dior wanted to free women from the repressive styles that had accompanied them to the fields and industrial jobs they worked while the men were away fighting. He accomplished this goal with suit jackets that tucked in at the waist and expanded at the hips, creating an inverted bellflower shape. As *Harper's Bazaar* editor Carmel Snow said, "It's quite a revelation, dear Christian. Your dresses have a new look."

At first, middle-class women were appalled by the New Look, as the Corelle line came to be known; it seemed wasteful. But Hollywood and the wealthy embraced the style. Stars Ava Gardner, Rita Hayworth, and Marlene Dietrich wore Dior creations to movie premieres and created the epitome of celebrity glamour. England's Princess Margaret wore them in private (King George VI forbade her and her sister, Princess Elizabeth, to wear such illustrious garments in public when common people were still participating in fabric rationing).

The New Look changed fashion, yet as Dior got bored and times changed, the designer did a complete overhaul and introduced the Flat Look. Think Audrey Hepburn in simple, skinny black pants; a matching cardigan; and flats. Dresses went from detailed and flowing to boxy flat sheets. The same people who had jeered the New Look couldn't believe that Dior was trying to hide the female form.

But of course, Dior didn't let the critics shake him; the Flat Look, like the New Look before it, eventually caught on. Dior's reputation was solidified in the fashion industry, and he began to make deals to produce ties and cosmetics. Tragically, Dior died of a heart attack at age 52 in 1957. Today, Dior is still a coveted name among young fashionistas and classic beauties all over the globe.

The Cola Claus

Although the Coca-Cola Company helped popularize Santa Claus, it cannot take credit for creating the ubiquitous Christmas image.

✳ ✳ ✳ ✳

NOTHING SAYS "CHRISTMAS" like the image of a white-whiskered fat man in a red suit squeezing down a chimney with a sack full of toys. But Santa Claus hasn't always looked that way. When the Coca-Cola Company used the red-robed figure in the 1930s to promote its soft drinks, the classic image of Santa was cemented in the public consciousness.

Santa Claus evolved from two figures, St. Nicholas and Christkindlein. St. Nicholas was a monk who became a bishop in the early fourth century and was a renowned gift-giver. Christkindlein (meaning "Christ child") was assisted by elfin helpers and would leave gifts for children while they slept.

Santa Claus originated from a Dutch poem called *"Sinterklaas."* Until the early 20th century, though, Santa Claus was portrayed in many different ways. He could be tall and clad in long robes like St. Nicholas or small with whiskers like the elves who helped Christkindlein.

In 1881, Thomas Nast, a caricaturist for *Harper's Weekly*, first drew Santa as a merry figure in red with flowing whiskers—an image close to the one we know today. Printer Louis Prang used a similar image in 1885 when he introduced Christmas cards to America. In 1931, the Coca-Cola Company first employed Haddon Sundblom to illustrate its annual advertisements, choosing a Santa dressed in red and white to match the corporate colors. By then, however, this was already the most popular image of Santa Claus, one that was described in detail in a *New York Times* article in 1927. If Coca-Cola had really invented Santa Claus, children would likely be saving the milk and leaving him soda with his cookies on Christmas Eve.

Why We Buy

Advertising executives know how to push our buttons.

✳ ✳ ✳ ✳

In the Kitchen

AD AGENCY MCCANN-ERICKSON Worldwide took a simple, two-sided slogan and turned Miller Lite into a top-selling brew in 1974. Actors, actresses, mystery authors, bronco riders, former and current athletes—all took a crack at debating whether Lite beer "Tastes great" or is "Less filling." The argument was never settled.

Candy-coated chocolate bits known as M&Ms were a blessing for moms who feared the dreaded "chocolate mess" on their children's hands. In 1954, the Ted Bates & Co agency informed America that M&Ms "Melt in your mouth, not in your hand." The candy was named after two executives at Hershey's—Forrest Mars and William Murrie.

Kellogg's Rice Krispies, a noisy breakfast favorite introduced in 1928, offered three cute elves named "Snap!, Crackle!, and Pop!" courtesy of the Leo Burnett ad agency. Worldwide favorites, they're known as "Piff!, Paff!, and Puff!" in Sweden, "Pim!, Pum!, and Pam!" in Mexico, and "Knisper!, Knasper!, and Knusper!" in Germany.

In the Bathroom

In 1957, Clairol, a leading manufacturer of hair-care products, focused on the vanity of women when they asked, "Does she ... or doesn't she?" Foote, Cone & Belding was the agency that boldly questioned the real hair color of the women of post-war America.

Benton & Bowles was an agency that developed clever slogans that brought booming sales for Crest toothpaste in 1958. A beaming boy flashed his smile following a successful visit to the dentist and cried, "Look, Ma! No cavities!" The agency also brought us the grouchy grocer Mr. Whipple, famous for the line "Please don't squeeze the Charmin!" in 1964.

Portly actor Jack Somack sat stone-faced, having wolfed down way too much dinner. Thanks to ad agencies like Jack Tinker & Partners; Doyle Dane Bernbach; and Wells Rich Greene, the overstuffed eater had Alka-Seltzer in the '60s and '70s. Somack claimed, "I can't believe I ate the whole thing," and the effervescent antacid tablets replied with, "Plop, Plop, Fizz, Fizz, Oh, what a relief it is."

Fast Food

A three-way tussle for the food dollar outside the home rumbled through the '70s and '80s. McDonald's told America, "You deserve a break today," while Burger King insisted that customers could "Have it your way." Late arrival Wendy's Hamburgers countered with a feisty old lady named Clara Peller who demanded that an invisible cashier answer this famous question: "Where's the beef?"

Soda Pop

In a soft drink battle that waged for decades, Pepsi-Cola, with the help of agency BBD&O, assured America that it belonged to "The Pepsi Generation" in 1964. Atlanta's Coca-Cola, with a typically top-notch jingle, responded that Coke was "The real thing." Also-ran 7-UP, however, was not caught lying down, as it cleverly positioned itself as "The Uncola" in the 1970s.

Transportation

Avis Rent-A-Car, trailing the industry leader Hertz, admitted their work was cut out for them as they proudly stated, "We try harder," courtesy of agency Doyle Dane Bernbach in 1963. As America built its interstate highway system in the mid-1950s, Chevrolet invited everyone to "See the USA in your Chevrolet." Meanwhile, the Greyhound Bus Company responded by suggesting that travelers "Leave the driving to us."

Hip, Happening Florence

The following fictionalized account offers a glimpse into a day in Renaissance life.

✳ ✳ ✳ ✳

NICOLO PEERS FROM the fifth-story bedroom window of his townhouse overlooking the streets of mid-15th century Florence. It's early morning, and Europe's most vibrant city is jumping.

Florence is the epicenter of the Renaissance. The city-state of 60,000 people is thriving as it sets the tone for Europe commercially, politically, and artistically. And Nicolo, a wealthy Florentine merchant, embarks on another day as the quintessential man of his times.

At Work at Home

Nicolo's townhouse also accommodates his prosperous cloth manufacturing business. Nicolo is a leading member of Florence's influential textile guild, and the exquisite goods he produces are among the finest in a city that dominates Europe's cloth industry.

Nicolo spends the morning in the ground-floor store, arranging displays and tending to customers. At mid-morning, he retreats to the fourth floor for the first of the two daily meals Florentines typically eat. He, along with his wife, Leonarda, and their two children eat fruit, salad, cheese, and pasta—a new culinary delight that's all the rage in Florence.

Hanging with the Movers and Shakers

After, Nicolo changes into an outfit befitting a man of his stature. Over his green long-sleeve collarless shirt he wears a burgundy velvet doublet, a long vest belted at the waist to create a skirt effect. White hose leggings and brown leather boots round out the ensemble. He also dons his *cioppa*, a red, full-length, fur-lined velvet gown worn by influential Florentine men.

Nicolo hires a horse-drawn carriage to take him to the Palazzo Vecchio, where 12 powerful merchant guilds conduct the business of Florence. Here, Nicolo makes his real money as he haggles with other textile merchants, arranging for the purchase of 300 wool bales from England and Spain and sales of finished cloth for export all over Europe.

Later, Nicolo and members of other guilds transform into political powerbrokers. In Florence, those who create the city's wealth also run it, and the 5,000 guild members, led by the powerful Medici banking clan, provide Florence with an enlightened form of government unseen in Europe since the ancient Greeks—one that emphasizes republicanism, democracy, and the welfare of the city.

Nicolo Gets Cultured

With the day's business done, Nicolo returns home for dinner. As on most days, Nicolo and Leonarda are entertaining. They serve up the usual guest-impressing cuisine: fruit and cake appetizers, a main course featuring roast lamb (only the well-to-do serve meat), a cheese plate, and dessert pastries.

After, Nicolo proudly shows off a recently purchased painting by a young emerging local artist named Botticelli. Nicolo, like many wealthy Florentines with the money and time to explore the arts, is a devoted patron of the city's flourishing arts scene.

Later, Nicolo reads aloud from Plato's *Republic*, reflecting on Europe's rediscovery of classic Greek and Latin writings triggered by the humanist movement, the intellectual driving force of the Renaissance. He is enthralled by Plato's philosophy, which stresses man's interaction with his world and the idea of determining one's own destiny.

Nicolo, a man of his times in Renaissance Florence, not only believes the hype—he lives it.

High Demand

This flowering poppy-plant-turned-addictive-narcotic shaped much of the Western world.

✳ ✳ ✳ ✳

THINK DRUGS ARE a modern scourge? Think again. The ancient Sumerians used opium and, if Greek and Roman texts are to be believed, so did Homer, Hesiod, and Hippocrates.

Opium has a long history in the United States. While George Washington was growing marijuana (granted, for hemp), other esteemed Americans were growing poppies. Thomas Jefferson grew the little red flowers at Monticello. For a time, visitors could purchase a packet of seeds descended from Jefferson's poppy plants at the Thomas Jefferson Center for Historic Plants gift shop. That is, until the University of Virginia ordered the plants be ripped up and the seeds destroyed after an unrelated 1991 campus drug bust made the board of directors jumpy.

In Victorian Britain, opium was a common ingredient in many medicines. Parents purchased concoctions to administer to their colicky, sick, or just plain fussy children. One of the most popular was Godfrey's Cordial, which contained a good bit of opium. Many children ended up addicted to the drug or dead from opium poisoning.

They Was Robbed!

It's reasonable to assume that Superman's creators made millions off their Spandex-clad hero. Unfortunately, that was not the case.

✳ ✳ ✳ ✳

I S THERE ANYONE in the world who isn't familiar with Superman? Over the years, the character has graced countless comic books, appeared in several movies, and seen his iconic "S" emblazoned on everything from underwear to snack cakes.

The "Man of Steel" Was a Real Steal

In 1932, Jerry Siegel and Joe Shuster were barely out of their teens when they created Superman, which they hoped to sell as a syndicated comic strip. When that didn't pan out, they presented Superman to the editors at DC Comics (known then as Detective Comics).

Their timing couldn't have been better. DC was getting ready to launch a new title called Action Comics, and it desperately needed a lead feature—something new and different. Superman fit the bill perfectly.

Amazingly, Siegel and Shuster sold all rights to Superman for a paltry $130. Such an arrangement was standard at the time, and the boys didn't mind because they were making good money writing and drawing the Man of Steel. Indeed, those were heady times for the science-fiction geeks from Cleveland. Every comic book in which Superman appeared sold through the roof, and Siegel and Shuster became minor celebrities.

Up Against the Big Guys

In 1947, it became apparent to the boys just how much money Superman was raking in for DC. They took the company to court for a much bigger piece of the pie.

Their plan was destined to fail. Despite the boys' best hopes, the suit was settled in DC's favor. Siegel and Shuster were fired from the company and spent the following years doing piecemeal work for a variety of lesser comic-book publishers. Eventually, Shuster developed vision problems that prevented him from drawing, and Siegel was forced to take a $7,000-per-year civil-service job for the health benefits. By the early 1970s, both men were living in near poverty.

In 1975, months after Siegel had mailed out a thousand copies of an angry, ten-page press release he had written, the national media finally started reporting how horribly the creators of Superman had been treated.

Siegel was first interviewed by a Los Angeles arts newspaper called *Cobblestone*, and in October the *Washington Star* came calling. An appearance on *The Tomorrow Show* with Tom Snyder followed, and shortly after that, the National Cartoonists Society took up the men's cause, enlisting the aid of such literary lions as Norman Mailer, Jules Feiffer, and Kurt Vonnegut. All demanded that Warner Communications, which owned DC Comics, do the right thing for the men who had helped make the company wealthy.

After weeks of negotiation, Warner Communications finally acquiesced. The company offered Siegel and Shuster $20,000 per year with built-in cost-of-living increases, provisions for their heirs, and—most important—creator credit on almost everything on which Superman appears. As the character made money, so did the men who created him. In their final years, it is estimated that Jerry Siegel and Joe Shuster were each pulling in approximately $100,000 annually.

✳ **The good fight continues. In March 2008, again after years of litigation, a federal court ruled that Siegel's family was entitled to a share of the Superman copyright—and a chunk of the cash the character has made in recent years. Most agree it was a big win for truth, justice, and the American way. The rights of the Shuster estate are expected to be revisited in 2013.**

What's in a Phrase?

They're part of our everyday language, but what are the origins some of these popular phrases?

✳   ✳   ✳   ✳

Blue Bloods—In the Middle Ages, the veins of the fair-complexioned people of Spain appeared blue. To distinguish them as untainted by the Moors, they referred to themselves as blue-blooded.

Catherine Wheel—This popular firework was named after St. Catherine, who, according to legend, was martyred by being tied to a spiked wheel and rolled down a hill.

Rob Peter to Pay Paul—In the mid-1550s, estates in St. Peter's, Westminster, were appropriated to pay for the new St. Paul's Cathedral. This process revived a phrase that preacher John Wycliffe had used 170 years before in *Select English Works*.

Humble Pie—While medieval lords and ladies dined on the finest foods, servants had to use leftovers (the "umbles" or offal) when preparing their meals. To eat humble pie means to exercise humility or self-effacement.

White Elephant—Once upon a time in Siam, rare albino elephants were to receive nothing but the best from their owners. Therefore, no one wanted one.

Touch and Go—English ships in the 18th century would often hit bottom in shallow water, only to be released with the next wave. The phrase indicated that they had narrowly averted danger.

By Hook or by Crook—This phrase describes a feudal custom that allowed tenants to gather as much wood from their lord's land as they could rake from the undergrowth or pull down from the trees with a crook.

I, Claudia: Trophy Wife

*The following is a fictionalized firsthand account of what a
day in the life of an ancient Roman might have been like.*

✳   ✳   ✳   ✳

I
T IS EARLY morning in ancient Rome. Claudia, matron of her
aristocratic household, finishes her breakfast: bread, cheese,
dried fruit, and honey. Her husband, a Roman senator, has left
for the day. She now assumes her daily role as the consummate
2nd century B.C. Roman wife.

Only 27, Claudia possesses the virtues esteemed Roman men
most want in a wife—fertility, impeccable housewifery skills,
and loyalty to her man and family. In 12 years of marriage, she
has produced five children, and most importantly, three sons.
She excels in household management, including supervising the
slaves. And as a woman in a staunchly patriarchal society, she
accepts her husband's legal and social control of her private life
and obligingly dons her public persona as adoring trophy wife.

Developing Future Claudias

During the day, Claudia manages the house and cares for the
kids—working outside the home is forbidden for women of
Republican Rome's elite. After checking on things and instructing the slaves, she summons her two young daughters. It's time
to school the girls in the fine art of being Claudia.

Claudia's sons attend schools outside the home; they learn the
classics and martial arts in preparation for political or military
careers. The girls are trained at home in how to be the ideal
housewife. Today, Claudia teaches them wool working—
spinning, sewing, and weaving—skills necessary for every
Roman woman.

Claudia takes her daughters' education very seriously. Their
performance as wives will be one of the standards by which her
success in life will be measured.

Keeping Up Appearances

After lessons and a light lunch—generally leftovers—Claudia readies herself for some personal time outside the home.

Even a casual stroll requires getting all dolled up. Claudia puts on an immaculate white *stolla*, the female version of the ubiquitous toga, which is usually cloaked by a *palla*. A slave styles her hair, elaborately raised, layered, and accented with cascading ringlets. She bedecks herself in ornate jewelry and accessories. She slips into her *calcei*, standard leather shoes that typically accompany the *stolla*.

Claudia leaves escorted by a slave who carries a parasol to shade her from the sun. Her first stop is the luxury goods market. Her slave then totes her purchases home as Claudia makes her way to visit a friend. From there, Claudia stops at the public baths to relax and gossip before heading home.

Claudia on Display

The baths reinvigorate Claudia for tonight's engagement—attendance with her husband at a grand banquet. As with any outing with her husband, Claudia will be on display as the perfect wife.

The banquet lasts for hours and becomes a gluttonous affair. A first course of eggs, salads, vegetables, and shellfish is followed by a main course featuring meat ranging from beef, lamb, and pork to wild goat, porpoise, and ostrich. Fruit, cake, and pudding are offered as dessert.

During dinner, Claudia's husband reclines on his left elbow while picking food off the table with his fingers. She remains upright. He downs goblets of wine. She abstains. She is careful not to upstage him in any way.

Her acquiescence earns her the life reward she desires most—a place of reverence in ancient Roman society.

Words for the Ages

"Beer is proof that God loves us and wants us to be happy."

—Benjamin Franklin

"Commitment is what transforms a promise into reality."

—George Hopkins

"If I could save the Union without freeing any slave I would do it; and if I could save it by freeing all the slaves, I would do it; and if I could save it by freeing some and leaving others alone I would also do that."

—Abraham Lincoln

"It's too bad, but the way American people are, now that they have all this capability, instead of taking advantage of it, they'll probably just piss it all away."

—Lyndon B. Johnson, on the Apollo program

"It's a recession when your neighbor loses his job; it's a depression when you lose yours."

—Harry S. Truman

"It is apparent to me that the possibilities of the aeroplane . . . have been exhausted."

—Thomas Edison, 1895

"Blessed is the man who, having nothing to say, abstains from giving wordy evidence of the fact."

—George Eliot

"I am always doing that which I cannot do, in order that I may learn how to do it."

—Pablo Picasso

"Justice is incidental to law and order."

—J. Edgar Hoover

"Greatness lies not in being strong, but in the right use of strength."

— Henry Ward Beecher

Working for the Man in Olde England

An average day for a serf in medieval England involved working land allotted to him by his master, the manor lord. In the following account, we take a look at what a "day in the life" may have been like.

✳ ✳ ✳ ✳

IT'S NOT YET daybreak, but Thomas is getting ready for the workday. Flickering rush-lights illuminate his tiny wood-frame, mud-walled cottage, which is topped with a straw thatched roof—much like the other dwellings in the small, mid-14th century English village Thomas calls home.

Thomas has a bit of oatmeal porridge and his usual breakfast drink: tepid ale poured from an earthenware jug. The same brew will quench Thomas's thirst throughout the day.

At sunup, Thomas, along with his wife and children, trudge to the plots of land allotted to him by the lord of the manor on which Thomas's village is located. Ostensibly, Thomas works the land for himself, but in reality most of the fruits of his labor go to his lord.

Thomas, like more than half of his fellow citizens, is a serf. He is socially and legally indentured to his lord for life, unless he can buy his freedom or his lord grants it.

Slogging Away in Fields of Dreams

The latter isn't likely to happen. So Thomas works his own fields of dreams hoping that his toiling will earn him a ticket to freedom.

Thomas dresses for the hard work ahead: a tattered shirt tucked into well-worn wool breeches; a ragged knee-length hooded coat; thick-soled leather shoes. It is standard serf garb, and Thomas wears it pretty much every day.

First task is weeding and watering the onions, cabbages, beans, leeks, and herbs sprouting in the gardens near the cottage. The two hogs in the cottage-side sty are thrown scraps and waste. The rooster, hens, and geese are fed while eggs are collected.

Next it's off to scratch out a living from the ten half-acre strips of land Thomas holds outside the village. Today, wheat and rye are harvested from the first strip. Thomas cuts the sheaves by hand with a sickle while his wife and children gather them onto an ox-pulled wooden cart that carries the crop home.

Sticking It to The Man

After harvesting, Thomas uses the little remaining daylight to surreptitiously procure some necessities at the expense of his lord.

First, he forages for dung, an activity done on the sly since all droppings on manor grounds are the exclusive property of his lord. Then he treks to the woods to poach his lord's forests and streams. Poaching usually involves late-night fishing for eels or salmon, but today Thomas goes to a well-hidden rabbit snare where tonight's dinner struggles vainly to get free. It's his lucky day—meat at supper is an infrequent treat.

Refuge at the Ale House

After dinner, Thomas walks to the village alehouse to escape the monotony of his dreary daily existence. There he spends the evening quaffing ales, socializing, singing, and gambling.

Thomas chats with a mate about the prospect, however bleak, of buying his freedom. What Thomas doesn't know is that freedom will come shortly, but at a terrible cost. The approaching scourge of the Black Plague will quickly wipe out a third of England's population and suddenly make Thomas's labor an extremely valuable commodity.

Thomas will soon have the economic leverage he needs to get out from under his lord's thumb.

Neanderthal Man

Daily life for Neanderthal man was no picnic, but it wasn't all about clubbing and bludgeoning thy neighbor either. Europe's Ice Age residents were social creatures, and this helped make their stark existence tolerable until their disappearance 30,000 years ago. The following depicts what was likely a typical day in the life of a Neanderthal.

❋ ❋ ❋ ❋

DAWN BREAKS, AND a cave on the edge of a forest in prehistoric Europe begins to stir with life. Neanderthal man rises along with his family and the rest of the communal group of cave dwellers that form the basis of his world.

Shucking aside the animal skins that kept him warm during the night, Neanderthal man readies himself for the one activity most critical for the group's survival: the hunt.

Bringing Home the Bacon

Neanderthal man gathers with other men and women from the group to embark on the day's hunt. If it's a cold day or if inclement weather looms, he will clad himself in animal skins—being no more hairy than humans are today, he needs to protect himself from the elements. If it's hot and sunny, he'll go completely naked. Modesty is of no concern to him.

The hunting party heads into the woods in search of their daily bread, or more accurately, meat. A voracious carnivore, Neanderthal man will eat almost nothing but meat, and in a typical day he'll devour twice the amount of food that his present-day counterpart normally consumes.

Neanderthal man brings with him a short wooden thrusting spear tipped with a sharp-edge stone. As he and his colleagues stalk bears, wolves, deer, wild horses, or cattle, he keeps an eye open for obsidian stones suitable for making highly effective cutting tools. Neanderthal man is an expert tool maker, though not a very innovative one: The stone and wooden tools he has forged will remain basically unchanged throughout 250,000 years of existence.

Taking One for the Team

Today the hunt goes well for Neanderthal man. He and the others have strategically trapped a small herd of deer in a natural enclosure. Together they carry out an ambush-style attack against their quarry, thrusting their spears into the animals' flesh at close range.

Ideally, they would have driven the herd over a cliff or steep embankment to lessen the risk of injury. But Neanderthal man has to get his food while the getting is good, so he braces himself for the blows often accompanying close-quarter hunting—a stiff kick of a hoof, a painful bite, or an unpleasant goring from a pointed antler.

After a brief but frenzied flurry, the animals are subdued. Neanderthal man emerges from the kill bloodied, but the pain from his wounds is tempered by the thrill of a successful hunt and the promise of a full belly tonight.

An Evening of Frivolity

Tired and sore but happy nonetheless, Neanderthal man returns with the hunting party to the communal caves with the evening meal for the group.

The fresh meat is cooked over an open fire, and Neanderthal man and the group dig in. Later, his hunger sated and his spirits soaring, he joins the group in an evening of frivolity and social bonding that includes singing, clapping, dancing, body slapping, and stick banging. The songs mimic birdsongs or other sounds of nature. The melody is nothing like anything we know today, but it's music to his ears.

Before finally falling asleep, Neanderthal man contemplates a way of life that is often harsh, but considerably less brutish than modern stereotypes suggest.

"Coco"

* Coco was the nickname for revolutionary fashion designer Gabrielle Chanel.

* Chanel's father was a traveling salesman. Her mother died when Coco was 12 years old, and Coco was reared at an orphanage. The nuns who ran the orphanage taught Coco to sew.

* With the help of her lover, Etienne Balsan, Chanel opened her first shop in Paris in 1909, where she sold hats. In 1910, she moved to the Rue Cambon, where the House of Chanel remains to this day.

* The concept we have of the classic little black dress is credited to Coco, in addition to sweater sets, pleated skirts, triangular scarves, and fake pearls.

* Coco once returned from vacation with a dark tan, and tanning quickly became fashionable. Chanel also produced the first artificial suntan lotion.

* Chanel No. 5 perfume was introduced in 1921. The number was chosen because it was the fifth sample presented to Chanel and the one she liked best.

* Although France was occupied by the Germans during much of World War II, Chanel was able to stay at the Paris Ritz because she was having an affair with German officer Hans Gunther von Dincklage.

* The average cost of a Chanel suit today is $5,000, and they are available only at Chanel boutiques or exclusive department stores.

* The haute couture House of Chanel now produces clothing designed by Karl Lagerfeld.

Days Consumed by War

*The Civil War cast a long shadow over the lives of all
Americans. The following is an account of what a day in
the life of a Civil War woman might have been like.*

✳   ✳   ✳   ✳

IT'S 7:30 A.M. on a late June morning in Philadelphia. Rebecca
looks in the mirror at her outfit. It's modest but fashionable 1863 attire: A navy blue ankle-length gown tapered at the
waist to create a full pleated skirt (sans the hoop—she needs
something functional, not fancy) and accentuated with long
wide sleeves and a jewel neckline covered with a white collar.
Satisfied with her appearance, the 20-year-old patriot leaves
her family's working-class home in the Spring Garden District
to do her part for the Union war effort.

Rebecca takes a horse-drawn cab through a city fully engaged
in war. The factories near her home continuously pump out
war goods. The Baldwin Locomotive Works employed all the
men in her family until her two older brothers quit to join the
Union army, leaving her father and younger brother behind.
The streets crawl with soldiers, some heading to the fight,
others returning. They congregate in Philadelphia, now threatened by General Lee's Army of Northern Virginia standing
140 miles to the west.

By 8:00 A.M., she reaches the Union Volunteer Refreshment
Saloon on Swanson Street. Here, weary soldiers passing through
Philadelphia wash up, eat a hearty meal, and rest a bit. It's run
by the city's Volunteer Relief Association, and Rebecca donates
her time there most days of the week.

Rebecca eats the Saloon's breakfast of the day—cold ham,
bread and butter, tomatoes, and coffee—then begins serving
the men. She puts in eight hours at the Saloon then has a bit
of supper—broiled beef, cheese, fruit, and coffee.

Rebecca, the News Junkie

Throughout the day, Rebecca seeks out the latest news from the front. The news in the *Philadelphia Inquirer* isn't good. Lee's 70,000-strong rebel army continues to advance unabated. The Rebs occupied Gettysburg on June 26 and took York two days later. Harrisburg looks to fall next.

Rebecca also scans the paper's daily casualty list and sees the name of a boy from her neighborhood. She thinks back to the day last September when she saw her oldest brother's name on the list; he died at Antietam halting Lee's first invasion.

The Saloon rumor mill produces worse news. One colleague tells Rebecca that the Rebs are pillaging Pennsylvania towns and farms. Another claims that President Lincoln is secretly negotiating an armistice with Jefferson Davis.

There is one bit of good news though. The Union Army of the Potomac, now led by Philly's own Major General George Meade, is finally marching to stop Lee.

Soldiering on into the Evening

After departing the Saloon, Rebecca's personal war effort continues. She and some friends attend an early evening rally organized by the Union League Club at Independence Hall.

Rebecca returns home after the rally and helps her mother and younger sister assemble a care package for her brother at the front. Inside is a pair of newly knitted socks, a deck of playing cards, back issues of the *Inquirer*, and some sweets.

She reads his letter, which arrived earlier in the day, and then pens a reply. Her eyes well up as she writes. The war is going terribly for the North, and she worries about him.

In a few days, in fields near Gettysburg, the situation will change dramatically. Prospects for a Union victory, and her brother's safe return home, will suddenly brighten.

Pucker Up

Kissing is a pastime that garners a lot of cultural attention.

✳ ✳ ✳ ✳

WHETHER IT WAS good or bad, everyone remembers their first kiss. But did you ever wonder about the first kiss of all? Some researchers believe kissing possibly derived from the practice of mothers passing chewed food to their babies (think of it as an early form of puree). Anthropologists aren't all in agreement about humanity's very first kiss, but there are clues as to how ancient this practice really is. Kissing is often depicted in Egyptian art, leading many scholars to believe that the kiss has long signified a "giving of life" or "blending of souls" for people all around the world.

According to anthropologist Vaughn Bryant Jr., evidence has been found that dates the first romantic kiss to circa 1500 B.C. in India. Prior to this date, no one has found other examples that records the kiss.

Et Tu, Judas?

The New Testament tells of a highly controversial kiss involving Jesus and his apostle Judas, whom Jesus had prophesied as the one who would betray him. One version of the story says Judas led Jesus to the Romans, and then identified Jesus to his captors by giving him a kiss on the cheek. Thus Judas is cast as the ultimate betrayer.

Some scholars argue that Jesus and Judas were in on the whole thing together, and that Judas was simply helping Jesus fulfill the prophecy. Either way, that kiss, known as "The Betrayal of Christ," is one of the most reproduced kisses in all of art.

Kiss Me, I'm Sleeping!

When one thinks of the Sleeping Beauty fairy tale, usually the 1959 Disney movie version comes to mind. But the story is far older, going back to the 1697 edition of Charles Perrault's *Tales* of *Mother Goose*. In the story, a wicked fairy curses a beautiful princess and puts her to sleep for 100 years. A smooch from a handsome prince is the only way out of hibernation. See? Kissing is good for you!

More Than Meets the Lips

Auguste Rodin's famous marble sculpture *The Kiss* suggests sex, romance, and . . . eternal damnation? Unfortunately, the backstory of one of art's most amorous pieces is a lot less romantic than most people believe. Upon first glance, the piece seems to depict two innocent, carefree lovers locked in a passionate embrace. Instead, the kissing couple actually represent two damned characters from Dante's *Inferno*. The sculpture, created in 1889, was initially part of a colossal work by Rodin called *The Gates of Hell*, but the two lovers were eventually removed from the larger work to stand on their own.

I'm Ready for My (Really) Close-up

The first kiss to be recorded in a film occurred in Thomas Edison's 47-second-long film *The Kiss*. Recorded in the spring of 1896 for nickelodeon audiences, the smooch was between actors John C. Rice and May Irwin. Although the kiss lasts only about 20 seconds, it managed to outrage plenty of people. The long, hard battle between filmmakers and censors had begun.

The Timed Kiss

During the golden age of film censorship, on-screen kisses couldn't last too long or look too passionate. In the 1941 comedy *You're in the Army Now*, the characters played by Jane Wyman and Regis Toomey enjoy a full, three-minute kiss. Scandalous!

Girls Kissing Girls = Great Ratings

Many people remember the hullabaloo surrounding the 1997 episode of *Ellen*, when comedienne Ellen DeGeneres announced she was gay and shared an onscreen kiss with actress Laura Dern.

But there were other girl-girl kisses on television before that. In 1991, two women puckered up on *L.A. Law*, and a 1994 episode of *Roseanne* featured a kiss between Roseanne Arnold and Mariel Hemingway. Huge controversy occurred among conservative *and* liberal audiences in all the above incidences—conservative viewers thought networks had gone too far, while liberal groups thought the kisses weren't properly handled. Judging by the sky-high ratings garnered for these episodes, we're guessing that there will be more opportunities for the major networks to get it right.

Les Kisses Dangereuse

Of all the scandalous kissing that happened on the 1980s TV drama *Dynasty*, one topped them all in terms of controversy—more than a year after it happened. In 1984, Daniel Reece, played by Rock Hudson, planted a big kiss on Krystle Carrington, played by Linda Evans. Then in 1985, Hudson issued a press release stating that he was dying of AIDS. He had known he was infected with the HIV virus when he kissed Evans; since very little was known about the virus at that time, the public panicked. Unfortunately, Hudson died later that year. However, the panic did lead to more research and (eventually) a better understanding of the virus.

Black and White and Kissed All Over

In 1945, when it was announced that Japan had surrendered, Times Square erupted into joyous chaos. *LIFE* magazine photojournalist Alfred Eisenstaedt was there at the time, and he snapped a picture of a sailor throwing nurse Edith Shain back in a celebratory kiss. The picture became an icon of America's return to prosperity. The sailor in the photo has never been positively identified, but that hasn't kept the iconic shot from being one of the most reproduced pictures in the world.

Chapter 12

Food and Drink

12 Items at a Feast of Henry VIII

Henry VIII was known for his voracious appetite.

✳   ✳   ✳   ✳

1. **Spit-Roasted Meat:** Spit-roasted meat—usually a pig or boar—was eaten at every meal. It was an expression of wealth because only the rich could afford fresh meat year-round; only the very rich could afford to roast it, since this required a lot of fuel; and only the super wealthy could pay a "spit boy" to turn the spit all day.

2. **Grilled Beavers' Tails:** These morsels were particularly popular on Fridays, when Christians abstained from eating meat. (Medieval people classified beavers as fish.)

3. **Whale Meat:** Another popular dish for Fridays, whale meat was fairly common and cheap, due to the plentiful supply of whales in the North Sea. Each whale could feed hundreds of people, and it was typically served boiled or roasted.

4. **Whole Roasted Peacock:** This delicacy was served dressed in its own iridescent blue feathers (which were plucked, then replaced after the bird had been cooked), with its beak gilded in gold leaf.

5. **Internal Organs:** If you're squeamish, stop reading now. Medieval cooks didn't believe in wasting any part of an

animal, and, in fact, internal organs were often regarded as delicacies. Beef lungs, spleen, and even udders were preserved in brine or vinegar.

6. **Black Pudding:** This sausage is made by filling a length of pig intestine with the animal's boiled, congealed blood. It is still served in parts of England.

7. **Boar's Head:** A boar's head, garnished with bay and rosemary, served as the centerpiece of Christmas feasts.

8. **Roasted Swan:** Roasted swan was another treat reserved for special occasions, largely because swans were regarded as too noble and dignified for everyday consumption. The bird was often presented to the table with a gold crown upon its head.

9. **Vegetables:** Vegetables were viewed as the food of the poor; they made up less than 20 percent of the royal diet.

10. **Marzipan:** A paste made from ground almonds, sugar, and egg whites and flavored with cinnamon and pepper, marzipan was occasionally served at the end of a meal (desserts weren't popular in England until the 18th century).

11. **Spiced Fruitcake:** The exception to the no dessert rule was during the Twelfth Night banquet on January 6, when a spiced fruitcake containing a dried pea (or bean) was served. Whoever found the pea would be king or queen of the pea (or bean) and was treated as a guest of honor for the remainder of the evening.

12. **Wine and Ale:** All this food was washed down with enormous quantities of wine and ale. Historians estimate that 600,000 gallons of ale (enough to fill an Olympic-size swimming pool) and around 75,000 gallons of wine (enough to fill 1,500 bathtubs) were drunk every year at Hampton Court Palace.

The Earl of Sandwich's Favorite Snack

John Montagu named (but did not invent) the sandwich.

✳ ✳ ✳ ✳

LEGEND HOLDS THAT Montagu, the Fourth Earl of Sandwich, invented the tasty foodstuff that is his namesake. Montagu was a popular member of England's peerage in the 18th century, and it seems he had a knack for converting nouns into homage to his rank. The Hawaiian Islands were once known as the Sandwich Islands, thanks to explorer James Cook's admiration for the earl, who was the acting First Lord of Admirality at the time. And although it does seem likely that Montagu is responsible for dubbing the popular food item a "sandwich," he certainly was not the first to squash some grub between slices of bread.

A Sandwich by Any Other Name

It seems likely that sandwiches of one sort or another were eaten whenever and wherever bread was made. When utensils weren't available, bread was often used to scoop up other foods. Arabs stuffed pita bread with meats, and medieval European peasants lunched on bread and cheese while working in the fields. The first officially recorded sandwich inventor was Rabbi Hillel the Elder of the first century B.C. The rabbi sandwiched chopped nuts, apples, spices, and wine between two pieces of matzoh, creating the popular Passover food known as charoset.

In medieval times, food piled on bread was the norm—prior to the fork, it was common to scoop meat and other food onto pieces of bread and spread it around with a knife. The leftover pieces of bread, called "trenchers," were often fed to pets when the meal was complete. Primary sources from the 16th and 17th centuries refer to handheld snacks as "bread and meat" or "bread and cheese." People have eaten sandwiches for centuries—they just didn't call them that.

It Is Named . . . Therefore It Is?

Regardless of the sandwichlike foods that were eaten prior to the 18th century, it appears that the Fourth Earl of Sandwich is responsible for the emergence of the sandwich as a distinct food category—but how this happened is unclear. The most popular story relates to Montagu's fondness for eating salted beef between pieces of toasted bread. Montagu was also known for his gambling habit and would apparently eat this proto-sandwich one-handed during his endless hours at a famous London gambling club. His comrades began to request "the same as Sandwich," and eventually the snack acquired its name.

The source that supports this story is *Tour to London*, a travel book that was popular among the upper echelons of society at the time. In one passage, the author of the book, Pierre Jean Grosley, claimed that in 1765, "a minister of state passed four and twenty hours at a public gaming-table, so absorpt in play that, during the whole time, he had no subsistence but a bit of beef between two slices of toasted bread. This new dish grew highly in vogue . . . it was called by the name of the minister who invented it." According to this scenario, "sandwich" initially referred to Montagu's preferred beef-and-bread meal and was subsequently used as an umbrella phrase for a variety of sandwich types.

Hard Work and Hunger

N.A.M. Rodger, John Montagu's biographer, offers an alternate explanation for the rise of the sandwich. He argues that during the 1760s, when the sand-wich was first called a sandwich, the earl was actually busy with government responsibilities and didn't have much time to gamble. He did, however, spend many nights working at his desk, during which time he liked to munch on beef and bread. It is possible, Rodger argues, that the sandwich came to be as a reference to the earl's tireless work ethic and general fondness for late-night snacking.

Europe Falls for Chocolate

Ancient South Americans considered it no less than a gift from heaven, but in 1500, chocolate was still unknown to Europeans. The great age of exploration would soon change that, and a hundred years later the "food of the gods" had conquered Old World taste buds, inciting a culinary obsession that continues to this day.

✻ ✻ ✻ ✻

HUMANKIND'S TASTE FOR chocolate predates the dawn of recorded history. According to one Aztec legend, the seeds of the cacao tree, from which chocolate is made, were given to the Aztecs' ancestors by the god Quetzalcoatl.

Regardless of origin, chocolate was held in high regard not only by the Aztecs, but also by the Olmecs, Mayans, and other indigenous American peoples. Several cultures used cacao beans as currency. In fact, the seeds held as prominent a place in Montezuma's treasury as did gold; a slave could be had for the price of 100 pods. Cacao seeds were so valuable that an industry of counterfeiters trafficked in fake beans made of clay.

Some cultures reserved chocolate for consumption by royalty as an expression of power and wealth—after all, to eat it would be nothing less than swallowing money. So great were the perceived benefits of chocolate that it became a staple in the diets of some armies. In Mayan tradition, couples exchanged cacao seeds at their weddings as an expression of commitment.

Christopher Columbus was probably the first European to encounter the cacao bean: He captured a number of the seeds from a Mayan trading canoe on his fourth voyage in 1501. However, the significance of the find was overlooked in the expedition's zealous quest for gold and silver, and it was left to later Spanish visitors to recognize and capitalize on the potential of chocolate.

An Acquired Taste

For most of its history, chocolate has been consumed primarily in the form of a beverage rather than as the solid candy we know today. It was in the liquid form that Europeans became acquainted with its use. However, chocolate was not at all pleasing to the European palate when first encountered; in its purest form, chocolate is a bitter, alkaloid substance, and the native custom of spicing it with chili peppers and other exotic herbs did nothing to endear it to the Spanish. Early European tasters described it as an obnoxious "drink for pigs," rather than a treat for people.

Though it may not have initially been seen as a food, chocolate gained a reputation as a wonder medicine. It was said to be good for treating any number of ailments—from tired livers to flagging libidos—a reputation modern confectioners encourage us to remember every Valentine's Day.

Europeans were soon adding cane sugar, cinnamon, vanilla, and other flavors to make chocolate not just tolerable, but desirable. One addition of particular importance was milk, which made for a lighter, smoother treat and created the taste that's still the most popular flavor of chocolate today.

Chocolate Chicanery

As chocolate became more pleasing to European tastes, it spread from the Spanish explorers—and the Franciscan clergy that accompanied them—to the monasteries of Spain. There its production was kept a secret for years, causing a minor religious schism along the way, as theologians debated whether or not drinking chocolate violated mandatory periods of fasting.

Monks introduced chocolate to the Spanish nobility, who enjoyed it at pastimes as diverse as official court functions and bullfights. In a macabre twist, it was even served as refreshment for spectators viewing the infamous punishments of the Spanish Inquisition of the 16th century.

European aristocracy of the time was a very close group, and the fashion in one country was sure to spread to another. Such was the case with the drinking of chocolate. During the 17th century, the practice spread from Spain to Italy, and via Italian chefs to the palace of the Sun King, Louis XIV of France, who restricted its consumption to the nobility and served it at receptions three times a week. He also established a new position on the royal court: Royal Chocolate Maker to the King.

Chocolate for Everyone

The drink also gained favor as a tool in court intrigues when chocolate's strong taste was found to be an effective mask of poison. This sinister use aside, there was no keeping chocolate a secret. When an expatriate Frenchman opened the first chocolate house in London in 1657, chocolate was finally available to the masses—at least any of the masses that could afford the 50–75 pence per pound.

The chocolate craze has never left us. Though its place as a dominant drink was largely overtaken by coffee and tea, consumption of solid chocolate and use of it as a flavoring began to soar. Today, Americans spend about $13 billion a year on chocolate—and yet our per capita consumption is only robust enough to rank us 11th on the global list (Switzerland, Austria, and Ireland are 1, 2, and 3, respectively). Chocolate is truly a worldwide obsession. Montezuma would be proud.

✳ **The United States produces more chocolate than Switzerland.**

✳ **Milton Hershey established his soon-to-be-famous chocolate company in 1871 at age 19. The familiar Hershey's chocolate bar was first sold in 1900, and Kisses were introduced in 1907.**

The First War on Drugs

Sure, Prohibition didn't work, but a study of its roots shows why people thought an alcohol ban was feasible enough.

✳ ✳ ✳ ✳

DID YOU BRING your ax? Let's shatter a kegful of mythology! Did you know that...

... *the Prohibition movement actually began before the Civil War?* The temperance movement registered local victories as early as the 1850s.

... *one-third of the federal budget ran on ethanol?* This was before federal income tax became the main source of revenue.

... *Prohibition didn't ban alcohol consumption?* Clubs that stocked up on liquor before Prohibition legally served it throughout.

... *Prohibition didn't create gangs?* The gangs were already there—they just took advantage of a golden opportunity.

... *Eliot Ness's "Untouchables" really existed?* They were agents of the Bureau of Prohibition.

Temperance

Strictly speaking, *temperance* means moderation, not abstinence. By the early 1800s, most people realized that drunkenness wasn't particularly healthy. As the industrial age gathered steam, working while intoxicated went from "bad behavior" to "asking for an industrial maiming by enormous machinery." Immigration also factored in, for nativist sentiment ran high in the 1800s. Many Americans didn't like immigrants with foreign accents (many of whom saw nothing wrong with tying one on) and made alcohol an "us versus them" issue.

Women formed the backbone of the temperance movement. With a woman's social role limited to home and family, whatever disabled the home's primary wage-earner threatened home economics. Worse still, alcohol abuse has always gone fist-in-mouth with domestic violence.

In 1869, the Prohibition Party was formed to run antialcohol candidates. It typically polled 200,000+ popular presidential votes from 1888 to 1920 but never greatly influenced national politics in and of itself. The compressed political energy and intellect of American women (who were denied access to congressional seats and judgeships) found its outlet in 1873: the Woman's Christian Temperance Union (WCTU), which still exists today. By 1890, the WCTU counted 150,000 members.

Meanwhile, the male-dominated Anti-Saloon League (ASL) was founded in 1893 and achieved rapid successes due to smart campaigning. By appealing to churches and campaigning against Demon Rum's local bad guys, it drew in nonprohibitionists who disapproved of the entire saloon/bar/tavern culture. While the ASL would later hog the credit for the Eighteenth Amendment, the WCTU laid the foundation for credible temperance activism.

Only three states were "dry" before 1893. In 1913, the ASL began advocating Prohibition via constitutional amendment. By 1914, there were 14 dry states, encompassing nearly half the population; by 1917 another 12 had dried up. In that same year, the Supreme Court ruled that Americans didn't have a constitutional right to keep alcohol at home. Prohibition's ax, long in forging, now had a sturdy handle.

Eighteenth Amendment

By January 29, 1919, the necessary 36 states had ratified this amendment. In October of that year, Congress passed the Volstead Act to enforce the amendment. One year later, it would be illegal to manufacture, sell, or transport intoxicating liquors. Of course, everyone stopped drinking.

Okay, that's enough laughter! What we got was the Roaring Twenties. Alcohol went underground, corrupting police departments and providing limitless opportunity for law-breakers. The understaffed, oft-bought-and-paid-for Bureau of Prohibition couldn't possibly keep up. America's War on Alcohol worked no better than the later War on Drugs, which would so casually ignore history's lessons.

Enough Already

On December 5, 1933, the Twenty-first Amendment repealed the Eighteenth—the only such repeal in U.S. history. Prohibition was over.

Everyone had a few beers, and then got busy worrying about marijuana.

Highest Alcohol Consumption

Country	Gallons per Person per Year
1. Luxembourg	4.11
2. Ireland	3.62
3. Hungary	3.59
4. Republic of Moldova	3.48
5. Czech Republic	3.43
6. Croatia	3.24
7. Germany	3.17
8. United Kingdom	3.10
9. Denmark	3.09
10. Spain	3.08
11. Portugal	3.05
12. Cyprus	3.04

Coffee Culture

* Coffee is the most popular beverage in the world, with more than 500 billion cups consumed each year. Americans consume more than 400 million cups of coffee every day.

* About half of the people in the United States over the age of 18 (that's 107 million) drink coffee every day. On average, each coffee drinker consumes three and a half cups each day.

* The word *coffee* comes from Kaffa, a region in Ethiopia where coffee beans may have been discovered.

* As early as the ninth century, people in the Ethiopian highlands were making a stout drink from ground coffee beans boiled in water.

* Coffee is grown in more than 50 countries in South America, Central America, Asia, Africa, and the Caribbean.

* In 1971, a group of Seattle-based entrepreneurs opened a coffee shop called Starbucks. Today there are more than 6,700 Starbucks outlets in the United States. The chain also operates stores in 49 other countries.

* Nearly 25 million farmers worldwide depend on coffee crops for their economic livelihood.

* Coffee contains caffeine, the most popular drug in the world.

* Despite what many believe, dark-roast coffee has less caffeine than coffee that's been lightly roasted.

* Scandinavia boasts the highest per-capita coffee consumption in the world. On average, people in Finland drink more than four cups of coffee a day.

* After oil, coffee is the world's second most valuable commodity exported by developing countries. The global coffee industry earns an estimated $60 billion annually.

The Green-Eyed Muse

After a 95-year ban, absinthe is again legal in the United States.

✳ ✳ ✳ ✳

ABSINTHE: THE PERIDOT-GREEN liqueur is synonymous with the bohemian excesses of the turn of the 19th century. Artists often sought inspiration from the "green-eyed muse." Toulouse-Lautrec carried it in a hollow cane. Van Gogh, Manet, Degas, and Picasso not only drank "the green fairy," they painted haunting portraits of absinthe drinkers. Many claimed they found a heightened sense of clarity and invention from drinking it, different from the effects of any other alcohol.

Originally produced in Switzerland around 1790 as an herbal cure-all, absinthe became popular as an aperitif following the French invasion of Algeria in 1832. The bitter drink was issued as an anti-malarial to French soldiers, who mixed it in wine to make it more palatable. Along with other souvenirs of the North African campaign, returning soldiers brought back a taste for the bitter drink. With the rise of café culture in the 1870s, absinthe became an essential element in the Parisian boulevard stroll known as *l'heure vert* (the green hour).

At the height of its popularity, drinking absinthe involved as much ritual as a Japanese tea ceremony. The liqueur was poured into a special glass marked to measure the "dose." A sugar cube was placed on a flat slotted spoon over the glass, and then ice water was dripped onto the cube until it dissolved into the alcohol. As the alcohol was diluted, the essential oils came out, transforming the green liqueur into an opalescent white in a process called *louching*. Serious absinthe drinkers let the ice water fall drop by drop so they could watch trails of opal swirl through the green liquid.

The major ingredients in absinthe were wormwood essence and alcohol. The classical formulation of the liqueur was made from grand wormwood (*Artemisia absinthium*), green anise, and fennel, which were steeped in an alcohol base and then distilled. The process was completed with an additional infusion of Roman wormwood (*Artemisia pontica*), hyssop, and lemon balm. Once it was filtered, the result was a clear green liqueur with undertones of licorice.

The Ill Effects

From the late 1850s on, doctors were concerned with the effects of excessive drinking of absinthe. A condition known as "absinthism" was identified with symptoms that one French doctor described as "sudden delirium, epileptic attacks, vertigo, [and] hallucinatory delirium." Others speculated that there was an increased risk of madness and suicide among serious absinthe drinkers. Some pinned the blame on *thujone*, a chemical derived from wormwood.

Absinthe was banned in most countries after Jean Lanfray, a French farmer, killed his family in a supposed "absinthe rage"; what was overlooked, however, was that Lanfray had also ingested crème de menthe, a couple cognacs, and at least seven glasses of wine that day.

Absinthe's Return

Absinthe began to reappear in the European market in 1989, and as of 2007, it is again available in the United States. Some scientists still advise against ingesting it, but most believe it is no more dangerous than any other spirit. Some who were supposedly "driven mad" by it had preexisting mental imbalances or were alcoholics. Absinthe does have an extremely high alcohol content, though (50 to 70 percent), so experts advise having no more than a small portion.

"After the first glass, you see things as you wish they were. After the second, you see them as they are not. Finally you see things as they really are, and that is the most horrible thing in the world."

—OSCAR WILDE, ON ABSINTHE

1957 Grocery Store Prices

*Maybe Father knew best in 1957, but he probably didn't
have a clue about how much Mother forked over at the
grocery story for his tuna noodle casserole. He made
about $4,494 a year, paid about $20,000 for his house,
$2,500 for his Ford, and roughly 27 cents a gallon to
fill 'er up. Let's see how deep Mother had to dig into
her pocketbook at the grocery store checkout.*

✳ ✳ ✳ ✳

1. **Milk:** Back in 1957, milk was $1 per gallon.
   Today, we have a lot more choices when standing
   in the dairy aisle, but whether whole, 2 percent,
   1 percent, skim, or soy, milk sets us back about
   $3.49 when it's not on sale.

2. **TV Dinner:** A Swanson TV dinner cost just 75 cents
   in 1957. With classics like *Wagon Train* and *American
   Bandstand* shown in 39.5 million homes, TV trays were
   popping up all over the place. Today, a frozen chicken and
   corn tray will set you back $2.99.

3. **Tang:** Tang Breakfast Crystals were launched in America in
   1957 for around 50 cents a jar. In 1965, the *Gemini 4* astronauts got this powdered vitamin C powerhouse for free
   on their space mission and all of the following Gemini and
   Apollo missions. Today, anyone can buy Tang for $3.39 for
   a 12-ounce canister.

4. **Ground Beef:** To make that delicious meatloaf, Mother
   shelled out 30 cents for a pound of hamburger in 1957.
   Today, we pay considerably more for our ground beef—
   $4.09 per pound!

5. **Butter:** When they weren't cooking with lard or short-
   ening, American women of 1957 opted for butter at
   75 cents a pound. These days, we're more likely to count

fat grams and opt for margarine or other butter substitutes. In any case, at about $3.99 a pound, we don't pay with just our arteries to enjoy good old-fashioned butter today.

6. **Syrup:** In 1957, you could douse a stack of flapjacks with pure Vermont maple syrup because it cost only 33 cents for 12 ounces. At $9.36 for 12 ounces of the real stuff today, we have to go a little lighter on the sap. But these days it's much less expensive to grab an imitation. You can get 12 ounces of Aunt Jemima for $1.89.

7. **Campbell's Tomato Soup:** It's no wonder Campbell's tomato soup has always been a family favorite. People have been wallowing in its creamy comfort for generations. To make it even more soothing, in 1957 a can only set you back a dime! Today, it's still an affordable form of therapy, and it costs only a buck.

8. **Gum:** Gum chompers had a few choices back in 1957. There was Juicy Fruit, Wrigley's Spearmint, and Dubble Bubble, to name a few. You could pretty much chew until your jaw hurt at just 19 cents for 6 packs (30 pieces). Today, in addition to the dental bills, it costs about $1.19 for a 6-pack of gum.

9. **Broccoli:** In 1957, in a world in which the word *fiber* was mostly used to discuss fabrics, a bunch of broccoli cost only 23 cents. Today's health conscious crowd pays a little more to munch this super food—around $1.79 per bunch.

10. **Eggs:** In 1957, a dozen eggs cost a mere 55 cents. For those who aren't quite ready to pour an omelette from a pint-size container of artificial eggs, you can still crack the good old-fashioned, incredible, edible egg for $2.99 a dozen.

11. **Iceberg Lettuce:** Iceberg lettuce used to rule the refrigerator's produce bin—it cost only 19 cents per head in 1957! Salad makers these days reach for romaine, red leaf, and endive, just to name a few. Iceberg still has its loyal followers, but they can now plan on paying $1.49 per head.

12. **Nabisco Saltines:** Nabisco saltines can settle an upset stomach, and, at 25 cents for a 16-ounce package in 1957, that's better than medicine. Today, the same size box will set you back $2.69.

13. **Pot Roast:** Pot roasts brought families to the table most Sundays in 1957, and it cost 69 cents a pound for that roast. Today, it's harder to get busy families together, and when they do, the cook can expect to pay $4.59 per pound.

14. **Canned Corn:** The "Ho Ho Ho, Green Giant" jingle wasn't born until 1959, but cooks in 1957 reached for a can of corn with his jolly green likeness for about 14 cents per 27-ounce can. Today, 95 cents will get you a 15-ounce can.

✳ When they were first introduced, TV dinners were packaged in oven-ready aluminum trays. They are now usually packaged in microwave-ready plastic trays.

✳ The first TV dinners included meat, a side dish such as rice, and two vegetables. Desserts such as cobblers and brownies were added in 1960.

✳ Chewing gum might be good for dental hygiene, but in many parts of the world—particularly Luxembourg, Switzerland, and France—public gum-chewing is considered vulgar. In Singapore, most types of gum have been illegal since 1992, when residents grew tired of scraping the sticky stuff off their sidewalks.

Chapter 13

Crime

Yo Ho Ho and All That

During the late 17th and early 18th centuries, daring men (and a few women) struck fear into merchants whose ships plied the Caribbean and Atlantic. Here's a brief look at a few pirates who became legends.

✳　✳　✳　✳

Henry Morgan (active 1663–74) was one of the most successful pirate leaders, as well as one of the few who managed to retire with his fortune intact. Ostensibly acting under authority given him by the British crown to make war against Spain, Morgan's actions frequently exceeded the bounds of a privateer's commission.

Remarkable in that many of his raids targeted towns rather than ships, Henry Morgan showed a ruthlessness that respected little but the pursuit of treasure. On one occasion, he locked captured enemy soldiers in houses, then blew up the buildings. He also routinely tortured prominent residents of captured towns. Most infamously, during an attack in Panama, Morgan took advantage of the religious beliefs of his foes by forcing priests and nuns to the front of the assault, ensuring that the Spanish could not fire on his troops without killing the clergy.

Morgan's actions became so egregious that they threatened a peace treaty between England and Spain, and he was briefly arrested by his benefactors. The British had no real wish to punish Morgan, however, and he was released, knighted, and retired from the sea. The British government eventually saw to his appointment as lieutenant governor of Jamaica. Morgan died in 1688 of natural causes exacerbated by a life of hard drinking. Ironically, a fanciful version of his image lives on as the mascot of a popular brand of rum.

William Kidd (active 1695–1701) may have been the most misunderstood pirate of all time. A prominent citizen of New York, in 1695, Kidd was commissioned to hunt down pirates. Kidd dutifully outfitted a ship, the *Adventure Galley*, and set out for Madagascar, a pirate haven.

Shortly after his voyage began, many of his handpicked crew were pressed into service by a British naval ship, and Kidd was forced to replace them with common criminals. Discipline suffered, and Kidd struggled to maintain control. The *Adventure Galley* took a number of merchant ships as prizes over the protest of Kidd himself, who finally acceded to his crew's demands for plunder.

On encountering their first pirate ship, the *Adventure Galley* crew mutinied and joined the outlaw vessel, leaving Kidd and 13 loyal men to make their way back to the Americas, where Kidd was astonished to find that he was wanted as a pirate. He was charged with murder and the illegal seizure of English ships. Captured and sent back to England for trial, Kidd was sentenced to be hanged. More ignominy was in store: The executioner's rope broke on the first drop and required a second (successful) attempt. Kidd's corpse dangled from a gibbet over the River Thames for several years, as a warning to other pirates.

More infamously known as Blackbeard, **Edward Teach** (active 1713–18) was a privateer turned pirate whose success and reputation for cruelty made him a legend across the Caribbean. From his ship, *Queen Anne's Revenge*, Blackbeard terrorized the coastal waters of the West Indies and the American Atlantic coast for four years. Teach gained immense fame by successfully fighting off a Royal Navy ship, an encounter that most other pirate captains would have completely avoided.

Blackbeard was well aware that his public image of wickedness was a key to his success, and he took pains to cultivate the impression. Before battle, he embedded match cord in his beard and set it alight, giving his enemies the impression that he had arisen from the depths of hell. His unfortunate crews sometimes bore the brunt of his attempts to reinforce his image; on one occasion Teach shot his chief gunner, crippling the man for life. When asked his reason, Blackbeard replied that if he didn't kill one of his men now and then, they would forget who he was. Despite his capriciousness, Teach's achievements and his seeming invincibility made men eager to sail with him.

After a new Jamaican Royal Governor began clamping down on Caribbean pirateering in January 1718, Blackbeard retired and was pardoned by the governor of North Carolina (a man to whom Teach paid a number of bribes). Teach soon returned to his old ways, however.

Blackbeard's career came to an end in November 1718, when two Royal Navy sloops commanded by Lieutenant Robert Maynard came athwart of the outlaw. Although outnumbered by more than two to one, Blackbeard and his crew chose to battle their pursuers, fighting hand to hand on the deck of *Queen Anne's Revenge*. Teach had snapped Maynard's sword and was on the verge of killing the British officer when one of Maynard's men slashed Teach's throat. Teach fought on until his body succumbed to blood loss. Maynard decapitated the famous pirate and hung his head from the bowsprit for all to see.

Piracy was largely a man's trade, but two remarkable women, **Anne Bonny and Mary Read** (active ca. 1720), earned their places in the annals of the profession. Coincidentally, both were found on the same ship, the *Revenge*, captained by Calico Jack

Rackham. Bonny was the daughter of a wealthy Charleston planter and was something of a wild child. Mary Read had a long history of crossdressing, having posed as a boy to trick a relative out of an inheritance and also serving as a man in the British military. Read was on board a ship that was taken by Calico Jack and was pressed into service with his crew. One day, Anne Bonny happened to walk in on Read while she was undressing, and Mary's secret was out. The two naturally gravitated to each other and lived openly as women accepted by the crew, donning men's clothes only in times of battle.

Pirate hunters seized the *Revenge* in 1720. Accounts of the capture say that Bonny and Read fought ferociously while the men of the ship cowered below decks. Tried and sentenced to hang, the two women achieved a nine-month reprieve by "pleading their bellies"—both were pregnant. Mary Read eventually died in prison, possibly in childbirth. Anne Bonny disappears from the history books; legend claims she escaped justice through the auspices of her estranged father, who bought her freedom before she could be executed.

Bartholomew "Black Bart" Roberts (active 1719–22), the "Great Pyrate Roberts," was a man of contradictions. Although initially reluctant to sail under the black flag, he was forced into the role when brigands captured the vessel he was on.

Bartholomew Roberts had one of the greatest careers in history, capturing an estimated 400 ships and pocketing treasure beyond reckoning. Black Bart's reputation was such that many authorities refused to tangle with him, but his success ended in 1722 when pirate hunters surprised his ship, the *Royal Fortune*, as its crew lay drunk from celebrating a prize won the day before. Roberts died in the battle, his throat ripped open by grapeshot.

✳ **Researchers believe that a wreck found in 23 feet of water off the coast of North Carolina in 1996 is Blackbeard's *Queen Anne's Revenge*.**

Hollywood Versus History

*You may not be surprised to learn that Hollywood
doesn't always get history right.*

✳   ✳   ✳   ✳

**Seventy-five pirates came on board and stole all the deck
chairs**
The Crimson Pirate (1952)—An establishing shot of Burt
Lancaster's sailing ship near the end of the film inadvertently
reveals a 20th-century ocean liner on the horizon.

Sometimes being ahead of your time just doesn't pay off
Almost Famous (2001)—An Eastern Airlines plane has a wing
configuration that wasn't introduced to commercial jetliners
until after Eastern ceased to exist.

And who's the character with the checkered flag?
Ben-Hur (1959)—During the chariot race, tire tracks from the
camera cars are plainly visible in the dust.

Au revoir!
Messenger: The Story of Joan of Arc (1999)—A cannonball is
sent flying with "Hello" scrawled on it, but the word wasn't
coined until around 1889.

History lite: half the calories and all the distortion
Mississippi Burning (1988)—Although based on real-life
white persecution of blacks in the 1960s, the movie focuses
almost exclusively on a pair of white FBI agents; black characters are peripheral.

You can't undertake a journey to infinite truth without one
Dead Man (1995)—Teddy bears, one of which shows up in
this mystical 19th-century Western, weren't created until the
early 20th century.

The Bloody Countess

In the early 1600s, villagers in the Carpathian region of Hungary whispered amongst themselves about a vampire living in the local castle. An investigation brought to light the brutal atrocities of Countess Elizabeth Bathory, who was accused of torturing hundreds of young girls.

✳ ✳ ✳ ✳

ELIZABETH BATHORY (BORN Erzsébet Báthory in 1560) was the daughter of one of the oldest and most influential bloodlines in Hungary. Her wedding in 1575 to Ferenc Nadasdy was enough of an event to warrant written approval and an expensive gift from the Holy Roman Emperor himself.

There were rumors that a streak of insanity ran in Elizabeth's family; some rumors hinted that she may have been related to Vlad the Impaler. However, nobles of the time were given wide latitude when it came to eccentric behavior.

Ferenc would go on to become one of the greatest Hungarian military heroes of the age. He was a battle-hardened man, but his wife treated the servants even more harshly than he did—and he had no reservations when it came to punishing the help. He was known to place flaming oil-covered wicks between the toes of lazy servants. But Elizabeth's punishments exceeded even this brutality. One honey-covered servant had been tied to a tree and ravaged by ants as punishment for stealing food. Ferenc spent a great deal of time away at war, and someone had to manage his castle. Elizabeth took on the task willingly.

Initially, Elizabeth's punishments may have been no more harsh than those imposed by her contemporaries. However, with her husband's lengthy absences and eventual death, Elizabeth found that she had virtually no restrictions on her behavior. She dabbled in black magic and had a series of lovers (legend has it one was the devil himself!).

Elizabeth spent hours doing nothing more than gazing into a wraparound mirror of her own design, crafted to hold her upright so that she would not tire as she examined her own reflection. Always a vain woman, the exacting fashion of the day required Elizabeth to constantly worry over the angle of her collar or the style of her hair. She had a small army of servants constantly by her side to help maintain her appearance. If they failed in their duties, Elizabeth would strike out and pummel them to the ground. On one occasion, a servant pulled too hard when combing Elizabeth's hair; Elizabeth struck the offender in the face hard enough to cause the girl's blood to spray and cover the countess. Initially furious, Elizabeth discovered she liked the sensation and began to use it as part of her spells.

Crimes Most Foul

The incident led to egregious atrocities. One story has her inviting 60 peasant girls (selected for their youth, beauty, and soft skin) for a banquet, only to lock them in a room and slaughter them one at a time. The countess began torturing girls without restraint. Aided by two trustworthy servants who recruited a never-ending supply of hopeful girls from the poor families of the area, she would beat her victims with a club until they were scarcely recognizable. When her arms grew tired, she had her two assistants continue the punishment as she watched. She had a spiked iron cage specially built and would place a girl within it, shaking the cage as the individual bounced from side to side and was repeatedly impaled on the spikes. She drove pins into lips and breasts, sewed mouths shut, held flames to pubic regions, and once pulled a victim's mouth open so forcefully that the girl's cheeks split.

Perhaps most chillingly, allegations of vampirism and cannibalism arose when Elizabeth began biting her victims, tearing off the flesh with her bare teeth. On one occasion, too sick to rise from her bed, the countess demanded that a peasant girl be brought to her. She roused herself long enough to bite chunks from the girl's face, shoulders, and nipples. She forced one young woman to strip her own flesh. Elizabeth's chambers had to be covered with fresh cinders daily to prevent the countess from slipping on the bloody floor.

The Countess on Trial

Eventually, even the cloak of nobility couldn't hide Elizabeth's atrocities. The situation was compounded by the fact that she got sloppy, killing in such numbers that the local clergy refused to perform any more burials. Thereafter, she would throw bodies to the wolves in full view of local villagers, who naturally complained to the authorities. The final straw was when Elizabeth began to prey on the minor aristocracy as well as the peasants; the disappearance of people of higher birth could not be tolerated.

The king decided that something had to be done, and in January 1611, a trial was held. Elizabeth was not allowed to testify, but her assistants were compelled to—condemning themselves to death in the process—and they provided eyewitness accounts of the terrible practices of the countess. Especially damning was the discovery of a list, in Elizabeth's own handwriting, describing more than 600 people she had tortured to death.

Elizabeth Bathory was convicted of perpetrating "horrifying cruelties" and was sentenced to be walled up alive in her own castle. She survived for nearly four years but was finally discovered dead on August 21, 1614, by one of her guards who had risked a peek through a tiny food slot. The countess was unrepentant to the end.

"Cruelty may remain latent till, by some accident, it is aroused, and then it will break forth in a devouring flame."

—SABINE BARING-GOULD, ENGLISH AUTHOR

The Lizzie Borden Murder Mystery

Most people know the rhyme that begins, "Lizzie Borden took an ax and gave her mother 40 whacks…" In reality, approximately 20 hatchet chops cut down Abby Borden, but no matter the number, Lizzie's stepmother was very much dead on that sultry August morning in 1892. Lizzie's father, Andrew, was killed about an hour later. His life was cut short by about a dozen hatchet chops to the head. No one knows who was guilty of these murders, but Lizzie has always carried the burden of suspicion.

✳ ✳ ✳ ✳

Andrew Borden, an American "Scrooge"

ANDREW JACKSON BORDEN was one of the richest men in Fall River, Massachusetts, with a net worth of nearly half a million dollars. In 1892, that was enormous wealth. Andrew was a shrewd businessman: At the time of his death, he was the president of the Union Savings Bank and director of another bank and several profitable cotton mills.

Despite his wealth, Andrew was miserly. Though some of his neighbors' homes had running hot water, the three-story Borden home had just two cold-water taps, and there was no water available above the first floor. The Bordens' only latrine was in the cellar, so they generally used chamber pots that were either dumped onto the lawn behind the house or emptied into the cellar toilet. And, although most wealthy people used gas lighting, the Bordens lit their house with inexpensive kerosene lamps.

Worst of all, for many years, Andrew was an undertaker who offered some of the lowest prices in town. He worked on the bodies in the basement of the Borden home, and allegedly, he bent the knees of the deceased (and in some cases, cut off their feet) to fit the bodies into smaller, less expensive coffins in order to increase his business.

So, despite the brutality of Andrew's murder, it seems few people mourned his loss. The question wasn't why he was killed, but who did it.

Lizzie vs. William

In 1997, when psychic Jane Doherty visited the murder site, she uncovered several clues about the Lizzie Borden case. Doherty felt that the real murderer was someone named "Willie." There is no real evidence to support this claim, but some believe Andrew had an illegitimate son named William who spent time as an inmate in an insane asylum. His constant companion was reportedly his hatchet, which he talked to as though it were a friend. Also, at least one witness reportedly saw William at the Borden house on the day of the murders. William was supposedly there to challenge Andrew about his new will.

Was William the killer? A few years after the murders, William took poison and then hung himself in the woods. Near his swinging body, he'd reportedly left his hatchet on the ground. So with William dead and Lizzie already acquitted, the Borden murder case was put to rest.

Lizzie's Forbidden Romance

One of the most curious explanations for the murder involves the Bordens' servant Bridget Sullivan. Her participation has always raised questions. Like the other members of the Borden household, Bridget had suffered from apparent food poisoning the night before the murders. She claimed to have been ill in the backyard of the Borden home.

During the time Lizzie's stepmother Abby was being murdered, Bridget was apparently washing windows in the back of the house. Later, when Andrew was killed, Bridget was resting in her room upstairs. Why didn't she hear two people being butchered?

According to some theories, Lizzie and Bridget had been romantically involved. In this version of the story, their relationship was discovered shortly before the murders. Around this same time, Andrew was reportedly rewriting his will. His wife was now "Mrs. Borden," to Lizzie, not "Mother," as Lizzie had called her stepmother for many years. The reason for the estrangement was never clear.

Lizzie also had a strange relationship with her father and had given him her high school ring, as though he were her sweetheart. He wore the ring on his pinky finger and was buried with it.

Just a day before the murders, Lizzie had been attempting to purchase prussic acid—a deadly poison—and the family came down with "food poisoning" that night. Some speculate that Bridget was Lizzie's accomplice in the murders and helped clean up the blood afterward.

This theory was bolstered when, a few years after the murders, Lizzie became involved with actress Nance O'Neil. For two years, Lizzie and the statuesque actress were inseparable. This prompted Emma Borden, Lizzie's sister, to move out of their home.

At the time, the rift between the sisters sparked rumors that either Lizzie or Emma might reveal more about the other's role in the 1892 murders. However, neither of them said anything new about the killings.

Whodunit?

Most people believe that Lizzie was the killer. She was the only one accused of the crime, for several good reasons: Lizzie appeared to be the only one in the house at the time. She showed no signs of grief when the murders were discovered. During questioning, Lizzie changed her story several times. The evidence was entirely circumstantial, but it was compelling enough to go to trial.

Ultimately, the jury accepted her attorney's closing argument, that the murders were "morally and physically impossible for this young woman defendant." In other words, Lizzie had to be innocent because she was petite and well bred. In 19th-century New England, that seemed like a logical and persuasive defense. Lizzie went free, and no one else was charged with the crimes.

But Lizzie wasn't the only one with motive, means, and opportunity. The most likely suspects were family members, working alone or with other relatives. Only a few had solid alibis, and—like Lizzie—many changed their stories during police questioning. But there was never enough evidence to officially accuse anyone other than Lizzie.

So whether or not Lizzie Borden "took an ax" and killed her parents, she's the one most closely associated with the crime.

Lizzie Borden Bed & Breakfast

The Borden house has been sold several times over the years, but today it is a bed-and-breakfast—the main draw, of course, being the building's macabre history. The Victorian residence has been restored to reflect the details of the Borden home at the time of the murders, including the couch on which Andrew lay, his skull hideously smashed.

As a guest, you can stay in one of six rooms, even the one in which Abby was murdered. Then, after a good night's sleep, you'll be treated to a breakfast reminiscent of the one the Bordens had on their final morning in 1892. That is, if you got to sleep at all. (They say the place is haunted.)

As with all good morbid attractions, the proprietors at the Lizzie Borden B&B don't take themselves too seriously. Before you leave, you can stop by the gift shop and pick up a pair of hatchet earrings, an "I Survived the Night at the Lizzie Borden Bed & Breakfast" T-shirt, or an ax-wielding Lizzie Borden bobble-head doll.

History's Coldest Cases

They were gruesome crimes that shocked us with their brutality. But as time passed, we heard less and less about them because the killers left frustratingly few clues behind.

✳ ✳ ✳ ✳

1. **Jack the Ripper:** A brutal killer known as Jack the Ripper preyed on London prostitutes in the late 1880s. His first victim was 43-year-old Mary Ann Nichols, who was nearly decapitated. Days later, 47-year-old Annie Chapman had her organs removed before being left for dead. Three weeks later, the killer was interrupted as he tore apart Swedish prostitute Elizabeth Stride. He managed to get away, only to strike again that same night. This time the victim was Kate Eddowes. His final kill was the most gruesome. On the night of November 9, 1888, Mary Kelly was methodically cut into pieces in an onslaught that must have lasted for several hours.

   Dozens of potential Jacks (and even one Jill) have been implicated in the killings, including midwife Mary Pearcey and morgue attendant Robert Mann. But more than a century after the savage attacks, the identity of Jack the Ripper remains a mystery.

2. **Elizabeth Short:** Elizabeth Short, also known as the Black Dahlia, was murdered in 1947. Like thousands of others, Elizabeth wanted to be a star. Unlike the bevy of blondes who trekked to Hollywood, this 22-year-old beauty from Massachusetts was dark and mysterious. She was last seen alive outside the Biltmore Hotel in Los Angeles on the evening of January 9, 1947.

   Short's body was found on a vacant lot in Los Angeles. It had been cut in half at the waist and both parts had been drained of blood and then cleaned. Her body parts appeared to be surgically dissected, and her remains were suggestively posed. Despite receiving a number of false confessions and taunting letters that admonished police to "catch me if you can," the crime remains unsolved.

3. **The Zodiac Killer:** The Zodiac Killer was responsible for several murders in the San Francisco area in the 1960s and 1970s. His victims were shot, stabbed, and bludgeoned to death. After the first few kills, he began sending letters to the local press in which he taunted police and made threats, such as planning to blow up a school bus. In a letter sent to the *San Francisco Chronicle* two days after the murder of cabbie Paul Stine in October 1969, the killer, who called himself "The Zodiac," included in the package pieces of Stine's blood-soaked shirt. In the letters, which continued until 1978, he claimed a cumulative tally of 37 murders.

4. **Jimmy Hoffa:** In 1975, labor leader Jimmy Hoffa disappeared on his way to a Detroit-area restaurant. Hoffa was the president of the Teamsters Union during the 1950s and 1960s. In 1964, he went to jail for bribing a grand juror investigating corruption in the union. In 1971, he was released on the condition that he not participate in any further union activity. Hoffa was preparing a legal challenge to that injunction when he disappeared on July 30, 1975. He was last seen in the parking lot of the Machus Red Fox restaurant.

Hoffa had strong connections to the Mafia, and several mobsters have claimed that he met a grisly end on their sayso. Although his body has never been found, authorities officially declared him dead on July 30, 1982. As recently as November 2006, the FBI dug up farmland in Michigan hoping to turn up a corpse. So far, no luck.

5. **Bob Crane:** In 1978, Bob Crane, star of TV's *Hogan's Heroes*, was clubbed to death in his apartment. Crane shared a close friendship with John Carpenter, a pioneer in

the development of video technology. The two shared an affinity for debauchery and sexual excesses, which they often recorded on videotape. But by late 1978, Crane was tiring of Carpenter's dependence on him and had ended the relationship.

On June 29, 1978, Crane was bludgeoned to death with a camera tripod in his Scottsdale, Arizona, apartment. Suspicion immediately fell on Carpenter. A small spattering of blood was found in Carpenter's rental car, but police were unable to connect it to the crime. Examiners also found a tiny piece of human tissue in the car. Sixteen years after the killing, Carpenter finally went to trial, but he was acquitted due to lack of evidence.

6. **Swedish Prime Minister Olof Palme:** On February 28, 1986, Swedish Prime Minister Olof Palme was gunned down on a Stockholm street as he and his wife strolled home from the movies unprotected around midnight. The prime minister was fatally shot in the back. His wife was seriously wounded but survived.

In 1988, a petty thief and drug addict named Christer Petterson was convicted of the murder because he was picked out of a lineup by Palme's widow. The conviction was later overturned on appeal when doubts were raised as to the reliability of Mrs. Palme's evidence. Despite many theories, the assassin remains at large.

7. **Tupac Shakur:** On September 7, 1996, rapper Tupac Shakur was shot four times in a drive-by shooting in Las Vegas. He died six days later. Two years prior to that, Shakur had been shot five times in the lobby of a Manhattan recording studio the day before he was found guilty of sexual assault. The 1994 shooting was a major catalyst for an East Coast-West Coast feud that would envelop the hip-hop industry and culminate in the deaths of both Shakur and Notorious B.I.G. (Christopher Wallace).

On the night of the fatal shooting, Shakur attended the Mike Tyson-Bruce Seldon fight at the MGM Grand in Las Vegas. After the fight, Shakur and his entourage got into a scuffle. Shakur then headed for a nightclub, but he never made it. No one was ever arrested for the killing.

8. **JonBenét Ramsey:** On the morning of December 26, 1996, Patsy Ramsey found a ransom note that indicated that JonBenét, her six-year-old daughter, had been abducted from her Boulder, Colorado, home. Police rushed to the Ramsey home where, hours later, John Ramsey found his little girl dead in the basement. She had been battered, sexually assaulted, and strangled.

Police found several tantalizing bits of evidence—a number of footprints, a rope that did not belong on the premises, marks on the body that suggested the use of a stun gun, and DNA samples on the girl's body. The ransom note was also suspicious. Police found that it was written with a pen and pad of paper belonging to the Ramseys. The amount demanded, $118,000, was a surprisingly small amount, considering that John Ramsey was worth more than $6 million. It is also interesting to note that Mr. Ramsey had just received a year-end bonus of $118,117.50.

A number of suspects were considered, but one by one they were cleared. Finally, the police zeroed in on the parents. For years, the Ramseys were put under intense pressure by authorities and the public alike to confess to the murder. However, a grand jury investigation ended with no indictments. In 2003, a judge ruled that an intruder had killed JonBenét. Then, in August 2006, John Mark Karr confessed, claiming that he was with the girl when she died. However, Karr's DNA did not match that found on JonBenét. He was not charged, and the case remains unsolved.

A Wife Disappears

The story of Louisa Luetgert, the murdered wife of "Sausage King" Adolph Luetgert, is a gruesome tale of betrayal and death.

✳ ✳ ✳ ✳

ADOLPH LUETGERT WAS born in Germany and came to Chicago after the Civil War. He opened his first business—a liquor store—in 1872. Luetgert married his first wife, Caroline Roepke, that same year. She gave birth to two boys, only one of whom survived childhood. Just two months after Caroline died in November 1877, Luetgert quickly married Louisa Bicknese. He gave Louisa an unusual gold ring that had her initials inscribed inside the band. Little did Luetgert know that this ring would prove to be his downfall.

In 1892, Luetgert built a sausage factory, but just a year later, sausage sales declined due to an economic depression. Luetgert had put his life's savings into the factory—along with plenty of borrowed money—so creditors started coming after him.

Instead of trying to reorganize his finances, Luetgert answered a newspaper ad posted by an English millionaire and made a deal to sell him the majority of the sausage business. The Englishman proved to be a con man, and Luetgert ended up losing even more money in the deal. Luetgert eventually laid off many of his workers, but a few remained as he attempted to keep the factory out of the hands of creditors.

Luetgert's marriage seemed to be failing, as well. Neighbors frequently heard the Luetgerts arguing, and he began carrying on with several mistresses. When Louisa discovered that he was fooling around with a relative of hers, she became enraged. One night, Luetgert allegedly took his wife by the throat and began choking her. After noticing alarmed neighbors watching him through the parlor window, Luetgert reportedly calmed down and released his wife.

Louisa disappeared on May 1, 1897. When questioned about it days later, Luetgert stated that Louisa had left him and was possibly staying with her sister or another man. When Louisa's brother, Dietrich Bicknese, asked Luetgert why he had not informed the police of Louisa's disappearance, the sausage maker told him that he'd hired a private investigator to find her because he didn't trust the police.

When Bicknese informed the police of his sister's disappearance, Captain Herman Schuettler and his men began to search for Louisa. They questioned neighbors and relatives, who detailed the couple's violent arguments. Schuettler summoned Luetgert to the precinct house on a couple of occasions. Luetgert stated that he did not report Louisa's disappearance because he could not afford the scandal.

During the investigation, a young German girl named Emma Schimke told police that she had passed by the factory with her sister at about 10:30 P.M. on May 1 and remembered seeing Luetgert leading his wife down the alley behind the factory.

Police also questioned employees of the sausage factory. Frank Bialk, a night watchman at the plant, told police that when he arrived for work on May 1, he found a fire going in one of the boilers. He said Luetgert asked him to keep the fire going and then sent him on a couple of trivial errands while Luetgert stayed in the basement. When Bialk returned to the factory, he went back to the boiler fire and heard Luetgert finishing his work at around 3:00 A.M.

Later that morning, Bialk saw a sticky substance on the floor near the vat. He noticed that it seemed to contain bone, but he thought nothing of it because Luetgert used all sorts of waste meats to make his sausage.

On May 3, Luetgert asked another employee, Frank Odorofsky, to clean the basement and told him to keep quiet about it.

Odorofsky put the slimy substance into a barrel and scattered it near the railroad tracks per Luetgert's instructions.

On May 15, the police search was narrowed to the factory basement and a vat that was two-thirds full of a brownish liquid. Officers drained the vat and began poking through the residue. Officer Walter Dean found bone fragments and two gold rings—one a band engraved with the initials "L. L."

Prosecutors indicted Luetgert, and the details of the crime shocked Chicagoans. Even though he had been charged with boiling Louisa's body, rumors circulated that she had actually been ground up into sausage that was sold to local butcher shops and restaurants. Needless to say, sausage sales dropped dramatically in Chicago in 1897.

Luetgert's trial ended in a hung jury on October 21. A second trial was held in 1898, and Luetgert was sentenced to life.

Louisa's Revenge

By 1899, Luetgert was a shadow of his former self, often babbling in his cell. Neighbors reported seeing Louisa's ghost inside her former home, leading many to wonder if she visited Luetgert and drove him insane. Luetgert died in 1900.

The sausage factory stood empty for years; eventually, the Library Bureau Company purchased it for storage space. On June 26, 1904, the factory caught fire. Despite the damage, the Library Bureau was able to reopen.

By the 1990s, the factory stood empty. But in the late '90s, the factory was converted into condos, and a brand-new neighborhood sprang up. Fashionable homes appeared, and rundown taverns were replaced with coffee shops.

But one thing has not changed. Legend has it that each year on May 1, the anniversary of her death, the ghost of Louisa can still be spotted roaming near the old sausage factory, in remembrance of her final moments on this earth.

My Bloody Valentine

During the Roaring Twenties, Al "Scarface" Capone ruled Chicago. Be it gambling, prostitution, or bootleg whiskey, Capone and his gangsters controlled it. For a few years, George "Bugs" Moran and his North Side Gang had been muscling their way into Chicago in an attempt to force Capone out. As 1929 began, rumors started to fly that Capone was planning his revenge. As the days turned into weeks and nothing happened, Moran and his men began to let their guard down. That would prove to be a fatal mistake.

✳︎　✳︎　✳︎　✳︎

ON FEBRUARY 14, 1929, six members of the North Side Gang—James Clark, Frank Gusenberg, Peter Gusenberg, Adam Heyer, Reinhart Schwimmer, and Al Weinshank—were gathered inside the SMC Cartage Company on the North Side of Chicago. With them was mechanic John May, who was not a member of the gang but had been hired to work on one of their cars. May had brought along his dog, Highball, and had tied him to the bumper of the car while he worked. Supposedly, the men were gathered at the warehouse to accept a load of bootleg whiskey. Whether that is true or not remains unclear. What is known for certain is that at approximately 10:30 A.M., two cars pulled up in front of the Clark Street entrance of the building. Four men—two dressed as police officers and two in street clothes—got out and walked into the warehouse.

Once the men were inside, it is believed they announced that the warehouse was being raided and ordered everyone to line up facing the back wall. Believing the armed men were indeed police officers, all of Moran's men, along with John May, did as they were told. Suddenly, the four men began shooting, and, in a hail of shotgun fire and more than 70 submachine-gun rounds, the seven men were gunned down.

When it was over, the two men in street clothes calmly walked out of the building with their hands up, followed by the two men dressed as police officers. To any onlookers, it appeared as though there had been a shootout and police had arrived and were now arresting two men.

"Nobody Shot Me"

Minutes later, neighbors called police after reportedly hearing strange howls coming from inside the building. When the real police arrived, they found all seven men mortally wounded. One of the men, Frank Gusenberg, lingered long enough to respond to one question. When authorities asked who shot him, Gusenberg responded, "Nobody shot me." The only survivor was Highball the dog, whose howls first alerted people that something was wrong.

When word of the massacre hit the newswire, everyone suspected Capone had something to do with it. Capone swore he wasn't involved, but most people believed he had orchestrated the whole thing as a way to get rid of Moran and several of his key men. There was only one problem—Bugs Moran wasn't in the warehouse at the time of the shooting. Some believe that Moran may have driven up, seen the cars out front, and, thinking it was a raid, drove away. One thing is sure: February 14, 1929, was Moran's lucky day.

Police launched a massive investigation but were unable to pin anything on Capone, although they did arrest two of his gunmen, John Scalise and Jack "Machine Gun" McGurn. Scalise never even made it to the courthouse—he was murdered before the trial began. Charges against McGurn were eventually dropped, although he was murdered seven years later, on Valentine's Day, in what appeared to be retaliation for the 1929 massacre.

Publicly, Al Capone may have denied any wrongdoing, but it appears that the truth may have literally haunted him until his dying day. Beginning in 1929, Al Capone began telling several of his closest friends that James Clark, one of the men killed in the massacre, was haunting him. Several times, Capone's body-guards heard him scream, "Get out! Leave me alone!" in the middle of the night. When they burst into the room believing Capone was being attacked, they would always find the room empty except for Capone, who would say that Clark was after him. Some say Clark didn't rest until Capone passed away on January 25, 1947.

Ghosts Linger

The warehouse at 2122 North Clark Street, where the bloody massacre took place, was demolished in 1967 and is now a parking lot. The wall against which the seven doomed men stood, complete with bullet holes, was dismantled brick by brick and sold at auction. A businessman bought the wall and reassembled it in the men's room of his restaurant. However, the business failed and the owner, believing the wall was cursed, tried getting rid of it to recoup his losses. He sold the individual bricks and was successful in getting rid of many of them, but they always seemed to find their way back to him. Sometimes they would show up on his doorstep along with a note describing all the misfortune the new owner had encountered after buying the brick.

At the former site of the warehouse, some people report hearing the sounds of gunfire and screams coming from the lot. People walking their dogs near the lot claim that their furry friends suddenly pull on their leashes and try to get away from the area as quickly as possible. Perhaps they sense the ghastly aura of a massacre that happened more than 80 years ago.

"They blamed everything but the Chicago Fire on me."

—Al Capone

A Life for a Loaf of Bread?

Only one American was executed for desertion during World War II. This is his story.

✳   ✳   ✳   ✳

EDDIE SLOVIK WAS the fifth child of an immigrant family living in Michigan during the Depression. His father was frequently out of work. In an ill-guided effort to contribute, Eddie began stealing. When he was just 12, he became a focus of law enforcement after he broke into a factory.

Over the next few years, Eddie was arrested several times. At age 17, he was part of a gang that, among other crimes, had stolen a car and wrecked it. On that occasion, the diminutive young criminal turned himself in and received a two- to-eight-year sentence in the state reformatory.

Soon after the start of World War II, Eddie was released from prison and classified 4F (unfit for duty). Eddie got a factory job at the Montella Plumbing Company in Dearborn, Michigan, and married Antoinette Wisniewski. During their first year of marriage, the couple saved money, and Antoinette became pregnant. On the day of their first anniversary, however, Eddie received a letter informing him that he had been reclassified and was to report for military service. The young man, who had so recently had nothing to lose, now had everything to lose. Moreover, Eddie knew he would not make a good soldier.

During basic training in Texas, the young draftee was so nervous about handling weapons that his exasperated instructors gave him a wooden weapon. While Eddie was in Texas, Antoinette suffered a miscarriage, and her grief-stricken young husband wrote her 376 letters during his 372 days at the camp. This trend continued after he was sent to France.

Shortly after arriving in Europe, Eddie's unit became involved in the bloody fighting around the Hurtgen Forest, where the

Allies suffered 33,000 casualties. Eddie was miserable and requested to be removed from the front lines. Finally, after a terse exchange of words with his company commander, he deserted. Just as he did after stealing the car at age 17, Slovik turned himself in and handed the military police a written confession in which he promised he would desert again if forced to return to combat. He was imprisoned in Belgium, tried by a court-martial committee, found guilty, and sentenced to death.

"The Unluckiest Kid that Ever Lived"

Many men had been sentenced to death for desertion since the war began, but the United States had not executed one of its own soldiers since the Civil War. Eddie and most others involved with the case assumed he would remain in jail until the end of the war. Army authorities, however, felt it was time to make an example and decided to carry out Slovik's sentence. Eddie wrote to General Dwight D. Eisenhower begging for clemency; the letter reached the general at the height of the Battle of the Bulge, and Eisenhower (perhaps bitter that a coward such as Slovik should request leniency when so many soldiers were dying) refused to rescind the order.

On January 31, 1945, Eddie Slovik was executed by firing squad. Slovik spent his last hours rereading letters from his wife and was heard to say: "I'm okay. They're not shooting me for deserting the United States Army—thousands of guys have done that. They're shooting me for that loaf of bread I stole when I was 12 years old."

Antoinette never ceased her efforts to clear her husband's name. She referred to him as "the unluckiest kid that ever lived."

✳ After his execution, Eddie's remains were buried in Oise-Aisne Cemetery's Plot E, which was reserved for the dishonorable dead. His remains were flown to Michigan in 1987, and Eddie was reburied next to his beloved Antoinette.

The Japanese American Relocation

After the attack on Pearl Harbor, Americans were suspicious of anyone with ties to Japan.

✻ ✻ ✻ ✻

EVEN BEFORE PEARL Harbor, the U.S. government acted against persons suspected of loyalty to the Axis. In 1939, the FBI put together a Custodial Detention Index of individuals considered security risks. In June 1940, Congress passed the Alien Registration Act, which compiled the names, addresses, and fingerprints of millions of "resident aliens"—immigrants who were not naturalized citizens.

After the attack on Pearl Harbor, military concerns combined with economic interests, prejudice, and fear resulted in the internment of West Coast Japanese Americans. The public was apoplectic over the attack in Hawaii and by Japanese atrocities in the Philippines. Americans thought Japan would invade the West Coast; in February 1942, a Japanese sub had briefly shelled the California town of Goleta. "Unless something is done," said California Attorney General Earl Warren, the future U.S. Supreme Court Chief Justice, the Japanese in America "may bring about a repetition of Pearl Harbor."

In February 1942, President Franklin D. Roosevelt signed Executive Order 9066, which authorized the War Department to designate exclusion zones for "any or all persons." In March 1942, another executive order set up an office that froze the assets of many aliens, prohibiting possible attempts to funnel money to the Axis. The same month, the army imposed a curfew on "all persons of Japanese ancestry" and forbade travel apart from short work commutes.

On May 3, 1942, Lieutenant General John DeWitt ordered everyone of Japanese descent to move to "relocation camps" in the country's interior. DeWitt told Congress and the press,

"A Jap's a Jap...a dangerous element. There is no way to determine their loyalty... It makes no difference whether the Jap is a citizen or not."

The orders applied to about 120,000 people; about 62 percent were American citizens. Most of the others were resident Japanese aliens: Asian immigrants were not then allowed naturalization. All were excluded from California and from areas of Washington and Oregon within as much as 150 miles from the coast. Interestingly, such rules did not apply to Americans of German and Italian descent.

Prisoners in Their Own Country

From 80,000 to 110,000 Japanese Americans went first to temporary "assembly centers" before boarding trains or buses to the camps. The assembly points were located on fairgrounds and racetracks, the residents often housed in stables. About 17,500 people went straight to the relocation camps. Roughly 10,000 were fortunate to find sponsors and jobs in other parts of America outside the exclusion zones, allowing them to move about freely.

Once notices of evacuation were posted in public, internees had a week to ten days to report to the camps. They were allowed to bring with them only the personal effects they could carry. Farms, homes, and businesses had to be auctioned off quickly. "Automobiles were sold for less than half their worth," according to a history of Wyoming's Heart Mountain camp; "other belongings often went for ten cents on the dollar; pets were given away... Those who stored belongings often discovered, after the war, that those items had been stolen or vandalized." The Farm Security Administration and Federal Reserve Bank of San Francisco were supposed to guard against unfair purchases, but the agencies almost never intervened. Poor tenant farmers lost rights for tilling their plots. En route to the internment centers, many internees murmured *shikata ga nai*— "it cannot be helped."

The camps were administered by the War Relocation Authority (WRA), headed by Milton S. Eisenhower, brother of the supreme commander and a future president of Pennsylvania State and Johns Hopkins universities.

The approximately ten relocation camps were in remote parts of California, Arizona, Arkansas, Wyoming, Idaho, Utah, and Colorado. A few were located on American Indian reservations. The number of residents in each camp ranged from about 7,300 to 18,700.

The Department of Justice also operated a separate set of 27 camps. These held about 7,000 Japanese, including reporters and Buddhist priests. These internees were deemed to be higher security risks. Further, the facilities held 2,264 persons of Japanese descent from Latin America, mostly Peru.

Economic interests helped push the internments. After war broke out, the Los Angeles Chamber of Commerce demanded removal of Japanese from California. Austin Anson, head of a Salinas farmer association, claimed, "If all the Japs were removed tomorrow, we'd never miss them . . . because the white farmers can take over and produce everything." Mexican migrants filled many of the open labor slots.

Heart Mountain Camp

Camp conditions were a mix of crowded confinement and all-American bustle. At Heart Mountain, the guard force of 124 soldiers staffed nine guard towers, turning searchlights onto the barbed-wire fences enclosing the encampment. Barracks for the 10,000 internees consisted of 120-by-20-foot buildings that were covered in tarpaper and set out in long blocks. The size of single-room apartments ranged from 20-by-16 feet to 20-by-24. Each unit had one ceiling light, a pot-bellied stove, and a cot with two blankets.

Construction of the camp touched off an economic boom in nearby Powell and Cody, Wyoming. Yet buildings were shoddy;

open ceilings brought in the conversations of neighbors, and latrines and mess halls were public. Such conditions stripped residents of their dignity.

The camp had a hospital and a school, but the WRA fixed the annual salary of Japanese doctors and teachers at $228, a tenth of comparable Anglo salaries in the area. In contrast, internees were able to harvest the crops of local sugar-beet growers for the prevailing wage when the farmers faced a severe labor shortage. Merchants in Cody and Powell forced their city councils to issue visitor's passes for internees.

In spring 1943, a new camp high school was finished: It had a machine shop, a library, and a 1,100-seat auditorium for concerts and plays. Its boys and girls basketball teams traveled to other schools for games. The football team lost only one game in two years. Along with sports, Kubuki theater and the camp's two cinemas and two churches were popular. There were also active Boy and Girl Scout Troops, and the former marched its Drum and Bugle Corps outside the barracks on July 4.

Conflicts at the Camps

There was much disorder at some centers, especially at California's Tule Lake, where those deemed security risks were congregated. Many internees refused loyalty tests, and some were pro-Japan; strikes and protests were common. Among all the camps, 5,766 internees renounced their American citizenship, many of whom were first-generation immigrants; 4,724 were repatriated to Japan after the war.

After the draft was reinstated for internees in 1943, scores were indicted at Tule Lake and Heart Mountain for refusing induction. Believing they should not be forced to fight without having full rights of citizenship, most interned males of military age did not volunteer for the armed services. Yet 654 from Heart Mountain signed up; 63 were killed or wounded in combat. Some served in Europe with the very highly decorated Japanese-American 442nd Regiment.

The War Winds Down

Life in the camps tracked the progress of the war. The camps were set up in the spring of 1942. At that time, the Imperial Navy was threatening the Pacific and America. In 1944, as it seemed more likely the Allies would eventually subdue Japan, some internees were allowed to return to the West Coast.

On December 17, 1944, the White House ended the exclusion zones. By the end of 1945, most internees had left the camps, and the last structures were bulldozed in 1946. Each person released received a train ticket and $25 for the trip home.

Some authorities had opposed the relocations from the start, including FBI Director J. Edgar Hoover. In a memorandum to Attorney General Francis Biddle on charges of Japanese American disloyalty, Hoover wrote, "Every complaint in this regard has been investigated, but in no case has any information been obtained which would substantiate the allegation."

About half the internees, 54,127, returned to the West Coast; 52,798 wound up residing in the interior of the U.S.; and 4,724 moved to Japan, according to the book *Japanese-Americans: From Relocation to Redress*.

Many ex-internees paid a steep and lasting financial price for their forced internment. Some estimates peg the value of lost businesses and homes at $5 billion (in today's dollars). In 1948, Washington began payment of about $38 million in claims compensation. In 1989, the government issued a formal apology for the internment program and paid survivors reparations of $20,000 each—$1.2 billion in all.

Champions of the payments in Congress were Senator Alan Simpson and former internee Representative Norman Mineta. They had met as Boy Scouts at Heart Mountain.

Words for the Ages

"There is no room in this country for hyphenated Americanism."

—THEODORE ROOSEVELT

"That was a long time ago. I am now old and my mind has changed. I would rather see my people living in houses and singing and dancing."

—TWO MOON (CHEYENNE CHIEFTAIN WHO FOUGHT AT THE BATTLE OF THE LITTLE BIGHORN), ON WHY HE NO LONGER BELIEVES IN WAR, *MCCLURE'S MAGAZINE,* SEPTEMBER 1898

"It is better to be violent, if there is violence in our hearts, than to put on the cloak of nonviolence to cover impotence."

—MOHANDAS GANDHI

"In certain trying circumstances, urgent circumstances, desperate circumstances, profanity furnishes a relief denied even to prayer."

—MARK TWAIN

"The girl doesn't, it seems to me, have a special perception or feeling which would lift that book above the curiosity level."

—REJECTION LETTER FOR *ANNE FRANK: THE DIARY OF A YOUNG GIRL*

"The true measure of a man is how he treats someone who can do him absolutely no good."

—SAMUEL JOHNSON

"I cannot help it that my paintings do not sell. The time will come when people will see that they are worth more than the price of the paint."

—VINCENT VAN GOGH

"Trust one who has gone through it."

—VIRGIL

"Speak when you are angry and you will make the best speech you will ever regret."

—AMBROSE BIERCE

Ponzi: The Man and the Scam

Do you want to get rich quick? Are you charming? Do you lack scruples? If so, a Ponzi scheme may be for you!

✳ ✳ ✳ ✳

Yes, THERE WAS a real Mr. Ponzi, and here's how his scam worked. First, come up with a phony investment—it could be a parcel of (worthless) land that you're sure is going to rise in value in a few months or stock in a (nonexistent) company that you're certain is going to go through the roof soon. Then recruit a small group of investors, promising to, say, double their money in 90 days. Ninety days later, send these initial investors (or at least some of them) a check for double their investment. They'll be so pleased, they'll tell everyone they know about this surefire way to make a fast buck.

You use the influx of cash from the new investors to pay your initial investors—those who ask for a payout, that is. The beauty of it is that most of your initial investors will be so enchanted with those first checks that they'll beg to reinvest their money with you. Eventually, of course, your new investors will start to wonder why they aren't getting any checks, and/or some government agency or reporter might come snooping around . . . but by then (if you've timed it right) you'll have transferred yourself and your ill-gotten gains out of the reach of the authorities. Like related scams that include the Pyramid Scheme and the Stock Bubble, financial frauds like this one have been around for centuries, but only the Ponzi Scheme bears the name of a particular individual—Charles Ponzi.

As you might imagine—given that he was a legendary con man—Ponzi gave differing accounts of his background, so it's hard to establish facts about his early life. He was likely born Carlos Ponzi in Italy in 1882. He came to America in 1903 and lived the hardscrabble existence of a newly arrived immigrant. But the handsome, suave Ponzi was determined to rise in the world—by fair means or foul. The foul means included bank fraud and immigrant smuggling, and Ponzi wound up doing time in jails in both the United States and Canada.

The Check Is (Not) in the Mail

While living in Boston in 1919, the newly freed Ponzi more or less stumbled across the scheme that would earn him notoriety. It involved an easily obtained item called an International Postal Reply Coupon. In simple terms, the scam involved using foreign currencies to purchase quantities of a kind of international postal stamp, then redeeming the stamps for U.S. dollars. This brought a big profit because of the favorable exchange rate of the time, and it actually wasn't illegal. The illegal part was Ponzi's determination to bring ever-growing numbers of investors into the scheme...and just keep their money. Until the roof fell in, Ponzi became a celebrity. Before long, people across New England and beyond were withdrawing their life savings and mortgaging their homes to get in on the action.

The end came in the summer of 1920, when a series of investigative reports in a Boston newspaper revealed that the House of Ponzi had no foundations. By that time, he'd taken some 40,000 people for a total of about $15 million. In 21st-century terms, that's roughly $150 million. Ponzi spent a dozen years in prison on mail fraud charges. Upon release, he was deported and continued his scamming ways abroad before dying penniless in Brazil in 1948.

---

* **In December 2008, Bernard Madoff's $65 billion Ponzi scheme—the biggest financial swindle in history— began to unravel. In 2009, Madoff was sentenced to 150 years in a medium-security prison.**

Valachi Speaks

On June 22, 1962, in the federal penitentiary in Atlanta, Georgia, a man serving a sentence for heroin trafficking murdered another convict. The killer was Joseph "Joe Cargo" Valachi; the intended victim was Joseph DiPalermo—but Valachi got the wrong man and killed another inmate, Joe Saupp. This mistake touched off one of the greatest criminal revelations in history.

✳ ✳ ✳ ✳

JOE VALACHI, A 59-year-old Mafia "soldier," was the first member of the Mafia to publicly acknowledge that criminal organization—making *La Cosa Nostra* ("this thing of ours") a household phrase. He opened the doors to expose a conglomerate of crime families, the existence of which was repeatedly denied by the FBI. By testifying against his own organization, Valachi violated *omerta*, the code of silence.

Vito Genovese was the boss of New York's Genovese crime family. Valachi had worked for the family for much of his life—primarily as a driver, but also as a hit man and drug pusher. When Valachi was on his way to prison after having been found guilty of some of these activities, Genovese believed Valachi had betrayed him to obtain a lighter sentence. Genovese put a $100,000 bounty on Valachi's head. He and Valachi were actually serving time in the same prison when Valachi killed Joe Saupp—mistaking him for Joseph DiPalermo, whom he thought had been assigned by Genovese to murder him.

Why did Valachi turn informer? This isn't entirely clear. Most speculate that Valachi was afraid of a death sentence for killing Saupp and agreed to talk in exchange for a lighter sentence.

Valachi was a street-level miscreant whose knowledge of the workings of the organization was limited. However, when he was brought before John L. McClellan's Senate Permanent

Investigations Subcommittee in October 1963, he began talking beyond his personal experience, relaying urban legends as truth, and painting a chilling picture of the Mafia.

Valachi helped identify 317 members of the Mafia. His assistance gave Attorney General Robert Kennedy "a significant addition to the broad picture of organized crime." Unlike J. Edgar Hoover and the FBI, Bobby Kennedy had no problem acknowledging the Mafia.

The Cat Is Out of the Bag

Valachi's revelations ran the gamut from minor accuracies to babbling exaggerations, but the cat was out of the bag. Americans became fascinated with crime families, codes of honor, hit killings, and the wide reach of the Mafia. Very private criminals suddenly found their names splashed across headlines and blaring from televisions. During the next three years in the New York–New Jersey–Connecticut metropolitan area, more organized criminals were arrested and jailed than in the previous 30 years. Whatever safe conduct pass the Mafia may have held had expired.

On Screen and in Print

When journalist Peter Maas interviewed Valachi and came out with *The Valachi Papers*, the U.S. Department of Justice first encouraged but then tried to block its publication. Regardless, the book was released in 1968. This work soon became the basis of a movie that starred Charles Bronson as Joe Valachi. The novel *The Godfather* was published in 1969, and in the film *The Godfather: Part II*, the characters of Willie Cicci and Frank Pentangeli were reportedly inspired by Valachi.

The $100,000 bounty on the life of Joseph Valachi was never claimed. In 1966, Valachi unsuccessfully attempted to hang himself in his prison cell using an electrical cord. Five years later, he died of a heart attack at La Tuna Federal Correctional Institution in Texas. Valachi had outlived Genovese—his chief nemesis—by two years.

Murder in the Heartland

*If you ever find yourself in northwestern Kansas looking
for the village of Holcomb, don't blink or you'll miss it. It's
the kind of place where nothing ever seems to happen.
And yet, back in 1959, Holcomb became one of the most
notorious locations in the history of American crime.*

* * * *

IN THE 1940S, businessman Herb Clutter built a house on
the outskirts of Holcomb and started raising a family with
his wife, Bonnie. The Clutters were friendly and quickly
became one of the most popular families in the small village.

On the morning of Sunday, November 15, 1959, Clarence
Ewalt drove his daughter Nancy to the Clutter house so she
could go to church with the family as she did every week. She
was a good friend of the Clutters' teenage daughter, who was
also named Nancy. Nancy Ewalt knocked on the door several
times but got no response. She went around to a side door,
looked around and called out, but no one answered.

Mr. Ewalt drove his daughter to the Kidwell house nearby and
picked up Susan Kidwell, another friend. Susan tried phoning
the Clutters, but no one answered. So the three drove back to
the Clutter house. The two girls entered the house through the
kitchen door and went to Nancy Clutter's room, where they
found the dead body of their dear friend.

Sheriff Robinson—the first officer to respond—entered the
house with another officer and Larry Hendricks, a neighbor
of the Clutters. The three men went first to Nancy Clutter's
room, where the teenager was dead of a gunshot wound to the
head. She was lying on her bed facing the wall with her hands
and ankles bound. Bonnie Clutter was discovered in the master bedroom. Like her daughter, Bonnie's hands and feet were
bound, and she appeared to have been shot in the head.

Police found the bodies of Herb Clutter and his 15-year-old son, Kenyon, in the basement. Like his mother and sister, Kenyon had been shot in the head; his body was tied to a sofa.

Herb Clutter appeared to have suffered the most. He had also been shot in the head, but there were slash marks on his throat, and his mouth was taped shut. And although his body was lying on the floor of the basement, there was a rope hanging from the ceiling; between that and the marks on Herb's neck, investigators surmised Herb had been hung from the rope at some point.

Dewey's Task Force

Alvin A. Dewey of the Kansas City Bureau of Investigation (KBI) took charge of the investigation. The Clutter murders hit Dewey hard. The Dewey and Clutter families had attended the same church, and Dewey considered Herb a good friend.

At the press conference after the bodies were discovered, Dewey announced that his task force would not rest until they found the person or persons responsible for the horrific murders. He knew it was going to be a tough case, though. The gore at the scene suggested a motive of revenge. But the Clutters were loved by all, as evidenced by the nearly 600 mourners who showed up for the funeral service. The idea that the murders were the result of a robbery gone bad was also being pursued, but Dewey had his doubts about that. It just didn't fit that the entire Clutter family would have walked in on a robbery and then been killed the way they had. Dewey began to believe that there had been more than one killer.

There was not a lot of evidence. Not only was the weapon missing, the perpetrator had taken the time to pick up the spent shells. However, Dewey did have a secret ace up his sleeve: Herb Clutter's body had been found lying on a piece of cardboard, and on that cardboard were impressions from a man's boot. Both Herb and Kenyon were barefoot, which meant the boots may have belonged to the killer. It wasn't much, but it was a start. Still, as Christmas crept closer, the case was starting to come to a standstill. Then, finally, a big break came from an unlikely place: Lansing Prison.

An Inmate Talks

The man who would break the case wide open was Lansing Prison inmate Floyd Wells. Earlier in the year, Wells had been sentenced to Lansing for breaking and entering. His cellmate was a man named Richard Hickock. One night, Hickock mentioned that even though he was going to be released from prison soon, he had nowhere to go. Wells told him that back in the late 1940s, he had been out looking for work and stumbled across a kind, rich man named Clutter who would often hire people to work around his farm. Once Wells mentioned Herb Clutter, Hickock seemed obsessed with the man. He wouldn't stop asking questions: How old was he? Was he strong? How many others lived in the house?

One night, Hickock calmly stated that when he was released, he and his friend Perry Smith were going to rob the Clutters and murder anyone in the house. Wells said that Hickock even explained exactly how he would tie everyone up and shoot them one at a time. Wells further stated that he never believed Hickock was serious until he heard that the Clutters had been murdered in exactly the way Hickock had described.

On December 30, after attempting to cash a series of bad checks, Hickock and Smith were arrested in Las Vegas. Among the items seized from the stolen car they were driving was a pair of boots belonging to Hickock. When confronted with the fact that his boots matched the imprint at the crime scene, Hickock broke down and admitted he had been there during the murders. However, he swore that Perry Smith had killed the whole family and that he had tried to stop him.

When Smith was informed that his partner was putting all the blame on him, Smith gave a very detailed version of how Hickock had devised a plan to steal the contents of a safe in

Herb Clutter's home office. The pair had crept in through an unlocked door at approximately 12:30 A.M. Finding no safe, the pair went to the master bedroom, where they surprised a sleeping Herb Clutter. When told they had come for the contents of the safe, Herb told them to take whatever they wanted, but there was no safe in the house. Not convinced, Smith and Hickock rounded up the family and tied them up, hoping to get one of them to reveal the location of the safe. When that failed, Smith and Hickock prepared to leave. But when Hickock started bragging about how he had been ready to kill the entire family, Smith called his bluff, and an argument ensued. At that point, Smith said he snapped and stabbed Herb Clutter in the throat. Seeing the man in such pain, Smith said he then shot him to end his suffering. Smith then turned the gun on Kenyon. Smith ended his statement by saying that he'd made Hickock kill the two women.

The Verdict

The trial of Richard Hickock and Perry Smith began on March 23, 1960, at Finney County Courthouse. Five days later, the case was handed over to the jury, who needed only 40 minutes to reach their verdict: Both men were guilty of all charges. They recommended that Hickock and Smith be hanged for their crimes. After several appeals, both men were executed at Lansing Prison on April 14, 1965.

Several years after the murders, in an attempt to heal the community, a stained-glass window at the First Methodist Church in Garden City, Kansas, was dedicated to the Clutters. Despite an initial impulse to bulldoze the Clutter house, it was left standing and is a private residence today.

✳ **Truman Capote was present at the trial and wrote a series of *New Yorker* articles about the murders. Those articles later inspired his best-selling novel *In Cold Blood*.**

Mind Control

From the mid-1950s through the early 1970s, thousands
of unwitting North Americans became part of a bizarre
CIA research project code-named MKULTRA.

✳   ✳   ✳   ✳

MKULTRA began in 1953 under the orders of CIA
director Allen Dulles. The program was developed in
response to reports that U.S. prisoners of war in Korea were
being subjected to mind-control techniques.

CIA researchers hoped to find a "truth drug" that could be used
on Soviet agents, as well as drugs that could be used against
foreign leaders (one documented scheme involved an attempt
in 1960 to dose Fidel Castro with LSD). They also aimed to
develop means of mind control that would benefit U.S. intelligence. The CIA investigated parapsychology and such phenomena as hypnosis, telepathy, precognition, photokinesis, and
"remote viewing."

MKULTRA was headed by Sidney Gottlieb, a military psychiatrist and chemist who specialized in concocting deadly
poisons. More than 30 universities and scientific institutes
took part in MKULTRA. LSD and other mind-altering drugs
including heroin, mescaline, psilocybin, scopolamine, marijuana, and sodium pentothal were given to CIA employees,
military personnel, and other government workers, often without the subjects' knowledge or consent.

To broaden their subject pool, researchers targeted unsuspect-
ing civilians, often those in vulnerable or socially compromising
situations. Inmates, prostitutes, and the mentally ill were often
used. In a project code-named Operation Midnight Climax,
the CIA set up brothels in several U.S. cities to lure men as
unwitting test subjects. Rooms were equipped with cameras
that filmed the experiments behind one-way mirrors. Some

civilian subjects who consented to participation were used for more extreme experimentation. One group of volunteers in Kentucky was given LSD for more than 70 straight days.

Clandestine Research

Gottlieb conducted mind-control experiments on POWs held by U.S. forces in Vietnam. During the same time period, an unknown number of Soviet agents died in U.S. custody in Europe after being given dual intravenous injections of barbiturates and amphetamine in the CIA's search for a truth serum.

MKULTRA experiments were also carried out in Montreal, Canada, between 1957 and 1964 by Donald Ewen Cameron, a researcher in Albany, New York, who also served as president of the World Psychiatric Association. The CIA appears to have given him potentially deadly experiments to carry out in Canada so U.S. citizens would not be involved.

Cameron also experimented with paralytic drugs as well as using electro-convulsive therapy at 30 times the normal voltage. The subjects were often women being treated for anxiety disorders. Many suffered permanent damage. A lawsuit by victims of the experiments later uncovered that the Canadian government had also funded the project.

There was at least one American casualty of the experiments. Frank Olson, a biological weapons researcher, was found dead on a New York City sidewalk in 1953. A doctor assigned to monitor Olson claimed he jumped from the window of his 10th-floor hotel room. Understandably, Olson's family had trouble making sense of the events. Declassified documents later revealed that Olson had been secretly dosed with LSD prior to his untimely death. Olson's family had his body exhumed in 1994.

An autopsy revealed that Olson had been knocked unconscious before his fall, leading his family to believe that someone threw Olson out the window. His family believes Olson was considered a security risk because he had witnessed some unethical experiments and was no longer proud of his work.

The U.S. army also conducted experiments with psycho-active drugs. A later investigation determined most army experiments involved subjects who had given their consent, and army researchers largely followed safety protocols. Ken Kesey, who later wrote *One Flew Over the Cuckoo's Nest*, volunteered for LSD studies at an army research center in San Francisco in 1960.

The army's high ethical standards seem to have been absent in at least one case. Harold Blauer, a professional tennis player in New York City who was hospitalized for depression following his divorce, died from apparent cardiac arrest during an army experiment in 1952. Blauer had been secretly injected with massive doses of mescaline.

CIA researchers eventually concluded that the effects of LSD were too unpredictable to be useful, and the agency later acknowledged that their experiments made little scientific sense. Records on 150 MKULTRA research projects were destroyed in 1973 by order of CIA Director Richard Helms. A year later, *The New York Times* first reported about CIA experiments on U.S. citizens. In 1975, congressional hearings and a report by the Rockefeller Commission revealed details of the program. In 1976, President Gerald Ford issued an executive order prohibiting experimentation with drugs on human subjects without their informed consent. Ford and CIA Director William Colby also publicly apologized to Frank Olson's family, who received $750,000 by a special act of Congress.

---

* **LSD stolen from an army lab by test subjects was some of the first in the world used "recreationally" by civilians.**

* **Sirhan B. Sirhan, who is serving a life sentence for the assassination of Robert Kennedy, claims to have been drugged in the hours leading up to the shooting.**

Chapter 14

Strange but True

Beyond This Point Be Monsters!

Centuries ago, map details were often more creative than factual.

✳   ✳   ✳   ✳

WHETHER HAND-DRAWN OR printed for limited distribution, maps from the late-medieval and Renaissance world reflect the limited knowledge of their makers: Creations were equal parts accurate and fanciful. Lacking the ability to look down on land masses and seas from above, and unable to communicate quickly with far-away peers, mapmakers were forced to rely on the imaginative accounts of seafaring merchants and sailors.

The Carta Marina, a 1539 map by Olaus Magnus, makes "Scandia" (northern Europe) its center. The map is multicolored and highly detailed, with careful delineations of mountains, nations, and activities such as hunting and agriculture. And in a lively flourish, Magnus filled the seas with an array of monsters: ship-sized lobsters; blood-red snakes—even finned, web-footed terrors that were part fish, part warthog.

These fanciful imaginings are amusing today, but get this: Scholars discovered later that the depictions of sea monsters frequently coincide with areas of hazardous currents, hidden shallows, and other real-life dangers.

Were the monsters whispering in the mapmakers' ears?

Terribly Terrifying

The first all-powerful Russian ruler was terrible indeed.

✳ ✳ ✳ ✳

THE TERRIBLE ONE was terribly paranoid. It must have been his upbringing. As a child prince in Moscow, Ivan was under the thumb of *boyars* (Russian nobles). Feuding noble families such as the Shuiskis would break into young Ivan's palace, robbing, murdering, and even skinning alive one of the boy's advisors. The orphan (his mother had been poisoned) took out his frustrations on animals, poking out their eyes or tossing them off the palace roof. In 1543, at age 13, Ivan took some personal revenge, having Andrei Shuiski thrown to the dogs—literally. After other vile acts, he'd sometimes publicly repent by banging his head violently on the ground.

When his beloved wife Anastasia died in 1560 (Ivan beat his head on her coffin), the boyars refused allegiance to his young son Dmitri. Then Ivan became terrifying. He set up the *Oprichniki*, a group of handpicked thugs. After his forces sacked the city of Novgorod in 1570, he had its archbishop "sewn up in a bearskin and then hunted to death by a pack of hounds." Women and children fared no better; they were tied to sleds and sent into the freezing Volkhov River.

Over time, Ivan had the lover of his fourth wife impaled and his seventh wife drowned. Perhaps afflicted by encephalitis, and likely by syphilis, his behavior grew ever stranger. He beat up his son's wife, who then miscarried, and later beat his son Ivan to death with a royal scepter (then beat his head on the coffin).

Ivan the Terrible may well have been mad as a hatter, and by the same cause that drove 19th-century hatmakers insane— mercury poisoning. When his body was exhumed in the 1960s, his bones were found to have toxic levels of the metal.

German Goliaths

King Frederick William I of Prussia wanted only the best for his country: the best civil service, the best farms, and—most important of all—the best army. As Prussia came into its own, the king formed an exclusive club, the pride of his armed forces: a regiment of the tallest soldiers in Europe.

✳ ✳ ✳ ✳

FREDERICK WILLIAM I, nicknamed "The Soldier King," was in some ways a model (albeit eccentric) monarch. He lived frugally, encouraged farming and settlement, avoided wars, and reformed the country's civil service. He replaced mass conscription with a national sales tax (which he paid along with everyone else) and established primary schools. But he had one "huge" obsession.

A Regiment of Giants

After becoming king in 1713, Frederick William set out to create a regiment of unusually tall soldiers. Sending agents to scour the countryside for farmers, soldiers, craftsmen, and peasants who were at least five feet, eleven inches tall—and preferably much taller—Frederick William assembled his collection of abnormally tall men into an elite unit of grenadiers. Thus was born the Potsdamer Riesengarde, or "Giant Guards of Potsdam."

Ranging from "small" men who met the minimum height requirement to at least two 8-foot goliaths, the Potsdam Giants were the king's favorites. Clad in blue jackets, scarlet trousers, and tall red hats that exaggerated their already ponderous height, the guards enjoyed the best pay and the special attentions of their sovereign. Frederick William paraded them before foreign dignitaries and kept them out of combat. Pleased to the point of obsession with his unique regiment, he painted the men's portraits, reviewed them daily, and had them march behind their mascot (a bear) for his pleasure whenever he suffered from sickness or depression.

He once confessed to the French ambassador, "The most beautiful girl or woman in the world would be a matter of indifference to me, but tall soldiers—they are my weakness."

Hunting Tall Fellows

The obvious problem was how to keep a three-battalion regiment up to strength. Every army unit loses men to disease, age, accident, and desertion, and Frederick William had to search far and wide for men tall enough to fill out his ranks. He transferred tall soldiers from other regiments, promoted captains of other companies who recruited tall soldiers, and let it be known in the courts of Europe that the Prussian king's goodwill could be had by sending a few dozen impressively tall soldiers into his service.

When those sources failed to keep up with the king's demand for ever-taller specimens, he sent agents to other lands to recruit (or even kidnap) tall men—priests, innkeepers, even diplomats—for his regiment. He bypassed his diplomats and sent agents to hire giants directly from foreign armies. He even forced tall Potsdam women to marry tall men to ensure an ongoing supply of giants for his beloved grenadier guards.

Frederick William died in 1740, and his son, Frederick the Great—a five-foot, five-inch former major of the Potsdam Giants—disbanded the regiment after coming to the conclusion that it was a useless, ornamental expense. Men recruited or kidnapped from foreign lands were sent home, and lumbering giants, knapsacks over their shoulders, could be seen making their way along roads leading from Berlin.

✳ The world's tallest woman? That would be "Rodina-Mat," or "Motherland," towering over Kiev, Ukraine, at 203 feet. She's still pretty short compared to the world's tallest man, Japan's Ushiku Amida Buddha, nearly 394 feet tall—three times the height of the Statue of Liberty.

Ghost Ship Ahoy!

Pirates of the Caribbean movies have renewed interest in such folkloric figures as Davy Jones and The Flying Dutchman while simultaneously muddling their stories. At no time was Davy Jones captain of the famed ghost ship.

✳ ✳ ✳ ✳

Davy Jones

AN OLD SEAFARING term for the bottom of the ocean, "Davy Jones's Locker" is the grave of all those who perish at sea. There are numerous tales about the origin of the expression, most of which attempt to identify a real Davy Jones. One version has Jones running a pub in London, where he press-ganged unwary customers into serving aboard pirate ships by drugging them and then storing them in the pub's ale cellar or locker. Other stories relate Jones to Jonah, the biblical figure who spent three days and nights trapped in the belly of a big fish.

The Flying Dutchman

This term is often used to refer to a ghost ship that is doomed to sail the oceans forever, but it is more accurately a reference to the captain of the ghost ship. Legend holds that in 1680, Dutch captain Hendrik Van der Decken's ship was wrecked in a terrible storm off the Cape of Good Hope at the southern tip of Africa. As the ship sank, the captain's dying words were a vow to successfully round the infamous Cape even if it took him until doomsday.

Over the years, whenever there is stormy weather off the Cape, seafarers have reported seeing a phantom ship battling the waves, with a ghostly captain at  the wheel. In 1939, dozens of bathers on a South African beach reported sighting a 17th-century merchant vessel off the coast and then seeing it suddenly vanish into thin air.

Truth and Myth of the Ninja

Ninjas were the special forces of feudal Japan. Trained in assassination, espionage, and guerrilla warfare, ninjas inspired fear in both rulers and commoners.

❋   ❋   ❋   ❋

THE NINJA HAS taken on a mythical status. But like most myths, the story is filled with both fact and fiction.

Humble Beginnings

Ninjas got their start as priests living in the mountains of Japan. Harassed by the central government and local samurai, they resorted to using *Nonuse* (the art of stealth)—what we would call guerrilla warfare. Their use of secrecy and stealth didn't win them many friends, but it secured them a role in the coming civil wars.

From roughly 794 to 1192, local rulers fought to gain control of Japan. While the samurai fought the wars, it was left to the mountain priests to do those things that the samurai considered cowardly: spying and assassinating rivals. This is when the ninja (*nin*, meaning "concealment" and *sha*, meaning "person") was born.

From Priests to Ninjas

The ninja made their reputation during the Japanese civil wars. They worked for anybody—and often for both sides at the same time. In addition to being scouts, a favorite ninja job was to sneak into a castle under siege and cause chaos. Dressed like the enemy, they made their way into enemy camps to set fires, start rebellions, steal flags, and generally keep the pressure on their opponents so that when the army stormed the gates, the defenders would be forced to give up without a fight.

Ninjas used weapons uniquely suited to them. They wore claws on their gloves to help them fight and climb. Because the ownership of weapons was forbidden to all but the samurai, ninjas used a common farming tool called a sickle. And, of course, they used the throwing stars that everybody sees in the movies (though the real ninjas weren't nearly as accurate as their Hollywood counterparts). They also used invisibility weapons: usually an eggshell filled with an eye irritant or a bit of gunpowder with a fuse in case they had to make a quick getaway.

Eventually the civil wars came to an end, and the ninjas found themselves out of a job. The ninjas were gone but certainly not forgotten. The exploits of the ninja made their way into popular literature and eventually into legend.

Ninja Fact and Fiction

The ninja were feared for their ability to assassinate their rivals, but there was never a documented case of any ruler being killed by a ninja. They tried, of course, but they were never successful.

Although ninjas are typically thought to be male, there were female ninjas as well. Whether male or female, one thing is certain: Ninjas didn't run around in black pajamas as Hollywood would have you believe.

This misconception originated in Kabuki Theater. During shows, the prop movers wore all black to shift things around while the play was going on. Everybody was supposed to ignore the people in black, pretending they were invisible. So when ninjas were played in the theater, they wore the same black dress as the prop movers to symbolize their gift of invisibility. The crowds bought it, and the black ninja suit was born.

The exploits of the ninja came to the West mainly after World War II. Like the Japanese theater, Hollywood's version of the ninja portrayed them either as an almost unbeatable mystical foe or as a clumsy fighter that the hero of the movie could take on singlehandedly.

Although there are martial arts schools that teach ninja techniques, the ninja have faded into history and legend.

Big Signature. Tall Tale?

*Did John Hancock really do some big talking
to fire up the other signatories?*

✳ ✳ ✳ ✳

TAKE A LOOK at the Declaration of Independence: specifically, the 56 signatures affixed to the document. You'll surely notice that one name stands out from the rest. It's written in large, flamboyant script in the center of the page directly below the main body of text.

That signature, of course, belongs to John Hancock, and it is the most readily recognized autograph on one of the most revered pieces of paper in American history. Hancock's inscription is so well known that his name has become synonymous with the word *signature* (as in "put your John Hancock right here").

John Hancock's John Hancock is symbolic of the stout defiance of America's founders toward tyrannical King George III. Adding to the aura of Hancock's in-your-face signature was the verbal bravado that history says he used to impress his fellow signers. Some accounts say that Hancock brashly stated, "There, I guess King George will be able to read *that*!"

Hancock's audacious declaration is indeed rousing—too bad he never actually made it. Hancock, the first signatory, signed the document on July 4, 1776. Aside from colleague Charles Thomson, no one was around to witness the signing (the other signatories didn't begin signing the document until August 1776). Thomson never attributed any such statement to Hancock, and Hancock very likely signed in silence.

✳ **Hancock, who inherited his uncle's business, was the wealthiest merchant in New England at the time of the Revolutionary War. He risked much in siding with the patriots, but he did so because he had come to resent British taxation. Hancock later served as governor of Massachusetts.**

A Pleasant Afternoon Relaxing and Watching the War

Some Washingtonians got more than they expected at the First Battle of Bull Run.

✳   ✳   ✳   ✳

SOME CALLED IT a "picnic battle." The First Battle of Bull Run was supposed to be a walk in the park for Union forces. They were to put down the Confederate rebellion in a quick effort and then march back to Washington as heroes.

The Union soldiers were green—mostly fresh volunteers who signed on after the Confederates captured Fort Sumter. These men had joined up for 90 days of army duty, which almost everyone assumed would be plenty of time to take care of the pesky rebels. Some signed up because they figured this would be the only battle of the war, and they didn't want to miss the excitement.

They were led by General Irvin McDowell. McDowell, a West Point graduate and veteran of the Mexican War, was less sanguine. He knew his 30,000 soldiers were not a real army. He'd had minimal time to train them, they were not particularly well equipped, and there was virtually no military experience among them or their line officers.

Keep It Quick

The politicians in Washington (who wanted a quick end to the Southern uprising), urged McDowell to march his troops to meet the growing Confederate army near Manassas, a railroad junction in Virginia just 30 miles from Washington. McDowell fretted, but he knew he had to follow orders.

On July 16, 1861, he marched his force out of Washington. The soldiers were having a grand time. "They stopped every moment to pick blackberries or get water," McDowell later wrote. "They would not keep in the ranks." Another witness recalled "the waving banners, the inspiring strains of the numerous bands, the shouts and songs of the men."

Washingtonians didn't want to miss the excitement of the battle either; many of them followed the troops on horseback or in buggies loaded down with picnic baskets. "I noticed about twenty barouches and carriages," recalled a Massachusetts soldier, "that contained members of Congress and their friends."

The Opposition

The new Confederate army forming in Manassas was no better trained than the Union army. They were Southern farm boys who also heard the call of war after Fort Sumter and charged into the fray. They were led by General Pierre G. T. Beauregard, who, like McDowell, was a West Point grad and Mexican War veteran. Nearby was the Army of the Shenandoah, led by General Joseph Johnston. Together they had about the same number of troops as McDowell.

It took a couple of days for McDowell's troops to make the 30-mile march. He massed his force near the town of Centerville while he planned the attack.

Meanwhile, the Confederates were still in two groups. Beauregard's army was set up in defensive positions along Bull Run (a stream), while Johnston's force was guarding Harpers Ferry in the Shenandoah Valley. The two groups were 30 miles away from each other but were connected by the Manassas Gap Railroad.

And So It Begins

On July 18, McDowell sent one division to the southeast, trying to outflank the Confederates on their right flank. He figured this would draw their attention and allow him to concentrate his attack on the left flank, which he expected would lead to a collapse of the entire enemy line.

The battle began at Blackburn's Ford, where the right-flanking division encountered the Confederates. A Boston news reporter recorded the start of the first major battle of the Civil War: "Louder, wilder, and more startling than the volley which they had fired was the rebel yell. A thousand Confederates were howling like wolves." Describing the ambulance corps collecting the wounded, he wrote, "I recall the first man brought back on a stretcher, his thigh torn to pieces by a cannon shot ... The reflection came that this was war. All its glamour was gone in an instant."

Surely the Washingtonian picnickers wondered what they had gotten themselves into.

Beauregard correctly guessed that the attack on his right flank was a diversionary tactic when he got reports about its relative mildness. He soon learned that Union troops were massing near his left flank.

Meanwhile, Johnston was ordered to hurry his army to Manassas. His 6,000 fresh troops arrived at noon on July 20, just in time to help defend the left flank.

McDowell himself led the main attack on the Confederate left flank. At first it succeeded, driving the rebels back to a position called Henry House Hill.

"Rally Behind the Virginians"

This site is where Confederate General Thomas Jackson earned the nickname "Stonewall." His brigade was anchoring the Confederate line on the heights. "There is Jackson standing like a stone wall," cried Confederate General Bernard Bee, whose own troops were wavering. "Rally behind the Virginians."

Eventually the Confederates were reinforced by more of Johnston's troops. They pressed their advantage and drove the Yankees back across Bull Run, forcing them to retreat toward Washington.

The green soldiers on both sides got their fill of battle that day. "The air is full of fearful noises," wrote a witness. "Trees are splintered ... There is smoke, dust, wild talking, shouting, hissings, howlings, explosions. It is a new, strange, unanticipated experience to the soldiers of both armies, far different from what they thought it would be."

A Mad Dash

The picnic was certainly over. The remaining civilian sightseers fled along with their defeated army. "What a scene," wrote a reporter for the *World*, a New York paper. "For three miles, hosts of Federal troops ... all mingled in one disorderly rout—were fleeing ... Army wagons, sutler's teams, and private carriages choked the passage, tumbling against each other amid clouds of dust and sickening sights and sounds."

Fortunately for the Union, the Confederates were too tired to pursue them very far. Some have speculated that had they done so, they may have captured Washington.

When the armies finally stopped to survey the damage, they recorded about 2,900 killed, wounded, and missing among the Yankees and nearly 2,000 among the Confederates. It was a brutal end to the "picnic battle," and a dark sign of things to come.

❋ An army colonel and the grandson of a fur trader, John Jacob Astor III served as a volunteer aide-de-camp to General McClellan and attained the rank of brevet brigadier general. He brought with him to his Washington post his valet, chef, and steward.

❋ Theologian Horace Bushnell of Hartford, Connecticut, went on record as crediting God for every federal victory.

❋ Martha Washington was the great-grandmother of Robert E. Lee's wife, Mary Anna Custis Lee.

Greatest Missing Treasures

They were fantastic examples of opulence and
splendor. But what happened to them?

✳ ✳ ✳ ✳

1. **Blackbeard's Treasure:** The pirate Blackbeard spent only
   two years (1716–18) plundering the high seas. Within that
   time, however, he amassed some serious wealth. While the
   Spanish were busy obtaining all the gold and silver they
   could extract from Mexico and South America, Blackbeard
   and his mates waited patiently, then pounced on the treasure-
   laden ships as they sailed back to Spain.

   Blackbeard's reign of terror centered around the West Indies
   and the Atlantic coast of North America, with headquarters in the Bahamas and North Carolina. His end came in
   November 1718, when British Lieutenant Robert Maynard
   decapitated the pirate and hung his head from the bowsprit
   of his ship as a grisly trophy.

   But what happened to the vast treasure that Blackbeard had
   amassed? He acknowledged burying it but never disclosed
   the location. Blackbeard's sunken ship, *Queen Anne's Revenge*,
   is believed to have been discovered off the North Carolina
   coast in 1996, but the loot wasn't onboard. Possible locations
   for the hidden stash include the Caribbean Islands, Virginia's
   Chesapeake Bay, the North Carolina swamps, and the caves of
   the Cayman Islands.

2. **Treasures of Lima:** In 1820, Lima, Peru, was on the edge
   of revolt. As a preventative measure, the viceroy of Lima
   decided to transport the city's fabulous wealth to Mexico.
   The treasures included jeweled stones, candlesticks, and two
   life-size solid gold statues of Mary holding the baby Jesus.
   In all, the treasure filled 11 ships and was valued at around
   $60 million.

Captain William Thompson, commander of the *Mary Dear*, was put in charge of transporting the riches to Mexico. But the viceroy should have done some research on the man to whom he handed such fabulous wealth because Thompson was a pirate, and a ruthless one at that. Once the ships were well out to sea, he cut the throats of the Peruvian guards and threw their bodies overboard.

Thompson headed for the Cocos Islands, in the Indian Ocean, where he and his men allegedly buried the treasure. They then decided to split up and lay low until the situation calmed down, at which time they would reconvene to divvy up the spoils. But the *Mary Dear* was captured, and the crew went on trial for piracy. All but Thompson and his first mate were hanged. To save their lives, the two agreed to lead the Spanish to the stolen treasure. They took them as far as the Cocos Islands and then managed to escape into the jungle. Thompson, the first mate, and the treasure were never seen again.

Since then over 300 expeditions have attempted to locate the treasures of Lima, without success. The most recent theory is that the treasure wasn't buried on the Cocos Islands at all, but on an unknown island off the coast of Central America.

3. **Pharaohs' Missing Treasure:** When Howard Carter found King Tut's tomb in 1922, he was mesmerized by the splendor of the artifacts that the young king took to the afterlife. Attached to the burial chamber was a treasury with so many artifacts that it took Carter ten years to fully catalog them. However, when the burial chambers of more prominent pharaohs were unearthed in the late 19th century, their treasure chambers were virtually empty. It is common knowledge that tomb robbers had been busy over the centuries, but the scale of these thefts was beyond petty criminals. So, where is the vast wealth of the pharaohs?

Some scholars believe that the treasures were appropriated by the priests who conducted reburials during the period of the early 20th and late 21st Egyptian dynasties (425–343 B.C.). Pharaohs were not averse to reusing the funeral splendors of their ancestors, so this may have been carried out with official sanction. One particular ruler, Herihor, has been the focus of special attention. Herihor was a high court official during the reign of Ramses XI. Upon Ramses' death, Herihor usurped the throne, dividing up the kingdom with his son-in-law Piankh. Herihor placed himself in charge of reburial proceedings, affording himself ample opportunity to pilfer. His tomb has not been found. When and if it is, many scholars believe that the missing treasures of many of Egypt's pharaohs will finally see the light of day.

4. **The Ark of the Covenant:** To the ancient Israelites, the Ark of the Covenant was the most sacred thing on earth. The central and paramount object of the Hebrew nation, this ornate chest was, according to the Bible, designed by God. Measuring 44 inches long, 26 inches wide, and 26 inches high, the chest was made of acacia wood, overlaid inside and out with pure gold, and surrounded by a gold border. Mounted on the solid gold cover were two golden cherubs, one at each end and facing each other, with heads bowed and wings extending upward.

The Ark served as a holy archive for the safekeeping of sacred relics, including the two stone tablets of the Ten Commandments. As a historical and religious treasure, the Ark and its contents were priceless.

In 607 B.C., Jerusalem was besieged and overthrown by the Babylonians. More than a million people were killed, with the survivors taken into captivity. Seventy years later, when the Israelites returned to rebuild the city, the Ark of the Covenant was gone. What happened to this priceless relic has been the subject of intense speculation ever since.

It is widely believed that the Ark was hidden by the Hebrews to keep it from the Babylonians. Possible locations for its hiding place range from Mount Nebo in Egypt to Ethiopia to a cave in the heart of Judah. Yet, if the Ark was hidden, why was it not recovered when the Israelites returned to Jerusalem and rebuilt the temple? Others believe that the Ark was destroyed by the Babylonians. Still another explanation put forth by the faithful is that God reclaimed the Ark for safekeeping.

5. **Montezuma's Treasure:** The Spanish decimation of the Aztec empire in Mexico came to a head on July 1, 1520. After mortally wounding Emperor Montezuma, Hernán Cortés and his men were besieged by enraged Aztec warriors in the capital city of Tenochtitlán. After days of fierce fighting, Cortés ordered his men to pack up the treasures of Montezuma in preparation for a night flight, but they didn't get far before the Aztecs fell upon them. The ensuing carnage filled Lake Tezcuco with Spanish bodies and the stolen treasures of Montezuma. The terrified army had thrown the booty away in a vain attempt to escape with their lives. The hoard consisted of countless gold and silver ornaments, along with a vast array of jewels.

Cortés and a handful of his men got away with their lives and returned a year later to exact their revenge. When the inhabitants of Tenochtitlán got wind of the approaching invaders, they buried the remains of the city's treasure in and around Lake Tezcuco to prevent it from falling to the Spanish. Today, a vast treasure trove remains hidden beneath nearly five centuries of mud and sludge on the outskirts of Mexico City (modern-day Tenochtitlán). Generations of treasure seekers have sought the lost hoard without success. A former president of Mexico even had the lake bed dredged, but no treasure was found.

Vanished: The Lost Colony of Roanoke Island

Twenty years before England established its first successful colony in the New World, an entire village of English colonists disappeared in what would later be known as North Carolina. Did these pioneers all perish? Did Native Americans capture them? Did they join a friendly tribe? Could they have left descendants who live among us today?

✳   ✳   ✳   ✳

Timing Is Everything

TALK ABOUT BAD timing. As far as John White was concerned, England couldn't have picked a worse time to go to war. It was November 1587, and White had just arrived in England from the New World. He intended to gather relief supplies and immediately sail back to Roanoke Island, where he had left more than 100 colonists who were running short of food. Unfortunately, the English were gearing up to fight Spain. Every seaworthy ship—including White's—was pressed into naval service. Not a one could be spared for his return voyage to America.

Nobody Home

When John White finally returned to North America three years later, he was dismayed to discover that the colonists he had left behind were nowhere to be found. Instead, he stumbled upon a mystery—one that has never been solved.

The village that White and company had founded in 1587 on Roanoke Island lay completely deserted. Houses had been dismantled (as if someone planned to move them), but the pieces lay in the long grass along with iron tools and farming equipment. A stout stockade made of logs stood empty.

White found no sign of his daughter Eleanor, her husband Ananias, or their daughter Virginia Dare—the first English child born in America. None of the 87 men, 17 women, and

11 children remained. No bodies or obvious grave sites offered clues to their fate. The only clues—if they were clues—that White could find were the letters CRO carved into a tree trunk and the word CROATOAN carved into a log of the abandoned fort.

No Forwarding Address

All White could do was hope that the colonists had been taken in by friendly natives.

Croatoan—also spelled "Croatan"—was the name of a barrier island to the south and also the name of a tribe of Native Americans that lived on that island. Unlike other area tribes, the Croatoans had been friendly to English newcomers, and one of them, Manteo, had traveled to England with earlier explorers and returned to act as interpreter for the Roanoke colony. Had the colonists, with Manteo's help, moved to Croatoan? Were they safe among friends?

White tried to find out, but his timing was rotten once again. He had arrived on the Carolina coast as a hurricane bore down on the region. The storm hit before he could mount a search. His ship was blown past Croatoan Island and out to sea. Although the ship and crew survived the storm and made it back to England, White was stuck again. He tried repeatedly but failed to raise money for another search party.

No one has ever learned the fate of the Roanoke Island colonists, but there are no shortage of theories as to what happened to them. A small sailing vessel and other boats that White had left with them were gone when he returned. It's possible that the colonists used the vessels to travel to another island or to the mainland. White had talked with others before he left about possibly moving the settlement to a more secure location inland. It's even possible that the colonists tired of waiting for White's return and tried to sail back to England. If so, they would have perished at sea. Yet there are at least a few shreds of hearsay evidence that the colonists survived in America.

Rumors of Survivors

In 1607, Captain John Smith and company established the first successful English settlement in North America at Jamestown, Virginia. The colony's secretary, William Strachey, wrote four years later about hearing a report of four English men, two boys, and one young woman who had been sighted south of Jamestown at a settlement of the Eno tribe, where they were being used as slaves. If the report was true, who else could these English have been but Roanoke survivors?

For more than a century after the colonists' disappearance, stories emerged of gray-eyed Native Americans and English-speaking villages in North Carolina and Virginia. In 1709, an English surveyor said members of the Hatteras tribe living on North Carolina's Outer Banks—some of them with light-colored eyes—claimed to be descendants of white people. It's possible that the Hatteras were the same people that the 1587 colonists called Croatoan.

In the intervening centuries, many of the individual tribes of the region have disappeared. Some died out. Others were absorbed into larger groups such as the Tuscarora. One surviving group, the Lumbee, has also been called Croatoan. The Lumbee, who still live in North Carolina, often have Caucasian features. Could they be descendants of Roanoke colonists? Many among the Lumbee dismiss the notion as fanciful, but the tribe has long been thought to be of mixed heritage and has been speaking English so long that none among them know what language preceded it.

✳ A group of researchers is currently attempting to solve the Roanoke mystery through DNA analysis.

The U.S. Attack on Pearl Harbor

A U.S. rear admiral's attack plan is used against America.

✳ ✳ ✳ ✳

O N December 7, 1941, Japan bombed Pearl Harbor. This tragedy prompted President Roosevelt's "infamy" speech, which credited "naval and air forces of the Empire of Japan" with the surprise attack that ultimately launched the United States into World War II. However, as is often the case with pivotal moments in history, there's more to the story.

On February 7, 1932, U.S. Navy Rear Admiral Harry Yarnell sought to prove his theory that aircraft carriers, not battleships, should operate as the principal arm of a well-prepared navy. With a fleet comprised of two carriers and more than 150 warplanes, Yarnell positioned an armada 60 miles northeast of Oahu and commenced exercises.

"Attacking" Pearl Harbor before dawn on a Sunday morning, Yarnell's surprise assault hypothetically knocked stationary U.S. aircraft completely out of commission and sunk or damaged a multitude of warships. The exercise was so effective that a reporter from *The New York Times* observed that Yarnell's planes "made the attack unopposed by the defense, which was caught virtually napping." After the exercise, many admirals argued that Yarnell's victory prompted a reassessment of naval tactics, but a majority of admirals voted the notion down.

Japanese observers who had witnessed the American exercise forwarded a comprehensive report to Tokyo. By 1936, the revealing data found its way into a report entitled "Study of Strategy and Tactics in Operations Against the United States." It concluded: "In case the enemy's main fleet is berthed at Pearl Harbor, the idea should be to open hostilities by surprise attack from the air." Five years later—on a date that will live in infamy—the Japanese did just that.

The Aryan "Spring of Life"

The Third Reich created the Lebensborn *program
to ensure an influx of "racially pure" children.*

✳ ✳ ✳ ✳

H EINRICH HIMMLER, COMMANDER of the SS, unveiled the
Lebensborn ("Spring of Life") program on December 12,
1935. The program encouraged members of the SS to repro-
duce—whether they were married or not. The objective was to
carry on their bloodlines.

Himmler decreed that the minimum offspring expected of
a member of the SS was four boys. His rationale was that "a
nation which has an average of four sons per family can venture
a war; if two of them die, two transplant the name. The leadership of a nation having one son or two sons per family will have
to be fainthearted at any decision because they will have to tell
themselves, 'We cannot afford it.'"

Declining birth rates and a high abortion rate contributed to
Lebensborn's creation. One of the main goals of the program
was to provide "racially pure" unwed mothers the opportunity
to give birth to their children without scrutiny.

To be accepted for care at *Lebensborn* facilities, the mother had
to prove that the father of her child was "racially approved."
Many of the fathers were reported to be men of the SS.
Himmler encouraged unwed SS officers to marry the mothers
of their children. If the SS officer was already married, the society provided assistance to help the mother raise her offspring.

The first *Lebensborn* home opened in Steinhoring in 1936.
Other homes cropped up and were often located in refurbished
ski chalets or hotels. The society also operated homes outside
Germany, opening the first facilities in occupied Norway in
1941. Later it established maternity homes in Austria, Belgium,
Denmark, France, Luxembourg, and the Netherlands.

Some 15,000 to 20,000 children were born in *Lebensborn*-run homes in Germany and Norway. The number of children born in *Lebensborn* wards in other countries is not known.

Most *Lebensborn* documents were destroyed at war's end. When Nazi forces were driven from an occupied country, *Lebensborn* facilities were closed, and documents were transferred to the original home outside Munich. When the Americans entered Steinhoring in May 1945, SS officers fled and either burned or dumped the documents in the Isar River.

After Germany's Surrender

After the war, several former administrators of the *Lebensborn* program were charged with kidnapping children in occupied countries. Numerous children were taken from Poland, Ukraine, and the Baltic countries and resettled with German families. The defendants were found not guilty because most investigators thought the *Lebensborn* program was nothing more than a breeding program for Nazis. However, a 1970s investigation by journalists Marc Hillel and Clarissa Henry uncovered much more information about the program.

In the years following World War II, resentments toward Nazis were often taken out on the innocent *Lebensborn* children in formerly occupied countries because their fathers were presumed to have been SS officers. Some assimilated into their adopted cultures, but others were horribly mistreated; some were even victims of rape and other abuses. In 2005, the *Lebensspuren* (Traces of Life) society was formed to help children of the *Lebensborn* program. The society acts as a support network and helps survivors trace their genealogy.

✳ In 2007, Bad Arolsen, the world's biggest Holocaust archive, was opened to scholars, victims, and victims' families (the archive had been closed on the pretext of protecting victims' privacy). Researchers believe more information about the *Lebensborn* program will be gleaned from these files.

The Blonde Poison

From August 1943 through the end of the war, a striking young Jewish woman walked freely through the streets of Berlin. Unlike her fellow Jews, she had no fear of being discovered by the Nazis. They were already well aware of her presence. In fact, she worked for them.

✳ ✳ ✳ ✳

BEING JEWISH IN prewar Berlin was at best barely tolerable. Constant threats, physical harassment, and official speeches made it clear that German society had turned against Jews. The easiest targets were refugees from Eastern Europe. They had been driven to Germany by Czarist purges at the turn of the century, had never assimilated into the city's culture, and were easily identified by their attire and language. But there were others—self-described Germans of Jewish Origin. These patriotic families proudly traced their German heritage back centuries. They looked down on their Eastern cousins almost as much as their gentile neighbors did and took great pains to distance themselves from their brethren.

Stella Goldschlag was the daughter of one such family. About 20 years old, already with a reputation as being a bit wilder than other girls her age, she commanded the attention of all the young men around her. She was beautiful in a way that conformed to so-called Aryan standards: Her blue eyes and blonde hair made her the very picture of the German ideal. Stella's father couldn't believe that the new measures being enacted against Jews would ever apply to families such as his. Like many German Jews, he considered himself a valuable German citizen.

By 1940, however, Stella's father could no longer deny reality. He tried to emigrate to America, Palestine, Santo Domingo— anywhere. His applications met with no better success than those of tens of thousands of other Jews. The time to go into hiding had come.

Capturing a U-boat

Stella and her family became U-boats, as Jews living submerged beneath visible Berlin society called themselves. It was a harsh existence defined by a constant fear of capture, but about 1,400 of these courageous individuals managed to survive the war undetected. However, U-boats couldn't survive in complete isolation. They needed some resources, primarily ration books for food and identity papers in case they were stopped on the street. A veritable industry of forgery sprung up, with the difference between life and death hinging on the skill of the artist producing the documents.

Stella's papers looked authentic, and she managed to survive for a time. Her luck ran out on July 2, 1943, with a disastrous lunchtime visit to a café, considered a safe activity because of the large number of people such locations drew. As she sat at her table, Stella happened to smile at a friend, a plump woman named Inge Lustigo. The brief recognition was enough, and Gestapo operatives rushed in to seize Stella. Her acquaintance turned out to be a *Greifer*, a Jew employed by the Nazis to root out other Jews in hiding. *Greifers*, or catchers, were rewarded with a cash prize for every Jew turned in, but more importantly, they were exempt from being sent to the death camps—at least while they remained useful.

With typical subtlety, the Gestapo took Stella to a basement and beat her for days, until her bones were almost broken. Her torturers demanded to know the location of the forger of her papers. Stella didn't have the answer they wanted, and she managed to escape and return to her family. She was rearrested in less than 12 hours, and this time the Gestapo found her parents as well.

The Goldschlags were placed in a collection camp. Stella's questioning began again, but this time the Gestapo had new leverage: Her mother and father had been put on the list to be sent to Auschwitz. Stella still didn't have the information they wanted, but she quickly realized the semblance of cooperation could save her family. She pretended to know where her forger might be found and guided the authorities in their search. Stella's treatment improved, and she grew accustomed to her new status.

The Gestapo would only be stalled for so long, and Stella knew it. She could not deliver the source of her forged documents, but she could deliver other Jews. She had been a U-boat, had extensive prewar social contacts in the Jewish community, and a presence that caused men to lower their defenses. She put all her resources to effective use. Each capture bought a delay in her parents' date with the death camps—at least until February 1944, when they were put on the trains despite Stella's service.

The "Tigress"

Her parents' departure might have been the end of Stella's cooperation with the Nazis, but that was not the case. Acquaintances of the time report that she enjoyed her special status and served her masters faithfully, even with zeal. She seemed to hate Jews more than the Nazis did; whereas they viewed Jews as less than human, Stella took their existence as a personal affront. Stella roamed Berlin at will, armed with papers from the Gestapo asserting that she was working for them in the matter of "Jewish affairs." She often paired with a former boyfriend whom she personally recruited to the *Greifer* ranks.

Keeping no schedule other than her own, Stella frequented locations known to be visited by Jews, accompanied by a Nazi squad waiting to pounce when she made a catch. She would often net more than one victim at a time, once arresting an entire family in a theater lobby. On another occasion, she used her body to block a revolving door as Jews tried desperately to get past her while the Gestapo descended upon them. She even stooped to lying in wait at funerals of deceased Germans who had been married to Jews. She developed a reputation as being heartless, at one point telling a captured former friend, "You'll get out of here all right . . . as a corpse!"

Word spread quickly among the Jews of Berlin that a "Blonde Ghost" or "Blonde Poison" was among them, and they circulated a picture of her amongst themselves as a warning. The remaining resistance groups attempted to assassinate her, and at one point delivered to her a message bearing a sentence of death, the verdict to be "executed at the end of the war."

Aftermath

No such execution was to take place, however. After the war, Stella, pregnant by an unknown man, was captured by the Soviets and sentenced to ten years in a labor camp. Characteristically, she developed a reputation among the prisoners for cooperating with her Soviet guards. Stella underwent a second German trial at which spectators waited in line for hours, heckled her during the trial, and tried to assault her during a break in the proceedings. Her daughter was taken from her. Living in Israel, Stella's daughter grew to hate her mother.

After her legal difficulties were settled, Stella spent the rest of her life in relative obscurity, claiming the Jewish witnesses at her trial had hated her because she was blonde and pretty. Stella's end came in 1994, when she committed suicide.

✳ Adolf Eichmann once claimed that getting Jews to work against other Jews was "the very cornerstone" of the Nazis' Jewish policy.

✳ Peter Wyden, whose biography of Stella was published in 1992, was once a classmate of Stella's. He lost touch with her after 1937, when he and his family obtained visas and fled to the United States. Wyden began to research Stella's story during the 1980s.

Beware, Balloon Bombs!

In a last-ditch effort to attack the United States, Japan relied on the wind.

✳   ✳   ✳   ✳

BY LATE 1944, the United States had cut off much of Japan's supply of food, fuel, and other war materials. Despite a shortage of resources, the Japanese Ninth Research Division laboratory developed a new weapon.

The Japanese knew that a strong wind current swept across the Pacific from Japan to North America (later this current would be called the jet stream). Researchers supposed they could float a large number of missiles on the current to explode over the United States. They expected Japan could achieve indefensible terror and destruction similar to Germany's buzz bombs and V-1s in Britain.

Military brass called in their engineers and laid out the requirements:

✳ The missiles' prime purpose would be to burn America's food crops and forests.

✳ Originally, targeting major cities was an objective, but it was soon realized the guidance would rely on the whimsy of wind currents.

✳ The weapons would need to carry antipersonnel explosives to prevent anyone from interfering with the incendiary devices.

So began project Fu-go. Planners set about the task. They decided a hydrogen-filled balloon would be the best method of transportation. With rubber in short supply, the engineers created the balloon's skin using thick, impermeable paper called *washi*, made from mulberry trees.

Meteorologists agreed the plan was inherently feasible. The Japanese government evacuated large warehouses on the islands to provide assembly sites for this high-priority project. Several high schools near the plants were closed, and female students were sent to work gluing paper to create the balloons. In all, about 30,000 soldiers and an equal number of civilians were put to work on the weapon. The product was then sent to northern Honshu, where technicians attached explosives and incendiary devices. The weapons were called *fusen bakudan*, which means "balloon bomb" but has also been translated as "fire balloon."

Engineers refined the mechanisms to ensure the balloons would be carried along the jet stream at an optimum altitude of 30,000 feet. If they slipped below 30,000 feet, a mechanism would release a pair of sandbags, and the balloons would rise. If they got as high as 38,000 feet, a vent was activated to release some hydrogen from the balloons.

Released from northern Honshu, the balloons would take three days to cross the Pacific. With its sandbags spent, a mechanism would drop the bombs and light a fuse that would burn for 84 minutes before detonating a flash bomb that would destroy the balloon. By causing the balloons to self-destruct in midair, the Japanese hoped to add mystery to the source of the fires.

The Assault Begins

The first balloons were launched November 3, 1944, and one was spotted two days later off the coast of San Pedro, California. They continued to turn up throughout the northwest United States and western Canada, reaching as far east as Farmington, Michigan, and south to northern Mexico.

Rather than incite widespread panic, the balloons were largely ineffective and rarely discussed. *Newsweek* ran a report on the weapons in January 1945, but the Office of Censorship issued a notice to the media not to report further incidents for fear of inciting needless panic.

During January and February 1945, debris showed up as far inland as Arizona and Texas. One bomb exploded near the Boeing plant in Seattle that produced B-29s. Another shorted a high-tension wire, temporarily blacking out one of the Manhattan Project's reactors in Hanford, Washington.

A balloon killed a woman in Helena, Montana. One in Oregon claimed six lives: On March 5, 1945, Elyse Mitchell, a minister's wife, was on a fishing trip with children from the Sunday school. They discovered a grounded balloon and tried to move it, but it exploded. After this incident, the media ban was lifted so that people would be aware of the potential danger.

When the balloons arrived, they were indeed a mystery—no one knew where they had come from. Many people feared they could be used to carry biological weapons. Researchers examined some of the balloon bombs that were found unexploded and analyzed the sand in the sandbags. Finding that it was not from the United States or the mid-Pacific, they eventually isolated its origin as the beaches of northeast Japan. Troops flew photo reconnaissance missions over the area, and photo interpreters identified two of the three hydrogen plants near Ichinomiya. B-29s were sent to destroy the plants, grinding the balloon-bomb production to a halt.

The Japanese government suspended funding for project Fugo in April 1945. While Japanese propaganda had declared casualties as high as 10,000, the actual toll was seven dead. In all, of more than 9,000 bombs launched, approximately 300 are believed to have reached the United States.

✳ The workhorse C-46s that flew over the Himalayas into China were sometimes loaded by trained elephants, lifting 55-gallon fuel drums with their tusks.

The Ultimate Transformation

Can surgery lead to happiness?

✳   ✳   ✳   ✳

THE FRONT PAGE of the *New York Daily News* on December 1, 1952, screamed: "Ex-GI Becomes Blonde Beauty." In a country weary from the Korean War and the McCarthy hearings, it was just the sort of story Americans needed. It announced that George William Jorgensen of the Bronx had received the first sex-change operation, which took place in Denmark. It wasn't precisely true, but it made for great copy.

This pioneering surgery had actually first been performed in the 1920s by Dr. Magnus Hirschfeld at the Institute of Sexual Science in Berlin. But then Hitler and the Nazis came along, and such surgery disappeared.

Jorgensen was among the first of the postwar transgendered people. The new element in Jorgensen's surgery was the use of artificial hormones to enhance the physical change. In Copenhagen, Jorgensen had his male sexual organs removed. Several years later, he—now she—received an artificial vagina when that procedure became available. Jorgensen's doctor, Christian Hamburger, then supervised her hormone therapy. Jorgensen chose the name "Christine" to honor the man who had made a woman out of her.

William Jorgensen had been a frail, introverted boy who avoided contact sports and ran from fights at Christopher Columbus High School. Upon his graduation in 1945, he was drafted and spent a hitch in the U.S. Army before receiving an honorable discharge. But he was not happy. As he would later note, he was "a woman trapped in a man's body." He began to research the possibility of a sex change. He was on his way to Sweden to meet with doctors there when, during a stop in Copenhagen to visit friends, he learned about Dr. Hamburger.

A New Life

The press picked up on the sensationalism of the *New York Daily News* headline (the story had originally been leaked by an acquaintance of the Jorgensen family), and on her return to the United States two months later, Christine was met with intense curiosity. The notoriety could easily have been short-lived, but Christine was canny enough to stay in the public eye and build a career—both as a photographer-performer and as a spokesperson for transsexuality and transgendered people.

Jorgensen was usually a good sport in interviews, where she was inevitably confronted with jokes such as, "Christine went abroad and came back a broad." But an encounter with talk show host Dick Cavett didn't go so well. Cavett was curious about romance in her life, so he asked about her "wife." He later insisted that he hadn't intended to insult her, but Christine got up and walked out. Christine was never married, though she was engaged to a man. When it was discovered that her birth certificate identified her as a male, the authorities refused to issue a marriage license.

Showbiz Beckons

Christine soon moved into the entertainment world. Known for her sharp wit, she toured college campuses on the same circuit as stand-up comedians. In an era when civil rights took center stage, she was in the right place at the right time. She was the subject of a 1970 film, *The Christine Jorgensen Story*, and was the supposed inspiration for the movie *Glen or Glenda?*

In 1989, Christine said that she'd given the sexual revolution "a good swift kick in the pants." She died that same year, after a battle with bladder and lung cancers.

✳ In the decade leading up to her illness, Christine Jorgensen had become concerned that her continued hormone treatments could lead to cancer.

The Mystery of Oak Island

*Some people consider Oak Island—a small island off the
coast of Nova Scotia, Canada—the repository of one of
the world's most fantastic treasures. Others, however,
think it's a natural monument to human gullibility.*

✳ ✳ ✳ ✳

I**T'S ONLY A** short boat ride across the channel (and an even
shorter walk across the causeway) between the Nova Scotia
mainland and Oak Island. Aside from the oak trees that give
the island its name, there's little to distinguish the 140-acre
island from the nearly 400 others that dot Mahone Bay.
Nevertheless, boats are not permitted to land here, and the
causeway is fenced off with a "No Trespassing" sign (access is
reserved to those with digging permits).

If the casual visitor could set foot on the
island, they would find its surface per-
meated by hundreds of mine shafts.
Thanks to plenty of folklore, for over two
centuries Oak Island has been the focus
of spectacular digging operations, with
excavators using everything from pick
and spade to modern industrial equip-
ment. To date, these exertions have consumed millions.

Depending on the source, Oak Island is the final resting place
of any number of precious objects, including:

✳ Captain Kidd's pirate treasure

✳ Manuscripts proving that Sir Francis Bacon wrote
   Shakespeare's plays

✳ South American gold

✳ Marie Antoinette's jewels

* The Holy Grail

* The accumulated wealth of the Knights Templar and/or the Freemasons

The Legend Begins

As the story goes, in 1795 a boy named Daniel McGinnis ventured onto the island and gleaned from marks on a tree that rope and tackle had been used to lower something into the ground. The next day, he returned with two companions and initiated the first attempt to recover treasure from a vertical shaft that has since become known as the Money Pit.

Flooding in the shafts, which many believe to be caused by tunnels built as booby traps for treasure seekers, has always thwarted digging operations on Oak Island. Attempts to block these subterranean channels have been unsuccessful.

Despite the difficulties, treasure seekers continue to labor on Oak Island because the Money Pit, its auxiliary shafts, and the various features on the island's surface have yielded tantalizing indications that something of value lies beneath. Among the evidence: a stone inscribed with strange markings and piece of parchment bearing characters inscribed in India ink.

The Skeptics Have Their Say

Naysayers take issue with Oak Island's supposed treasure. They point out that while it may be likely that at one time pirates landed on the island, that doesn't necessarily spell buried treasure. And there's nothing weird about sinkholes and subterranean chambers in limestone. In fact, they're all over the region.

Moreover, skeptics note the lack of evidence of any digging on the island before the 1840s. They figure it's much more likely that a story about someone discovering a treasure cave got a few people excited. Legend built upon legend until, like the island itself, the story was muddied and mixed up by the passage of time. Either way, perhaps Oak Island's greatest treasure is simply the human imagination.

Biracial Prodigy

"You were an accident" are words a child should never hear. But it could be worse: "You were an experiment in hybrid vigor and miscegenation."

✳   ✳   ✳   ✳

BORN ON AUGUST 2, 1931, Philippa Schuyler made headlines in African American newspapers across the United States. Her parents, famed Harlem journalist George Schuyler and Josephine Cogdell, a white Texan from a wealthy family, were proud socialists who firmly believed in hybrid vigor. They thought that babies born of black-and-white couples would have the best characteristics of both parents and their races. Through this idea, George and Josephine believed they had found the answer to America's racial unrest.

From an early age, their daughter seemed to prove them right. Philippa was precocious, learning to read and write before age three and playing Mozart by age four. Josephine played doctor/nutritionist with Philippa's health. She believed firmly in a raw diet, so her daughter never ate anything that was cooked. Most modern raw foodists are vegan; Josephine included raw meat in Philippa's diet as well. The mother believed that liver and brains (washed under hot water) were the most nutritious. Besides raw flesh, they ate cod liver oil, wheat germ, and fruit. Sugar, tobacco, and alcohol weren't even allowed into their home, and Philippa never got sick.

There's no question the Schuylers loved Philippa, but what's unknown is whether George and Josephine loved each other. He was often traveling and writing to maintain their tony Harlem address, while Josephine threw herself into her daughter's development, bringing in private tutors and keeping intricate scrapbooks. When Philippa did attend school, she was advanced, but being of mixed race, she didn't feel like she fit in.

At age 11, Philippa began touring as a concert pianist, performing for foreign dignitaries. Although popular all over the United States (thanks mostly to her father's writing), her most notable fan was New York Mayor Fiorello La Guardia, who declared June 19, 1940, to be Philippa Duke Schuyler Day.

More Questions than Answers

By age 13, Philippa had written more than 100 compositions and seemed to be on route to becoming a famous pianist. But as she got older, her identity and race became an issue, and she was not the commodity she once was. And when she came across those developmental scrapbooks, Philippa was devastated. She felt that she was nothing more than a science experiment.

In adulthood, Philippa took after her father and became a journalist (writing in several languages for various publications), lecturer, and activist. Disdained in America, she toured the world again, all the while going through an identity crisis. She decided that she liked Latin America's lax attitudes toward race and eventually began using the alias Felipa Monterro y Schuyler, posing as a woman of Spanish descent. Unlucky in love, Philippa continued to throw herself into her work. She eventually ended up in Vietnam, covering the war there.

In 1967 at age 35, Philippa drowned after a helicopter crash. Her intelligence has been recognized at the Philippa Schuyler Middle School for the Gifted and Talented. Students at this advanced school in Brooklyn go through a rigorous curriculum, enhanced with a strong homeschool connection—much like its namesake. Even the motto, "To Whom Much Is Given, Much Is Required," is reminiscent of the unique Philippa Schuyler.

✳ Contemporary music critics compared Philippa Schuyler's teenage compositions to those of Mozart at a similar age.

Timeline

3.85 billion B.C.
Signs of Life! Carbon evidence of life dates back to 3.85 billion years ago, when single-cell bacteria begin forming in Earth's oceans.

1.8 billion B.C.
Multicellular organisms form, die, and are preserved for future paleontologists in fossil form. For the next one and a half billion years, life evolves into complex forms such as fish, reptiles, and reptilian protomammals. Earth's land consists of one supercontinent that we refer to as Rodinia.

540 million B.C.
Call Orkin! Segmented bugs develop legs and outer shells. The Cambrian Era bursts with genetic creativity as sponges, trilobites, snails, and more complex animals appear on the scene.

450 million B.C.
Rodinia breaks into large fragments, including the huge southern landmass Gondwana.

280 million B.C.
The supercontinent Pangaea forms from collisions of Earth's major landmasses, putting most land animals on the same mass. In a span of 10,000 years, about 90 percent of all life on Earth is snuffed out in the planet's greatest wave of extinctions.

248 million–65 million B.C.
Age of Dinosaurs. The Mesozoic Era puts dinosaurs in the evolutionary driver's seat. Pangaea begins breaking into separate continents. Early birds and mammals evolve on land. Cataclysmic extinctions at the end of the era put an end to dinodominance and give mammals the opportunity to become the new rulers of Earth.

65 million–33 million B.C.
Earth warms; tropics extend to the poles; and mammals, birds, and small reptiles dominate Earth's surface. The modern continents of Europe, Asia, and North America make up a loose northern landmass, while Antarctica, Africa, India, South America, and Australia hang together in the south. Sea levels drop, land bridges are exposed, and plants and animals spread over continents. Lemurlike primates make their first appearance; whales evolve from land mammals; and global cooling kills off 90 percent of animal species.

33 million–24 million B.C.
Going Ape. Grasslands proliferate and hoofed animals—including a 20-foot-tall Asian rhinoceros—spread. During this period, called the "Oligocene Epoch," apes debut, and Antarctica splits from South America and Australia.

24 million–5 million B.C.
Temperatures rise and drop; ice caps reform; and land bridges encourage migration among species. Mountain ranges—such as the Cascades, Andes, and Himalayas—

form as giant tectonic plates collide. Chimpanzees and early hominoids (proto-humans) coexist.

5 million B.C.
Happy Hunting. The Pliocene Epoch kicks off as woolly mammoths, saber-toothed cats, giant armadillos, and giant flightless birds roam Earth. Mammals grow in size and number as the planet cools off again. North and South America connect.

4.4 million B.C.
Let's Go for a Walk. Hominoid *Ardipithecus ramidus* walks on two legs around northeastern Africa. A short 300,000 years later, *Australopithecus anamensis* strolls around Lake Turkana, Kenya.

3.2 million B.C.
I Love Lucy: The original "Lucy," a hominoid (*Australopithecus afarensis*) inhabits Ethiopia; her kin spread throughout east Africa.

2.5 million B.C.
The Stone Age begins with *Homo habilis,* an apelike biped, using stone tools in Africa. Huge ice sheets cover Canada, Greenland, and northern Europe.

1.6 million B.C.
Homo habilis wanders into central Asia, but the big brains of the planet are found in Africa's *Homo erectus.* In another hundred thousand years, *Homo erectus* walks out of Africa and begins inhabiting the rest of the world.

200,000 B.C.
Neanderthal man, a close relative of modern humans, debuts on the Eurasian landmass. During the next 100,000 years, *Homo sapiens* appears in Africa.

100,000 B.C.
Regional characteristics begin to emerge among *Homo sapiens* in Australia, Asia, Africa, and Europe.

50,000 B.C.
Homo sapiens shows up in the Near East and spreads into Asia. Human development heats up: Man tames fire, but the rest of the world takes the news coolly as the last great Ice Age begins. Large mammals such as woolly mammoths and giant ground sloths die out.

49,000–15,000 B.C.
Move Over. Cro-Magnon man, a true *Homo sapiens,* begins displacing his smaller-brained Neanderthal neighbors in Europe. Bows and arrows are in vogue for hunting, and paintings show up in France's Chauvet and Lascaux Caves; painted rocks appear in southern Africa. Nomads cross the Bering Strait into the Americas. Before long, the "New World" supports populations from Alaska to South America's Tierra del Fuego.

15,000–10,000 B.C.
Dogs are domesticated in east Asia. Hunter-gatherers start building semipermanent settlements. Early Japanese settlers produce pottery.

10,000–6000 B.C.
Neolithic (New Stone Age) Period. The "Cradle of Civilization" springs up as primitive agriculture develops in the Fertile Crescent (Syria, Jordan, Iraq, and Turkey) and spreads to southern Europe and Asia. Cereals such as wheat and barley are

cultivated in the Fertile Crescent, while rice and millet are grown in China and India. Sheep, cats, goats, pigs, and cows are domesticated in western Asia and the Middle East. Farmers in Mesopotamia begin using tokens to keep track of farm products. Fishing villages spring up in coastal Africa. Middle Easterners make early attempts at metallurgy.

6000–5500 B.C.

Early agricultural settlements crop up in China, the Americas, and sub-Saharan Africa; soon after, these settlements become real cities. In Peru, settlers raise guinea pigs; domesticated chickens are bred in Thailand. The wheel, pottery, and systematic farming methods develop in Mesopotamia and slowly spread throughout most of the world. In China, an early form of symbol-writing appears on tortoise shells, and pottery makes its first appearance.

5500–4500 B.C.

Fertile river valleys give birth to clusters of towns as agricultural communities appear in the Tigris-Euphrates Valley (Iraq), in the Nile Delta (Egypt), near the Indus River (northern India), and along the Yellow River (northern China). In fact, farming communities appear everywhere except Antarctica and Australia. Staple crops include corn (Mexico), chilies (Central and South America), mangoes (southeast Asia), and wheat (Egypt).

Husbandry and planting allow fewer residents to feed greater populations—giving the nonfarming residents chances to specialize

in linguistics, theology, navigation, medicine, astronomy, metallurgy, and politico-military arts.

4500–3500 B.C.

Primitive Spanish tribes begin migrating to Britain. Over in Mesopotamia, copper is smelted for use in tools, pots, and weapons. Egyptians begin using oared boats for river and coastal travel; the invention of cotton sails soon follows. Animal domestication gallops along smoothly as horses are tamed on the central Asian steppes and silkworms are raised in China. People in the Caucasus worship multiple gods, perform burial rituals, farm, and drink fermented beverages.

3500–3000 B.C.

Bronze Age Begins. Mesopotamians develop primitive accounting systems; further south, Sumerians pioneer the city-state at Ur and develop cuneiform writing. From Egypt to Iraq, copper and other metals are used in production and for trade. Ancient Britons begin first-stage construction of Stonehenge. Groups migrate from the Caucasus to Europe and India. The ox-drawn plow stimulates farming and makes larger settlements possible. Pottery-making begins in Mesoamerica. Memphis, Egypt, is the world's largest city with more than 30,000 residents.

3000–2500 B.C.

In Mesopotamia, the wheel is used for making pottery before it is turned upright and used for transportation. King Menes unites Upper and Lower Egypt, and his successors build the Great Pyramid at Giza (the first "step" pyramid) and the Great Sphinx. Mummification, hieroglyphs, papyrus, ink, trade, and 365-day calendars also appear there, and meals are sweetened with honey from domesticated bees. Phoenician settlements appear in Lebanon and Syria. Minoan civilization in the Aegean takes root after settlers from Asia Minor sail over and decide to stay. Mathematics and serious astronomy are taken up in China, India, Babylon, and Egypt. Peruvians use the llama as a food source and beast of burden. Chinese mathematicians develop an early abacus. Large, permanent communities form in Japan.

2500–2000 B.C.
Groups from the Caucasus begin spreading into Europe. The "Gilgamesh" epic tells listeners (and later, readers) about legendary deeds of an ancient Sumerian king. Mesopotamian mathematicians prepare multiplication tables. Akkadian king Sargon carves out an empire from Syria to the Persian Gulf, but the fractious land splinters into a patchwork of competing city-states 200 years later. Ur becomes the world's largest city, with a population of around 65,000.

2000–1500 B.C.
Technology Boom. War erupts as the Hyksos invade Lower Egypt; King Amosis I will drive the interlopers out two centuries later. Surgery in Egypt reaches a sophisticated level; medical texts prescribe treatments for a variety of neurological, orthopedic, and internal ailments. Writing flourishes as the Hittites use cuneiform and the Minoans on Crete develop the earliest form of written Greek. Stone anchors are used to steady ships in Cyprus, and the Minoans dominate trade in the eastern Mediterranean and invent indoor plumbing. Babylonian mathematicians perform multiplication, fractions, squares, and square roots. Babylon's King Hammurabi puts writing to good use by developing a code of laws, and his subjects use early abacuses for calculating numbers. On the Indian subcontinent, metalsmiths begin smelting iron, which is weaker than bronze but much cheaper to produce. In the Far East, the yak is domesticated. The Xia Dynasty rises in China but falls to Shang rebels. Under the Shang Dynasty, the Chinese develop a writing system, bound books, fireworks, and sophisticated bronze metallurgy methods.

1500–1250 B.C.
Dawn of the Iron Age. Monotheism raises eyebrows in Egypt. The Hittites establish an empire in Anatolia, but in 1274 Egypt's King Ramses II roundly defeats them at the Battle of Kadesh; ten years later the Egyptian and Hittite empires sign the world's first recorded peace treaty. Moses leads Israelites out of Egypt and into Canaan. Nigerian metalworkers begin using iron. Phoenician seafarers settle on Cyprus. A massive volcanic eruption destroys royal palaces on Crete; Minoan dominance of the eastern Mediterranean comes to an abrupt end, and Greco-Phoenician sea trade flourishes.

1250–1000 B.C.

Greeks invade Troy and level it, inspiring Homer's epic, the *Iliad*, centuries later. In Palestine, King David rules an Israelite monarchy. Mexico's Olmecs produce stone monuments, obsidian tools, and picture-writing. Phoenicians develop an alphabet and begin colonizing Carthage and Spain. Mycenaean metallurgists develop bronze helmets and plate armor.

1000–800 B.C.

Solomon builds his temple in Jerusalem as Hebrew elders begin compiling the Old Testament. Assyrian power expands, and by 850, the empire extends from the Tigris River to the Mediterranean Sea. Egyptians develop the sundial to keep time. Etruscans migrate into the Italian peninsula. Homer composes the *Iliad*. Siberians raise reindeer in herds, and writing systems develop among the Olmecs in Mesoamerica. The Chinese develop gunpowder, an organized postal service, and an early feudal system under the ruling Zhou Dynasty.

800–700 B.C.

Rise of the Greeks. Greek mythology is described in Hesiod's *Theogeny*. Across the Aegean, 50-oared *pentekonter* boats—soon succeeded by their larger cousins, double-banked *biremes*—form the backbone of naval power in the Greek world. Greeks inaugurate the Olympic Games, build wooden temples on the Acropolis, and colonize Byzantium and Sicily. Etruscans dominate central Italy; Rome is founded by Romulus, and a Latin alphabet develops. The Brahmi writing system develops in India, and the oldest of the Hindu Upanishads are written.

700–600 B.C.

A tough set of Athenian laws is codified by the tyrannical Draco (giving us the word "draconian"). Assyria's King Sargon II conquers much of Palestine and Syria and defeats the Hittites, Chaldeans, and Samarians; his successors conquer much of Egypt but cannot hold it for long. The Assyrian Empire promotes art and culture and even assembles a great library at Nineveh, but it falls to the Medes (Persians) and succumbs to a Chaldean revolt in Babylonia. Babylon, the center of the Chaldean Empire, is the world's largest city, with a population exceeding 200,000; to beautify his imperial seat, King Nebuchadnezzar II builds Babylon's famed Hanging Gardens. In Japan, the Jimmu Dynasty begins, ushering in the island's legendary period.

600–500 B.C.

Babylonians capture and destroy Jerusalem but fall to Cyrus the Great and the Persian Empire 50 years later. Cyrus and his successors build the most powerful empire the world will see until the era of Alexander the Great. To the west, Carthage breaks away from Phoenicia and rules the western Mediterranean. In Greece, Anaximander draws the first map of the world, while primitive democracy, poetry, and Pythagorean mathematics flourish. Greek colonists battle the Carthaginians at sea and compete for dominance along the lucrative sea trade routes. Romans overthrow their Etruscan rulers. Taoism and Confucianism take root in China, which uses blast furnaces to produce iron and makes great advances in herbal medicine. Buddhism is founded in India.

500–479 B.C.
Three Strikes, You're Out. Persia invades Greece, losing its transport fleet in a storm off the Greek coast in 492, then losing to the Athenians at Marathon in 490. On their third try, the Persians sweep through Greece and destroy Athens, but are soundly defeated at sea by the Greeks at Salamis. Persia's King Xerxes returns to Persia in defeat, and the remnants of his army are destroyed at Platea a year later, ushering in the Golden Age of Greece. Herodotus, the "Father of History," is born. Elsewhere, Chinese astronomers document the planetary grouping as the region enters its period of the "Warring States." Sicilian Greeks repel a Carthaginian invasion.

476 B.C.
China's Zhou Dynasty collapses, and the empire's vast lands are carved up among petty kingdoms. The period of the Warring States will last until the rise of the Ch'in Dynasty in 221 B.C.

ca. 469 B.C.
Earthquake! Some 20,000 Spartans die in one of the most devastating earthquakes ever recorded. Sparta's growth is disrupted—but not halted.

431–403 B.C.
The Peloponnesian War pits the Athenian empire against Sparta and her allies. Athens takes the lead with early victories at sea, but the Peloponnesian coalition eventually defeats the Athenian fleet and breaks Athenian power in eastern Greece.

335 B.C.
It's All Greek to Me. Alexander the Great goes on a rampage across the Balkans, the Middle East, Asia Minor, and India, establishing the ancient world's greatest empire and spreading Hellenic culture across southern Asia. He dies, allegedly of a fever, in 323 B.C.—one month short of his 33rd birthday.

347 B.C.
An emerging Rome fights its Samnite neighbors for control of central Italy. After the defeat of coastal rival Tarentum in 272 B.C., Rome dominates nearly all of the Italian boot.

264 B.C.
Rome and Carthage (which was located in modern-day Tunisia) begin the First Punic War. The Romans win a sea battle that isolates the Carthaginian army, and Carthage surrenders in 241 B.C.

216 B.C.
In the Second Punic War, Carthage's top general, Hannibal Barca, defeats Rome's finest at Cannae with battlefield tactics that will be studied in perpetuity. But the Romans are a resilient bunch, and they come back to win Round Two.

146 B.C.
Mare Nostrum. After a three-year siege, Roman General Scipio Africanus takes the city of Carthage

to win the Third Punic War. This time, Rome destroys the rival capital for good. Rome dominates trade throughout the Mediterranean, a position it will enjoy for more than a quarter millennium.

61–52 B.C.
Hail Caesar (Part I). Julius Caesar's legions conquer Switzerland, France, Belgium, and Germany. Caesar makes a brief appearance on the shores of Great Britain before declaring victory and heading back to Rome.

51 B.C.
Egypt's Princess Cleopatra becomes Queen Cleopatra VII, ruling Egyptian lands jointly with her ten-year-old brother, King Ptolemy XIII. Around this time, Heron of Greece invents the steam engine, but no one seems to know what to do with it.

48 B.C.
Hail Caesar (Part II). Caesar defeats Pompey the Great and the Roman Senate at the Battle of Pharsalus, making Caesar the undisputed ruler of Rome.

44 B.C.
Caesar is assassinated. Resulting unrest quickly breaks into civil war.

31 B.C.
Hail Caesar (Part III). Julius Caesar's nephew, Octavian, defeats Marc Antony and Cleopatra at the Battle of Actium, ushering in the era of the Roman Empire.

ca. 4 B.C.
Jesus Christ is born in Bethlehem, Palestine.

ca. A.D. 1
Shintoism becomes the dominant religion in Japan.

ca. A.D. 29
Christ is crucified outside Jerusalem. Christianity quietly begins to spread throughout the Roman world.

A.D. 63
Joseph of Arimathea introduces Christianity to the British Isles.

A.D. 79
Mount Vesuvius erupts, wiping cosmopolitan Pompeii, Italy, off the map.

A.D. 135
The Diaspora. Jewish revolt leads to a brutal Roman crackdown followed by the dispersal of the Jewish peoples from Jerusalem and surrounding territories for nearly 1,900 years.

A.D. 220
After a nearly 400-year run, China's Han Dynasty comes to an end. China fragments into kingdoms for the next 81 years.

A.D. 306
Roman general Constantine becomes emperor; Christians are officially tolerated, and by Constantine's death in A.D. 337, Christianity has become a dominant religion in Rome.

A.D. 320
Gupta Kingdom replaces the Kushana Empire in northern and central India, opening the door to a golden age of Indian civilization. Poetry, medicine, and other cultural achievements mark Gupta rule for nearly a century.

A.D. 324–330

Constantine I moves the capital of the Roman Empire to Byzantium, at the border of Europe and Asia.

ca. A.D. 350

A small collection of tribes in Central America begins to form the Mayan civilization.

A.D. 395

After the death of Emperor Theodosius I, the Roman Empire is divided into eastern and western empires under the rule of his two sons. Barbarians continue to press the weakening empire from the north.

A.D. 407

Rome withdraws the last of its legions from Britannia, and Picts, Scots, and Saxons rush into the power vacuum. According to legend, King Arthur battles the Saxons toward the end of the 5th century.

A.D. 433–453

Attila, king of the Huns, runs wild from the Black Sea into France, threatening the dominions of the declining Roman Empire. Rome and the Visigoths team up to defeat Attila in 451 at the Battle of Chalons in France, saving western Europe from "the scourge of God," but Attila threatens Italy the next year. Attila's unexpected death after a banquet in 453 ends one threat to the Empire, but before long Attila's place is taken by other barbarian warlords.

A.D. 476

Look Out Below! Germanic leader Odocer topples the last Roman emperor in the west, and the fall of the Roman Empire is complete. Europe enters a period known as the Dark Ages. Franks, Vandals, Ostrogoths, and Huns, among other barbarian tribes, dismember the western empire's dominions.

A.D. 538

Korean missionaries introduce Buddhism to Japan; before long, "Shinto" is used to differentiate Japan's native religion from Buddhist and Confucianist imports. In 605, Buddhism and Confucianism become the state religions of Japan.

ca. A.D. 613

The prophet Muhammad begins preaching; seven years later, he speaks of a spiritual journey with the archangel Gabriel. In 622, he moves to Medina, marking a new phase of the Islamic calendar. Over the next hundred years, the Islamic faith drives an explosive campaign of conquest stretching from India to southern France.

A.D. 732

Charles Martel ("the Hammer"), ducal leader of the Frankish kingdom, halts the Muslim tide at Poitiers; Islamic gains in the west are held to the Iberian Peninsula.

A.D. 751

In return for military protection and service, Pope Zachary confirms Pepin the Short, son of Charles Martel, as the first Carolingian king of the Franks, creating a dynasty that will rule France until the early 10th century.

ca. A.D. 862

According to tradition, Byzantine missionary Saint Cyril invents the Cyrillic alphabet to spread the gospel among Slavonic peoples.

ca. A.D. 867

Doctrinal arguments between Roman Pope Nicholas I and Byzantium's Patriarch Photius deepen estrangement between East and West. A full-blown schism divides Roman and Eastern churches in A.D. 1054.

A.D. 871

Viking settlers establish villages in Iceland.

ca. A.D. 900

Mass migration into Mexico's Yucatán peninsula leads to the emergence of a new Mayan kingdom.

A.D. 919

Frankish noble Henry of Saxony becomes King of Germany, which at the time is little more than a hodge-podge collection of duchies sharing a common language.

A.D. 929

Abd-al-Rahman III declares himself Caliph of Spain, formalizing a Moorish kingdom in which literature, architecture, and medicine thrive.

A.D. 961

Otto of Saxony (son of King Henry I) marches to the rescue of the pope and is crowned the first Holy Roman Emperor. Before long, the Holy Roman Empire becomes one of the most powerful political forces in Europe.

A.D. 987

Frankish noble Hugh Capet is crowned King of France and establishes the Capetian Dynasty; branches of the Capetian Dynasty, such as the Bourbons, will rule France until revolution hits in 1789.

A.D. 988

Vladimir I, Grand Prince of Kiev and Novgorod, orders his subjects to convert to Orthodox Christianity, establishing what will become Russia's dominant religion.

ca. A.D. 1000

Viking captain Leif Eriksson travels across the Northern Atlantic to Greenland and down the Canadian coast into Newfoundland nearly a half-century before Christopher Columbus reaches the "New World."

1066

The last successful invasion of England reaches its climax at the Battle of Hastings, where William the Conqueror trounces King Harold Godwinson to claim the English throne.

1095

It Is God's Will! Pope Urban II calls for a crusade to retake Jerusalem from its Islamic conquerors. The campaign is the first of eight major crusades (and a smattering of smaller crusades) to the Holy Land.

ca. 1125

In Cambodia, Kambuja's King Suryavarman II embarks on a building project that includes Angkor Wat, the world's largest temple.

ca. 1150

Peru's Inca tribes begin to expand into one of the three great Western empires, creating a state that will last until 1533. Meanwhile, the Aztecs of central Mexico begin replacing the Toltec civilization and build their capital at Tenochtitlán.

ca. 1200

Mayan leader Hunac Ceel and his allies fight a "Mayan Trojan War" against the empire's government at Chichén Itzá.

1204

Crusaders Behaving Badly. Unruly Crusaders sack the Orthodox capital of Constantinople, unleashing an orgy of violence and looting that feeds animosity between Western and Eastern Christians that survives to this day.

1206

An even more unruly Mongol named Temujin takes the title Genghis Khan and launches an empire that will reach from the Pacific Ocean to Eastern Europe.

1215

An Offer He Can't Refuse. Menacing English barons force King John to sign the Magna Carta, a document that acknowledges the king's fealty to the rule of law.

1242

Novgorod's Prince Alesandr Nevskii defeats the Teutonic Knights on a frozen Lake Peipus, turning back Germanic threats to western Russia. He pays tribute to the Mongol khans to the east to preserve Russian society throughout his domains.

1260

Kublai Khan, grandson of Genghis Khan, becomes the first foreigner to rule China as emperor, founding the Yuan Dynasty.

1271

Spaghetti Eastern. Marco Polo visits China; he is happy to sample local pasta dishes, which Italians have enjoyed for generations. On his return, Polo's writings spark Western interest in trade that continues through the early 20th century.

1337–1453

The Hundred Years' War drains England and France. France wins by a nose, although England holds on to a bit of the French coastline around Calais.

1346–1351

Aw, Rats! The Black Death sweeps across Western Europe, killing an estimated 25 million people; about a third of Europe's population is wiped out (60 percent of Venetians died within 18 months). No one makes the connection with the hordes of flea-laden rats that infest European cities.

1368

Rebellion in China leads to the eventual overthrow of Mongol rule. The Ming Dynasty, which would rule China until 1644, leads the country into a period of scientific, military, and cultural enlightenment.

1370

For 35 years, Samarkand noble Timur-i Lang cuts a bloody swath of conquest from Syria to India. But dreaded Tamerlane (as he is known in Europe) dies before he can begin his conquest of China. Eight years later, Mongolian rule in China collapses as the Ming emperors take power for the next three centuries.

1378–1413

The Roman Catholic papacy is torn by influences from France and the Holy Roman Empire. The Western Schism, in which competing popes claimed the throne of Saint Peter, weakens the influence of the pope.

ca. 1380

Geoffrey Chaucer begins work on *The Canterbury Tales,* a monumental tome that takes nearly 20 years to complete.

1440

"Start the Presses!" German inventor Johannes Gutenberg changes the world with the invention of the printing press, making written knowledge available to the masses.

1453

It's Getting Late. The Ottoman capture of Constantinople marks the end of the Middle Ages. The Orthodox church moves to Moscow, and Greek scholars head west to start a humanist movement that flowers into the Renaissance.

1455

Pruning Flowers. The three-decade Wars of the Roses begins when England's House of York (symbolized by a white rose) rises up against the House of Lancaster (symbolized by a red rose) over the succession of King Henry VI, a Lancastrian noble.

1461

Wallachia's Prince Vlad Tepes turns back an Ottoman force at Tirgoviste by treating the invaders to the sight of some 20,000 prisoners impaled on sharp stakes before his castle walls. Some 430 years later,

author Bram Stoker will turn Vlad the Impaler into one of Western literature's most enduring villains: the vampire Dracula.

1475

Good Fences Make Good Neighbors. Leaders of China's Ming dynasty bulk up the Great Wall to some 4,100 miles of walls and watch-towers to guard against Mongol incursions.

1478

"Nobody Expects the Spanish Inquisition!" To solidify their Catholic kingdom, Spain's King Ferdinand and Queen Isabella begin a program of religious persecution that becomes the Spanish Inquisition, a tool of repression to persecute Jews and Protestants. Some 2,000 Spaniards would be executed under the administration of Inquisitor-General Tomas de Torquemada.

1485

"My Kingdom for a Horse." At the Battle of Bosworth Field, Henry Tudor of England defeats King Richard III and claims the English throne. As Henry VII, he inaugurates the Tudor dynasty, which rules England for the next 118 years.

1489

Italian genius Leonardo da Vinci begins detailed drawings of the human skull, building a body of work that makes him history's best-known "Renaissance Man."

1492

Under the Spanish flag, Christopher Columbus crosses the Atlantic Ocean to land at San Salvador in the New World. If sailors had known how to calculate longitude back then, American natives would not have been called "Indians."

1497–1499
Out of Africa. Portuguese explorer Vasco da Gama circumnavigates Africa to reach the lucrative Asian trade market.

1508–1512
Italian painter Michelangelo paints the ceiling of the Vatican's Sistine Chapel.

1512
"What Goes Around..." Polish astronomer Nicolaus Copernicus begins popularizing the theory of heliocentrism, arguing that the earth revolves around the sun. Scientists scoff at what is obviously an incorrect theory.

1517
Irascible Catholic monk Martin Luther nails his famous "95 Theses" to the door of Castle Church in Wittenberg, Germany, calling for an end to established papal practices such as the sale of indulgences. His crusade to reform the Catholic Church sparks the Reformation, as well as the eventual splintering of Western Christians into various Protestant denominations.

1519
Rude Houseguests. Spanish conquistador Hernán Cortés visits the Aztec capital of Tenochtitlán and repays the courteous welcome of King Montezuma by taking the king hostage and extorting gold and silver from his subjects—a true "king's ransom." That same year, Portuguese navigator Ferdinand Magellan sets sail with five ships and 270 men to circumnavigate the globe. When his sole surviving ship returns to Spain three years later, Magellan is not among the sailors left to tell the tale.

1520
Süleyman the Magnificent presides over the zenith of the Ottoman Empire, ruling territory from the Persian Gulf to the Polish frontier.

1526
The Apple Doesn't Fall Far from the Tree. Babar, a descendant of Genghis Khan and Tamerlane, marches southwest into India and declares himself emperor of Hindustan after defeating the Sultans of Delhi and Bengal.

1533
Spanish conquistador Francisco Pizarro captures the Inca king, murders him after receiving a ransom, and loots the Inca capital at Cuzco. One Old World gift to the Inca peoples, smallpox, kills somewhere between 70 to 94 percent of the native population.

1534
Messy Divorce. England's King Henry VIII splits with the Roman church over political and personal issues. The Act of Supremacy makes Henry the head of the Church of England, and his kingdom becomes the rallying point in the Protestant struggle against Catholicism.

1552
Russia's Ivan IV defeats the Tatars in southeastern Russia and expands

the Muscovite Empire deep into Crimean, Caspian, and Siberian lands.

1571

The Battle of Lepanto, the last naval battle between galleys, halts the tide of Ottoman conquest in central and southern Europe.

1582

Mark Your Calendars. Concerned that discrepancies between the civil and solar calendars was pushing Easter too far into the spring, Pope Gregory XIII junks the Julian Calendar for the "Gregorian" version. Gregory declares October 4, 1582, to be October 15, 1582. Orthodox countries will continue to use Julius Caesar's system into the 1900s.

1588

Bad weather and crafty English seamanship combine to defeat the Spanish Armada. Britannia begins her ascension to the title of World's Greatest Maritime Power.

ca. 1590

No Cliff Notes Here. Shakespeare pens *Henry VI*, his first play. *Henry VI* will be followed by 37 other major plays, topping off the Bard's writing credits, which include 154 sonnets and two long poems.

1592

Japan's Hideyoshi Toyotomi invades Korea. Impressive Japanese gains are offset when China comes to Korea's aid.

1595

Dutch lens maker Zacharias Janssen develops the compound microscope, paving the way for advances in medicine and microbiology.

1600

Victory at the Battle of Sekigahara concentrates Japanese military and political power in the hands of *shogun* Tokugawa Ieyasu and his successors. The Tokugawa Shogunate will last until 1868, and during much of that time the *shogun* rules Japan as emperor in all but name.

1605

Tilting at Windmills. Miguel de Cervantes, a veteran of the Battle of Lepanto, publishes the first part of his novel *Don Quixote*, one of Western literature's great tales of misguided chivalry.

1606

Dutch explorer Willem Janzsoon discovers New Holland, a continent that will later be known as Australia.

1607

English colonists land at Jamestown, Virginia. Another band of colonists, at Plymouth, Massachusetts, will set up shop 13 years later.

1608

The East India Company sets up shop under a royal charter, leading the way to British domination of India that lasts until 1947.

1613

Tsar Mikhail Romanov founds Russia's longest-running dynasty, one that will last until revolution topples the monarchy in 1917.

1618

Catholics and Protestants go at each other's throats during the Thirty Years' War. By the time the Peace of Westphalia settles matters in 1648, about a third of present-day

Germany and Czechoslovakia is killed off in bitter fighting.

1641

"I Think, Therefore I Am." René Descartes publishes *Meditations on First Philosophy,* setting forth some of the questions over which future philosophers will wrestle.

1642–1649

The first and second English Civil Wars pit King Charles I against Parliament. Charles loses more than just his throne in 1649 when an executioner's ax gives him a close shave.

1672

A Bit over the Top. France's King Louis XIV moves his court into his fantastic new palace at Versailles, outside Paris. While the palace was a stunning achievement, its cost to the nation and the in-your-face opulence set the stage for revolution just over a century later.

1682

The Apple Still Doesn't Fall Far from the Tree. England's Isaac Newton publishes his *Principia,* a monumental work that defined human understanding of gravitation and mechanics until the early 20th century.

1692

Salem witch trials result in the hanging of 19 accused witches. The chief prosecutor, a hard-nosed witch hater, refuses to admit he was wrong and becomes the next governor of Massachusetts.

1701

Old World, New Wars. The War of Spanish Succession engulfs western Europe. Catholic France and Spain battle Protestant England and Holland on land and at sea over the religion of the to-be-named Spanish monarch. When the conflict ends in 1714, French hegemony over the western continent is sharply curtailed.

1707

The Acts of Union merge England, Wales, and Ireland with Scotland to create the Kingdom of Great Britain.

1709

Growing Bear. Russia's Peter the Great defeats Sweden's Charles XII at the Battle of Poltava, establishing Russia as the dominant kingdom in Eastern Europe and the Baltic region. Peter founds the city of St. Petersburg as his new administrative capital.

1740

The eight-year War of Austrian Succession pits Prussia, France, Spain, Sweden, and Bavaria against Austria, Britain, Holland, Saxony, and Russia. The war commences a rivalry between Prussia and Austria over dominance of the German-speaking lands.

ca. 1750

The African slave trade reaches its peak, filling fields in the Caribbean and North America with kidnapped laborers.

1756–1763

The Seven Years' War. Largely a struggle between Britain and France, this first "world war" sees Britain take control of New France (Canada).

1760s

Such inventions as an efficient steam engine lay the foundations for the Industrial Revolution—in which Britain takes an early lead.

1762

French philosopher Jean-Jacques Rousseau publishes *The Social Contract,* a key document of the Enlightenment—an intellectual movement skeptical of organized religion and favoring individual freedom.

1775–1783

Colonists in Britain's 13 North American colonies successfully throw off British rule after a long military struggle. The new United States of America draws up a constitution in 1787; George Washington is elected president in 1789.

1782–1801

Revolution spreads to the Caribbean and Latin America. A revolt against Spanish rule fails, but a former slave, Toussaint-Louverture, establishes Haiti's independence from France.

1789–1795

The storming of the Bastille prison in Paris begins the French Revolution. The movement descends into widespread bloodshed (including the execution of King Louis XVI and his queen, Marie Antoinette, in 1793).

1803–1848

Territorial expansion in the United States; the Louisiana Purchase (1803), war with Mexico (1846–48), and other acquisitions see the nation expand to the Pacific coast.

1804

Napoleon Bonaparte declares himself emperor of France; over the next eight years, he conquers much of Europe.

1808–1830

Spain's South American colonies achieve independence after much struggle by leaders such as Simón Bolívar, Bernardo O'Higgins, and José de San Martín.

1812–1815

Napoleon's European empire founders after a disastrous invasion of Russia and defeat at the hands of a British-led coalition at the Battle of Waterloo in Belgium.

1848

A Year of Revolutions. Nationalist and democratic movements take to the streets in Prussia, Italy, France, and Hungary. Most are unsuccessful. Karl Marx and Friedrich Engels publish *The Communist Manifesto.*

1857–1858

Britain asserts control of the Indian subcontinent following a failed "rebellion." India becomes the "jewel in the crown" of a rapidly expanding British Empire.

1860–1871

Nationalist movements establish the modern states of Italy and Germany.

1861–1865

The American Civil War. After four years and 600,000 deaths, the Union defeats a confederacy of southern states and outlaws slavery in the United States.

1867–1868

Canada achieves dominion status within the British Empire. Japan begins to modernize under the rule of Emperor Meiji.

ca. 1880–1900

The "Scramble for Africa"; by the end of the 19th century practically the entire continent is under European colonization.

1884

The first automobile goes on sale in Germany—just one invention in a century that sees the introduction of the telegraph, photography, the telephone, recorded sound, the electric light, radio, and motion pictures.

1900–1914

Austrian psychoanalyst Sigmund Freud publishes *The Interpretation of Dreams.* Henry Ford produces the Model T automobile. Japan defeats Russia in a 1904–05 war.

1914–1918

World War I sweeps Europe and then the world. It ends with an Allied victory, the fall of the German and Austro-Hungarian empires, and the establishment of Bolshevik (Communist) rule in Russia.

ca. 1920–1940

Various forms of totalitarian government emerge in Europe—Fascism in Benito Mussolini's Italy, Nazism in Adolf Hitler's Germany, and Josef Stalin's regime in the Soviet Union.

1927

Height of the Roaring Twenties in the United States. Charles Lindbergh makes the first solo flight across the Atlantic; Italian-American radicals Sacco and Vanzetti are executed; and *The Jazz Singer* is the first successful "Talkie" movie.

1928

Alexander Fleming discovers mold on an old petri dish full of staph bacteria. The *Penicillium notatum* mold had inhibited the growth of the bacteria, and Fleming's observation will lead to the rise of antibiotics to fight disease.

1929–1939

The stock market crash in October 1929 and international financial jitters plunge much of the world into the Great Depression.

1936–1939

Civil war in Spain serves as a dress rehearsal for World War II. Japanese forces push deep into China. Stalin imprisons and executes millions in the Soviet Union.

1939–1941

World War II begins with a joint German-Soviet invasion of Poland. Most of continental Europe comes under German domination. Britain fights on alone.

1941–1945

Germany attacks the Soviet Union in June 1941. The United States enters the war after a Japanese attack on Pearl Harbor, Hawaii, on

December 7, 1941. Germany surrenders in May 1945, and the Japanese surrender after the atomic bombings of Hiroshima and Nagasaki in August 1945. Worldwide death toll: 50–60 million.

1946–1953

Start of the Cold War between the West and the Soviet Union. India achieves independence, and the nation of Israel comes into existence. People's Republic of China is established in 1949. The Cold War turns hot in Korea in 1950.

1954

Communist Viet Minh rebels defeat French colonial forces in Vietnam. The U.S. Supreme Court overturns segregation in public education sparking the movement for civil rights for African Americans.

1957–1961

"Space Race" begins with the Soviet Union's launch of the first satellite, *Sputnik*. Yuri Gagarin of the Soviet Union becomes the first man in space.

1962–1963

The Cold War almost boils over when the Soviet Union installs nuclear missiles in Cuba. U.S. President John F. Kennedy is assassinated on November 22, 1963.

1968

A Year of Worldwide Unrest: Students riot in Paris; civil-rights leader Martin Luther King Jr. and presidential candidate Robert Kennedy are assassinated in the United States; and Soviet forces crush a pro-democracy uprising in Czechoslovakia.

1969

The U.S. *Apollo 11* space mission lands men on the moon.

1973–1974

The United States withdraws from the Vietnam War, and President Richard Nixon resigns in disgrace following the Watergate Scandal.

1979–1981

U.S. diplomatic personnel are held hostage in Tehran, Iran, for 444 days. The Soviet Union invades Afghanistan.

1983

Soviet jet fighters shoot down Korean Airlines flight 007 over the Sea of Japan after it veers off course into Soviet airspace. Of the 269 individuals aboard the unarmed passenger plane, none survive. Confusion reigns in the days after the tragedy, however, as investigators from various countries fail to share information and few bodies and significant wreckage turn up.

1985–1991

Endgame in the Cold War: Soviet leader Mikhail Gorbachev liberalizes Communist rule in the Soviet Union; the Berlin Wall falls in 1989, ending Soviet domination of Eastern Europe.

1991

British computer scientist Tim Berners-Lee develops the World Wide Web, fueling the massive growth of the Internet.

1991–1992

A multinational coalition led by the United States drives occupying Iraqi forces from Kuwait.

1994

Former political prisoner Nelson Mandela is elected president of South Africa in the country's first multiracial elections after nearly 50 years of apartheid (official seg-regation). More than 500,000 Tutsis and their sympathizers are hacked to death in the Rwandan genocide after UN troops are pulled out of the area.

2001

On September 11, Islamic funda-mentalist terrorists attack New York City and Washington, D.C., killing nearly 3,000 people. The U.S. government announces a "war on terror."

2003

Claiming Iraq possesses "weapons of mass destruction," the United States invades the country and topples Saddam Hussein's regime, leading to a controversial and costly occupation of the country. The Darfur conflict between Africans and Arabs begins in Sudan; more than 300,000 will die during years of strife in the region.

2004

Pakistani nuclear scientist Abdul Qadeer Khan admits that he sold weapon designs to North Korea and Iran. A 9.0 magnitude earthquake unleashes an Indian Ocean tsunami that claims the lives of approxi-mately 225,000 people.

2005

Hurricane Katrina comes ashore off Louisiana, leaving 80 percent of New Orleans flooded in its wake. Nearly 2,000 lives are lost in the disaster.

2006

The International Astronomical Union reclassifies Pluto as a dwarf planet.

2007

The Great Recession begins, sparked by a slumping stock mar-ket and the burst of the housing bubble.

2008

Fidel Castro resigns as president of Cuba and hands the reins of power over to his brother Raúl.

2009

Barack Obama, the first African American commander-in-chief, assumes the presidency of the United States of America.

2010

Haiti and Chile suffer devastating earthquakes. An offshore oil rig in the Gulf of Mexico explodes, leaving many with concerns about future offshore drilling.

Index

* * * *